FROMMER'S

COMPREHENSIVE TRAVEL GUIDE

BERMUDA &
THE BAHAMAS '92-'93

W9-BNK-584

by Darwin Porter
Assisted by Danforth Prince

PRENTICE HALL TRAVEL

NEW YORK • LONDON • TORONTO • SYDNEY • TOKYO • SINGAPORE

FROMMER BOOKS

Published by Prentice Hall General Reference
A Division of Simon & Schuster Inc.
15 Columbus Circle
New York, NY 10023

ISBN 0-13-335035-5
ISSN 1044-2383

Manufactured in the United States of America

BERMUDA & THE BAHAMAS '92–'93

Editor-in-Chief: Marilyn Wood
Senior Editors: Judith de Rubini, Pamela Marshall, Amit Shah
Editors: Alice Fellows, Paige Hughes, Theodore Stavrou
Assistant Editors: Suzanne Arkin, Ellen Zucker, Peter Katucki
Contributing Editors: Robert Daniels, Lisa Renaud
Managing Editor: Leanne Coupe

CONTENTS

PART THREE

TURKS & CAICOS ISLANDS

MAPS

A Disclaimer

I don't have to tell you that whatever the level of inflation, prices do rise. In researching this book, I have made every effort to obtain up-to-the-minute prices, but even the most conscientious researcher cannot keep up with the constantly changing prices of the travel industry. As this guide goes to press, I believe I have obtained the most reliable data possible. Nonetheless, in the lifetime of this edition—particularly in its second year (1993)—the wise traveler will add 15% to the prices quoted throughout these pages.

What the Symbols Mean

Travelers to The Bahamas and Bermuda may at first be confused by classifications on rate sheets. I've used these same classifications in this guide. One of the most common rates is **MAP,** meaning modified American plan. Simply put, that usually means room, breakfast, and dinner, unless the room rate has been quoted separately, and then it means only breakfast and dinner. **CP** means Continental plan—that is, room and a light breakfast. **EP** is European plan, which means room only. **AP** (American plan) is the most expensive rate of all because it includes not only your room but also three meals a day. To make matters even more confusing, travelers to Bermuda often see **BP** (Bermuda plan) rates quoted. That means a room and a full Bermudian breakfast.

BERMUDA

GETTING TO KNOW BERMUDA

Less than two hours from the U.S. coastline, another world unfolds very different from the shores you left behind. Horse-drawn carriages are still seen on the streets of Hamilton (although strictly for tourists), "bobbies" and businessmen go around in Bermuda shorts, judges still wear powdered wigs as they head to Sessions House, and miles and miles of pink-sand beaches await your swimsuit-clad body.

Bermuda has been called one of the "most attractive and civilized places on earth," and it certainly is one of the world's most sophisticated resorts.

It is appropriate that Bermuda and The Bahamas should be linked in one book. Although they lie 800 miles apart, they are spiritually linked in climate and culture, even though both are separate countries with different governments.

Both Bermuda and The Bahamas were settled in recent history by people from the British Isles, and certain ties to Britain still exist in both countries. (Today, Bermuda is a self-governing colony of Great Britain, and the Commonwealth of The Bahamas is a member of the Commonwealth of Nations, of which the British monarch is the symbolic head.) The histories of these two island entities reveal striking similarities in their loyalty to Britain at the time of the American Revolution: in their sympathy with the Confederacy at the time of the American Civil War, which led to involvement in blockade-running, and in their prosperity from rum-running when Prohibition was supposed to de-alcoholize the United States.

Most early landowners in both Bermuda and The Bahamas were also slave-owners until the government of Great Britain ordered emancipation. The islanders of African racial stock long ago outnumbered the white population, and in fairly recent years have become leaders in their countries.

They're alike, yet the little Bermuda island chain and the big Bahamian archipelago are not really twins. The difference in size makes a visit to one subtly unlike a visit to the other. I find both of them inviting and rewarding in either winter or summer.

1. Geography

Bermuda is far north of the Tropic of Cancer, which cuts through the Bahamian archipelago, but Bermuda, like The Bahamas, has a pleasant climate year round, with sunshine prevailing almost every day. The chief source of Bermuda's mild weather is the Gulf Stream, that broad belt of warm water formed by equatorial currents, whose northern reaches separate the islands of Bermuda from North America and, with the prevailing northeast winds, temper the wintry blasts that sweep across the Atlantic from west and north.

Until the 17th century the islands of Bermuda were known to seafarers as the "Isles of Devils." They probably had contributed to the popular pre-Columbian belief that ships sailing too far west from Europe fell over the edge of the earth into a monster-filled pit. Many ships sailing too close to these remote and uninhabited islands came to grief on the treacherous reefs close to the surface of the turquoise Atlantic. Even Shakespeare was familiar with the reputation of the Isles of Devils, making "the still-vex't Bermoothes" the setting for *The Tempest.*

Bermuda is based on the upper parts of an extinct volcano, which may date from 100 million years ago. Through the millennia, wind and water have brought limestone deposits and formed the islands far from any land mass—the closest is Cape Hatteras, almost 600 miles away. (Early residents soon learned that the limestone base of their land made excellent building stone, easily sawed soon after being quarried but gaining hardness and durability upon exposure to the sun.)

The first recorded discovery of the islands was made in 1503 by a Spanish mariner, Juan de Bermúdez, for whom they were named. The uncharted islands were a navigational menace to ships following the trade routes of the Atlantic, as Spanish vessels did on voyages from the New World. Bermuda's location is at a point in the ocean where galleons from New Spain could easily run into trouble in less than perfect weather, and the eroded wreckage of many ships scattered on the ocean floor amid reefs and shoals bears mute testimony to tragedies, some dating from four or five centuries ago.

ORIENTATION

This tiny fishhook-shaped archipelago is made up of some 150 small islands, only 20 of which are inhabited. The chain is about 22 miles long and less than 2 miles across at the widest point, so that no residents live more than a mile from the sea. The seven largest islands are now joined by causeways and bridges, presenting a connection of land that is known simply as the island of Bermuda.

Combined, the islands form a land mass of 20.59 square miles. Great Bermuda, often called the mainland, is the largest island, about 14 miles long, containing the capital city of Hamilton. Linked by bridge and causeway, the other islands bear such names as Somerset, Watford, Boaz, and Ireland in the west, and St. George's and St. David's in the east.

This chain of islands encloses the archipelago's major bodies of water, which include Castle Harbour, St. George's Harbour, Harrington Sound, and Great Sound. Most of the other, smaller islands, or islets, lie within these bodies of water.

The Parishes

The islands of Bermuda are divided into parishes.

SANDYS PARISH In the far-western part of the archipelago, Sandys Parish is centered around Somerset Village. This parish takes in the islands of Ireland, Boaz, and Somerset, and is named for Sir Edwin Sandys, one of the major shareholders of the origi-

BERMUDA

□ PARK

St. George's Parish

Fort St. Catherine
St. Catherine Beach
Fort Albert
St. George's
St. George's Harbour
FERRY RD.
KINDLEY FIELD RD.
CAUSEWAY
Int'l Airport
Castle Harbour

ATLANTIC OCEAN

Hamilton Parish

Bermuda Pottery
Blue Grotto
Leamington Caves
Crystal Caves
Harrington Sound
Flatts
Devil's Hole
Shelly Bay Beach
Aquarium, Museum & Zoo

Smith's Parish

Pink Beach
Spanish Rock

ATLANTIC OCEAN

Pembroke Parish

NORTH SHORE RD.
MIDDLE RD.
Ft. Hamilton
Hamilton

Devonshire Parish

Paget Parish

SOUTH RD.
Coral Beach
Flamingo Beach

Warwick Parish

HARBOUR RD.
MIDDLE RD.
SOUTH RD.

Maritime Museum
Grassy Bay
Mangrove Bay
Cambridge Beaches

Sandys Parish

Somerset
Ely's Harbour
SOMERSET RD.

Ferry
Great Sound
Hamilton Harbour
Little Sound

Southampton Parish

MIDDLE RD.

Miles
Kilometers
0   4
0   6

N

nal Bermuda Company. Somerset Long Bay is the biggest and best public beach in Bermuda's west end.

SOUTHAMPTON PARISH   Going east, Southampton Parish (named for the third Earl of Southampton) stretches from Riddells Bay to Tucker's Island, site of the U.S. Naval Air Station Annex. This parish is split by Middle Road and is celebrated for its public beach stretching along Horseshoe Bay. The parish is the site of such major resorts as the Southampton Princess.

WARWICK PARISH   Named in honor of another shareholder in the 1610 Bermuda Company, the second Earl of Warwick, this parish lies between Southampton and Paget parishes. Known for its golf courses and hotels, it offers Warwick Long Bay, along the South Shore, one of Bermuda's best public beaches.

PAGET PARISH   East of Warwick Parish, Paget Parish begins at Hamilton Harbour in the east and lies directly south of the capital city of Hamilton. Named after the fourth Lord Paget, it has many residences and historic homes. It is also the site of the 36-acre Botanical Gardens.

PEMBROKE PARISH   This parish contains the capital city of Hamilton (the only full-fledged city in Bermuda), which is most often viewed as passengers arrive aboard a cruise ship in Hamilton Harbour. Named after the third Earl of Pembroke, the parish shelters one-quarter of Bermuda's population.

DEVONSHIRE PARISH   Lying east of both Paget and Pembroke parishes, near the geographical center of the archipelago, Devonshire Parish is lush, green, and hilly. It has some housekeeping apartments, a cottage colony, and one of Bermuda's oldest churches, the Old Devonshire Parish Church, which dates from 1716. Named for the first Earl of Devonshire, the parish can be traversed by three of the major roads of Bermuda—the aptly named South Road, Middle Road, and North Road.

SMITH'S PARISH   Directly east of Devonshire Parish, Smith's Parish opens onto Harrington Sound along its eastern flank. Its northern and southern coasts face the Atlantic. Named after Sir Thomas Smith, another member of the Bermuda Company, the parish takes in charming Flatts Village, along with two bird sanctuaries.

HAMILTON PARISH   Not to be confused with the city of Hamilton (which is in Pembroke Parish), Hamilton Parish lies directly north of Harrington Sound, opening onto the Atlantic. Named for the second Marquis of Hamilton, the parish ropes itself around Harrington Sound, a saltwater lake stretching some 6 miles. On its eastern periphery, it opens onto Castle Harbour.

ST. GEORGE'S PARISH   In Bermuda's extreme eastern part, this historic parish is composed of several different islands, the largest of which are St. George's Island and St. David's Island. St. George's Island was the site of the *Sea Venture*'s wreck in 1609. Its major settlement, St. George's, was founded in 1612 and was once the capital of Bermuda. Filled with historic buildings, it contains St. Peter's Church, the oldest continuously used Protestant house of worship in the Western Hemisphere. The parish is flanked by Castle Harbour on the western and southern edges and bisected into two halves by St. George's Harbour. St. David's Island is linked to the rest of

Bermuda by the Severn Bridge, which lies near the U.S. Naval Air Station and the country's international airport. The people who inhabit this most easterly part of Bermuda are longtime sailors and fishermen. St. George's Parish also includes Tucker's Town, founded in 1616 by Governor Daniel Tucker on the opposite shore of Castle Harbour.

FLORA & FAUNA

Decorating the gently rolling Bermudian landscape are oleander, hibiscus, royal poinciana, poinsettia, bougainvillea, morning glory (convolvulus), and other flowering plants, shrubs, and trees. Bananas, grapefruit, lemons, oranges, and limes grow profusely. Among trees, you'll see pine, palm, casuarina (Australian pine), fiddlewood, and bay grape. Nearly all the important plants of the islands can be seen in the government's Botanical Gardens in Paget Parish. Indigenous trees are the Bermuda cedar, the Bermuda olivewood bark, and the palmetto. Indigenous flowers include the Bermudiana (sometimes called the Bermuda iris), Darrell's fleabane (a plant of the daisy family), and the maidenhair fern.

The animal life found here includes several species of small harmless lizards and the tiny whistling frogs heard making cricket-like sounds on summer nights. There are no snakes on any of the islands. Cardinals and bluebirds make their home here.

2. History

THE EARLY YEARS

Although the discovery of the Bermuda Islands (as they are also called) is attributed to the Spanish, they made no territorial claim. The archipelago was probably discovered in 1503 by the Spanish navigator Juan de Bermúdez, for whom it was later named. A 1511 map published in the *Legatio Babylonica* includes "La Bermuda" among the Atlantic islands. It was a little more than 100 years after Bermúdez wrote about this place that the English staked a claim and began colonization. Spain's archives reveal that during that century some Spaniards survived shipwrecks in the waters off Bermuda, but they devoted their energies to building boats to take them home. It took an English shipwreck to initiate permanent settlement here.

In 1609 the flagship of British admiral Sir George Somers, the *Sea Venture,* en route to the struggling Jamestown settlement in Virginia with much-needed supplies, was wrecked on Bermuda's reefs. The dauntless Englishmen built two new ships and sailed on to the American colony, but three sailors hid out and stayed on Bermuda. From that point on, the islands have been inhabited.

Just three years after the wreck of the *Sea Venture,* the islands of Bermuda were included in the third British charter of the Virginia Company, and 60 colonists were sent there from England. St. George's Town was quickly founded.

Bermuda's status as a colony dates from 1620, when the first Parliament sat, making it the oldest in the British Empire in continuous operation. It became a Crown Colony in 1684, under King Charles II.

Slaves became a part of life in Bermuda shortly after the official settlement. The majority of these were from Africa, but a few were Native Americans. Later brought to the islands were Scots imprisoned for fighting against Cromwell and, in 1651, Irish slaves. The lot of these bond servants was never as cruel as that of plantation slaves in America and the West Indies, the very nature and size of Bermuda causing them to be used in less strenuous capacities. All slaves were freed by the United Kingdom Emancipation Act of 1834, which provided compensation for the former owners.

After early whaling and tobacco-growing ventures of the islanders failed, the Bermudians turned their attention to shipbuilding, using the cedar trees that grew in abundance on the islands. The expertise gained led to cabinetmaking, and fine furniture was turned out, using the indigenous cedarwood and the skills developed through the building of tight ships.

DEALINGS WITH AMERICA

Although Bermuda is 1,000 miles north of the West Indies and more than half that distance from the American mainland, it was inevitable that close links would be maintained in the early colonial days with both those outposts of Great Britain. With their own ships, the islanders set up a thriving mercantile American trade on the eastern seaboard, especially with Southern ports, and with all the Bahamian and other West Indian islands. The major commodity sold by Bermuda's merchant ships was salt from Turks Island, which they controlled before losing it to The Bahamas around 1800.

The American Revolution dealt a blow to Bermuda's prospering economy, the rebellious colonies on the mainland being unwilling to trade with their former business associates because of their close link with Britain, despite the fact that many Bermudians and Americans had family connections and close friendships. The seafaring islanders, never much for farming, had depended heavily on America for food and reached a point of near starvation after trade was cut off.

The mainland colonies, meanwhile, had a great need for gunpowder. After certain discreet communications, a powder magazine in St. George's was left carelessly "guarded" one dark night in August 1775, and a number of kegs of gunpowder were stolen. Those kegs next appeared in Boston, where they arrived aboard American ships and were later used to oust the British from that area in early 1776. A large shipment of food arrived in Bermuda shortly thereafter. This little breach of the rules of war did not, however, alter Bermuda's loyalty to England.

With a complement of "wooden ships and iron men," a natural step for some owners or captains of seagoing vessels was to turn their skill to privateering and even to piracy in those "happy days of yore" when those pursuits were flourishing in The Bahamas and throughout the Caribbean. Privateering had a certain aura of respectability, as it was legal then to prey on enemy ships. It was an easy sail into piracy, and the lack of speedy communications often persuaded sea captains that all ships were enemies.

The successful revolt of the colonies and establishment of the United States of America forced more of Bermuda's seafarers, now lacking trade routes, to look for economic aid. They found it in privateering, piracy, and wrecking. Wrecking was the name given the business of salvaging goods from wrecked or foundered ships, a highly lucrative venture in these shoal- and reef-filled waters. Unfortunately, if business lagged, some wreckers would lure vessels onto the rocks by placement of beacons, presumably promising safety, in such positions as to doom storm-tossed ships.

Britain's loss of its important American colonial ports on the eastern seaboard led to a naval buildup in Bermuda, beginning with a dockyard from which ships and troops sailed in 1814 to burn Washington, D.C., and the Executive Mansion, renamed the White House after an emergency repainting.

Bermuda got a new lease on a healthy economic life during America's War Between the States, or Civil War. With Bermuda sympathetic to the Confederacy, it was perhaps natural that the island business and government, with approval of the government in London, would participate in running the blockade the Union placed on exports, especially of cotton, by the southern states. St. George's Harbour was a principal Atlantic base for the lucrative operation of sending manufactured goods into Confederate ports and bringing out cotton and turpentine cargoes.

When the Confederacy fell, so did Bermuda's economy, although on a less permanent basis. Seeing no immediate source of money from the Atlantic in the last quarter of the 19th century, the islanders turned their attention to agriculture and found that the colony's fertile soil and salubrious climate produced excellent vegetables—chief among them, onions. Portuguese people were brought in as farmers, and soon celery, potatoes, and tomatoes were being shipped to the New York market. During this period Bermuda came to be called the "Onion Patch" because of the abundance of big sweet onions shipped to the United States—onions that Americans found superior to home-grown products.

(Enterprising Texas farmers learned how to duplicate the island product through additions to and fertilization of their soil. They registered the name "Bermuda onions," and aided by a high tariff placed on imported produce, they virtually put Bermuda out of the export-farming business.)

Bermudians again profited by problems of the United States during the Prohibition era, from passage of the 18th Amendment in 1919 to its repeal in 1933, when rum-running was a lucrative business. Although the distance from the islands to the mainland was too great to allow a quick crossing in small booze-laden boats, as was the case from The Bahamas and Cuba, Bermuda played a part in transporting alcoholic beverages to America.

Bermuda has many connections—historic and present—with the United States. U.S. Air Force and Navy ties date from World War II.

WORLD WAR II ESPIONAGE

Bermuda had an important role in World War II, beginning with the establishment of the Imperial Censorship Headquarters at the Hamilton Princess hotel in 1940, when Britain, under Churchill, was in the darkest days of the war.

The story is most dramatically related in *A Man Called Intrepid,* the 1976 bestseller (more than two million copies sold) by William Stevenson about "the secret war" (you may recall the film with Michael York, Barbara Hershey, and David Niven). Curiously, although written by William Stevenson, the book was about Sir William Stephenson (no relation), the master superspy. An aide to Stephenson (alias Intrepid) was Ian Fleming, who later created the James Bond character.

Under the Hamilton Princess, Britain employed men and women to decode Nazi signals picked up by "radio nets." Unknown to the Germans, the British early in the war had broken the Nazi code. The German coding-decoding machine was called "Enigma," and it was vastly complicated, which explained Hitler's reliance on it. (Knowledge of its workings was so valuable to Churchill that he failed to order the evacuation of Coventry—even though he knew it was slated for aerial bombardment. To have evacuated Coventry presumably would have tipped off the Nazis that the British had broken their precious code.)

The commanders of the dreaded U-boats, which were, at least in 1942, efficiently destroying Allied shipping across the Atlantic, relied heavily on radio signals. This proved to be an Achilles' heel. They also believed in the integrity of Enigma, foolishly unaware that their code had been broken. Even when German submarines with their Enigma unharmed were captured by Allied vessels, the Nazi hierarchy did not become overly alarmed. The powers in Berlin believed that the Allies, even with an Enigma sitting in front of them, would be unable to figure out the intricate workings of the coding-machine drums, and how they could be continually altered.

In a different operation, a carefully trained British staff, working in Bermuda in cramped, stifling conditions under the Hamilton Princess hotel, intercepted and examined mail between Europe and the United States.

Bermuda was also used as a refueling stop between the two continents. While airplane pilots were entertained at the Yacht Club in Bermuda, the mail was taken off the carriers and examined by experts. An innocent-appearing series of letters from Lisbon, for example, often had messages written in invisible ink. These letters were part of a vast German spy network. The British became skilled at opening carefully sealed envelopes, examining the written material, then resealing them, without the person at the other end knowing that his or her mail had been tampered with.

This highly skilled crew was called the "trappers." In his account, William Stevenson wrote: "And by some quirk in the law of averages, the girls who shone in this work had well-turned ankles." The author quotes a medical official as reporting that it was "fairly certain that a girl with unshapely legs would make a bad trapper." Therefore, amazingly, women seeking recruitment in Bermuda as trappers were asked to display what World War II men called their "gams."

These women with shapely ankles discovered the "Duff" method of transporting secret spy messages. This was a reference to a microdot. An important military secret could be hidden under a punctuation dot such as a comma. It was possible to shrink a regularly typed page to so small a size. The British likened these secret messages to a plum duff, a popular English dessert. According to author Stevenson, they were "punctuation dots scattered through a letter like raisins in the suet puddings." The nickname Duff stuck throughout the war.

J. Edgar Hoover sent his FBI agents to Bermuda to join in these intelligence operations, which continued until 1945.

British officials in Bermuda often took bolder steps than opening the mail. They sometimes confiscated stolen art from Europe. The Nazis—Goebbels, in particular—intended to sell the stolen treasures in New York to help finance the Nazi war effort. An example cited in *A Man Called Intrepid* concerns the *Excalibur*, an American Export Lines vessel. The captain of the ship refused to allow the authorities to enter a strong room that had been sealed off like a bank vault. Like a safecracker, the British broke into the room, only to discover 270 works by French impressionists. At the end of the war these impressionist paintings were returned to their rightful owner in Paris, who in all probability thought he'd never see his art again.

A RENDEZVOUS FOR WORLD LEADERS

Churchill, taking great risks, flew to Bermuda even during some of the most dangerous aerial and sea bombardment over the North Atlantic in World War II. Perhaps the balmy shores of Bermuda were worth the risk. They were certainly far better than war-torn London.

In 1953 Churchill requested that Bermuda be used as the setting for "the Big Three conference," which brought not only Churchill but President Eisenhower and Joseph Laniel, the prime minister of France. Eisenhower, who seemed to like Bermuda (especially its golf courses), returned in 1956. This time it was for "the Big Two talks," between Ike and Harold Macmillan, the prime minister of Britain.

In 1961 it was another American president, John F. Kennedy, who met with Harold Macmillan for a second "Big Two conference."

Shortly before Christmas in 1971, another "Big Two summit conference" was held, this time between President Richard Nixon and Prime Minister Edward Heath, and most recently it was the turn of their 1991 counterparts, George Bush and John Major.

MODERN TIMES

In 1957, after nearly two centuries of rule, Great Britain withdrew its forces from its oldest colony, Bermuda. An agreement made with the British, extending to 2040, gave the U.S. Navy a rent-free lease at Kindley Field in St. George's Parish. Nearby, on Cooper's Island, a space-traking network of the National Aeronautics and Space Administration operates quietly and discreetly.

Although racial segregation in hotels and restaurants ceased in 1959, it wasn't until 1971 that schools were integrated. Women received the right to vote in 1944, but the law still restricted suffrage only to property holders. However, this was rescinded in 1963, when voter registration became open to all citizens. Bermuda was given rather sweeping powers of self-government in the constitutional changes of 1968. It established and still retains a two-house Parliament, made up of a House of Assembly and a Senate (the upper house); the cabinet is headed by the premier, who is appointed by the royal governor. The governor, the queen's representative, fills in this and other areas the same function as the monarch.

Judicial responsibility falls to the Supreme Court, headed by a chief justice. English law is the fundamental guide, and the court wears traditional wigs and robes.

During the rocky road to independence, there have been problems in this "colony." Rioting broke out in 1968, a matter so serious that British troops were called in to restore order. Then, in 1973, Sir Richard Sharples, the governor, was assassinated. In 1977 men believed to have been the assassins were themselves executed, an event marked by more rioting.

In 1970 Bermuda was "expelled" from the sterling currency area, and Bermudians hitched their currency to that of the U.S. dollar, a practice that continues to this day.

It was during the 1970s that the phenomenon of the Bermuda Triangle—if such a thing exists—gained great media attention. Ships or planes entering this mysterious area of the Atlantic Ocean, bounded by Melbourne (FL), Bermuda, and Puerto Rico, allegedly vanished without a trace.

The 1990s have brought talk about what role Bermuda will play in the future. There are those who talk of complete independence, and others who want to retain firm connections to the Crown (meaning Britain). The issue is far from being resolved.

TOURISM

Winter holidays to Bermuda from England came into fashion during Queen Victoria's reign, with VIPs, including royalty, going there. In the early 1900s steamships brought wealthy visitors seeking a place in the sun during American winters. The industry now accounts for by far the major portion of Bermuda's economy.

If you take many sightseeing tours of Bermuda, especially in the eastern parishes, you'll constantly encounter the name of Thomas Moore (1779–1852). He was, in many ways, the archipelago's most famous first tourist. Moore, of course, was the Irish poet known for both his *Irish Melodies* and his biography of Byron. Some of his songs include "The Last Rose of Summer" and "The Harp That Once Through Tara's Halls."

Moore arrived in St. George's in the winter of 1804, only 24 years old. He was to spend four months in Bermuda, working as a registrar in the Court of the Vice-Admiralty (and in that sense he was not, technically, a tourist). During his stay in Bermuda he wrote a total of 13 odes to Nea. Nea was in fact the wife of William Tucker, then governor of Bermuda. Her real name was Hester, and she was already seven months pregnant when Moore became infatuated with her. However, the dashing, romantic poet didn't confine his attention only to Hester. He turned out to be a philanderer, and it is said that many a foolish young girl lost her heart to him.

Moore made several visits to see the Trott family, and their old house in Hamilton Parish is now known as Tom Moore's Tavern (see "Hamilton Parish" in Chapter IV). He wrote under the now-famous calabash tree on the Trott estate. One of his odes was a farewell to Bermuda: "Long may the bloom of the lemon and myrtle its vallies perfume."

Since Moore actually had a job in Bermuda, the title of "most famous first tourist" might go to Mark Twain. Unlike Moore, Twain needs no introduction to today's visitors. In spite of his intense dislike of the sea voyage, he felt that once he had reached Bermuda it was worth the "hell" of getting there. Twain's 1877 trip on the steamer *Quaker City* was vividly recalled in *Innocents Abroad*.

Like many of today's tourists, Twain was a repeat visitor, and for Bermuda that was gratifying. Twain spent several winters here, staying in the Pitts Bay area with a well-to-do family. Either walking in his white suit or riding in a donkey cart, the American humorist became a familiar figure on the streets of Hamilton. (Twain was joined by another famous figure in 1908, Woodrow Wilson, in signing a petition against bringing the automobile to Bermuda. Someone, somewhere, must have listened, because it wasn't until 1946 that the automobile was introduced.)

Finally, and sadly, he left Bermuda in 1910. Already ailing, he was heading back to his home in Connecticut, where he was soon to die.

The most flattering thing Twain ever wrote about Bermuda was "Americans on their way to heaven call at Bermuda and think they have already arrived."

---

3. The People

Some Bermudians can trace their ancestry back to the first settlers and some to successful privateers and to slaves. Today's 57,000 residents—mostly of African, British, and Portuguese derivation—have a high standard of living, with no personal income tax and virtually no unemployment. The color bar, which was there long after slavery was abolished, has almost disappeared, and blacks have assumed a prominent place in Bermudian civic and government affairs. Interracial unity among the Bermudians is excellent today, except for pockets of dissidents. There is no illiteracy here, and you won't see any slums or poverty.

You'll be strongly aware of the British influence in Bermuda, what with predominantly English accents, police wearing helmets like those of London bobbies, and cars driving on the left. Americans, however, have made an impact as well (which is more obvious to visitors from the United Kingdom than to us).

Schools here are run along the lines of the English system, providing a high standard of preparatory education. Children 5 to 16 years of age must attend school. The Bermuda College offers academic and technical studies and boasts a renowned hotel and catering program.

---

4. Sports & Recreation

Twenty-one square miles of year-round action: that's what the outdoor sports enthusiast finds in and around Bermuda. A wide array of water sports is pursued here, with plenty of equipment, instructors, and facilities offered. You can go boating, windsurfing, sailing, waterskiing, and shore, reef, or deep-sea fishing on top of the water. The Bermuda-fitted dinghy is one of the world's most distinctive sailing craft, carrying up to 1,000 square feet of sail. At only 14 feet 1 inch in length, this dinghy carries more sail for its size than any other craft.

If you prefer to disport yourself underwater, you have a choice of helmet diving, scuba diving, or snorkeling. Or you can just swim around, in the sea or in a pool. The fine pink-sand beaches of Bermuda are legendary.

Not a water buff? Then you may want to play tennis on one of the more than 90 courts in Bermuda, or perhaps you'd like to golf on one of the eight fine courses, which support the claim that Bermuda has more golf per square mile than any island on earth. Pedal cycling, bowling, walking, and jogging are engaged in by many Bermudians and visitors alike.

If you'd rather be a viewer than a doer, you'll find a wide variety of spectator sports too. These include such traditional British games as cricket, rugby, and soccer, plus lacrosse, field hockey, softball, cycle scrambling, and track-and-field events, among other pursuits.

Most of the large hotels have their own water-sports facilities and equipment for the use of hotel guests, which may also be available to guests of other hotels on request. Ask at your hotel.

SPECIAL SPORTS EVENTS

Besides the day-to-day sports activities you can engage in, there's always something going on in Bermuda or its surrounding waters that will be of interest to many sports enthusiasts. The annual **Bermuda Game Fishing Tournament** is held from May 1 to November 30, with special prizes for top catches of 17 species of game fish. All amateur anglers are eligible. You'll learn all about it if you go around any of the docks from which fishing boats depart, or any of the marinas.

Yachtsmen from the United States, the United Kingdom, Canada, and other countries compete with Bermudians in a week of races in April or May. This is called the **Invitational International Week.** Other boat-racing events take place in alternate years. The **Blue Water Cruising Race** from Marion, Massachusetts, to Bermuda is held in June in odd-numbered years, as is the **Multi-Hull Ocean Yacht Race** from Newport, Rhode Island, to Bermuda. In June of even-numbered years, some 180 of the world's finest yachts compete in the **Bermuda Race,** from Newport to Bermuda.

The **Invitation Tennis Weeks** are held in November, when more than 100 visiting players vie with Bermudians in two weeks of matches.

In December a week of golfing activity is held. The **Bermuda Goodwill Tournament** attracts 70 to 80 pro/amateur foursomes from international golf clubs to play over 72 holes on four of Bermuda's eight courses.

The **Bermuda International Marathon and Ten Kilometre Race,** with international and local runners participating, is held in January.

Two **international dog shows** are held here, one in March and the other in November. A **regional bridge tournament,** in January or February, is interesting to watch for the ferocity with which some people participate.

SPECIFIC SPORTS

Boating

Bermuda is one of the world's sailing capitals. Sail-yourself boats are available on a half-day (4-hour) or full-day (8-hour) basis. **Salt Kettle Boat Rentals, Ltd.,** Salt Kettle, P.O. Box PG 201, Paget PG BX, Bermuda (tel. 809/236-4863), rents craft such as Sunfish, daysailers, and motorboats. Sunfish are rented at $50 (4 hours) or $80 (8 hours), and a 17-foot O'Day Daysailer costs $75 (4 hours) or $120 (8 hours). Sailing instruction is also given, a 2-hour beginner course costing $75 for an O'Day Daysailer.

Blue Hole Water Sports, Grotto Bay Beach Hotel, 11 Blue Hole Hill, Hamilton Parish (tel. 809/293-3328), rents Sunfish for $50 (4 hours) or $80 (8 hours). A 13-foot Boston Whaler with a Bimini top rents for $90 (4 hours) or $130 (8 hours). It also has a wide range of other equipment for rent as well, including Hobie Cats and water bikes.

Yachts for charter with a licensed skipper can be rented at a number of places, including **Bermuda Caribbean Yacht Charter,** 2A Light House Rd., Southampton Parish (tel. 809/238-8578). The 52-foot ketch *Night Wind* costs $225 for a half day, $450 for a full day. Operating from April to November, it charges these prices for six passengers. Any person above that pays an extra $10.

Deep-Sea Fishing

In these waters are wahoo, amberjack, blue marlin, white marlin, dolphin, tuna, and more. Fishing is considered best from May through November. One of the world's finest fishing centers, Bermuda offers a wealth of equipment. The **Bermuda Department of Tourism,** P.O. Box HM 465, Hamilton, Bermuda (tel. 809/292-0023), can assist with general inquiries about fishing.

Bermuda Sportsfishing, Creek View House, 8 Tulo Lane, Pembroke, HM 02, Bermuda (tel. 809/292-5535), is run by the De Silva family, who have been in business for many years. They charge $575 for a half day of fishing and from $650 to $700 for a full day. If given enough notice, the family can compose groups of fishermen into units of six. If so, the charge then is only $95 per person for a half day and

$108 per person for a full day, with all equipment included in the price. Boats include a 50-foot all-wood vessel with two bathrooms, a kitchenette, three "fighting chairs," and space for up to 20 persons. There is also a 36-foot sportfishing boat available.

Golf

Since the first course was laid out in Bermuda in 1922, golf has become one of its most popular sports. It can be played year round; early spring, winter, and fall offer near-perfect seaside golf conditions. At the eight courses, it is necessary to arrange your starting time in advance through the management of your guesthouse or hotel. Women's and men's clubs, either right- or left-handed, are available at each course, and most leading stores in Bermuda sell golf balls.

Tournaments are held throughout the year, with top players participating. For information, get in touch with the **Bermuda Golf Association,** P.O. Box HM 433, Hamilton HM BX, Bermuda (tel. 809/238-1367), or the **Bermuda Department of Tourism** (see "Information" in the "Fast Facts" section of Chapter II).

The Castle Harbour Hotel golf course is considered one of the most scenic courses on the island, while the Port Royal, designed by Robert Trent Jones, is a challenge to your golfing expertise. Two famous courses, the Mid Ocean Club at Tucker's Town and the Riddells Bay Golf and Country Club, are private, requiring introduction by members before you can play there. One of the most photographed golf courses in Bermuda is at the Southampton Princess hotel, where rolling hills and flowering shrubs add to a player's enjoyment.

The golf courses listed below that are part of a hotel complex also allow nonguests to use their facilities. All of these golf courses have pros, and you can take lessons if you wish.

Belmont Hotel, Golf & Country Club, between Harbour and Middle Roads, Warwick Parish (tel. 809/236-1301). This course has 18 holes, par 70, 5,745 yards. Greens fees are $30 for hotel guests, $35 for others. A full set of golf clubs rents for $15; gas golf carts cost $30, handcarts $5. This can also be played as a 9-hole course.

Port Royal Golf Course, Southampton Parish, (tel. 809/234-0974). This is a public course with 18 holes, par 71, 6,565 yards. Greens fees are $32 (reduced rates are available after 4pm). There are no caddies. A full set of clubs rents for $13; golf carts cost $22, handcarts $4. The clubhouse overlooks the ocean and the 9th and 18th greens. It boasts a bar and a restaurant, serving breakfast and lunch.

Southampton Princess Golf Club, Southampton Parish (tel. 809/238-0446). This course has 18 holes, 2,684 yards, par 54. Greens fees for hotel guests are $20, $24 for visitors. There are no caddies. Rental of clubs costs $12 per 18 holes; gas golf carts rent for $20.

Castle Harbour Golf Club, Tucker's Town, Hamilton Parish (tel. 809/293-0795). This course has 18 holes, par 71, 6,440 yards. Greens fees are $70 for 18 holes. There are no caddies. A full set of clubs rents for $22; gas golf carts cost $32 for 18 holes (mandatory use of golf carts); and shoe rental is $6.

Queen's Park Golf Course, Ocean View Golf and Country Club, Inc., Devonshire Parish (tel. 809/236-6758). This course has 9 holes, par 35, 2,956 yards. Greens fees are $22 (for 9 holes or the course played for 18 holes). There are no caddies. A full set of clubs costs $10; gas golf carts cost $11 for 9 holes, $22 for 18 holes; handcarts cost $5 for 9 or 18 holes.

St. George's Golf Club, Park Road, St. George's Parish (tel. 809/297-8067). This course has 18 holes, par 64, 4,502 yards. Greens fees for 9 or 18 holes are $25 (reduced rates are available after 4pm). There are no caddies. A full set of clubs costs $12; gas golf carts rent for $22, handcarts for $4.

Horseback Riding

At the **Spicelands Riding Centre,** Middle Road, Warwick Parish (tel. 809/238-8212), you'll find trail rides for $25 per person for 1 hour. The popular early morning ride, a 2-hour jaunt with a full breakfast following, costs $37.50 per person. From May to September, weekly evening rides and lunch rides costing $30 are offered.

Lee Bow Riding Stables, Tribe Rd., Devonshire Parish (tel. 809/236-4181), is especially for children aged 6 to 18. However, riders of all ages are accommodated, often in small groups of no more than four. Instruction is available. Lessons and trail rides are given for $25 per hour.

Parasailing

Enthusiasts can find this sport at **Skyrider Bermuda, Ltd.,** Robinson's Marina, Somerset Bridge (tel. 809/234-1034), going to the sheltered waters off Little Sound 10 months of the year, daily from 9am to 7:30pm. The charge per flight is $36 per person. Closed January and February.

Swimming & Beaches

Bermuda is one of the world's leading beach resorts, with its miles of pink-sand shoreline, broken now and then by cliffs that form sheltered coves. Many stretches have shallow water for some distance out and sandy bottoms, making them safe for children and even nonswimmers. Hotels and private clubs often have their own private beaches, but there is no shortage of public facilities in Bermuda, under the supervision of the Parks Division of the Department for Agriculture and Fisheries.

At most of the public beaches you'll find public rest rooms and usually a place nearby for drinks or snacks. **Shelly Bay,** North Shore, Hamilton Parish, for instance, even has a beach house, with changing rooms, towels, lounging and snorkeling equipment for rent, and a shop where you can buy souvenirs and film. There's a place also to have a hot lunch or a cold drink. The **Shelly Bay Beach House** (tel. 809/293-1327) is open daily from 10am to 7pm. Take bus no. 10 or 11 from Hamilton.

Other good beaches are **John Smith's Bay,** South Shore, Smith's Parish, where there are a lunchwagon and rest rooms; **Tobacco Bay** beach, North Shore, St. George's Parish, which has changing rooms and refreshments; **Church Bay and West Whale Bay** beaches, both on the South Shore in Southampton Parish, which have rest rooms; and **Warwick Long Bay,** South Shore, Warwick Parish, with rest rooms.

Bermuda's most famous beach is the one at **Horseshoe Bay,** South Shore, Southampton Parish, where the Beach House (tel. 809/238-2651) contains lockers, changing rooms, toilets, and showers, as well as food and drink and rental equipment for the beach or water. You can also buy magazines, suntan lotion, and other sundries you may need.

Tennis

Nearly all the big hotels, and many of the smaller ones, have courts, which are usually lit for night play. It's best to come to Bermuda with your own tennis clothing and sneakers because such an outfit may be required to play the game. Colored tennis togs, so popular in America, have now arrived in Bermuda. Before that, outfits were restricted to white.

Each of the facilities described below has a tennis pro on duty, and lessons can be arranged. In case you didn't come prepared, you can rent rackets and buy balls at each place.

There are six clay and two asphalt courts at the **Government Tennis Stadium,** Cedar Avenue, Pembroke Parish (tel. 809/292-0105 for court reservations and to arrange lessons). Charges for clay are $4 for adults, $2.50 for juniors; for asphalt, $3 for adults, $1.50 for juniors. An extra $5 is charged for lit play at night. Tennis attire is mandatory. Rackets rent for $4 per hour, balls for $6 per can. Hours are Monday through Friday from 8am to 10pm, on Saturday and Sunday from 8am to 7pm.

The previously mentioned **Port Royal Golf Course,** off Middle Road, Southampton Parish (tel. 809/234-0974), also has tennis facilities. The four Plexipave courts cost $5 in daytime; night plays are $5 extra for the lights.

At the **Elbow Beach Hotel,** Paget Parish (tel. 809/236-3535), there are five LayKold courts (one only for lessons). Hotel guests are charged $5 (others pay $12) to play here. Two of the courts are lit for night play, when hotel guests pay an extra $2 while visitors pay $3.

The **Southampton Princess,** Southampton Parish (tel. 809/238-1005), has Bermuda's largest tennis court layout, with 11 True-Flex courts, 3 of them lit for night play. Hotel guests pay $10 per hour, and outsiders are charged $12 per hour, with a $2 surcharge for lights. Rackets rent for $6 per hour, and balls cost $6 per can.

Underwater Sports

Bermuda's waters are considered the clearest in the western Atlantic. Hence it's ideal for scuba diving and snorkeling as well as for helmet diving. Many of the hotels, as mentioned, have their own water-sports equipment. If not, there are several independent establishments that rent equipment.

Bermuda's oldest and largest full-service scuba-diving operation, **Blue Water Divers Co. Ltd.,** Somerset Bridge, Sandys Parish (tel. 809/234-1034), offers introductory lessons and dives at $75 for a half-day experience from March to December. Daily one- and two-tank dive trips cost $50 and $75 each, respectively, with a $15 reduction if you have equipment. Snorkeling trips are $25 per half day. Full certification courses are available through PADI, NAUI, and SSI. All equipment is provided. Reservations are necessary.

South Side Scuba Ltd., Sonesta Beach Hotel, Southampton, P.O. Box HM 1070, Hamilton HM EX, Bermuda (tel. 809/238-1833), and the Grotto Bay Beach Hotel, 11 Blue Hole Hill, Hamilton Parish CR 04, Bermuda (tel. 809/293-2915), is known for its daily two-tank wreck and reef dives, costing $65. A Resort Course lesson, plus dive, is $70. A single-tank dive goes for $50, and you can snorkel off the boat for $20. There is a $10 reduction if you have your own diving gear, except for Resort Courses; otherwise, the rates include all equipment. The company has two fully equipped, custom-built fiberglass dive boats, with the latest approved safety gear.

Bermuda Water Sports, Grotto Bay Beach Hotel, Hamilton Parish (tel. 809/293-8333), operates *Sundeck Too,* a 60-foot cruise vessel that makes glass-bottom, sightseeing, and snorkeling cruises at various times during the week, costing $29.50 per person. All snorkeling gear and buoyancy aids are provided. The cruise, lasting 3 to 3½ hours, first takes its passengers to water shallow enough to stand up in, where instructions are given. Passengers are then taken to where more underwater wonders can be seen. Service is from May to November.

Bermuda Cruises, P.O. Box DV 385, Devonshire DV BX (tel. 809/234-7038), picks up passengers from Albuoy's Point, at the dock of the Hamilton Princess hotel, and Darrell's Wharf, taking them aboard the 55-foot powerboat *Big Dipper* for a 3½-hour snorkeling experience, costing $30 per person. Masks, flippers, snorkels, floats, and buoyancy aids are provided. The boat operates May to mid-November from 9am.

Note: Spearfishing is not allowed within 1 mile of any shore, and spearguns are not permitted in Bermuda.

Waterskiing

You can waterski in the protected waters of Hamilton Harbour, Great Sound, Castle Harbour, Mangrove Bay, Spanish Point, Ferry Reach, Ely's Harbour, Riddells Bay, and Harrington Sound. May through September is the best time for this sport. Bermuda law requires that waterskiers be taken out by a licensed skipper. Only a few boat operators participate in this sport, and charges fluctuate with fuel costs. Rates include the boat, skis, safety belts, and usually an instructor. Hotels and guesthouses can assist with arrangements.

Bermuda Water Sports, Grotto Bay Beach Hotel, Hamilton Parish (tel. 809/293-2640), operates March to November, weather permitting, from 9am to 5pm. Up to three persons are taken for skiing on board a Ski Nautique. You pay $30 for 15 minutes, $50 per half hour.

The **Bermuda Waterski Centre,** Robinson's Marina, Somerset Bridge (tel. 809/234-3354), operates daily from 8:30am to 6:30pm from April to the end of October (periodically the rest of the year). Up to four people can go waterskiing with a specially designed Mastercraft. Lessons are available. The per-person charge is $40 for a half hour of skiing, $75 for one hour.

Windsurfing

For this exciting sport, **Watlington's Windsurfing Bermuda** operates at Old Cellar, Front Street, Hamilton HM 11 (tel. 809/295-0808). This is the finest windsurfing school in Bermuda. Hugh Watlington taught himself to windsurf and brought the sport to the island in 1977. He competed in the 1984 Olympics. He operates seasonally, weather permitting, daily from 9am until sunset. He makes a promise to pupils: they'll have the knack after a single 1½-hour lesson at $35. That lesson is conducted on both land and water.

---

5. Food & Drink

For years Bermuda was not considered the island of grand cuisine. Food was too often bland, lacking in flavor. In the past 20 years, however, there has been a remarkable change. Bermuda has shared the revived interest in fine cuisine that swept across America beginning in the 1970s. Chefs seem better trained than ever, and many top-notch, albeit expensive, restaurants dot the archipelago, from Sandys Parish in the west to St. George's Parish in the east.

Italian food currently enjoys much vogue. The Chinese have also landed. And fast food is available, including Kentucky Fried Chicken.

In recent years some Bermudians have shown an interest in their "roots," and many of the old-time dishes and recipes have been revived and published in books devoted to Bermudian cookery. One of these books might make an interesting souvenir.

Today Bermuda imports most of its foodstuffs from the United States. Because of the high population density, much farmland has now given way to the construction of private homes. Nevertheless, private gardens are still cultivated, and at one Bermudian home I was amazed at the variety of vegetables grown on just a small plot of land. These plants included sorrel, from which a good-tasting soup was made, along with oyster plants and Jerusalem artichokes.

As related in any history of Bermuda, Admiral Sir George Somers and his 150 castaways arrived on the shores of Bermuda from their ill-fated *Sea Venture*. Within 30 minutes they set about fishing for food. They named the fish they caught "rockfish," and later wrote about how sweet and very fat it was.

These early settlers also found wild hogs roaming the island. These swine were believed to have swum to the shore when some ship (or ships) were wrecked off the coast of Bermuda. The settlers captured these boars and fed them cedarberries. That way, when they didn't want to go fishing or the weather was too choppy, they could roast a pig.

FISH & SEAFOOD

Around the coastline of Bermuda more species of both shore and ocean fish are found than in any other place—that is, if you can believe what any local fisherman is likely to tell you. These include grunt, angel fish, yellowtail, gray snapper, and the ubiquitous rockfish. Rockfish is similar to the Bahamian grouper, and it appears on nearly every menu.

This popular fish weighs anywhere from 15 to 135 pounds (or even more). Steamed, broiled, baked, fried, or grilled, rockfish is a challenge to any chef. There's even a dish known as "rockfish maw," which I understand only the most old-fashioned cooks—a handful still left on St. David's Island—know how to prepare. It's the maw, or stomach, of a rockfish that has been stuffed with a dressing of force-meat and simmered slowly on the stove.

The most popular dish on the island is Bermuda fish chowder. It allows the cook to use the heads and fins of a fish, so nothing is wasted. Nearly every waiter will pass around a bottle of sherry peppers and some black rum for you to lace your own soup. This adds a distinctive Bermudian flavor.

Shark used to be more popular than it is today. One old-time cook confided to me, "The young kids who get married today wouldn't know how to cook shark. I grew up on it." Many traditional dishes are still made from shark, including hash, which I first enjoyed on St. David's Island many long years ago. (Shark oil, extracted from the fish, is still used by a lot of old-timers to tell the weather. It's said to be more reliable than the weatherperson.)

The Bermuda lobster—or "guinea-chick," as it is known locally—has been called a first cousin of the Maine lobster. It is the same spiny lobster that one encounters in The Bahamas, the Caribbean, or the Florida Keys. Fresh lobster is in season only from September to March. The measure of how much of a delicacy it is locally is in the high price tag that accompanies it.

The conch is not as available or as popular as it is in The Bahamas, the Caribbean, or the Florida Keys. But occasionally you can still get a good conch stew in Bermuda at one of the local restaurants.

Sea scallops, while still available, have become increasingly rare. Mussels are cherished in Bermuda. Often they are steamed, but one of the most popular dishes, and one of the most traditional, is mussel pie Bermuda style.

FRUITS & VEGETABLES

In the latter part of the 19th century, Bermuda enjoyed good revenue from such fresh vegetables as potatoes and onions, which were sold to New York markets during the nongrowing season there. To help till the land, farmers were brought in from the Azores. The Portuguese seemed to have left very little of their cuisine on the island, with one exception. In both restaurants and private homes, Portuguese red-bean soup precedes many a meal.

The Bermuda onion was once so common on the island that people of Bermuda were called "onions." Although the so-called Bermuda onion is most likely from Texas today, the onion still figures in a lot of Bermudian recipes, including onion pie. Bermuda-onion soup has kept many a family happy on a chilly night in January. It's most often flavored with Outerbridge's Original Sherry Peppers. The old people used to consume this dish around a cedarwood fire before a 1940 blight destroyed those trees.

Bermudians grow more potatoes than any other vegetable, chiefly the Pontiac red and the Kennebec white potato. At some homes in Bermuda, the Sunday breakfast of codfish and banana cooked with potatoes is still served. It is eaten all year by some residents, but it is the most traditional breakfast that can be consumed on Easter Sunday morning.

"Peas and plenty," as it is called, is a Bermudian tradition. It is still consumed at New Year's, but can be eaten on any occasion. It is black-eyed peas cooked in onions and salt pork, to which rice can be added. Old-fashioned cooks added dumplings or boiled sweet potatoes to the concoction at the last minute.

The familiar peas 'n' rice dish that is so widely consumed in The Bahamas is called Hoppin' John in Bermuda. Many locals eat this as a main dish. It can also accompany a meat or poultry plate. A pig's tail or snout was once commonly used to flavor the dish.

Bermudians and Bahamians share the same tradition of Johnny Bread, or johnnycake. This bread dates from the early settlers. It is, basically, a pan-cooked bread made with butter, milk, flour, sugar, salt, and baking powder. (Originally it was called "Journey Cake," which was eventually corrupted to johnnycake.) Fishermen could make this simple bread on the deck of their fishing vessels. They'd build a fire in a box that had been filled with sand to keep the flames from spreading to the craft itself.

The cassava was once more important in Bermuda than it is today. Nowadays it is used chiefly at Christmas to make the traditional cassava pie. Cassava is a major source of tapioca and farina.

Many legends grew up around cassava pie, which, before the advent of modern kitchen equipment, used to be very difficult to make. For example, the root of the cassava takes two years to grow, and its pulp has to be squeezed, as the juice is poisonous. There were other hazards too. Because pork was put into the pie, and in the days before refrigeration that meat could turn quickly, many diners were stricken with ptomaine poisoning at Christmas festivities.

Another dish that has a festive holiday connection is sweet-potato pudding, which was traditionally eaten on Guy Fawkes Day. People ate this pudding as if it were cake, as they'd watch the fireworks on this holiday. Because matters got out of hand, the Bermudian government has banned the use of fireworks on this holiday, but the sweet-potato pudding remains.

Bermuda grows many fresh fruits, including strawberries, Surinam cherries, guavas, avocados, and, of course, bananas. Guavas are made into jelly, which in turn is often used to make the famous Bermuda syllabub. Traditionally it is accompanied by johnnycake. Because of the British influence, you'll often see an English trifle on the menu.

The plumlike loquat also grows in Bermuda and can be made into a pie, but most often will find its way into a chutney. Introduced by Governor Reid in the mid-19th century, it was said to have come from Malta, and before that, from Japan.

My favorite springtime dessert is a Bermuda cherry pie made with orange-red Surinam cherries that have been allowed to ripen on the tree. Grenada is considered the source of the Surinam cherry, which eventually found its way to Bermuda.

A seedless navel orange—once used to pay rents on Bermuda—is still grown there. One local cook recently combined it with a sweet Bermuda onion to make a delectable and refreshing salad.

The papaya is called pawpaw here, the same as it is in the Caribbean. It is consumed either as a fresh fruit or cooked as a vegetable. The green pawpaw is prepared in ways similar to how the Americans cook squash.

Another favorite dish is pumpkin stew, which is made with many kinds of meat or poultry. Sea captains brought in curry powder, and that was often used to give the stew added flavor.

The banana is the favorite fruit of Bermudians. Recently when I arrived to visit an old friend, I was offered a banana from the tree in the backyard. It was a dwarf Cavendish banana, with a wonderfully sweet taste. The banana is not only eaten raw but used to flavor meat, fish, poultry, and desserts. Everybody has had a slice of banana bread, but what about banana pumpkin pie or banana-flavored meatloaf made with chopped meat?

DRINKS IN BERMUDA

Tap water is safe in Bermuda, but use it sparingly—it is scarce. Bermuda does not have springs or rivers to supply fresh water, and there have been shortages. The islanders must rely on rainwater. Each house has a whitewashed roof constructed to channel water into an underground cistern for later use. To cover shortages, Bermuda also has a desalinization plant.

Before bottled drinks, ginger beer—made with green ginger and lemons—was an island favorite. Some people still make it from the locally grown citrus.

Once Bermudians made their own beer from cedarberries. Nowadays beer is more likely to be "tinned" or bottled.

Many herb-based teas are still made on the island. However, with the coming of modern times these old home remedies no longer enjoy the popularity they used to. The flowers or leaves of such plants as Father John, periwinkle, and Strong Back have traditionally been used to make herbal teas.

For some 300 years rum has been considered the national drink of Bermuda. Especially popular is Bacardi rum (they have a headquarters in Bermuda) and Demerara rum (also known as black rum).

A rum swizzle is perhaps the most famous alcoholic drink in Bermuda. One version includes a mixture of Barbados rum and Demerara rum, with a dash of Angostura bitters, some lime juice, sugar, and some falernum (a sugar syrup with an almond taste).

An interesting drink is loquat liqueur, which is now exported. In its simplest form, it is made with loquats, rock candy, and gin. In more elaborate concoctions, the gin gives way to brandy and there are such spices as cinnamon, nutmeg, cloves, and allspice.

Both European and California wines are sold in Bermuda, most often at inflated prices. On the whole, wine costs more than it does in New York. If you're saving money, pick and choose your way carefully across a wine carte.

All the name-brand alcoholic beverages are sold in Bermuda, but prices on such a typical drink as scotch and soda can run as high as $5 in some places. You have to watch where you drink or else you can run up some huge bar tabs if you like more than one libation in the evening.

---

6. Recommended Books

For the most part, these titles are available at bookstores in Bermuda, but hard to find in the United States.

HISTORY

Ives, Vernon A., ed. *The Rich Papers—Letters from Bermuda* (Bermuda National Trust and University of Toronto Press, 1984).

Kennedy, Sister Jean de Chantal. *Biography of a Colonial Town* (Bermuda Bookstores Publisher, 1961).

Smith, James E. *Slavery in Bermuda* (Vantage Press, 1976).

Tucker, Mrs. Terry. *Bermuda's Story* (Bermuda Bookstores Publisher, 1959).

Zuill, W. S. *The Story of Bermuda and Her People* (Macmillan Caribbean, 1983).

GENERAL

Hyde, Bryden Bordley. *Bermuda Antique Furniture and Silver* (Bermuda National Trust, 1971).

Robinson, Dr. Kenneth E. *Heritage* (Macmillan Education and Berkeley Educational Society, 1979).

FLORA & FAUNA

Brown, Ann B., and Outerbridge, Jean M. *Bermuda Houses and Gardens* (Garden Club of Bermuda, 1979).

Collett, Jill. *Bermuda: Her Plants and Gardens, 1609–1850* (Macmillan Caribbean, 1987).

Mowbray, Louis S. *A Guide to the Reef, Shore and Game Fish of Bermuda* (published by the author; third edition, 1976).

PLANNING A TRIP TO BERMUDA

Getting to Bermuda has now become easier than ever, thanks to more frequent flights, often direct ones, from such gateway cities as New York, Boston, and Washington, D.C., among others.

For those who'd like to relive the glamorous days of "cruising down to Bermuda," several cruise lines sail there from spring until late autumn.

In this chapter I'll survey some of the most popular air carriers and their routes from the American mainland, as well as some vacation alternatives, and provide advice about many practical details for those contemplating a foreign trip.

1. Information, Entry Requirements, Customs & Money

INFORMATION

Before you go, you can obtain much valuable information by writing to various tourist offices on the U.S. mainland. In the **United States,** they are located in New York, Suite 201, 310 Madison Ave., New York, NY 10017 (tel. 212/818-9800, or toll free 800/223-6106); Boston, Suite 1010, 44 School St., Boston, MA 02108 (tel. 617/742-0405); Chicago, Suite 1070, Randolph Wacker Building, 150 North Wacker Dr., Chicago, IL 60606 (tel. 312/782-5486); and Atlanta, Suite 2008, 235 Peachtree St. NE, Atlanta, GA 30303 (tel. 404/524-1541). In **Canada,** it's at Suite 1004, 1200 Bay St., Toronto, Ontario, Canada M5R 2A5 (tel. 416/923-9600).

Other useful sources are, of course, newspapers and magazines. You may also want to contact the State Department for background bulletins. Write to **Superintendent of Documents, U.S. Government Printing Office,** Washington, DC 20402 (tel. 202/783-3238), for a list of what's available.

ENTRY REQUIREMENTS

A U.S. or Canadian citizen does not need a passport to enter Bermuda, although one will serve as your required identification.

Otherwise, visitors entering from the United States are required by Bermuda Immigration authorities to have in their possession any one of the following items: a birth certificate or certified copy, a U.S. naturalization certificate, a U.S. Alien Registration card, a U.S. reentry permit, or a U.S. voter registration card bearing the signature of the holder.

Visitors entering from Canada who do not have a valid passport in their possession must have a birth certificate or certified copy, a Canadian certificate of citizenship, or a valid passport plus proof of their Landed Immigrant status.

If you stay longer than three weeks from your arrival date, you must apply to the Chief Immigration Officer for an extended stay. You must have a return or onward ticket.

All travelers are taxable under the Passenger Tax Act of 1972. For air and ship passengers, see "Taxes" under "Fast Facts" later in this chapter.

CUSTOMS

Bermudian Customs

Visitors may bring into Bermuda duty-free apparel and articles for their personal use, including sports equipment, cameras, 200 cigarettes, 1 quart of liquor, 1 quart of wine, and approximately 20 pounds of meat. Other foodstuffs may be dutiable. All imports may be inspected on arrival. Visitors entering Bermuda may claim a duty-free gift allowance.

U.S. Customs

When you return home, you may take $400 worth of merchandise duty free if you've been outside the United States for 48 hours or more and have not claimed a similar exemption within the past 30 days. Articles valued above the $400 duty-free limit but not over $1,000 will be assessed at a flat duty rate of 10%. Gifts for your personal use, not for business purposes, may be included in the $400 exemption. Unsolicited gifts totaling $50 a day may be sent home duty free. You are limited to 1 liter of wine, liqueur, *or* liquor. Five cartons of cigarettes can be brought home duty free. U.S. Customs preclearance is available for all scheduled flights. Passengers leaving for the U.S. must fill out written declaration forms before clearing U.S. Customs in Bermuda. The forms are available at hotels, travel agencies, and airlines in Bermuda.

Collect receipts for all purchases made abroad. Sometimes merchants might suggest a false receipt for you, understating the value of the goods. *Beware:* You could be involved in a "sting" operation, and the merchant might be an informer to U.S. Customs. In addition, you must declare on your Customs form the nature and value of all gifts received during your stay abroad. If you carry expensive cameras and/or jewelry with you, it's prudent to carry proof that you purchased them within the borders of the U.S. mainland.

If you need more specific guidance, write to the **U.S. Customs Service,** 1301 Constitution Ave., P.O. Box 7407, Washington, DC 20229, requesting the pamphlet *Know Before You Go,* which is mailed free. If you use prescription drugs, carry your medication in clearly marked containers from a pharmacy. A handwritten prescription from your doctor is also good evidence.

Canadian Customs

For total clarification, write for the booklet *I Declare,* issued by **Revenue Canada Customs Department,** Communications Branch, Mackenzie Avenue, Ottawa, Ontario K1A 0L5. Canada allows its citizens a $300 exemption, and they are allowed to bring back duty free 200 cigarettes, 2 pounds of tobacco, 40 ounces of liquor, and 50 cigars. In addition, they are allowed to mail gifts into Canada from abroad at the rate of $40 (CDN) a day, provided they are unsolicited and aren't alcohol or tobacco. On the package, mark "Unsolicited gift, under $40 value."

MONEY

Cash/Currency

Legal tender is the Bermuda dollar (BD$), which is divided into 100 cents. Prior to 1972, the Bermuda dollar was pegged to the pound sterling. Since then, it has been pegged through gold to the U.S. dollar on an equal basis. That is, BD$1 equals U.S. $1. U.S. currency is generally accepted at par in shops, restaurants, and hotels. Currencies from the United Kingdom and all other foreign countries are not accepted. However, such currencies can be exchanged for Bermuda dollars at banks. Canadian, British, and all other currencies are liable to daily fluctuations. Banking and credit-card transactions in all foreign currencies involving currency exchange are subject to exchange rates. U.S. traveler's checks are cashed almost anywhere, and credit cards are accepted in many shops and restaurants and in some, certainly not all, hotels. When booking a room at a hotel, check to see if it accepts credit cards.

Traveler's Checks

Before leaving home, purchase traveler's checks and arrange to carry some ready cash. U.S. citizens should usually take about $200 in cash as a safeguard against unforseen problems and inconvenience.

American Express (tel. toll free 800/221-7282 in the U.S. and Canada) is the most widely recognized traveler's check abroad. Other agencies include **Bank of America** (tel. toll free 800/227-3460 in the U.S., or 415/624-5400 collect in Canada), **Citicorp** (tel. toll free 800/645-6556 in the U.S., or 813/623-1709 collect in Canada), **MasterCard International** (tel. toll free 800/223-9920 in the U.S., or 212/974-5696 collect in Canada), **Barclays Bank** (tel. toll free 800/221-2426 in the U.S. and Canada), and **Thomas Cook** (tel. toll free 800/223-7373 in the U.S., or 212/974-5696 collect in Canada).

Credit Cards

Credit cards are in wide use in Bermuda. VISA and MasterCard are the major cards used, although American Express and, to a lesser extent, Diners Club are also popular.

2. When to Go

Bermuda enjoys a mild climate, and the term "Bermuda high" has come to mean sunny days and clear skies. Bermuda, being farther north in the Atlantic than The Bahamas, is much cooler in winter. Its slow season, or off-season, begins in December, lasting until around the first of March, when business starts to pick up. Many hotels, therefore, quote their low-season rates in winter. During the autumn and winter, many hotels also quote some very attractive package deals. Other hotels, because of lack of business, shut down for a week or two, maybe even a month or two, in winter.

The off-season (that is, fall to spring) hotel reductions in Bermuda—which could range anywhere from 20% to as much as 60% in some extreme cases—are emphasized in this guide by being set in *italics*. It's a bonanza for cost-conscious travelers, especially those without children, who are free to travel to Bermuda from November to March.

CLIMATE

Bermuda is a semitropical island, and the Gulf Stream, flowing between it and North America, keeps the climate temperate. There is no rainy season, and no normal month of excess rain. Showers may be heavy at times, but the skies clear quickly. Summer temperatures are recorded from May to mid-November, with the warmest weather in July, August, and September. The thermometer rarely rises above 85° Fahrenheit. There's nearly always a cool breeze in the evening, and accommodations that require it are air-conditioned. Springlike temperatures prevail from mid-December to late March, with the average ranging from the low 60s to 70°. It's usually warm enough for swimming in December and January. From mid-November to mid-December and from late March through April, either spring or summer weather can occur, so visitors should be prepared for both.

Hurricanes do sometimes churn up the Atlantic, bringing high winds to the area, but they do not often actually strike Bermuda. At any rate, the people know how to prepare for a big blow, and they'll see to it that you don't suffer. An efficient warning system gives ample notice of the approach of a storm.

A look at the official chart on temperature and rainfall will show you what to expect during the time you plan to visit Bermuda.

AVERAGE TEMPERATURE & RAINFALL: BERMUDA

Month	Average Temperature	Average Inches of Rainfall
January	64.8°F (18.3°C)	4.06
February	63.5°F (17.5°C)	5.05
March	64.0°F (17.8°C)	4.63
April	65.4°F (18.5°C)	3.01
May	70.0°F (21.1°C)	3.86
June	75.1°F (24.0°C)	5.17
July	78.6°F (25.9°C)	3.98
August	80.0°F (26.6°C)	5.27
September	78.5°F (25.8°C)	5.25
October	74.8°F (23.8°C)	6.02
November	69.1°F (20.6°C)	4.48
December	65.4°F (18.5°C)	3.82

HOLIDAYS

The following public holidays are observed in Bermuda (the ones listed without a date change from year to year): New Year's Day (January 1), Good Friday, Easter, Bermuda Day (May 24), the Queen's Birthday (first or second Monday in June), Cup Match Days (cricket; Thursday and Friday preceding first Monday in August), Labour Day (first Monday in September), Christmas Day (December 25), and Boxing Day (December 26). Public holidays that fall on a Saturday or Sunday are usually celebrated on the following Monday.

SPECIAL EVENTS

Bermuda College Weeks

Beginning March 2 and lasting till April 13, Bermuda College Weeks is an annual spring odyssey for lots of American and Canadian youth. It is estimated that at least 10,000 students flock here every year for this spring ritual. College Weeks is actually run under the auspices of the Bermuda Department of Tourism, although they try to discourage some of the more exuberant excesses of previous years, like putting goats in elevators and bottles of laundry detergent in swimming pools.

Bermuda, as everybody knows, is an upmarket resort. Many hoteliers have told me that the island likes to attract families who make a beginning salary of $40,000 to $50,000 a year. Why then is there such an official endorsement of these hell-raising College Weeks? The Bermudians wisely know that if the young people flock to Bermuda while they are still in college, they are likely to return with their emerging families when they establish themselves in careers.

These weeks began in 1933 as Rugby Weeks. Rugby teams from such Ivy League schools as Yale came to compete against British or Bermudian teams. "Where the Boys Are," to borrow the popular song title, led to "Where the Girls Are." A tradition was born.

Complimentary beach parties, boat cruises, and various events are arranged by the Department of Tourism. Those who have a valid college identification card are issued a College Week Courtesy Card. That has been called a springtime passport to a week of beach parties, lunches, boat cruises, dances, and entertainment. And it's all free, a gift of the Bermudian government.

A big beach bash is always staged at the Elbow Beach Surf Club, one of the most popular student hangouts. There's also a party at Horseshoe Bay, where students enjoy limbo dancers and engage in such events as tugs-of-war.

Bermuda Rendezvous Time

If you need to escape from the cold of winter but feel that you don't fit the Florida scene, Bermuda may be just the place for you. If you are not expecting to bake on the beach but do want to be outside and active, walking, playing tennis or golf, or just reading a book on the lawn, Bermuda is perfect.

As the weather is not always favorable, the government knows that to keep tourists happy, amusements must be provided. Therefore, they created Rendezvous Time, November 15 to March 31. During this time, walking tours of the historic towns of Hamilton and St. George's (which is as old as Williamsburg) are sponsored, plus a tour of the Botanical Gardens. Pipe and drum music with Scottish dancers, a fashion show and tea, a thriving craft market, a skirling ceremony, a treasure hunt, and many other special events are offered free to the winter visitor. Specific dates for these and other events cited below can be obtained in advance from the offices of the **Department of Tourism** (see "Information" under "Fast Facts" later in this chapter), from your hotel or guesthouse management, or from local publications when you are in Bermuda.

Bermuda Festival

During the winter months, the Bermuda calendar is jam-packed with such events as golf and tennis invitationals, an international marathon race, a dog show, open house and garden tours, and, of course, **the Bermuda Festival,** the six-week International Festival of the Performing Arts, held during January and February, in Hamilton, featuring drama, dance, jazz, classical and popular music, and other entertainment. The best of artists come from Europe, England, Canada, and the U.S. Some tickets are reserved until 48 hours before curtain time for visitors. For details, write the **Bermuda Festival,** Box HM 297, Hamilton HM AX, Bermuda (tel. 809/ 295-1291).

Homes & Gardens

Each spring, usually from the end of March to mid-May, the **Garden Club of Bermuda** lays out the welcome mat at a number of private homes and gardens that are open to view. Admission, payable on the viewing day only, is $10. A different set of houses, conveniently located in the same parish, is open every Wednesday during this springtime viewing.

Normally a total of 20 homes participate in the program, many dating back to the 17th and 18th centuries. One year, a tour included Blackburn Place, a stately 1730 home that features extensive cedarwork throughout and is set in acres of lush gardens. Other houses of note were Spanish Grange, once the home of the English playwright Sir Terrence Rattigan, and Inwood, built in 1700 and recently restored to its original splendor. Knapton House (circa 1720), whose first owner was one of Bermuda's early silversmiths, was also included on the tour, but participants vary from year to year.

Bermuda's homes have always had a special character and atmosphere, and these spring tours afford a marvelous glimpse into the history of the island.

Other Events

The **Beating of Retreat** ceremony of the Bermuda Regiment and massed pipes and drums is held on the last Wednesday in every month except August, from April through October. This takes place on Front Street in Hamilton at 9pm. Periodically it's also held in Somerset and St. George's.

A historic and traditional event takes place in April—the **Peppercorn Ceremony,** when His Excellency the governor collects the annual rent of one peppercorn for use of the island's Old State House in St. George's.

An **agricultural show** in April comprises a three-day exhibit of Bermuda's best fruits, flowers, vegetables, and livestock, as well as featuring equestrian and other ring events.

May is **Bermuda Heritage Month,** when cultural and sporting activities are held, culminating in **Bermuda Day,** May 24, which is a public holiday.

The **Queen's Birthday** (first or second Monday in June) is celebrated by a parade on Front Street in Hamilton.

A truly festive time is had by all during **Cup Match and Somers Days** (held on Thursday and Friday before the first Monday in August). The spectacular match pits the east and west end of the island in that great traditional English sport, cricket.

If you're here in November, you may want to see the traditional ceremony and military guard of honor connected with the **opening of Parliament** by His Excellency the governor as the queen's personal representative.

On **Remembrance Day,** November 11, a gala parade is held, with Bermudian police, British and U.S. military units, Bermudians, and veterans' organizations taking part.

There are numerous **sports events,** ranging from marathon racing to yacht competition to tennis and golf tournaments. For information on the particular field of your choice, ask at your hotel or at the Department of Tourism. (See also "Sports & Recreation" in Chapter I.)

---

3. Health, Safety, Insurance & Other Concerns

HEALTH

Traveling to Bermuda need not impair your health in any way. But if you need treatment while there, finding a good doctor is no real problem (and all of them speak English). See "Fast Facts," below, for specific locations and addresses.

It's a good idea to carry all your vital medicines and drugs (the legal kind) with you in your carry-on luggage, in case your checked luggage is lost.

Water

Although tap water is generally considered safe to drink, if you have a delicate stomach it is better to avoid it and drink mineral water instead. This applies even to iced drinks. Stick to beer, hot tea, or soft drinks. Why risk a vacation with a stomach upset?

Sunburn

Actually, one of the most dangerous elements in Bermuda is the very thing you might have gone there to enjoy: the sun. It can be brutal, especially if you're going from a winterly climate and haven't been exposed to it in some time.

Take such precautions as wearing sunglasses, a hat (wide-brimmed if possible), a coverup for your shoulders, and a sunscreen lotion. Experts also advise that you should limit your time on the beach the first day.

Insects & Pests

Mosquitoes exist, but rarely are they the dangerous malaria-carrying kind. Nevertheless, they are still a nuisance. One of the biggest menaces is the "no-see-ums." Even if you can't see these gnats, you sure can "feel-um," as any local will agree. These biting little insects appear mainly in the early evening. Even screens can't keep these critters out. You'll have to spray yourself with your favorite bug repellent.

Vaccinations

Vaccinations aren't required to enter Bermuda if you're coming from a "disease-free" country such as the United States or Canada.

SAFETY

There is no need for any particular crime alert for Bermuda. Occasionally every few years racial tensions explode, and there are acts of violence. But for the most part the Bermudians are a peaceful people, whites coexisting harmoniously with blacks, especially now since blacks are taking more and more active roles in politics.

However, don't be lulled into any false security. Crime does exist. Protect your valuables, especially when you're at the beach. Lock your moped each time you come to visit a place. Extreme valuables should be placed in your hotel safe (if your hotel is big enough to have one) and never left carelessly in your room.

It is usually safe to go anywhere in Bermuda, but, here again, caution should be exercised, particularly late at night and especially if you're a woman traveling alone.

INSURANCE

Before purchasing any additional insurance, check your homeowner's, automobile, and medical insurance policies. Also check the membership contracts of automobile and travel clubs and credit cards.

Many homeowners' insurance policies cover theft of luggage during foreign travel and loss of such documents as your passport or your airline ticket. Coverage is usually limited to about $500 U.S. To submit a claim on your insurance, remember that you'll need police reports or a statement from a local medical authority.

Many credit-card companies insure their users in case of a travel accident, provided that the travel cost was paid with their card. Sometimes fraternal organizations have policies that protect members in case of sickness or accidents abroad.

Often flight insurance against a canceled trip is written into tickets paid for by credit cards from such companies as VISA and American Express. Many tour operators or insurance agents provide this type of insurance for a reasonable additional supplement.

Among the companies offering insurance policies for travel abroad are **Travel Guard International,** 1100 Center Point Dr., Stevens Point, WI 54481 (tel. toll free 800/634-0644 in Wisconsin, or toll free 800/826-1300 outside Wisconsin); **Travel Insurance Pak,** Travelers Insurance Co., 1 Tower Sq., 15 NB, Hartford, CT 06183-5040 (tel. 203/277-2318, or toll free 800/243-3174); **Mutual of Omaha (Tele-Trip),** 3201 Farnam St., Omaha, NB 68131 (tel. 402/345-2400, or toll free 800/228-9792); **HealthCare Abroad (MEDEX),** 243 Church St. NW, Suite 100D, Vienna, VA 22180 (tel. 703/255-9800, or toll free 800/237-6615); **WorldCare Travel Assistance Association,** 605 Market St., Suite 1300, San Francisco, CA 94105 (tel. 415/541-4991, or toll free 800/666-4993); and **Access America,** 600 Third Ave., P.O. Box 807, New York, NY 10163-0807 (tel. 212/490-5345, or toll free 800/284-8300).

---

4. What to Pack

CLOTHING

Cotton slacks or shorts are just fine for going around during the day. Some women wear skirts and shifts, either with a T-shirt or a polo shirt. Both men and women who burn easily should wear long-sleeved shirts and long-legged pants.

Summer travelers don't need suits, but men in winter might want to wear a jacket with an open neck if they're dining in one of the more famous spots. Don't forget that evenings tend to be cooler, especially from October to March, and sometimes restaurants and bars are overly air-conditioned.

Try to fashion a wardrobe of lightweight cotton wherever possible, avoiding nylon and other synthetics, which become hot and sticky in these climes. Khaki pants are acceptable for men in most places. Of course, anything that doesn't have to be ironed or dry-cleaned is always a good idea.

LUGAGGE

Always pack as light as possible. Airlines are increasingly strict about how much luggage you can bring abroad. Checked luggage should not measure more than a total of 62 inches (width plus length plus height) and weigh no more than 70 pounds. Carry-on luggage should measure no more than 45 inches (width plus length plus height) and fit under your seat or in the overhead bin.

---

5. Tips for the Disabled, Seniors, Students & Families

FOR THE DISABLED

Hotels rarely give much publicity as to what facilities, if any, they offer the handicapped, so it's always better to contact the hotel directly. You can also write the **Society for the Advancement of Travel for the Handicapped,** P.O. Box HM 449, Hamilton HM BX, Bermuda.

Before you go, there are many agencies that provide advance data to help you plan your trip. The **Travel Information Service,** Moss Rehabilitation Hospital, 12th Street and Tabor Road, Philadelphia, PA 19141 (tel. 215/456-9600), provides names and addresses of accessible hotels, restaurants, and attractions, often based on firsthand reports of travelers who have been there. It charges $5 per package for this information.

You may also want to subscribe to *The Itinerary,* P.O. Box 2012, Bayonne, NJ 07002-2012 (tel. 201/858-3400), at $10 a year. This travel magazine, published bimonthly, is filled with news about travel aids for the handicapped, special tours, information on accessibility, and other matters.

You may also want to consider joining a tour specifically for disabled visitors. Names and addresses of such tour operators can be obtained by writing to the **Society for the Advancement of Travel for the Handicapped,** 26 Court St., Brooklyn, NY 11242 (tel. 718/858-5483). Yearly membership dues in this society are $40, or $25 for senior citizens and students. Send a self-addressed envelope.

One such tour company is **Whole Person Tours,** P.O. Box 1084, Bayonne, NJ 07002-1084 (tel. 201/858-3400, or toll free 800/462-2237 outside New Jersey).

You might also consider the **Federation of the Handicapped,** 211 W. 14th St., New York, NY 10011 (tel. 212/206-4200), which offers summer tours for members, who pay a yearly fee of $4.

For the blind, the best source is the **American Foundation for the Blind,** 15 W. 16th St., New York, NY 10011 (tel. toll free 800/232-5463), which offers information on travel and various requirements for bringing in seeing-eye dogs. For those legally blind, it also issues identification cards for $6.

FOR SENIORS

Many discounts are available for seniors, but be advised that you have to be a member of an association to obtain certain discounts.

For your initial source of information, obtain *Travel Tips for Senior Citizens* (publication #8970), distributed for $1 by the **Superintendent of Documents, U.S. Government Printing Office,** Washington, DC 20402 (tel. 202/783-5238). Another booklet—and this one is distributed free—is called *101 Tips for the Mature Traveler.* Write or phone **Grand Circle Travel,** 347 Congress St., Suite 3A, Boston, MA 02210 (tel. 617/350-7500, or toll free 800/221-2610).

SAGA International Holidays, 120 Boylston St., Boston, MA 02116 (tel. toll free 800/343-0273), is also well known for its all-inclusive tours for seniors. They prefer that joiners be at least 60 years old or older. Insurance is included in the net price of any of their tours. Membership is $5 a year.

The **American Association of Retired Persons,** 1909 K St. NW, Washington, DC 20049 (tel. 202/872-4700), offers members discounts on car rentals, hotels, and airfares, even sightseeing in some cases. Its affiliate, **AARP Travel Service,** 100 North Sepulveda Blvd., Suite 1020, El Segundo, CA 90024 (tel. toll free 800/227-7737), offers tours and, for those traveling independently, a list of discounts available on the road.

Information is also available from the **National Council of Senior Citizens,** 925 15th St. NW, Washington, DC 20005 (tel. 202/347-8800). A nonprofit organization, the council charges $12 per person to join (couples pay $16), for which you receive a monthly newsletter, part of which is devoted to travel tips. Discounts on hotel and auto rentals are also featured.

FOR SINGLES

One company that has made heroic efforts to match single travelers with likeminded companions is now the largest and best-listed such company in the United States. Jens Jurgen, the German-born founder, charges $36 to $66 for a six-month listing in his well-publicized records. New applicants desiring a travel companion fill out a form stating their preferences and needs. They then receive a minilisting of the kinds of potential partners who might be suitable for travel. Companions of the same or opposite sex can be requested. For an application and more information, write to **Jens Jurgen,** Travel Companion, P.O. Box P-833, Amityville, NY 11701 (tel. 516/454-0880).

Singleworld, 401 Theodore Fremd Ave., Rye, NY 10580 (tel. 914/967-3334, or toll free 800/223-6490), is a travel agency that operates tours geared to solo travel. Two basic types of tours are available, either a youth-oriented tour for people under 35 or else jaunts for any age. Annual dues are $25.

Another agency to check is **Grand Circle Travel,** 347 Congress St., Boston, MA 02210 (tel. 617/350-7500, or toll free 800/221-2610), which offers escorted tours and cruises for retired people, including singles. Once you book one of their trips, membership is included; in addition, you get vouchers providing discounts for future trips.

FOR STUDENTS

Bona fide students can avail themselves of a number of discounts in travel. The most wide-ranging travel service for students is the **Council on International Educational Exchange (CIEE),** 205 E. 42nd St., New York, NY 10017 (tel. 212/661-1414). This outfit runs the spectrum on travel-related services for students, providing details about budget travel, study abroad, working permits, and insurance. It also sells a number of helpful publications, including the *Student Travel Catalogue* ($1). To bona fide students, it issues an International Student Identity Card for $10.

To keep costs trimmed, membership in the **International Youth Hostel Federation (IYHF)** is recommended. Many countries have branch offices, including **American Youth Hostels (AYH),** P.O. Box 37613, Washington, DC 20013-7613 (tel. 202/783-6161). Membership costs $25 annually unless you're under 18, then only $10.

FOR FAMILIES

Bermuda contends for top position on the world list of places for vacations for the entire family. The smallest toddlers can spend blissful hours on sandy beaches and in the shallow seawater or pools constructed with them in mind. There's no end to the fascinating pursuits offered for older children too, ranging from boat rides to shell collecting to horseback riding, hiking, even discoing. Perhaps yours are old enough to learn to snorkel and explore the wonderland of underwater Bermuda.

There are important pointers to keep in mind when you're planning a family vacation so that your trip is plagued with a minimum of worry. Most resort hotels will advise you as to what there is in the way of fun for all, and many have play directors and supervised activities for the young of various age groups. However, there are some tips for making the trip a success that parents should attend to in advance.

☐ **Take along a "security blanket" for your child.** This might be a pacifier, a favorite toy, or books the child likes especially—something to make him or her feel at home. An older offspring might take along a treasure such as a baseball cap, a favorite T-shirt (even though there'll be plenty to buy down there), or some special trinket or good-luck piece.

☐ **Take protection from the sun.** For tiny tots, this should include a sun umbrella, while the whole family will need sunscreen (a 15 is a good idea) and sunglasses.

☐ **Take along anti-insect lotions and sprays.** You'll probably need both of these to repel such little unwanted island denizens as mosquitoes and sand fleas as well as to ease the itching and possible other aftereffects of insect bites.

☐ **Arrange ahead for necessities,** such as a crib and a bottle warmer, as well as for cots in your room for larger children. Find out if the place where you're staying stocks baby food, and if not, take it with you.

☐ **Draw up rules** for your family to follow during your holiday. These should be flexible, of course—after all, this trip is for fun. But guidelines on bedtime, eating, keeping tidy, being in the sun, even shopping and spending, can help make everybody's vacation more enjoyable.

Babysitters can be found for you by most hotels. Talk with the sitter yourself, and introduce her or him to those to be cared for before you leave the hotel room or nursery.

In addition to fundamentals that you should take along whenever you travel with children—such as a thermometer, basic first-aid supplies, and medications your doctor may suggest—don't forget swimsuits, beach and pool toys, waterwings for tiny mites, flip-flops for everybody, and terrycloth robes.

For $35, **Family Travel Services** will send you 10 issues of a newsletter about traveling with children. Subscribers to the newsletter can also call in with travel questions, but only from 10am to noon Monday through Friday. Contact **TWYCH,** which stands for Travel With Your Children, 80 Eighth Ave., New York, NY 10011 (tel. 212/206-0688).

---

6. Alternative/Adventure Travel

Offbeat, alternative modes of travel often cost less and yet are far more enriching ways to travel. Some of the organizations arranging such travel are listed below.

EDUCATIONAL TRAVEL

The best information is available at the **Council on International Educational Exchange (CIEE),** 205 E. 42nd St., New York, NY 10017 (tel. 212/661-1414). This outfit not only arranges low-cost travel opportunities, but offers information about working or studying abroad. It's best to request a copy of their 455-page *Work, Study, Travel Abroad: The Whole World Handbook,* costing $11.95 if you'd like it mailed. Outlined are some 1,000 study opportunities abroad.

One of the most dynamic organizations offering postretirement studies for senior citizens is **Elderhostel,** 75 Federal St., Boston, MA 02110-1941 (tel. 617/426-7788), established in 1975. Most courses last for two or three weeks and are a good value, considering that airfare, hotel accommodations in student dormitories or modest inns, all meals, and tuition are included. Courses involve no homework, are ungraded, and center mostly on the liberal arts. Participants must be age 60 or older. However, if two members go as a couple, only one member need be 60 or over. Write for their free newsletter and a list of upcoming courses and destinations.

For persons over 50 years of age, **Interhostel,** developed by the University of New Hampshire, offers two-week programs escorted by a university faculty or staff member, arranged in conjunction with a host college, university, or cultural institution. Participants can extend a stay beyond two weeks if they wish. Programs consist of cultural affairs and intellectual activities, with field trips to museums and other centers of interest. For information, get in touch with the **University of New Hampshire,** Division of Continuing Education, 6 Garrison Ave., Durham, NH 03824 (tel. 603/826-1147). It's best to phone between 1:30 and 4pm EST.

HOMESTAYS OR VISITS

The international, interfaith **Servas** ("to serve" in Esperanto), 11 John St., Suite 706, New York, NY 10038 (tel. 212/267-0252), is a nonprofit, nongovernmental network of travelers and hosts whose goal is to help build world peace, goodwill, and understanding. They do this by providing opportunities for deeper, more personal contacts among people of diverse cultural and political backgrounds. Servas travelers are invited to share living space in a privately owned home, staying without charge for visits lasting a minimum of two days. Visitors pay a $45 annual fee, fill out an application, and are interviewed for suitability by one or more than 200 Servas interviewers throughout the country. They then receive a Servas directory listing the names and addresses of Servas hosts who allow (and encourage) visitors in their homes. This program embraces 112 countries, including Bermuda and The Bahamas.

Friendship Force, 575 S. Tower, 1 CNN Center, Atlanta, GA 30303 (tel. 404/522-9490), is a nonprofit organization existing for the sole purpose of fostering and encouraging friendship among people worldwide. Dozens of branch offices throughout North America arrange en masse visits, usually once a year. Because of group bookings, the airfare to the host country is usually less than you'd pay if you bought an individual APEX ticket. Each participant is required to spend two weeks in the host country, one full week of which will be as a guest in the home of a family. Most volunteers spend the second week traveling in the host country.

For $5.95, the **International Visitors Information Service, 733** 15th St. NW, Suite 300, Washington, DC 20005 (tel. 202/783-6540), will send you a directory listing opportunities for contact with local residents in foreign countries. It's called *Meet the People.*

Experiment in International Living, Kipling Road (P.O. Box 676), Brattleboro, VT 05301 (tel. 802/257-7751), often provides a chance to sample another culture by actually living with a family in one of the 40 participating countries. Students aged 16 to 22 are placed with families for two to four weeks, during which time they, in essence, "become one of the family," taking part in daily activities. After the program ends, many students stay on and plan a tour of their own.

WORK CAMPS

If you're 16 to 18 years of age, you may want to involve yourself in an increasingly popular method of travel. Joining with other worldwide volunteers, you pay your own airfare or boat fare; but once you arrive at a destination, you work for your keep, often in a group of 6 to 30 other like-minded volunteers, for periods of about two or three weeks. Since the work week is limited to 30 hours, you have plenty of free time to explore your surroundings.

The work you engage in has been called "socially significant," but that doesn't mean you'll have to go and carry out someone's garbage. One of the work tasks, for example, might be restoring a national park whose hiking trails have been badly damaged in a hurricane. The lodgings and communal meals are of the "boot camp" variety.

For more information, contact the already mentioned **Council on International Educational Exchange (CIEE), 205** E. 42nd St., New York, NY 10071 (tel. 212/661-1414). For those 18 or over, it offers a booklet detailing the possibilities in international work camps. Applications cost $125.

HOME EXCHANGES

If you don't mind "staying put," you can avail yourself of a "house swap"—as it's often called. It certainly keeps costs low if you don't mind a stranger living in your mainland home or apartment. Sometimes the exchange includes use of the family car.

Many directories are published detailing the possibilities for this type of service. Sometimes it's a straight house exchange for vacation purposes; at other times it's more complicated. For example, your teenage child might be housed free in exchange for free room and board when the host child visits your hometown. In this day of increased crime, sometimes the deal is for a "house-sitter." One problem is, there can be no guarantee you'll find a house or apartment in the area you're seeking if you subscribe to one of the following programs.

International Home Exchange Service, P.O. Box 190070, San Francisco, CA 94119 (tel. 415/435-3497), has a network spread over three dozen countries, with about 8,000 listings. For a $35 fee, you can obtain copies of a trio of annual directories, and you're given a chance to list your house on the exchange market. A photograph of your house can be printed for $8.50 extra, and senior citizens (65 or older) are given a 10% discount.

Although it has fewer listings, **Vacation Exchange Club,** 12006 111th Ave., Suite 12, Youngtown, AZ 85363 (tel. 602/972-2186), offers the same service for less. For $24.70, you get two directories a year and you're listed in one. Or else for $16 you can get both booklets without a personal listing.

World Wide Exchange, 1344 Pacific Ave., Suite 103, Santa Cruz, CA 95060 (tel. 408/476-4206), will, for a yearly membership fee of $45, give you one listing for your house, apartment, or motorhome. For the fee you also get a trio of their annual booklets with plenty of listings.

SPA TREATMENTS

Full-fledged spa facilities are available at the **Sonesta Beach Hotel and Spa,** Southampton (tel. 809/238-8122, or toll free 800/766-3782 in the U.S.), which is recognized by some experts as one of the top 10 health-and-beauty spas of the world. European-staffed, it combines the health-and-fitness regimes so popular at American spas. Here they offer many exotic and beneficial treatments, one being Ionithermie, the inch-reducing treatment from Europe, as well as deluxe facial care from Paris, ancient forms of therapeutic and relaxing massage such as aromatherapy and reflexology, and Swedish massage. Some people check into the hotel on calorie-controlled four- or seven-day programs. From that moment on, the client's time each day will be almost totally occupied from 8:30am to 7pm with the likes of aerobics, skin and body care, supervised indoor and outdoor stretching exercises, massages, facials, and beauty regimes.

The facilities can also be used by hotel guests or outsiders who opt for pin-pointed treatments rather than the full spa treatments. The up-to-date accoutrements include Universal gym equipment, saunas, steambaths, and massage rooms. The staff directs five-times-a-day exercise classes, which outsiders can join for $6 per lesson. Each procedure is priced separately for nonpackage participants. For example, a 55-minute body massage costs $45 plus tip. For after-workout pick-me-ups, there's a beauty salon adjacent to the health spa for those crowning final touches.

---

7. Getting There

BY AIR

From North America's East Coast, you can be in Bermuda in 2 hours by plane, which is not only the fastest but also the most economical means of transport there.

The Regular Fares

The best strategy for securing the lowest airfare is to shop around. Keep calling the airlines. Most of them make their best deals for tickets ordered at least seven days before a traveler's anticipated departure, with stopovers of at least two days. Prices fluctuate with the season, but tend to remain competitive among the companies as they vie for shares of the lucrative Bermuda runs.

Peak season, which means summer in Bermuda, is the most expensive time to go; **basic season,** during the winter months, offers the least expensive fares. **Shoulder season** refers to the spring and fall months in between.

Most airlines offer an assortment of **fares** from **first class,** the most expensive, through **business class** to **economy.** The latter is the lowest-priced regular airfare carrying no special restrictions or requirements. Most airlines also offer promotional fares, which carry stringent requirements such as advance purchase, minimum stay, and cancellation penalties. The most common such fare is the **APEX (Advance Purchase Excursion).** Land arrangements (that is, prebooking of hotel rooms) are often tied in with promotional fares offered by airlines.

Choice of Airline

Several airlines fly from North America into Bermuda, but one that seems especially committed to the efficient servicing of the island is **American Airlines** (tel. toll free 800/433-7300), which flies in daily nonstop from two of its most modern and busiest hubs, Raleigh/Durham, North Carolina, and New York's John F. Kennedy International Airport. From Raleigh/Durham (which lies on almost the same latitude as Bermuda), the airline offers convenient connections to at least 50 North American destinations (including the three airports of the New York City region), as well as connections to such European destinations as Paris, Zurich, and Brussels.

Other airlines servicing the archipelago include the well-recommended **United Airlines** (tel. toll free 800/241-6522), which recently introduced its first-ever service to Bermuda, offering daily nonstop flights from Washington, D.C.'s Dulles Airport. Through the Dulles flight, easy linkages are available to other parts of United's vast North American network, which includes such cities as Denver, Los Angeles, Cleveland, New Orleans, and Chicago. Especially popular are United's daily flights to Bermuda, via Washington, from Buffalo, New York, and its easy access to nearby Windsor, Ontario.

Delta (tel. toll free 800/241-6522) offers daily nonstop service from both Boston and Atlanta, with easy connections to the rest of its network through its hubs in those two cities.

Continental Airlines (tel. toll free 800/525-0280) offers daily nonstop service to Bermuda from New Jersey's Newark Airport, which is considered one of the airline's hubs for transfers to many other North American cities.

British Airways (tel. toll free 800/247-9297) operates approximately four nonstop flights to Bermuda per week, depending on the season, from London's Gatwick Airport, with connections to the rest of Britain and Europe. Residents of south Florida also appreciate the frequent service this U.K. airline offers from Tampa to Bermuda (between three and four times a week).

From Toronto, **Air Canada** (tel. toll free 800/776-3000) offers nonstop flights six days a week into Bermuda, with connections to Montréal and virtually every other Canadian city.

Despite its fiscal woes, at presstime **Pan American** (tel. toll free 800/221-1111) offered daily direct flights from Boston that touch down at New York's JFK International Airport before continuing nonstop on to Bermuda. (Pan Am was one of the first U.S.-based airlines to service Bermuda with its celebrated "flying boats," which landed in the calm waters off Darrell Island, in Bermuda's Great Sound.)

Charter Flights

Charters were once severely restricted in Bermuda. However, a more relaxed situation has led to increased charter traffic to the island chain, which means that many more Canadians and U.S. citizens can now visit Bermuda than in the past. In general, charter flights are not allowed from "gateway" cities such as New York or other points where major international carriers service Bermuda. If the gateway is not serviced by a nonstop flight, then charters can also be permitted. It is an extremely complicated situation that changes yearly or even monthly, and it's best to take your problems to a good travel agent, who should know the least expensive and most direct route you can fly from your home to Bermuda.

A long time ago charter flights were extended to the general public. Essentially, they allow visitors to Bermuda to fly at a less expensive fare than on a regularly scheduled flight. In some cases a charter flight is 30% or more cheaper than a regular airfare. But that's only a general rule and can vary considerably from flight to flight.

It's not a completely rosy picture, however, as charter flights have several drawbacks. One is the long advance booking often required. For example, many require that you make reservations and purchase your ticket at least 45 days or more before your actual trip. That certainly takes the spontaneity out of going to Bermuda.

Should you be forced by unforeseen circumstances to cancel your flight, you could lose most of the cash you've advanced. To avoid such a disaster, there is cancellation insurance you can now take out, and you should ask your travel agent about it.

The charter flight always requires that you go to Bermuda and come back on a certain date. Again, this allows for no flexibility in your scheduling.

Some of the charter flights also require that you prebook hotel rooms and pay for what are called certain "ground arrangements."

Travel Clubs

Yet another possibility exists for low-cost air travel, the travel club, with Bermuda heavily featured in the discounted offerings. A club supplies an unsold inventory of tickets discounted in the usual range of 20% to 60%. Some of the deals involve cruise ships and complete tour packages.

After you pay an annual fee to join a club, you are given a hot line number to call when you're planning to go somewhere that sounds attractive. Many of the discounts become available several days in advance of an actual departure. Many of them give you at least a week, and sometimes you might have as much as a month. Because you're limited to what's available, you have to be fairly flexible.

Some of the best of these clubs nationwide include the following.

Discount Travel International, Ives Building, 113 Forest Ave., Suite 205, Narberth, PA 19072 (tel. 215/668-2182, or toll free 800/334-9294), charges an annual membership of $45.

Last Minute Travel Club, 132 Brookline Ave., Boston, MA 02215 (tel. 617/267-9800, or toll free 800/LAST-MIN). One person pays $30 annually to belong, or two can join for the discounted fee of only $35.

Moment's Notice, 40 E. 49th St., New York, NY 10017 (tel. 212/486-0503), is considered one of the best, with a members' hotline (regular phone toll charges) and a yearly fee of $45 per member.

Vacations to Go, 2411 Fountain View, Houston, TX 77057 (tel. toll free 800/624-7338), charges an annual membership fee of $19.19, or you can save money by paying $50 and joining for three years.

Worldwide Discount Travel Club, 1674 Meridian Ave., Miami Beach, FL 33139 (tel. 305/534-2082), presents a "travelogue" listing with about 200 discount possibilities about every three weeks. Single travelers pay $40 annually to join, but family membership is only $50.

BY CRUISE SHIP

Conditions have improved remarkably since that "Innocent Abroad," Mark Twain, used to take a rough sea trip to Bermuda. He considered the place "hell to get to," but thought the charms of Bermuda were worth the tough sea voyage. The American humorist would surely be amazed at the luxurious way today's seagoing passengers can go from East Coast seaports to sunny Bermuda.

Even so, the cruise-ship trip to Bermuda isn't as highly developed or as important as it is to Nassau, which is the big cruise-ship port of this guide. Cruise ships, because of the island's lack of facilities and other reasons, have been deliberately kept limited in Bermuda.

There is an increased movement to divide the cruise-ship business between Hamilton Harbour (the city of Hamilton) and the old capital of St. George's in the eastern part of Bermuda. That way it is hoped that the island's limited facilities will not be so taxed, and that congestion and other problems can be alleviated.

Cruise ships aren't for many people, and they may not be for you. However, if you'd like to try this method of travel, Bermuda is a good choice for the first-timer because of the short time involved. Since you can sail from the East Coast to Bermuda and back in just a few days, you won't be locked into a long time on the sea, the way you'd be if you took an extended trip to, say, the Caribbean.

The cruise-ship season today is from April to November, the reverse of what snobbish New York once viewed as "the season" in Bermuda. As one woman wrote in her memoirs of New York society, "No one thought of going to Bermuda in the summer. It just wasn't done." Now the seasons are reversed, and the spring, summer, and fall are the cruise-ship months for Bermuda. In winter, as one industry spokesman said, "It's quiet."

Once only the wealthy could afford to sail from New York Harbor to Bermuda, and such a trip in winter enjoyed a high social status in its heyday before World War II. Because of many factors in the travel industry, cruise ships are no longer to be enjoyed just by the affluent. Many package deals and other cost-saving methods in the industry have opened the doors of the cruise ship to today's middle-income voyager.

Once you've decided to go by cruise ship, selecting your line becomes the next big problem. Some cruise-ship operators want their passengers to have a total vacation—one filled with activities from "sunup to sundown." Others see time lodged at sea as a period of tranquillity and relaxation, with less emphasis on "fun, fun" organized activities (which tend to get a little corny anyway).

To keep your costs trimmed, you can ask for one of the more cramped, inside cabins, which are considered less desirable and thus are much cheaper. If you plan to be active during most of the day, spending little time in your cabin, this might be ideal for you. Most cabins today have a private shower and toilet, regardless of how confined the space is, so you're not reduced to having to use shared facilities. Many readers report that in a midship cabin they are less likely to experience severe rolling and pitching. Modern vessels have more standardized accommodations. It is usually on the older vessels that the cabins come in such widely different sizes, beginning with deluxe stateroom suites, a throwback to the old days of oceangoing transatlantic voyages to beloved in the era of Douglas Fairbanks and Mary Pickford.

Gone too, for the most part, are the "white tie and tails" days of yesterday. However, it's still a good idea for a man to take along a dark suit, and women should bring along at least one cocktail dress. It's not necessary to dress up every evening on most lines. Men often wear sport coats and slacks with open shirts, and women appear in sport dresses or pant suits.

On cruises to Bermuda you'll usually need a sweater, especially if you're traveling in the spring and autumn. A sun hat or scarf will do nicely for women as well. Once you arrive in Bermuda, dress tends to be more formal than it is in The Bahamas. If you're planning to go out at night, patronizing some of the more elegant restaurants or clubs, men are required to wear a jacket and tie in some places. Otherwise, for actual touring in Bermuda, or participating in the deck activities there and back, men can wear sport shirts, slacks, walking shorts (certainly Bermuda shorts), and a comfortable pair of walking shoes. Women will need sun dresses, blouses, shifts, culottes, and shorts. Walking shoes are preferred for touring the island. Naturally, you should take along a bathing suit or bikini.

Finally, and in some ways unfortunately (considering the investment of your capital), the one ingredient needed for a successful cruise is the hardest to know in advance. That's the list of your fellow passengers. The right crowd can be a lot of fun. A group incompatible with your interests can leave you sulking in your cabin.

Economy tip: You are granted considerable savings on these seven-day cruises by booking early. See a travel agent or call the ship line itself.

Celebrity Cruises, 900 Third Ave., New York, NY 10022 (tel. 212/750-0044, or toll free 800/223-0848), operates two ships on its U.S. to Bermuda schedule. The *Meridian* has a varied schedule of six- or seven-night sailings from Baltimore, Boston, Charleston (S.C.), Philadelphia, and Wilmington (N.C.) to Bermuda. In summer, the *Meridian* sails every Sunday from New York to Bermuda. The *Meridian* docks at Kings Wharf in the newly restored Royal Navy Dockyard. From May to October, the *New Horizon* sails to Hamilton and St. George's, offering seven-night sailings every Saturday from New York.

A popular cruise is aboard the *Nordic Prince,* the handsome 1,038-passenger liner of the **Royal Caribbean Cruise Line,** 903 South America Way, Miami, FL 33132 (tel. 305/379-2601). The ship leaves New York on Sunday, arriving in Bermuda on Tuesday. The departure from Bermuda is on Friday, with New York arrival on Sunday. Docking on Tuesday is at Hamilton.

Featuring "breakaway cruises" to Bermuda, the *Royal Viking Star* began service to Bermuda in the spring of 1989. For those who desire shorter vacations, the vessel sails on Saturday from New York to Bermuda. Visitors enjoy four nights at sea and three nights in Hamilton, the capital. The ship, which has a spa and a casino, berths at Front Street, the main shopping drag of the capital. The *Royal Viking Star* heads back to New York on the following Saturday. The ship has a capacity of 900 passengers. For more information, contact the **Royal Viking Line,** 2 Alhambra Plaza, Coral Gables, FL 33134 (tel. 305/447-9660).

BY PACKAGE TOUR

If you want everything done for you, and want to save money as well, you might consider traveling to Bermuda on a package tour. General tours appealing to the average voyager are commonly offered, but many of the tours are very specific—tennis packages, golf packages, scuba and snorkeling packages, and, only for those who qualify, honeymooners' specials.

Economy and convenience are the chief advantages of a package tour, in that the costs of transportation (usually an airplane fare), a hotel room, food (sometimes), and sightseeing (sometimes) are combined in one package, neatly tied up with a single price tag.

If you booked your flight or hotel separately, you could not save as much as on a package tour—hence their immense and increasing appeal. Also, because tour operators can mass-book hotels and make volume purchases, transfers between your hotel and the airport are often included. Of course, there are disadvantages: You may find yourself in a hotel you immensely dislike, yet you are virtually trapped there because you've already paid for it. The single traveler, regrettably, usually suffers too, since nearly all tour packages are based on double occupancy.

Choosing the right package tour can be a bit of a problem, but your travel agent might offer one, and certainly all the major airline carriers will.

One company that has specialized in marketing travel to Bermuda since 1978 is the **Bermuda Travel Company, Ltd.,** 420 Lexington Ave., Suite 401, New York, NY 10017 (tel. toll free 800/323-2020), which represents almost 50 of the island's hotels, ranging from modest and out-of-the-way guesthouses to deluxe palaces. Especially popular are the company's wedding packages (which aficionados cite as especially appropriate for "second-time arounders"), where, for a net (and sometimes very attractive) price, everything a couple needs is prearranged. Ranging from simple to elaborate, and depending on the desires of the couple, these arrangements include airfare, discounted hotel accommodations, a wedding cake, champagne, a minister, paperwork and arrangement of all legalities, and arrangements for up to 50 wedding guests (or none at all). Bermuda Travel also arranges vacation packages for horseback riders, scuba enthusiasts, golf and tennis players, and honeymooners.

Other companies that offer well-organized packages to Bermuda include **American Express Vacations,** P.O. Box 5014, Atlanta, GA (tel. toll free 800/241-1700; 800/282-0800 in Georgia); **Delta Dream Vacations,** 110 Broward Blvd., Fort Lauderdale, FL 33301 (tel. 305/522-1440, or toll free 800/872-7786); and **Go-Go Tours,** 69 Spring St., Ramsey, NJ 07446 (tel. 201/934-3500, or toll free 800/821-3731).

8. Getting Around

The national speed limit is 20 mph in Bermuda, 15 mph in busier areas. Cars are limited to one per family—and to none at all for visitors. In such a far-off Eden, the most popular form of transportation is the motorized bicycle, called a "putt-putt," and the most romantic means of transport is the colorful fringe-topped surrey.

AIRPORT TRANSFER SERVICE

Shuttle service, if prearranged in advance, is provided between the airport and virtually anywhere in Bermuda by the **Airport Transport Department of the Bermuda Aviation Service,** P.O. Box HM 719, Hamilton HM CX (tel. 809/293-0513). The company operates a dozen 26-seat buses, charging one-way per-person fares that are determined by the distance from the airport of each final destination. Transit within zone 1, between the airport and Hamilton Parish, costs $4; to zone 2 (Smith's Parish), $6; to zone 3 (Paget Parish), $12; to zone 4 (Southampton Parish), $16; and to zone 5, the extreme western tip of Bermuda (within Sandys Parish), $21.

BY TAXI

Every cruise ship or incoming flight is met by a fleet of taxis. A typical ride from the airport to, say, a hotel right outside Hamilton costs about $20. Taxis are metered and are allowed to carry a maximum of four passengers. The meter begins at $2.60 for the first ½ mile, with each additional ⅖ mile costing 20¢.

Light packages and bags can be carried inside the taxi free, but baggage that has to be placed in the trunk or on the roof costs 25¢ per item, maximum $3 per trip. There's a 25% surcharge for taxi travel between midnight and 6am.

The hourly charge for taxis is $20, but if you want to take one on a sightseeing tour, the minimum is 3 hours. When a taxi driver, man or woman, has a blue flag on the hood of the vehicle (the locals refer to it as the "bonnet"), that means that the driver is qualified to serve as a tour guide. This is the type of driver, checked out and tested by the government, that you should use if you're planning to take the expensive method of touring Bermuda by taxi. "Blue bonnet" drivers charge no more than regular taxi drivers, who are not qualified to serve as guides.

To reach Bermuda Taxi Operators, call 292-5600.

BY CYCLE & SCOOTER

If you're looking for a lot of exercise, you may want to try a pedal bicycle, the old Bermudian way to travel around the island, although some of the hills may be a real challenge to your stamina.

Many people prefer a motor-assisted cycle—moped, motor scooter, whatever —which you can rent on an hourly, daily, or weekly arrangement. The operator of such a vehicle must be at least 16 years of age, although younger persons may be carried as passengers. Some are large enough for two adults. Both driver and passenger are required by law to wear a helmet, which will be furnished by the place from which you rent your machine. Straps must be securely fastened. *Warning:* Visitors on mopeds have a high accident rate, but no one seems to talk about that. Exercise extreme caution.

Don't forget: You must *drive on the left,* as in England.

Astwood Cycles Ltd. (tel. 809/292-2245) has shops where you can rent either mopeds or 50-cc scooters on Front Street in Hamilton; at Flatts Village; at The Princess, Sonesta Beach, and Belmont hotels; and at Horizons and Cottages. Scooters rent for $39 per day, $70 for two days. A $20 deposit and a $10 one-time insurance payment are required.

Charging comparable prices, and also renting either type of vehicle, is **Wheels Ltd.,** Trott Road, Hamilton (tel. 809/295-0112), or at the Southampton Princess (tel. 809/238-3336).

For motorized vehicles, you can also try **Ray's Cycles, Ltd.,** Middle Road, Southampton, West (tel. 809/234-0629), or at the Lantana Club, Somerset (tel. 809/234-0141). Open daily from 8am to 5pm, the company rents two kinds of vehicles. A small moped costs $25 for the first day and $39 for two days. Helmets and locks come with each rental. The insurance charge, which is part of each rental, is $8 for the moped and $12 for the scooter. This is a one-time charge levied against each rental regardless of how many days you keep the vehicle. There's sometimes a 20% discount in the winter season.

One of the best rental companies on the island is **Eve's Cycle Livery,** 114 Middle Rd., Paget Parish (tel. 809/236-6247). Named after a now-legendary matriarch who founded it 40 years ago, it rents men's and women's pedal bicycles (usually 12-speed mountain bikes well suited to the island's hilly terrain) for $15 for the first day, $10 for the second day, and $5 for each supplemental day. A $10 deposit is required. The shop lies within a 10-minute drive (or a 20-minute leisurely cycle) west of Hamilton. The company also rents a selection of motorized pedal bikes or scooters for between $20 and $36 for the first day, depending on the model, with a descending tier of prices for each additional day.

Oleander Cycles Ltd., Valley Road, P.O. Box 114, Paget Parish (tel. 809/236-5235). A single moped rents for $20 per day in season, and for only $16 per day in winter. However, a Puch Lido scooter will cost $36 daily in summer, $29 in winter. Scooters and mopeds tend to be reliable and well maintained. There is another location on Gorham Road in Hamilton (tel. 809/295-0919). Both locations are open daily. Rentals require a $20 deposit and a supplemental charge of $12 for an insurance policy that lasts for the duration of your rental (a day or a week), at least until you cause any damage to your rented moped.

BY BUS

You can't have a car. Taxis are expensive. You may not want or be able to ride a bicycle or a motor bike. What's left for getting around Bermuda? Buses, of course. All major routes are covered by the bus network, but be prepared for waits. There's even a do-it-yourself sightseeing tour by bus and ferry, and regularly scheduled buses go to most of the destinations that tourists find of interest in Bermuda. However, some routes are not operated on Sunday and holidays, so be sure to find out about the trip you want to make.

Bermuda is divided into 14 zones of about 2 miles each. At presstime, fare for adults was $1.25 for the first 3 zones, $2.50 for any longer trip. You can save some nickels by purchasing tokens, which are $1 for the first 3 zones you travel, $1.75 for more than 3 zones. *Note:* You must have the exact fare, either in coins or a token, ready to deposit in the farebox as you board the bus. Drivers do not make change.

You can also purchase tickets at sub-post offices or at the **Central Terminal** on Washington Street in Hamilton, where all routes begin and end. It's just off Church Street a few steps east of City Hall. You can get there from Front Street or Reid Street by going along Queen Street or through Walker Arcade and Washington Mall. Tickets are sold in booklets of 15. You pay $9 for a 3-zone booklet or $16 for a 14-zone packet. Children under 13 pay 55¢ in cash for all zones or $5 for a 15-ticket booklet. Children under 3 ride free.

A **Mini-Bus Service** also traverses the island. It begins its operation in St. George's at 7 in the morning, continuing late into the evening. From Town Square in St. George's, it branches out to the outlying areas. Fares for this service are $2 for a one-way ride, and you should phone 809/297-8492 for times of departures.

A **do-it-yourself sightseeing tour** might be taken as follows:

Leave Hamilton at 10:15am on a bus marked "Dockyard," enjoying views of Great Sound en route. At 11:25am you will arrive at the Maritime Museum, where the driver will drop you off at the entrance on request. After your visit to the museum, you leave the Old Royal Naval Dockyard main gate at 12:35pm on a bus marked "Hamilton." Ask the driver to point out the Watford Bridge Ferry Dock. At 12:45pm you arrive at Mangrove Bay, where you have a choice of restaurants or a pub for lunch and can browse in the local shops. You leave Watford Bridge by ferry at 2:55pm, going via Cavello Bay and Somerset Bridge, with views of Somerset homes and harbor islands en route, arriving back at the Hamilton Ferry Terminal at

3:45pm. The total cost of this expedition is about $10.75, with fares divided between bus and ferryboat tickets.

For more **information** regarding the bus service, telephone 809/292-3854. Nearly all hotels, guesthouses, and restaurants have bus stops close by.

BY FERRY

One of the most interesting methods of transportation is the government-operated ferry service. Ferries crisscross Great Sound between Hamilton and Somerset, charging a $2 fare one way, and they also take the harbor route, going from Hamilton to the parishes of Paget and Warwick, where so many hotels are concentrated. From Hamilton to Paget costs only $1. Motorcycles are allowed on the Hamilton to Somerset run (you must pay $2 for your cycle, however). For ferry service **information,** telephone 809/295-4506.

BY HORSE-DRAWN CARRIAGE

Being romanticists, Bermudians have retained at least some of their horse-drawn carriages. They once were plentiful, but now only about a dozen are left. Drivers congregate on Front Street in Hamilton, adjacent to the No. 1 passenger terminal near the cruise-ship docks. Before 1946 the horse was the principal mode of transport. After that, the first automobiles came to the island. For a tour of the island's midriff, you can book one of these four-wheeled rigs for a chauffeured ride. Rates range from about $15 to $20 for the first 30 minutes and from $10 to $15 for each additional 30 minutes. If you want to take a ride lasting more than 3 hours, the fee is negotiable. Unless you make arrangements for night rides, you aren't likely to find any carriages after 4:30pm.

BY SEA

From Hamilton Harbour you can strike out in almost any direction on almost any tour. **BDA Water Tours Ltd.,** P.O. Box 1572, Hamilton (tel. 809/295-3727), offers 2- and 3-hour trips, most of which include the sea gardens, where passengers board glass-bottom boats to view the wonders of coral reefs and fish. Also available are a variety of water trips, ranging from 2-hour sea-garden tours to snorkeling and dinner cruises.

---

9. Where to Stay

Accommodations in Bermuda basically fall into these major categories:

RESORT HOTELS

These often sprawling properties are Bermuda's best, offering many facilities, services, and luxuries—but also charging the highest prices, especially in summer. It's usually cheaper to check into them on MAP rates (breakfast and dinner) than it is to order all your meals à la carte. They charge the lowest rates from mid-November to April, usually about 20% less. Most of the large resorts have their own beaches or beach clubs, along with swimming pools. Some even offer their own golf courses.

COTTAGE COLONIES

A unique Bermudian offering, these colonies are usually a series of bungalows constructed around a main clubhouse, which is the center of social life, drinking, and dining. The cottages are usually placed scenically on landscaped grounds. Most of them have been built to give guests maximum privacy, and nearly all have their own kitchenettes (used mainly for preparing light meals). Most of the colonies have either their own beaches or swimming pools.

HOUSEKEEPING COTTAGES & APARTMENTS

These accommodation units are usually called efficiencies in America. Most of them lie on landscaped estates, containing swimming pools, and usually they are built around a main clubhouse. All of them offer kitchen facilities, and some are designed as wings or modern apartment-style units surrounding a pool or else opening onto a beach. Most of them offer minimal daily maid service.

GUESTHOUSES

These accommodations are the cheapest means of living in Bermuda. Most of the large ones are in old Bermuda homes, with garden settings. Some of them have their own pools. Generally, they have been modernized, with comfortable guest rooms. A number of these guesthouses are modest, small places, offering breakfast only; the bath is often shared with other guests. You will usually have to commute to the beach if you stay in one of these places.

HOME EXCHANGES & HOMESTAYS

See the discussions in "Alternative/Adventure Travel," above.

RENTAL VILLAS & VACATION HOMES

You might rent a big villa, a good-sized apartment in someone's condo building, or even a small beach cottage (more accurately called a "cabaña").

Private apartments are also available with or without maid service. This is more of a no-frills option than the villas and condos. The apartments may not be in buildings with swimming pools, and they may not have a front desk to help you.

Cottages, or cabañas, offer the most freewheeling life-style available in these categories of vacation homes. Many ideally open onto a beach, although others may be clustered around a communal swimming pool. Most of them are fairly simple, containing no more than a simple bedroom plus a small kitchen and bath. In the peak summer season, reservations should be made at least five or six months in advance.

Several agents throughout the United States and Canada offer these types of rentals.

To get you going, try **Rent-a-Home International,** 7200 34th Ave. NW, Seattle, WA 98117 (tel. 206-789-9377), or **Travel Resources,** P.O. Box 935, Coconut Grove, FL 33133 (tel. 305/444-8583, or toll free 800/327-5039), which specializes in condos and villas and arranges both daily and weekly tariffs, although longer bookings are preferred.

---

10. Where to Dine

Whenever possible, it is best to stick to local food; for a main dish, that usually means Bermuda lobster or fish caught in the deep sea. But let me state at the beginning that food is not one of the reasons people go to Bermuda. So-called "gourmet fare" often isn't, although the prices charged would make you think that you're getting something special. To find the many dishes that *are* truly worthy, pick and choose your way carefully through the menu.

In general, it is unwise to order too many meat dishes. Red meats have probably been flown in, and may have been resting on the island for some time.

Dining in Bermuda also is generally more expensive than it is in the United States and Canada. Because virtually everything has to be imported except the fish or

Bermuda lobster, restaurant prices are more in tune with those of Europe than with those of America. Service is automatically added to most restaurant tabs, usually 10% to 15%. Even so, if service has been good, it is customary to leave something extra.

If you're booked into a hotel on MAP rates (half board), which hotels sometimes require in the peak summer season, you can sample some of the local restaurants at lunch. That way, your stomach won't become completely "hotel bound."

In some establishments, men are required to wear jackets. An open-neck shirt usually suffices instead of a tie. If in doubt, check the policy of a restaurant before going there.

At the better places, women will always want to appear casually chic in the evening. During the day, no matter what the establishment, it is proper to wear a coverup instead of arriving for lunch attired in a bikini.

Because of the lack of inexpensive transportation on the island, many economy-minded people eat at their hotel at night to avoid adding an expensive taxi fare to their already overburdened dinner cost. It's a good idea to find a hotel in and around Hamilton that has a number of restaurants. That way, you can walk to and from the restaurant and save the cab fare.

---

11. Fast Facts: Bermuda

A number of situations, such as a medical emergency, might arise during your vacation, and there are various customs, such as tipping, you'll need to know about. The desk personnel at your hotel are usually reliable dispensers of information. If you're staying at a guesthouse, your host or hostess will probably be able to supply any information you need on the immediate vicinity of your parish.

AMERICAN EXPRESS: The representative in Hamilton is **L. P. Gutteridge, Ltd.,** Bermudiana Road, P.O. Box HM 1024 (tel. 809/295-4545). The office provides complete travel service, sightseeing tours, airport transfers, hotel reservations, traveler's checks, and emergency check cashing.

AREA CODE: The area code for Bermuda is **809.** It can be dialed directly from the mainland.

BABYSITTING: Arrangements can often be made at your hotel, but never at the last minute. Always ask as far ahead as possible, and be prepared to be turned down. Each financial arrangement has to be personally negotiated.

BANKS: There are three banks, all with their main offices in Hamilton:

The **Bank of Bermuda Ltd.,** Front Street, Hamilton (tel. 809/295-4000), has branches on Church Street, Hamilton; Par-la-Ville Road, Hamilton; King's Square, St. George's; in Somerset; and at the airport.

The **Bank of N. T. Butterfield Ltd.,** Front and Reid Streets, Hamilton (tel. 809/295-1111), has branches on Church Street West, Hamilton; in St. George's; in Somerset; and at the Southampton Princess.

The **Bermuda Commercial Bank Ltd.** is at 44 Church St., Hamilton (tel. 809/295-5678).

All banks and their branches have the same hours (with the exception of the airport branch of the Bank of Bermuda). They are open Monday through Thursday from 9:30am to 3pm, on Friday from 9:30am to 3pm and 4:30 to 5:30pm (9:30am to 4:30pm at the Bank of Bermuda). The Bank of Bermuda airport branch is open Monday through Friday from 11am to 12:30pm and 1 to 4pm. All banks are closed Saturday, Sunday, and on public holidays.

Many of the big hotels will cash traveler's checks.

BOOKSTORES: **Bermuda Book Store (Baxters) Ltd.,** Queen Street (tel. 809/295-3698), stocks everything that is in print about Bermuda. Some books are available only through this store. There are books on gardening, flowers, local characters, and poets, among other subjects. There are also many English publications not easily obtainable in the United States, as well as a fine selection of children's books. You can also buy maps and prints here. The store has an extensive stationery department.

BUSINESS HOURS: Most businesses are open Monday through Friday from 9am to 5:30pm. Stores are generally open Monday through Saturday from 9am to 5:30pm. Several shops open at 9:15am, closing at 5pm. A few shops are also open in the evening, but usually only when big cruise ships are in port.

CAR RENTALS: See "Getting Around" earlier in this chapter.

CLIMATE: See "When to Go" earlier in this chapter.

CURRENCY: See "Information, Entry Requirements, Customs & Money" earlier in this chapter.

CURRENCY EXCHANGE: Because the U.S. dollar and the Bermudian dollar are on par, both currencies can be used. It is unnecessary to convert U.S. dollars into Bermudian dollars. However, because of different valuations, it will be necessary to convert Canadian dollars into local currency.

DENTIST: Try **Dr. David Roblin,** Outerbridge Building, Pitts Bay Road, Pembroke Parish (tel. 809/292-7676).

DOCTOR: Try **Dr. Gordon Campbell,** Sea Venture Building, Parliament Street, Hamilton (tel. 809/295-8106).

DRIVING REQUIREMENTS: There are no specific automobile-driving requirements for visitors for a very simple reason—there are no car-rental agencies in Bermuda. However, motor-assisted cycles are available (see "Getting Around," above), but they may not be operated by children under 16. All cycle drivers and passengers are required by law to wear safety helmets that are securely fastened.
Driving is on the left side of the road. The speed limit is 20 mph.

DRUGS: Importation of, possession of, or dealing with unlawful drugs, including marijuana, is an offense under Bermuda laws, with heavy penalties levied for infraction. Customs officers, at their discretion, may conduct body searches for drugs or other contraband goods.

DRUGSTORES: In Hamilton, try **Bermuda Pharmacy,** Church Street West (tel. 809/295-5815). It's in the Russell Eve Building, and is open Monday through Saturday from 8:30am to 5:30pm. Under the same ownership is the **Phoenix Drugstore,** 2 Reid St. (tel. 809/295-3838), open Monday through Saturday from 8am to 6pm, on Sunday from noon to 6:30pm.
In Paget Parish, you can go to **Paget Pharmacy,** 130 South Rd. (tel. 809/236-7275), open Monday through Saturday from 8:30am to 8:30pm.
At Mangrove Bay, the **Somerset Pharmacy** (tel. 809/234-2484) is open Monday through Saturday from 8:15am to 6pm.

ELECTRICITY: Electricity is 110 volts, 60 cycles, AC. American appliances are compatible without converters or adapters.

EMBASSIES/CONSULATES: Except for Portugal, no European government, including Great Britain, maintains an embassy or consulate in Bermuda. Nor does Canada. However, the United States has a representative. You'll find the **United States Consulate General** in Hamilton, in the Vallis Building on Bermudiana Road (tel. 809/295-1342).

EMERGENCIES: To call the **police** in an emergency, dial **292-2222;** if it's not an emergency, dial **295-0011.** To report a **fire,** dial **900;** to summon an **ambulance,** call **236-2000.** For **Air-Sea Rescue,** dial **297-1010.**

ETIQUETTE: Well-tailored Bermuda shorts are acceptable on almost any occasion, and many men wear them with jackets and ties at rather formal gatherings. But aside from that, the people are rather conservative in their attitude toward dress— bikinis are banned more than 25 feet from the water.

EYEGLASSES: **Argus Optical Company** (Henry Simmons, O.D.), Parliament Street, Hamilton (tel. 809/292-5452), works with both prescription glasses and contact lenses.

FIREARMS: Bringing in any firearm, part of a firearm, or ammunition is forbidden except under a license granted by the commissioner of police. Such a permit will not usually be granted except to visiting rifle club members attending a sports meeting in Bermuda. Spearguns and a variety of dangerous weapons are treated as firearms, but antique weapons made 100 or more years ago may be imported if you can show that they are antique. Breaches of the firearms import law are punishable by imprisonment or heavy fines.

HAIRDRESSER/BARBERS: Bermuda is well supplied with beauty shops and hairdressers. Nearly all the major hotels, such as the Southampton Princess, have them on the premises.

You can always head for the **Bosun's Chair,** Front Street, Hamilton (tel. 809/295-5743). Open Monday through Saturday from 9am to 5:30pm, the store is sometimes so busy that an advance appointment is necessary. Call the shop for an appointment there or at any of the other Bosun's Chair locations: Flatts Village, St. George's, Marriott's Castle Harbour Resort, the Elbow Beach Hotel, or the Southampton Princess (Beauty Salon and Health Club). The company also owns and operates the famous spa at the Sonesta Beach Hotel.

Women can also head for **BerSalon,** Front Street West, Hamilton (tel. 809/295-4804), for an array of hair and skin treatments. Open from 9am to 6pm, it too requests appointments.

HITCHHIKING: There are no special restrictions that I know of. It's usually a safe thing to do. However, don't expect to get "picked up" too easily. Taxis, of course, will stop only if you pay them. The only people allowed to have cars other than taxi drivers are local residents, and they are limited to one to a household. Because of that restriction, family cars are often filled with friends or relatives. Better count on using public transport in Bermuda instead of your thumb.

HOLIDAYS: See "When to Go" earlier in this chapter.

HOSPITAL: **King Edward VII Memorial Hospital,** Point Finger Road, Paget Parish (tel. 809/236-2345), has a staff of many nationalities and high qualifications. It has Canadian accreditation.

HOTLINES: Call **Helpline** at **295-5159** for personal crisis; **Lifeline** at **236-0224**

from 9am to 5pm or **236-3770** from 5pm to 9am, for any life-threatening emergency.

INFORMATION: For information before you go, refer to "Information, Entry Requirements, Customs & Money" earlier in this chapter. For information while you're in Bermuda, the following data will prove helpful: headquarters of the **Bermuda Department of Tourism** is at 113 Front St., Hamilton 5-23 (tel. 809/295-1480), which is open Monday through Friday from 9am to 4:45pm. However, you can get answers to most of your questions at the **Visitors Service Bureau** at the Ferry Terminal, Hamilton (tel. 809/295-1480); King's Square, St. George's (tel. 809/297-1642); or in Somerset (tel. 809/234-1388). The Visitors Service Bureau is open Monday through Saturday from 9am to 4:45pm.

LAUNDRY/DRY CLEANING: If you're staying at a hotel, service will be provided in most cases—but with a very expensive price tag.

One sure bet is **Coral Cleaners,** Victoria Street, Hamilton (tel. 809/292-4059), open Monday through Friday from 9am to 5pm, and Saturday from 9am to 1pm.

If you're saving money, try one of the local laundries, such as the **Quickie Lickie Laundromat,** 74 Serpentine Rd., Pembroke Parish (tel. 809/295-6097). It is open Monday through Saturday from 7am to 10pm, on Sunday from 8am to 7pm.

Another convenient laundromat is called **Soaps,** The Market Place, Shelly Bay Plaza (tel. 809/293-2303), open Monday and Thursday through Saturday from 8am to 10pm; Sunday from 8am to 5pm. Closed Tuesday and Wednesday.

If you're out in Somerset, try **Sandy's Laundromat,** Market Place Plaza (tel. 809/238-9426).

Pembroke Laundry, 18 Parsons Rd., Pembroke Parish (tel. 809/292-9055), is open daily from 6am to 10pm. It maintains a branch, the **West End Laundry,** at 57 Main Rd., Somerset Parish (tel. 809/234-3402), which is open Monday through Friday from 7am to 10pm; Saturday from 6am to 10pm; and Sunday from 6am to 7pm.

LIBRARIES: The **Bermuda Library,** Queen Street, Hamilton (tel. 809/295-2905), is open Monday through Friday from 9:30am to 6pm (on Saturday to 5pm). It stands in Par-la-Ville, occupying the former house of the celebrated postmaster, W. B. Perot. There are two branch libraries—one in Somerset (tel. 809/234-1980) and another in St. George's (tel. 809/297-1912). The branches are open on Monday, Wednesday, and Saturday from 10am to 5pm.

LIQUOR LAWS: Persons must be 21 years of age to order alcoholic drinks in Bermuda.

LOST PROPERTY: Call the police with a full description of your lost property.

LUGGAGE STORAGE/LOCKERS: There are no facilities unless private arrangements are made with a hotel.

NEWSPAPERS/MAGAZINES: One daily newspaper is published in Bermuda, the *Royal Gazette.* Two weekly papers, the *Bermuda Sun* and the *Mid Ocean News,* are issued on Friday. Major U.S. newspapers and magazines (such as *Time* and *Newsweek*) are delivered to Bermuda on the day of publication on the mainland.

PETS: If you want to take your pet with you to Bermuda, you'll need a special permit issued by the director of the **Department of Agriculture, Fisheries & Parks,** P.O. Box HM 834, Hamilton HM CX, Bermuda (tel. 809/236-4201). Dogs and cats entering Bermuda from any country other than the United Kingdom, Australia, or New Zealand must have received a vaccination against rabies at least one month and not more than one year before the date of their intended arrival. Some guesthouses and hotels will permit you to bring in small animals, but others will not, so be sure to know about this in advance.

PHOTOGRAPHIC NEEDS: Many hotels, gift shops, camera dealers, and drugstores offer 24-hour service on Kodacolor, Ektachrome, and black-and-white film. Kodacolor 110, 120, 126, 127, and 135 pocket Instamatic film sizes can be developed and printed in Bermuda on Kodak quality-controlled equipment. In most cases, you can get same-day service on color prints (except Saturday, Sunday, and holidays) if you bring in your film before midmorning. Most varieties of film are available in Bermuda. **Camera Store,** Queen Street (tel. 809/295-0303), is Hamilton's leading camera store and has been for quite a while. Here you can find the source of your photographic needs. Kodak and Fuji film comes in all formats (including disk), and such name brands as Konica, Nikon, and Hasselblad are for sale. They also sell a complete range of binoculars, and offer fast-film developing and printing. The staff will even repair your camera.

POLICE: See "Emergencies," above.

POST OFFICES: The **General Post Office** is on Church Street in Hamilton (tel. 809/295-5151), open Monday through Friday from 8am to 5pm, on Saturday from 8am to noon. Post office branches and the Perot Post Office, Queen Street, Hamilton, are open Monday through Friday from 8am to 5pm. Some take a lunch break from 11:30am to 1pm. Regular mail can also be deposited in **red pillar boxes** on the streets. You'll recognize them by the monogram of Queen Elizabeth II.

Airmail service for the United States and Canada closes at 9:30am in Hamilton, leaving daily. The postage rates for airmail letters up to 10 grams and for postcards is 55¢ to the United States and Canada. Sea mail costs 40¢ for letters up to 20 grams and for postcards.

RADIO AND TV: News is broadcast on the hour and half hour over AM stations 1340 (ZBM), 1230 (ZFB), and 1450 (VSB). FM stations are 89 (ZBM) and 95 (ZFB). Tourist-oriented programming, island music, and information on activities and special events are aired over AM station 1160 (VSB) daily from 7am to noon.

The television channel, 10 (ZBM), is affiliated with CBS.

RELIGIOUS SERVICES: Nobody can call Bermuda the "Isles of Devils" today. It's an archipelago of churches. In this relatively small area, with 57,000 in population, the following religions are represented, several by more than one congregation:

African Methodist Episcopal, Anglican, Apostolic Faith, Baha'i, Baptist, Brethren, Christian Science, Church of Christ, Church of God, Church of God in Christ, Church of God of Prophecy, Church of Jesus Christ of Latter Day Saints, Church of the Nazarene, Ethiopian Orthodox, Evangelical, Jehovah's Witnesses, Jewish, Lutheran, Methodist, Muslim, New Testament Church of God, Pentecostal Assemblies of Canada, Presbyterian, Roman Catholic, Salvation Army, Seventh Day Adventist, Twentieth Century Gospel Crusade, United Holy Churches of America, Unity, and Worldwide Church of God. If you're contemplating attending a Sunday service, go to the tourist office Friday or Saturday. Inform the staff of the particular denomination with which you'd like to worship, as well as the location of your hotel, and someone there will direct you to the nearest place of worship and provide the various times of services. You may have to show up on a moped, however.

REST ROOMS: Hamilton (the city) and St. George's provide public facilities, but only during business hours. In Hamilton, toilets are found at City Hall, in

Par-la-Ville Gardens, and at Albouy's Point. In St. George's, they are at Town Hall, Somers Gardens, and Market Wharf. Outside of these towns, you'll find rest rooms at the public beaches, the Botanical Gardens, in several of the forts, at the airport, and at service stations, but often you'll have to use the facilities in hotels, restaurants, and whatever else you can find.

SAFETY:　You are probably safer in Bermuda than you are in your hometown. Violence and crimes against tourists are rare. That doesn't mean that you won't get your wallet picked in Hamilton. Take the usual precautions you would anywhere. Never leave valuables unguarded, especially on the beach. Lock your moped each time you come to visit a place.

SHOE REPAIR:　One of the most popular establishments is **Reid Johansen,** Washington Mall, Hamilton (tel. 809/295-2151).

TAXES:　Air passengers must pay a passenger tax of $15, collected at Bermuda Airport on departure. For ship passengers, the steamship company collects $40 in advance. Children under 2 are exempt from the tax, but children 2 to 11 pay $5.

All room rates, regardless of the category of accommodation or the plan under which you stay, are subject to a 6% Bermuda government tax, to be paid when you check out of your hotel.

TAXIS:　See "Getting Around" earlier in this chapter.

TELEGRAMS/TELEX/FAX:　Worldwide cable and overseas phone service is available, and charges may be reversed. Direct dialing is possible from Bermuda to the United States and Canada. To send telegrams, telexes, or faxes, go to the **Cable and Wireless Office** on Church Street in Hamilton, open Monday through Friday from 8am to 7pm, on Saturday and Sunday from 9am to 5pm; or else telephone 809/295-1815.

TIME:　Standard time in Bermuda is Greenwich Mean Time minus four hours (one hour ahead of Eastern Standard Time). Daylight Saving Time is in effect from the first Sunday in April to the last Sunday in October, as it is in the United States. Thus when it's 6am in New York, it's 7am in Bermuda.

TIPPING:　In most cases, a service charge is added to your hotel and/or restaurant bill. In hotels, this is in lieu of tipping the various individuals such as the bellman, maids, and restaurant staff (for meals included in a package or in the daily rate). Otherwise, a 15% tip for service is customary.

TRANSIT INFORMATION:　For information about **ferry service,** call 809/295-4506. For **bus** information, call 809/292-3854.

USEFUL TELEPHONE NUMBERS:　For **time and temperature,** call **909.** To learn **"What's On in Bermuda,"** dial **974.**

WEATHER:　This might be an all-important consideration for your Bermuda plans. In addition to the newspaper and the radio, you can call **977** at any time of the day or night for the latest forecast covering the next 24-hour period.

YELLOW PAGES:　All Bermuda telephone numbers appear in one phone book, revised annually, with the helpful Yellow Pages in the rear outlining all the goods and services you are likely to need.

III

WHERE TO STAY IN BERMUDA

1. BIG RESORT HOTELS
2. SMALL HOTELS
3. COTTAGE COLONIES
4. HOUSEKEEPING UNITS
5. GUESTHOUSES

Bermuda offers a wide selection of lodgings, ranging from small guesthouses to large luxury hotels. You'll find variations in size and facilities in each category. The Bermuda Hotel Association requires two nights' deposit within 14 days of confirmation of a reservation; full payment 30 days prior to arrival; and cancellation advice 15 days prior to scheduled arrival or loss of your deposit.

Some smaller hotels and other accommodations levy an energy surcharge. This is a good point to check in advance when you are making your travel arrangements.

All room rates, regardless of what plan you're staying on, are subject to a 6% Bermuda tax, which is added to your bill. A service charge is added to your room rates in lieu of tips, ranging from 10% to 15%. Service charges do not cover bar tabs. Third-person rates are lower for those occupying a room with two other people, and children's tariffs vary according to their ages.

Generally, there are two major seasons in Bermuda, winter and summer. Bermuda has the reverse of the Bahamian or Caribbean high season, with its major season in spring and summer. Most establishments start to charge their high-season tariffs in March (Easter is the peak period), lowering their rates again around mid-November. A few hotels have all-year rates, and others charge in-between, or "shoulder," prices in spring and autumn. If business is slow, many smaller places will shut down in winter.

EMERGENCY ACCOMMODATION

If you haven't time to reserve rooms, there is a solution. Throughout the islands there are private homes in which the owners rent out a room or two to earn a few extra dollars. The staff at the Visitors Service Bureau has screened the island to find these hospitality homes, where your room rate sometimes includes a Bermudian breakfast. The bath is generally shared, and rooms are adequately furnished, as these selected homes are in pleasant residential areas. Some rooms are for single

What the Symbols Mean

AP (American plan): Includes three meals a day (sometimes called full board or full pension).

BP (Bermuda plan): Popularized first in Bermuda, this option includes a full American breakfast (sometimes called an English breakfast).

CP (Continental plan): A Continental breakfast (that is, bread, jam, and coffee) is included in the room rate.

EP (European plan): This rate is always cheapest, as it offers only the room—no meals.

MAP (modified American plan): Sometimes called half board or half pension, this room rate includes breakfast and dinner (or lunch if you prefer).

or double occupancy; other homes offer studio apartments or one- and two-bedroom guest cottages. The rates run $35 to $45 per person per day, based on double occupancy.

This service, at no extra cost to you, is available at the airport, at the Visitors Service Bureau (tel. 292-0030), open daily from 9am to 5pm. The office is immediately behind the point where newcomers clear customs. Unless someone has a prebooked hotel reservation and a return airplane ticket, they will not be allowed in Bermuda. Therefore, newcomers without a reservation will be required to have the Visitors Service Bureau book them a room before their passport is returned to them. If you don't want to take a chance, arrangements can be made ahead by writing the **Visitors Service Bureau,** P.O. Box HM 655, Hamilton HM CX, Bermuda, or by calling them at 809/295-1480. Jackie Garcia, who is in charge of the office, must know the exact dates of your arrival and departure, the number of people in your party, the type of accommodations you prefer, and the maximum rate you can pay per person.

1. Big Resort Hotels

The big resort hotels can promise their patrons enough amenities to make it unnecessary to leave the premises, although most visitors tend to want to see what's on the outside. Most of the large hotels have their own beaches or beach clubs and swimming pools. Some have their own golf courses. Most hotels in this category offer luxury resort facilities such as porter and room service, planned activities, sports facilities, shops (including a cycle shop), beauty salons, bars, nightclubs, entertainment, and taxi stands.

Few hotels or guesthouses include taxes and service charges in the prices quoted, so be aware that they will be added to your bill.

Southampton Princess, P.O. Box HM 1379, Hamilton HM FX, Bermuda (tel. 809/238-8000, or toll free 800/223-1818 in the U.S.), is perhaps *the* most desirable hotel in Bermuda. You receive superlative service and sumptuous accommodations at this 100-acre resort, the biggest and best maintained on the island. It was built on top of a verdant knoll between two views of the sea, at a point where Bermuda narrows to a spit of rock and sand. Since its erection, a team of landscape architects have turned the grounds into the most idyllic large-scale gardens on the island. Guests who check in here are often interested in convention facilities (many international companies hold annual get-togethers here). Other occupants of the resort's 600 rooms are lured to the executive 18-hole golf course (see "Sports & Recreation" in Chapter I).

The main building is rich in theme restaurants and entertainment facilities (covered separately in this guide). But some of the best parts of this resort are scattered throughout the gardens of the surrounding acreage. The athletic and agile might choose to walk to the 11 outlying tennis courts or to the crystalline sweep of the scenic beach whose private harbor lies within a 5-minute walk. The hotel maintains a shuttlebus, which makes almost nonstop runs among the various facilities. Clients who want to sightsee or shop in Hamilton can board one of the hotel's ferryboats, which make runs along Little Sound into the capital. Guests who never want to leave the shelter of the beautifully paneled public rooms enjoy a self-contained village of bars, restaurants, shops, and athletic facilities. These public rooms, scattered over three plushly carpeted or tile floors, are connected by baronial staircases, the intermediate landings and well-crafted angles of which provide absorbing vantage points for looking out over the well-dressed clientele. What might be the most dramatic chandelier in Bermuda—a glass, brass, and wrought-iron Spanish-inspired piece especially designed for the space—illuminates three floors of festivities. The furnishings throughout the hotel are well-upholstered pieces reflecting a restrained kind of 18th-century English dignity.

As for swimming, the hotel contains both an indoor and an outdoor pool. Although the terrace pool is ideal for a tropical drink in the sunlight, my preferred pool is a re-creation of a Polynesian waterfall, where streams of heated water spill off an artificial limestone cliff, while cascades of flowering vines bloom above the foaming waterjets of the swirling basin. Swimming is possible here even during colder weather because of the greenhouse constructed above. If you crave the salty waters of the sea, the hotel beach is sheltered in a jagged cove, flanked by cliffs and studded with rocky outcroppings lashed by the tides. Bar and restaurant facilities are available on the beach.

The hotel's design allows each of the luxurious bedrooms to incorporate a private veranda with a sweeping view of the water. The rooms are arranged around a weblike design that includes three soaring wings that radiate more or less symmetrically from a central core. In summer, MAP rates range from $252 to $422 daily for a single and from $305 to $475 for a double. *In winter, guests pay MAP rates ranging from $160 to $195 daily for a single and from $200 to $235 for a double.* Meals are taken in one of the hotel's restaurants (see "Southampton Parish" in Chapter IV). Dining rooms include Windows on the Sound, a three-tiered palace that seems like a happy medley of London's Mayfair of the 1930s and New York's Rainbow Room. Arched windows rising 20 feet look out upon the islands of Great Sound. It's almost a nostalgic re-creation of the grand dining of an earlier era.

The Princess, P.O. Box HM 837, Hamilton HM CX, Bermuda (tel. 809/295-3000, toll free 800/223-1818 in the U.S., toll free 800/268-7176 in Canada), on the edge of Hamilton Harbour, is a regal pink "wedding cake" landmark. Often called the Hamilton Princess, it's been graced with a history spanning decades of visits from British aristocrats, Hollywood and European movie stars, and countless discreetly wealthy yachting enthusiasts since it was named after Princess Louise, Queen Victoria's daughter. She stayed here shortly after the hotel opened with international fanfare in 1887. Today it's the flagship hotel of the Princess Hotel chain, and undoubtedly the one with the most glamorous history. When it was initially designed, it was a wintertime palace for the very wealthy. It boasted an all-wood construction to "guarantee against dampness." Before 1932 it had been reconstructed no fewer than four times. By World War II its role as a deciphering center and mail-inspection headquarters for each piece of mail transported from Europe to North America ensured its place in history.

Its elegantly colonial core is flanked by sprawling but well-designed modern wings, each of which is pierced with row upon row of balconied loggias. One of the hotel's more unusual salons is the gray-and-white Adam Lounge, the central lounge of this prestigious hotel where prewar weekly balls were *the* social event of the colony. The property was designed around a concrete pier extending into the harbor, off of which lies a Japanese-style floating garden, complete with lily ponds, waterfalls, fountains, and towering trees. The theme is repeated in the lobby, where a rivulet of water cascades past rock-climbing orchids near the huge windows.

There are two pools (one a heated freshwater pool, the other an unheated saltwater pool) set into flagstone terraces. Guests who yearn for tennis, sailing, whitesand beaches, or golf are invited to take one of the frequent ferryboats that the hotel operates between the Hamilton Princess and her younger chain partner, the Southampton Princess. The hotels lie only a scenic boatride from each other. In addition to the balustraded terraces on the waterfront, the hotel maintains a wide array of drinking and dining facilities. Some 40% of the guests are repeat visitors. For more information, refer to "The City of Hamilton" in Chapter IV and "Evening Entertainment" in Chapter V.

Management poured $15 million into renovating the tastefully decorated bedrooms and public salons, making a good property even better. Many of the funds were spent on the accommodations, each of which was designed "to create the feeling that you'd choose the same kind of bedroom if you owned a home here." Most of the units have private balconies, and all of them have air conditioning, TVs, and phones. In summer, single or double rooms range from $170 to $225 daily, EP. *In winter, between early December and the end of March, single or double accommodations range from $120 to $155 daily, also EP.*

Marriott's Castle Harbour Resort, Tucker's Town, P.O. Box HM 841, Hamilton HM CX, Bermuda (tel. 809/293-2040, or toll free 800/268-9250 in the U.S.), is on a hilltop overlooking Castle Harbour and Harrington Sound. Originally built of coral blocks in the 1920s, this prestigious property had fallen into disrepair before Marriott poured $60 million into one of the loveliest renovations in Bermuda late in 1986. The renovation added more than 100 bedrooms, landscaped the gardens, and enhanced the public rooms into one of the most strikingly elegant array of spaces of any hotel on the island. The 250 acres of prime real estate surrounding the property are maintained by at least 50 gardeners. From the outside the place looks almost severe, a bit like a modernized version of a Tuscan fortress with abruptly angular outbuildings. One of these is connected to the main building by an elevated concrete catwalk. The most dramatic wing slopes like a modern version of a Mayan pyramid down to the sea.

The 1929 era core was entirely transformed. What might be the most glamorous room in Bermuda is an 18th-century salon, much like what you'd find in an English country house. Filled with copies of Chippendale and Queen Anne furniture, and sheathed with mahogany paneling, it's a showplace for morning coffee, afternoon fish chowder, four o'clock tea, six o'clock hot hors d'oeuvres (to the playing of a live pianist), and after-dinner dance music. Adjacent to it is an elegant dining room where copies of the original Castle Harbour china from the 1920s are part of the meal service. Throughout the property are such refined touches as the Cascade Terrace, stone moongates, and formal garden terraces built around a Bermuda cedar. For sporting diversion, there's a health club, a sauna, a golf course, a beach club (accessible by minivan), a disco, and several restaurants (the Mikado is reviewed separately).

Depending on your tastes, your room might be within one of at least three different buildings on the property. The 402 accommodations are either predominantly pink or predominantly yellow, and they are invariably furnished with a sense of tradition, usually with good copies of English furniture. In summer, single or double occupancy is $220 to $350 daily. *In winter, singles or doubles cost $125 to $210 daily.* MAP is $50 extra per person per day year round.

Sonesta Beach Hotel and Spa, Southampton Parish, P.O. Box HM 1070, Hamilton HM EX, Bermuda (tel. 809/238-8122, or toll free 800/343-7170 in the

U.S.), is a long-established luxury resort set on 25 acres of prime seafront property that has benefited from a massive multimillion-dollar restoration. It was built in an even crescent that curves along the spine of a rocky peninsula whose jagged edges provide views of the Bermudian coastline. Benefiting from its status as the only major hotel in Bermuda built directly on the beach, it boasts a trio of sandy beaches, ample lengths of oceanside walkways, and well-trimmed hedges of sea grape, which separate the gardens from the limestone cliffs dropping the short distance to the Atlantic. The property is approached from a winding road that descends the hill from the road above it. A uniformed doorman greets visitors in front of a glass tunnel stretching over a flowering ravine and eventually opening into the tastefully art deco —inspired lobby. With its big windows, blond-wood trim, and pastel shades, the lobby is like a 1920s interpretation of the view from a sailboat. In addition to an upmarket restaurant, Lillian's (see my dining recommendations in Chapter IV), the hotel contains a spa facility. Many clients check in on a weight-reduction and muscle-toning regime, which is strictly supervised by the staff.

Besides the outdoor swimming pool, the hotel contains a complete dive shop for snorkelers and scuba divers, along with six foliage-concealed tennis courts, each illuminated for night play. The full-time tennis pro offers complimentary group lessons twice weekly. The resort also incorporates a favorite beach on the island, Boat Bay, into its facilities. Shaped like an almost-perfect circle and flanked by limestone cliffs and sandy beaches, the bay was used long ago by gunpowder smugglers and later by rum-runners because of its well-camouflaged entrance. From the sea, the rocky coastline almost conceals the narrow inlet that supplies the bay's waters. With its encircling palm-covered cabañas and bars, and soft sandy bottom, the bay looks like a small corner of Polynesia transported onto the buccaneer sands of Bermuda. For cold-weather bathing, there is an indoor pool covered with a symmetrical plastic bubble for a hothouse effect of year-round warmth.

Rates in the 403 air-conditioned accommodations are based solely on the view. Each room contains a radio alarm, TV, phone, and private terrace, plus a floral kind of charm and all the conveniences you'd expect. In summer, EP rates range from $190 to $340 daily for a single or double. *In off-season, EP rates go from $120 to $155 daily for a single or double.* For MAP (half board), add another $40 per person daily, year round. MAP clients are served well-prepared evening meals in the Port Royal dining room. Be sure to ask about the reduced honeymoon packages, if applicable, when you call.

Belmont Hotel, Golf & Country Club, P.O. Box WK 251, Warwick WK BX, Bermuda (tel. 809/236-1301, 416/363-6152 in Toronto, or toll free 800/CALL-THF in the U.S.), overlooking Hamilton Harbour with views over Great Sound, is an exclusive country-club resort situated on 110 acres of manicured grounds. Trusthouse Forte, the managing company, poured millions of dollars into creating one of the most desirable properties in Bermuda. Less than a minute's walk from the hotel is the first tee of the Belmont's 18-hole championship golf course, designed by Robert Trent Jones. Tennis is available day and night on three floodlit courts, and the outdoor pool completes the resort's sporting life. There is a pier that serves as the stopping point for the government ferryboat, which goes every 45 minutes to and from Hamilton. Saltwater lovers can catch the hotel shuttlebus, which frequently wends its way to the hotel's facilities at the Discovery Bay Beach Club. The full-time social director answers questions and assists with the many planned activities.

The hotel's exterior is a modern interpretation of a Bermuda colonial building. Wide latticed porches flank the entrance portico leading into a formal reception area paneled in Virginia cedar and dotted with Sheraton and Chippendale reproductions. Plushly upholstered English sofas and comfortable wing chairs are illuminated by light streaming through big windows looking out over the lawn and the scattered cays of the Bermuda coast. You'll find a garden with a limestone moongate, plus a handful of outdoor bars. However, my favorite place for a drink is the Harbour Bar, off the main lobby, one of the most elegant modern bars in Bermuda. Its decor features beautifully finished hardwoods, and there are panoramic views—all adding up to a sophisticated ambience.

The 142 luxurious rooms and 10 suites feature designer decor and Queen Anne–style furniture. Each unit contains air conditioning, a phone, and TV. EP prices in summer are $170 daily for a standard single, $200 to $250 for a superior or deluxe single, with higher rates for suites. Doubles go for $190 to $270, depending on the room's category, and again suites are more expensive. *In winter, singles range from $125 to $180 daily, with doubles costing $140 to $195.* A third person in a room is charged $55 per day, and children under 17 can stay in their parents' room free. Guests enjoy their meals in the main dining room, called The Gallery, with a view over the golf course; all the hotel's restaurants offer Continental cuisine and Bermudian specialties. The Belmont has a beauty salon and a handful of boutiques. Services include laundry, baby-sitting, and room service (breakfast and dinner only).

Elbow Beach Hotel, P.O. Box HM 455, Hamilton HM BX, Bermuda (tel. 809/236-3535, or toll free 800/223-7434 in the U.S.), is a self-contained resort set in 34 acres of gardens, with its own quarter-mile pink-sand beach on the South Shore, 10 minutes by taxi from downtown Hamilton. (You can also take bus no. 1 or 2.) Tennis is played on five all-weather courts, and in addition to the beach, there is a large swimming pool with controlled temperatures.

The hotel accommodates up to 600 guests in a choice of 220 well-furnished air-conditioned rooms and 80 suites. An array of special package rates is likely to be offered. In summer, MAP tariffs for singles are $224 to $396 daily, with doubles costing $256 to $428. *MAP rates for singles from November to mid-March are $152 to $214 daily, with doubles costing $184 to $246.* Suites, also MAP, range in summer from $436 to $506 daily for a single and from $468 to $538 for a double, *lowered in winter to $302 for a single and $334 for a double.* Children under 12 share their parents' room free. Service is included, but taxes are added to the bill.

At Elbow Beach, you can expect five-course dinners and American and English breakfasts, with Sunday brunches and barbecues providing a change of pace. In the evening, guests listen to music and dance either at the Surf Club under the stars or at the Peacock Club, or perhaps gravitate to the English-style Seahorse Pub, where guests are entertained with comedy and song. The Seahorse Grill restaurant is recommended separately.

The resort usually attracts the tradition-minded guest, but during the spring College Weeks it draws the largest concentration of young students in Bermuda.

Grotto Bay Beach Hotel & Tennis Club, 11 Blue Hole Hill, Hamilton Parish CR 04, Bermuda (tel. 809/293-8333, or toll free 800/225-2230 in the U.S.). The only major complaint any guest could have about this top-notch resort is that it's slightly isolated from the rest of the island. The natural and other advantages of this place, however, make up for any inconvenience this might cause, and buses no. 1, 3, 10, and 11 service the hotel.

The resort is named after the subterranean caves that perforate the 21 acres surrounding it. The organizers have turned these caves into their best advantage, conducting tours, communal swimfests, and spelunking expeditions through them, creating one of the most unusual hotel attractions in Bermuda. One of the caves has been turned into a disco, Prospero's. The property is rife with tropical fruit trees, which permit clients to eat loquats, oranges, papayas, and a local kind of kiwi called "locust and wild honey."

The swimming pool is blasted out of natural rock and ringed with serpentine edges, much like a grotto in its own right. Under a peaked Bermuda roof, swimmers enjoy the swim-up bar, where a handful of underwater chairs permit guests to "sip and dip." A sandy beach nearby offers a view of an unused series of railroad pylons, leading onto forested Coney Island across the bay. There, what used to be a lighthouse was demolished for one of the explosion scenes in the film *The Deep.*

There is a good social program. Guests are invited to participate in the resort's nature walks, the twice-weekly "cave crawls," and a daily cave swim, plus a complete program for children. There are frequent tennis clinics, daily "Jazzercise" in the Rum House Lounge before breakfast, and such activities as scavenger hunts, communal croquet near the bar, fish feeding, bridge competitions, afternoon tea, a daily happy hour, and organized activities for teenagers. Nightly live entertainment is provided in the Rum House Lounge, and there are a handful of other bars on the property.

From the sea side, the airy public areas look like a modernized version of a mogul's palace, with big windows, thick white walls, and a trio of peaked roofs with curved eaves. The hotel's stylishly lighthearted decor includes quilted wall hangings and pendulous macramés.

The 201 air-conditioned double accommodations are contained in 11 three-story "lodges" (actually modern buff-colored buildings with prominent balconies and sea views). Each room has a phone. Several package rates are available for those who remain more than six nights and for families who stay more than four. Scuba-diving, tennis, and golf packages are also available for stays of more than five nights. In summer, EP singles or doubles cost $198 to $240 daily. *In winter, EP rates range from $98 to $130 daily, single or double occupancy.* MAP costs another $40 per person daily in any season.

Palm Reef Hotel, P.O. Box HM 1189, Hamilton HM EX, Bermuda (tel. 809/236-1000, or toll free 800/221-1294 in the U.S.), on Harbour Road where Paget and Warwick parishes meet, has had a loyal following for more than three-quarters of a century. The resort overlooks Hamilton Harbour, with Hamilton only a 10-minute ride by the frequent ferries. The landscaped grounds contain a large open-air, temperature-controlled swimming pool. The main buildings, in Bermuda pink, have a decorative style originally set by Dorothy Draper.

A total of 94 well-furnished bedrooms, many with their own separate dressing rooms, coffeemakers, and refrigerators, have walls of sliding glass opening onto private terraces or balconies. Each room has a phone, and the hotel has central air conditioning.

Doubles in summer go for $170 daily, with singles renting for $140. *Doubles in winter rent from $90 daily, with singles costing from $69.* Golf, honeymoon, and family plans are featured.

Facilities include a cocktail lounge, a dining room, and a nightclub called Le Cabaret. Good food is served in the waterfront Great Sound House, and an English afternoon tea is offered daily. The Marine Terrace features outdoor dining, dancing, and entertainment under a night sky. The hotel's own ferry takes visitors back and forth to Hamilton.

2. Small Hotels

More informal than the big luxury and first-class hotels are the places in the small-hotel category. Many of these establishments have their own good dining rooms and bars, and some feature their own beaches or beach clubs. All of these hotels have their own pools and patios.

Pompano Beach Club, 32 Pompano Beach Rd., Southampton SB 03, Bermuda (tel. 809/234-0222, 617/237-2242 in the Greater Boston area, or toll free 800/343-4155 in the U.S.; in Massachusetts and Canada, 508/358-7737 collect), on the southwest shore, is said to be the only hotel in Bermuda wholly owned by Americans. It's also one of the most delightful smaller hotels on the island. Part of its allure stems from its setting on the side of a limestone hill. Years ago it was cut in a stair-shaped series of terraces to accommodate the various buildings of this well-maintained property. Each of these is painted in a shade of rose that local paint merchants call "Pompano pink," which other homeowners around the island have tried to emulate. Arizona-born David Southworth and his wife, Aimee, are the owners and managers of this attractive property. Many aspects of the interior design were chosen by Aimee herself, including the original design of the carpeting in the dining room. Not satisfied with the patterns that were commercially available, she commissioned a design from a swatch of antique fabric, varying the colors to match the environment created by the dining room's sweep of bay windows. Opposite these are hand-painted murals depicting a Bermudian village on a sunlit seacoast. The result is a pleasingly spacious eating area furnished with difficult-to-obtain Bermuda cedar tables and chairs. Most new construction in Bermuda uses Virginia cedar, which is redder than Bermuda cedar, since local cedar was almost universally afflicted by a blight in 1940.

From the terraced beach below the clubhouse, it's possible for water lovers to walk waist-deep along a clean sandy bottom for the length of 2½ football fields before finally reaching deep water. The renovated accommodations present this view to its best advantage, offering balconies or terraces from each of the hillside villas scattered over the landscaped property. For guests who prefer to admire the sunlit ocean from the edge of a pool, the resort offers a crescent-shaped freshwater oasis with an adjacent bar, Tea by the Sea, and a mosaic depiction of a pompano, the fish that made these waters famous. There's also an oceanside Jacuzzi. Other extras provided by this resort include a cold-weather fire (built every evening when needed in one of the stone-trimmed lounges), a honeymoon gate, a tennis court, and easy access to the government-owned Port Royal Golf Course. Designed by Robert Trent Jones, it has a par of 71. Six of its holes lie immediately adjacent to the hotel.

In summer, MAP singles ranges from $246 to $286 daily, with doubles costing $266 to $306. *In off-season, MAP singles range from $170 to $210 daily, with doubles costing $190 to $230.*

Meals in the dining room are international. Nonresidents can reserve a place for the fixed-price evening meal, which offers a wide selection of courses. Each dish is prepared by a team of five chefs. The price of dinner is from $30 per person.

Glencoe, Harbour Club, P.O. Box PG 297, Paget PG BX, Bermuda (tel. 809/236-5274, or toll free 800/468-1500 in the U.S., toll free 800/268-0424 in Canada), lies in Salt Kettle on the harbor's edge. During racing season this clublike hotel is likely to be filled to capacity with yachting enthusiasts. It's built at the edge of a cove lined with private houses and filled with boats in any season. Reggie Cooper, who runs the place, was captain of Bermuda's yachting team in the 1964 and 1968 Olympics. Today Reggie and his wife, Margot, welcome nautically minded guests, many of whom reserve the best rooms months in advance.

The oldest core of this property dates from 1744. (Some of the ceiling beams of the original house are visible below the billiard tables.) When it was still a private residence, it was visited many times by Woodrow Wilson, who stayed here before he became president. The Coopers have expanded it to include pink-walled extensions containing a total of 41 rooms. Each of the public rooms faces a waterfront terrace, where a black ebony tree blooms every year on May 1, according to Reggie. The sophisticated decor includes a paneled bar with a working fireplace. There's entertainment nightly from calypso bands or a live pianist.

Soon after the house was built, it was sold to Josiah Darrell for 10 shillings, two peppercorns, and three hogs heads of rum. Today, in summer, doubles range from $180 to $250 daily, MAP. Singles pay $15 less per category. A third person staying in any double is charged another $60 year round, MAP. *In winter, MAP doubles cost $150 to $185 daily.* Singles pay $15 less per category in any season. Each accommodation has a veranda, as well as air conditioning and a phone. Tariffs do not include service and taxes.

Reggie has also rebuilt his dock and added a nautically inspired conference room whose windows open onto views of Hamilton Harbour and The Princess hotel. The government ferryboat makes frequent stops nearby on its way into the capital.

Harmony Club, P.O. Box PG 299, Paget PG BX, Bermuda (tel. 809/296-

3500, or toll free 800/CALL-THF in the U.S.). Early in 1987, Trusthouse Forte transformed a well-furnished and well-landscaped resort into the first all-inclusive couples-only hideaway in Bermuda. Using a touristic format that has been frequently employed in the Caribbean, the package includes all meals, drinks, and diversionary activities, giving participants the advantage of knowing exactly what their vacation will cost in advance.

Visitors walk beneath a pink-and-white portico, leading them inside the reception area, where the daily activities are listed. On the premises is a freshwater pool, along with tennis courts, Jacuzzis, a sauna, a video library, complimentary beach club privileges, and the unlimited use of a double-seat motorscooter (one per couple) during a week's stay. Guests are granted reduced greens fees at the nearby Belmont golf course.

The resort contains only 70 bedrooms, each furnished with reproductions of Queen Anne furniture. Units are contained in a series of rambling pink-sided wings, which usually encircle formal gardens containing gazebos and well-tended roses.

Only couples are admitted to this hotel. The cost is $390 per couple per day in summer. *In off-season, the price is reduced to $274 per couple per day.* The hotel closes from mid-December to mid-February. No children are accepted. Included in the prices are all taxes and gratuities, plus such extra features as champagne, bathrobes, French toiletries, full English tea every afternoon, an array of constantly available snacks, free and open-bar privileges, carefully prepared evening meals served by candlelight on fine china and crystal, and nightly cocktail parties. There is daily entertainment.

The Reefs, 56 South Rd., Southampton SN 02, Bermuda (tel. 809/238-0222, or toll free 800/223-1363 in the U.S., toll free 800/268-0424 in Canada), is a lanai colony on Christian Bay, arranged along a low coral ridge. The uncrowded cluster of salmon-pink cottages faces a private beach of pink-flecked sand surrounded by palm trees and jutting rocks. On a ledge with an ocean view is a kidney-shaped swimming pool, and there are two all-weather tennis courts on the property. The main clubhouse has a beam-ceilinged nautical lounge offering entertainment seven nights a week, ranging from calypso to pub-style sing-along favorites.

The Reefs offers 65 lanais decorated with rattan furniture and island colors, all with private sundecks and ocean views. Each room has a phone and air conditioning. In summer, the rates for a single or double is $258 to $338 daily, MAP. *In winter, one or two persons can stay here on the Bermuda Plan for $126 to $186 daily.* Services include laundry, baby-sitting, and room service. There is a choice of dining in either the plant-filled dining room or al fresco at Coconuts, the popular waterside beach deck between palm trees. No credit cards are accepted for rooms or at the restaurant.

Stonington Beach Hotel, P.O. Box HM 523, Hamilton HM CX, Bermuda (tel. 809/236-5416, or toll free 800/223-1588 in the U.S., 800/268-0424 in Canada; or for reservations and information, get in touch with Reservations Systems, 500 Monroe Turnpike, Monroe, CT 06468; tel. 203/459-0900). Overlooking South Shore in Paget Parish, the hotel is set in what used to be a grape arbor. The $6-million structure is owned and operated by the Bermuda Department of Hotel Technology, whose classrooms and headquarters lie at the top of a nearby knoll. Some of the employees are students, supervised by professional international staff and trainers. Few deluxe hotel resorts can offer such a high standard of service, and the students are likely to be more helpful than some battle-trained, jaded personnel in the hotel field. A lamplit drive leads visitors through foliage up to the buff-colored façade. A stucco passageway follows a trail to an inner octagonal courtyard where a palm tree grows as a centerpiece. The reception area is high-ceilinged, its dark pine beams alternating with white plaster.

The 64 air-conditioned accommodations are contained in four outlying buildings. Rooms are comfortably spacious, each with a wide balcony or patio, plus a view of the ocean. They are furnished with Drexel-Heritage pieces, and have ceiling fans, private phones, small refrigerators, and love seats that become extra folding beds. In summer, singles cost $225 to $245 daily, while doubles go for $288 to $318. *In winter, singles are charged $105 to $115 daily, and doubles pay $135 to $145.* A full American breakfast is included in the rates. A third adult in a room pays another $55 daily, and children 5 to 12 are charged $40 per day. MAP rates are also available. Service charges are included in the room tariff.

The hotel's sandy beach is reached via steps cut through foliage and limestone. There's also a freshwater pool with an adjacent terrace bar. A library bar with a fireplace is most inviting, as is a very attractive restaurant, the Norwood Room (see "Paget Parish" in Chapter IV).

Waterloo House, Pitts Bay Road, P.O. Box HM 333, Hamilton HM BX, Bermuda (tel. 809/295-4480, or toll free 800/468-4100 in the U.S., 800/268-9051 in Canada), on the edge of Hamilton Harbour in Pembroke Parish, is a remake and an extension of a 19th-century house, lying on the outskirts of town center, right at harborside. Terraced gardens descend to the water in the style of the Italian Riviera. Behind salmon walls, the gardens are filled with palms, magnolia, poinsettia, urns of ivy, and a splashing fountain, and white iron garden furniture with fringed parasols. Guests can observe the British custom and take afternoon tea at the water's edge on the lawn. There are nooks for drinks and sunbaths. Shade trees stand on the fringe of an open-air, freshwater swimming pool. There are, as well, a private dock, a water-side barbecue area, and a terrace for rum-swizzle parties. Inside, the drawing room is furnished with English antiques and decoratively tiled floors. The main dining room, overlooking the terrace and harbor, is dignified with Queen Anne chairs. On the lower terrace level is a bar lounge, with eclectic decorations, Moorish arches, English armchairs, and hand-woven pillows.

The 34 bedrooms vary in size and decorative treatment, each with its own flair, suggesting a country-house guest room. In summer, MAP rates range from $130 to $173 daily for a single, rising to $220 to $335 for a double. *In off-season, MAP singles cost $92 to $130 daily, with doubles renting for $150 to $230.*

Palmetto Hotel & Cottages, P.O. Box FL 54, Flatts FL BX, Bermuda (tel. 809/293-2323, or toll free 800/982-0026 in the U.S. for reservations), in Flatts Village, Smith's Parish, was the ancestral home of the Bermudian Tucker family, whose best-known member is Teddy Tucker. He became famous in the 1950s for dredging up treasure from wrecked ships of the 17th century. The walls of the hotel are pink, and there's a cluster of cottages and outbuildings that are also pink. The main building's reception area is paneled in Bermuda cedar.

Palmetto's location is on the waters of Harrington Sound, about 4½ miles from Hamilton. A raised beach rests on the side of the sound, with access for both swimming and snorkeling to the sandy bottom of the bay. A swimming pool on the grounds also overlooks the water. Complimentary taxis take guests to a beach, 5 minutes away on the South Shore.

The air-conditioned rooms are attractively furnished. In addition to 26 double rooms with bath in the hotel, there are 16 double units with bath in separate cottages, all with views of the water and private pools. MAP singles range from $159 to $199 daily in summer, rising to $213 to $253 for a double. *In off-season, AP singles cost from $98 to $124 daily, with doubles renting for $148 to $198.* The hotel also offers a number of special package plans. Dinner can be taken on an à la carte basis or booked for your entire stay at the rate of $25 per person extra daily.

The Inlet Restaurant (see "Smith's Parish" in Chapter IV) overlooks the moongate, which frames a view of Harrington Sound. The Ha'Penny Pub is a darkly intimate hideaway with big windows behind the dark-grained bar. In summer, barbecues are held on the terrace.

Rosedon, P.O. Box HM 290, Hamilton HM AX, Bermuda (tel. 809/295-1640; or for information and reservations, contact Jenkins-Gibson, Ltd., P.O. Box 10685, Towson, MD 21285; tel. 301/321-1219, or toll free 800/225-5567). Situated on the outskirts of the city of Hamilton in Pembroke Parish, this old manor house is just across the lawn from the Hamilton Princess, surrounded by extensive gardens and lawns. The formal entry hall is dominated by an open staircase, and a midway landing window. There is a tastefully appointed lounge with a fireplace, plus another lounge. Guests can sit on a flagstone terrace under parasol tables around the large, temperature-controlled pool.

Altogether, 42 individually decorated bedrooms with private baths are rented out. The back modern veranda rooms—called lanai suites—open onto a pool, and there are, as well, fully air-conditioned rooms in the main house; each unit has a private phone and refrigerator. The Bermuda Plan rates include a full breakfast, room service, English afternoon tea, and unlimited tennis and beach use at Elbow Beach, with free round-trip taxi service (10 minutes). In high season, the daily tariffs are $110 to $178 for a single, $135 to $188 for a double, BP. *Off-season (December to April), these daily rates are reduced to $104 to $130, BP, single or double.* No credit cards are accepted.

Newstead, P.O. Box PG 196, Paget PG BX, Bermuda (tel. 809/236-6060, or toll free 800/468-4111 in the U.S.), on Harbour Road in Paget Parish, overlooking Hamilton Harbour, is owned by a prominent local family. It is a Bermuda landmark, with a long and colorful history. The original guesthouse accommodated only 12 guests when it opened in 1923, but nowadays there is room for 107 guests in 50 units. Part of the property, Lyndham, was the former home of Sir Richard and Lady Fairey. It was long ago expanded to include adjoining properties, forming a waterfront resort on a flowering hillside overlooking Hamilton Harbour. (From the estate, it's a 10-minute ferry ride to Hamilton.) The ancestral home, painted in three shades of green, has become the hub of social activities. It is popular with the sailing set, and it's impossible to get in here during race week in Bermuda. The setting is traditional, with drawing rooms, a library, and lounges, furnished in part with English antiques, a true country-house flavor, and many informal touches.

Extended from the manor are a sun-pocket swimming pool and a sauna room. Swimming is also possible from two private docks, and the hotel has two clay tennis courts. The privileges of the Coral Beach Tennis Club are also extended to guests of Newstead; a nine-hole mashie golf course at Horizons is also available to guests. At an outdoor terrace, they can enjoy waterside barbecue buffets, rum-swizzle parties, calypso music, and dancing, according to the season.

On the extensive grounds are well-designed and furnished bungalows, with a view either of the harbor or of the garden with its flowering hibiscus, coconut palms, and cut-flower beds. Air-conditioned accommodations are in either the main house or the garden bungalows. Each unit has a phone. In summer, MAP double occupancy costs $196 to $275 daily; single residents on MAP pay $156 to $220. *In winter, MAP rates in a single are $140 daily, rising to $180 in a double.*

Dining is available through the Bermuda Collection, a fraternity of seven different properties, allowing you to dine at a different hotel every night for seven days, all part of the MAP plan of the hotel. No credit cards are accepted.

---

3. Cottage Colonies

These are considered uniquely Bermudian. Each has a main clubhouse with a dining room, lounge, and bar, plus its own beach and/or pool. The cottage units are spread throughout landscaped grounds and offer privacy and often luxury. Most have kitchenettes suitable for beverages and light snacks, but not for full-time cooking.

The St. George's Club, P.O. Box GE 92, St. George's GE, BX, Bermuda (tel. 809/297-1200), is an all-suite resort featuring clusters of traditionally designed Bermudian one- and two-bedroom cottages. On 18 acres atop Rose Hill in St. George's, the resort has much to offer. An elegant restaurant called the Margaret Rose, the Sir George Pub, and a convenience store, the Ample Hamper, are in the spacious clubhouse. There are three freshwater swimming pools, one of which is heated, and also a tennis facility. The beach club at Achilles Bay is connected by a short shuttlebus ride. Golfers receive preferential tee times at reduced rates on the adjacent 18-hole Robert Trent Jones–designed golf course.

The luxurious accommodations offer private balconies or patios, comfortable living and dining areas, fully equipped kitchens, baths with sunken tubs and marble vanities, cable TVs, and air conditioning. The 61 cottages have a choice of ocean, pool, or golf-course views. Cottages (EP) cost the same year round: $250 daily for a cottage big enough for four, or $450 for a cottage suitable for up to six.

Lantana Colony Club, P.O. Box SB90, Somerset Bridge SB BX, Bermuda (tel. 809/234-0141, or toll free 800/468-3733 in the U.S.), is like a private club where dining is a strong asset. Overlooking Great Sound, this fashionable 64-unit cottage colony lies in a far-out location, attracting those seeking peace more than action (a 25-minute ferry ride to Hamilton). It is spread over 23 acres of cultivated gardens, with both poolside and bay swimming, along with tennis courts.

Mr. and Mrs. Young have guided the destiny of Lantana for more than 40 years. Their son-in-law, Paul Leseur, is managing director. A popular rendezvous point is the clubhouse with its large fireplace. A superb dinner is served in the midst of much greenery and flowers. The chef skillfully prepares a Continental cuisine, and the staff is well trained.

Placed around the main building are clusters of Bermudian cottages and lanai suites. Accommodations are restrained and traditional in decor, with the emphasis on comfort; you'll even find an iron and hairdryers. Each unit is air-conditioned and has a private phone. One cottage has its own private swimming pool. On the MAP, a single costs $230 to $330 daily in summer, and a double costs $265 to $365. *In off-season (that is, from November 16 until the end of March), an MAP single rents for $150 to $245 daily, and a double goes for $185 to $280.*

Cambridge Beaches, 26 King's Point, Sandys MA 02, Bermuda (tel. 809/234-0331, or toll free 800/468-7300 in the U.S.), on a peninsula overlooking Mangrove Bay in Somerset, has qualities no other cottage colony has, and for that reason heads the desirability list in its category. Its position is one of a kind, occupying the entire western tip of the island—25 acres of semitropical gardens, lush green lawns, and a choice of five palm-fringed private beaches. As the pioneer of Bermudian cottage colonies, Cambridge Beaches has at its center an old sea captain's house. The main lounges are tastefully furnished with some antiques, and a country-estate flavor prevails. One lounge has a beamed pitched ceiling, chintz-covered sofas, and chairs placed around a fireplace. Informal lounges for drinks include the Port O'Call Pub and the residents' piano bar. Calypso and other entertainment are often offered six nights a week. Dining is in the air-conditioned main room or else out on the terrace, where barbecues are held.

The hotel has three all-weather tennis courts, and a Robert Trent Jones–designed golf course, Port Royal, is 7 minutes away; the resort has its own putting green. Guests swim in a temperature-controlled pool or from the many beaches. Cambridge Beaches has a full marina with Boston whalers and various kinds of sailboats. Water sports include windsurfing with instruction, canoeing, kayaking, snorkeling, and fishing with equipment available. Parasailing, sailing, and snorkeling trips, plus glass-bottom boat excursions and fishing voyages, are offered from the property. Adjacent to the colony are two bonefishing flats. There is also a health, beauty, and exercise facility on the premises. The hotel's ferry will take you directly to Hamilton or else you can take the Somerset bus from Hamilton.

Scattered throughout the gardens are some 59 well-furnished, air-conditioned pink-and-white units, some of which are nearly 300 years old and retain Bermudian architectural features. There are also 18 suites. The restrained furnishings are color- and fabric-coordinated, and each unit has a phone and air conditioning. All cottages, several of which were once private homes, have sun-and-breakfast terraces, mostly with unmarred views of the bay and gardens. The MAP rate ranges from $260 to

$360 daily in summer, with two persons in a suite paying from $390 to $424. *In winter, 30% discounts are granted.*

Pink Beach Club & Cottages, P.O. Box HM 1017, Hamilton HM DX, Bermuda (tel. 809/293-1666, or toll free 800/372-1323 in the U.S.), on South Road, Smith's Parish, is a luxurious colony of pink cottages surrounding two private South Shore beaches. The largest cottage colony on the island, with 81 units, it enjoys an 18-acre garden setting, filled with bay grape trees and flowering hibiscus bushes.

The heart of the colony is the limestone clubhouse, painted pink, with its natural-wood dining room where "backyard vegetables" and fresh seafood are served. Every table has a view of the ocean and the South Shore breakers. The drawing room is harmoniously decorated with mahogany wooden pieces. On extensive landscaped grounds are found a large saltwater pool, a sun terrace, and two tennis courts, one of which is lit for nighttime play. A maid will come around to one of the little kitchenettes located just outside your door and prepare breakfast for you (just as you requested it the night before). The staff is one of the best on the island, including many who have been with Pink Beach since right after World War II.

Attracting a loyal list of international habitués, since its inception in 1947, the resort offers a wide range of cottages from a studio (bed-sitting room, bath, and patio) to an individual unit (living room, two bedrooms, two baths, and two private terraces), the latter suitable for four people. In summer, MAP single-occupancy ranges from $275 to $330 daily, with doubles paying $285 to $340. Four people can stay in one of the cottages for $610 to $635, MAP. *In winter, the single MAP rate is $176 to $213 daily, with doubles costing $186 to $224. The MAP rate in a cottage for four is $393 to $403.*

Horizons and Cottages, South Road, P.O. Box PG 198, Paget PG BX, Bermuda (tel. 809/236-0048, or toll free 800/468-0022 in the U.S.), has as its core a converted manor farm (circa 1690) where much of the romantic atmosphere of the past has been retained. A Relais & Châteaux member, it is set on a 25-acre estate with terraced gardens and lawns, on a hilltop overlooking Coral Beach. It has its own 9-hole mashie golf course, an 18-hole putting green, tennis courts, and a heated freshwater swimming pool. The manor house has fine reception rooms, containing old Bermudian architectural details. Throughout are some antiques from England and the Continent, and several drawing rooms have open fireplaces. The main dining room serves superb French *cuisine naturelle* that uses all fresh products, as guests sit on country chairs before an open fireplace. The buffet suppers are popular. Lunch can be served on a terrace furnished with white garden furniture. In the evening, that terrace is transformed into an entertainment area, with informal dancing and often calypso music.

The complex consists of 50 double accommodations in either the cottages or the main building. All are handsomely furnished, with separate dressing areas and private terraces overlooking the ocean, as well as ceiling fans, Italian terra-cotta tile floors, scatter rugs, and traditional tray ceilings. Some units are split-level. All accommodations are air-conditioned and have private phones; minibars and TVs can be arranged on request. In summer, MAP tariffs for a double range from $260 to $375 daily. *In off-season, two persons pay from $196 to $280 daily for MAP.* Lunches and dinners, by reservation, can be exchanged at Newstead and Waterloo House. Reservations for dinner by nonguests at Horizons and Cottages are limited, so you should book as far in advance as possible. No credit cards are accepted.

Ariel Sands Beach Club, South Road, Devonshire, P.O. Box HM 334, Hamilton HM BX, Bermuda (tel. 809/236-1010, or toll free 800/468-6610 in the U.S., collect from Canada), is one of the best-established cottage colonies in Bermuda. You'll reach it by driving down a winding lane leading through a park, which eventually deposits you near a lime-green clubhouse with forest-green shutters.

The grounds are well landscaped with flowering trees and coconut palms, each with a view of the ocean. Water lovers can swim in an oval freshwater pool, in a rectangular saltwater pool whose waters are replenished every day by rising tides, or at a sandy beach. One of the most original sculptures on the island is the stainless-steel statue of Ariel, who dances like a water sprite on the surf. The statue was made in Princeton, New Jersey, by Seward Johnson. The resort contains three tennis courts, two of them floodlit, plus a series of public rooms where a double-hearth fireplace throws cold-weather light and heat into both a reception lounge and a conservatively attractive bar area designed in cardinal red to look like an English library. Those who want to explore Hamilton can take a public bus, which stops nearby. The 2½-mile ride takes about 15 minutes.

The accommodations each have a private entrance, air conditioning, and a simple but attractive decor of white walls, Bermudian flower paintings, and bentwood furniture. Most of them have private porches as well. Each lies adjacent to other units, which can be connected to create units of up to eight rooms, ideal for large families or reunions of old friends. The club rents 48 rooms with bath. In summer, MAP for one or two persons costs from $220 to $308 per day. *In off-season, MAP for one or two costs from $184 to $260 per day.*

---

4. Housekeeping Units

Housekeeping apartments, Bermuda's efficiency units, vary from modest to superior. Most have kitchens or kitchenettes and minimal daily maid service. Housekeeping cottages all have fully equipped kitchens, are either on or convenient to a beach, and are air-conditioned. The cottages offer privacy and casual living.

Fourways Inn, Middle Road, P.O. Box PG 294, Paget PG BX, Bermuda (tel. 809/236-6517, or toll free 800/962-7654 in the U.S.). Pink-sided, airy, and stylish, this cluster of Bermudian cottages was added to the garden of one of the best restaurants on the island. Its core is a former private home that dates from 1727. Each of five cottages contains two accommodations, offering views of Hamilton Harbour or of Great Sound, a patio, private safe, minibar, air conditioning, fully equipped kitchenette, conservatively comfortable furniture, satellite-connected TV, and lots of extra touches. The cottages ring a communal swimming pool and a well-maintained garden. The beaches of the South Shore lie nearby. In summer, singles or doubles on the CP plan (with a Continental breakfast included) rent for $225 to $325 daily. A cottage for four guests on the CP rate is priced at $550 per day. *In winter, CP singles or doubles cost from $205 per day. A two-bedroom cottage for four goes for $480 per day.*

Surf Side Beach Club, P.O. Box WK101, Warwick WK BX, Bermuda (tel. 809/236-7100, or toll free 800/553-9990 in the U.S.), was terraced into a steeply sloping hillside that descends, after passing through gardens, to a crescent-shaped sweep of private beachfront. The property was purchased by Norway-born Erling D. Naess and his wife, Elisabeth, who designed it nearly a quarter of a century ago and who still maintain the varied array of flowering trees and panoramic walkways. The stone masons added several quiet vantage points at various places in the gardens, from which visitors can see grouper and other fish swimming among the distant rocks of the shallow sea.

Accommodations include one-bedroom apartments near the terrace pool. Other lodgings are in hillside buildings. Each of the units is simple and sunny, furnished in bright colors with comfortable accessories; and each of the 36 accommodations is self-contained, with a kitchenette, air conditioning, phone, and private balcony or patio. Linens and towels are provided. There are also two hillside penthouses, one of which contains a fireplace. In summer, apartments cost from $150 to $175 daily for two persons; three or four guests can rent a penthouse at rates ranging from $240 to $280. *In winter, apartments cost two persons $90 to $120 daily, with penthouses for three or four ranging from $180 to $200.* All tariffs quoted are EP (no meals). These tariffs do not include taxes and service. Mr. and Mrs. Naess host

Tuesday-night swizzle parties in summer. Also in summer, an à la carte coffeeshop serves breakfast and lunch at open-air tables beside the pool. No credit cards are accepted.

Longtail Cliffs, P.O. Box HM 836, Hamilton HM CX, Bermuda (tel. 809/236-2864), is in a scenic spot in Warwick Parish. Birdwatchers will enjoy the dozens of longtails (a form of seagull) that nest in the cliffs below this establishment. A swimming pool is set into a lawn, and a row of hedges signals the beginning of a steep drop-off toward the sea. Beachcombers can walk a short distance to one of the neighboring coves.

The façade that you'll see from the road might not appear very dramatic, but once you're inside one of the rooms, especially those on the upper floor, you'll be rewarded with lots of space, cathedral-like ceilings, and comfortable accommodations. Each unit has a kitchen, phone, radio, TV, wall safe, and air conditioning, along with a panoramic view over the sea. Twelve of the 50 units contain two bedrooms and two baths. In summer, one to two persons pay $110 daily EP for a one-bedroom apartment, and three to four guests are charged $215 to $250 for a two-bedroom unit. *In winter, a one-bedroom apartment for one or two guests costs $75 daily EP, and a two-bedroom apartment for three or four persons goes for $150.* No credit cards are accepted. Bus no. 7 from Hamilton runs by the hotel.

Pretty Penny, P.O. Box PG 137, Paget PB BX, Bermuda (tel. 809/236-1194, or toll free 800/541-7426 in the U.S.), is a charming home in an excellent neighborhood.

The owner and manager of this retreat is a Bermudian citizen, Stephen Martin. You'll be welcomed into a bright and airy living room, his personal residence, for a weekly cocktail party. A fire usually burns in a stone hearth during cooler weather, but in summer Mr. Martin entertains on an outdoor terrace. A food market is within easy reach so that guests can replenish their supplies. The ferryboat to Hamilton is just a 2-minute walk from the front desk. A selection of beaches lie within a 10-minute walk of the premises, and there's a deck-ringed pool right on the grounds.

Some of the names of the accommodations evoke a smile: Tuppence, Thruppence, Sixpence, Playpenny, and Sevenpence. In all, there are nine apartments. Each is contained in its own hillside bungalow, with kitchenette, air conditioning, private phone, and attractive furnishings; one unit contains a fireplace. Each of the units is suitable for at least two guests, and a third person can also be added at another $35 per person daily. In summer, EP rates range from $95 to $105 daily, *lowered off-season to $70 to $80 on the EP.*

Astwood Cove, 49 South Rd., Warwick WK 07, Bermuda (tel. 809/236-0984, or toll free 800/225-2230 in the U.S.). Nigel (Nicky) and Gabrielle (Gaby) Lewin own this homestead, built in 1720, on a dairy farm. The cove house has tradition. Three Astwood sisters, Maude, Ada, and Mary, willed the house with the stipulation that it always carry their name. The apartment resort enjoys a peaceful setting overlooking lightly wooded meadows and the South Shore, with such extra features as a sauna, pool, and gas-fired barbecue stations. The pool opens onto a subtropical garden where you can help yourself to papayas, grapefruit, bananas, and oranges, depending on the season.

Each of the 18 self-contained, fully air-conditioned rental units has a private bath with shower (no tubs), phone (no charge for local calls), radio, ceiling fans, and a terrace or porch, and some of them have sitting rooms as well. They all have compact, fully equipped kitchenettes, with English bone china, wine glasses, even salt-and-pepper shakers. An all-apartment building added in 1985 has a communal terrace and pavilion with TV and an exercise cycle. One or two people can rent an apartment on the EP from April 1 to November 15 at a cost ranging from $96 to $120 daily. Children 15 and under pay $25 year round, that tariff reduced to $20 year round for those 4 and under. *In the winter months, one or two people are charged $70 to $86 daily on the EP.* No credit cards are accepted. From here, the closest large beach, Long Bay, is a quarter of a mile away; however, Astwood's beach and Mermaid beach are only a 3-minute stroll from the compound. Take bus no. 7 from Hamilton.

Somerset Bridge Hotel, P.O. Box SB 149, Sandys SB BX, Bermuda (tel. 809/ 234-1042, or toll free 800/468-5501 in the U.S.), was skillfully designed to fit into its hillside terrain and is almost completely hidden from the road on which it sits. Consequently, you climb down, rather than up, a flight of steps after registering at the upper-level reception area. This establishment is owned by the Roberts family, whose head serves in the Bermudian Parliament. The property is managed by the owner's charming daughter, Karen. A swimming pool is set between the hotel and Ely's Bay, where guests can swim. A government ferryboat stops at a nearby wharf five or six times a day on its way to Hamilton.

Each unit is like an urban studio apartment, complete with kitchenette, private bath, air conditioning, and phone. At night, a pair of Murphy beds (one double and one single) folds down from one of the closets. There's also a double bed contained in one of the foldaway couches. When the beds are folded up and out of sight, the rooms become comfortably furnished living rooms, with large glass doors opening onto private balconies. In summer, MAP rates are $98 per person for double occupancy. A single, also on the MAP, pays $139 daily. Additional guests, up to four per unit, are charged another $49 per person for MAP. Clients who prefer BP (breakfast only) pay about $25 less per person per day. *In winter, tariffs are reduced by about 10%.* The Blue Foam Restaurant (see "Sandys Parish (Somerset)" in Chapter IV) is the establishment's dining hideaway, opening onto the water.

Sky-Top Cottages, South Shore Road, P.O. Box PG 227, Paget PG BX, Bermuda (tel. 809/236-7984). Set on a hilltop above Paget's southern shoreline, opposite the Elbow Beach Hotel, this white-walled collection of cottages provides some of the most comfortably isolated accommodations in their price bracket. The 11 units are contained in four cozy English-style cottages, two dating from early this century, which were assembled into one administrative unit by the English-born wives of two local doctors, Marion Stubbs and Susan Harvey. Each is air-conditioned, containing a tastefully conservative decor of well-chosen furniture, thick carpeting, and, in most cases, a small private terrace. Each has a private bathroom, minibar, and phone, and nine of the units contain fully equipped kitchenettes. In summer, EP singles pay from $67.50 to $99 daily, with EP doubles ranging from $75 to $110. *In winter, EP singles are charged $49.50 to $67.50 daily, with EP doubles costing $55 to $75.*

The units take their names from some of the flowers in the gardens, so you might find yourself staying in Morning Glory, Pink Corallita, or Allamanda. On all sides of the property, emerald-colored lawns encompass shrubs and trees whose sightlines stretch down to a sweeping view of the sea. Few social activities are planned, except for an occasional rainy-day party to cheer everybody up. Nonetheless, a kind of English-inspired camaraderie sometimes permeates the consciously private accommodations. The sands of Elbow Beach are only 5 minutes' walk away, and Hamilton can be reached in about 10 minutes by cab, bus, or moped.

Paraquet Guest Apartments, P.O. Box PG 173, Paget PG BX, Bermuda (tel. 809/236-5842), is a buff-colored collection of Bermudian houses attractively landscaped into a gentle knoll a 5-minute walk from Elbow Beach. Built in the mid-1970s and owned by the Portuguese-born Correia family, they contain 11 apartments, 8 of which have kitchenettes. Each unit has a private bath, TV, maid service, air conditioning, and functional but comfortable modern furniture. In summer, two persons pay $100 daily for a room or $125 for an efficiency; single rooms cost $95. *In winter, both EP singles and doubles rent for $75 daily, with efficiencies going for $98.* The focal point here is a restaurant and coffeeshop, recommended separately. There's also a small swimming pool on the premises.

Marley Beach Cottages, P.O. Box PB 278, Paget PG BX, Bermuda (tel. 809/ 296-8910, or toll free 800/541-7426 in the U.S.). Pink-walled and beautifully located, these 14 cottages are set in a steep but verdantly landscaped plot of land that was used for some scenes in the film *The Deep*. A trio of narrow beaches lie at the bottom of the slope that leads to the sea, and there are also a curved swimming pool and a whirlpool on the premises. Each attractively airy cottage has its own sea-view patio and sense of spaciousness, as well as air conditioning and a fully equipped kitchen. Each cottage offers both a suite and a studio apartment, which can be rented as one unit or two, depending on your needs. In summer, EP singles or doubles cost $148 to $222 daily, with a cottage for four going for $265 to $300. *In off-season, EP rates for one or two persons range from $104 to $210 daily; a cottage for four costs $255 to $282.*

Rosemont, 41 Rosemont Ave., P.O. Box HM 37, Hamilton HM AX, Bermuda (tel. 809/292-1055, or toll free 800/367-0040 in the U.S.), is a gray-walled 47-unit cottage cluster set on a flowered hillside a short distance from the Hamilton Princess hotel. The harbor, with its passing ships, is visible from the raised terrace beside the small L-shaped swimming pool. The policy of the hotel is to "keep it quiet" so that the commercial travelers, families, and mature couples who stay here won't be disturbed. In fact, this hotel usually doesn't accept college students or large groups. A grocery store is within a few minutes' walk, and the heart of the city lies only 10 pedestrian minutes away. Elbow Beach, a 15-minute ride, provides saltwater swimming, and a motorscooter can be delivered.

Each of the well-furnished rooms has lots of sunlight, a kitchenette, air conditioning, radio/alarm, full bath, and cable TV. It's possible to connect as many as three rooms together, which some families prefer to do. In summer, daily EP rates (no meals) range from $114 to $120 for a single or double. *In off-season, EP singles or doubles cost $86 to $92 daily.* In addition to the regular rooms, the hotel offers three deluxe penthouse suites, with private entrances and luxurious furnishings. Two persons can enjoy these luxurious units at year-round rates ranging from $200 to $250 per day. These tariffs do not include service and taxes. Credit cards are not accepted.

Sandpiper Apartments, South Shore, P.O. Box HM 685, Hamilton HM CX, Bermuda (tel. 809/236-7093), built in 1979 and frequently upgraded, is a 14-unit apartment complex. An excellent choice for a budget-conscious vacation, it is within a short walk of several beaches. You can also relax in the outdoor whirlpool and swimming pool, or lounge in the inviting gardens. Nine of the units are studios suitable for single or double occupancy. The studios have bedrooms with two double beds, baths, and fully equipped kitchenettes. Five of the units have bedrooms with king-size or twin beds, kitchens, baths, and living/dining areas with two double pull-out sofa beds. All of the apartments have air conditioning, phones, radios, TVs, and balconies, plus daily maid service. Year-round single or double occupancy costs $75 to $108 EP daily, with triples priced at $95 to $150 and quads at $105 to $176. The Sandpiper is only minutes from restaurants and the supermarket.

5. Guesthouses

Guesthouses are usually comfortable old converted manor houses in garden settings. Some have pools and terraces. The smaller ones have fewer facilities and are much more casual. Most guesthouses serve only breakfast. Those taking fewer than 12 guests are usually small private homes, some having several housekeeping units, while others provide shared kitchen facilities for the preparation of snacks.

Royal Heights Guest House, Lighthouse Hill, P.O. Box SN 144, Southampton SN BX, Bermuda (tel. 809/238-0043, or toll free 800/247-2447 in the U.S.; 201/835-1672 in New Jersey and from Canada). The strange thing about this amply proportioned guesthouse is that it isn't better known. Set at the top of a steeply inclined driveway near the summit of Lighthouse Hill, it's convenient to the Southampton Princess hotel and its assorted nightlife and restaurant facilities. This is a modern turquoise-trimmed building whose pair of wings embrace either side of the front entryway. Terraced near the foundation, a sparkling swimming pool encompasses a view of the passing ships of Great Sound. Guests are welcome to congregate in the stylish modern living room of the owners, Russel Richardson and his wife Jean, who will suggest activities for you, although guests here tend to be independent types. Each of the seven very clean bedrooms has air conditioning, TV, balcony, and comfortable furniture. In summer, with breakfast included, singles and doubles cost $100 daily, and triples go for $150. *In winter, BP singles and doubles rent for $90 daily, triples for $120.* Children under 12 sharing a room with their parents pay $40 in any season.

Loughlands, 79 South Rd., Paget PG 03, Bermuda (tel. 809/236-1253), is a stately, once-private residence built in 1920 as the home of Mr. Lough, president of the Staten Island Savings Bank in New York. It is now the largest guesthouse in Bermuda, with 25 bedrooms. Set on 9 acres of landscaped grounds in the center of the island, it is plantation chalk-white, its entry hall containing a large portrait of Queen Victoria. Loughlands was purchased in 1973 by Mary Pickles, who sold her large country house in Cornwall, England, shipping many of her antiques to Bermuda. The bedrooms at Loughlands are handsomely decorated, some with high-post beds and antique chests; they are air-conditioned, with private baths as well. Rates here include a Continental breakfast with such Bermudian touches as fresh citrus fruit or bananas and homemade preserves. In summer, an EP twin rents for $105 daily, *dropping to $70 off-season.* EP singles range from $75 daily in summer to *$55 off-season.* On the grounds are a swimming pool and a tennis court, and bus service (buses no. 2 and 7 stop nearby) to all parts of the island is available. Elbow Beach is just a short walk away. No credit cards are accepted.

Greenbank & Cottages, Salt Kettle Road, P.O. Box PG 201, Paget PG BX, Bermuda (tel. 809/236-3615), on the water's edge in Salt Kettle, stands across the bay from Hamilton, reached by a 10-minute ferry ride. It's an old Bermuda home, hidden under pine and palm trees, with shady lawns and flower gardens. The manager extends hospitality to guests, welcoming them to an antiques-filled drawing room with its original floor, a fireplace, and a grand piano. The atmosphere is relaxed and personalized. Greenbank offers nine accommodations with private entrances, baths, and kitchens—either waterside cottages or garden-view apartments. EP rates are $90 to $100 daily for two persons in summer. *Winter EP prices are $80 to $90 daily for one or two.* There is maid service daily. Greenbank has a private dock for swimming, plus a boat rental and charter operation on the property, where sailing, snorkeling, motorboats, and sailboats are offered.

Royal Palms Club Hotel & Restaurant, 24 Rosemont Ave., P.O. Box HM 499, Hamilton HM CX, Bermuda (tel. 809/292-1854, or toll free 800/441-7087 in the U.S.), in Pembroke Parish, is one of the most sought-after guesthouses in the city. Residents of nearby houses often walk by its gardens just to admire the masses of marigolds and zinnias that bloom in the front yard. The house is one of the prettiest around, with ocher-colored walls, gold shutters, and a white roof, plus a wraparound front porch dotted with rocking chairs and sofas. The 12 rooms were converted from the living rooms, parlors, and bedrooms of what used to be a very grand private house. Today each of them is spacious, sunny, and comfortably if simply furnished. Ten units are equipped with private baths, air conditioning, and phones. In summer, single accommodations on EP rent for $99 to $109 daily, and doubles go for $119 to $129. *EP charges in winter are $76 daily for a single, $92 for a double.*

Serenity, 29 St. Michael's Rd., P.O. Box PG 34, Paget PG BX, Bermuda (tel. 809/292-7419, or toll free 800/852-4553 in the U.S.), is a small guesthouse. Sun worshippers sometimes regret the short trek to the nearest beach, but few other guesthouses offer such reasonable rates and such an intimate view of Bermudian life. Owned and operated by Mrs. Celia Dawkins, this buff-colored house sits within a development behind a circular driveway ringed with flowers. Each of the seven rooms has a private bathroom, air conditioning, and access to a comfortable guest lounge that is like a Bermudian family's private living room. A few of the units have verandas and kitchenettes. Depending on the accommodation, singles in summer range from $70 daily, with doubles going for $98 and triples for $123. *Winter rates are $55 daily for a single, $80 for a double, and $100 for a triple.* Children under 4 stay free, and children 4 to 12 pay $25 per person daily, year round.

The Oxford House, Woodbourne Avenue, P.O. Box HN 374, Hamilton HM BX, Bermuda (tel. 809/295-0503, or toll free 800/548-7758 in the U.S.), is one of the most centrally located—and one of the best—guesthouses in the city of Hamilton. It lies on a side street leading into Front Street near the Bermudiana Hotel. It was built in 1938 by a doctor and his French wife, who requested that some of the architectural features follow French designs. The white- and cream-colored entrance portico is flanked by Doric columns, corner mullions, and urn-shaped balustrades. Inside, a curved stairwell sweeps upward to the 12 spacious, well-furnished bedrooms, each of which is named after one of Bermuda's parishes. There's even an upstairs sitting room bathed in sunlight. Each accommodation gives the feeling of a private home, containing air conditioning, a direct-dial phone, color TV, and private bath. In summer, EP singles cost $89 daily; doubles go for $105, triples for $132, and quads for $154. *In winter, EP singles are $79 daily; doubles, $95; triples, $125; and quads, $140.* The Bermudian breakfast, included in all rates, has fresh-fruit salad (in season), made with oranges and grapefruit grown in the yard. The gracious manager of the establishment is Ann Smith.

Greene's Guest House, 71 Middle Rd., P.O. Box SN 395, Southampton SN BX, Bermuda (tel. 809/238-0834), overlooks Great Sound. The outside of this place appears well maintained, clean, and unpretentious. A look on the inside reveals a pleasant and conservatively furnished environment that's even better than you might have initially supposed. The entryway is flanked by a pair of lions resting on stone columns. The dining room, which can be closed off from the adjacent kitchen by a curtain, is set with a full formal dinner service throughout the day. Wall-to-wall carpeting covers the floors of the entrance lobby as well as the spacious and well-furnished living room. Guests are free to use this room, as well as the sun-washed terraces in back. A swimming pool is in the back garden. The owners are Walter ("Dickie") Greene and his wife, Jane.

Of the six bedrooms, four contain full baths, ironing boards with irons, coffee makers, TVs, phones, refrigerators, and air conditioning. Year-round daily rates, with breakfast included, are $100 for a double and $75 for a single. No credit cards are accepted. There's even a cozy bar facing the sea, where guests use the honor system to record their drinks. Dinners can be prepared upon request. A public bus stops at the front door for runs into Hamilton. The beach and the Port Royal Golf Course are both about 5 minutes away.

Edgehill Manor, Rosemont Avenue, P.O. Box HM 1048, Hamilton HM EX, Bermuda (tel. 809/294-7124), outside the city limits in a quiet residential area that is nevertheless convenient to restaurants and shopping in Hamilton, might just become "your little home in Bermuda." Your landlady is British-born Bridget Marshall, who still observes the custom of English tea in the afternoon. Some of her nine well-lit, airy units are cooled by ceiling fans and some have air conditioning; at least two are equipped with kitchenettes. All come with TVs and small balconies or patios. Singles cost $95 daily in summer, and doubles go for $98 to $106. An extra $10 is charged year round for children under 12 sharing their parents' room. *In winter, daily prices are $50 for a single, $60 to $68 for a double.* All tariffs are on the CP. If you're interested, ask Bridget Marshall about her special honeymoon rates. No credit cards are accepted.

Hillcrest Guest House, Nea's Alley, P.O. Box GE 96, St. George's GE BX, Bermuda (tel. 809/297-1630), is a green-and-white early 18th-century home, spread on the rise of a hill off Old Maid's Lane. With its wide verandas, lawns (with a moongate), and trees, it has a homelike look, and the interior is pleasant and comfortable. (Tom Moore, the Irish poet, roomed here in 1804 for many weeks. He was quite taken with Hester Tucker next door, and wrote her some romantic verse.) The small entry hall has Edwardian furnishings, and the bedrooms are on two levels. All 10 accommodations have private bathrooms. The year-round EP rate is $45 daily for a single, $65 for a double. All are air-conditioned and have clock-radios. Hillcrest is 3 to 5 minutes from restaurants, shops, golfing, the bus route, and all points of interest in the historic town of St. George's. Write to Mrs. E. Trew Robinson at the address given above for a reservation. No credit cards are accepted.

IV

DINING IN BERMUDA

1. THE CITY OF HAMILTON
2. PAGET PARISH
3. WARWICK PARISH
4. SOUTHAMPTON PARISH
5. SANDYS PARISH (SOMERSET)
6. ST. GEORGE'S PARISH
7. ST. DAVID'S ISLAND
8. HAMILTON PARISH
9. SMITH'S PARISH

Wahoo steak, shark hash, mussel pie, fish chowder laced with rum and sherry peppers, Hoppin' John (black-eyed peas and rice), and the succulent spiny Bermuda lobster (called "guinea-chick") are some of the unusual dining experiences awaiting you in Bermuda. Trouble is, you'll have to search hard to find these off-beat dishes. Many hotels and a large number of restaurants serve typical international resort cookery. For a more detailed description of Bermudian cookery, refer to the "Food & Drink" section in Chapter I.

Bermudian food has been much improved in recent years, although dining out is still not the major reason to visit these islands. British dishes such as steak-and-kidney pie are common, as are American ones. Most of the meat has to be imported, so whenever possible it's best to stick to selections from the briny. Fish is generally excellent, especially Bermuda rockfish.

Most restaurants, at least the better ones, insist on a dress code, preferring men to wear a jacket and tie after 6pm.

Sunday brunch is a Bermuda tradition. Hot and cold dishes are served buffet style at several restaurants recommended below. My preferred choice for brunch is the Waterlot Inn in Southampton Parish (see below).

Note that all prices quoted are per person.

1. The City of Hamilton

VERY EXPENSIVE
   Romanoff Restaurant, 34 Church St., just west of Burnaby (tel. 809/295-0333). In the last few years it has established itself as the most prestigious gourmet

restaurant in Bermuda. In an atmosphere evoking the style of Old Vienna, the haute cuisine of the Continent is dispensed, after you're greeted by the manager, Antun Duzevic. Some $250,000 in renovations was poured into rejuvenating the site, and fine Wedgwood china, Damask linen, brass lamps, and crystal accompany your elegant repast. The smoked-glass mirrors deceivingly make you think the burgundy-colored room is larger than it is.

You get splendid French and Continental dishes—not only Russian, as the name implies—along with impeccable service. Appetizers include snails in garlic butter and smoked rainbow trout. The chef prepares crêpes filled with assorted seafood and also makes tempting kettles of soup, including the traditional Russian borscht and also lobster bisque and French onion soup. Dover sole is prepared in classic ways, but if you want something fresh from local waters, try either the broiled wahoo filet or the Bermuda lobster. Shashlik is served Georgian style (that is, flambéed with vodka), or you might prefer chicken Kiev or duckling à l'orange. However, the chef's pièce de résistance is his tournedos flambé Alexandra, which is beef tenderloin flamed with cognac and served with a superb sauce made at your table. Each night you can also select the chef's creation of the evening from a silver trolley. For dessert, there are marvelous soufflés and crêpes, or perhaps a zabaglione.

Lunch is served Monday through Friday from noon to 2:30pm, a business repast with six choices going for $11.95. Dinner is served Monday through Saturday from 7 to 10pm and is likely to cost $60 per person; closed Sunday. Men are asked to wear jackets and ties to dinner.

Tiara Room, Hamilton Princess (tel. 809/295-3000). The gourmet choice of this posh hotel, this modernized restaurant focuses its decor around elaborate tiara-shaped chandeliers and the sweeping panoramic view over Hamilton Harbour. The illumination is enhanced by the dozens of flickering candles that seem to set fire to the fine crystal and heavy silver. Flambé dishes are a specialty here, each of which adds a touch of theatricality to the decor.

The cuisine is classic French. For an appetizer you have a choice of such dishes as terrine du chef or antipasto. Among the soup selections are chilled soup of the day and Bermuda fish soup. The chef is superb at preparing fish dishes and is said to search the eastern seaboard for unique aquatic catches. From this Atlantic bounty, try the scampi provençale or a brochette of scallops broiled with cherry tomatoes and mushrooms. Among the main poultry and meat dishes, you are likely to find such fare as roast quail served with a cherry sauce, roast rack of lamb with herbs of Provence, and filet mignon with a béarnaise sauce. Of course, menus change, but you get an idea of what to expect. Full meals cost from $55 per person. Dinner only is served Monday through Saturday from 6:30 to 10:30pm. Reservations are necessary, and in such a setting, men are requested to wear jackets and ties.

EXPENSIVE

Once Upon a Table, 49 Serpentine Rd., west of City Hall (tel. 809/295-8585). I think I'd come here because of the charming name. Fortunately, it has a lot more going for it than that. If Bermuda ever had a belle époque period, it's here in a restored and richly decorated Victorian island home, furnished in part with antiques. An old island buggy in the front yard sets the tone of the place. Inside, you are shown to a table in one of the intimate rooms, where you'll notice the delicate lace curtains at the windows.

A small family of hospitable Bermudians operate this place, serving candlelit dinners nightly from a French menu, from which you can choose hors d'oeuvres from either the *froids* or the *chauds* column. These might include bay scallops in a saffron wine sauce, or locally caught wahoo marinated with herbs and juniperberries. You might also begin with a soup such as Bermuda fish chowder flavored with black rum and sherry peppers. When it's available, you are given an entree choice of fresh Bermuda fish—broiled, grilled, or pan-fried with banana or lemon butter sauce. Wahoo Doris is poached wahoo in a white-wine sauce with capers and grapes. Rack of lamb coated with herbs and Dijon mustard must be ordered for two guests, or you might select tournedos à la maison (beef tenderloin with pâté and a madeira sauce). Desserts might include crêpes Alexandra or a homemade sorbet of the day. One section of the menu—called "spa cuisine"—is for those who are paying careful attention to calories. Expect to spend from $40 and up for a really superb and memorable meal. Dinner only is served nightly from 6:30 to 9 or 9:30pm. (Closed in January.) Jackets are required for men.

New Harbourfront Restaurant, Front Street (tel. 809/295-4207). In the center of town, across from the ferry station, on the second floor of an old Hamilton building, this spacious restaurant was stylishly renovated with marine-blue-and-pink Italian-inspired accents. The menu is French and Italian, with specialties including such dishes (for two) as chateaubriand and young lamb with an apricot sauce, as well as poultry and veal dishes. Fresh swordfish in garlic-and-white-wine sauce is a standard, as are veal Oscar, broiled Bermuda lobster (in season), and an array of other seafood dishes. Lunches cost from $15 each, while dinners run from $40. Formally dressed waiters serve lunch Monday through Saturday from 11:45am to 3pm, dinner from 6:30 to 10:30pm Monday through Saturday. Melodies from a shiny black piano accompany your meal and dancing after dinner.

MODERATE

Lobster Pot & Boat House Bar, Bermudiana Road (tel. 809/292-6898), is the island's oldest fish eatery. It specializes in local seafood cooked just right, and with flair. With its nautical decor, it attracts visitors and 'Mudians alike to its location off Front Street. The Bermuda fish chowder is laced with black rum and sherry peppers. It's very good, but you can get that elsewhere. A unique appetizer is the curried Bermuda rockfish (delicately seasoned and rolled in a thin crêpe). Fresh oysters are available all year and priced according to the season. I suggest the baked Bermuda fish for two—fresh fish that has been seasoned and stuffed. Perhaps you'll try the lobster potpourri, the deep-fried tiger shrimp and scallops, or the wahoo steak (a game fish). Bermuda lobster (the so-called guinea chick) is available in season (that is, from mid-September until the end of March). The typical Bermuda banana fritter is a popular finish to a meal. Expect to pay from $30 for a complete meal. Lunch is served Monday through Saturday from 11:30am to 5pm; dinner Monday through Saturday, is from 6 to 11pm. Dress is casual. This place is extremely popular, and with good reason, so always reserve a table.

The Conch Shell, Emporium Building, 69 Front St. (tel. 809/295-6969), is a sophisticated nighttime rendezvous. Its most desired tables are outside on a balcony overlooking Hamilton Harbour. The ambience is stylish, with salmon-colored walls, gray-clothed tables, ceiling fans, and aquariums with exquisite fish. The chef specializes in Asian- and Western-style seafood. You could begin with one of the hot appetizers such as a crispy egg roll or perhaps shrimp "legs" Nori (raw shelled shrimp with ginger, wine, water chestnuts, and scallions). The most exotic soup is shark's fin, or you might prefer to start with a conch salad. For your main course, try fried abalone with oyster sauce, New Orleans–style chicken (that is, with a lemon-and-orange sauce and chopped almonds), or fresh Bermuda fish seasoned with a touch of Pernod and served papillote style. Prime sirloin steaks are also offered. Dinner, served nightly from 6:30 to 10:30pm, costs from $30 per person. Lunch is also served daily from noon to 3pm, offering an array of soups, sandwiches, and salads, costing from $12.

Rum Runners, Front Street (tel. 809/292-4737). Lined with bricks and aged paneling, this warmly decorated restaurant contains a pub that is a popular hangout in its own right. Both establishments lie at the top of a steep flight of steps. Filled with antique rifles and bowsprits, the main dining room, the Nonsuch Room, is open daily from 11:45am to 4:45pm and 6:30 to 10pm. The menu offers standard English, American, and European fare, with beef and veal dishes predominating. You may want to try the prime sirloin steak (10 ounces) or the prime roast rib of beef with Yorkshire pudding, perhaps the chicken Cordon Bleu or the seafood brochette. Full dinners cost from $35, but lunches are less expensive, going for $12 and including sandwiches, salads, fresh fish, crab cakes, burgers, and oysters.

The same menu is served in the nearby pub within view of the harbor. Called the Load of Mischief Pub, it has cedar trim, a beamed tray ceiling, and a somewhat less formal ambience than its neighbor. Meals tend to be less expensive, and no one minds if you order pub grub to supplement your tankard of English ale. Live music is a special event almost every night from 10pm to 1am.

Fisherman's Reef, Burnaby Hill (tel. 809/292-1609), in the heart of Hamilton, lies above the Hog Penny Pub, and is a deserving choice for fine local seafood and typically Bermudian dishes. It offers a nautical setting and a separate bar and cocktail lounge. For seafood, you can order wahoo, one of Bermuda's most popular game fish. It's cut into steaks and topped with banana and bacon strips. Bermuda rockfish is also served. When available, a whole Bermuda fish is seasoned, stuffed, and baked in the island's typical way. Also, Bermuda guinea chicks—that is, small lobsters—are broiled on the half shell in season. Ask the waiter about the daily catch —snapper, grouper, shark, or yellowtail—which can be pan-fried, broiled, or poached. Although most people come here for fish, the chef is also adept at preparing meat courses. He does an excellent peppersteak flambé and a number of classic veal specials, including Oscar, marsala, and français. Banana fritters laced with black rum is a favorite dessert. Expect to spend from $30 for dinner, $12 for lunch. Dress is informal, and hours are daily noon to 2:30pm and 6:30 to 10:30pm. Reservations are needed.

Little Venice, Bermudiana Road (tel. 809/295-3503), is definitely Italian, as you might guess. The owner likes to introduce you to his specialties—casseruola di pesce dello chef (a variety of Bermuda lobster, shrimp, fresh fish, mussels, and clams cooked in white wine with herbs and tomatoes) and tournedos Rossini. The pasta dishes are varied, beginning with homemade ravioli filled with spinach and ricotta cheese. Among the soups I'd suggest the fish chowder. The veal dishes featured on my last visit were properly seasoned and prepared. If you have room for dessert, you might try the zabaglione. Good Italian, German, and French wines are featured, and wine is also available in carafes.

An abbreviated menu is offered at lunch, with meals costing from $15. Dinner is likely to average around $30, but a $16.75 special is served before 7pm. The restaurant is open for lunch Monday through Friday from 11:45am to 2:30pm, and for dinner nightly from 6:30 to 10:30pm. Dress is "smart casual."

Loquats, Bermuda House, 95 Front St. (tel. 809/292-4705). Some visitors to Bermuda immediately claim this as their preferred dining and drinking hangout. It occupies a long, narrow second-story room whose entrance lies off an alleyway a few paces from the main artery of Front Street. You dine beneath a high sloping ceiling whose widely spaced rafters reveal slabs of Bermuda limestone laid in layers as roofing shingles. There's a narrow veranda overlooking the harbor and a long and well-used bar designed a bit like a Victorian antique.

The cuisine is international. Lunches, costing from $15, include a large selection of flame-broiled burgers, broiled Bermuda fish, and salads. Dinner, from $30, features English-style fish and chips and Bermuda fish en papillote. Spit-roasted specialties include duckling Indonesia with mango slices and green peppercorns, along with a mixed grill from the skewer. Charbroiled main dishes feature everything from veal Dutch style to meaty barbecued pork ribs. Several dishes are combination platters such as a rack of barbecued baby back ribs with jumbo shrimp. A variety of seasonal fruit and cake desserts are available from the chef's special menu; otherwise, you can settle happily for Apple Brown Betty. Drinks are generously poured, and seem the appropriate accompaniment to the live music featured here on most evenings. The establishment is open Monday through Saturday from 11:30am to 11pm, but mealtimes last from noon to 2pm for lunch and 6 to 10pm for dinner.

Harley's, Hamilton Princess, Hamilton (tel. 809/295-3000). Named after the bearded bon vivant who established The Princess a century ago, this is the popular restaurant of this previously recommended landmark hotel. In warm weather, tables are extended outside to the edge of the swimming pool, creating an effect a bit like a flowering terrace on the Italian Riviera. The restaurant—serving breakfast from 7 to 11am, lunch from noon to 4:30pm, and dinner from 6 to 10pm—is open daily but only in high season (usually from May to October).

You might want to dine on a two-handed sandwich or one of the fresh-tasting salads at lunch, when full meals cost from $15. Salads include a Greek version of chicken with cashews and oranges, and low-calorie and vegetarian selections are also available. Full dinners, costing from $35, include an array of beef, lamb, and poultry dishes. The cuisine is essentially Mediterranean. Try the catch of the day, veal marsala, or Asian-style chicken with peppers and teriyaki. Fresh Bermuda chowder, laced with black rum, usually begins most meals. The chef also prepares a number of fish dishes, including fresh imported Pacific salmon. There is also a selection of familiar pasta dishes such as cannelloni or fettuccine Alfredo.

Primavera, Pitts Bay Road (tel. 809/295-2167), lies in Hamilton West between Front Street and the Hamilton Princess. It is one of the finest classic Italian restaurants in town, often viewed as an alternative to the more traditional fare served in many of the island's restaurants. You might begin with a selection of either hot or cold antipasti, including a cold seafood salad or hot baked clams served in a marinara sauce. You can follow with a soup, perhaps pasta e fagioli in the Venetian style, or a salad, most likely a Caesar. The array of pasta dishes features ravioli Primavera (the chef's surprise), or chicken breast filled with garlic butter and cheese, or osso buco (the veal shank dish that is a specialty of Milan). Naturally, you'll want to finish such a satisfying meal with either an Italian espresso or a cappuccino. Lunch is served Monday through Friday from 11:45am to 2:30pm, when tabs average around $18. Dinner, costing from $30, is served nightly from 6:30 to 11pm.

Royal Palms Club, 24 Rosemont Ave. (tel. 809/292-1854), in the city of Hamilton, is contained in a well-maintained guesthouse with the same name. This restaurant isn't well frequented by tourists, even though it does a thriving business with the local community at lunchtime. It contains a simple bar area, where drinks are a bargain at $2 each during the afternoon happy hour from 5 to 7pm. Lunch is offered daily from noon to 2:30pm, either inside the simple and somewhat old-fashioned interior or on the outdoor terrace. At lunch, you're offered a choice of sandwiches at $6.50 each. More substantial platters of food, such as chicken Cordon Bleu, are available as well. At dinner, served nightly from 6 to 10pm, a more elaborate menu has such elegant fare as chicken Kiev, veal scallops with zucchini, U.S. choice sirloin steak, and the catch of the day prepared "the way you like it." Meals cost from $30. Summer barbecues are an island event. Special features of the place are a Wednesday steak and lobster night, costing $28, and a Friday seafood buffet, also $28. It includes shrimp and salmon, among other offerings. For more information about this place, refer to "Guesthouses" in Chapter III.

Show Bizz, Reid and King Streets (tel. 809/292-0676), is a small restaurant with a jazzy decor and a pianist who often keeps things lively at night. The kitchen turns out good pasta dishes, salads, hamburgers, seafood, soups, Bermuda fish, sandwiches, and steaks. Look also for their blackboard specials. The charbroiled beef ribs and barbecued ribs are also popular. Dinners cost from $25, with lunches going for around $12. The place is open Monday through Saturday from noon to midnight, on Sunday from 6pm to midnight; there is full bar service until 1am.

Red Carpet Bar and Restaurant, Armoury Building, 37 Reid St. (tel. 809/292-6195), serves many Italian dishes even though the atmosphere is evocative of an English pub. This place does a thriving lunch business from the many office workers who fill the buildings nearby. Later, after work, its wood-trimmed bar is popular as a place to relax with a beer amid a decor of dark-red carpeting, dim lights, and darkly stained trim. Meals are served daily from 11:30am to 2:30pm for lunch and 6:30 to 10pm for dinner. Lunches cost from $12 to $15 and include sandwiches, cold platters, and a few hot dishes such as pan-fried fish. Dinners, from $25 to $35, feature a wide selection, including veal scaloppine, veal marsala, chicken cacciatore, filet mignon, and New York–strip sirloin.

INEXPENSIVE

M.R. Onions, Par-le-Ville North (tel. 809/292-5012), is an enormously popular restaurant and bar. The name of the place is a colloquialism. Bermudians are known as onions, and the "M.R." stands for "em are," or "they are." Hence the name means, "They are Bermudians." Designed like an Edwardian-era bar, it's done up with lots of brass, potted palms, leaf-green walls, and miles of oak trim. Many caricatures of Bermudians hang on the walls. A different portrait is picked each month, first shown at the entrance and then moved into the restaurant. If you go early, have a drink at the large rectangular bar that fills most of the establishment's front room. It's especially popular during happy hour, daily from 5 to 7pm, when it is a favorite rendezvous for office workers in the neighborhood. The bar is open daily from 11:30am to 1am.

Well-prepared meals are served in a rear dining room, with specialties including house onion soup, french-fried breaded mushrooms, escargots, barbecued chicken or ribs, shish kebab, steak teriyaki, fish steak of the day, deep-fried scallops, and charbroiled fresh Bermuda wahoo and tuna. You can also order an array of burgers and beer by the pitcher or the glass. The dessert specialties are mud pie and cheesecake, or you can choose from the elaborate sweet trolley. There is also a bakery featuring onion bread and curried onion bread. Lunch is served Monday through Friday from noon to 3pm, costing $10.75. Dinner, served nightly from 5:30 to 10pm, goes for around $12 to $25. Snacks are available in the bar until 10pm. Closed Monday in January and February.

Portofino, Bermudiana Road (tel. 809/292-2375), is an Italian trattoria. Chianti bottles hang from the ceiling, and the decor is in typical tavern style. The place offers well-prepared and reasonably priced specialties, including four kinds of spaghetti and all the famous pastas, such as lasagne, ravioli, and cannelloni. There are 13 kinds of 9-inch pizza offered, along with a classic minestrone. Standard and familiar Italian dishes include Venetian-style liver, veal parmigiana, chicken cacciatore, and beefsteak pizzaiola. Snails are prepared with "a secret recipe." Meals cost from $12 at lunch and from $18 at dinner. Lunch is served Monday through Friday from noon to 3pm, with dinner offered Monday through Saturday from 6pm to 1am and on Sunday from noon to 5pm.

Hog Penny, Burnaby Hill (tel. 809/292-2534), is Bermuda's most famous pub, built and decorated in the British style with dark paneled rooms and draft beer and ale. Old fishing and farming tools make up part of the decor, along with bentwood chairs and antique mirrors. At lunch you can order pub specials, including shepherd's pie and seafood crêpes, or a tuna salad. The kitchen prepares a number of curries, including chicken and lamb. Fish and chips and steak-and-kidney pie are the perennial favorites. Dinner is more elaborate. You can always order a fresh fish of the day, perhaps Bermuda yellowfin tuna. The Angus beef is excellent, and you may want to precede your meal with Bermuda onion soup. Lunch costs from $15 and is served daily from 11:30am to 5:30pm. Dinner costs $25 and up and is served nightly from 6 to 11pm. There is nightly entertainment, and dress is casual.

Chopsticks Restaurant, 65 Reid St. East (tel. 809/292-0791), although off the beaten track, offers some of Bermuda's best Chinese cuisine, including spicy soup, tangy pork ribs, and seafood. Mr. Luk, the chef, specializes in Szechuan and Cantonese dishes with an accent on fresh vegetables and delicate sauces. This two-story restaurant, with dining upstairs and downstairs, gives you the best of two worlds. The fine food is served by a Bermudian staff. Lunch costs from $15, and dinner costs around $25. Meals are served daily from noon to 2:30pm and 6 to 11pm. Reservations are advised.

The Bombay Bicycle Club, Rego Furniture Building, Reid Street (tel. 809/ 292-0048). Indian haute cuisine is expertly cooked and served in an upstairs hideaway where you can enjoy lunch or dinner in a relaxed atmosphere. For lunch, they offer A Taste of India buffet, with a different selection daily, and a variety of à la carte dishes ranging from mulligatawny soup to chicken, beef, lamb, and seafood either served with a choice of sauces, in a spicy curry, or roasted in the tandoori oven. Indian vegetarian dishes and Continental selections are also available. Lunches cost from $10, dinners from $25. The place, on the third floor of the building between Court and King Streets, serves lunch Monday through Friday from noon to 2:30pm, dinner Monday through Saturday from 6:30 to 11pm. It's closed Sunday. Dress is smart casual.

The Pub, Hamilton Princess (tel. 809/295-3000), is a pleasantly informal eatery off the lobby of this famous hotel. The blue-and-green plaid carpets and the dark paneling give you a feeling of a Scottish pub. It offers temptingly fragrant tropical drinks whose colors include the full spectrum of a sunset. From noon to 2:30pm daily, one of Hamilton's better bargains is the pub's buffet luncheon, whose tempting array of salads and platters draws a busy midday crowd. The price is from $13. Dinners, served from 6:30 to 10pm, are à la carte and cost from $25. The roast prime rib of beef is served with the classic Yorkshire pudding and is well flavored. Always ask about the fish du jour if you're interested. The food is good and hearty, also familiar, and that means roast country chicken, English fish and chips, and pork chops. The salads are fresh, and you might begin your meal with a French onion soup.

BUDGET

MacWilliams, 75 Pitts Bay Rd. (tel. 809/295-5759). Set on the waterfront road leading into the most congested part of Hamilton, this informal restaurant is sheathed in light-colored brick and neutral-colored paneling. Clean and bright, and designed in a coffeeshop decor, it serves breakfast, lunch, and dinner, as well as coffee and snacks, daily from 7:30am to 10:30pm. Lunch, costing from $10, includes an array of sandwiches, hamburgers, soups, and salads. The evening meal, from $20, features such dishes as Bermuda fish dinners, fisherman's platter, sirloin steak, liver with onions, spaghetti with meatballs, and barbecued ribs.

Fourways Pastry Shop, Washington Mall, Reid Street (tel. 809/295-3263), lies on the ground floor of a shopping and office complex whose bustling crowds remind visitors of London. Yet, its array of very fresh pastries, tartlets, ice creams, petit fours, quiches, and croissant sandwiches evoke a Viennese or Milanese coffeehouse. You can order espresso or cappuccino while waiters dressed in Bermuda shorts bustle to serve the dozens of cramped, tiny tables. Coffee with a pastry costs from $3.50. The establishment does a thriving business Monday through Saturday, from 8am to 5:30pm.

Botanic Garden, Trimingham's, Front Street (tel. 809/295-1183), is housed on the third floor of the most famous department store in Hamilton. Naturally the place is filled with shoppers, most of whom know good value when they see it (that's why they're here). The place is informal and self-service, and ideal for morning coffee or a British afternoon tea. The pastries, pies, and cakes are excellent, especially the banana bread and the gingerbread. There is an array of European sandwiches as well. The luncheon specials are likely to include macaroni and cheese or barbecued chicken, along with a tossed salad and coffee (or tea), all for only $8.50. Food is served daily from 9:30am to 4:30pm; however, if you're going for a hot lunch, the hours are only from 11:30am to 3pm.

2. Paget Parish

VERY EXPENSIVE

Fourways Inn, Middle Road (tel. 809/236-6517), is considered by many to be the best restaurant in Bermuda. It was once an 18th-century Georgian house built of coral stone and cedar, which has been tastefully converted into a dining room offering Continental specialties and local seafood dishes. In the conversion, the traditional Bermudian character was observed. The glow of candlelight shines on the old mahogany beams. Guests have a choice in season of dining inside or out. On most nights a pianist plays, and the atmosphere is graceful and relaxed, the service good. The popularity of the place makes reservations essential. The old kitchen has been turned into the Peg Leg Bar with a whitewashed fireplace.

Sunday brunch is an elaborate buffet, costing from $30 and served from 11:30am to 1:30pm (no lunch is served Monday through Saturday). At night, a more ambitious menu is featured, beginning with the chef's specialty, cold smoked-salmon soup with dill. Main-dish specialties of the chef are tender filet of beef wrapped in light pastry and offered with a truffle–and–foie gras sauce, filet of lamb in a raspberry-vinegar sauce, and roast prime rib of beef carved to order and served with the traditional Yorkshire pudding. An unusual dish is called le tartare de poissons, which is prepared at your table with fresh raw Bermuda fish. A superb selection is the roast duck in its own gravy accompanied by a fresh pear poached in red wine. For dessert, the chef is known for his soufflés (which should be ordered in advance). Try the black-rum soufflé. I find that the most delectable is the chocolate, but you may prefer the strawberry or Grand Marnier. The wine cellar is among the finest on the island. The establishment is one of quality, as reflected by its price scale, which is likely to set you back more than $60 for dinner. In summer, dinner is served nightly from 6:30 to 9:30pm, but in winter, hours are from 7 to 9pm. Men should wear coats and ties in the evening.

EXPENSIVE

Newstead Restaurant, Newstead, Harbour Road (tel. 809/236-6060). Contained in one of the most quietly elegant manor-house hotels in Bermuda, this attractively dignified dining room welcomes nonresidents who telephone for a reservation. Guests dine beneath a beamed tray-style ceiling in a conservative dining room whose chintz-filled decor could have been transported from Britain. While you dine, a view of the lights of Hamilton Harbour slowly emerges as twilight falls. Between May and October, an outdoor barbecue is held every Tuesday and Thursday, accompanied by live dance music and by water splashing from a dolphin-shaped fountain above the swimming pool. Regardless of where they are served, full fixed-price dinners cost $42.50 per person without drinks; they are served every night from 7:30 to 9pm. The chefs offer a frequently changing array of Continental-inspired food, including roast leg of lamb with mint sauce, grilled sirloin steak with savory butter, and roast chicken Grand Mère.

Norwood Room, Stonington Beach Hotel, Paget (tel. 809/236-5416), offers stately dining in a large sun-washed room with tartan carpets, spidery iron chandeliers, Spanish-style stucco arches, and fan-shaped windows looking out over the foliage and the water. The restaurant is contained within a state-run hotel training school (see "Small Hotels" in Chapter III). The service and attitude among the youthful employees are most attractive. A piano provides music in the evening, when men should wear jackets and ties.

Lunch is served daily in the dining room or on the patio from noon to 2pm and costs from $15 per person. At dinner, an à la carte menu is presented, but many guests prefer the $35 table d'hôte, whose last order is taken at 8:15pm. Dinner is at specific seatings nightly at 7, 7:30, and 8pm.

Appetizers might include scallops in lobster sauce or a cold plate of marinated beef with onions, perhaps mushrooms stuffed with crabmeat or Bermuda fish chowder. Main courses feature fresh filets of Bermuda fish with prawns and mushrooms, and grilled sirloin with herb butter, the all-time favorite. The cooks have a deft Continental flair, as reflected in their veal steak with duxelles of mushrooms and melted cheese and their Hungarian chicken in, naturally, a paprika sauce. The restaurant adjoins the Overplus Bar, where you may want to stop for a before-dinner drink.

MODERATE

Terrace Room, Elbow Beach Hotel, South Shore, Paget (tel. 809/236-3535). Enormous, stately, and with a view of the sea, this coral-colored dining room is the most formal area in this previously recommended hotel. Only dinner is served in its conservatively decorated confines at two daily seatings: 6:30 and 8:45pm. The establishment offers a fixed-price menu for $25, usually with a choice of five different main dishes. Regular à la carte dinners cost from $35. Menu choices include a well-selected medley of such Continental dishes as roast veal loin with a walnut cream sauce, grilled wahoo sautéed in lemon butter, and Long Island duck with a bing cherry sauce. You might begin with snails in puff pastry with garlic butter or a vegetable soufflé with a raspberry sauce. Desserts tend to be elaborate, as reflected by the mint cream parfait, frozen hazelnut soufflé, and traditional English trifle. Bus no. 7 runs by the hotel. The restaurant is closed in December.

INEXPENSIVE

Paraquet Restaurant, P.O. Box 173, Paget (tel. 809/236-5842). Set near an important traffic junction on the South Shore, this unpretentious restaurant is the center of a previously recommended apartment cluster with the same name. Its decor of lime-colored Formica, tiles, metal chairs, and plants is definitely coffeeshop, but some of the menu items include substantial restaurant fare. The chef specializes in home-style Bermudian fare. As you dine, you overlook a circular formal flower garden, which the Portuguese owners created. The establishment has one of the largest sandwich menus on the island, both hot and cold, as well as omelets, homemade soups (which always include a fish chowder), and salads. You can order mixed platters such as turkey breast and crabmeat, or such grilled dishes as T-bone steak, fried liver and onions, and roast chicken. Full meals range from $12 to $30 per person, and they are served daily from 9:30am to 1:30am.

Seahorse Grill, Elbow Beach Hotel, South Shore, Paget (tel. 809/236-3535), is in a previously recommended hotel that permits a view of the sea and an old-fashioned colonial setting. Lunch includes such fare as seafood, pita-bread sandwiches, Bermuda fish cakes, and a selection of burgers, pizzas, salads, and ice cream. Dinner menu choices include fettuccine Saragossa, escargots in crêpes, lobster bisque, Oriental chicken platter, New York sirloin steak, and various preparations of shrimp and scallops, topped off by such desserts as banana fritters with black rum. Lunch, served daily from 11:30am to 3pm, costs from $8; dinner, served nightly from 6:30 to 9:30pm, costs $15 and up per person.

---

3. Warwick Parish

INEXPENSIVE

Herman's Restaurant, South Shore, Paget (tel. 809/238-9635), could be considered a snackbar, a coffeeshop, or a full-fledged restaurant, depending on your needs and the time of day. Its clientele includes the inhabitants of many of the surrounding guesthouses, as well as a healthy percentage of local residents and their children. Behind a low wall, just off the road, it contains a collection of parasols set on the outside terrace. If you prefer to dine indoors, there's a lunch counter with padded stools, plus an inner room filled with plants and wooden tables and chairs. Sometimes it's so crowded you can't get in.

The polite staff will tell you that the "open menu" allows them to accept orders for breakfast specialties throughout the day, so if you've a fancy for ham and eggs, Herman's will serve them to you day and night. In addition to the early-morning breakfasts, you can get lunches consisting of specialties such as burgers, sandwiches, omelets, "three-alarm" chili, and many kinds of salad, including pasta, at $12 for a full meal. For dinner, you get a bigger choice, and also a bigger price, around $20 and up. You might select fish and chips, one of six kinds of pasta, barbecued chicken, or sirloin steak (cooked to order). To begin your meal, try either the red-bean soup or Bermuda fish chowder. Herman's is open Sunday through Thursday from 9am to 11pm, on Friday and Saturday from 9am to midnight.

---

4. Southampton Parish

VERY EXPENSIVE

Newport Room, Southampton Princess, South Shore Road (tel. 809/238-8000). There is no restaurant in Bermuda where the decor is as sumptuously understated as at this one. It's French cuisine rates among the best in Bermuda as well. But none of this elegance comes cheap. Full meals begin at $75 per person, and can easily stretch upward. But if you're interested in yachts, boating, or competitive sailing, the cost will be worth the visual effects that a decorator worked hard to produce. Everything about the place re-creates the expensive interior of a well-maintained yacht. The theme is highlighted by the pair of exact miniature replicas of two of the winning sailing craft in the Newport to Bermuda race, each reportedly costing $15,000. These act as the illuminated centerpieces of a room that is entirely paneled in teak and rosewood and where any of the meticulously appropriate brass accents could grace the sleekest of world racing craft. Large illuminated paintings of the windblown regattas add the only real touch of vibrant color to an otherwise austerely somber yet immensely appealing room. Even the sophisticated overhead lighting was designed to simulate patterns of a starlit sky.

You'll be greeted at the entrance by a formally polite maître d'hôtel, stationed beside a gleaming ship's compass. The plush leather armchairs help you settle comfortably for dinner, which might include gourmet variations of *cuisine moderne* such as venison medallions with orange sauce. The menu is frequently changed. A wide array of international wines, served in Irish crystal, complements each dinner. The restaurant is open for dinner only, nightly beginning at 7pm, the last orders are accepted at 9:15pm. Reservations are suggested, and men are required to wear jackets and ties. The restaurant usually closes during January and February, depending on business.

Waterlot Inn, Middle Road, Southampton (tel. 809/238-0510). Three hundred years ago, merchant sailors unloaded their cargoes directly into the basement of this historic inn and warehouse, which sits within a few feet of the wharves. Today the best way to approach it is still by water, and that's precisely what many Bermudians do, mooring their sailing craft in the sheltered cove that has seen so many dozens of similar boats come and go. At one time the Darrell family owned this house and all the land stretching from Jew's Bay to the Atlantic on the other side of Bermuda. The land was parceled out to subsequent generations of Darrells until its most famous occupant, Claudia Darrell, ran one of the island's best-known eateries from the house until she died. She became the subject of international media attention. Over the years the inn has attracted such patrons as Mark Twain, James Thurber, Eleanor Roosevelt, and Eugene O'Neill. After the landmark building was devastated by a gas explosion in 1976, the Southampton Princess had it renovated and today it's one of their gourmet restaurants. Guests are transported from the hotel in a shuttle to this waterside inn.

Diners enjoy a drink in an upstairs bar entertained by the resident classical pianist. After descending a colonial staircase with white balustrades, they sit in one of a trio of conservatively nautical rooms. Each is filled with captain's or Windsor chairs, oil paintings of old clipper ships, and lots of exposed wood. From the outdoor terrace, you can view the movement of pleasure craft to the yacht mooring alongside the dock. Dinner, ranging from $55 per person, is served nightly from 7 to 10pm, when jackets and ties are required for men. The Sunday brunch, from noon to 1:30pm, is considered the best on the island, drawing not only hotel guests but lots of Bermudians as well; the cost is from $30. The cuisine is both French and classically Bermudian. Main courses are likely to include filet of pan-fried Bermuda rockfish, roast duck with black-currant sauce, lamb roasted with herbs and butter, and a *pave* of beef with freshly cracked pepper, cognac, and a cream sauce.

EXPENSIVE

Henry VIII, South Shore (tel. 809/238-1977), located below Gibb's Hill Lighthouse, is a pub restaurant lying between the Southampton Princess and the Sonesta Beach Hotel that has been given the royal treatment. The pubby atmosphere is enhanced by solid oak furnishings, brass railings, ornaments, and lighting fixtures in keeping with a Tudor flavor. The place is red-carpeted throughout. Even if you're just passing through, you might want to drop in at the split-level Oak Room Bar for some English beer on draft.

The cuisine is French and English. Hot pub lunches, served Monday through Saturday from noon to 2:30pm, cost from $10 and include such fare as steak-and-kidney pie, mussel pie, and plain old hamburgers. Sandwiches are available from 2:30 to 3:30pm. The popular Sunday brunch, costing from $18, is served from noon to 3pm. In the evening, from 6:45 to 10:30pm, the chef gets more elegant, turning out such whimsically named dishes as "Court Jester" (broiled combination of seafood) and "Steak Anne Boleyn" (flavored with cognac and simmered in a madeira sauce). The chef also prepares an English mixed grill, peppersteak, and a chateaubriand. Count on spending around $40 for dinner. Reservations are needed at night, when there is entertainment. Take the Southshore bus.

Whaler Inn, Southampton Princess, South Shore Road (tel. 809/238-0076), is an eagle's-nest restaurant positioned high above the boulders and jagged outcrops jutting from the soft sands of the beach at this well-known hotel. The multicolored tiles of the restaurant's cliff-bordered terraces sprout with landscaped clusters of sea grape, Norfolk Island pine, and comfortably padded iron armchairs. These offer lookout posts over the sunsets that redden the lapping waves of one of the island's most secluded beaches. If you want to dine on the terrace, someone will bring you a menu shaped, understandably, like a whale. If you prefer indoor dining, the interior's huge windows provide an airy setting where the panoramic view is the main decor. The timeless views of the Atlantic evoke the era when Bermuda's early colonizers complained about being disturbed during their sleep by the whistling of the hundreds of whales that migrated twice a year along the island's coastline.

The chef specializes in seafood. Fixed-price items are chosen from a three-course table d'hôte menu with a wide selection of choices. To "bait your appetite," you can begin your repast with tiger prawns in a cocktail sauce, shrimp bisque, or oysters on the half shell. The chef's special main courses will be well-seasoned portions of whatever game fish the local fishermen brought in that day, including yellowfin tuna, barracuda, shark, wahoo, or dolphin (the fish). Main courses that are not dependent on the whims of the tides or ocean currents include a kettle of seafood St. David's style, mussels marinière, and a deep-fried fisherman's platter, along with pan-fried local fish with almonds and bananas. You'll get a full array of Bermuda fish, either broiled or sautéed in butter. Your "happy ending" could include banana fritters with black-rum sauce, or Armagnac ice cream with prunes. Meals cost from $35. The restaurant is closed in January and February. Otherwise, it's open nightly for dinner from 7 to 9:30pm. Dress is casual.

Lillian's, Sonesta Beach Hotel and Spa, South Shore Road (tel. 809/238-8122), has an elegant art nouveau ambience and superb Continental cuisine. The seafood is also excellent here and is served by an international brigade of waiters. Classic dishes such as rack of lamb are prepared, along with such nouvelle cuisine dishes as veal Atlantic—that is, sautéed veal medallions served with sea scallops in a lime-and-champagne sauce. Reservations are essential, and meals are offered nightly from 7 to 10:30pm, costing from $45. From Tuesday through Thursday, there is piano bar entertainment, and classic chamber music is played on weekends.

Rib Room Steak House, Southampton Princess, South Shore Road (tel. 809/238-8000), offering international cuisine, sits atop the golf pro shop, near the tee-off point for the first hole. As you sit in the midst of panoramic windows and upholstered armchairs, the staff might suggest a "Dark and Stormy" (black rum with ginger beer) to get you started. Your drink might be followed by a main course such as baby pork spareribs, several kinds of beef broiled over charcoal, or roast prime rib of beef with Yorkshire pudding. If you don't want beef, you can have a catch of the day as a substitute or one of 10 other choices, such as chicken with short ribs or broiled lamb chops. Meals cost about $40. The restaurant is open every night from 7pm, with the last orders taken at 9pm.

---

5. Sandys Parish (Somerset)

EXPENSIVE

Lantana Colony Club, Somerset Bridge (tel. 809/234-0141), is the elegant restaurant contained within this exclusive hotel. Guests sometimes prefer a drink near the fireplace of the huge salon before climbing the short flight of steps into the pastel-colored dining room. The decorator probably spent time in Venice before receiving the commission to design the place. The ceiling trusses have been painted a pastel shade of spring green, and the neobaroque floral stencils were applied between garlands of Italian-style ornamentation. If you prefer a greenhouse effect, a second room has been glassed over with a solarium-style roof and surrounded with plants. A uniformed staff member will usher you to a table where a hibiscus has been placed at each place setting.

The frequently changing menu might on the night of your visit include such specialties as fresh salmon steak with dill sauce, prosciutto with melon, fish terrine, fish soup Lantana, grilled sirloin Delmonico style, breast of chicken with a whisky cream sauce, Bermuda fish meunière, veal Cordon Bleu, and grilled jumbo shrimp, any of which might be accompanied by grilled tomatoes provençale. Dinner is served table d'hôte style, nightly from 7:30 to 9pm, with a fixed price of $39 per person, plus 15% service. There is a large choice under each heading (appetizers, main courses, desserts, etc.). Jackets and ties are required for men. Live music is offered for dancing on certain nights of the week; call for information.

MODERATE

La Plage, Lantana Colony Club, Somerset Bridge (tel. 809/234-0141). Walking toward this charming restaurant will give you a chance to admire the sculpture scattered throughout the gardens of the most exclusive hotel in Sandys Parish. In many ways, it's the perfect luncheon stopover during a tour of Bermuda's west end. The urn-shaped balustrades that separate the terrace from the cove, fresh flowers, and impeccable service are much like something you might find at the edge of a lake in the north of Italy. An endearing statue of an elfin girl gleefully experimenting with her mother's necklaces and lipstick stands guard beside the Roman-style pool where a stone cherub spurts water high into the air. A pier and a dock area a few steps away from the restaurant create the impression that a yacht might pull up for a Bloody Mary at any moment. You'll be able to choose a table near the flowers of the sundeck, or one inside the pink-and-white summertime interior.

The international luncheon menu advises that the price of a main course will include a complete meal. You might begin with a Bermuda fish chowder, then follow with an array of dishes, which include items from ordinary sandwiches (peanut butter and bacon) to elaborate fantasies such as salmon mousse, crêpes stuffed with beef and cheese, Bermuda mussel stew, and coquilles St-Jacques. Several salads are offered as well, including a traditional chef's salad or one made with tropical fruit. Lunch only is served, daily from 1 to 2:30pm; closed January 4 to March 1. Full meals range from $15 to $25 per person.

Il Palio, Main Road (tel. 809/234-1049), is named after the famous horse race in Siena, Italy. In the center of Somerset in the west end of Bermuda, it lies on the Main Road and near several outstanding attractions that I'll document later. Currently, it's the only restaurant in the western sector specializing in the rich Italian cuisine, and it does so exceedingly well. If you arrive early, you can enjoy a drink in the bar downstairs before going upstairs to your well-set table. In a cozy, intimate decor, you might order from the menu a specialty such as fettuccine Alfredo, named after the famed restaurateur of Rome, or roasted quails with rosemary and sage. You might also order conchiglia di mare (lobster, scallops, shrimp, fish, and mushrooms, cooked in a light brandy cream sauce). A selection of 9-inch pizzas is also presented nightly. The Italian owners serve Tuesday through Sunday from 6 to 10pm, with an early-bird dinner special from 6 to 7pm costing $13; otherwise, count on spending $25 and up for dinner.

Village Inn, Watford Bridge (tel. 809/238-9401). What looks like a private vacation house sits a few feet above a boat dock. If you want to dine indoors, you'll have the run of the unpretentious paneled interior. The bar at one end of the room is a good place to share a drink with one of the local residents. Many diners prefer a table, at least for a cocktail, on a series of terraces that have been cut or inserted into the slope of the terrain leading down to the harbor. There, some of the tables have been fashioned from halves of barrels that rest on crisscrossed legs and that are usually sheltered from the sun with a parasol. This restaurant announces that its specialties include both Bermudian and European cuisine, as well as a "native" barbecue. The polite staff will recommend Bermuda seafood, such as fish chowder, rockfish, and, when available, lobster. The fine food represents value for money. Lunches cost from $12, and dinners range from $25 apiece. Food is served from noon to 3:30pm and 7 to 10pm. The inn is closed on Monday and holidays, and the yearly closing is in January and February.

Loyalty Inn, Mangrove Bay, Somerset Village (tel. 809/234-1398), is a 250-year-old converted home overlooking Mangrove Bay. A white-painted building, it looks vaguely like a church. The bar, in a separate building, is filled with captain's chairs and a mock fireplace. The restaurant with its decor of cedar paneling and small-paned windows attracts both visitors and locals who prefer its uncluttered atmosphere. The menu of steak, chicken, sandwiches, and seafood is not elaborate, but dishes are well prepared and the portions are generous. The fish chowder is superb, followed by either the fish plate or tasty scallops and a salad. In the evening, if you have the appetite, you can ask for a seafood dinner. Expect to spend from $25 per head. The bar is open from 10am to 1am daily, and food is served in the restaurant from 11:45am to 10pm. The restaurant lies about a 5-minute walk from the Watford Bridge ferry landing.

Blue Foam Restaurant, Somerset Bridge Hotel, Somerset Bridge, Sandys (tel. 809/234-2892), sits about 100 yards from the entrance to the Somerset Bridge Hotel, down the road. The entrance path, indicated by a sign, winds down the hillside until you reach the pleasantly panoramic restaurant, whose view encompasses the bobbing moorings of Ely's Harbour. Lunches are pleasantly informal, with a full array of burgers, salads (including one of pasta and a chef's salad), chicken, fish, and shrimp with chips. Such sandwiches as roast beef with onions and horseradish are offered, and the pizzas are 12 inches wide. At dinner, a more expensive menu is presented. It includes fresh wahoo steak, filet mignon in a mushroom sauce, homemade fish chowder, and other uncomplicated yet savory fare. Full lunches cost around $12, and dinners cost from $25. Breakfast is served from 8 to 10am, lunch from 11:30am to 2:30pm, and dinner from 6:30 to 9:30pm seven days a week. Take bus no. 7 or 8.

INEXPENSIVE

The Somerset Country Squire Tavern, Mangrove Bay (tel. 809/234-0105). You'll pass through a moongate arch to reach the raised terrace of this waterside restaurant in the center of town. It's a good choice during your tour of Somerset. If you don't want to eat within the confines of the limestone blocks and hedges that ring the terrace, you can choose the interior dining room downstairs. The restaurant, which can be visited on a trip to the Old Royal Naval Dockyard on Ireland Island, is open Monday through Saturday from 10am to 1am, on Sunday from noon to 1am, if you'd like to drop in for drinks. Lunch, however, is served from noon to 4pm and dinner from 6:30 to 10pm. With meals costing from $20, the bill of fare ranges from "pub grub" to fresh fish caught in local seas or else the traditional roast beef with Yorkshire pudding. Local Bermudian favorites include curried mussel pie and fresh Bermuda tuna or wahoo. Look for the specialties of the day, but count on charbroiled and barbecued meals. There is light entertainment six evenings a week.

---

6. St. George's Parish

EXPENSIVE

The Margaret Rose, St. George's Club, Rose Hill, St. George's (tel. 809/297-1200), is stylishly designed, one of the most appealing restaurants in the east end of Bermuda. Named after both Princess Margaret and Rose Hill (on which it sits), the fashionably decorated restaurant overlooks the harbor and the old part of town. Candlelight adds to the romantic ambience. The cuisine is international. You might begin with the award-winning Bermuda fish chowder or else enjoy an endive–and–rose-petal salad with a pine-nut–and–raspberry dressing. The wild-mushroom ravioli served in a thyme butter sauce is also an excellent appetizer. For your main selection, you might choose Bermuda fish Picasso (with a mosaic of fresh fruit and ginger), loin of lamb with an herb-and-garlic stuffing, or breast of Barbarie duckling, pink-roasted. Several pasta specialties are also featured. Dinner only, served from 7 to 9pm, goes for around $40 per person. Reservations are required.

MODERATE

Carriage House, Water Street, Somers Wharf (tel. 809/297-1730), specializing in beef as well as seafood, is housed in an old waterfront storehouse in the same building as the Carriage Museum in St. George's. After careful restoration, it keeps its 18th-century-warehouse look with two rows of bare brick arches, the effect softened by hanging baskets of greenery. After placing your order for dinner, you can help yourself at a large salad bar in the rear of the restaurant. But before that, you may want to enjoy an unusually good selection of hot and cold hors d'oeuvres. The chef specializes in prime ribs, the cost depending on the size of your beef, which is always cut to order and served with a ramekin of creamed horseradish in the British tradition. A different soup is offered every day, and a baked Idaho potato, Carriage fries, or rice is included with your main course. At lunch, a large selection of hamburgers is offered. A choice of excellent desserts is always available. A light luncheon should set you back no more than $13. Expect to spend from $30 for dinner. The Carriage House serves daily from noon to 2:30pm and 7 to 9:30pm, and Sunday brunch, buffet style, is also available from noon to 2:30pm. Casual dress is accepted.

Wharf Tavern, Somers Wharf (tel. 809/297-1515), is a nautically minded, modern restaurant built on the ground floor of a building with a veranda. It's situated among the cluster of buildings that make up Somers Wharf. Only pedestrians are allowed nearby, which might account for the popularity of the porch, of the window seats, and of the darkly paneled bar area inside. Dinners could include curried mussels, Bermuda fish cakes with peas and rice, pan-fried or broiled rockfish, broiled wahoo, oysters on the half shell, steak-and-kidney pie, both Bermuda and Maine lobsters in season, or steamers (fresh clams in a pot). Lunch, costing about $12, is served daily from 11:30am to 2:30pm; dinner is offered nightly from 6 to 10pm and costs from $25. The bar stays open throughout the day.

San Giorgio, Water Street (tel. 809/297-1307), is a charming little Italian restaurant that serves only dinner, Monday through Saturday from 6:30 to 10:15pm, costing from $30. To reach it, guests climb a short flight of steps from a point opposite Somers Wharf. The location is next to the Tucker House Museum. Most guests begin with a selection of antipasto, while others prefer a Caesar salad. Several well-prepared pasta dishes tempt diners, including cannelloni and lasagna. For your main course, you can select from such elegant dishes as breast of chicken sautéed with black-cherry–and–rum sauce. The chef also does a good veal marsala. Broiled grouper is also regularly featured on the menu. Reservations are recommended.

White Horse Tavern, King's Square (tel. 809/297-1838), is St. George's oldest tavern, a restaurant and cedar bar with a terrace jutting into St. George's Harbour. In fair weather (which is most of the time), guests prefer to sit on this terrace Venetian style, feeding breadcrumbs to the sparrows. A white building with green shutters, it is one of the most popular taverns in all of Bermuda. First, its location is so central you can't miss it. The most ordered item here is fish and chips, cooked in the manner of St. David's Island. The Bermuda fish chowder is also good. You can order such dishes as seafood combo, stuffed flounder, and marinated chicken. At lunch, a selection of Tavern burgers, fresh salads, and open-faced sandwiches are served. Lunches are from $12, with dinners costing around $25. The tavern is open daily from 10am to 1am (on Sunday it doesn't open until noon).

INEXPENSIVE

Pub on the Square, King's Square (tel. 809/297-1522), is a British pub with a rustic atmosphere serving an American and Bermudian cuisine. On a good evening the fun here has been compared to that of a prewar English music hall. The sing-along can keep St. George's rocking. The pub and restaurant are on two levels. After a mug of beer downstairs, guests can climb a spiral staircase to the tavern dining room with a veranda bar overlooking the square. Washed down with draft beer, the fish and chips is the most popular item, and sandwiches are also available. Other good dishes include Bermuda fish chowder laced with rum and sherry peppers, and pub-style chicken. Lunch is served daily from noon to 3pm, with meals costing from $9 to $15. Dinner is served nightly from 6 to 10pm for around $25. Closed in February.

Clyde's Café & Bar, Duke of York Street (tel. 809/297-0158), rarely visited by the cruise-ship crowd, is a secret address known among local residents who come here for some of the best home cooking in the east end. You enter through a bar with a jukebox usually blaring, then head for the family dining room in the rear. If you visit at lunch, you might want to settle for one of their well-stuffed sandwiches served with homemade cole slaw. But you can also order from an array of hot dishes at both lunch and dinner. Clyde's is known for its pork chops, Bermuda fish, shrimp, scallops, roast beef, and lobster. Lunches cost from $10, with dinners priced from $20. Service is Monday and Wednesday through Saturday from 11am to 1am, on Sunday from noon to 1am (closed Tuesday). The location is across from Somers Garden.

7. St. David's Island

MODERATE

Dennis's Hideaway, Cashew City Road (tel. 809/297-0044). In the eastern-most parish of St. George's, Dennis Lamb, a burly St. David's Islander, is one of the treasures of Bermuda. So is his quaint little eatery. As you approach it, you're likely to see Dennis (part Irish, part Mohawk) working in his garden in front (he even grows the cabbage he uses in his coleslaw and the beets for pickling). He'll show you into his fisherman's cottage by one of the island's little coves. Once inside, you'll feel you've left Bermuda and are visiting some little pocket-size country with a distinctive personality.

The descendant of whalers and pilots—"wooden ships and iron men"— Dennis and his son will offer you a cuisine that has virtually disappeared in Bermuda's restaurants, practiced only in private homes these days. Dinner, nightly from 7 to 10pm, is the only meal served. For about $28.50, he'll give you "the works," an array of dishes, including conch stew, dolphin (the fish), even herb-flavored shark hash, shrimp, conch fritters—you name it (but please don't order turtle, an endangered species). You bring your own wine. If you don't want to eat so much, request the fish dinner for $18. The fisherman's cottage is accessible by land or sea, and don't dress up. Always call in advance.

(This Pa Kettle ambience is not for everybody, it must be frankly pointed out. Reactions of readers have varied tremendously. Some repeat visitors give it high marks, claiming they've made at least 20 pilgrimages here during their annual visits to Bermuda. Some first-time visitors, however, claim that travel writers who send diners here should be tarred and feathered. So go only if you're a bit adventurous.)

Black Horse Tavern, St. David's Island (tel. 809/293-9742). If you should land here, in a section of the island that Bermudians call "the country," you won't be disappointed at all. The exterior looks like a dusty-rose–colored version of a private home, complete with green shutters and a rear glassed-in porch that looks over Smith's Sound. The bar might be your preferred place here. Hanging above the bar are two stuffed fish—one a Mako shark, the other a marlin. There's even a section of a whalebone with a rusty knife embedded in it from some long-ago struggle. Over the years the tavern has been host to many celebrities, including Robert Stigwood, the Australian movie producer. Many of the guests show up in yachts, but others, by far the majority, come from the nearby U.S. naval base, especially on pay day.

You might begin your meal with curried conch stew, shark hash, fish chowder, or curried mussels. This could be followed by one of a choice of sandwiches or burgers, perhaps a platter of fish and chips or chicken and chips. The chef also does a good sirloin steak and will also prepare you a chicken dinner. The house drink, especially if you're in love, is a honeymoon special. It combines rum, apricot brandy, and tequila in one potent drink. Lunch costs from $10; dinner, from $22. The establishment is open Monday through Saturday from 10am to 1am. Sunday hours are noon to 1am.

8. Hamilton Parish

EXPENSIVE

Tom Moore's Tavern, Bailey's Bay (tel. 809/293-8020), is Bermuda's oldest eating house, built in 1652. Once it was a private home, and was visited in 1804 by

Tom Moore, the romantic Irish poet who wrote some of his verses here, making reference to a calabash tree that still exists some 200 yards from the tavern. The location is on Walsingham Bay near the Crystal Caves in Hamilton Parish. The tavern is also the most famous dining room in Bermuda, which has known many incarnations. In 1985 two Italians, Bologna-born Bruno Fiocca and his Venetian partner, Franco Bortoli, opened it for dinner, quickly establishing it as one of the most popular upmarket restaurants in Bermuda. Fortunately, they have maintained the old character of this landmark place, with its four fireplaces. A bar and lounge are found upstairs.

The darkened cedar walls are a backdrop for the classical French and Italian cuisine served here. Seafood, impeccably prepared, is the specialty. A lobster tank is found outside during the season for Bermuda lobster (in the off-season months Maine lobster is served). The Bermuda fish from local waters is likely to be tuna, swordfish, rockfish, or yellowtail. Try quails in puff pastry or duck with a raspberry-vinegar dressing. The setting, the English silver, and the general ambience can help make for a memorable visit. The cost is about $55 per person for dinner. Dinner only is nightly from 7 to 9:30pm, with seatings every half hour.

The Plantation, Bailey's Bay (tel. 809/293-1188), is a charming oasis on the site of Leamington Caves along Harrington Sound Road. It is a yellow colonial-style building with steep white roofs and fireplaces. There are three rooms inside, with plush carpeting, ceiling fans, and rattan furniture, making for a warm, inviting ambience. In fair weather, guests dine al fresco in the tropical garden shaded by a giant marquee. The bar with its Bermuda cedar base is ideal for a drink.

The cuisine is French, Continental, and Bermudian. Lunches include an array of sandwiches and salads, such as an intriguing warm chicken liver–and–spinach salad. From the charcoal grill comes everything from a hamburger to the fresh filet of Bermuda fish. At night, the French chef shows his excellence by turning out such dishes as shrimp-and-wahoo cocktail and a chilled soup of the day, or better yet, one of the special hors d'oeuvres that are based on the availability of fresh produce. Local fish courses are offered, including one fish filet with bananas and almonds in a local style, another gently coated with Pommery mustard and topped with sliced tomatoes. One of the main specialties is charcoal-grilled mignon of lamb served with chutney. Lunches cost from $15, dinners from $45 per person, including wine and tips.

Christopher and Carol West, your hosts, welcome you daily for lunch from noon to 2:30pm and for dinner from 6:45 to 9:30pm. (They are closed from mid-December to mid-February.) Bar service is from 10am, and dinner reservations are suggested. Buses no. 1 and 3 go by.

Mikado, Marriott's Castle Harbour Resort, Tucker's Town (tel. 809/293-2040). Contained in the lower level of this previously recommended hotel, this is one of the most imaginatively stylish rooms in Bermuda. You pass through lacquered gateways to reach a whimsically art deco version of a Japanese tea garden. An experienced chef is assigned to each group of eight diners, preparing his cuisine much like an actor would prepare theater. Grills placed as the main distraction near each table permit diners to view whatever is cooking. Rare imported fish are used for the sushi bar, and these are mixed with very fresh Bermuda fish such as wahoo. All the traditional Japanese specialties, along with an aromatic sake, are available. À la carte meals go for around $45 each. Only dinner is served, nightly from 6:30 to 10:30pm (the restaurant is closed on Monday from December to March). Reservations are needed, and dress is smart casual.

BUDGET

Swizzle Inn, Blue Hole Hill, Bailey's Bay (tel. 809/293-9300), the home of the Bermuda rum swizzle, lies west of the airport, near the Crystal Caves and the Bermuda Perfume Factory. This is one of the most venerable bars in Bermuda, some 300 years old. As for food, the meaty Swizzleburger is most popular. Soups are offered, and fish and chips with coleslaw is a standard. Of course, you can have the traditional English bangers and mash. The inn makes an ideal "watering spot" if you're touring the island and want a drink, a lunch (light meals cost from $10), even a game of darts. It's customary to plaster your business card on a wall here—then attempt to find it on your next visit to Bermuda. The inn is closed Monday in the off-season, but otherwise meals are served continuously during its open hours, 11am to 1am.

Bailey's Ice Cream & Food D'Lites Restaurant, on the corner of Wilkinson Avenue and Blue Hole Hill (tel. 809/293-9333), at Bailey's Bay, stands across from the just-recommended Swizzle Inn. For "all-natural" ice cream, there is no comparable place in Bermuda. Forty different flavors are made in the 40-quart ice-cream maker, under the supervision of owner Frank T. Powers. The parlor is in a small Bermuda cottage, with a convenient parking lot. You can eat your butterscotch crunch, almond delight, or piña colada ice cream, whatever you choose, at one of the outdoor tables or else take it away. A sandwich nook, which uses fresh-baked breads, is a popular attraction. Also featured are fresh-fruit ices, frozen yogurts, and natural juices. Light meals cost from $6. They're closed in January and February; otherwise, hours vary depending on the time of year, but in summer the place is open daily from 11am to 7pm.

The establishment has one other location, 95 Front St., Hamilton (tel. 809/292-3703), featuring sit-down tables, waiter service, old-fashioned ice-cream-parlor glassware, and exotic creations made from their homemade ice creams, sherbets, and low-fat yogurts. It has a spectacular view of the harbor. Menus here feature light, healthful food at reasonable prices—lunches and dinners from $8. A separate section caters to fast take-out ice cream and lunches on the run. Hours are 11am to 10pm from April to October. Otherwise, off-season it closes at 6pm.

---

9. Smith's Parish

MODERATE

Inlet Restaurant, Palmetto Hotel and Cottages (tel. 809/293-2323), at Flatts Village, in Smith's Parish. In creating this attractive restaurant, the owners added a slope-roofed modern addition onto what had been a lushly paneled lounge lined with Bermuda cedar. If you choose to dine here, you can select a seat either near the big windows, which look over the moongate, the swimming pool, and the harbor, or you can sit in the darker and more intimate recesses of the back. Lunches are pleasing. You might start with mussels Casino, spinach or Caesar salad, or Bermuda fish chowder. Seafood courses include a platter of shrimp, scallops, fish and chips, seafood Rockefeller (scallops, crab, and other seafood in a cheese sauce on spinach), and perhaps fresh Bermuda fish, broiled or pan-fried. Meat dishes include sirloin steak, Bermuda chicken, and pan-fried liver. Other tempting main courses are steak-and-kidney pie, lasagne, and quiche. There is also a good selection of sandwiches and burgers available for lunch, and light snacks can be taken on the outside patio when the weather is fine. Dinners are more elaborate, with a more detailed menu containing a wider selection of dishes. The price averages around $8 for lunch and $35 for an evening repast. Meals are served daily from noon to 2:30pm and 7 to 10pm. Light snacks are served in the pub until 10pm.

BERMUDA—DAY & NIGHT

1. ATTRACTIONS
2. WHERE TO SHOP
3. EVENING ENTERTAINMENT

Bermuda is for fun! Even the major attractions are "lightweight," not designed to tax one. Because of the island's small size, it's easy to get to know Bermuda parish by parish on your trusty moped. After 20 miles or so, you'll run into the sea —so don't rush anywhere. At no point on the island are you allowed to go more than 20 mph anyway.

Even though a lot of people have been fitted into a tiny land mass, Bermuda doesn't appear to be as populated as some of the more crowded islands in the Caribbean. Although its population density is higher, it doesn't look that way, mainly because houses have been fitted quite naturally into the landscape. And there are no jarring billboards or neon signs to spoil the countryside. Because there are no car-rental companies, you'll encounter no traffic jams and no polluted air.

Bermuda seems like a perpetual festival, as it has something going on all the time. Sports are always a star attraction, especially golf and tennis. Sailing, horseback riding, and especially the pink-sand beaches are potent lures.

In this chapter we'll go on a guided do-it-yourself tour, taking in Bermuda parish by parish. After that, we'll go on a shopping expedition along Front Street in Hamilton, ending the day with some evening entertainment.

1. Attractions

From the western tip of Somerset to the eastern end of St. George's, there is much to see in Bermuda, either by bike, ferry, bus, or taxi. Just allow plenty of time. You'll need it, as the pace is slow. Chances are, you'll either be on a bicycle, on a moped, or in a private taxi. Cars can only travel 15 mph in Hamilton and St. George's, 20 mph outside these towns. This speed limit is rigidly enforced, and penalties for violation are severe.

Bermuda is divided into nine parishes (or counties), including Sandys Parish (in the far-western end of the island), Southampton Parish, Warwick Parish, Paget

Parish (center of the greatest concentration of hotels), Pembroke Parish (seat of the government at Hamilton), Devonshire Parish, Smith's Parish, Hamilton Parish (not to be confused with the city of Hamilton), and St. George's Parish (at the far eastern extremity; it also takes in the U.S. naval base and the little seafaring island of St. David's).

In the early days these districts, encompassing 21 square miles, were called "Tribes." By the early 17th century the term "Tribe Road" had come into use to describe the boundaries between the parishes. Pembroke, because it encloses the city of Hamilton, is the largest parish in population, and St. George's has the most land area.

Many local guidebooks are fond of pointing out that "you can't get lost in Bermuda." Don't you believe them. Along narrow, winding roads—originally designed for the horse and carriage—you can get lost, several times, especially if you're looking for an obscure guesthouse along some long-forgotten lane. I've been with taxi drivers of 25 years' experience who have gotten lost in Bermuda.

Fortunately, you won't stay lost for long. Bermuda is so narrow that if you keep going in either an easterly or westerly direction, you'll eventually come to a main road. At its fattest "waistline" Bermuda is only 1½ miles wide. The principal arteries are the North Shore Road, the Middle Road, and the South Shore Road, and with such marvelously descriptive names as those, you'll at least have some indication as to what part of the island you're in.

Sometimes the rain comes almost without warning in Bermuda. Never attempt to stay on your vehicle in drizzly weather. It's better to pull off the road and wait under some shelter. Usually the skies clear rapidly and the road dries quickly, but it's easy to have an accident on Bermuda's slippery roads after a rain, especially if you're not accustomed to using a motor scooter as your principal means of transport.

Gasoline stations—called "petrol stations" by the resident British—appear fairly frequently in Bermuda. But if you "tank up" at the beginning of your run, chances are you'll have plenty of energy to get you to your destination. For example, one tank of gas in a motorbike will take you from Somerset in the west to St. George's in the east.

A THREE-DAY ITINERARY

After you've landed and rested in Bermuda, recuperating by spending a day on its pink-sand beaches, you may be eager to explore the island. For the first three days, I have a suggested itinerary. I hope you'll be around for at least a week so you can break up your sightseeing trips with plenty of time for relaxing, either enjoying the beach, going boating, or engaging in some of the other sports activities offered.

Day 1

If you've only got one day to devote to sightseeing attractions, I suggest you spend it in the historic capital of **St. George's.** It has everything from a ducking stool to narrow, alleyway-like streets with quaint names: Featherbed Alley, Duke of York Street, Petticoat Lane, Old Maids' Lane, Duke of Kent Street. You can spend a day exploring British-style pubs, seafood restaurants, shops (several major stores along Front Street in Hamilton have branches here), old forts, museums, and churches. You'll even see stocks and a pillory once used to humiliate wrongdoers. Serious offenses were dealt with more severely, of course.

Day 2

For a second day of sightseeing, I suggest you take the ferry from Hamilton across Great Sound to **Somerset.** Your cycle can be carried on the boat (you'll need it later). You'll be let off at the western end of Somerset Island in Sandys Parish, where you'll find the smallest drawbridge in the world. It's easy to spend an hour walking around Somerset Village. After that, you can head east until you reach a beach on Long Bay along the northern rim of the island. There are several places for lunch in Sandys Parish (see Chapter IV). The Somerset Country Squire Tavern, a typical village inn, is the best of many of them. It's near the Watford Bridge ferry stop at the eastern end of the island.

After lunch you can go across Watford Bridge to Ireland Island, home of the important Maritime Museum. On your return to Somerset Bridge and the ferry back to Hamilton, you might take the turnoff to Fort Scaur. From Scaur Hill you'll have a commanding view of Ely's Harbour. You'll also have an excellent view over Great Sound. Or if you don't want to traverse Somerset again, you can board a ferry at Watford Bridge that will take you back to Hamilton.

Day 3

Reserve a third day for sightseeing and shopping in **Hamilton.** It's likely you'll be staying in one of the hotels in Paget or Warwick that we've already visited two chapters ago. If so, a ferry from either parish will take you right into Hamilton (the city, not the parish).

In Hamilton, you can always blend sights with shops. For many visitors, the shops are more compelling. Try to time your visit to avoid the arrival of cruise-ship passengers. On those days, facilities in Hamilton can get cramped.

The seat of the government of Bermuda since 1815, Hamilton was once known as the "Show Window of the British Empire." Both Mark Twain and Eugene O'Neill, who lived in places opening onto Hamilton Harbour, cited the beauty of the place. On little islands in the harbor, prisoners-of-war and victims of plagues were held either in prison or in quarantine.

A stroll along Front Street will take you by some of Hamilton's most elegant stores, but you'll want to branch off along the little alleyways to check the shops and boutiques to be found there. If you get tired of walking or shopping (or both), you can also take one of the boats or catamarans waiting to show you the treasures of Little Sound and Great Sound.

On some days you'll be lucky and get to see locals buying their fresh fish—that is, that part of the catch not earmarked for restaurants—right from the fishermen who sell the "catch of the day" at Front Street docks. That catch always seems to turn up more rockfish than any other, although you'll also see snapper, grouper, and many other species. In the 1930s, seaplanes would land passengers right in Hamilton Harbour.

Most Bermudians consider the winter months too cold to wear the shorts, although you'll see plenty of them. But in May, all the businessmen along Front Street seem to don a pair. The British military introduced these shorts to Bermuda in the early part of the 20th century. By the 1920s and 1930s the garment had become very fashionable. However, they were not worn to dinner parties or to church services. These shorts were originally worn with a white shirt, a tie, and a jacket, along with knee stockings. It was considered "daring" to wear the shorts 5 inches above the knee. And to go beyond that and wear Bermuda short-shorts could have gotten you ticketed by the police in the years after World War II. For some, Bermuda shorts, at least at summer cocktail parties, remain de rigueur.

ST. GEORGE'S PARISH

Settled in 1612, the town of St. George's was once the capital of Bermuda, before losing that position to Hamilton in 1815. The town was settled three years after Admiral Sir George Somers and his shipwrecked party of English colonists came ashore. A band of settlers, led by Richard Moore, of the newly created Bermuda

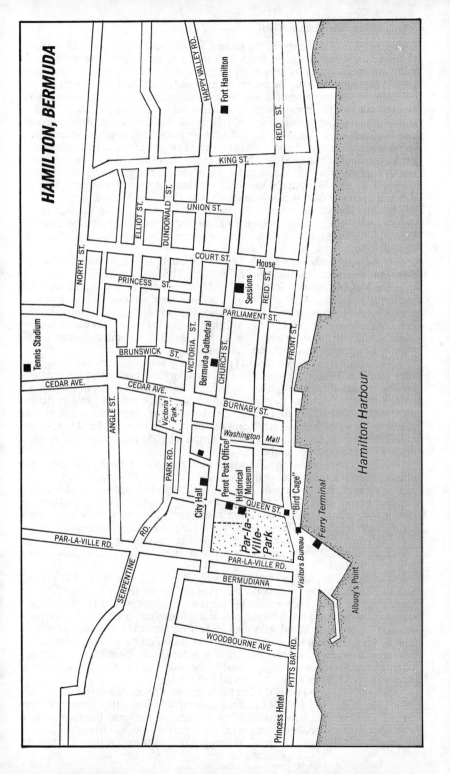

Company, founded the town, the second English settlement in the New World (Jamestown, Virginia, was the first). The town was named after England's patron saint, and its coat-of-arms depicts St. George and the dragon. Sir George Somers died in Bermuda in 1610, and his heart was buried in the St. George's area.

Almost four centuries of history come alive here, and generations upon generations of sailors have set forth from its sheltered harbor. St. George's even played its role in the American Revolutionary War. Bermuda depended on the American colonies for food. When war came, food ran dangerously short. Loyalties were divided in Bermuda, as many of the people had kinsmen living on the American mainland. A delegation headed by Col. Henry Tucker went to Philadelphia to petition the Continental Congress for food and supplies, for which the Bermudians were willing to trade salt. George Washington had a different idea, however. He needed gunpowder, and a number of kegs of it were stored at St. George's. Without the approval of the British/Bermudian governor, a deal was consummated that resulted in the gunpowder's being trundled aboard American warships waiting in the harbor of Tobacco Bay under cover of darkness. In return, the grateful colonies supplied Bermuda with food.

St. George's is about an hour's run east of Hamilton. To reach any of the attractions outlined below, take bus no. 1, 3, 8, 10, or 11 from Hamilton.

The **Visitors Service Bureau** (tel. 809/297-1642), King's Square, will give you a map and any information you need before you set out for exploration on your own, invariably on foot. King's Square is also called Market Square or King's Parade. It is the center of life in St. George's. Opposite the Town Hall, the center is open Monday through Saturday from 9am to 1pm and 2 to 4:45pm in summer. Off-season, it's open only on Wednesday and Saturday.

The square contains two colorful pubs where you may want to stop for a drink after your tour. Also on the square you'll see a pillory and stock where honeymooners like to have themselves photographed. These instruments of humiliation are treated as a joke today, but they were deadly serious at the time. Sometimes victims were placed in the pillory for a certain number of hours—sometimes with one ear nailed to the post! Victims were burnt on the hand or branded, fined in tobacco, nailed to the post, declared "infamous." Often they had their ears cut off or were made to "stand in a sheet on the church porch."

Offenses for which Bermudians were punished in the early days of settlement offer an illuminating glimpse of the social life of the time. Along with such "usual" acts as treason, robbery, arson, murder, and "scandal," records of the assizes (courts) of the early 1600s include concealing finds of ambergris, exporting cedarwood, railing against the governor's authority, hiding tobacco, being "notorious cursers and swearers," leading an "uncivil life and calling her neighbor an old Bawd and the like," neglecting to receive Holy Communion, the acting of any stage play of any kind whatsoever, and playing at such unlawful games as dice, cards, ninepins, and "such like."

The **Town Hall,** King's Square (tel. 809/297-0526), stands near the Visitors Service Bureau. Headed by a mayor, officers of the Corporation of St. George's meet here. There are three aldermen and five common councillors. The Town Hall has a collection of Bermuda cedar furnishings, along with photographs of previous mayors. You can go inside Monday through Friday from 9am to 5pm, on Saturday from 9am to 4pm. A multimedia, audiovisual presentation on the history, culture, and heritage of the colony, *Bermuda Journey,* is presented in the Town Hall several times a day. The half-hour show was produced by the makers of *The New York Experience.* Admission is $3.50 for adults, $2 for children.

Behind the Town Hall is the **Old State House,** Princess Street (tel. 809/297-1260), Bermuda's oldest stone building, constructed with turtle oil and lime mortar in 1620. The Old State House, where meetings of the legislative council once took place, was eventually turned over to the Freemasons of St. George's. The government asked the annual rent of one peppercorn, insisting on the right to hold meetings there upon demand. The Masonic Lodge members, in a ceremony of pageantry, still turn over one peppercorn in rent to the Bermuda government every April. (Peppercorns were sometimes a form of payment in the old days. In the late 18th century, two small islands off King's Square were sold for a peppercorn apiece: in 1782 Henry Tucker bought Ducking Stool Island, and in 1785 Nathaniel Butterfield bought Gallows Island. Several years later Simon Fraser purchased both for 100 peppercorns and built them into one, making what is today Ordnance Island.)

For the information of those who have never witnessed the 45-minute spectacle, it begins around 11am with the gathering of the Bermuda Regiment on King's Square and the subsequent arrival of the premier, mayor, and other dignitaries amid the bellowing introductions of the town crier. As soon as all the principals have taken their places, a 17-gun salute is fired, as the governor and his lady make a grand entrance in their open horse-drawn landau. His Excellency inspects a military guard of honor, while the Bermuda Regiment Band plays. The stage is, of course, now set for the center of attention—a peppercorn, which sits on a silver plate atop a velvet cushion. Payment is made in a grand and formal manner, after which the Old State House is immediately used for a meeting of Her Majesty's Council.

The Old State House is open to the public. Visiting is possible only on Wednesday from 10am to 4pm. No admission is charged.

Across from St. George's town square and over a bridge, visitors head for Ordnance Island to see *Deliverance II* (tel. 809/297-1459), a full-scale replica of *Deliverance I*, a Bermuda-built pinnace constructed in 1609 by the shipwrecked survivors of the *Sea Venture. Deliverance I* was the ship that carried these settlers on to Virginia. Admission is $2 for adults and 50¢ for children. There's a tape recording to guide visitors through the ship, which is open daily from 10am to 4pm. Alongside *Deliverance II* is the **ducking stool,** a replica of a horrible contraption used in 17th-century witch trials. Its use is demonstrated on Wednesday only.

Back on King's Square, head east to the Duke of York Street. Here **St. Peter's Church** (tel. 809/297-8359) is believed to be the oldest Anglican place of worship in the Western Hemisphere. The original church on this spot, built by the colonists in 1612 almost entirely of cedar with a palmetto-leaf thatch roof, was almost destroyed by a hurricane in 1712. Some of the interior, including the original altar from 1615 (still in daily use) was salvaged, and the church was rebuilt in 1713. It has been restored many times since and provides excellent examples of the architectural work of the 17th to the 20th centuries. The tower was added in 1814. On display in the vestry is a silver communion service given to the church by King William III in 1697. Before the Old State House was constructed, the colony held public meetings in the church. The first assize convened in 1616, and the first meeting of Parliament was in 1620. Sunday and weekday services are conducted here. Otherwise, it is open daily from 10am to 4:30pm, and a guide is on hand Monday through Saturday. There is no admission charge, but the church always needs donations to help maintain the building.

The **graveyard of St. Peter's** is also an attraction. The entrance is opposite Broad Alley. Some of the tombstones in the graveyard are more than three centuries old. Many tombs mark the graves of slaves. Here you'll find the grave of Midshipman Richard Dale, an American who was the last victim of the War of 1812. The churchyard also contains the tombs of Gov. Sir Richard Sharples and his aide, Capt. Hugh Sayers, who were murdered while walking the grounds of Government House in 1973. Even the governor's dog, Horsa, was killed. A state of emergency was declared in Bermuda following the assassinations.

The **Confederate Museum,** 32 York St. (tel. 809/297-1423), was once the Globe Hotel, headquarters of Maj. Norman Walker, the Confederate representative in Bermuda, and contains relics from the island's involvement in the U.S. Civil War. St. George's was the port from which ships carrying arms and munitions ran the Union blockade. There is a replica of the Great Seal of the Confederacy fitted to a

Victorian press so that visitors can emboss copies as souvenirs. The museum is open Monday through Saturday from 10am to 5pm; closed public holidays. Admission is $2 for adults; $1 for children under 12 years; free for children under 5 years.

Tucker House, 5 Water St. (tel. 809/297-0545), was the home of distinguished members of the well-known Tucker family of England, Bermuda, and Virginia. It displays a notable collection of Bermudian furniture, portraits, and silver. Also in the Tucker House is the Joseph Rainey Memorial Room, where the first black elected member of the House of Representatives in Washington, D.C., a refugee during the U.S. Civil War, practiced barbering. Admission is $2 for adults; $1 for children under 12 years; free for children under 5 years. Hours are Monday through Saturday from 10am to 5pm; closed public holidays.

Next to the restaurant is the **Carriage Museum,** 22 Water St. (tel. 809/297-1367), which offers "admission by donation." Transportation in Bermuda was only by carriage until 1946, when the "automobile age" arrived. But many of these old conveyances were preserved to delight present-day visitors, some of whom go for carriage rides in Hamilton. The site is a renovated old Royal Engineers warehouse. It's open Monday through Friday from 10am to 4:30pm; closed public holidays.

At **Somers Garden,** on Duke of York Street, the heart of Sir George Somers was buried in 1610. A stone column perpetuates the memory of Bermuda's founder. The garden was opened in 1920 by the Prince of Wales (later King of England, and subsequently Duke of Windsor). It is open daily from 7:30am to 4:30pm. Admission is free.

It's called the **Unfinished Cathedral.** After leaving Somers Garden, head up the steps to the North Gate, opening onto Blockade Alley. This structure is also known as the "folly of St. George's." The plan was that this cathedral, begun in 1874, would replace St. Peter's. But the planners ran into money troubles, a schism developed, and as if that weren't enough, a storm caused more damage.

In Featherbed Alley, **St. George's Historical Society Museum** (tel. 809/297-0423) is housed in a former home built around 1700, containing an original 18th-century Bermuda kitchen complete with utensils from that period. Exhibits include a 300-year-old Bible, a letter from George Washington, and American Indian ax heads. (Some early settlers on St. David's Island were Native Americans, mainly Pequot.) It's open Sunday through Friday from 10am to 4pm for a $1 admission for adults, 50¢ for children.

Also in Featherbed Alley stands the **Featherbed Alley Printery** (tel. 809/297-0009). It contains a working press in use for some 350 years. The alley gets its name because featherbeds were placed here for drunks to sleep on until they could sober up. Admission is free, and the shop can be visited Monday through Saturday from 10am to 4pm.

Petticoat Lane (sometimes called Silk Alley) got its name because two recently emancipated slave girls were said to have paraded up and down the lane rustling their new and flamboyantly colored silk petticoats.

Like Petticoat Lane, **Barber's Lane** is an alley named for a former slave. It honors Joseph Hayne Rainey, mentioned above, a freedman from the Carolinas who fled to Bermuda aboard a blockade runner during the Civil War. He was a barber in Bermuda for the rest of the war. Upon its conclusion he returned to the United States and was elected to Congress, becoming the first black member of the House of Representatives.

At the head of Broad Alley, behind St. Peter's Church, stands the **Old Rectory** (tel. 809/297-0879), built by a reformed pirate in 1705. A charming old Bermuda cottage, it is administrated by the Bermuda National Trust. It was later inhabited by Parson Richardson, who was nicknamed the "Little Bishop." Now a private home, it's open to the public only on Wednesday and Friday from 10am to 5pm. Admission is free, but donations are welcomed.

St. George's Library, 5 Queen St. (tel. 809/297-1912), is in an 18th-century Bermuda home, Stuart Hall. Cedar-beamed rooms and Bermuda furniture provide a cozy atmosphere in this circulation library, a branch of the Bermuda Public Library. It's open Monday and Wednesday from 10am to 1pm and 2 to 6pm, on Saturday from 10am to 1pm and 2 to 5pm. No admission is charged.

Bridge House Art Gallery, 1 Bridge St. (tel. 809/297-8211), is one of the best known in Bermuda, displaying only works by Bermudian artists, including Alfred Birdsey. Owned by the National Trust, the house was constructed in the very early years of the 18th century. It was home to several of the colony's governors. Perhaps its most colorful owner was Bridger Goodrich, a Loyalist from Virginia, whose privateers once blockaded Chesapeake Bay. So devoted was he to the king that he also sabotaged Bahamian vessels trading with the American colonies. The house is called Bridge because a bridge used to stand over a muddy creek (it's been filled in now). The art gallery is open daily from 10am to 5pm in summer, only on Wednesday and Saturday in winter.

From its earliest days St. George's has been fortified, and although it never saw much military action, the reminders of those former days are interesting to explore. On the outskirts of the town, the sights are reached by Circular Drive.

The first is **Gates Fort,** open daily from 10am to 4:30pm, built by Sir Thomas Gates, one of the original band of settlers on the *Sea Venture.* The fort dates from 1609. Gates was governor-designate for the Colony of Virginia. Nearby, along the coast, is **Building Bay,** where the shipwrecked victims of the *Sea Venture* built their vessels, including the *Deliverance* in 1610.

Towering above the beach where the shipwrecked crew of the *Sea Venture* landed in 1609 is **Fort St. Catherine,** Barry Road (tel. 809/297-1920), first completed in 1614 and named for the patron saint of wheelwrights and carpenters. The fortifications were upgraded over the years, the last major reconstruction being undertaken from 1865 to 1878, so that the fort's appearance today is largely the result of work done in the 19th century. Now a museum, visitors begin their visits by seeing a series of dioramas, "Highlights in Bermuda's History." Museum figures are used to show various activities taking place in the Magazine of the fort, restored and refurnished as it was in the 1880s. Large Victorian muzzle-loading cannons can be seen on their original carriages. In the Keep, which served as the living quarters of the fort, you can see information on local and overseas regiments that served in Bermuda, a fine small-arms exhibit, a cooking-area display, and an exhibition of replicas of the crown jewels of England. A short audiovisual show on the St. George's defense systems and the forts of St. George's can be seen here. Fort St. Catherine is open daily from 10am to 4:30pm; closed Christmas Day. Admission is $2.50 for adults, free for children under 12.

HAMILTON PARISH

Around Harrington Sound, the sights differ greatly from those of St. George's —more action, less history. A public bus from Hamilton goes here in about an hour. Hamilton Parish is bordered on the east by St. George's and on the southwest by Smith's Parish. The parish encloses **Harrington Sound,** a landlocked saltwater lake that is 1½ miles at its most expansive width and 2⅛ miles long. It was named for John, first Lord Harrington of Rutland, England.

Some experts believe that in unrecorded times Harrington Sound was a cave that fell in. Its gateway to the ocean is through an inlet at Flatts. However, it is believed that there are underwater gateways as well. Several deep-sea fish have been caught in the sound.

The **Bermuda Perfumery,** 212 North Shore Rd., Bailey's Bay (tel. 809/293-0627), is where Lili Perfumes are made. Visitors are given guided tours showing the perfume-making process, including the old method of extracting scents from native flowers. Among the fragrances produced are passion flower, Bermuda Easter lily, oleander jasmine, and sweet pea. A small botanic garden with a seating area and walkways provides an attractive resting place. You can also visit the orchid house, with more than 500 orchids, and the nature trail that passes through a large area of the property planted with tropical flowers, shrubs, and trees. The perfumery has a gift shop, the Cobweb. The perfumery is open Monday through Saturday from 9am to 5pm, on Sunday from 10am to 4pm. Admission is free.

Across Flatts Bridge, the **Bermuda Aquarium, Zoological Garden, and Natural History Museum,** North Shore Road (tel. 809/298-2727), is home to an amazing collection of tropical marine fish, turtles, harbor seals, and other forms of sea life. In the museum you can see exhibits on the geological development of Bermuda, deep-sea exploration, and humpback whales. The complex also has a zoo with Galápagos tortoises, alligators, and monkeys, along with an outstanding collection of birds, including parrots and flamingos.

You can bring a picnic lunch or choose from one of several restaurants in Flatts Village. There is parking for cycles and cars across the street from the Aquarium. To reach it by public transport, take bus no. 10 or 11 running from Hamilton, or bus no. 10 or 11 from St. George's. All these lines stop at the complex. By motorcycle from Hamilton, follow Middle Road or North Shore Road east to Flatts Village; or from St. George's, once over the causeway, follow North Shore Road or Harrington Sound Road west to Flatts Village. The Bermuda Aquarium, Zoological Garden, and Natural History Museum is open daily from 9am to 5pm; closed Christmas. Admission is $4 for adults, and $1 for children ages 5 to 12 (those under 5 are admitted free).

Crystal Caves, 8 Crystal Caves Rd., Bailey's Bay (tel. 809/293-0640), is composed of translucent formations of stalagmites and stalagtites, a setting including the crystal-clear Cahow Lake. Discovered in 1907, the cave is reached by a gently sloping path and a few steps. At the bottom, 120 feet below the surface, is a floating causeway that follows the winding cavern, where hidden lights illuminate the glistening interior. All tours through Crystal Caves are guided. Admission is $3 for adults, $1.50 for children 5 to 11. Closed during January, the caves are open February, March, November, and December from 10am to 4pm; April through October from 9:30am to 4:30pm (closed Saturday from the middle of November to the end of March, otherwise, open daily).

Another grotto, this one attached to the Plantation Club, is **Leamington Caves,** 46 Harrington Sound Rd., Bailey's Bay (tel. 809/293-1188). This grotto has stunning crystal formations and underground lakes. It was first discovered by a young boy, who noticed a small opening on the rocky hillside that he and his father were clearing for plowing in 1908. He slipped through the hole with a rope and candles and found a wonderland of natural cave splendors some 1½ million years old. Guided tours take you along lighted walkways with hand rails, through the high-vaulted, amber-tinted grotto. It's open Monday through Saturday from 9:30am to 4pm; admission is $3 for adults, $1 for children 4 to 12 (under 4 free). It is closed from December to February. Take bus no. 1 or 3.

Also at Bailey's Bay, **Tom Moore's Jungle** consists of wild woods. The poet Tom Moore is said to have spent many hours writing poetry under a still-standing calabash tree. Since the jungle is held in private trust, permission has to be obtained to enter it. However, it's much easier to pay your respects to the Romantic poet by calling at the Tom Moore Tavern (see "Hamilton Parish" in Chapter IV).

Devil's Hole, 96 Harrington Sound Rd. (tel. 809/293-2072), is a former cave. The pool is fed by the sea through half a mile of subterranean passages. Used as a natural aquarium since 1847, it's stocked with some 400 individual fish, including moray eels, sharks, giant groupers, and massive green turtles. Visitors can tempt the pond's inhabitants with baited but hookless lines. The attraction is open daily in summer from 9am to 5pm; from September to March, hours are 10am to 4:15pm. Admission is $5 for adults, $3 for children 6 to 12, $1 for tots under 5. Take bus no. 1 or 3.

For the best sightseeing view of the parish, visitors head for **Crawl Hill,** right before they come to Bailey's Bay. At this point, the highest place in Hamilton Parish, you can enjoy a view of the North Shore. Crawl is a corruption of the word "kraal," where turtles were kept before slaughter. Shelly Bay, named for one of the passengers of the *Sea Venture,* is the longest beach along the North Shore.

The **Hamilton Parish Church** can be reached by going down Trinity Church Road. It stands on Church Bay and dates from 1623, when it was just a one-room structure. Much work and many alterations have gone into it in just over 3½ centuries.

SMITH'S PARISH

Smith's Parish, named for Sir Thomas Smith, a member of the Bermuda Company, faces the open sea on both its northern and southern borders. To the east is Harrington Sound, and to the west, bucolic Devonshire Parish.

The parish takes in **Flatts Village,** one of the most charming little parish towns of Bermuda. This was a smugglers' port for about 200 years. The origin of the name is lost to history. Once it was the center of power for a coterie of successful "planter politicians" and landowners. Their government ranked in importance second only to that of St. George's, then the capital. People gathered at the rickety Flatts Bridge to "enjoy" such public entertainment as a hanging on the gallows. A so-called blasphemer in 1718 had his tongue bored through with a fire-hot poker. If the offense was serious enough, victims were drawn and quartered here.

From Flatts Village you'll have good views of both the inlet and Harrington Sound.

At the top of McGall's Hill (which you can visit after seeing the Verdmont mansion) is **St. Mark's Church.** Another church, built in 1746, once stood near the site of St. Mark's. When it became unsafe, a local family, the Trotts, donated land for the construction of St. Mark's, on which construction began in 1846. It is reported that the first services were conducted here on Easter Sunday in 1848. However, work on the church had not been completed, and subsequent additions, such as the chancel, were made. Work continued until the closing years of the 19th century. St. Mark's Church was based on the same designs as the Old Devonshire Parish Church.

Verdmont, 6 Verdmont Lane, Smith's Parish (tel. 809/236-7369), is an 18th-century mansion that holds a special significance to U.S. citizens interested in colonial and Revolutionary War history. It stands on property owned in the 17th century by William Sayle, who left Bermuda to found South Carolina on the American mainland, becoming its first governor. The house was built before 1710 by John Dickinson, a prosperous ship owner who was also Speaker of the House of Assembly in Bermuda from 1707 to 1710. Verdmont passed to Mr. Dickinson's granddaughter, Elizabeth, who married the Hon. Thomas Smith, Collector of Customs, whose oldest daughter, Mary, married Judge John Green, a Loyalist who came to Bermuda in 1765 from Philadelphia. During and after the American Revolution, Green was judge of the Vice-Admirality Court and had the final say on prizes brought in by privateers. Many American shipowners lost their vessels through his decisions. The house is now administrated by the National Trust. It contains many antiques, china, and portraits, along with the finest cedar stair balustrade in Bermuda. Open Monday through Saturday from 10am to 5pm; closed public holidays. Admission is $2 for adults, $1 for children under 12 years, free for children under 5 years. Bus no. 1 from Hamilton or St. George's serves Verdmont.

On the South Shore Road, turn right for **Spittal Pond,** Bermuda's largest wildlife sanctuary. The most important of the National Trust's open spaces, it is 60 acres in extent, containing about 25 species of waterfowl, which can be seen annually from November to May. Visitors are asked to keep to the scenic trails and footpaths provided. Birdwatchers, in particular, visit in January, when as many as 500 species of birds can be observed wintering on the pond. In general, migrating birds can be spotted anytime from November to April. The pond is open daily from sunrise to sunset.

Spittal Pond also shelters **Spanish Rock,** on a cliff facing the sea. It contains a cipher dating from 1543, probably carved by an Iberian mariner who may have been shipwrecked here. Historians still debate if it was placed here by a Portuguese or a Spanish seafarer.

At the western end of Mangrove Lake, just across the road from Pink Beach, is the **North Nature Reserve,** an area of living mangroves growing in a brackish pond. The pond is of interest to students of water fauna and flora. It attracts several species of birds. The reserve is open daily from 9am to 5pm; free.

DEVONSHIRE PARISH

As you wander its narrow lanes, with some imagination you can picture yourself in the original Devon in England. The parish takes its name from the first Earl of Devonshire. It is a lush, hilly parish, rarely spoiled by commercial intrusions.

Devonshire is not rich in accommodations, but it has some (see Chapter III).

Along the North Shore Road, you reach **Devonshire Dock,** long a seafarer's haven. It's near the border to Pembroke Parish. Fishermen still bring in such catches as grouper and rockfish here. You can shop for dinner if you've been fortunate enough to get a nearby cottage with a kitchen. British soldiers in the War of 1812 came here to be entertained by local women.

On Middle Road stands the **Old Devonshire Parish Church** (tel. 809/292-1348). A house of worship is said to have been built on the site in 1624, although the present foundation is from 1716. An explosion virtually destroyed the church on Easter 1970, and it was reconstructed. It is very tiny, looking almost more like a vicarage than a church. Some of the church relics survived the blast, including church silver from 1590, said to be the oldest on the island. The Old Devonshire Parish Church stands northeast of the "new" Devonshire Parish Church, which dates from 1846. It's built of limestone, with a high-pitched roof, constructed in the early English style. It was designed by Sir George Grove.

At the **Arboretum** on Middle Road, you'll discover one of the most tranquil oases in Bermuda, an open space with a wide range of some of the island's plant and tree life. It was created by the Department of Agriculture and Fisheries.

Along the South Shore Road, you can visit the **Edmund Gibbons Nature Reserve,** west of the junction with Collector's Hill. This portion of marshland, owned by the National Trust, provides living space for a number of birds and rare species of Bermuda flora. It's open daily at no charge. Visitors must keep out of the marshy area.

Also along the South Shore Road, heading to Hamilton, you'll come to **Palm Grove,** 38 South Shore Rd. (tel. 809/236-9079), a private estate 2½ miles east of Hamilton. It has some stunning flower gardens, opening onto a view of the ocean. A map outline of Bermuda is set into a spacious pond. The place is open Monday through Thursday from 8am to 5pm; free.

PEMBROKE PARISH

The city of Hamilton is not in Hamilton Parish but in Pembroke Parish, which is a peninsula that opens at its northern rim onto the vast Atlantic Ocean and on its southern side onto the beautiful Hamilton Harbour. Its western border edges Great Sound. The parish is named after the third Earl of Pembroke, who was a power in the Bermuda Company of 1616. Nearly one-fourth of Bermuda's population lives in Pembroke Parish, most of them in the capital of Hamilton.

The ideal way to see Hamilton or the parish itself for the first time is to sail in through Hamilton Harbour, past the offshore cays. You'll be joining everything and everybody from fishermen to the yachting set to cruise ships.

Earlier we've paid our respects to the Irish poet Tom Moore, and to the American humorist Mark Twain, for publicizing the glories of Bermuda. But for the British at least, the woman who put Bermuda on the tourist map was Princess Louise. The daughter of Queen Victoria, she spent several months in Bermuda in 1883. Her husband was the governor-general of Canada, and he allowed her to spend some time in Bermuda to escape the fierce cold up north.

Although in the 20th century Bermuda was to play host to a string of royal visitors, including Queen Elizabeth II, Princess Louise was the first royal personage to set foot in the colony. And set foot she did, turning up all over the island, visiting and chatting with its friendly people and winning their respect and admiration. Upon reaching Canada, she told reporters that she'd found the Shangri-La of tourist destinations.

In the beginning, guests could stay only at the Hamilton Hotel on Church Street, which was destroyed by fire in 1955 long after it had been turned into government offices.

The Hamilton Princess hotel, still in existence and named in honor of Princess Louise, opened in 1884. Over the years it has had a colorful history, none more dramatic than when it was taken over by Allied agents in World War II.

If Princess Louise or her equivalent were to visit today, she would most likely be housed at **Government House,** which stands on North Shore Road and Langton Hill. Not open to the public, it is the magnificent residence of the queen-appointed governor of the island. The large and beautiful grounds may be viewed on request to the governor's aide-de-camp. A Victorian residence, it has sheltered many notable guests, including Queen Elizabeth II and her husband, Prince Philip, as well as Prince Charles, Sir Winston Churchill, and President John F. Kennedy. The saddest moment for Government House was in 1973, when Gov. Sir Richard Sharples and his aide, Capt. Hugh Sayers, along with the governor's dog, Horsa, were assassinated while walking on the grounds. This led to a state of emergency in Bermuda.

While touring Pembroke Parish, visitors are fond of looking at **Black Watch Well** at the junction of North Shore Road and Black Watch Pass. Excavated by a detachment of the Black Watch Regiment, the well was ordered dug in 1894, when Bermudians suffered through a long drought.

After skirting the environs, it's time to zero in on the capital itself.

City of Hamilton

Since 1815 Hamilton has been the capital of Bermuda. Most people go here to shop, but the city also contains a number of sightseeing attractions. Named for a former governor, Henry Hamilton, it was incorporated as a town in 1793, and in 1815, because of its central location and its large, protected harbor, it was chosen as the capital, which was moved from St. George's. It occupies only 182 acres of land in its entirety, so it is most often explored on foot.

Today Hamilton is the hub of the island's economy, but long before it got such fancy labels as "showcase of the Atlantic," it was a modest outlet for the export of Bermuda cedar and fresh vegetables.

Hamilton boasts the largest number of eating and drinking establishments in Bermuda, especially on or near Front Street. These restaurants charge a wide range of prices, and there are many English-style pubs if you'd like to go on a pub crawl. Although there is a huge conglomeration of bars, religion isn't neglected—there are 12 churches within the city limits, one or two of which merit a sightseeing visit.

Hamilton should be seen not only on land but also from the water, and there are frequent boating tours of the harbor and its coral reefs. If you're visiting from other parishes, the ferry will let you off at the western end of Front Street, which is ideal if you'd like to pay a call to the **Visitors Service Bureau** and pick up a map. The location is near the Ferry Terminal. The staff here also provides information and helpful brochures. Hours are 9am to 5pm Monday through Saturday.

To return to the parishes of Paget, Warwick, and Sandys, ferries leave daily between 6:50am and 11:20pm. On Saturday and Sunday, there are fewer departures.

Opposite the Visitors Service Bureau stands the much-photographed **"Bird Cage,"** where it used to be possible to see a policeman (or woman) directing traffic. Now it's rare. Visitors wondered for years if the traffic director was for real or else placed there for tourist photographs.

Nearby is **Albuoy's Point,** site of the Royal Bermuda Yacht Club, founded in 1844. The point, named after a 17th-century professor of "physick," is a public park overlooking Hamilton Harbour.

After leaving the harbor, proceed up Queen Street to the Public Library and the **Bermuda Historical Society Museum,** Par-la-Ville, 13 Queen St. (tel. 809/295-2487), which has a collection of old cedar furniture, antique silver, early Bermuda coins (hog pennies), and costumes, plus the sea chest and navigating lodestone of Sir George Sommers, whose shipwrecked crew colonized Bermuda. You'll find portraits of Sir George and Lady Sommers, as well as models of the ill-fated *Sea Venture,* along with the *Deliverance* and *Patience,* other vessels important in the colonization of Bermuda. The museum is open daily except Wednesday and Sunday from 9:30am to 12:30pm and 1:45 to 4:30pm. Admission is free.

The library and museum lie in **Par-la-Ville Park** on Queen Street, which still dwells in the 19th century. It was designed by William Bennett Perot, Hamilton's first postmaster, and an eccentric one at that. As he delivered mail around the town, he is said to have placed letters in the crown of his top hat, so as to preserve his dignity. You enter by the landmark rubber tree, planted in 1847.

The **Perot Post Office,** on Queen Street at the park entrance (tel. 809/295-5151), is a landmark building where Bermuda's first stamp was printed. Beloved by collectors from all over the world, the stamps, signed by Perot, are considered priceless. It is said that Perot and his friend, Heyl, who ran an apothecary shop, conceived of the idea of the first postage stamp to protect the post office from cheaters. People used to stop off at the post office and leave letters but not enough pennies to send them. The postage stamp was conceived to make them honest. Of French Huguenot ancestry, Perot held his post from 1818 to 1862. The postage stamps were printed in either black or carmine.

In this same post office, philatelists can purchase Bermuda stamps of today. For its 375th anniversary Bermuda issued stamps honoring its 1609 discovery. One stamp portrays the admiral of the fleet, Sir George Somers, along with Sir Thomas Gates, the captain of the *Sea Venture.* Another depicts a building in the settlement of Jamestown, Virginia, which was on the verge of extinction when Sir George and the survivors of the Bermuda shipwreck finally arrived with supplies in late 1610. A third shows the *Sea Venture* stranded on the coral reefs of Bermuda. Yet another shows the entire fleet, originally bound for Jamestown, leaving Plymouth, England, on June 2, 1609. The old post office is open Monday through Friday from 9am to 5pm.

Hamilton City Hall, 17 Church St. (tel. 809/292-1234), is an imposing white structure with a giant weather vane and wind clock to tell maritime-minded Bermudians which way the wind is blowing. Completed in 1960, the building is headquarters for Hamilton's municipal government. The theater on the first floor is the scene for stage, music, and dance productions throughout the year, as well as being the site of the Bermuda Festival. It's open Monday through Friday from 9am to 5pm, with no charge for admission.

An art gallery upstairs in City Hall (tel. 809/292-3824) is where the **Bermuda Society of Arts** holds rotating exhibits of both Bermudian and foreign artists, much of whose work can be purchased. The Bermuda Society of Arts boasts a membership of 500, including many of the island's foremost amateur and professional artists. It is concerned with the promotion of all the visual arts. Besides exhibits, activities include slide shows, workshops, and dinner/film show evenings. For information about coming shows contact the Curator, Bermuda Society of Arts, P.O. Box HM 1202, Hamilton HM FX, Bermuda. The gallery is open Monday through Saturday from 10am to 4pm April to November and for limited hours on Saturday from December to March. Admission is free.

A short distance away, the **Bermuda cathedral** on Church Street (tel. 809/292-4033) is the seat of the Anglican Church of Bermuda. It was consecrated in 1894 on the site of Holy Trinity Church, which was destroyed by an arsonist in

1844. The cathedral is in the Gothic style, and inside it contains an interesting reredos. It is open daily from 8am to 7pm.

The **Sessions House,** opening onto Parliament Street (tel. 809/292-7408), built in the 1820s, is an Italian Renaissance–style structure with the **Jubilee Clock Tower,** built in the jubilee year of Queen Victoria. The House of Assembly meets on the second floor. Visitors are allowed in the gallery (you can call to learn the time of assemblies). On the lower floor, the chief justice presides over the Supreme Court. Again, there is a visitors' gallery. For times of court, telephone 809/292-1350. The building is open Monday through Friday from 9am to 5pm.

The **Cabinet Building,** occupying the block of Front Street between Court and Parliament Streets (tel. 809/292-5501), is a Hamilton landmark, fronted by the **Cenotaph,** a memorial to Bermuda's dead in the two world wars. The Cabinet Building houses the Cabinet Office, which includes the office of the premier. Parliament convenes here every fall. Visitors are allowed into the Senate Chamber, where Bermuda's upper house meets every Wednesday at 10am except during summer recess. The handsome oak throne dates from 1642. The building is open for free visits Monday through Friday from 9am to 5pm.

On the outskirts of Hamilton on Cedar Avenue stands **St. Theresa's** (tel. 809/292-0607), the Roman Catholic cathedral in Bermuda. Unlike the other parish churches of Bermuda, the architecture of St. Theresa's is in the Spanish Mission style. The church dates from 1927, and contains a chalice left by Pope Paul VI when he visited Hamilton in 1968.

Fort Hamilton, 6 Happy Valley Rd. (tel. 809/292-1234), is a massive Victorian fortification overlooking Hamilton and its harbor. It was ordered built in the 19th century by the Duke of Wellington, who had grand plans to turn Bermuda into the Gibraltar of the West. However, the fort was never called into active duty to defend Hamilton. It was allowed to fall into ruins, but is now restored and visitors can wander through its ancient passages and labyrinths. The dry moat is filled with plants and shrubbery, and there is a tea shop. From the fort there is a panoramic view of Hamilton and its harbor, and also of Great Sound. It is reached by Victoria and King Streets and Happy Valley Road. The admission-free fort is open from 9:30am to 5pm Monday through Friday.

PAGET PARISH

Chances are good that your hotel will be in this desirable residential section, across from Hamilton Harbour. It is a virtual "bedroom" of the city of Hamilton. Visitors flock here not so much for its many sightseeing attractions, but for its beautiful South Shore beaches, among the most beautiful on the chain of islands. Named after the fourth Lord Paget, the parish has a lot of historic homes and gardens, but most of them are not open to public view, except on special occasions. During the springtime College Weeks, the Elbow Beach Hotel is the center of most activities.

Most visitors who stay here in one of the section's many hotels use the ferry service, with landing docks at Salt Kettle, Hodson's, and Lower Ferry. It's also possible to "commute" by ferry to Warwick Parish or Sandys Parish to the west.

The Bermuda National Trust, which works to maintain the charm of the parish and its natural settings, is housed at **Waterville,** 5 The Line, Paget (tel. 809/236-6483), an 18th-century building. It's open Monday through Friday from 9am to 4:30pm.

Paget Parish is also the setting of **Chelston,** on Grape Bay Drive, the official residence of the U.S. consul-general (which is open only during the Garden Club of Bermuda's open houses and gardens program in the spring). It stands on 14½ acres of landscaped grounds overlooking South Shore.

At Bermuda's **Botanical Gardens,** South Shore Road (tel. 809/236-4201), you'll find hundreds of flowers, shrubs, and trees, all clearly identified. Guided tours leave from the main parking lot at 10:30am on Tuesday, Wednesday, and Friday (only Tuesday and Friday in winter). Buses no. 1, 2, and 7 run nearby.

Paget Marsh, on Middle Road, is 18 acres of unspoiled woods and marshland, with vegetation of ecological interest. It can be visited only when special arrangements are made with the National Trust (tel. 809/236-6483) from 9am to 5pm Monday through Friday.

One of Bermuda's best-known painters, Alfred Birdsey, invites visitors to his gallery, the Birdsey Studio, Stowe Hill (tel. 809/236-6658). His son-in-law, Tony Davis, will probably be there to answer questions and quote prices for original works in watercolor and oils by the painter who has exhibited around the world. Birdsey is known for sun-washed land- and seascapes with Bermuda settings.

Birdsey's daughter, Antoinette, exhibits some of her flower paintings, while another daughter, Joanne, displays whimsical and amusing versions of animals for children. The shop is open Monday through Friday from 9am to 4pm.

WARWICK PARISH

Famed for its two golf courses, this western parish of Bermuda was named after the second Earl of Warwick, a shareholder in the Bermuda Company of 1610.

It is quite likely that you will stay in this parish, as it boasts a number of hotels and housekeeping cottages, including the Belmont Hotel Golf & Country Club.

Warwick Long Bay, on the South Shore, with public conveniences, is one of the finest beaches of Bermuda and forms the major attraction of the parish.

In the vicinity, you can go inside Christ Church, across from the Belmont Hotel on Middle Road, daily from 9am to 4pm. Built in 1719, it is one of the oldest Scottish Presbyterian churches in the New World.

If you're in the parish on a Sunday morning, it seems that nearly everyone heads for Herman's Restaurant, a popular place serving local Bermudian food (see "Warwick Parish" in Chapter IV).

SOUTHAMPTON PARISH

This parish is a narrow strip of land opening at its northern rim onto Little Sound and on its southern shore onto the wide Atlantic Ocean. It is bordered by Warwick Parish in the east and Sandys Parish in the west. The U.S. Naval Air Station Annex is here, and you'll sometimes see red flags hoisted in the area, warning of aerial firing—so take care.

Celebrated for its beaches, the parish was named after the third Earl of Southampton. It is the setting for two of Bermuda's poshest resort hotels, the Southampton Princess and the Sonesta Beach Hotel and Spa, both reviewed in Chapter III.

The main attraction of this parish is the Gibbs Hill Lighthouse, Gibbs Hill, Lighthouse Road between South Shore and Middle Road (tel. 809/238-0524). Built in 1846, it is the oldest cast-iron lighthouse in the world. The magnificent view of the Bermuda islands and the sweeping shoreline from the lookout balcony at the top is worth the 185-step climb. The workings of the machinery are explained by the lighthouse keeper. In spring, visitors may see migrating whales beyond the South Shore reefs. The climb costs $2. You can see a collection of artifacts from shipwrecks recovered by Teddy Tucker, free. The lighthouse is open daily (closed Christmas) from 9am to 4:30pm. Take bus no. 7 or 8.

Also in the parish, Horseshoe Bay is one of Bermuda's most attractive public beaches, with changing rooms, a snackbar, and space for parking.

SANDYS PARISH

There are those who visit Bermuda by flying into the airport and then heading directly for Sandys Parish, which they never leave until it's time to go home. For many, the far-western tip of Bermuda is that special, with its rolling hills, lush countryside, and pleasant bays. The parish is actually made up of a group of islands, and was named in honor of Sir Edwin Sandys, one of the shareholders of the original Somers Island (Bermuda) Company, as well as a director of the Virginia Company and the East India Company.

Somerset Island, the largest of the Sandys group, where the village of Somerset lies, was named to pay tribute to Sir George Somers of *Sea Venture* fame. Sandys Parish is often called Somerset. Somehow it has always stood apart from the rest of Bermuda. For example, during the U.S. Civil War, when most of Bermuda sympathized with the Confederate cause, Sandys Parish stood firmly in the Union camp.

To explore this western end, the tip of the fishhook of Bermuda, it is best to take a ferry (fare of $2) plying Great Sound, a 45-minute run from Hamilton to Watford Bridge. Bikes can be taken aboard the ferry (motor-assisted cycles are assessed $2). Ferries also stop at Cavello Bay, Somerset, and the Royal Naval Dockyard. The **Visitors Service Bureau** is on the main road near St. James' Church (tel. 809/234-1388). It's open Monday through Saturday from 10am to 4pm from April to November.

Fort Scaur, Somerset Road (tel. 809/234-0908), was part of a ring of fortifications constructed in the 19th century during the troubled relations between Britain and the United States. Built as a last-ditch defense line for Old Royal Naval Dockyard, the fort stands on the highest hill on Somerset Island and is skillfully constructed to take advantage of the land contours so that it's well camouflaged from the sea. There are subterranean passages and a dry moat that stretches across the land from Ely's Harbour to Great Sound. Fort Scaur was opened to visitors in 1957 and has become one of Somerset's most popular tourist attractions. The fort offers views of Ely's Harbour and Great Sound, and points as far away as St. David's Lighthouse and Fort St. Catherine can be seen with the free telescope. Picnic tables, benches, and rest rooms are provided in the fort. Surrounding it are 22 acres of parkland filled with interesting trails, picnic areas, a rocky shoreline for fishing, and a public dock for access from the sea. Fort Scaur is open daily (closed Christmas) from 10am to 4:30pm. Admission is free, and visitors are welcome to picnic and photograph the many scenic views it offers.

After leaving the fort, you can continue on the **Somerset Bridge,** the world's smallest drawbridge. When open for marine traffic, the space between the spans is a mere 22 inches at road level. Much photographed, it is just big enough to allow the mast of a sailboat to pass through. The bridge dates from the early 17th century.

In the center of the island is the **Springfield Library and Gilbert Nature Reserve,** Main Road, Somerset. In it stands **Springfield,** an old plantation home restored by the National Trust that today houses Somerset Library (tel. 809/234-1980), a branch of the Bermuda Public Library. The nature reserve consists of 5 acres of unspoiled woodland, and bears the name of the family who owned the property from the beginning of the 18th century until it was acquired by the Bermuda National Trust in conjunction with the Bermuda Audubon Society in 1973. No admission is charged for either the nature reserve, the home (the branch library), or the outbuildings (used as a nursery school). The Nature Reserve is open daily from dawn until dusk. The library is open Monday, Wednesday, and Saturday from 9am to 1pm and 2 to 5pm.

On Somerset Road is the **Scaur Lodge Property,** an open area that includes the site of Scaur Lodge, a Bermuda cottage that was severely damaged by a waterspout, which moved up on land, turning into a tornado and driving across this neck of Somerset Island. This typical Bermuda steep-shoreline hillside is open daily at no charge.

Sandys Parish has areas of great natural beauty, including **Somerset Long Bay,** a public beach, which the Bermuda Audubon Society is developing into a nature preserve, and **Mangrove Bay,** a protected beach right in the heart of **Somerset Village.** From the public wharf, you can take pictures. If time remains, try to walk around the old village; it's filled with typically Bermudian houses and contains some interesting shops.

St. James' Anglican Church, open daily, in the village was built on the site of a structure that was destroyed by a hurricane in 1780. The present church was built nine years later, although the north and south aisles were added in 1836, the entrance gates in 1872, and the spire and chancel in 1880. The church was struck by lightning in 1939 but has been restored.

IRELAND ISLAND

A multimillion-dollar cruise-ship dock and tourist village has grown up in this historic area, which was used by the British navy until 1951. The site also shelters the Bermuda Maritime Museum, a theater, the Crafts Market, and the Bermuda Arts Centre. Ferries from Hamilton stop at Ireland Island, in the extreme west end of Bermuda, once per hour from 7am to 6pm. The fare is $2 each way. A bus leaves Hamilton for the Royal Naval Dockyard every 15 minutes from 8am to 8pm Monday through Saturday. The journey takes one hour and costs $2.50 for adults, half price for children.

The **Royal Naval Dockyard** has been transformed into a park, with Victorian street lighting and a Terrace Pavilion and bandstand for concerts. Vendors can be found pushing carts filled with food, dry goods, and local crafts. A full-service marina with floating docks is in operation along with a marina clubhouse and showers.

In a large 19th-century fortress, the **Bermuda Maritime Museum,** Old Royal Navy Dockyard, Ireland Island (tel. 809/234-1333), is open daily from 10am to 4:30pm, costing $5 for adults and $1 for children under 12. The museum continues to improve exhibits about Bermuda's nautical heritage. Its most famous exhibit is in the Treasure House, which was opened in 1979. It is devoted to various exhibits, including artifacts such as gold bars, pottery, jewelry, silver coins, and other items recovered from 16th- and 17th-century shipwrecks, including the *Sea Venture*. But most visitors come here to gaze at the Tucker Treasure.

A well-known local diver, Teddy Tucker, is credited with making the most significant marine archaeological find of this century when, in 1955, he uncovered one of the richest caches of underwater wealth in the Western Hemisphere. He discovered the wreck of the *San Antonio,* a Spanish vessel that went down off the coast of Bermuda in a violent storm in 1621. One of the great treasures of this find, the Pectoral Cross, was stolen only minutes before Queen Elizabeth II opened the museum in 1975. The priceless original cross had been replaced by a fake. To this day, the original cross has never been recovered, and its mysterious disappearance is still the subject of much discussion.

The museum is located in the enormous fortress, which was built by convict labor. The massive buildings of fitted stone, with their vaulted ceilings of English brick, are alone worth a visit. So are the 30-foot defensive ramparts; the underground tunnels, gunports, and magazines; and the water gate and pond for entry by boat from the sea. Exhibits in four exhibition halls illustrate the island's long, intimate connection with the sea, from Spanish exploration to 20th-century ocean liners, from overcanvassed racing dinghies to practical fishing boats, from shipbuilding and privateering to naval exploits. The 1837 Shifting House contains shipwreck exhibits, including the earthenware and pewter of the English colonists aboard the *Sea Venture,* wrecked in 1609.

As you enter the Parade Ground, at the entrance to the museum, you'll notice a 10-foot-high figure of King Neptune. This is a figurehead from the HMS *Irresistible,* recovered when the ship was broken up in 1891. The **Queen's Exhibition Hall** houses general maritime exhibits, including those on navigation, whaling, cable and wireless, and "Bermuda in Five Hours," this last a reference to the advertisements touting Pan American's early "flying boats." Under a vaulted brick ceiling (the bricks came from England), the building was constructed in 1850 for the storage of 4,860 barrels of gunpowder.

The **Forster Cooper Building** of the museum, from 1852, illustrates the history of the Royal Navy in Bermuda, including the Bromby Bottle Collection. This exhibit was opened in 1984 by Princess Margaret. The Boatloft houses part of the museum's boat collections, including the century-old fitted dinghy *Victory,* the 17-foot *Spirit of Bermuda,* and the *Rambler,* the only surviving Bermuda pilot gig. The original dockyard clock is a working exhibit on the upper floor, and chimes the quarters and the hours.

In the **Cooperage Building,** opposite the Maritime Museum entrance, is "The Attack on Washington," an audiovisual presentation about Bermuda's unusual role in the War of 1812 between Great Britain and the United States. The film graphically re-creates the burning of the Executive Mansion (repainted white after the smoke cleared), plus the eventual British defeat at Fort McHenry. Admission is $2.50 for adults and $1.50 for children and senior citizens. There are continuous shows daily every half hour from 10am until the last show at 4pm. Call 809/238-9432 for more information.

The **Crafts Market,** also in the Cooperage Building, 4 Freeport Rd. (tel. 809/234-3208), is the place to watch local artists at work and to buy their wares. It is open daily from 10:30am to 4pm, and admission here is free.

The **Bermuda Arts Centre,** next door, features works and lectures by local and international artists. New exhibits are installed every month. Admission is $1 for adults and 50¢ for children under 12 years. For more information, call 809/234-2809.

On a historical note, when this dockyard, which had been British Admiralty land, was sold in 1953 to the Bermudian government, it marked the end of British naval might in the western Atlantic.

SPECIALTY SIGHTSEEING

One of the major popular sightseeing attractions in Bermuda is a ride aboard one of the **Looking Glass Cruises,** Ferry Dock, Hamilton (tel. 809/236-8000), daily from 8am to 10pm. One of the most interesting is the Reef & Wreck Adventure, lasting 2 hours and costing $20. Departures are daily at 10am and 1:30pm. Passengers can see the wreck of the HMS *Vixen,* observing reef fish and coral formations. Guests can see 50 islands of the west end of Bermuda, and are provided with a lively commentary. Unlimited complimentary bar is included. The Cruise of Lights is also popular. It lasts 1¾ hours, costing $25 per person, and departs Tuesday through Saturday at 10:30pm, with a special cruise on Monday at 8:30pm. Honeymooners are especially fond of this one.

The vessel goes through the islands of Great Sound, as a nocturnal world unfolds, complete with the coral reef and a sunken wreck. The glass-bottom boat is specially lit for the best viewing. Music is also played, and the commentary includes talk of the constellations of the zodiac. The Sea Garden Dinner Cruise takes four hours, costs $55 per person, and departs Tuesday through Sunday at 6pm. Providing unlimited complimentary drinks, it takes guests along 50 islands, with good views of the sea gardens. A four-course meal of Bermudian dishes is included at the waterside terrace of Somerset's Village Inn. A calypso guitarist adds to the amusement.

The original **undersea walk** offered by Bronson Hartley can be arranged by writing or calling Mr. Hartley at P.O. Box FL 281, Flatts Fl BX, Bermuda (tel. 809/292-4434). Anybody can take part in this adventure, featured twice in *Life* magazine. It's as simple as walking through a garden, and you won't even get your hair wet. A helmet is placed on your shoulders as you stand on the ladder of the boat and begin your guided walk. It is an ideal underwater experience for nonswimmers and those who must wear glasses. Safe and educational, the walk takes you to see the feeding of corals and breathing of sponges, as well as the feeding of sea anemones. The skipper and host, Mr. Hartley, personally conducts the tours. His ability to train fish in their natural habitat has been acclaimed in many publications. His 50-foot boat, *Carioca,* leaves Flatts Village daily at 10am and 2pm. The underwater wonderland walk costs $35 per person.

One of the most unusual sightseeing adventures in Bermuda is to walk the **Bermuda Railway Trail,** which stretches along the old train right-of-way for 21 miles across three of the interconnected islands that make up Bermuda today. The railway is, of course, long deserted. It opened in 1931 but in 1948 was abandoned. The railroad was sold to what was then British Guiana (now Guyana). Before setting out on this trek, arm yourself with a copy of the *Bermuda Railway Trail Guide*, obtainable at the Bermuda Department of Tourism in Hamilton, or at the Visitors' Service Bureau in Hamilton or in St. George's. With it, you're ready to hit the old trail of the train system that was affectionately called "Rattle and Shake." Once the rail line was the island's main source of transportation, but it gave way to the automobile. The line follows the road between St. George's in the east and Somerset in the west, except for a section stretching for about 3 miles. That section, where the train whistle was once heard, was lost to roads in and around the capital city of Hamilton.

In some parts the trail connects with main arteries, but for the most part it winds along an automobile-free route left over from the "good old days." Rattle and Shake was considered the most costly rail line, per mile, ever constructed. In many places the views of Bermuda have not been seen by the general public since the end of World War II. To explore the trail, you face a choice of options: horseback, bike, moped, or your trusty feet. The trail cuts through the 5-acre Springfield Library and Gilbert Nature Reserve (recommended separately). You'll also spot the rare Bermuda cedar, which nearly vanished in the blight that struck the island in the early 1940s. Along the trail, you'll take in much greenery and semitropical vegetation such as the poinsettia, oleander, and hibiscus. At some point you can take time out to visit Fort Scaur, the 1870s fortress.

A nucleus of **bird watching** enthusiasts exist on Bermuda, but there are not many organized tours. Visiting birdwatchers are advised to make arrangements directly with the local people involved or find their own way around using David Wingate's *Check List and Guide to the Birds of Bermuda*, which is available at Hamilton bookstores and at the Bermuda Book Store (Baxter) Ltd., Queen St., Hamilton (tel. 809/295-3698). Use this in conjunction with standard American field guides.

Get in touch with David Wingate, Conservation Officer (tel. 809/236-4201). Mr. Wingate will occasionally—but not always—accompany interested birdwatchers as part of his conservation work. More frequently, he'll advise them by phone of the island's best retreats, walkways, and hideaways.

You can also contact the **Bermuda Audubon Society,** c/o Bermuda National Trust, P.O. Box HM 61, Hamilton HM AX, Bermuda (tel. 809/293-7394), for information about any organized field trips.

To help find a solution for a threatening world problem, the **Bermuda Biological Station for Research, Inc.,** has been given a grant to study the "greenhouse effect" by the U.S. National Science Foundation. Some $500,000 will be used every year to study this menace.

The Bermuda Biological Station is best equipped to measure changes in the oceanographic absorption of man-released carbon dioxide, having tracked levels of CO_2 for more than 35 years 15 miles southeast of Bermuda. The station also has kept extensive data on acid rain for the North American atmosphere.

Now vacationers to Bermuda can learn firsthand what Bermuda-based scientists are studying at the station by taking a free hourlong guided tour of the station's grounds and laboratory in St. George's. Tour leaders explain what scientific studies are being conducted in Bermuda and how they relate to the overall world environment.

The educational tours on Wednesday at 10am are conducted by scientists involved in the station's special projects and specially trained volunteers. Visitors should assemble in the Biological Station's main building. Coffee and snacks are served, and participants are asked to give a donation for the refreshments.

Some of the other topics that are discussed on the tour include the island's natural areas, including the coral reefs, protected by strict conservation laws, and how people have caused changes in the fragile ecological environment.

For information on the tours, contact the Bermuda Biological Station for Research, Inc., 17 Biological Lane, Ferry Reach, St. George's (tel. 809/297-1880).

2. Where to Shop

Most of Bermuda's best shops are along Front Street in Hamilton. Shopping is relaxed and casual here, no hysterical hustling to sell you merchandise the way you'll experience in many lands to the south. The best buys are usually imports from Great Britain and Ireland. For example, Shetland and cashmere sweaters cost less in Hamilton than in Britain, certainly less than in the States. You're likely to find good buys in Harris tweed jackets, all kinds of Scottish woolen goods, tartan kilts, as well as fine china and crystal.

Other good buys are the quality merchandise known as "Bermudiana," items either made here or produced exclusively for local stores. These include Bermuda cedar gifts, original Bermuda carriage bells, 375th-anniversary coins, Bermuda flower plates by Spode, pewter tankards, handcrafted gold jewelry, traditional-lines handbags with cedar or mahogany handles, miniature Bermuda cottages made in ceramics or Bermuda limestone, Bermuda sharks' teeth hand-polished and mounted in 14-karat gold, decorative kitchen items, Bermuda shorts, and silk scarves, as well as watches with Bermuda-map or longtail faces.

Liquor is also a good buy. You're allowed one quart duty free. But even with U.S. tax and duty, you can save between 35% and 50%, depending on the brand. Liqueurs offer the largest savings.

Stores in Hamilton, as well as those in St. George's and Somerset, are generally open Monday through Saturday from 9am to 5:30pm. When large liners are in port, stores often open in the evening.

HAMILTON SHOPPING A TO Z

Antiques
Heritage House, Front Street West (tel. 809/295-2615), sells nautical prints, English antiques, old maps, modern porcelain, and the largest collection of fine art on the island. There's also a collection of greeting cards by local artists, printed in Bermuda, plus top-of-the-line gifts.

Pegasus, 63 Pitts Bay Rd. (tel. 809/295-2900), is where to go if you're looking for antique prints, engravings, or magazine illustrations. You'll find no better anywhere in Bermuda. The inventory is varied, with old maps of many different regions of the world and more than 3,000 medical and legal caricatures from *Vanity Fair,* published between 1869 and 1914. These cost $20 to $200, depending on the subject. The hand-colored engravings of birds, fruits, and flowers are worth framing and sometimes cost as little as $40 each. Owner Robert Lee and his wife, Barbara, scour the print shops of the British Isles to stock this unusual store. Most prints range from the late 1700s to the late 1800s and are carefully grouped according to subject. The authenticity of whatever you buy is guaranteed in writing. They also offer ceramic house signs, costing from $40 each, made at a small pottery in England. Each is unique, based on any design a buyer chooses, then hand-painted together with the house name or a number and street. The shop also has a wide range of English greeting cards, many with botanical designs. Everything purchased here is duty free and will not affect your take-home quota. The shop is across the street from the Hamilton Princess.

Timeless Antiques, 26 Church St. (tel. 809/295-5008), opposite the bus terminal. You go down terra-cotta tile steps to spacious display rooms where you can look over carved early English oak tables, chests, and chairs, clocks of all types and ages, icons, candelabra, pictures, what have you. The shop also provides expert clock repair and restoration services. Packing and shipping of larger items are arranged for you.

Art

Windjammer Gallery, corner of Reid and King Streets (tel. 809/292-7861), housed in a charming yellow cottage, exhibits paintings and bronze sculptures by local and international artists. It also has an extensive selection of cards, prints, and limited editions, including photographs and signed silk-screen prints. The gallery has the last private garden in Hamilton, adjacent to the gallery and used for the display of life-size sculpture.

Asian Art

Tolaram's, 101 Front St. East (tel. 809/295-2826), truly is, as it claims, the "treasure house of the East." It has carved jade, soapstone, Chinese cloisonné, gold and silver jewelry, Chinese porcelain, Indian brassware, and a host of other objects. You can also purchase Seiko and Pulsar watches here at considerable savings over U.S. prices. Another Tolaram shop is in St. George's on Duke of York Street.

Beachware

Calypso, 45 Front St. (tel. 809/295-2112), has the largest and most comprehensive selection of beachwear in Bermuda. The shop is the exclusive island retailer of Louis Vuitton luggage and accessories, and it is Bermuda's only store that manufactures its own fashions. Exclusive and exotic designs by Polly Hornburg are available in a variety of internationally collected fabrics. There are branches at both Princess hotels and the Coral Beach and Tennis Club.

Boutiques

Bananas, Front Street West, opposite the Bank of Bermuda (tel. 809/295-1106), offers "Bermuda signature" items that are of good quality and colorful. You'll find T-shirts, jackets, beach bags, and beach umbrellas to take back home and let your friends know where you've been. The store has several other branches in Bermuda.

27th Century Boutique, Chancery Lane (tel. 809/292-2628), has long been known as a stylish and trend-setting boutique in the heart of Hamilton on one of the most charming shopping streets. It offers a fashionable selection of designer clothing, as well as shoes and accessories, for both women and men.

Casual Wear & Sunglasses

Sail on Bermuda, Old Cellar, Front Street (tel. 809/295-0808), offers everything from bright bathing suits to accessories and children's wear. It also has clothes for the leisure-minded—arguably the best T-shirts in Bermuda. A small addition, called Shades of Bermuda, has the finest collection of sunglasses on the island.

China & Glassware

Bluck's, 4 Front St. (tel. 809/295-5367), established in 1844, is well known for some of the finest names in china and crystal. Its wide selection includes Royal Worcester, Spode, Anysley, Royal Doulton, and Herend porcelain from Hungary, to name just a few. The choice in crystal is equally impressive: Waterford, Baccarat, Daum, and of course, Lalique, exclusive with Bluck's. Upstairs, you'll find a superb Antiques Room filled with fine English furniture, antique Bermuda maps, and an impressive array of old English silver. Bluck's has branch shops on Water Street in St. George's and in the Southampton Princess and Sonesta Beach hotels.

A. S. Cooper & Sons, 59 Front St. (tel. 809/295-3961), is Bermuda's oldest and largest china and glassware store, family-owned since 1897. It offers a broad range of fine bone china, earthenware, oven-to-table cookware, and jewelry. Among the famous names represented are Coalport, Minton, Royal Doulton, Belleek, Aynsley, and Royal Copenhagen. The Crystal Room contains Orrefors, Waterford, Royal Brierley, and Kosta Boda among other selections. The Collector's Gallery is known for its limited editions by Bing & Grondahl, Beswick, and Lladró. A perfume department has selections from the world's greatest perfumiers.

Department Stores

H.A. & E. Smith Ltd., 35 Front St. (tel. 809/295-2288), has been selling top-quality merchandise since 1889, at substantial savings over U.S. prices. Smith's comprehensive stock includes sweaters for men and women in cashmere, lambswool, and Shetland, plus cottons as well as superb British sportswear. Lladró porcelain and English bone china from Royal Crown Derby, Royal Doulton, Royal Worcester, and Aynsley are featured along with sparkling crystal from Waterford, Thomas Webb, Baccarat, and Swarovski. The perfume room features an outstanding collection from the top French *parfumeurs,* as well as cosmetics. Smith's is also noted for an excellent selection of handbags, gloves, fabrics by the yard, and children's clothing.

Trimingham's, 37 Front St. (tel. 809/295-1183), family-owned since 1842, specializes in fine European imports at savings of up to 40% and more over U.S. prices. Spode, Aynsley, and Royal Worcester china are featured along with Waterford and Galway crystal. The cashmere, lambswool, and specialty knitwear collection is unrivaled in Bermuda, and Trimingham's own lines of men's and women's wear are famous for their quality. French perfumes and European accessories are best buys here, as are fine jewelry, paintings, and gifts. Trimingham's Hamilton store is open daily. Branch shops are to be found throughout the island and at major hotels.

Fashions

Cécile, 15 Front St. West (tel. 809/295-1311), lies near the Visitors Service Bureau and the Ferry Terminal. It's well stocked with merchandise and is a center for high fashion in Bermuda. Cécile's claims that a visit to the shop is like a visit to the fashion capitals of the world—from France, Tiktiner; from West Germany, Mondi; from Hong Kong, Ciao and Ciaosport; from Israel, swimwear from Gottex. Its sweater and accessory boutique is outstanding as well, with many hand-detailed and hand-embroidered styles. Prices are sometimes 35% less than you'd pay in the States. Cécile has branches at the Southampton Princess, Marriott's Castle Harbour, and Sonesta Beach hotels.

St. Michael (Bermuda) Ltd., the brand name of Marks & Spencer, Reid Street (tel. 809/295-0031), brings you reliable quality merchandise from Marks & Spencer in England. You'll find men's, women's, and children's fashions in everything from resortwear to sleepwear, including lingerie. There are also well-tailored dresses and suits, dress shirts, blazers, and British-tailored trousers, as well as swimwear, toiletries, and English sweets and biscuits.

Footwear

W. J. Boyle & Son, Queen Street (tel. 809/295-1887), in business since 1884, specializes in selling brand-name footwear made in such countries as England, Spain, Brazil, and the United States. These include Clarks of England, Bally, and Loake Brothers. Footwear for men, women, and children is offered.

Gifts

Vera P. Card, 11 Front St. (tel. 809/295-1729), is known for its superb offerings of "gifts from around the world." These include the island's largest collection of ship's clocks, mantle clocks, and table clocks. Famous-name watches include Nivada, Girard Perregaux, and Michel Herbelin. The dinnerware collection features such famous names as Rosenthal, and the crystal department offers works also by Rosenthal among others. Hummel and Lladró figurines are also on sale. Look for Coalport English bone china, and also for a collection of jewelry in exquisite designs.

Jewelry

Astwood Dickinson Jewellers, Front Street (tel. 809/292-5805), has a treasure trove of famous-name watches, including Patek Philippe, Concord, Tissot, Omega, Chopard, and Movado, plus designer jewelry, all at prices generally below U.S. retail. From its original Bermuda collection, you can select a gold memento of the island. Other Astwood Dickinson shops are in the Walker Arcade and at the Sonesta Beach, Hamilton Princess, and Southampton Princess hotels.

E.R. Aubrey, Jeweller, Front Street West (tel. 809/295-3826), opposite the Ferry Terminal, has a rich collection of gold chains, rings with precious and semiprecious stones, and charms, including the Bermuda longtail.

Bermuda Jewellery Centre, Church Street (tel. 809/292-4199), opposite City Hall, carries a good selection of gold and silver jewelry, and it's also the authorized dealer for Citizen watches. The Ana-Digi-Temp will even tell you the temperature as well as the time.

Crisson Jewellers, Queen Street (tel. 809/295-2351), sells such top-name Swiss watches as Ebel, Rolex, Baume & Mercier, and Vacheron & Constantin, plus Les Must de Cartier selection of watches, jewelry, and accessories. You'll also be able to purchase gold and silver jewelry for men or women, as well as Bermuda charms.

Leather Items

The Harbourmaster, Washington Mall (tel. 809/295-5333), is your best bet for luggage and leather goods. Many items in its leather collection are often sold at prices 30% less than in the United States. Items include leather handbags from Italy and France, leather manicure sets, an extensive collection of wallets, and a large selection of nylon and canvas tote bags.

Linens

The Irish Linen Shop, 31 Front St. (tel. 809/295-4089), stands at Heyl's Corner, near the "Bird Cage" policeman or -woman. The shop stocks not only table fabrics of pure linen from Ireland, but a wide-ranging selection of other merchandise from Europe, everything from quilted placemats to men's shirts in French cotton from Souleiado of Provence. European linens purchased in Bermuda can often realize you as much as 50% in savings over American prices. The owners go over to Europe twice a year to bring back imports, including Madeira hand embroidery and Belgian lace. The shop has other branches at Somers Wharf in St. George's and on Cambridge Road, Mangrove Bay, in Somerset.

Liquors & Liqueurs

Burrows, Lightbourn Ltd., whose main store is at 87 Front St. (tel. 809/295-0176), is recommended for liquor purchases. The people here have been in business since 1808. You can make your own combination of liquors by asking for a "Select-a-Pac," consisting of any five fifths or two half gallons. Orders must be placed 24 hours prior to departure, except on Sunday, when 48 hours before departure is required. The store will deliver your liquor packages to the airport or else aboard ship. There are actually three stores in Hamilton, one in St. George's, one in Flatts Village, yet another in Paget, and one in Somerset.

Needlepoint Patterns

The Knit Shop, 48 Reid St. (tel. 809/295-6722), is the place to go if you knit, embroider, or sew. There is a good choice of needlepoint and cross-stitch patterns with Bermudian themes, which are available in kits.

Perfumes

Peniston-Brown Co., 23 Front St. West (tel. 809/295-0570), opposite the Ferry Terminal, carries almost all of the world's most popular perfumes, and you may learn something about the art of choosing and wearing perfume you didn't know from the shop's helpful "fragrance specialists."

Silver

Otto Wurz Co., 2 Vallis Building, 3 Front St. (tel. 809/295-1247), lies at the western end of Front Street past the Ferry Terminal and the Bank of Bermuda between Parlaville Road and Bermudiana Road. It specializes in articles made of silver, including jewelry, charms, and bracelets. It also sells a large selection of pewter tankards and flasks from England.

Stamps & Coins

Philatelists and numismatists will enjoy the **Bermuda Coin & Stamp Co. Ltd.,** Walker Arcade, Front Street (tel. 809/295-5503), where they can browse among stamps and coins, some of them real treasures, including commemorative groupings.

Woolen Goods

Archie Brown & Son, 49 Front St. (tel. 809/295-2928), features sweaters for men and women in cashmere, cotton, lambswool, and Shetland. For women, there are matching skirts as well. From neutrals to spectaculars, the color scope is wide. This shop has been in business for more than half a century.

Constable's of Bermuda, "Emporium," 69 Front St. (tel. 809/295-8060). Stepping into this spacious and well-carpeted store has induced culture shock in the hardiest travelers. Everything inside has been hand-woven or -knitted in Iceland. The inventory ranges from thick woolly blankets to patterned sweaters, both cardigan and pullover, for men and women. If you think you might need a pair of mittens or a wool cap during your vacation in the sun, Constable's will have them, although probably you'll prefer to have them packaged to take back for a cold winter back home.

The English Sports Shop, 95 Front St. (tel. 809/295-2672), was established in 1918 and is credited as one of the island's leading retailers of quality classic and British woolen items for men, women, and children, with branch shops in major hotels.

The Scottish Wool Shop, 7 Queen St. (tel. 809/295-0967), carries a wide range of tartans for men, women, and children—all imported from Great Britain. It also has a wide selection of woolens and cottons made especially for this shop. Merchandise includes an array of women's accessories, children's toys, Shetland, cashmere, and lambswool sweaters, plus cotton sweaters.

SHOPS AROUND THE ISLAND

As you leave Hamilton and tour the island, you may want to continue your shopping expedition, especially for typical Bermudian items, at one of the following addresses:

The Old Market, Main Road, Mangrove Bay (tel. 809/234-0744), in the village of Somerset, occupies premises dating from 1827, when it was a private home. For 65 years, however, it was a meat market. This unusual shop offers everything from old coins, brass, and crystal, to costume jewelry and casual clothes.

Globe Gift Shop, King's Square, St. George's (tel. 809/297-1670), in a historic old building, offers a good selection of items for souvenirs and gifts. You'll find T-shirts, charms, Bermuda cedar objects, and straw bags. The shop, which also sells stamps, bus tokens, cigarettes, ice cream, sodas, and candy, is open daily from 9am to 11pm.

Bridge House Straw Market, King's Square, St. George's (tel. 809/297-1853), has a wide array of straw products such as hats, bags, and calypso dolls. Bermuda pottery and cedar items, T-shirts, charms, and other costume jewelry are also offered.

Art House, 80 South Shore Rd., Paget (tel. 809/236-6746), specializes in original Bermuda paintings and hand-signed lithographs by artist Joan Forbes. The store also carries a range of selected handmade island crafts. It is open Monday through Saturday from 10am to 4pm.

The Chameleon, South Shore Road, Paget (tel. 809/236-8675), with branches at major hotels, is the exclusive agent in Bermuda for Iceland's oldest knit-wear manufacturer, Alafoss. The shop has both traditional styles and new fashion colors in Alafoss Icewool.

---

3. Evening Entertainment

Nightlife has never been the primary reason that visitors flocked to Bermuda. However, there is a surprising lot of it. Trouble is, it seems to float from hotel to hotel. Among the independents, it's hard to predict which pub or nightspot will have the best steel-drum band, calypso, whatever. Many of the local pubs feature sing-alongs at the piano bar, a popular form of entertainment in Bermuda. Most of the big hotels offer shows after dinner, with combos filling in between shows for couples who like to dance.

CULTURAL ENTERTAINMENT

Bermuda's major cultural season is the **Bermuda Festival,** staged for a two-month period in January and February, when outstanding artists, including both classical and jazz, perform on the island, along with major theatrical entertainments. Tickets for these events range in price from $18 to $25, and most of the performances are at City Hall Theater, City Hall, Church Street, Hamilton (tel. 809/295-1727). For more information and reservations, you can write Bermuda Festival, P.O. Box 297, Hamilton HM AX, Bermuda (tel. 809/295-1291).

At different times of the year the **Bermuda Philharmonic Society** performs. Often, students of the Menuhin Foundation participate (named for the virtuoso violinist Yehudi Menuhin). Concerts take place in the City Hall Theatre, City Hall, Church Street, Hamilton (tel. 809/295-1727).

Ask at the tourist office if the **Gombey Dancers** will be appearing at any time during your stay. This local dance troupe of highly talented men and women often performs in winter. This is the island's single most important cultural event with African influences, a tradition dating from the mid-1700s and once considered part of the "slave culture." On all holidays, you'll see the "gombeys" dancing through the streets of Hamilton in their colorful costumes.

In addition, the **Bermuda Civic Ballet** presents classical ballets at different venues on the island. Again, ask at the tourist office if any performances are scheduled at the time of your visit.

THE CLUB & MUSIC SCENE

For sheer glitz and glamour, the **Empire Room** in the lower lobby of the Southampton Princess (tel. 809/238-8000) offers the only Las Vegas–style revue in Bermuda. It's open from April to September. At 7pm Monday through Saturday, a dinner is served with a fixed-price menu costing $54 per person. Then, at 9pm, the doors reopen for a Broadway-style show, costing from $29 per person; the price includes two drinks. Shows start at 9:30pm.

The carefully choreographed revues are presented on a revolving stage in an amphitheater, where the predominant color is red and where the shows are tastefully provocative. Greg Thompson, the Seattle-based choreographer, combines humor with feathers, and lots of flash and glitter.

Touch Club, Southampton Princess (tel. 809/238-8000), is the most elegant disco on the western side of the island. In the lower lobby of the hotel, the spacious room is decorated like a warmly colored version of a London club. You'll find dozens of intimate corners in which to create your own party, each softly illuminated and containing plushly upholstered English sofas. Each conversation area has its own shaded candle, although if you're looking for more of an electronic thrill, the octagonal dance floor is ringed with batteries of colored lights that flash in synchronized patterns with the music. There's a cover charge of $15, which includes two drinks. Functioning only between April and November, the club is open daily from 10pm to 1am, except on Friday and Saturday, when it shuts down at 3am.

At **Prospero's,** Grotto Bay Beach Hotel, 11 Blue Hole, Hamilton Parish (tel. 809/293-8333), few guests are really prepared for what they'll find once they pass the ancient calabash tree that flanks the entrance. Even if you brought your couture silks to Bermuda, don't wear them here, since dripping water might dampen your outfit even more than your spirits. The entrance leads you down a flight of narrow stone steps to a dimly illuminated concrete walkway that carries you over Bermuda's version of the River Styx, out of which rises a single enormous stalagmite whose base was formed before the grotto was ever flooded with seawater. The cave is said to be 500,000 years old, although the electronic rhythms reverberating around the rock formations are unmistakably 20th century. Musical styles run the gamut from the 1940s to today.

You can chat on the bridge, eying newcomers looking furtively for Cerberus, stand at the bar, dance under stalactite spears, or select one of several table groupings spread under a plastic Napoleonic tent. The occasional dripping from the ceiling is hardly noticed by the crowd, which has been known to become gregariously rowdy during College Weeks. If you're transported to the point where a jump in the deep subterranean lake seems to be in order (you won't be the first to do so), remember that if the waters haven't been disturbed for a while, there's a layer of freshwater about 5 inches thick floating on top of a saltwater base. There are no cover charge and no minimum for eerily intimate evenings that begin at 9pm and finish around 1am. Drinks cost from $4.60. Buses no. 1, 3, 10, or 11.

Gazebo Lounge, Hamilton Princess, Hamilton (tel. 809/295-3000), is one of the most stylish nightclubs in the capital. This beautiful hotel lounge with a magnificent view over the harbor presents acts of international and local renown. From April to November, doors open Monday through Saturday at 9:30pm for an all-star steel-band performance that lasts one hour. A cabaret and Las Vegas–style revue, developed by Bermuda's most famous choreographer, Greg Thompson, begins at 10:45pm, lasting until just before midnight. With two drinks included, the cabaret costs $29. For clients wanting to create a full evening celebration, the hotel offers a dinner/cabaret package for $52 per person, reasonably priced by Bermudian standards. This includes a four-course meal at either of its most upscale restaurants (Harley's or the Tiara Room, depending on a client's choice), followed by access to the cabaret.

The Club, Bermudiana Road (tel. 809/295-6693), is the most sophisticated place in Hamilton for late-night viewing of the island's nighttime elite. It's above the Little Venice restaurant, which has a discreetly understated mirrored entrance that reflects the four stone lions at its portals. Jackets are required for men. Dancing is from 10pm to 3am. Nonmembers pay a cover charge of $8, after which drinks cost extra. The Club is open seven nights a week. Complimentary admission is granted after you dine at the Little Venice, the Harbour Front, or La Trattoria restaurant.

For the most authentic show on the island, I recommend **Clay House Inn,** North Shore Road, Devonshire Parish (for reservations, telephone 809/292-3193). There's a $15 cover charge, and it's well worth that, as you're likely to be entertained by folkloric dancers, a "real-thing" steel band, limbo dancers, and calypso artists. In all, it's a package of island entertainment. Show time is nightly at 10:30pm.

Oasis Club, Emporium Building, 69 Front St., Hamilton (tel. 809/292-3379). Acknowledged as the leading disco on the island, it requires that guests ride a glass-cased elevator to the second floor of a stylishly angular commercial building in the center of Hamilton. Although there's a restaurant within its chic interior, the establishment is better known for its dancing facilities upstairs. You can drink at a black-lacquer bar amid a high-tech decor. The establishment is thoughtfully designed to permit normal conversation in one area while a high-volume acoustical system emits some of the best sounds of Bermuda in another part. The club is divided into two sections, one called The Lounge and the other The Disco. One admission entitles guests to enter both precincts. Hours are nightly from 9pm to 3am. The cover charge ranges from $9 to $10. From October to January, that admission price includes one drink. In season, however, no drinks are included and are priced separately, beginning at $4.50.

Ye Olde Cock and Feather, 29-31 Front St., Hamilton (tel. 809/295-2263). Local wits sometimes debate whether it's more painful to climb up to this pub at the beginning of a long evening or to fall down the stairs after a few drinks. The steps leading up from the street, like much of the rest of the establishment, are flanked with cedar paneling. This multiroom hideaway offers seating on the streetside balcony with a view over carriages lining up under a shade tree, or at the long bar, where you can get draft beer from the old English taps.

If you want a meal, you can choose between a duo of dark-paneled rooms, one of which lies under the soaring eaves, with a view of the exposed structural elements of the limestone roof. At midday, meals include hamburgers, sandwiches, deep-fried Bermuda fish, steak-and-kidney pie, "bangers and mash," and salads. Evening meals are more formal, featuring any of the above items, as well as curried seafood Madras style, prime sirloin, and wienerschnitzel. The house's special drink is a blend of secret ingredients with orange juice and coconut milk called a Cock-a-doodle-doo. This might whet your appetite for lunch, which costs from $12, or dinner, from $25. Lunch is served daily from 11am to 5:30pm, after which you can order dinner. There's a dartboard for competition in the pub, and live music is presented every evening from 9pm to 1am. You can also watch sports events on large-screen TV via satellite.

MOVIES

The Little Theater, Queen Street, Hamilton (tel. 809/292-2135), is a 173-seat theater open seven days a week, with films shown at 2:15pm, 7:15pm, and 9:30pm.

Neptune Theater, Royal Naval Dockyard, Ireland Island (tel. 234-2923), offers shows Monday through Saturday at 7 or 7:30pm and again at 9 or 9:30pm. Sunday shows are only at 7:30pm. Most tickets cost $6.

PART TWO

THE BAHAMAS

GETTING TO KNOW THE BAHAMAS

After George Washington visited the Bahama Islands, he wrote that they were the "Isles of Perpetual June," and I can't improve on that capsule comment by the first president of the United States.

Today the 760-mile-long chain of islands, cays, and reefs collectively called The Bahamas, is designated by many as the playground of the Western world and the "South Sea Islands of the Atlantic." The chain stretches from Grand Bahama Island, whose western point is almost due east of Palm Beach, Florida, about 75 miles away, to Great Inagua, southernmost of The Bahamas, lying some 60 miles northeast of Cuba and less than 100 miles north of Haiti. (The self-proclaimed Haitian king, Henri Christophe, is believed to have built a summer palace here in the early 19th century.)

There are 700 of these islands, many of which bear the name *cay,* pronounced *key.* (*Cay* is the Spanish word for small island.) Some, such as Andros, Grand Bahama, Great Abaco, Eleuthera, Cat Island, and Long Island, are fairly large, while others are tiny enough to seem crowded if more than two persons visit at a time.

Rising out of the Bahama Banks, a 70,000-square-mile area of shoals and broad elevations of the sea floor where the water is relatively shallow, The Bahamas are flat, low-lying islands. Some are no more than 10 feet above sea level at the highest point, with Mount Alvernia on Cat Island holding the height record at just over 200 feet. In most places the warm, shallow water is so clear as to allow an easy view of the bottom, although cuts and channels are deep. The Tongue of the Ocean between Andros and the Exumas, for example, has depths of many thousands of feet.

1. Geography

As mentioned, there are some 700 hundred islands in The Bahamas, although some observers raise the count to 3,000. It depends on what you want to count as an "island." If the count were raised to thousands, then that would include rocks sticking up from the water. Geographically, the archipelago includes the Turks and Caicos Islands in the south (see Part Three). But these are constitutionally separate from The Bahamas.

The total land area of the major Bahamian islands is estimated at 5,000 square miles. Of all the islands, Andros is the largest, with 2,300 square miles; it's rather sleepy, however. Bimini, with only 8½ square miles and easily reached from Miami, is far livelier.

Most of the population is centered on the major islands of New Providence (Nassau) and Grand Bahama (Freeport). Other major population centers are the islands of Eleuthera (including the offshore Harbour Island and Spanish Wells) and Andros. Long Island and the Exuma Islands are small population centers.

Emerging from relatively shallow water, The Bahamas also contain major channels. The Straits of Florida separate the northwestern islands from Florida. Two major channels—Northwest Providence Channel and Northeast Providence Channel—separate Andros and New Providence from Grand Bahama and the Abaco Islands. The deep depression called the Tongue of the Ocean, already mentioned, separates Andros from the Exuma Cays. The Old Bahama Channel separates The Bahamas from Cuba.

The Tropic of Cancer, extending through the Great Bahama Bank, crosses Great Exuma. South of the Tropic of Cancer are relatively minor islands, including Ragged Island, Crooked Island, Great Inagua, Acklins Island, and Mayaguana Island.

To the east of The Bahamas is the North Atlantic Ocean, which means that The Bahamas are definitely not part of the Caribbean, as many visitors commonly assume.

THE ISLANDS IN BRIEF

NEW PROVIDENCE ISLAND   This island is better known as Nassau, after its largest city and capital of the Commonwealth of The Bahamas. Forty air minutes from Miami, it is home to some 125,000 residents. Nassau is separated from **Paradise Island** by a toll bridge. Formerly Hog Island, Paradise Island is the site of glittering hotels and casinos, but **Cable Beach** on New Providence is equally important—hailed as "the Bahamian Riviera."

GRAND BAHAMA ISLAND   A flat, 65-mile-long island in the northern Bahamas, Grand Bahama is the center of **Freeport/Lucaya,** which has the largest population, hotel development, and tourist infrastructure outside of New Providence. Famed for its palm beaches and its International Bazaar, it offers a half-dozen championship golf courses. It is also the industrial center of The Bahamas, with steel and oil works, and has cement and pharmaceutical plants.

The Family Islands

These islands, which constitute all but New Providence (Nassau/Cable Beach) and Grand Bahama Island (Freeport/Lucaya), are scattered like pearls in the Atlantic, and form the part of the long Bahamian archipelago that has only gradually been awakening from a long somnolence in the subtropical and tropical sun and begun to play a part in the drama of tourism developing throughout their country.

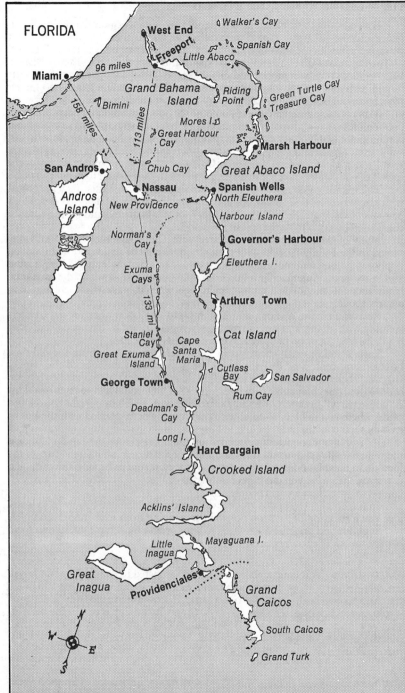

THE BAHAMAS AND TURKS AND CAICOS

For centuries these bits of land lying varying distances away from New Providence and the Bahamian capital were called the Out Islands. However, in recent years, perhaps with the aim of making them feel more a part of what is now a nation —The Bahamas—the government has changed the appellation to Family Islands. With modern transportation methods—airplanes, helicopters, and speedier boats —and with modern communications systems, the former Out Islands no longer seem so far out of the mainstream of everyday life in The Bahamas.

Many of these areas have already become the homes of modern resorts. Airstrips provide lifelines once supplied only by the infrequent mailboat runs from Nassau. All the major island chains are now serviced by regularly scheduled airplane flights, some from Nassau and Freeport/Lucaya, others from such Florida cities as Miami, Fort Lauderdale, and West Palm Beach. Of course, if you're of a mind to flip back the calendar, you can still take the mailboat or one of the interisland passenger ferries.

The islands come in every conceivable shape and size. Often they're fringed with sandy beaches and coral reefs, and hundreds of them are deserted or have no permanent residents. Swimming, boating, snorkeling, diving, and fishing here are considered by many to be the best in the world.

Many of the characteristics associated with The Bahamas of old are still preserved in the Family Islands, with their sleepy villages of pastel and whitewashed clapboard houses, a number of which were built by Loyalists who fled here during and just after the American Revolution. People move more slowly in the Family Islands, and you can soon realize that they're right when they ask what there is to be in a hurry about.

Relaxation is the keynote, and it is this, plus the boon of sunny days, waters teeming with sea life, and languid moonlight nights cooled by the trade winds, that has drawn the attention of more and more tourists to the Family Islands.

Each island or small chain has its own character, ranging from the old-time boatbuilding centers of the Abacos to the flaming-red flamingos of the remote Inaguas. Therefore it's necessary to read the descriptions of the resorts referred to in order to find one compatible with your interests. Often you'll find yourself in almost a "house party" situation or in an isolated outpost, so it's important to seek out places where you're likely to fit in with the crowd—or be pleased with the lack of crowds.

An important consideration for visitors planning to tour the Family Islands is the welcome they can expect from the local inhabitants. Hospitality is part of the lifestyle in these islands, and the reception is almost sure to be far more open and charming than what you can expect in Nassau or Freeport/Lucaya. The Family Islanders in general are a warm people.

In further chapters in this guide, I will review the inhabited Family Islands and give you a selection of vacation possibilities, ranging from lively resorts complete with nightlife and organized activities, to comfortable but simple guesthouses and cottages in out-of-the-way places.

ABACO ISLANDS This long, arching archipelago attracted Revolutionary War Loyalists, who settled at Hope Town and New Plymouth. Extending for some 130 miles, the chain takes in both Great Abaco and Little Abaco—often called the "mainland" —plus a necklace of other islets and cays. **Green Turtle Cay** is one of the most attractive centers for tourism, and **Great Guana Cay** is the longest offshore island. **Marsh Harbour,** on the Abaco "mainland," is the third largest town in The Bahamas, with an estimated population of 3,500.

ELEUTHERA Long and slender, this island with its satellite islands of **Spanish Wells** and **Harbour Island,** has more tourist facilities than any of the Family Islands. Its resorts stretch along the Queen's Highway for some 100 miles, and there are three airports: Rock Sound, Governor's Harbour, and North Eleuthera. Harbour Island, centering around Dunmore Town, is its chief touristic allure, with a 3-mile pink beach.

EXUMA ISLANDS Favored by the yachting set, this 100-mile necklace of islands, islets, and cays extends from Hog Cay, lying off Long Island, north to Sail Rocks near New Providence. Most of these islands are uninhabited. The largest number of people live in George Town, the capital, on the island of Great Exuma. A bridge known as "The Ferry" connects Great Exuma to Little Exuma at the Tropic of Cancer.

ANDROS The most "mysterious" island in The Bahamas, Andros is the largest of them, with a great coral reef running the length of the island. A mecca for snorkelers and scuba divers, this reef—called a "fringing reef"—is equaled only by that of the Red Sea. It embraces the drop-off point, called Tongue of the Ocean, a favorite cruising ground for submarines.

BIMINI Beloved by Hemingway, this island is called the "fishing capital of the world." Most of the population lives in and around Alice Town on North Bimini, which is flat and sandy, a 7-mile strip separated from South Bimini by a narrow channel. The location is just 50 miles due east of Miami.

Other members of the archipelago, of much less importance, include the following.

BERRY ISLANDS An archipelago within an archipelago, these islands, some 30 miles northeast of Nassau, make up only 30 square miles of land. The land is divided among about 30 islets and cays, with minor tourist facilities.

CAT ISLAND Many Cat Islanders claim that Columbus landed on their island—not San Salvador. Remote and with wide, open beaches, it remains yet to be developed. It may have gotten its name from an English sea captain whose name was spelled Catt. Its Fernandez Bay beach is considered one of the most beautiful in the Commonwealth.

SAN SALVADOR Claimed as the site of the "discovery of America," this island is the focus of the 500th anniversary of the Columbus arrival in America in 1992. Cockburn Town is its major settlement, and it is an outstanding scuba-diving center, but Columbus failed to put it on the tourist map. However, the worldwide publicity of 1992 may lead to another discovery.

LONG ISLAND In 1492 Columbus pronounced this island as the most beautiful he'd ever seen, and called it Fernandina, in honor of the king of Spain, Ferdinand. Containing about 58 miles, it is known for its fishermen and boatbuilders, with minor tourist facilities on its northern coast. It is a popular spot with divers.

ACKLINS ISLAND AND CROOKED ISLAND Lying southeast of Nassau and relatively forgotten by the world, these former pirate havens are among the sleepiest islands in this guide. With scheduled but infrequent transportation connections, they are some 225 miles southeast of Nassau. Once they were settled by American Loyalists, who established plantations here, all of which failed.

MAYAGUANA ISLAND This island is separated from Acklins and Crooked by the Mayaguana Passage. It is sliced from the Turks and Caicos Islands by the Caicos Passage. With a population of some 500, it sits amid the Windward Passage completely undeveloped and visited only by an occasional yacht.

INAGUA ISLANDS The most southerly and the third largest island of The Bahamas,

Great Inagua is some 40 miles long and 20 miles wide. It is a flat land, lying 325 miles southeast of Nassau. It does have some tourist facilities, but is only for escapists seeking "hideaways." Little Inagua lies between Great Inagua and Mayaguana Island.

---

2. History & Politics

HISTORY

The Early Years

The shallow waters of the Bahama Banks are believed to be the basis of the name of the island chain. After Columbus made his first landfall in the New World somewhere in The Bahamas, perhaps San Salvador, and subsequently visited elsewhere in the archipelago in his futile hunt for the Indies and China, Ponce de León voyaged here looking for the legendary Fountain of Youth. This journey, incidentally, led to the European discovery of Florida and the Gulf Stream—but not the magic fountain. The historian for Ponce de León described the waters of the Little Bahama Bank—just north of Grand Bahama—as *bajamar* (pronounced "bahamar") Spanish for shallow water. This seems a reasonable source of the name Bahamas.

It was Columbus, landing on October 12, 1492, who met the island residents, Arawak Indians called Lucayans. He renamed the island, which its inhabitants called Guanahani, declaring it to be San Salvador. Over the years there has been much dispute as to just which island this was. Long ago, it was decided that the discoverer's first landfall in the New World was a place known as Watling Island, supposedly after one of the buccaneers of the freebooters' era, and the name of that spot of land was changed (back?) to San Salvador in 1926. Recent obviously well-founded claims, however, place the first landing on Samana Cay, 65 miles southeast of San Salvador. In 1986 *National Geographic* propounded and supported this island as the true Columbus landfall, calling it "a small outrider to the sea lying in haunting isolation in the far eastern Bahamas."

The Lucayans who lived in the archipelago are believed to have emigrated here in about the 8th century A.D. from the Greater Antilles (but originally from South America), seeking refuge from the savage Carib Indians then living in the Lesser Antilles. The Lucayans were peaceful people. They welcomed the Spaniards and taught them a skill soon shared with the entire seagoing world—the making of hammocks from heavy cotton cloth. Sailors adapted the swings to shipboard use as beds.

The Spanish who claimed the Bahamian islands for their king and queen did not repay the Lucayans kindly. They did not even establish any settlements on the verdant cays surrounded by clear, warm waters. Finding neither gold nor silver mines nor fertile soil, the conquistadors simply cleared the islands of the Indians, taking some 40,000 doomed Lucayans to other islands in New Spain to work mines or dive for pearls. References to the islands first discovered by Columbus are almost nil after that time for about the next 135 years. They appear somewhat sketchily on maps, but the only actual written mention of the area is when King Ferdinand sent Ponce de León in the early 16th century "to find and settle the island of Bimini," where Indian legend placed a fountain of perpetual youth.

The Coming of the English

England formally claimed The Bahamas, by then destitute of population, in 1629, beginning with a succession of grants by Charles I and Charles II to territories in America and "Bahama and all other Isles and Islands lying southerly there or nearer upon the foresayd continent." Until 1717 the islands were governed by appointees of the lord proprietors given the king's grants. No settlement took place, however, until the 1640s, and it resulted from religious disputes that arose in Bermuda (as in England). A group called the Company of Eleutherian Adventurers was formed in London "for the Plantation of the Islands of Eleutheria, formerly called Buhama in America, and the Adjacent Islands."

English and Bermudian settlers sailed to an island called Cigatoo, changed the name to Eleuthera (from the Greek word for freedom), and launched a tough battle for survival. Many became discouraged and went back to Bermuda, but a few hardy souls hung on, living on the products of the sea—fish, ambergris, and shipwreck salvage.

Other people from Bermuda and England followed the Eleutherian Adventurers, and New Providence Island (first named Sayle's Island for the Eleutherians' leader) was settled in 1656. Crops of cotton, tobacco, and sugarcane were soon being grown, with Charles Towne, honoring Charles II, being established at the harbor.

Pirates & Privateers

The promising agricultural economy was short-lived. Several governors of The Bahamas of that era were corrupt, and soon the islands became a refuge for buccaneers. These were English, Dutch, and French seafaring adventurers who organized as the "Brethren of the Coast" and harried the ships of Spain, which thought it controlled the seas at that time. With the Spaniards repeatedly ravaging New Providence for revenge, many of the settlers left, the remainder apparently finding the pirates a good source of income. Privateers, a slightly more respectable type of freebooter (they had their sovereign's permission to prey on enemy ships), also found the many islets, tricky shoals, and secret harbors of the Bahama Islands to be good hiding places from which to stage their forays on ships sailing between the New and Old Worlds.

Late in the 17th century the name of Charles Towne was changed to Nassau at the instigation of the governor and inhabitants, to honor King William III, then on the British throne, who also had the title of Prince of Nassau (a former German province). But the name change didn't ease the troubled capital, as some 1,000 pirates still called New Providence their home base.

Finally the appeals of merchants and law-abiding islanders for Crown control were heard, and in 1717 the lord proprietors turned over the government, both civil and military, of The Bahamas to King George I, who commissioned Capt. Woodes Rogers as the first royal governor of the Bahama Islands.

Rogers got rid of the pirates. A former privateer in the War of the Spanish Succession, he dealt harshly with the lawless marauders of the sea, seizing many hundreds. Some were sent to England to be tried. Eight were hanged, and others received the king's pardon, promising thereafter to lead law-abiding lives. Rogers was later given authority to set up a representative assembly, the precursor of today's Parliament of the Commonwealth of The Bahamas. Despite such interruptions as the capture of Nassau by the fledgling U.S. Navy in 1776 (over in a few days) and the surrender of the Crown Colony to Spain in 1782 (of almost a year's duration), the government of The Bahamas since Rogers's time has been conducted in an orderly fashion. The Spanish matter was settled in early 1783 in the Peace of Versailles, when Spain permanently ceded The Bahamas to Britain, ending some 300 years of disputed ownership.

From Loyalists to Blockade-Runners

Following the American Revolution, several thousand Loyalists from the former colonies emigrated to The Bahamas. Some of these, especially southerners, brought their black slaves with them and tried their luck at planting sea island cotton in the Out Islands, as the land masses other than New Providence were called. Cotton growing was not a lasting success, as the plants fell prey to the chenille bug, but by then the former Deep South planters had learned to fish, grow vegetables, and by other means provide for their families and servants.

The first white settlers of The Bahamas had also brought slaves with them, and the early years of the 19th century saw dissension as to the treatment of those in bondage, ending in the United Kingdom Emancipation Act of 1834, which freed the slaves and provided for the government to compensate the former owners for their property loss. A fairly peaceful transition was achieved, although it was many years before any real equality of blacks and whites was discernible.

For a number of years shipwrecking was a profitable industry in The Bahamas —the unmarked shoals and reefs became graves for many ships. But the erection of lighthouses along major shipping lanes and the issuance of accurate charts made this unprofitable after the 1860s.

The War Between the States, or Civil War, in America brought a transient prosperity to The Bahamas through blockade-running. Nassau became a vital base for the Confederacy, with shallow-draft vessels taking manufactured goods to Charleston, South Carolina and Wilmington, North Carolina, and bringing out cotton. Union ships were banned from island harbors, even to take on drinking water. The victory of the Union ended blockade-running and plunged Nassau into economic depression. Some Americans who had supported the Confederacy emigrated to The Bahamas after their cause was lost, many bringing their slaves with them, even though they were forced to make the blacks free on arrival.

From Rum-Running to Drug-Smuggling

The next real boom enjoyed by the islands through troubles of their American neighbor was that engendered by U.S. Prohibition. As with the blockade-runners— but this time with faster boats and more of them—rum-runners churned the waters between The Bahamas and the southeastern United States. From passage of the 18th Amendment in 1919 to repeal of that law in 1933, Nassau, Bimini, and Grand Bahama were used as bases for running contraband alcoholic beverages across the Gulf Stream to assuage the thirst of Americans. The Coast Guard and the new generation of freebooters battled ceaselessly over the years and the seas. Repeal saw another shattering blow to the Bahamian economy.

World War II healed the wounds of the bootlegging days, as The Bahamas served as an air and sea way-station in the Atlantic. From this, they inherited two airports built for U.S. Air Force use during hostilities with the Germans. The islands were of strategic importance when Nazi submarines intruded into the Atlantic coastal and Caribbean waters. Today U.S. missile-tracking stations exist on some of the outlying islands.

In recent years a new and sinister problem has arisen for the United States through its proximity to The Bahamas—drug-smuggling. The same shoal waters, narrow inlets, and small, uninhabited islands that provided safe havens for pirates, blockade-runners, and rum-runners are now used for drug transport, with modern, small airfields compounding the problem. The U.S. Coast Guard is diligently pursuing the almost-impossible goal of ending this menace. Unfortunately, the Bahamian government has neither the manpower nor the money to police the 70,000 square miles of its domain, so this is an ongoing trouble.

POLITICS

The Commonwealth of The Bahamas came into being in 1973, becoming the world's 143rd sovereign state, with a ministerial form of government and a bicameral legislature. The end to some 250 years of colonial rule was signaled in 1964, when The Bahamas were granted internal self-government pending drafting of a constitution, adopted in 1969. By choice, the island nation did not completely sever its ties with Great Britain, preferring to remain in the Commonwealth of Nations with the

British monarch as its head of state. The queen appoints a Bahamian governor-general to represent the Crown.

In the British tradition, The Bahamas have a two-house Parliament, a ministerial cabinet headed by a prime minister, and an independent judiciary.

Power in The Bahamas is held by Lynden Oscar Pindling, the elected prime minister and head of the Progressive Liberal Party. His party is the most important, although there are four other major challengers.

The hub of government is on Parliament Square in Nassau, with its old pink government buildings. There, the archipelago is run with a strong emphasis on tourism, which generates some 70% of the island country's annual income.

---

3. The People & the Economy

THE PEOPLE

No descendants of the early inhabitants of The Bahamas, the Lucayans (Arawak Indians), survive. A few of today's Bahamians can trace their ancestry back to the Eleutherian Adventurers, others to Loyalists of American Revolution times and to southern Americans who fled after the Civil War, all of whom brought slaves to the islands. Some Bahamians of today can claim descent from pirates and privateers. Of the overall population of some 200,000 people, blacks are in the great majority, holding positions of leadership in all areas.

The language of The Bahamas is English. Bahamians speak it with a lilt and with more British Isles influence than American. There are some words left from the Arawak Indian tongue (like *cassava* and *guava*), and African words and phrases add to the colorful speech patterns.

THE ECONOMY

Despite many efforts over the decades since the Eleutherian Adventurers first settled in The Bahamas, it has only been in this century that a seemingly lasting and lucrative economic base has been discovered—tourism. Earlier entrepreneurs had a vision of this possibility, and the first positive step was taken in 1860, when the Royal Victoria Hotel was built in Nassau for winter visitors. The early years of this hostelry's existence, however, saw it filled with blockade-runners and their cohorts, who made its corridors ring with their spirited high jinks and then left it to silence and empty rooms when the Civil War ended. Henry Flagler, who was so successful with his posh hotels and his railroad construction to transport guests to them in Florida, tried to establish a steamer link with Nassau, built a hotel here, and failed. A few wealthy Canadians and Americans found their way to what they enjoyed as a winter paradise, but they weren't much interested in seeing The Bahamas become a lure for just anybody who could afford to come.

After World War II, tourism in The Bahamas really began to catch on. Since that time it has grown fantastically, not just in Nassau but throughout the archipelago, with nearly three million visitors coming here annually. United States and Canadian residents top the list, but thousands come from England, Germany, France, wherever, to this year-round tourist mecca. Sunshine, soft breezes, casino gambling, water sports—these attractions and others draw visitors. The capital of the Commonwealth, Nassau, is a city of old charm and modern resorts, and the second major tourist destination is Freeport/Lucaya, with its casino and plush resorts on Grand Bahama Island. Many North Americans flock to both places in summer or winter, as they lie less than an hour's flight from the United States.

Only a few Bahamian products are suitable for export, such as salt, frozen crawfish (Florida lobster), pulpwood, and vegetables. There is a favorable banking structure, which has proved attractive to investors.

4. Flora & Fauna

In this gentle climate, a staggering number of plants abound. At least 34 vegetables grow here, ranging from potatoes, corn, beans, and broccoli to more exotic-sounding produce such as eddoe, cho-cho, and breadfruit. To read a list of the flora found in the islands is like dipping into a botany textbook on tropical and subtropical plants. It would be impossible to name them all in this guide. Suffice it to say that among the more common are 53 trees, 29 shrubs, 21 climbers and vines, 3 grasses, 3 lilies, 1 tuberous plant, 2 succulents, 43 fruit trees, 4 fruit vines, and 6 herbs, in addition to the array of vegetables. At least those are the ones I was able to identify. If you count more—or less—I won't argue. Note that most of these plants are not indigenous to The Bahamas. My count paled into insignificance when I was told there are 950 naturalized and native flowering plants and ferns in the islands, plus 7 indigenous palm trees.

The Bahamas are deficient in mammals, most having been exterminated early in the islands' history. Hutia, a ratlike rodent found only on Atwood Cay, is the only native mammal found today. It was once thought to be extinct. There are donkeys, hogs, and horses in the Abacos and cattle in Inagua, and bats are common throughout the archipelago.

Special mention should be made of the Bahamian iguana, which is considered rare or endangered. One of the reasons for this is that since the days of the Lucayan Indians until modern times, the iguana was considered a food delicacy. However, David Blair, founder of Cyclura Research Center, which is dedicated to the conservation and captive propagation of West Indian rock iguanas, states, "The reason for their drastic decline in recent years is, in part, due to habitat loss, the introduction of domestic animals, and the attitude that anything that moves is fair game for food or just target practice."

Today the Bahamian iguana is protected by law. It is forbidden to capture or kill an iguana. Upon conviction, the penalty is a fine of up to $300 and/or imprisonment for a term not exceeding six months. Mr. Blair states that the three species of Bahamian iguanas belong to the genus Cyclura, and that some species of Cyclura are considered to be perhaps the rarest lizards on earth. His research has shown that virtually all iguanas on inhabited islands in The Bahamas have been exterminated and those few remaining are restricted to small uninhabited cays difficult to reach by private boat. He considers the iguana of San Salvador to be the most endangered, and states that the population there is believed to number less than 100 iguanas.

Of course, a vast amount of fish and other sea life thrives in Bahamian waters. A wealth of sports fish (many of them also edible) draws anglers to these islands, so that season limitations have been placed on some. Fishermen seek out tuna—Allison, blackfin, and bluefin (or giant). Other coveted denizens of the deep or not-so-deep waters around The Bahamas are white marlin, wahoo, bonefish, dolphin (the fish), tarpon, sailfish, barracuda, amberjack, blue marlin, kingfish, and grouper. Strict prohibitions control the taking of sponges and turtles from Bahamian waters. A close eye is kept by the Ministry of Agriculture, Fisheries and Local Government on catches of crayfish (spiny lobster), and export of conch meat is prohibited. Stone crab cannot be caught within 2 miles off Bimini or Grand Bahama.

Birds come to The Bahamas from the United States, Cuba, and the Caribbean, but there are also a few indigenous species, such as the Bahamian swallow, the Bahamian parrot, and the woodstar hummingbird. Inagua National Park is a 287-square-mile bird sanctuary where the flamingo breeding ground has a population of up to 40,000 birds, including reddish egrets and roseate spoonbills. The mangrove swamps of The Bahamas are visited by cattle egrets and various species of herons, which are among migrants from America. You may also see the magnificent (that's part of its name) frigate bird from the tropics and the Caribbean, which sometimes soars as high as 8,000 feet.

Other birds you may observe in The Bahamas, some of which may be hunted in open season, are the bobwhite quail, ring-necked pheasant, white-crowned pigeon, wood dove, mourning dove, whistling duck, Bahama duck, ruddy duck, white-jaw duck, jack snipe, coot, chuckar partridge, Wilson's snipe, guinea fowl, and both the black-crowned and the yellow-crowned night heron, as well as other migratory ducks and geese.

Among the less desirable classes of animals, insects have their representatives. Mosquitos are normally bothersome only on the less-populated islands, but you might run into the pesky "no-see-um," a tiny insect that takes a big bite. However, you don't have to worry about poisonous snakes, because there aren't any.

WILDLIFE PRESERVES

The Bahamas National Trust has under its protection several areas of the islands. Its aims are to conserve wildlife and aesthetic values while maintaining recreation facilities and educating people in the need to protect and encourage the life on land and in water.

The **Exuma Cays Land and Sea Park,** a 176-square-mile preserve, is some 40 nautical miles from New Providence Island. Here you'll find good anchorages among the small islands, which are dedicated to boating, snorkeling, walking, and looking at the flora and fauna of the land and sea. More than 40 species of birds indigenous to The Bahamas and many migratory birds have been reported in the park. Strict laws allow fishing, with limitations on the number of conchs, crayfish, and other sea creatures that may be brought in.

The National Trust is also in charge of **Inagua Park,** which encompasses some 300 square miles of nesting area of flamingos; Peterson Cay off Grand Bahama; and the Abacos' Pelican Cays. The breeding ground of an endangered species, the Bahamian parrot, is protected in a woodland area of the Abacos. A stop-off for migratory birds and a breeding ground for turtles are maintained near Rum Cay, at Conception Island.

The Ministry of Agriculture, Fisheries and Local Government is also in the business of protecting certain sites on land and at sea.

---

5. Sports & Recreation

The 700 islands in the Bahamian archipelago—fewer than 30 of them inhabited—are surrounded by gin-clear waters ideal for fishing, sailing, and scuba-diving holidays. Since sports and recreation are one of the major reasons visitors come to The Bahamas, detailed recommendations and often the costs of these activities will be previewed under the individual destination listings. A few general comments follow.

Fishing begins at Bimini, about 50 miles from Miami, Florida, and goes all the way to Great Inagua, southernmost Bahamian island on the northern edge of the Caribbean. You can try your hand at fly fishing, deep-sea fishing, and shore fishing, with all the variations of each. If you are skillful enough you may want to participate in the fishing tournaments that abound.

Among the catches, large and small, that you can hook into there are tuna, bonefish, marlin, grouper, dolphin (the fish), sailfish, kingfish, amberjack, barracuda, and even the lowly grunt. Charter boats and guides are available at most of the resort islands.

Golf facilities range from 9- to 18-hole courses and are found from Grand Bahama and New Providence to the Family Islands, where resorts have been built. You can play year round.

Some of the best **tennis** in the world is found in The Bahamas. Almost all those islands that have tourist facilities have tennis courts connected with one hotel or more. Many are lit for night play.

Boating in The Bahamas, whether you bring your own craft or charter one, is great. Getting out on the water—by motor or sail—is a way of life here. Good marinas and yacht clubs are found all over. You can usually rent boats to travel around the islands. Motorboats, sloops, speedy catamarans, even rowboats are available at most docks and waterfront resorts.

Parasailing and **waterskiing** are enjoyed at many places in the Bahamian islands.

Deep or shallow **diving** in the unpolluted warm waters is an experience most visitors find memorable. Snorkeling and scuba diving open up a beautiful new world of undersea life, along coral reefs or amid the remnants of wrecked ships. Equipment for these activities and expert training are offered at dive centers, clubs, shops, hotels, and marinas.

Swimming is available in many hotel pools, although most visitors prefer the warm waters off sun-drenched, sandy beaches.

---

6. Food & Drink

You're sitting in a plush restaurant reading a menu and you spot radicchio di treviso alla Cesare listed. If any lettuce today could be called "chic," it is this red endivelike delight. You read on, taking in such gastronomic wonders as tagliatelle alla vodka, osso buco alla milanese, saltimbocca alla romana. Have you been suddenly transplanted from the sunny Bahamas to sunny Italy?

No, you're on Paradise Island, where escargots forestières and strip sirloin of beef Café de Paris are familiar fare in the deluxe restaurants and hotel dining spots.

Suddenly, on this same menu your eyes focus on Bahamian conch chowder. It rests somewhere between the printed lines touting lobster bisque and chilled cream of avocado soup "with a hint of nutmeg."

You realize there is a Bahamian cuisine after all. But except for this Continental-inspired chef's one concession to his native cuisine, you will sometimes have to leave the deluxe hostelries of Freeport/Lucaya, New Providence (Nassau and Cable Beach), or Paradise Island to find it. Once you reach the Family Islands, it's a different story. Of course, they too have Continental chefs, along with their beef Wellington and crêpes Suzette, but in many places, especially at the little local restaurants previewed in this guide, you get to eat what the Bahamians eat.

To put it bluntly, the Bahamian cook is a thief. By that, I mean the local cooks have not only borrowed from the Caribbean cultures to the south (to which their cuisine has a similarity), but have also taken whatever "tasted good" from the kitchens of the United States, Great Britain and other European countries, and Africa. The Bahamian imagination came into play when they couldn't get hard-to-obtain items that were prevalent in the countries where the recipes originated.

Therefore the Bahamian cooks had to adapt these recipes to what was available locally, and in so doing they developed their own natural talents and ingenuity. The end result is what is called "Bahamian flavor."

THE UBIQUITOUS CONCH

In Nassau, as well as in Freeport, there are many small local places serving a Bahamian cuisine that is very similar to the fare offered in the Family Islands. In honor of the nation's cookery skills, I have lifted forks on many occasions in the best of these, and perhaps you will too. Economy is just one of the reasons. That $50 dinner on Paradise Island becomes only $15 at the Bahamian Kitchen once you traverse the bridge heading back to Nassau.

Conch (pronounced "konk") is the national food of The Bahamas. The firm white meat of this mollusk—called the "snail of the sea"—is enjoyed throughout the islands. Actually, its taste is somewhat bland, but not when Bahamian chefs finish with it. Locals eat it as a snack (usually served at happy hour in taverns and bars), as a main dish, as a salad, or as an hors d'oeuvre. So far, to my knowledge, it hasn't been made into a dessert.

The Pacific Coast resident will look upon it as having the taste of abalone. The conch does not have a fishy taste, like halibut, and it has a chewy consistency, which means that a chef must pound it to tenderize it, the way one might pound wiener-schnitzel.

Every cook has a different recipe, or so it would seem, for making conch chowder. A popular version includes tomatoes, potatoes, sweet peppers, onions, carrots, salt pork or bacon, bay leaf, thyme, and (of course) salt and pepper. One local cook in Eleuthera revealed to me her secret for conch chowder. She uses a bit of barbecue sauce and poultry seasoning instead of the usual spices.

Conch fritters, shaped like balls, are served with hot sauce, and are made with finely minced sweet peppers, onions, and tomato paste, among other ingredients. Like most fritters, they are deep-fried in oil.

Conch salad is another local favorite, and again it has many variations. Essentially, it is uncooked conch that has been marinated in Old Sour (a hot pepper sauce) to break down its tissues and to add extra flavor. It is served with diced small red (or green) peppers, along with chopped onion. The taste is tangy.

Cracked conch (or fried conch, as the old-timers used to call it) is like a breaded veal cutlet in preparation. Pounded hard and dipped in batter, it is then sautéed. Conch is also served steamed, in a Créole sauce, curried, "scorched," creamed on toast, and stewed. Instead of conch chowder, you might get conch soup. You'll also see "conchburgers" listed on menus, including that of the Palms Restaurant in Nassau.

Even after you've eaten conch, there are two more advantages to the mollusk: its chewy meat is said to have aphrodisiac powers, and if not that, then you can take along the delicate pink-lined shell as a souvenir of your stay in The Bahamas. The shell of the conch also makes a fine piece of jewelry, as you'll see as you stroll through the shops along Bay Street in Nassau. Even the Queen of England has been photographed wearing her matching set of conch pearl earrings and a necklace from The Bahamas.

MORE FROM THE SOUP KETTLE

Ranking next to conch chowder in popularity is Bahamian fish chowder. Again, this tasty soup can be prepared in any number of ways. Old-time Bahamian chefs tell me that it's best when made with grouper. To that they add celery, onions, tomatoes, and an array of flavorings that might include A-1 sauce (or Worcestershire, or both), along with thyme, cooking sherry, a bit of dark rum, and lime juice. To thicken the soup, one chef I know uses a layer of Crown Pilot chowder crackers, which he puts along with sliced potatoes at the bottom of his stew kettle. Hot pepper is added to taste.

Increasingly rare these days, turtle soup was for years a mainstay of the Family Islands (called Out Islands back then). Turtle soup and other turtle dishes still appear on some local menus. However, if you have alternatives, it would be better to choose another dish. Turtles are considered an endangered species by environmentalists.

They are rare and endangered precisely because they are a favorite food of islanders and tourists. Add the pressures of habitat destruction and it becomes clear why turtles are in trouble. We of the industrialized West have such a variety of foods from which to choose that we can afford to pass up some items. If we can also work to preserve natural habitat, we might save an ancient, important, and interesting animal.

OTHER FRUITS OF THE SEA

The most expensive item you'll see on nearly any menu in The Bahamas is the spiny local lobster. A tropical cousin of the Maine lobster, it is also called crayfish or rock lobster. Only the tail is eaten, however. You get fresh lobster only when it's in season, from the first of April until the end of August. Otherwise it's frozen.

Bahamian lobster, in spite of its cost, is not always prepared well. Sometimes a cook leaves it in the oven for too long, and the meat becomes tough and chewy. But when prepared right, such as is done by the famed Graycliff Restaurant in Nassau, it is perfection and worth the exorbitant cost.

The Bahamian lobster lends itself to any international recipe for lobster, including Newburg or thermidor. It can also be served in a typical local style: curried, with lime juice and fresh coconut among the other ingredients.

After conch, grouper is the second most consumed fish in The Bahamas. It's served in a number of ways, often batter-dipped, sautéed, and called "fingers" because of the way it's sliced. At Family Island inns, you sometimes must decide by noon what you'll want for dinner, since supplies are limited. I've been asked several times "How do you want your grouper done?" It was just assumed that I'd be ordering grouper.

The fish is often steamed and served in a spicy Créole sauce. Sometimes it comes dressed in a sauce of dry white wine, mushrooms, onions, and such seasonings as thyme. Because the fish has a mild taste, the extra flavor of the other ingredients is needed.

Baked bonefish is also common, and it's very simple to prepare. The bonefish is split in half and seasoned with a hot pepper sauce, Old Sour and salt, then popped into the oven to bake until ready.

Baked crab is one of the best-known dishes of The Bahamas. A chef mixes the eggs and meat of both land or sea crabs with seasonings and breadcrumbs. The crabs are then replaced in their shells and baked.

You'll also encounter yellowtail, "goggle eyes," jacks, snapper, grunts, and margot, plus many more sea creatures.

PEAS 'N' RICE & JOHNNYCAKE

If mashed potatoes are still the "national starch" of America, then peas 'n' rice perform that role in The Bahamas. Peas 'n' rice, like mashed potatoes themselves, can be prepared in a number of ways. A popular method is cooking pigeon peas (which grow on pods on small trees) or else black-eyed peas with salt pork, tomatoes, celery, uncooked rice, thyme, green pepper, onion, salt, pepper, and whatever special touch a chef wants to add. When served as a side dish, Bahamians most often sprinkle hot sauce over the concoction.

Johnnycake, another famed part of the Bahamian table, dates from the early settlers, who most often were simple folk and usually poor. They existed mainly on a diet of fish and rice, supplemented by johnnycake. This is a pan-cooked bread made with butter, milk, flour, sugar, salt, and baking powder. (Originally it was called "Journey Cake," which was eventually corrupted to johnnycake.) Fishermen could make this simple bread on the decks of their fishing vessels. They'd build a fire in a box that had been filled with sand to keep the flames from spreading to the craft.

BIRDS, BOARS & WHATEVER

Chicken is grown locally in The Bahamas, especially Eleuthera. A popular method of cooking it is to make "chicken souse." This is a dish made with chicken, onion, sweet peppers, bay leaves, allspice, and other ingredients left up to a cook's imagination. It's simmered in a pot for about an hour, then lime juice is added and it's simmered a little longer. Pig's feet souse is also a favorite dish. Naturally, the souse in whatever variety of meat or fowl is served with johnnycake.

Goats and sheep are also raised in the Family Islands. Somehow either meat on a menu appears as "mutton," and it's often curried.

Wild boar is caught on some of the Family Islands, and game birds such as ducks and pigeons are shot. Raccoon stew is also eaten.

Most meats, including pork, veal, and beef, are imported. However, even here, Bahamian cooks show their ingenuity by giving these meats interesting variations. For example, at a Family Island inn, I recently enjoyed pork that had been marinated with vinegar, garlic, onion, celery tops, cloves, mustard, and Worcestershire sauce, then baked and served with gravy. Even a simple baked ham is given a Bahamian touch with the addition of fresh pineapple, coconut milk, and coconut flakes, along with mustard, honey, and brown sugar.

Many vegetables are grown in The Bahamas; others are imported. If it's a cucumber, you can be almost certain it's from one of Edison Key's farms in North Abaco. They not only supply cucumbers to their own country, but it's estimated that they have captured about 5% of the Stateside market for that vegetable as well. Bahamians also grow their own sweet potatoes, corn, cassava, okra, and peppers (both sweet and hot), among other produce.

GUAVA DUFF

Guava duff is the dessert specialty of The Bahamas, although one cook confided to me, "It takes too long, and we don't like to make it anymore unless there's a special call for it."

The dessert, resembling a jelly roll, is made with guava pulp that has been run through a food mill or sieve. Nobody seems to agree on the best method of cooking it. One way is to cream sugar and butter and add eggs and such spices as cinnamon and cloves, or nutmeg. The flour is made into a stiff dough and mixed with the guava pulp, which is then placed in the top of a double boiler and cooked over boiling water for hours. It can also be boiled or steamed, and there are those who insist it should be baked. The guava duff is served with hard sauce.

In addition to guava duff, there is a large array of other tasty desserts and breads, including coconut tarts, coconut jimmie, benne seed cakes, and potato bread.

TROPICAL FRUITS

Bahamians are especially fond of fruits, and they make inventive dishes out of them, including soursop ice cream and sapodilla pudding. Guavas are used to make their famous guava duff dessert, which has already been described. The islanders also grow and enjoy melons, pineapples, passion fruit, mangoes, and other varieties.

Perhaps their best-known fruit is the papaya, which is called pawpaw or "melon tree." It's made into a dessert or a chutney, or else eaten for breakfast in its natural state. It's also used in many luncheon or dinner recipes. An old Bahamian custom of using papaya as a meat tenderizer has, at least since the '70s, invaded the kitchens of North America. Papaya is also used to make fruity tropical drinks such as a Bahama Mama shake. And if you see it for sale in a local food store, take home some "Goombay" marmalade, made with papaya, pineapple, and green ginger.

THAT OL' DEBBIL RUM

Rum was known to the ancient Romans, even the ancient Chinese as far as that goes. But it is today mostly associated with the islands in the sun, stretching from The Bahamas to the Caribbean.

It's traced back to Columbus. From the Canary Islands, he brought sugarcane cuttings, which his men planted in Jamaica in 1494. These plantings took to Jamaican soil the way a fish does to water. It is said that slaves on plantations were the first to distill the molasses that led to the production of rum.

Although rum came north from Cuba and Jamaica, the people of The Bahamas quickly adopted it as their national alcoholic beverage. And using their imagination, they "invented" several local drinks, including the Yellow Bird, the Bahama Mama, and the Goombay Smash.

The Yellow Bird is made with crème de banana liqueur, Vat 19 rum, orange juice, pineapple juice, apricot brandy, and Galliano; whereas a Bahama Mama is made with Vat 19, citrus juice (perhaps pineapple as well), bitters, a dash of nutmeg, crème de cassis, and a hint of grenadine.

A favorite—and potent—libation, well suited to the tropical and subtropical climate of The Bahamas, is the Goombay Smash. I don't know the precise origin of this drink, but its fame seems to have spread from the Blue Bee Bar at New Plymouth, Green Turtle Cay, where "Miss Emily" for years concocted the tasty combination of rums and other ingredients. Miss Emily's version has three kinds of rum, and she was always reticent to say what all else. However, throughout the islands it is usually made with coconut rum, pineapple juice, lemon juice, Triple Sec, Vat 19, and a dash of simple syrup. Try it that way, and then go see if you like Miss Emily's better.

Nearly every bartender in the islands has his or her own version of planter's punch. A classic recipe is to make it with lime juice, sugar, Vat 19, plus a dash of bitters. It's usually served with a cherry and an orange slice. Bartenders in The Bahamas are also skilled at making daiquiris, especially the banana and strawberry varieties. The piña colada is firmly entrenched here, just as much as it is in the Caribbean.

In addition to these special rum and fruit-juice concoctions, the old standbys such as scotch, bourbon, gin, and vodka are also sold. Drinks in the Nassau and Freeport/Lucaya area tend to be expensive, however.

If you want a typically Bahamian liqueur, try Nassau Royale. Nassau Royale is used to make an increasingly famous drink, the C. C. Rider, which won an international contest in 1983. Other ingredients in this prize-winning drink include Canadian Club, apricot brandy, and pineapple juice, served with crushed ice.

Curiously enough, Bahamians are especially fond of ending a dinner with a small glass of Scotland's Drambuie. After the bottle is emptied, they retain it for use as a container for tropical flowers, because they like the bottle it comes in.

DRINKING WATER

The Bahamians don't need to post "Please Don't Drink the Water" signs, although in some outlying areas it might be in short supply. New Providence and Grand Bahama have ample pure water, filtered and chlorinated. In other islands, only Marsh Harbour on Great Abaco Island has chlorinated and piped water, but you will find potable water at all resorts. In addition, bottled water is available at all tourist facilities and at stores and supermarkets.

On many of the Family Islands, ever since the first settlers arrived, rainfall has been a main source of water for drinking and other household uses. This is caught and kept in the cisterns that most houses have. The roofs are white or very light in color. The drainpipe systems are such that the first of a rainfall washes off the roof impurities that may have gathered and runs off to the ground. After that cleansing, the remaining rain is piped into the cisterns. In this land of no factories and no polluted air, you can be sure it's safe to drink the water.

---

7. Recommended Books

HISTORY

Albury, Paul. *The Story of the The Bahamas* (Macmillan Caribbean, 1975). The checkered past of these islands—from the pirates to the ship-wreckers, from the blockade-runners to the rum-runners, from "hard times" to the coming of tourism —is all found in this 294-page book, the best of its kind.

Fuson, Robert H. *The Log of Christopher Columbus* (International Marine Publishing, 1987). Read in the words of the explorer himself the first impressions of The Bahamas ever recorded by a European. From his log of 1492 comes the following: "I made sail and saw so many islands that I could not decide where to go first."

GENERAL

Barrat, Peter. *Grand Bahama* (Caribbean Macmillan, 1989). This town planner in charge of the development of Freeport on Grand Bahama (second most populated island of The Bahamas) writes of how a barren pine-covered island was turned into a major tourist center.

Hannau, Hans W. *The Bahama Islands* (Argos, Inc.). A photographer and writer prepared the first large pictorial volume about the islands with 68 color photographs. Somewhat of a coffee-table book, it does contain 76 pages of text with much general information about The Bahamas. It is often for sale in local book stores.

The Yachtsman's Guide to The Bahamas (Tropic Isle Publishers, revised annually). Even aerial surveys by float planes are used to collect the enormous amount of information that goes into this guide, which is essential for all visitors contemplating boat tours of The Bahamas. Each edition has hundreds of revisions.

PLANNING A TRIP TO THE BAHAMAS

The Bahamas, as a country, are completely different from the United States. You are indeed "going abroad." But unlike a trip from the U.S. mainland to Europe, you can be in The Bahamas after only a 35-minute jet hop, provided you use Miami as your gateway. Even if you live in New York, it's easy to wing your way south to The Bahamas. In just a matter of hours you can flee the north winds and be lying on the beach, sipping a Goombay Smash.

Travel agents who keep up-to-the-minute schedules and rates can inform you about the latest package deals if you're contemplating either a summer or winter holiday. Fortunately, many of these package deals aren't offered just in the slow season, the summer, but appear frequently throughout the winter, except during the heavily booked Christmas period.

1. Information, Entry Requirements, Customs & Money

INFORMATION

Before you go, you can obtain much valuable information by writing to various tourist offices, often on the U.S. mainland. For further information on The Bahamas, see your travel agent or **The Bahamas Tourist Office** nearest you. In the United States, offices are found in **Atlanta:** 2957 Clairmont Rd., Suite 150, Atlanta, GA

30345 (tel. 404/633-1793); **Boston:** 1027 Statler Office Building, Boston, MA 02116 (tel. 617/426-3144); **Charlotte:** 1000 Independence Tower, 4801 E. Independence Blvd., Charlotte, NC 28212 (tel. 704/532-1290); **Chicago:** 875 N. Michigan Ave., Suite 1816, Chicago, IL 60611 (tel. 312/787-8203); **Cincinnati:** 1500 Chicquita Center, 250 E. 5th St., Cincinnati, OH 45202 (tel. 513/762-7863); **Dallas:** World Trade Center, 2050 Stemmons Frwy., Suite 186, P.O. Box 581408, Dallas, TX 75259-1408 (tel. 214/742-1886); **Detroit:** 26400 Lahser Rd. Suite 112A, Southfield, MI 48034 (tel. 313/357-2940); **Houston:** 5277 Richmond Ave., Suite 755, Houston, TX 77056 (tel. 713/626-1566); **Los Angeles:** 3450 Wilshire Blvd., Suite 208, Los Angeles, CA 90010 (tel. 213/385-0033); **Miami:** 255 Alhambra Circle, Suite 425, Coral Gables, FL 33134 (tel. 305/442-4860); **Philadelphia:** Lafayette Building, 437 Chestnut St., Suite 212, Philadelphia, PA 19106 (tel. 215/925-0871); **San Francisco:** 44 Montgomery Center, Suite 503, San Francisco, CA 94104 (tel. 415/398-5502); **St. Louis:** 555 North New Ballas, Suite 310, St. Louis, MO (tel. 314/569-7777); and **Washington, D.C.:** 1730 Rhode Island Ave. NW, Washington, D.C. 20036 (tel. 202/659-9135).

In Canada, offices are found in **Montréal:** 1255 Phillips Square, Montréal, Québec H3B 3G1 (tel. 514/861-6797); and **Toronto:** 121 Bloor St. East, Suite 1101, Toronto, Ontario M4W 3M5 (tel. 416/968-2999).

You may also want to contact the State Department for background bulletins. Write to **Superintendent of Documents, U.S. Government Printing Office,** Washington, DC 20402 (tel. 202/783-3238) for a list of the backgrounds available.

ENTRY REQUIREMENTS

To enter The Bahamas, citizens of the United States coming in as bona fide visitors for a period not to exceed eight months need bring only proof of citizenship, such as a passport, a birth certificate, or a voter registration card. The latter two require a photo ID. Onward or return tickets must be shown to immigration officials in The Bahamas. Canadians and British citizens need a passport.

The Commonwealth of The Bahamas does not require visas. On entry to The Bahamas, you'll be given an Immigration Card to complete and sign. The card has a carbon copy that you must keep until departure, at which time it must be turned in. Also, a departure tax is levied before you can exit the country (see "Taxes" under "Fast Facts" later in this chapter).

Visitors leaving Nassau or Freeport/Lucaya for most U.S. destinations clear U.S. Customs and Immigration before leaving The Bahamas. Charter companies can make special arrangements with the Nassau or Freeport flight services and U.S. Customs and Immigration for preclearance. No further formalities are required upon arrival in the United States once the preclearance has taken place in Nassau or Freeport.

CUSTOMS

Bahamian Customs

Customs requires only an oral baggage declaration, unless you're bringing in something on which duty must be paid. However, your baggage is subject to Customs inspection. Each adult visitor coming to The Bahamas is allowed 50 cigars, 200 cigarettes, or 1 pound of tobacco; 1 quart of spirits; and personal effects, articles that have been in the possession and use of the visitor before arrival. These include personal jewelry, two still cameras with a reasonable quantity of film, one pair of binoculars, one portable musical instrument, one portable phonograph with a reasonable quantity of records, one portable radio and television, portable sound-recording apparatus, a portable typewriter, a baby carriage, personal sports equipment (including a bicycle, surfboard, Sunfish, a moped, and fishing rods), an iron, a clock, and a hairdryer.

The Bahamaian government has enacted strict laws regarding possession of dangerous drugs or firearms. The Dangerous Drugs Act makes it illegal for any person (other than a qualified individual) to import, export, or be in possession of marijuana, LSD, morphine, cocaine, or opium in the Bahama Islands. A qualified person is one who has special permission to have such drugs for medical or scientific purposes (for instance, a licensed pharmacist, medical practitioner, dentist, or veterinary surgeon). Penalties for infractions of this act are severe.

Licenses are required for all firearms in The Bahamas. The Firearms Act cites three categories of licenses: revolvers, rifles and other firearms and ammunition, and guns (smooth bore, such as shotguns with barrels 20 inches or more long). If you wish to bring a firearm with you to The Bahamas, inquire in person at the office of the police commissioner on New Providence or the district commissioner of any of the Family Islands before bringing in the firearm. Special authorization is necessary.

U.S. Customs

When U.S. citizens return home, they may take $400 worth of merchandise duty free if they've been outside the country for 48 hours or more and have not claimed an exemption in the past 30 days. Articles valued in excess of $1,000 will be assessed at a flat duty rate of 10%. Gifts for your personal use, not for business purposes, may be included in the $400 exemption. Unsolicited gifts may be sent home duty free at the rate of $50 in value per day. You are limited to 1 liter of wine, liqueur, or liquor. Five cartons of cigarettes can be brought home duty free. Collect receipts for all purchases made abroad.

If you carry expensive cameras or jewelry with you, it's prudent to carry proof that you purchased them within the borders of the United States mainland. If you purchased such an item during an earlier trip abroad, you should carry proof that you have already paid Customs duty on the item at the time of your previous re-entry.

Canadian Customs

Canada allows its citizens a $300 exemption, and they are allowed to bring back duty free 200 cigarettes, 2 pounds of tobacco, 40 ounces of liquor, and 50 cigars. In addition, they are allowed to mail gifts into Canada from abroad at the rate of $40 (CDN) a day, provided they are unsolicited and aren't alcohol or tobacco. On the package, mark "Unsolicited gift, under $40 value." *Caveat:* The $300 exemption can be used only once a year and then after an absence of at least seven days.

MONEY

Cash/Currency

The legal tender is the Bahamian dollar (B$1), which is on a par with the U.S. dollar. Both U.S. and Bahamian dollars are accepted on an equal basis throughout The Bahamas. There is no restriction on the amount of foreign currency brought into the country by a tourist. Currency transfers must be handled through banks, as there are no provisions for Western Union–type money cabling. If you wish to send home for funds, you can do so by telephoning, cabling, or writing to your Stateside bank with the request that a specified sum be transmitted to a bank in The Bahamas. Traveler's checks are accepted by most large hotels and stores, but you may have trouble getting a personal check honored.

Traveler's Checks

Before leaving home, purchase traveler's checks and arrange to carry some ready cash. (U.S. citizens should usually take about $200 in cash as a safeguard against unforeseen problems and inconvenience.)

American Express (tel. toll free 800/221-7282 in the U.S. and Canada) is the most widely recognized traveler's check abroad. Other agencies include **Bank of America** (tel. toll free 800/227-3460 in the U.S., or 415/624-5400 collect in Canada), **Citicorp** (tel. toll free 800/645-6556 in the U.S., or 813/623-179 collect in Canada), **MasterCard International** (tel. toll free 800/223-9920 in the U.S., or 212/974-5696 collect in Canada), **Barclays Bank** (tel. toll free 800/221-2426 in the U.S. and Canada), and **Thomas Cook** (tel. toll free 800/223-7373 in the U.S., or 212/974-5696 collect in Canada).

Credit Cards

Credit cards are in wide use in The Bahamas. VISA and MasterCard are the major cards used, although American Express and, to a lesser extent, Diners Club are also popular.

---

2. When to Go

More and more, The Bahamas are becoming a vacation goal for all seasons. Although the islands have more rain in the late spring and summer, The Bahamas have so little variation in temperature that you can enjoy a visit there at any time. Installation of air conditioning in many accommodations, plus the whirling ceiling fans in almost every room you'll see, make for personal comfort everywhere.

IN WINTER

"The season" in The Bahamas runs roughly from the middle of December to the middle of April. Hotels charge their highest prices during this peak winter period, when visitors fleeing from the cold north winds crowd into the islands. Winter is generally the dry season in the islands, but there can be heavy rainfall regardless of the time of year.

During the winter months, make reservations two months in advance if you can, and if you rely on writing directly to the hotels, know that the mail service is unreliable and takes a long time. At certain hotels it's almost impossible to secure accommodations at Christmas and in February. Instead of writing to reserve your own room, it's better to book through one of the many Stateside representatives all major and many minor hotels use, or else to deal directly through a travel agent. If you don't want to do that, you should telephone the hotel of your choice, agree on terms, and rush a deposit to hold the room.

This can be done by calling the **Bahamas Reservation Service** on their toll-free number: 800/327-0787. In Dade County, Florida, call 305/443-3821.

Air-conditioned by trade winds, the temperature in The Bahamas varies to a surprisingly slight degree, averaging between 75° and 85° Fahrenheit in both winter and summer, although there can be really chilly days, especially in the early morning and at night. However, the Bahamian winter is usually like a perpetual May.

THE "OFF-SEASON"

For many travelers the islands of The Bahamas simply do not exist except when fearsome winds beat around corners and ice and slush pile up on the sidewalks up north. Regrettably, because everybody wants to visit the islands at these times, "the season" developed. Knowing they have a hot item to sell—warm, sandy beaches when much of North America is hit by blizzards—hotel entrepreneurs charge the maximum for their accommodations in winter, "the maximum" meaning all that the traffic will bear.

When North America warms up, vacationers head for Cape Cod or the Jersey shore or the beaches of California, forgetting the islands in the sun, thinking perhaps that The Bahamas are a caldron. This is not the case. The fabled Bahamian weather is balmy all year. The mid-80s prevail throughout most of the region, and trade winds make for comfortable days and nights, even in cheaper places that don't have air conditioning. Truth is, you're better off in The Bahamas than suffering through a roaring August heat wave in Chicago or New York.

20% to 60% Reductions

The so-called off-season in The Bahamas—roughly from mid-April to mid-December (although this varies from hotel to hotel)—amounts to a summer sale. Except that summer in this context is eight months long, stretched out to include spring and autumn, often ideal times for travel.

In most cases, hotel rates are slashed a startling 20% to 60%, and these rate reductions are emphasized in this guide by being set in *italics*. It's a bonanza for cost-conscious travelers, especially families who like to go on vacations together.

In the chapters ahead, I'll spell out in dollars the specific amounts hotels charge during the off-season.

Other Off-Season Advantages

In addition to price slashes at hotels, there are some other important reasons for visiting The Bahamas in spring, summer, and autumn.

□ After the winter hordes have left, a less hurried way of life prevails. You'll have a better chance to appreciate the food, the culture, and the local customs.

□ Swimming pools and beaches are less crowded—perhaps not crowded at all.

□ Because summer business has grown, year-round resort facilities are offered, often at reduced rates. This is likely to include, among other activities, snorkeling, boating, and scuba diving.

□ To survive, resort boutiques often feature summer sales, hoping to clear the merchandise they didn't sell in February. They've ordered stock for the coming winter, and must clean their shelves and clear their racks. Duty-free items in free-port shopping are draws all year too.

□ You can often walk in unannounced at a top restaurant and get a seat for dinner, a seat that would have been denied you in winter unless you'd made reservations far in advance. Also, when the waiters are less hurried, you'll get far better service.

□ The endless waiting game is over in the off-season: no waiting for a rented car (only to be told none is available); no long tee-up for golf; more immediate access to the tennis courts and water sports.

□ The atmosphere is more cosmopolitan in the off-season than it is in winter, mainly because of the influx of Europeans. You'll no longer feel as if you're at a Canadian or American outpost. Also, the Bahamians themselves travel in the off-season, and your holiday becomes more of a people-to-people experience.

□ Some package-tour fares are as much as 20% cheaper, and individual excursion fares are also reduced between 5% and 10%.

□ All accommodations, including airline seats and hotel rooms, are much easier to obtain.

□ Summer is the time for family travel, which is not possible during the winter season. Or else parents can travel while children are away at camp.

□ Finally, the very best of wintertime attractions remain undiminished—sea, sand, and surf, usually with lots of sunshine.

THE HURRICANE SEASON

The curse of Bahamian weather, the hurricane season lasts—officially at least —from June 1 to November 30. But there is no cause for panic in that. More tropical cyclones pound the U.S. mainland than hurricanes devastate The Bahamas. Hurricanes are, in fact, infrequent in The Bahamas. However, when one does come, islanders hardly stand around waiting for it to strike. Satellite forecasts generally give adequate warnings so that precautions can be taken in time.

If you're heading for The Bahamas during the hurricane season, you can call your nearest branch of the National Weather Service. In your phone directory, look it up under the U.S. Department of Commerce listing. Actually, radio and TV weather reports keep you posted from the **National Hurricane Center** at Coral Gables, Florida.

You can obtain current weather information on many destinations, including The Bahamas, by calling **WeatherTrak.** To obtain the telephone number for your particular area, dial 900/370-8725. What you get is a taped message informing you to call the three-digit access code for the place you're interested in.

CLIMATE

The Tropic of Cancer crosses the Bahamian archipelago at about the halfway mark, passing through Great Exuma and the northern part of Long Island. Thus there is some variation between the mean temperatures in the northernmost and southernmost of the islands, but the climate overall is mild. The Gulf Stream sweeps along the western shores with its clear, warm waters, and the prevailing trade winds blow steadily in from the southeast. As a result, temperatures seldom drop below 60° Fahrenheit, even in the islands farthest north, or rise above 90°.

A look at the official government chart on temperatures and rainfall will let you know what to expect during the time you plan to visit The Bahamas.

AVERAGE TEMPERATURE & RAINFALL: THE BAHAMAS

Month	Average Temperature	Average Inches of Rainfall
January	70°F (21°C)	1.9
February	70°F (21°C)	1.6
March	72°F (22°C)	1.4
April	75°F (24°C)	1.9
May	77°F (25°C)	4.8
June	80°F (27°C)	9.2
July	81°F (27°C)	6.1
August	82°F (28°C)	6.3
September	81°F (27°C)	7.5
October	78°F (26°C)	8.3
November	74°F (23°C)	2.3
December	71°F (22°C)	1.5

HOLIDAYS

Public holidays observed in The Bahamas are New Year's Day, Good Friday, Easter Monday, Whit Monday (seven weeks after Easter), Labour Day (the first Friday in June), Independence Day (July 10), Emancipation Day (the first Monday in August), Discovery Day (October 12), Christmas Day, and Boxing Day (the day after Christmas). When a holiday falls on Saturday or Sunday, it is usually marked on the following Monday by the closing of stores and offices.

FESTIVALS

Your choice of when to go might coincide with a special festival. Bahamians believe in having a good time, and they have a variety of holidays during which great festivities are carried on. The outstanding national celebration is **Junkanoo,** held on Boxing Day (December 26) and New Year's Day.

Junkanoo begins two or three hours before dawn on both days, when the goat-skin drums begin to throb, with shak-shak gourds, cowbells, lignum vitae sticks, horns, and whistles adding to the beat of African rhythms. A carnival of cavorting, crêpe-paper-costumed figures prances through the Nassau streets, the Freeport/ Lucaya bazaars, and on Family Island beaches and narrow lanes. Elaborate head-dresses and imaginative fringed masquerade apparel are worn by throngs of men, women, and children.

Junkanoo is believed to have come down through the centuries from West Africa and the Ivory and Gold Coasts, where free people celebrated their festivals. In slavery, they kept the tradition alive for a long time, although changes crept in. The observance, attacked by Christian clergymen and missionaries, died out among American and Caribbean slaves, but Bahamian blacks have preserved the custom.

Authorities differ on the origin of the name Junkanoo, but the general belief is that it derives from John Canoe, a West African folk hero reputed to have presided over tribal rituals as master of the revels. He is supposed to have worn wild costumes and masks at the festivals, while fellow tribesmen danced around him and made loud noises.

Whatever the truth is, the Junkanoos of The Bahamas celebrate the African heritage in music, dancing, and costumes. Visitors and townspeople alike share in this holiday fun. Mini-Junkanoos in which visitors can participate are regular events.

The **Goombay Summer Festival** incorporates the sounds of Junkanoo and the rhythm of Goombay in a round-the-clock celebration for the enjoyment of summer visitors. Goombay is a word derived from the Bantu language of the Kongo people of the lower Congo River. Their *nkumbi* ceremonial drum gave the Bahamians the word, which is now applied to calypso music as it developed in the islands. The date of the Goombay Festival varies, so check with the Bahamas Tourist Office nearest you.

Independence Week is marked throughout the islands by festivities, parades, and fireworks in July to celebrate the independence of the Commonwealth of The Bahamas, with the focal point being **Independence Day,** July 10.

Emancipation Day is a public holiday on the first Monday in August, when the freeing of the slaves is commemorated in all The Bahamas. But there's another emancipation celebration, **Fox Hill Day,** observed in Nassau. Because of their isolation from the day-to-day life of Bay Street to its west, the people of Fox Hill, now the east section of Nassau, didn't get the word that they were free until some days after the official date. Therefore Fox Hill Day is celebrated on the second Tuesday of August.

October 12 is the date the history of the New World began with the landing of Christopher Columbus supposedly on an island that the Arawak Indian residents called Guanahani, which the explorer renamed San Salvador. This date is marked annually throughout The Bahamas as **Discovery Day.** San Salvador has a parade on that day.

Other festive events are an **Easter Egg Hunt** in Nassau and **Guy Fawkes Day** on or around November 5. Nighttime parades through the streets are held on many of the islands, culminating in the hanging and burning of Guy Fawkes, an effigy of the British malefactor who was involved in the Gunpowder Plot of 1605 in London. The effigy is hauled through the streets in a wheelbarrow or carried by festival participants for a long parade before being taken to the funeral pyre prepared for him earlier.

---

3. Health, Safety, Insurance & Other Concerns

HEALTH

Medical facilities in The Bahamas are considered excellent for an island group so small in population and so diverse in distribution. Physicians and surgeons in private practice are readily available in Nassau, Cable Beach, and Freeport/Lucaya.

In the Family Islands, there are 13 Health Centres. Satellite clinics are held periodically in small settlements by health personnel, and there are 36 other clinics, making a total of 49 health facilities throughout the outlying islands. For the names and telephone numbers of specific clinics, refer to the individual island listings. Where intensive or urgent care is required, patients are brought by the Emergency Flight Service to Princess Margaret Hospital in Nassau.

There is a government-operated hospital, Rand Memorial, in Freeport, plus government-operated clinics on Grand Bahama Island. Nassau and Freeport/Lucaya also have private hospitals.

Dentists are plentiful in Nassau, somewhat less so on Grand Bahama. You'll find two dentists on Great Abaco Island, one at Marsh Harbour and another at Treasure Cay, and there's one on Eleuthera.

Some of the big resort hotels have in-house physicians or can quickly secure one for you. Staffs are also knowledgeable as to where to go for dental care.

Before you go, review the "Health" section under "Health, Safety, Insurance & Other Concerns" in Chapter II. The same advice applies for The Bahamas.

SAFETY

When going to Nassau (New Providence), Cable Beach, Paradise Island, or Freeport/Lucaya, exercise the kind of caution you would if visiting an American metropolis such as Miami. Whatever you do, if you're approached by people peddling drugs, view them as if they had the bubonic plague. Americans have gotten into much trouble in The Bahamas by purchasing illegal drugs.

Women, especially, should take caution if walking alone on the streets of Nassau after dark, especially if those streets *appear* to be deserted. Pickpockets (often foreigners) work the crowded casino floors of both Paradise Beach and Cable Beach. See that your wallet or money, or whatever, is secured.

If you're driving a rented car, always make sure your car door is locked, the same way you'd do in Los Angeles or New York City. If you have valuables with you, don't leave them unguarded in hotel rooms. That most definitely includes jewelry. Many of the bigger hotels will provide safes.

You're less likely to get mugged in the Family Islands, where life is generally more peaceful. There are some resort hotels that—even today—don't have locks on the doors (never a good policy, in my opinion).

However, there can easily be trouble in paradise. Drug dealers frequent many of the Family Islands, especially Bimini, because of its proximity to Miami. Take special care if you plan to vacation there. Transporting illegal drugs between Bimini and the Florida coastline is so commonplace that every day the boating set sees bales of marijuana floating on the water as they make the crossing. The marijuana is dumped when vessels are spotted by the Coast Guard as they approach American territorial waters.

Will I be safe in The Bahamas? This is one of the questions most often asked by the first-time visitor, and it's one of the most difficult to answer. Can a guidebook writer safely recommend traveling to New York or any major American city? Are you, in fact, free from harm in your own home?

In general, whenever you're traveling in an unfamiliar country, stay alert. Be aware of your immediate surroundings. Wear a moneybelt, carry your traveling funds in traveler's checks, and keep your check numbers in a separate place. Don't sling your camera or purse over your shoulder; wear the strap diagonally across your body. Store valuables in the hotel safe and keep your hotel-room doors locked. Besides always locking car doors, never leave possessions in view in an automobile. And don't leave valuables such as cameras and cash-stuffed purses lying unattended on the beach while you go for a swim. Bahamian tourist officials often warn visitors, "If you've got it, don't flaunt it." This will minimize the possibility of your becoming a victim of crime. Every society has its criminals. It's your responsibility to be aware and alert even in the most heavily touristed areas.

Attitudes Toward Visitors

Many tourist boards are increasingly sensitive to the treatment of visitors because their fragile economies depend on how many people their islands attract. Rudeness, room burglaries, anything that results in unfavorable publicity can cause damage. As a result, many islands are taking steps to make their own people more aware of the importance of tourism, and to treat their guests as they themselves would want to be treated if traveling in a foreign land.

Of course, many of the problems have come from the tourists themselves. A white person arriving in a predominantly black society may feel threatened—or worse, superior—and that can create difficulties. The people of The Bahamas must be given their respect and dignity. A smile usually wins a smile.

In addition, many of the islanders are deeply religious, and they are offended by tourists who wear bikinis on shopping expeditions in town. Know that most of the people in The Bahamas are proud, very proper, and most respectable, and if you treat them as such, they will likely treat you the same way. Others—certainly the minority, but a visible minority—can be downright antagonistic. Some, in fact, are not to be trusted. But every country on earth has its share of that type.

Some islands are more hospitable to tourists than others. Your greeting is likely to be friendlier on Harbour Island than on more jaded Nassau. But, then, Harbour Island doesn't have five cruise ships a day docking at its harbor.

INSURANCE

Before you go, review the "Insurance" section under "Health, Safety, Insurance & Other Concerns" in Chapter II. The same conditions apply to The Bahamas.

---

4. What to Pack

In this day and age, when dress is such a personal statement, it is hard to present checklists of what to pack—hard, but not impossible. Many beachcombers arrive in The Bahamas carrying little more than what they have on their backs, perhaps a toothbrush and a bikini. But that is an extreme situation.

On the other hand, the dress code in some places is much stricter than in others. It's much more formal at certain upper-bracket resorts, not only on Paradise Island but in the Family Islands as well. One resort in particular shuns the idea of women appearing in slacks.

In general, however, most travelers are aware of clothing needed in subtropical or tropical climates. You'll want to dress casually to stay cool, and you'll want to select apparel that is easy to clean, of course.

If you're living at deluxe and first-class hotels, women should be prepared with at least an evening cocktail dress. Some restaurants and hotels—and admittedly it's a hopeless battle—still require men to wear a jacket and tie in the evening. Others, in despair, have taken to posting signs suggesting that clients should be "casual but chic." You are allowed to interpret that according to your wishes. I have attempted to give clues in individual writeups when hotels have set particular standards of dress.

Obviously, you should take coordinated clothing so that you can travel lightly.

---

5. Tips for the Disabled, Seniors, Students & Families

FOR THE DISABLED

Some 30 hotels and resorts have made provisions for the physically handicapped that allows full or limited use of the accommodations and facilities. Many of these have been built or restored so that free access to the public rooms and some or all of the bedrooms is within the capacities of handicapped persons. This includes bathroom access, as well as easy use of the dining rooms, nightclubs, pool areas, and the like.

Such accommodations can be found in Nassau and Cable Beach, and on Paradise Island, Grand Bahama, the Abacos, Andros, Cat Island, Eleuthera, Great Inagua, Long Island, and Spanish Wells, according to a survey conducted by The Bahamas Paraplegic Association in Nassau.

Some other small hotels, guesthouses, and cottages have also made provisions for comfortable stays by the physically handicapped. Ask your travel agent or inquire about Family Island accommodations at the Bahamas Reservation Service (tel. toll free 800/327-0787 in the U.S., or 305/443-3821 in Dade County and Miami).

Other sources of information—obtainable before you go—are reviewed under "Tips for the Disabled, Seniors, Students & Families" in Chapter II. The same data applies to The Bahamas.

FOR SENIORS, STUDENTS & FAMILIES

Refer to these sections in Chapter II under "Tips for the Disabled, Seniors, Students & Families." The same organizations or information detailed under Bermuda also applies to The Bahamas.

---

6. Alternative/Adventure Travel

Offbeat, alternative modes of travel often cost less and yet are far more enriching ways to travel.

Some of the organizations listed under "Alternative/Adventure Travel" in Chapter II also offer programs that cover The Bahamas. Under "Educational Travel," refer specifically to the Council on International Educational Exchange (CIEE), Elderhostel, and Interhostel; and under "Homestays or Visits," review the offerings of Servas, Friendship Force, and International Visitors Information Service. Also of interest might be the information provided in this section under "Work Camps" and "Home Exchanges."

PEOPLE-TO-PEOPLE

Visitors to Nassau on New Providence Island and Freeport/Lucaya on Grand Bahama Island are in for a unique happening. A potential idea called People-to-People, thought up by the Bahamas Ministry of Tourism, gives visitors a chance to sample some "real" Bahamian culture.

It's a program meant to bring people together and make your stay more meaningful and enjoyable. You will be introduced to a Bahamian family or couple, and they will show you how they live, take you to their churches and social functions, introduce you to their special cuisine, such as soursop ice cream (a real taste sensation), as well as give you a chance for some good conversation. The staff tries to match you up with a host or hostess who might have interests similar to yours. The program works, from all reports, and I suggest that you try it for an unusual and pleasurable experience. Not to mention adding a few friends to your list.

The Bahamians participating in the program represent a cross-section of the community. They volunteer for the program because they enjoy meeting people from other countries and are glad to show visitors a closer view of their life in The Bahamas. Expenses are borne by the individual Bahamians.

To coordinate a People-to-People visit often takes several days, so visitors or their travel agents are encouraged to request the adventure before arrival. However, arrangements can also be made through the hotel where you are staying. If you want to participate in the program, you can get a form in advance of your visit by writing to the Ministry of Tourism, P.O. Box N-3701, Nassau, The Bahamas. If you're already in Nassau, go to one of the Tourist Information Centres, which are at the airport, at Prince George Dock, and at Rawson Square, or telephone 809/326-5371. If you are planning to go to Freeport/Lucaya, the form can be mailed to the Ministry of Tourism, P.O. Box F-251, Freeport/Lucaya, The Bahamas. In Freeport/Lucaya, you can fill out the form at the Tourist Information Centre at the International Bazaar or phone 809/352-8044.

INTERNATIONAL UNDERSTANDING

Many of the world's travelers hold a concern for the future of less wealthy societies whose borders are invaded annually by floods of big-spending tourists. One highly reputable organization, the **Center for Responsible Tourism,** 2 Kensington Rd., San Anselmo, CA 94960 (tel. 415/258-6594), tries to raise the consciousness of travelers as to the unhappy effects that cultural conflicts can bring to fragile third-world societies. Although it doesn't actually sponsor tours into The Bahamas, its newsletter and the schedules of its meetings might be of interest to visitors who are motivated by humanitarian feelings of concern for less developed societies. This group, in its own words, "exists to change the attitudes and practices of North American travelers and to persuade North Americans to be part of the struggle for justice in tourism in the Third World." The organization thrives on contributions and for a small fee will send new members its newsletter and information about upcoming seminars.

A YOGA RETREAT

Unusual for Paradise Island is **Sivananda Ashram Yoga Retreat,** P.O. Box N-7550, Paradise Island, The Bahamas (tel. 809/363-2902). One of the island's most extraordinary establishments is made even more extraordinary because of its location near some of the most glitteringly expensive real estate anywhere in The Bahamas. Its organizers call it the "last outpost" on a hectic tourist island and stress that it is the only ashram in The Bahamas or the Caribbean that practices authentic Indian yoga. It was established when a wealthy benefactor willed the land in a 99-year trust to the Swami Vishnu Devananda in gratitude for his having assisted her daughter during withdrawal from a drug dependency. Today the spirit and soul of this place is very distant from that of other resorts on the island.

The central core here is a clapboard building that used to be a private beach house. It contains dormitories, the kitchen, and the roughly constructed al fresco dining area, with long rows of communal sinks where guests are expected to wash their own dishes after the simple vegetarian meals. Some of the accommodations are in a series of redwood huts built on stilts above the sands of the beach. Some of the huts are whimsically capped with onion domes and Asian-style gingerbread, but other than that they are quite Spartan. Many guests sleep in their own tents set up under the trees of the "cathedral of palms," whose walkways are lined by pools of water and leafy vegetation.

The schedule of activities includes mandatory participation by all guests of the ashram. Communal meditation every day at 6am takes place either on the beach or at an open-air temple by the bay. Guests are expected to attend 8am and 4pm yoga classes. Breakfast at 10am is followed by free time until 4pm, when additional yoga lessons are held. An early dinner (6pm) is followed by an evening of meditation or an inspirational film.

About 75% of the guests here are North Americans, many of whom check in for one of the specialized clinics or workshops. These workshops include fasting clinics and four-week yoga seminars, which offer all levels of instruction. No smoking, drinking, or drugs are allowed here, since one of the major goals is the detoxification of the guests within a strongly developed support system. Rates here are the cheapest on the island. In any season, rooms for double occupancy in beach huts cost $60 per person daily, with meals and classes included. Shared rooms holding up to six persons rent for $45 to $55 per person daily for bed, meals, and classes. If you bring your own tent, you are charged $30 per day, again with meals and classes. Single rooms cost from $70 to $75 per day. In high season (November to Easter in April), all units are usually booked, and since the policy of the retreat is to give as many individuals as possible the opportunity to participate in the yoga program, they prefer occupancy by two or more persons. In summer, there is more chance to obtain a single room. If you phone the ashram upon your arrival in Nassau, someone will pick you up at the Mermaid Dock there.

---

7. Getting There

BY AIR

More than a dozen international airlines fly into Nassau International Airport from the United States. (Freeport is another important gateway to The Bahamas from the United States.)

Flights are available from New York, Chicago, and Atlanta. But Florida, because of its proximity, has the most flights, leaving from such cities as Miami, Fort Lauderdale, Tampa, and Palm Beach. If you're coming from such major American cities as Dallas, Los Angeles, Houston, or wherever, Miami is still your best gateway because of its elaborate air links with the rest of the mainland. Most foreigners who visit from abroad come through Miami as well, unless they can get on a direct flight, such as ones offered by Air Canada or British Airways.

Of course neither Nassau nor Freeport may be your final destination in The Bahamas. If you're headed for one of the Family Islands (formerly known as the Out Islands), refer to the "Getting There" section that appears at the beginning of my review of each island chain.

You face a choice of booking a seat on a regularly scheduled flight or a charter plane, the latter being cheaper of course. On a regular flight you can cancel your ticket without penalty. On a charter you do not have such leeway.

Flight time from Miami to Nassau is about 35 minutes; from New York to Nassau, 2½ hours; from San Francisco to Nassau, under 6 hours; from Houston to Nassau, 2½ hours; and from Toronto to Nassau, 3½ hours.

The Regular Fares

The best strategy for securing the lowest airfare is to shop around. Keep calling the airlines. **Peak season,** which means winter in The Bahamas, is the most expensive time to go; **basic season,** during the summer months, offers the least expensive fares. **Shoulder season** refers to the spring and fall months in between.

Most airlines offer an assortment of **fares** from **first class,** the most expensive, through **business class** to **economy.** The latter is the lowest-priced regular airfare carrying no special restrictions or requirements. Most airlines also offer promotional fares, which carry stringent requirements such as advance purchase, minimum stay, and cancellation penalties. The most common such fare is the **APEX (Advance Purchase Excursion).** Land arrangements (that is, prebooking of hotel rooms) are often tied in with promotional fares offered by airlines.

Choice of Airlines

From the U.S. mainland, about a half-dozen major international carriers fly nonstop to the country's major air hub, Nassau International Airport, and about half that number fly either direct or nonstop to The Bahamas' second major city of Freeport. By far the greatest influx of visitors to the country, however, land at Nassau before funneling out by air or by sea to the dozens of islands that comprise the country's far-flung archipelago.

Airlines flying nonstop into Nassau from the United States include **Delta** (tel. toll free 800/221-1212), and **American Airlines** and **American Eagle,** (tel. toll free 800/433-7300), **Midway Airlines** (tel. toll free 800/621-5700), **USAir** (tel. toll free 800/428-4322), **Pan Am** (tel. toll free 800/221-1111), **Air Canada** (tel. toll free 800/776-3000), and **Bahamasair** (tel. toll free 800/222-4262).

One highly specialized airline, established during the 1980s, is **Carnival Airlines** (tel. toll free 800/222-7466), an affiliate of Carnival Cruise Lines. It flies planeloads of clients in close cooperation with the country's biggest hotel, the 1,559-room Crystal Palace, whose rooms the airline is specifically designed to fill. Air-only airfare is also available, especially from Newark, New Jersey.

Flying to the Family Islands Directly from Florida

Many frequent visitors do everything possible to avoid the congestions and uncertain connections of Nassau International Airport. Four airlines catering to that trade include **Aero Coach** (tel. toll free 800/327-0010), **Paradise Island Airlines** (tel. toll free 800/432-8807), **Chalk's International Airlines** (tel. toll free 800/432-8807), and the best recommended of them all, **American Eagle,** an affiliate of American Airlines (tel. toll free 800/433-7300).

Aero Coach, a small airline established in 1981 and based in Fort Lauderdale, operates a fleet of aircraft never holding more than 18 passengers. It offers dozens of scheduled daily flights to Grand Bahama Island and the Family Islands from its four Florida gateways: West Palm Beach, Fort Pierce, Fort Lauderdale, and Miami.

Another unusual airline directly associated with a resort complex is the Fort Lauderdale–based Paradise Island Airlines operating a trio of 50 passenger deHavilland Dash 7 four-engine turboprop planes, it makes daily runs to the company's private landing strip on Paradise Island, a 5-minute drive from the island's hotels, from Palm Beach, Fort Lauderdale, and Miami.

Chalk's International Airline, founded in 1919 by World War I pilot Arthur Burns ("Pappy") Chalk, stakes a claim as the oldest airline in the world in continuous service, and has carried a list of celebrity clients including Judy Garland, Errol Flynn, and Howard Hughes. Containing between 17 and 28 passengers, the planes are amphibious aircraft that take off and land in calm waters near each of the company's portside terminals. In addition to its flights to Paradise Island from Florida, the airline offers service from both Miami's Watson Island Terminal and Fort Lauderdale to Bimini; twice-a-week service from Miami to the privately held Cat Cay, south of Bimini; and a host of charter operations to all parts of the archipelago.

American Eagle offers frequent and probably the most reliable service from Miami's International Airport (site of the touchdowns of aircraft from around the world) to some of the outlying Bahamian islands, including the Abacos and Eleuthera as well as Nassau and Freeport.

Charter Flights

Now open to the general public, charter flights allow visitors to The Bahamas to travel at rates cheaper than on regularly scheduled flights. Many of the major carriers offer charter flights to The Bahamas at rates that are sometimes 30% (or more) off the regular fare.

There are some drawbacks to charter flights that you need to consider. Advance booking, for example, of up to 45 days or more may be required. You could lose most of the money you've advanced if an emergency should force you to cancel a flight. However, it is now possible to take out cancellation insurance against such an eventuality.

Unfortunately, on the charter flight you are forced to depart and return on a scheduled date. It will do no good to call the airline and tell them you're in the hospital with yellow fever! If you're not on the plane, you can kiss your money goodbye.

Since charter flights are so complicated, it's best to go to a good travel agent and ask him or her to explain to you the problems and advantages. Sometimes charters require ground arrangements, such as the prebooking of hotel rooms.

The most visible agent for the booking of charter flights to The Bahamas is **Paradise Island Express,** 545 Eighth Ave., Suite 16N, New York, NY 10018 (tel. 212/947-3440, or toll free 800/722-4262). Prices, as always, fluctuate with the season and day of travel, but represent some savings over most traditional tickets on conventional carriers. Airfare can be sold alone, but it's usually sold in conjunction with hotel packages in one of 20 different hotels scattered between Paradise Island and New Providence (Nassau). At presstime, the company did not represent any hotels within the Family Islands.

Bucket Shops (Consolidators)

The name originated in the 1960s in Britain, where mainstream airlines gave that (then perjorative) name to sellers of blocks of unsold tickets consigned to them by major carriers. "Bucket shops" has stuck as a label, but it might be more polite to refer to them as "consolidators." They exist in many shapes and forms. In their purest sense, bucket shops act as clearinghouses for blocks of tickets that airlines discount and consign during normally slow periods of air travel. In the case of The Bahamas, that usually means from mid-April to mid-December.

Charter operators (see above) and bucket shops used to perform separate functions, but their offerings in many cases have been blurred in recent times. Many outfits perform both functions.

Tickets are sometimes—but not always—priced at up to 35% less than the full fare. Terms of payment can vary—anywhere, from, say, 45 days prior to departure to last-minute sales offered in a final attempt by an airline to fill a disturbingly empty craft. Tickets can be purchased through regular travel agents, who usually mark up the ticket 8% to 10%, maybe more, thereby greatly reducing your discount. A survey conducted of flyers who use consolidator tickets voiced only one major complaint. Use of such a ticket doesn't qualify you for an advance-seat assignment, and you are therefore likely to be assigned a "poor seat" on the plane at the last minute.

Bucket shops abound from coast to coast, but just to get you started, here are some recommendations. Look also for their ads in your local newspaper's travel section. They're usually very small and a single column in width.

Maharaja Travels, Inc., 393 Fifth Ave., New York, NY 10016 (tel. 212/213-2020, or toll free 800/223-6862); **Access International,** 101 W. 31st St., Suite 1104, New York, NY (tel. 212/333-7280, or toll free at 800/827-3633); **Sunline Express Holidays, Inc.,** 607 Market St., San Francisco, CA 94105 (tel. 415/541-7800, or toll free 800/877-2111); and **Euro-Asia, Inc.,** 4203 East Indian School Rd., Suite 210, Phoenix, AZ 85018 (tel. 602/955-2742, or toll free 800/525-3876).

Rebators

To confuse the situation even more, in the past few years rebators have also competed in the low-cost airfare market. Rebators are outfits that pass along part of their commission to the passenger, although many of them assess a fee for their services. Although they are not the same as travel agents, they can sometimes offer roughly similar services. Sometimes a rebator will sell you a discounted travel ticket, and also offer discounted land arrangements, including hotels and car rentals. Most rebators offer discounts averaging anywhere from 10% to 25% (but this could vary from place to place), plus a $20 handling charge.

Some rebators include **Travel Avenue,** 641 W. Lake St., Suite 201, Chicago, IL 60606-3691 (tel. 312/876-1116, or toll free 800/333-3335); **The Smart Travel-**

ler, 3111 SW 27th Ave., Miami, FL 33133 (tel. 305/448-3338, or toll free 800/226-3338 in Florida and Georgia only); and **Blitz Travel,** 8918 Manchester Rd., St. Louis, MO 63144 (tel. 314/961-2700).

Standbys

A favorite of spontaneous travelers with absolutely no scheduled demands on their time, a standby fare leaves your departure to the whims of fortune, and the hopes that a seat will remain open for you to claim at the last minute. With only rare exceptions, most airlines don't offer standbys.

Going as a Courier

This cost-cutting technique has lots of restrictions, and tickets may be hard to come by, so it's not for everybody. Basically, you go as both an airline passenger and a courier. Couriers are hired by overnight air-freight firms hoping to skirt the often tedious Customs hassles and delays on the other end that regular cargo faces. With a courier, the checked freight sails through Customs just as quickly as your luggage would. Don't worry—the courier service is absolutely legal: you won't be asked to haul in illegal drugs, for example. For the service, the courier gets a greatly discounted airfare or sometimes even flies free.

You're allowed one piece of carry-on luggage only; your baggage allowance is used by the courier firm to transport its cargo. As a courier, you don't actually handle the merchandise you're "transporting." You just carry a manifest to present to Customs.

Upon arrival, an employee of the courier service will reclaim the company's cargo. Incidentally, you fly alone, so don't plan to travel with anybody. (A friend may be able to arrange a flight as a courier on a consecutive day.) Most courier services operate from Los Angeles and New York, but some operate out of other cities such as Chicago and Miami.

Courier services are often listed in the Yellow Pages or in advertisements in travel sections of newspapers.

To get you going, check with **Halbart Express,** 147-05 176th St., Jamaica, NY 11434 (tel. 718/656-8189 from 10am to 3pm daily).

Another firm to try is **Now Voyager** (named for the old Bette Davis movie), 74 Varick St., Suite 307, New York, NY 10013 (tel. 212/431-1616). Call daily from 11:30am to 6pm; at other times you'll get a recorded message. It has an automatic telephone answering system announcing last-minute specials for round-trip fares.

You can also send $5 and a stamped, self-addressed envelope to **Pacific Data Sales Publishing,** 2554 Lincoln Blvd., Suite 275F, Marina del Rey, CA 92091. You'll be sent a list of courier outfits, along with the destinations to which they fly.

Promotional Fares

Since they are now deregulated, expect airlines to announce promotional fares to The Bahamas. This means that you'll have to have a good travel agent or do a lot of shopping or calling around yourself to learn what's currently available at the time of your intended trip.

Travel Clubs

Yet another possibility exists for low-cost air travel, the travel club, with The Bahamas heavily featured in the discounted offerings. A club supplies an unsold inventory of tickets discounted in the usual range of 20% to 60%. Some of the deals involve cruise ships and complete tour packages.

After you pay an annual fee to join a club, you are given a hotline number to call when you're planning to go somewhere. Many of these discounts become available several days in advance of an actual departure. Many of them give you at least a week, and sometimes you might have as much as a month. Because you're limited to what's available, you have to be fairly flexible.

Some of the best of these clubs nationwide include the following.

Discount Travel International, Ives Building, 113 Forest Ave., Suite 205, Narberth, PA 19072 (tel. 215/668-2182, or toll free 800/334-9294), charges an annual membership of $45.

Last Minute Travel Club, 132 Brookline Ave., Boston, MA 02215 (tel. 617/267-9800, or toll free 800/LAST-MIN). One person pays $30 annually to belong, or two can join for the discounted fee of only $35.

Moment's Notice, 40 E. 49th St., New York, NY 10017 (tel. 212/486-0503), is considered one of the best, with a members' hotline (regular phone toll charges) and yearly fee of $45 per member.

Vacations to Go, 2411 Fountain View, Houston, TX 77057 (tel. toll free 800/624-7338), charges an annual membership fee of $19.19, or you can save money by paying $50 and joining for three years.

Worldwide Discount Travel Club, 1674 Meridian Ave., Miami Beach, FL 33139 (tel. 305/534-2082), presents a "travelogue" listing with about 200 discount possibilities about every three weeks. Single travelers pay $40 annually to join, but family membership is only $50.

Private Pilots

Many private pilots fly to The Bahamas from the U.S. mainland, especially from Florida. Of the dozens of airports and airstrips, many in private hands, 20 are designated as official ports of entry by the Bahamian government. This means that someone from the Bahamian government, representing Customs and Immigration, will be there to process you. Many other airstrips, of course, are used illegally by drug smugglers.

However, legitimate private pilots coming for a holiday can write the nearest Bahamas tourist office (see the "Information" section under "Information, Entry Requirements, Customs & Money" earlier in this chapter) for a fact-filled "flight planner and air navigation chart," or in the United States call the Pilot Hotline toll free at 800/327-3853.

BY CRUISE SHIP

If you'd like to sail The Bahamas, having a home with an ocean view, a cruise ship might be for you. It's slow and easy, and it's no longer to be enjoyed only by the idle rich who have months to spend away from home. Most cruises today appeal to the middle-income voyager who probably has no more than one week (or two at the most) to spend cruising at sea. Some 300 passenger ships sail the Caribbean and The Bahamas all year, and in January and February that figure may go up another hundred or so.

Most cruise-ship operators suggest the concept of a "total vacation." Some promote activities "from sunup to sundown," while others suggest the possibility of "having absolutely nothing to do but lounge." Cruise ships are self-contained resorts, offering everything on board but actual sightseeing once you arrive in a port of call.

If you don't want to spend all your time at sea, some lines offer a fly-and-cruise vacation. Terms vary widely under this arrangement. You spend a week cruising, another week staying at an interesting hotel at reduced prices. These total packages cost less (or should!) than if you'd purchased the cruise and air portions separately.

On yet another interpretation of "fly and cruise," you fly to meet the cruise and to leave it. Although multifarious in nature, most plans offer a package deal from the principal airport closest to your residence to the major airport nearest to the cruise departure point. Otherwise, you can purchase your air ticket on your own—say, from Kansas City to Fort Lauderdale—and book your cruise ticket separately as well, but you'll save money by combining the fares in a package deal.

Miami is the "cruise capital of the world," and vessels also leave from New York, Port Everglades, Los Angeles, and other points of embarkation.

As in a hotel, if you're keeping costs at a minimum, ask for one of the smaller, inside cabins when booking space on a cruise ship. If you're the type who likes to be active all day and for most of the night, spending little time in your cabin except to sleep or whatever, you need not pay the extra money, which can be considerable, to rent luxurious suites aboard these seagoing vessels. Nearly all cabins rented today have a shower and a toilet, regardless of how cramped and confining the bathroom is. If you get a midship cabin, you are less likely to experience severe rolling and pitching. Most of the modern vessels have standardized accommodations, and the older vessels offer cabins of widely varying sizes, ranging from deluxe stateroom suites to "steerage."

Dress is more casual on cruise ships than it used to be in the "white tie and tails" days. Men still can use a dark suit occasionally, and women should have at least one cocktail dress. Most passengers on cruise ships don't dress up every evening, and some don't dress up at all. Men often wear sport coats and slacks with open shirts; women, pant suits or sport dresses.

Some evenings may be cool and you'll need a sweater. For women, a sun hat or scarf will do nicely. Plenty of casual, comfortable clothes are suggested for the day. For actual touring in the islands, or participating in the deck activities, men wear sport shirts, walking shorts, slacks, and a comfortable pair of walking shoes. Women will need sun dresses, skirts, blouses, shifts, culottes, and shorts. Walking shoes are preferred to city footwear.

Naturally, you'll need a bathing suit or a bikini. For women, even that kooky dress may be worn too, as Bahamian cruises lend themselves to masquerades.

Most of the cruise ships prefer to do their traveling at night, arriving the next morning at the day's port of call, as anyone who has ever been trampled underfoot in Nassau's Straw Market will testify. In port, passengers can go ashore for sightseeing and shopping. It's also possible to have lunch at a local restaurant of your choice to sample some of the island specialties and break the monotony of taking every meal aboard ship.

Prices vary so widely that I cannot possibly document them here. Sometimes the same route, stopping at the identical ports of call, will carry different fares.

Unfortunately, the one ingredient needed for a successful cruise is the hardest to know in advance—and that's the list of your fellow passengers. The right crowd can be a lot of fun. A group incompatible with your interests can leave you sulking in your cabin.

If you've never taken an ocean cruise before, you may find the Miami-to-Nassau cruise, lasting three to four days, a good and proper introduction to cruising. Not only that, it's far kinder to your pocketbook than the more extended cruises to the Caribbean.

One cruise line in a class by itself is the **American Canadian Caribbean Line, Inc.,** P.O. Box 368, Warren, RI 02885 (tel. 401/247-0955 in Rhode Island, or toll free 800/556-7450 outside Rhode Island). Recognized for the quality of its ecological and historical tours by both the National Geographic Society and the Library of Congress (which participated in one of its cruises in 1990 as part of a film documentary), the company was founded in 1965 by shipbuilder Luther H. Blount, who designed and built a trio of highly specialized (and highly idiosyncratic) cruise ships. Designed with a shallow draft of only 6 feet, each contains space for no more than 80 passengers and can land on isolated shorelines without the pier and wharf facilities required for the disembarkation of larger cruise ships. Thanks to a specially designed 40-foot bow ramp, passengers can disembark directly onto the sands of some of the most obscure but pristine islands in The Bahamas—places that would otherwise require the chartering of a private yacht to reach.

Tours through The Bahamas are offered only in March, April, and November (when the weather is supposedly perfect for this type of expedition). They always last for 12 days, begin and end in Nassau, and include stopovers at outlying islands, which usually include San Salvador, Norman's Cay, Sampson's Cay, Crooked Island, Staniel Cay, the Exumas, and Provo in the Turks and Caicos Islands. Priced at from $1,190 to $2,045 per person, double occupancy, the cruise is entitled "The Columbus Discovery Tour" and follows in the footsteps of the 15th-century explorer, with lots of birdwatching, snorkeling, nature appreciation, and conviviality thrown in as part of the experience. Appealing to mature and worldly travelers of greater than usual sophistication, the line is proud of its lack of on-board casinos, flashing lights, and disco music. Its B.Y.O.B. policy, where passengers' private supplies of liquor are marked for their exclusive use, is cited as one of the greatest incentives for enhanced socializing on the high seas. The line enjoys a 65% repeat business, one of the highest in the industry, so it must be doing something right.

Carnival Cruise Lines, 5225 NW 87th Ave., Miami, FL 33178 (tel. 305/599-2600, or toll free 800/327-7373), one of the newest cruise lines, is also the world's largest, with both Holland America Line and Windstar Cruises (two of the most experienced lines within their particular markets anywhere) now set firmly within its orbit. Although many of the company's nine ships occasionally include stops in Nassau as part of their regular Caribbean itinerary, four of them specialize exclusively in excursions through The Bahamas. Departing either from Miami or Port Canaveral, Florida, these four include two well-maintained and well-upholstered older ships, carrying around 1,200 passengers each—the *Carnivale* and the *Mardi Gras* (formerly the *Empress of Britain* and the *Empress of Canada,* respectively). The other two ships are among the largest and most impressive passenger ships in the world, the *Fantasy* and the *Ecstasy,* luxurious floating hotels designed for 2,600 passengers each.

These custom-built ships each contain casinos, one or two dining rooms, swimming pools, and an on-board branch of the Nautica Spa Program, and one of the most staggering collections of entertainment and participatory activities in the cruise-ship industry. Designed for singles, honeymooners, families, and senior citizens, these activities almost never stop and offer guests something interesting to do throughout the course of the cruise. (They don't call them "fun ships" for nothing.) There are eight meals or snacks a day (including 24-hour free room service). Those Bahamian cruises last between three and seven days, and are priced from $395 each, double occupancy, with airfare from many North American cities included. However, there are seasonal variations.

One of the most affordable cruises is offered by **Admiral Cruises,** a division of Royal Caribbean Cruises Ltd., 1050 Caribbean Way, Miami, FL 33132 (tel. 305/373-7501, or toll free 800/327-0271). Said to be the oldest cruise line operating out of Miami, it operates a seaworthy but not-overly-glamorous converted World War II troop ship variously known during its lifespan as the *General W. P. Richardson* and the *President Roosevelt,* and today dubbed the *Emerald Seas.* The ship offers four-day, three-night cruises beginning (depending on the season) at a very reasonable $365 per person, double occupancy. They always include stops in either Nassau or Freeport (or both), as well as a beach stop at Little Stirrup Cay in the sparsely settled Berry Islands. (For more information on the Berry Islands, see Chapter XI.)

Dolphin Cruise Lines, 901 South America Way, Miami, FL 33132 (tel. toll free 800/222-1003), sails the *Dolphin IV,* a small, 588-passenger vessel with an outdoor pool and casino. From Miami, it makes three-day cruises to Nassau and Blue Lagoon Island (a sparsely inhabited cay with bathing, barbecue, and snorkeling facilities), which depart every Friday. It also makes four-day cruises (departing every Monday) to visit the bastions of Victorian architecture at Key West, Florida, before continuing to Nassau and Blue Lagoon Island.

Norwegian Cruise Line, 2 Alhambra Plaza, Coral Gables, FL 33134 (tel. 305/445-0866, or toll free 800/327-7030), operates popular three- and four-day cruises out of Miami, stopping first at Nassau, then at a private Family Island, then Freeport, before eventually returning to Miami. The line carries more passengers than any other cruise line in North America. Its "Bahamarama cruises," as they are called, are among the most popular in the industry. Passengers sail from Miami to Nassau aboard the M/S *Sunward II,* a white 14,100-ton cruise ship. Their Family Island stopover is at Great Stirrup Cay in the relatively uninhabited Berry Islands. Year-round departures from Miami are on Monday or Friday at 4:30pm. Passengers arrive in Nassau the next morning. The four-day cruise adds Freeport to the ports of call.

Premier Cruise Lines, 400 Challenger Rd., Cape Canaveral, FL 32920 (tel. toll free 800/327-7113), was established in 1985 with three cruise ships: the *Oceanic,* the *Atlantic,* and the *Majestic.* The two largest and best accessorized are the *Oceanic,* and the *Atlantic,* each with space for 1,600 passengers, which cruise for three or four nights to Nassau and to a sparsely inhabited nearby island, Salt Cay, with extended shore leaves in Nassau for gambling (there's also an on-board casino), shopping (there are also boutiques on board), barbecues, and snorkeling parties. The more unusual and the smallest of the three ships is the *Majestic,* with space for only 950 passengers, which specializes in cruises to the Abaco Islands. Two of the cruise's four days are spent moored in a deepwater harbor while smaller craft (known as "tenders") carry participants on day tours to the Abacos' most important settlements. These include Green Turtle Cay, Man-O'-War Cay, Great Guana Cay, and Treasure Cay.

Sun-Line Cruises offers transatlantic cruises that stop in Nassau. The 21-day eastbound cruises are on the five-star Sun Line flagship, the *Stella Solaris.* Information can be obtained from Sun Line's office, 1 Rockefeller Plaza, Suite 315, New York, NY 10020 (tel. 212/397-6400, or toll free 800/872-6400).

BY CHARTERED BOAT

For those who can afford it (or else who know friends who can), this is one of the most luxurious ways to arrive in The Bahamas. On your private boat, you can island-hop at your convenience. Well-equipped marinas are on every major island and many cays. There are designated ports of entry at Great Abaco (Marsh Harbor), Andros, the Berry Islands, Bimini, Cat Cay, Eleuthera, Great Exuma, Grand Bahama Island (Freeport/Lucaya), Great Inagua, New Providence (Nassau), Ragged Island, and San Salvador.

Vessels must check with Customs at the first port of entry and receive a cruising clearance permit to The Bahamas. Carry it with you and return it at the official port of departure.

You should buy *The Yachtsman's Guide to The Bahamas,* which is available from Tropic Isle Publishers, P.O. Box 610935, North Miami, FL 33161 (tel. 305/893-4277). The cost is $22.95 postpaid in the United States (add $4 postage and handling to orders outside the U.S.).

Experienced sailors and navigators, with a sea-wise crew, can charter "bareboat," a term meaning a rental with a fully equipped boat but with no captain or crew. You're on your own, and you'll have to prove you can handle it before you're allowed to take out such craft. Even if you're your own skipper, you may want to take along an experienced yachtsman familiar with local waters, which may be tricky in some places. (The company that insures the craft will definitely want to know that the vessel in question is in safe hands.)

Four to six people, maybe more, often charter yachts varying from 50 to more than 100 feet, and split the cost among them. Often a dozen people will pitch in to finance the sail.

The Bahamas, as will be pointed out many times, offer among the most beautiful and romantic cruising grounds in the world, especially around such island chains as the Exumas, the Abacos, and Eleuthera.

Most yachts are rented on a weekly basis, with a fully stocked bar, plus equipment for fishing and water sports. More and more people taking bareboat charters are learning that they can save money and select menus more suited to their tastes by doing their own provisioning, rather than relying on the yacht company that rents them the vessel.

Sunsail, 2 Prospect Park, 3347 NW 55th St., Ft. Lauderdale, FL 33309 (tel. toll free 800/327-2276), specializes in yacht chartering from one of its bases in Marsh Harbour, Great Abaco, The Bahamas. Bareboat and crewed yachts between 32 and 80 feet are available from a well-maintained fleet of sailing craft. The charter manager suggests that four- to six-month advance reservations (which require a $500 deposit) are a good idea for locked-in dates. Clients whose schedules are more flexible usually need give only about a month's notice to arrange a reservation. Insurance and full equipment will be included in the rates quoted to you.

BY PACKAGE TOUR

If you want everything done for you, and want to save money as well, consider traveling to The Bahamas on a package tour. General tours appealing to the average voyager are commonly offered, but many of the tours are very specific—tennis packages, golf packages, scuba and snorkeling packages, and, only for those who qualify, honeymooner specials.

Economy and convenience are the chief advantages of a package tour in that the costs of transportation (usually an airplane fare), a hotel room, food (sometimes), and sightseeing (sometimes) are combined in one package, neatly tied up with a single price tag.

If you booked your flight or hotel separately, you could not come out as cheaply as on a package tour—hence their immense and increasing appeal. Also, because tour operators can mass-book hotels and make volume purchases, transfers between your hotel and the airport are often included. This is more of a financial break than it sounds at first, as some airports are situated a $20 taxi ride from a resort. (In one case in The Bahamas, a $100 taxi ride!) Many packages carry several options, including the possibility of low-cost car rentals. There are disadvantages too. First, you generally have to pay the cost of the total package in advance. Then, you may find yourself in a hotel you dislike immensely, yet you are virtually trapped there because you've already paid for it. The single traveler, regrettably, usually suffers too, since nearly all tour packages are based on double occupancy.

Personally, I find one of the biggest drawbacks to taking a package tour to The Bahamas to be the hotel selected. I am especially fond of local inns—small, family-run places—and you don't get those on package tours. Rather, tour operators who have to deal in block bookings can get discounts only at the larger, more impersonal resorts.

Also, I find that many package deals to The Bahamas contain more hidden extras than they should. The list of "free" offerings sometimes sounds better than it is. Forget about that free rum punch at the manager's cocktail party and peruse the fine print to see if your deal includes meals and other costly items.

Everybody from Idaho potato growers to birdwatchers of Alcatraz seemingly offers package tours to The Bahamas. Choosing the right one can be a bit of a problem. Your travel agent may offer one. Certainly all the major airline carriers will. It's best to go to a travel agent, tell him or her what island (or islands) you'd like to visit, and see what's currently offered.

Some of the leading companies offering tours to The Bahamas include the following:

American Express Vacations, P.O. Box 5014, Atlanta, GA 30302 (tel. toll free 800/241-1700 nationwide, or 800/282-0800 in Georgia); **Delta Dream Vacations** (tel. 305/522-1440, or toll free 800/872-7786); **Go-Go Tours,** 69 Spring St., Ramsey, NJ 07446 (tel. 201/934-3500, or toll free 800/821-3731); and **Globetrotters,** 124 Mt. Auburn St., Cambridge, MA 02138 (tel. 617/661-4555, or toll free 800/999-9696).

---

8. Getting Around

If your final destination is Paradise Island, Freeport, or Nassau (Cable Beach), and you plan to go there by air, you'll have little trouble in reaching your destination.

However, if you're heading for one of the Family Islands, you face more exotic choices, not only of airplanes but of other means of transport, including a mailboat, the traditional connecting link among the old Out Islands in days of yore.

As mentioned, each section on one of the Family Island chains in the Bahamian archipelago will have a specific breakdown of transportation, but in the meantime, I'll give you a general overview.

BY AIR

The national airline of The Bahamas, **Bahamasair** (tel. toll free 800/222-4262), provides service to the major Family Islands.

Many of the Family Islands have either airports or airstrips, or are within a short ferry ride's distance of one.

Besides carrying passengers, as a government-owned airline Bahamasair has another responsibility—to serve the people of The Bahamas by providing transportation of medical supplies, food, and cargo of all kinds to remote areas such as Cat Island and Long Island.

More specific air connections will be provided under the individual island listings.

BY MAILBOAT

Before the advent of better airline connections, the traditional way of exploring the Family Islands—in fact, about the only way of getting to them unless you had your own boat—was by mailboat. This 125-year-old service is still available, but it's recommended only for those who have unlimited time and a sense of adventure—and who don't mind sharing a seat with an odd assortment of cargo headed out to the islands. You may ride with cases of rum and/or beer, oil drums, crawfish pots, live chickens, even an occasional piano.

The boats, 19 of them comprising the "Post Office Navy," under the direction of the Bahamian Chief of Transportation, are often fancifully colored, high-sided, and somewhat clumsy in appearance, but the little motor vessels chug along, serving the 29 inhabited islands of The Bahamas. Schedules can be thrown off by weather and other causes, but most morning mailboats depart from Potter's Cay (under the Paradise Island Bridge in Nassau) or from Prince George Wharf. The voyages last from 4½ hours to most of a day, sometimes even overnight. It's advisable to check the schedule of the particular boat you wish to travel on with the skipper at the dock in Nassau.

Tariffs charged on the mailboats are considerably less than for air travel (more about this later). Many of the boats offer two classes of passenger accommodations, first and second. In first class you get a bunk bed and in second you may be entitled only to deck space. The bunk beds are actually usually reserved for the seasick, but first-class passengers sit in a fairly comfortable enclosed cabin, at least on the larger boats.

For information about mailboats to the Family Islands, get in touch with the **Dockmasters Office** in Nassau, under the Paradise Island Bridge (tel. 809/323-1064).

BY RENTED CAR

Some judicious research may reveal that renting a car is less expensive than you may have thought, especially if you consider the high cost of transportation by taxi or the inconvenience of traveling by bus. Blithe spirits will also appreciate the freedom afforded only by a car for reaching that out-of-the-way beach or secluded cove. Many visitors rent cars just to circumnavigate their island, with no particular destination in mind, wishing only to sightsee, to take in the landscape and the sunshine, interrupting the transit only for lunch or a tropical drink.

Of all the locations in The Bahamas, the airports at Nassau (New Providence Island) and Freeport (Grand Bahama Island) are the most hotly contested as sales territories by North America's car-rental companies. Of course, they compete with a handful of local car-rental companies, some of which may charge a few dollars less.

Most readers, however, when faced with a choice prefer to do business with one of the major firms. This is because they offer toll-free reservation services, and because the maintenance level of the vehicles, while never perfect, tends to be better than those of most local outfits.

Reserving a car in Nassau or Freeport is just a matter of making a toll-free phone call from wherever you live in the United States or Canada. Renting a car in the Family Islands, however, may be more difficult. If you plan to remain near your hotel, limiting your excursions to an offshore reef in a scuba or snorkeling outfit, you'll probably be better off relying on one of the dozens of unmetered taxis that await the arrival of incoming airplanes.

At the time of my latest inquiry, each of the major firms quoted an unlimited-mileage rate, which varied slightly with the time of year. Each company's system was slightly different, although after the first week the per-day rate was usually less expensive than the daily rate for rentals of less than a week. Of course, there are extra charges, which the fine print of a rental contract will reveal. These sometimes include a small refueling service charge, which applies if the renter returns the car with less fuel than when he or she originally rented it. More important, a renter is able to arrange additional insurance in the form of a collision damage waiver (CDW). Without the waiver, depending on the company, a renter is liable for the first several hundred dollars' worth of damage to the car in the event of an accident. If the waiver is purchased, the driver waives all financial responsibility in the event of an accident. The amount of liability varies from company to company. If in doubt, I suggest you purchase the waiver.

As for driving requirements, each company has a different age limit for its drivers. All require a minimum age of between 21 and 25, and some won't rent a car to anyone over 70. This varies with the company. Underage drivers can sometimes rent from one or another of the agencies upon payment of a substantial cash (not credit card) deposit. Of course, a valid driver's license must be presented when the rental contract is issued.

For more information about rentals in Nassau or Freeport, you can call the international departments of **Budget Rent-a-Car** toll free at 800/527-0700, **Hertz** at 800/527-0700, **Avis** at 800/331-2112, and **National** at 800/227-7368.

Driving Requirements

A visitor may drive on his or her home driver's license for up to three months. Longer stays require a Bahamian driver's license. Insurance against injury or death liability is compulsory.

A word of warning: British tradition lives on in The Bahamas. *You must drive on the left!*

Gasoline

"Petrol" is easily available in Nassau and Freeport. In the Family Islands, where the cost of gasoline is likely to vary from island to island, you should plan your itinerary based on information as to where you'll be able to get fuel. Usually the major towns of the islands have service stations. You should have no problems on New Providence or Grand Bahama unless you start out with a nearly empty tank.

BY TAXI

Taxis are plentiful in the Nassau/Cable Beach/Paradise Island area and in the Freeport/Lucaya area on Grand Bahama Island. These cabs, for the most part, are metered. See "Getting Around" in the section on each island.

In the Family Islands, however, you will not be so richly blessed. In general, taxi service is available at all air terminals, at least if those air terminals are of the status of "port of entry" terminals. They are also available in the vicinity of most marinas.

Taxis are usually shared, often with the local residents. Family Island taxis aren't metered, so you must negotiate the fare before you get in. Cars are often old and badly maintained, so be prepared for a bumpy ride over some rough roads if you've selected a particularly remote hotel.

---

9. Where to Stay

The Bahamas offer a wide selection of accommodations, ranging from small private guesthouses, where only lodging is available, to large luxury resorts, cottage colonies, housekeeping units, apartment hotels, and apartment cottage units.

Hotels vary in size and facilities, from deluxe (offering room service, planned activities, sports, shops, beauty salons, swimming pools, entertainment, even private beaches, golf courses, and tennis courts) to fairly simple hostelries (which still may have swimming pools, a restaurant, a bar, and sports activities). Apartments, either in a hotel format or as cottages, may have kitchens and sometimes maid service, but many do not have restaurant and bar facilities. Cottage colonies are usually of the luxury type, surrounding a main clubhouse with a bar, lounge, and dining room, plus a private beach and/or swimming pool and sports facilities. These are designed to offer maximum privacy.

If you live in the United States, it's not recommended that you call one of the hotels in the Family Islands to confirm a hotel reservation. Service is spotty, and numbers are sometimes vague if they exist at all. In some cases you communicate with an island by use of a walkie-talkie. If you're not using a travel agent, then dial a toll-free number in Coral Gables, Florida, to reach the **Bahamas Reservation Service.** Dial from anywhere in the U.S. by calling 800/327-0787. If you live in Dade County (Miami), dial 305/443-3821. The service is a fully computerized reservation system that provides instant confirmation and confirmed reservation vouchers for all hotels throughout The Bahamas. Call anytime from 9am to 7pm Monday through Friday, from 9:30am to 2:30pm on Saturday, Eastern Time.

One of the most galling experiences you can have in The Bahamas is to run into someone from your hometown and learn that he or she is staying in the same hotel that you are, even enjoying an ocean view as opposed to your "garden view," and paying some $200 to $300 less per week than you are.

That happens more often than you might imagine. A lot of it stems from a zeal among hoteliers, especially during the slow months, to promote business. There are package deals galore, and though they have many disadvantages, they are always cheaper than rack rates. (A rack rate is what an individual pays who literally walks in from the street.) Therefore it's always good to go to a reliable travel agent to find out what, if anything, is available in the way of a land-and-air package before booking into a particular accommodation.

There is no rigid classification of hotel properties in the islands. The word "deluxe" is often used—or misused—when "first class" might have been a more appropriate term. First class itself often isn't. For that and other reasons, I've presented fairly detailed descriptions of the properties, so that you'll get an idea of what to expect once you're there. However, even in the deluxe and first-class resorts and hotels, don't expect top-rate service and efficiency. "Things," as they are called in the islands, don't seem to work as well here as they do in certain fancy resorts of California, Florida, or Europe. Life here has its disadvantages. When you go to turn on the shower, sometimes you get water and sometimes you don't. You may even experience power failures.

Facilities often determine the choice of a hotel. If scuba diving is your goal, then head, say, for Small Hope Bay Lodge on Andros. Regardless of your particular interest, there is probably a hotel for you. All the big first-class resort hotels have swimming pools. Usually a beach is nearby if not directly in front of the hotel property. If you want to save money, you can book into one of the more moderate accommodations less desirably located. Then, often for only a small fee, you can use the facilities of the larger and more expensive resorts. However, don't try to "crash" a resort. It's better to be a paying customer. Often if you have lunch or patronize the bar, you can stick around and enjoy the afternoon. Policies vary from resort to resort: some are stricter than others.

In the modern properties of The Bahamas, your hotel room is likely to look like one you had in Florida or California—that is, two standard oversize beds, a private bath, sometimes a TV, and perhaps a balcony or small terrace. The larger hotels are likely to have more than one choice for dining, perhaps a "gourmet" restaurant as well as a coffeeshop. The chain hotels are highly reliable.

Some islands, such as Paradise Island, have a deluxe property, for example, the Ocean Club, that is even more luxurious than your typical first-class chain operation. These accommodations are always listed at the top of my recommendations. If economy is one of the major requirements for your holiday, then read the recommendations from the bottom up.

Many Family Islands in The Bahamas, such as the Exumas, Cat Island, Long Island, the Berry Islands, and Andros, have very limited tourist facilities, but many readers prefer to seek out these offbeat retreats. Others, wishing to be in the center of the tourist hustle-bustle, will head to such old reliable meccas as Nassau, Freeport, Cable Beach, and Paradise Island.

THE BAHAMIAN GUESTHOUSE

The guesthouse is where many Bahamians themselves stay when they're traveling in their own islands. In The Bahamas, however, and to a very limited extent in the Turks and Caicos Islands, the term "guesthouse" can mean anything. Sometimes so-called guesthouses are really like simple motels built around swimming pools. Others are small individual cottages, with their own kitchenettes, constructed around a main building in which you'll often find a bar and restaurant serving local food.

Giving fair warning, I'll point out that many of these guesthouses are very basic. You must remember that nearly every piece of furniture must be imported, often at outrageous costs to the owner of the establishment. Salt spray on metal or fabric takes a serious toll, and chipped paint is commonplace. Bathrooms can fall into the vintage category, and sometimes the water isn't heated. But when it's 85° to 92° Fahrenheit outside, you don't need hot water.

On the other hand, some of these establishments are quite comfortable. Some are almost luxurious: and in addition to giving you the opportunity to live with a local family, they boast swimming pools, private baths in all rooms, and air conditioning. The rooms are sometimes cooled by ceiling fans or trade winds blowing through open windows at night.

Of course, don't expect the facilities of a fabulous resort hotel, but for value the guesthouse can't be topped. Staying in a guesthouse, you can journey over to a big beach resort, using its facilities for a small charge.

In the Family Islands of The Bahamas, the guesthouses are not as luxurious for the most part as those of Bermuda. Although bereft of frills in general, the Bahamian guesthouses I've recommended are clean, decent, and safe for families or single women. Many of the cheapest ones are not places you'd like to live in all night and day, because of their simple, modern furnishings (often worn) and other amenities (or lack of them). However, many of today's new breed of traveler to The Bahamas don't want to spend more than eight hours in their rooms anyway.

Guesthouses are rarely built on the best beaches, but sometimes they lie across the street or perhaps a 5- to 10-minute stroll from the sands. That's why they can afford to charge such low prices.

Although not said to disappoint, these comments are made to anyone experiencing cultural shock or to a first-time visitor to The Bahamas who may never have encountered such a leisurely, beachcombing life as prevails there.

Having said that, let me add another word about the hospitality and convivial atmosphere often created in these small places, which not only attract locals, but are themselves most often locally owned and run. Staying in a guesthouse is for the serious tourist who'd like to meet some of the local people as well as fellow visitors with similar interests. Often, spontaneous barbecues are staged, and even in some of the smaller places a steel band is brought in on a Saturday night for a "jump-up."

HOUSEKEEPING HOLIDAYS

Particularly if you're a family or a congenial group, a housekeeping holiday can be one of the least expensive ways to stay in The Bahamas. These types of accommodations are now available on all the islands discussed in this guide. Sometimes you can rent individual cottages; other accommodations are housed in one building. Some are private homes rented when the owners are away. All have small kitchens or kitchenettes where you can do your home cooking after shopping for groceries, including freshly caught grouper or some Bahamian lobster. Life this way is easy and pleasant. You can get up anytime you choose and prepare your own breakfast with eggs just as you like them. You can even turn shopping into an adventure, particularly at a local marketplace, where you may see fresh vegetables such as christophine (a kind of squash) that you've never tried before. The fruits, such as soursop, are luscious as well.

A housekeeping holiday, however, doesn't always mean you'll have to do maid's work. Most of the self-catering establishments have maid service included in the weekly rental, and you're given a supply of fresh linen as well.

Cooking most of your meals yourself and dining out on occasion, such as when a neighboring big hotel has a beachside barbecue with entertainment, are the surest ways of keeping holiday costs at a minimum.

HOME EXCHANGES & HOMESTAYS

See the entry under "Alternative/Adventure Travel" in Chapter II. The same possibilities exist for The Bahamas.

RENTAL VILLAS & VACATION HOMES

You might rent a big villa, a good-sized apartment in someone's condo, or even a small beach cottage (more accurately called a "cabaña").

Private apartments are also available, with or without maid service. This is more of a no-frills option than the villas and condos. The apartments may not be in buildings with swimming pools, and they may not have a front desk to help you.

Cottages, or cabañas, offer the most freewheeling lifestyle available in these categories of vacation homes. Many ideally open onto a beach, although others may be clustered around a communal swimming pool. Most of them are fairly simple, containing no more than a simple bedroom plus a small kitchen and bath. In the peak winter season, reservations should be made at least five or six months in advance.

Several agents throughout the United States and Canada offer these types of rentals. (Sometimes maid service and a part-time cook are included in the offerings.) **Island Services, Inc.,** 750 SW 34th St., Suite 105, Fort Lauderdale, FL 33315 (tel. 800/825-5099), and **WHR Worldwide,** 235 Kensington Ave., Norwood, NJ 07648 (tel. 201/767-9393, or toll free 800/NEED-A-VILLA).

GOOMBAY PACKAGES

Every year several hotels in The Bahamas offer a value-packed Goombay package, which is usually available from mid-April right up to December 16, the beginning of the high winter season prices.

In Nassau/Paradise Island/Cable Beach, the Great Goombay packages are usually for three days and two nights. All rates, incidentally, are per person, based on double occupancy. Air fare is extra.

On Grand Bahama Island, the Goombay packages are for four-day/three-night stays. And Goombay Getaway packages in the Family Islands are often for four days and three nights.

---

10. Where to Dine

The bad news is that dining in Nassau/Paradise Island or Freeport/Lucaya is generally more expensive than it is in the United States and Canada. Virtually everything has to be imported except locally caught fish. Service is automatically added to most restaurant tabs, usually 10% to 15%. Even so, if service has been good, it is customary to leave something extra.

If you're booked into a hotel on MAP rates (half board), which hotels sometimes require in the peak winter season, you can sample some of the local restaurants at lunch. That way, your stomach won't become completely "hotel bound."

In a very few establishments, men are required to wear jackets, but only in winter. An open-neck shirt usually suffices instead of a tie. If in doubt, always ask the restaurant or check with the policy of the establishment before going there.

At the better places, women will always want to appear casually chic in the evening. During the day, no matter what the establishment, it is proper to wear a coverup instead of arriving for lunch attired in a bikini.

In general, it is unwise to order too many meat dishes. Red meats have probably been flown in and may have been resting on the island for some time. Whenever possible, it is best to stick to local food; for a main dish, that usually means grouper or conch caught in the deep sea.

Before you start writing in letters of complaint, let me state at the beginning that food is not one of the reasons people go to The Bahamas. So-called "gourmet fare" often isn't, although the prices charged would make you think that you're getting something special. To find the many dishes that *are* truly worthy, pick and choose your way carefully through the menu.

In the Nassau/Paradise Island area, you can get a taxi to take you where you want to go for dinner. The same holds true for Freeport/Lucaya. However, if you're staying on one of the Family Islands, it is better to sample local island restaurants for lunch and then stay near your hotel at night, because driving on bad, unmarked, and poorly lit roads is hazardous.

---

11. Fast Facts: The Bahamas

A number of situations, such as a medical emergency, might arise during your vacation, and there are various customs you'll need to know about. The desk personnel at your hotel are usually reliable dispensers of information. If you're staying at a guesthouse, your host or hostess will probably be able to supply any information you need on the immediate vicinity of your parish.

AMERICAN EXPRESS: Representing American Express in The Bahamas are **Playtours,** Shirley Street, Nassau (tel. 809/322-2931), and **Mundytours,** Building

4 Regent Centre, Suite 20, Freeport (tel. 809/352-4444). At either of these offices you can receive assistance with all American Express services, including customer services, cardmember personal check cashing, traveler's check sales and refunds, emergency card replacement, and all travel and tour arrangements. Hours are 9am to 5pm Monday through Friday. Traveler's checks are issued upon presentation of a personal check and an American Express card.

AREA CODE: The area code for The Bahamas is **809**. It can be dialed directly from the mainland.

BABYSITTERS: At the largest resort hotels and in Nassau, Cable Beach, and Freeport/Lucaya, your hotel desk will help you arrange for the services of a reliable person to stay with your child or children while you are absent. At practically every accommodation in the Family Islands, you'll find it easy to secure someone for this purpose by simply asking your host or hostess, or inquiring at a store or post office on the island.

BANKS: For Nassau, Cable Beach, and Freeport/Lucaya, commercial banking hours are 9:30am to 3pm Monday through Thursday, 9:30am to 5pm on Friday. Hours are likely to vary widely in the Family Islands. Ask at your hotel.

BUSINESS HOURS: Most government offices are open Monday through Friday from 9am to 5pm. Most shops are open Monday through Saturday from 9am to 5pm.

CAR RENTALS: See "Getting Around" earlier in this chapter.

CLIMATE: See "When to Go" earlier in this chapter.

CURRENCY: See "Information, Entry Requirements, Customs & Money" earlier in this chapter.

CURRENCY EXCHANGE: Many of the big hotels will cash traveler's checks, or else you can go to the nearest bank. Because the U.S. dollar and the Bahamian dollar are on par, both currencies can be used. It is unnecessary to convert U.S. dollars into Bahamian dollars. However, because of different valuations, it will be necessary to convert Canadian dollars into local currency.

DRIVING REQUIREMENTS: See "Getting Around" earlier in this chapter.

DRUGS: Importation of, possession of, or dealing with unlawful drugs, including marijuana, is a serious offense under the laws of The Bahamas, with heavy penalties levied for infraction. Customs Officers, at their discretion, may conduct body searches for drugs or other contraband goods.

ELECTRICITY: Electricity is normally 120 volts, 60 cycles, AC. American appliances are compatible.

EMBASSIES/CONSULATES: The **U.S. Embassy** is on Queen Street, P.O. Box N-8197, Nassau (tel. 809/322-4753); and the **Canadian Consulate** is on the ground floor of the Out Island Traders Building, East Bay Street, Nassau (tel. 809/323-2123), near the foot of the Paradise Island Bridge. The **British High Commission** is in the BITCO Building (third floor), East Street, Nassau (tel. 809/325-7471).

EMERGENCIES: In Nassau, call the **police** at **919**. You can report a **fire** at the same number. In the Freeport/Lucaya area, call the **police** at **911**, or dial 352-

8888 to report a **fire**. In the Family Islands, ask at your hotel—or the first responsible-looking person you see—to summon the nearest available help. If you are near a phone, call the operator and ask to be connected to the nearest police station.

ETIQUETTE: It is customary to greet people in the Family Islands with a hello or some acknowledgment of their existence as you pass them on the road. People are often shy and will wait for you to make the first overture in conversation. In dress, never appear in a bathing suit, much less a bikini, in a restaurant. Always wear a coverup.

EYEGLASSES: Opticians are readily available in Nassau and Freeport, but if you're traveling through the Family Islands, it is always best to carry a spare set of glasses or contact lenses.

FILM: Purchasing film in Nassau/Paradise Island or Freeport/Lucaya is relatively easy. However, it might be well to stock up if you're going to some of the remote Family Islands and need a special kind of film.

FIREARMS: Licenses are required for all firearms in The Bahamas. The Firearms Act cites three categories of licenses: revolvers; rifles and other firearms and ammunition; and guns. If you wish to bring a firearm with you to The Bahamas, inquire in person at the office of the police commissioner on New Providence or the district commissioner of any of the Family Islands before bringing in the firearm. Special authorization is necessary.

GAMBLING: Casino gambling is legal in The Bahamas for visitors. Bahamians and Bahamas residents are prohibited from gambling, although they can enter the casinos in the company of friends from elsewhere. Games offered are dice, roulette, blackjack, baccarat, wheel of fortune, and slot machines. There is a casino at Cable Beach on New Providence, one on Paradise Island, and two at Freeport/Lucaya on Grand Bahama Island.

HAIRDRESSERS/BARBERS: The major resorts, Nassau, Cable Beach, and Freeport/Lucaya have beauty salons and barbershops that are easy to find. Just ask at your hotel desk. However, in some of the Family Islands you may have to inquire around a bit, perhaps settle for someone to take care of such services in his or her own home.

HITCHHIKING: Even though technically illegal, this is a commonplace method of travel, particularly in the Family Islands, where there is a scarcity of vehicles. It's a less desirable practice in Nassau, Cable Beach, and Freeport/Lucaya, and it's unheard of on Paradise Island. At any rate, you do so at your own risk.

HOLIDAYS: See "When to Go" earlier in this chapter.

HOSPITALS: See "Health, Safety, Insurance & Other Concerns" earlier in this chapter.

INFORMATION: For tourist information before you go, see "Information, Entry Requirements, Customs & Money" earlier in this chapter. For information while you're in The Bahamas, see the individual island listings.

INSECTS: In The Bahamas, they are called "no-see-ums." But they're for real all right. Bites by insects can cause skin irritation, itching, or whatever. Carry insect repellent with you, and don't become dinner for a colony of mosquitoes. It's commonplace to have insects invade your room—and that goes for the deluxe establishments as well as the beachside bungalows. Carry along some insect spray—it might come in handy. If you've booked that secluded cottage in one of the remote Family Islands, remember that you are retreating from civilization, not from nature.

LAUNDRY/DRY CLEANING: These matters present no problem in Nassau, Cable Beach, and Freeport/Lucaya, or at the large resorts, where such service is part of the amenities. You could face difficulties on some of the smaller, remote islands, but usually, just by asking around, you can find someone who is willing to do your laundry. A number of professional services exist on the more populated Family Islands.

LIQUOR LAWS: Persons must be 21 years of age to order alcoholic drinks in The Bahamas.

LOST PROPERTY: Call the nearest police station with a full description of your lost property.

LUGGAGE STORAGE/LOCKERS: There are no professional facilities. If you're going to tour some of the Family Islands, you might make an arrangement with your hotel—say, in Nassau—but only if you plan to return to Nassau for your international flight, of course.

MAIL/POSTAGE RATES: Only Bahamian postage stamps are acceptable for the payment of postage in The Bahamas. To send that postcard back home to the United States or Canada by airmail will cost 40¢. Airmail letters cost 45¢ per half ounce to the United States or Canada, but 50¢ to Europe.

From the United States, mail to the Family Islands is sometimes slow. Airmail may go by air to Nassau and by boat to its final destination. If a resort has a U.S. or Nassau address, it is preferable to use it.

MARRIAGE/DIVORCE: Want to have a romantic Bahamas wedding? If nonresidents wish to tie the knot here, one member of the couple must spend 15 days in the country and submit proof of presence. A waiver may be granted if one of the couple has been in The Bahamas at least three days. If either party has been divorced, proof of divorce must be produced. Applications for marriage licenses are obtainable on New Providence Island at the Registrar General's Office, East Hill Street, P.O. Box N-532, Nassau. No blood test is required. Minimum age without parental consent is 21. Minors may be married with the consent of all parents. Nothing special is required of widows or widowers; the Registry will take your word for it that your spouse is dead.

Regardless of nationality, couples can get a divorce in The Bahamas if the husband is a bona fide resident, but it's not easy. Don't think you can fly in, get a decree, and fly right home. Better consult a Bahamian attorney if you're eligible and if you really want to take this route. Otherwise, do it at home.

NEWSPAPERS/MAGAZINES: Two newspapers are published in Nassau and circulated there and in Freeport: the *Nassau Guardian,* a morning paper, and the

Tribune, printed in the afternoon. Both publish Monday through Saturday. Circulation in the Family Islands is limited and likely to be slow. The *Freeport News* is published Monday through Friday.

You can find the *New York Times,* the *Wall Street Journal,* the *Miami Herald, The Times* of London, and the *Daily Telegraph* at newsstands in your hotel and elsewhere in Nassau, usually the day after they are published but sometimes later. Such U.S. magazines as *Time* and *Newsweek* are flown in from the mainland and are for sale at the major resorts.

PETS: A valid import permit is required to import any animal into The Bahamas. Application for such a permit must be made in writing, accompanied by a $10 processing fee, to the **Director of Agriculture, Department of Agriculture,** P.O. Box N-3028, Nassau, The Bahamas (tel. 809/325-7502), a minimum of three weeks in advance.

POLICE: In Nassau, call the police at **919;** in Freeport/Lucaya, dial **911.**

RADIO/TV: Government-owned Radio Bahamas is run by the Broadcasting Corporation of The Bahamas and supported by advertising. ZNS-1, the most powerful of the three, is located in Nassau but can be heard throughout the country. ZNS-2 also operates out of Nassau, and ZNS-3 is based in Freeport. ZNS-1 broadcasts 24 hours a day.

ZNS TV transmits on Channel 13 in full color, for 6 hours a day Monday through Friday. On Saturday it transmits for 16 hours, on Sunday for 12. The Bahamas Broadcasting Company handles all programming. Most large hotels have cable television and can receive U.S. telecasts via Miami from all major networks. Islands nearest the United States receive TV without cable.

RELIGIOUS SERVICES: You'll find many houses of worship in The Bahamas, with denominations including Anglican, Assembly of God, Baptist, Christian Science, Church of God, Church of God of Prophecy, Greek Orthodox, Jehovah's Witnesses, Jewish, Lutheran, Methodist, Presbyterian, Roman Catholic, Seventh-Day Adventist, and several smaller sects. Local tourist offices will provide locations and times of services.

REST ROOMS: Adequate toilet facilities can be found at hotels, restaurants, and air terminals in The Bahamas that are frequented by the public, although they may turn out to be in short supply at some of the points of interest you may go to see. Also, if you're in some of the more remote Family Islands not well supplied with public places, you may have difficulty finding a comfort station.

SAFETY: See "Health, Safety, Insurance & Other Concerns" earlier in this chapter.

SHOPPING: Plan your shopping sprees for Nassau, Cable Beach, and Freeport/Lucaya if you can. You'll also find boutiques and gift shops at the major resorts, but in smaller places not much is offered. For information on the best places to shop, see the chapters on Nassau, Cable Beach, and Freeport/Lucaya in this book. In the Abacos, both Marsh Harbour and Treasure Cay have fully equipped shopping centers, while most of the resorts have gift shops for their guests. On Andros there's a shopping center in Nicholl's Town and additional shops in other towns on the island. You'll be able to purchase food at markets on practically all the Family Islands, and you can find T-shirts all over.

TAXES: Departure tax is $7. International airline and steamship tickets issued in The Bahamas are subject to a nominal tax, which is written into the cost of the ticket.

A 4% tax, plus a "resort levy" of either 4% or 6%, is imposed on hotel tariffs. There is no sales tax in this country.

TAXIS: See "Getting Around" earlier in this chapter.

TELECOMMUNICATIONS: Communications by telephone and cable to resorts in The Bahamas have improved recently, although some of the Family Islands are difficult to reach because of distance and equipment. The Bahamas Telecommunications Corporation operates phone, cable, teletype, and leased circuits, as well as mobile-phone service. It's also in charge of licensing marine radio and other private radio-phone stations. Service between Florida, Nassau, Freeport, and some of the major resort islands is available 24 hours a day. Other radio-telephone systems link the Family Islands to Nassau and through Nassau to the world. Not all radio-phone stations in the outlying areas are connected to telephones in homes and offices. In such cases it is necessary to call the operator at the nearest radio station to the person being called and arrange to have him or her summoned to the station to complete the call. Such stations close at 9pm and are on an emergency basis during the night.

Direct Distance Dialing between North America and Nassau, Grand Bahama, the Abacos, Andros, the Berry Islands, Bimini, Eleuthera, Harbour Island, Spanish Wells, the Exumas, and Stella Maris on Long Island is available. The **area code** for The Bahamas is 809. Cables to The Bahamas are usually delivered by phone or by citizens' band radio. Urgent telegrams are charged at double the full rate, although no urgent-rate messages to the United States mainland are accepted.

TIME: Eastern Standard Time is used throughout The Bahamas. In recent years, Eastern Daylight Time has been adopted during the summer to avoid confusion in scheduling transportation to and from the United States. April to October, EDT; October to April, EST.

TIPPING: Many establishments add a service charge, but it's customary to leave something extra if service has been especially fine. If you're not sure whether service has been included in your bill, ask. Unfortunately, in most places you have to pay the 15% service charge even if an incompetent waiter has spilled soup on you.

Bellboys and porters, at least in the upper-bracket hotels, have come to expect a tip of $1 per bag. It's also customary to tip your chambermaid at least $2 per day—more if she or he has performed special services such as getting a shirt or blouse laundered. Most service personnel, including taxi drivers, waiters, and the like, expect 15% (perhaps 20% in deluxe restaurants).

WEATHER: Thanks to the Gulf Stream currents and balmy tradewinds, The Bahamas are blessed with a semitropical climate. Typical temperatures range from 70° to 80°F. Rarely does the temperature climb above 90°F in midsummer, or fall below 60°F on a winter's night.

YELLOW PAGES: All Bahamian telephone numbers appear in one phone book, revised annually, with a helpful Yellow Pages in the rear outlining all the goods and services you are likely to need.

NEW PROVIDENCE (NASSAU/CABLE BEACH)

The capital of the Bahamas, the historic city of Nassau, stands on the island of New Providence, less than an hour's flight from the United States and a favorite cruise-ship port of call. It offers the charm of an antique, and has a tropical indolence, yet it boasts up-to-date tourist facilities and modern hotels. Nassau lies on the north side of New Providence, which is 21 miles long and 7 miles wide at its greatest point.

Horse-drawn surreys still wind down narrow streets, and faded pastel-colored homes look out onto the sea. The waterfront, too, still looks much the same as it did when Winslow Homer painted it. The major difference now is that an arched bridge joins Nassau with Paradise Island (described in the next chapter), with its hotels, Continental-style restaurants, and gambling casino.

Before getting involved in city life, it's customary to purchase a straw hat at the market on Rawson Square and then begin your journey of discovery.

Much has changed in this Bahamian capital, once the haunt of pirates and rum-soaked sailors. Whitewashed and latticed houses evoke memories of a colonial past. But today's Nassau is alive and bustling, forging its own destiny as a contemporary resort city.

Once it was known as a mecca for the rich and socially secure of the world, particularly when the Duke and Duchess of Windsor were in residence. (He was governor of The Bahamas from 1940 to 1945, living at Government House.) As a honeymoon haven, it rivaled (and rivals) Bermuda. However, today's visitors are more broad-based in lifestyles and pocketbooks, ranging from yachting people to underwater explorers on a budget. The rich are still very much in evidence, discreetly so. Because of its tax advantages, Nassau is such a center of international banking that some refer to it as the Switzerland of The Bahamas.

Nassau is the heart of The Bahamas, the hub from which sea and air roads fan outward. Unless Freeport is your gateway, chances are you'll be stopping here even if your ultimate destination is the Family Islands. You may want to linger long enough to get to know it.

1. Getting Around

After you land at the Nassau International Airport, you immediately face the problem of transportation to your hotel. If you're renting a car, you can drive there. If not, you'll find no inexpensive bus service waiting for you, and must take a taxi instead, unless you're being met by a special van. (Nassau taxi drivers years ago blocked the major traffic arteries of New Providence when the government attempted to inaugurate bus service from the airport to the hotels of Cable Beach, downtown Nassau, and Paradise Island.)

FINDING AN ADDRESS

In Nassau, and especially in the rest of The Bahamas, you will seldom if ever find street numbers on hotels or other businesses. Sometimes in the more remote places, you won't even find street names. Always get directions before heading somewhere in particular. You can always ask, as Bahamians tend to be very helpful in showing you the way.

GETTING AROUND

Public Transportation

The elegant, traditional way to see Nassau was in a **horse-drawn surrey**—the kind with the fringe on top and a wilted hibiscus stuck in the straw hat shielding the horse from the sun. But these aren't as plentiful anymore and, when available, are usually too expensive for the average visitor. (Before you get in, you should negotiate with the driver and agree on the price. The average price is $8 to $10 for one or two people for a 30-minute ride.) The maximum load is three adults plus one or two children under the age of 12. The surreys are generally available seven days a week from 9am to 4:30pm, except when horses are rested, from 1 to 3pm from May to October and from 1 to 2pm from November to April. If you want to go on a short trip, you'll find the surreys at Rawson Square, off Bay Street.

Taxis are more practical, at least for longer island trips, as their rates for New Providence, including Nassau, are set by the government. When you get in, you should find a working meter, as this is a requirement. For the first quarter mile, one or two passengers are charged $1.20, and 20¢ for each additional quarter mile. Each additional passenger is assessed another $1.50. Typical fares are $8 from the airport to Cable Beach, $10 to downtown Nassau, and $18 (plus the $2 bridge toll) to Paradise Island. Taxis can also be hired on the hourly rate of $20 to $23 for a five-passenger cab. Luggage is carried at a cost of 30¢ per piece. The radio taxi call number is 809/323-5111.

The least expensive means of transport is by **jitney,** really VW minibuses, which leave from the downtown Nassau area to outposts on New Providence, costing from 50¢ to $1 per ride. They operate daily from 6:30am to 7:30pm. Some hotels on Paradise Island and Cable Beach run their own jitney service free. However, jitneys and buses are not allowed to operate from the airport to Cable Beach, Nassau, or Paradise Island (the taxi union saw to that).

Water taxis operate daily from 8:30am to 6pm at 20-minute intervals between Paradise Island and Prince George Wharf at a round-trip cost of $3 per person.

There is also **ferry** service from the end of Casuarina Drive on Paradise Island across the harbor to Rawson Square for a round-trip fare of $2 per person. The ferry operates daily from 9:30am to 4:15pm, with departures every half hour from both sides of the harbor.

Scooters & Bicycles

Motor scooters have become a favorite mode of transportation among tourists. The little mopeds with their identifying white license tag and helmeted riders scoot all over New Providence. Unless you're an experienced moped rider, it's wise for you to stay on quiet roads until you feel at ease with your vehicle. Don't start out on Bay Street. Many hotels have rental vehicles on the premises. Average rental is $28 per day.

Besides walking, **bicycles** are certainly the most economical means of getting around. Most hotels can arrange bicycle rentals for you. If your hotel doesn't have these rentals, check with **Bowe's Scooter Rentals,** Prince George Wharf (tel. 809/326-8326), or **B&S Scooter Rentals,** Union Dock, Bay Street (tel. 809/322-2580).

Car Rentals

Four of the biggest U.S.-based car-rental companies—**Avis** (tel. toll free 800/331-2112), **Budget Rent-a-Car** (tel. toll free 800/527-0700), **Hertz** (tel. toll free 800/654-3001), and **National** (tel. toll free 800/326-4567)—maintain well-equipped branches at the Nassau International Airport, across the street from the main terminal. Avis also maintains branches at the cruise-ship docks, at the Paradise Island Holiday Inn, and in downtown Nassau. National has a branch at the Cable Beach Hotel and one in downtown Nassau. Hertz has an office at Wyndham's Ambassador Beach Hotel.

Budget will send a driver anywhere on New Providence or Paradise Island to pick you up and deliver you to its headquarters at the airport. If you're arriving by seaplane at Paradise Island, Budget has a kiosk at Chalk's Airline Terminal.

Rates among the various companies are roughly similar. Weekly prices are usually calculated at six times the daily rate, so keeping a car for the seventh day usually works out free, although that gives you a price break only if you declare your intention to rent for a full week when you sign your rental contract.

At presstime, among the four rental firms, Budget offered the least expensive rate, $42 a day, and some of the most lenient restrictions, with an advance-reservation requirement of only 48 business hours. (The car in question was a peppy, unglamorous, but very serviceable Volkswagen "Beetle.") Drivers at Budget need to be between 21 and 70, although a surcharge of $3 a day is added for clients between 21 and 24, inclusive. The rental of a Budget car with automatic transmission and air conditioning (a Toyota Corolla) costs $54 a day, still less than the daily rate for the cheapest manual-transmission, nonair-conditioned car at some of the other companies.

Each of the companies offers additional insurance for between $9.50 and $11 per day. Purchase of a collision damage waiver (CDW) will waive a customer's financial responsibility in the event of an accident. Without arranging a CDW, unless a customer has private insurance (perhaps a policy connected to the credit card that was imprinted upon the original car-rental contract), he or she will be responsible for up to the full value of any damage caused accidentally to the vehicle.

There's no tax on car rentals in Nassau. Drivers must present a valid driver's license, plus a credit card or a cash deposit.

Drive on the left, don't drink and drive, and pay extra attention when driving at night.

2. Fast Facts: New Providence (Nassau/Cable Beach)

Much factual information regarding Nassau is also applicable to the rest of The Bahamas and appears under "Fast Facts: The Bahamas" in Chapter VII. The data presented here should help you on matters pertaining specifically to the capital.

AMERICAN EXPRESS: The local representative is **Playtours,** Shirley Street, Nassau (tel. 809/322-2931). Hours are Monday through Friday from 9am to 5pm.

AREA CODE: The area code for Nassau is **809,** which can be dialed directly from North America.

BOOKSTORES: The largest on the island is the **United Bookstore,** with its major branch located 2 miles east of the center of town, at the Madeira Street Shopping Centre (tel. 809/322-8597). Another branch, almost as big, lies in the heart of Nassau, within the Marathon Mall, at the corner of Robinson and Marathon (tel. 809/393-6166).

BUSINESS HOURS: See "Fast Facts" in Chapter VII.

CAR RENTALS: See "Getting Around" above.

CLIMATE: See "When to Go" in Chapter VII.

CURRENCY: See "Information, Entry Requirements, Customs & Money" in Chapter VII.

CURRENCY EXCHANGE: Americans need not bother to exchange their dollars into Bahamian dollars, because the currencies are on par. However, Canadians will need to convert their dollars, and Britishers their pounds, which can be done at local banks or sometimes at a hotel. Hotels, however, offer the least favorable rates.

DENTISTS: There are numerous dentists in Nassau, all of whom speak English, but for the most modern facilities and equipment, use one of the half dozen or so dentists in the dental department of the Princess Margaret Hospital (see "Hospitals," below).

DOCTORS: For the fastest and best services, use a member of the staff at the Princess Margaret Hospital (see "Hospitals," below).

DRUGS: The strict drug law of The Bahamas was cited under "Fast Facts" in the preceding chapter, but the warning bears repeating. The authorities do not smile on visitors possessing or selling marijuana or other narcotics, and offenders are speedily and severely punished. A normal lapse of three days between arrest and sentencing can be expected. Penalties are harsh.

DRUGSTORES: Try **Lighbourn's Pharmacy,** Bay and George Streets (tel. 809/322-2095), which is open Monday through Saturday from 9am to 5pm.

EMBASSIES/CONSULATES: See "Fast Facts" in Chapter VII.

EMERGENCIES: For **police,** dial **919;** for the **fire department,** dial **919;** and for an **ambulance,** dial **322-2221** (if busy, an alternate number is **322-2861).**

EYEGLASSES: Both large and convenient to the center of Nassau is **Optical Services Ltd.,** inside the British Colonial Arcade, off Bay Street (tel. 809/322-3910).

HAIRDRESSERS/BARBERS: Try **Cliffie's Unisex Beauty Salon,** Frederick Street (tel. 809/323-6253), a short walk south of Bay Street, for both men and women.

HOLIDAYS: See "When to Go" in Chapter VII.

HOSPITALS: If you need medical attention, Nassau has a large number of qualified persons, ranging from general practitioners to specialists in obstetrics and gynecology, surgery, psychiatry, ophthalmology, orthopedics, psychology, dermatology, pediatrics, internal medicine, and radiology. As far as medical facilities are concerned, the **Princess Margaret Hospital** on Shirley Street (tel. 809/322-2861) is the leading hospital in The Bahamas. Its bed capacity is 455, and it has departments with well-qualified staffs in medicine, surgery, maternity, pediatrics, intensive care, eye, and chest, as well as an emergency ward, a dialysis unit, a laboratory with a blood bank, X-ray facilities, and a pharmacy. It is a government-operated hospital. The privately owned doctors' **Rassin Hospital,** with 26 beds, is at the corner of Shirley Street and Collins Avenue, P.O. Box N-972 (tel. 809/322-8411).

HOTLINES: For the **Drugs Action Service,** dial **322-2308.**

INFORMATION: Assistance is available at a booth at the Nassau International Airport. Otherwise, you'll find an **Information Booth** at Prince George Wharf (tel. 809/325-9155) and at Rawson Square (tel. 809/325-9171).

LAUNDRY/DRY CLEANING: One site that combines laundry and dry-cleaning facilities is at the corner of Nassau Street and Boyd Road. There, you'll find the **Laundromat Superwash** (tel. 809/323-4018). (Insert tokens, which you buy from the attendant, to make the machines work.) In the same building is the **New Oriental Dry Cleaner** (tel. 809/323-7249). Another dry cleaner lies a short drive north of the center of town, the **Jiffy Quality Cleaner,** at the corner of Blue Hill Road and Cordeaux Avenue (tel. 809/323-6771).

LIBRARY: The **Nassau Public Library and Museum,** Bank Lane (tel. 809/322-4907), is housed in the former Nassau Gaol. Dating from 1797, the library and museum are open Monday through Friday from 10am to 9pm, on Saturday from 10am to 5pm. Admission is free. The museum has many historic prints and colonial artifacts, especially documents.

LOST PROPERTY: There is no office for this. You must call the police station and report your loss.

LUGGAGE STORAGE/LOCKERS: There are no facilities for this, but arrangements can possibly be made at your hotel.

NEWSPAPERS/MAGAZINES: See "Fast Facts" in Chapter VII.

PHOTOGRAPHIC NEEDS: **John Bull,** Bay Street (tel. 808/322-3328), one block east of Rawson Square, is the largest camera store in Nassau. It sells such top brand names as Nikon, Vivitar, Hasselblad, and Minolta. It also sells lenses, binoculars, film, and other accessories. Camera experts there are available for advice.

POLICE: See "Emergencies," above.

POST OFFICE: The **Nassau General Post Office** is at the top of Parliament Street on East Hill Street (tel. 809/322-3344), and it is open Monday through Friday from 9am to 5pm, on Saturday from 9am to 1pm.

RADIO/TV: See "Fast Facts" in Chapter VII.

RELIGIOUS SERVICES: Bahamians tend to be religious people, with a history of religious tolerance. The number and variety of houses of worship around Nassau may surprise you. Of the major faiths, the following churches are established here. **Anglican**—Christ Church Cathedral, King and George Streets (tel. 809/322-4186); St. Matthews, Shirley Street and Church Lane (tel. 809/325-2191). **Baptist** —Zion, East and Shirley Streets (tel. 809/325-3556). **Roman Catholic**—St. Francis Xavier's Cathedral, West and West Hill Streets (tel. 809/323-3802); Sacred Heart Church, East Shirley Street (tel. 809/326-6274). **Methodist**—Trinity, Fredrick Street (tel. 809/325-2552); Ebenezer, East Shirley Street (tel. 809/323-2936). **Presbyterian**—St. Andrew's Kirk, Princes Street (tel. 809/322-4085). **Lutheran**—Lutheran Church of Nassau, John F. Kennedy Drive (tel. 809/323-4107).

REST ROOMS: These are generally inadequate. Visitors often have to rely on the facilities available at airports and terminals, hotels, restaurants, cafés, and other commercial establishments, although their use in some of these places is restricted to customers.

SAFETY: Women should avoid walking along the often nearly deserted streets of Nassau at night. Cable Beach and Paradise Island are much safer places to be in the evening. For more details, see "Health, Safety, Insurance & Other Concerns" in Chapter VII.

SHOE REPAIR: Virtually everyone in town heads for **Wilson's Shoe Repair,** at the corner of East Street and Wulff Road (tel. 809/323-4250).

TAXES: There is no city tax, other than the national 4% tax already mentioned, which is imposed on hotel rates. All visitors leaving Nassau also pay a $7 departure tax.

TAXIS: See "Getting Around" above.

TELEGRAMS/TELEX/FAX: Nearly all major hotels send telexes and faxes, although yours may be too small to offer such services. If so, go to the main post office (see above). To send a telegram, you can either call from your hotel (paying over the phone with a valid credit card) or visit in person the **Bahamas Telecommunications Corp.,** Poinciana Drive, Nassau (tel. 809/323-6414), located beside the main seafront road leading to the resort hotels of Cable Beach.

TRANSIT INFORMATION: To summon a taxi, call 323-5111. There is no central information number for the Nassau International Airport. If you want flight information, it is necessary to call individual airlines directly.

WEATHER: New Providence, which is fairly centrally located in The Bahamas, has temperatures in winter that vary from about 60° to 75° Fahrenheit daily. Summer variations are 78°F to the high 80s.

YELLOW PAGES: All the phone numbers for The Bahamas are condensed in one annually revised book. Nassau has the most extensive listing of goods and services in the Yellow Pages at the back of the book.

---

3. Where to Stay & Dine in Nassau

Many visitors prefer to find lodgings or to dine in historic downtown Nassau. Accommodations generally tend to be more reasonably priced in this area, and there are many good places to eat, whether you're in the mood for elegance or just for a quick meal to stave off hunger. First, I'll recommend a number of places to stay and follow with my dining selections.

WHERE TO STAY

Many old properties, such as the British Colonial Beach Resort downtown, have been considerably revamped and refurbished. The legendary Royal Victoria couldn't keep up and was gutted. The accommodation picture is brighter than ever, as new managements have pumped fresh energy into tired properties.

If you're economizing, you'll find moderate and, in some cases, bargain price tags, but you'll have to "commute" to the beaches on Paradise Island or at Cable Beach.

Incidentally, the hotels of The Bahamas are known for quoting package rates that are cut-rate discounts. These change frequently, so I've given only regular room tariffs, called "rack rates" in the travel industry. In booking, however, always inquire about honeymoon specials, golf packages, summer weeks, and other discounts.

Hotels add a 4% room tax and a 4% to 6% "resort levy" to your rate. Sometimes this is quoted as part of the tariff, and at other times it is added when your final bill is presented. Always ask if the tax is included when you are quoted a rate. Many hotels also add a 15% service charge to your bill as well—so check these items out in advance so you won't be shocked when the final tab is presented.

What the Symbols Mean

AP (American plan): Includes three meals a day (sometimes called full board or full pension).

CP (Continental plan): A Continental breakfast (that is, bread, jam, and coffee) is included in the room rate.

EP (European plan): This rate is always cheapest, as it offers only the room—no meals.

MAP (modified American plan): Sometimes called half board or half pension, this room rate includes breakfast and dinner (or lunch if you prefer).

Expensive

Graycliff, West Hill Street, P.O. Box N-10246, Nassau, The Bahamas (tel. 809/322-2796, or toll free 800/423-4095 in the U.S.), stands deep in the heart of Old Nassau, an exceptionally well-preserved colonial villa across the street from Government House. It's the only Relais & Châteaux hotel in The Bahamas. The main house of Graycliff is some 250 years old, built by Capt. John Howard Graysmith, a pirate who was noted for his exploits against Spanish shipping and who was commander of the notorious *Graywolf*, which was scuttled off New Providence in 1726. Captain Graysmith settled in Nassau and used some of his riches to build Graycliff. There is no written history on the use to which this fine example of Georgian colonial architecture was put after the captain's death in 1734, but it may once have housed the British West Indies Regiment. It is believed that the cellars, with their low thick walls and bars, may indicate that a garrison occupied the house. By 1844 Graycliff was a hotel for "gentlefolk and invalids."

Over the years since then, when the house was sometimes a hotel, sometimes a private residence, a handsome swimming pool was added and extensive additions and renovations were made to the property while keeping the main house intact. Both as hotel and home, the place has hosted the rich and famous. The Duke and Duchess of Windsor often visited here while he served as governor of The Bahamas and lived across the street. Sir Winston Churchill used to enjoy the swimming pool, paddling around with a cigar in his mouth. Lord Mountbatten, Aristotle Onassis, even the Beatles were guests at Graycliff at one time or another. In 1966 the Earl and Countess Dudley of Staffordshire purchased the house and occupied it as a winter home. Since that time it has been sold and changed again to a 14-room hotel. It is furnished with exceptional and luxuriously styled antiques. Here you're likely to run into Paul Newman, Perry Como, Michael Caine, Brooke Shields, or Kenny Rogers, among the celebrities who come to relax in this gracious ambience. In winter, a single costs $170 daily, a double rents from $255 to $280, and a poolside cottage (double occupancy) is priced at $290. *In summer, a single costs $120 daily, a double ranges from $165 to $210, and a poolside cottage (double occupancy) goes for $210.* In any season, a Continental breakfast is included in the price. The present owner, Enrico Garzaroli, brings his own aristocratic ways and tastes to this chic oasis. The hotel boasts one of the finest restaurants in Nassau—also called Graycliff—certainly the most elegant (see my recommendations for dining out). Always reserve well in advance.

Coral World Villas, Silver Cay, P.O. Box N-7797, Nassau, The Bahamas (tel. 809/328-1036, or toll free 800/328-8814 in the U.S.), lies isolated on the private island of Silver Cay (site of the underwater attraction Coral World, reviewed later), midway between downtown Nassau and Cable Beach. It promotes secluded luxuries in this 22-villa property, which opened in 1988, making Silver Cay the 21st of the inhabited islands of the archipelago. You can cross a small bridge to the "mainland" (New Providence), but many guests find this little world sufficient unto itself. They can roam about the private island, which becomes quite tranquil after the Coral World sightseeing crowds have departed.

These villas, furnished in a light Caribbean motif with wicker furniture and tropical accents, come with a private swimming pool for each villa. All of them open onto ocean views. Decorator designed, each villa has a king-size bed and a pull-out queen-size sleeping sofa, ideal if the unit is shared with children. The villas also contain their own kitchens, complete with microwaves, and bars. A complimentary Continental breakfast will be delivered to your private pool patio. The bathrooms are sheathed in marble, and from your oval bathtub you can take in a view of the waves through a picture window as you make your own waves. Amenities include remote control color cable TV and phones. In winter, a villa (single or double) on the EP rents from $245 daily, *falling in summer to $195 daily*. However, there is no charge for children 12 years or younger sharing with an adult (a maximum of two children per room). Guests can dine at the Conch Club terrace restaurant at the hotel or else lunch at Coral World's oceanfront Clipper Restaurant.

Moderate

British Colonial Beach Resort, 1 Bay St., P.O. Box N-7148, Nassau, The Bahamas (tel. 809/322-3301, or toll free 800/528-1234 in the U.S.), is on 8 tropical acres in the heart of Nassau, the only major hotel in the downtown area and just steps away from the shopping area of Bay Street, it is a regenerated ruler of Nassau's

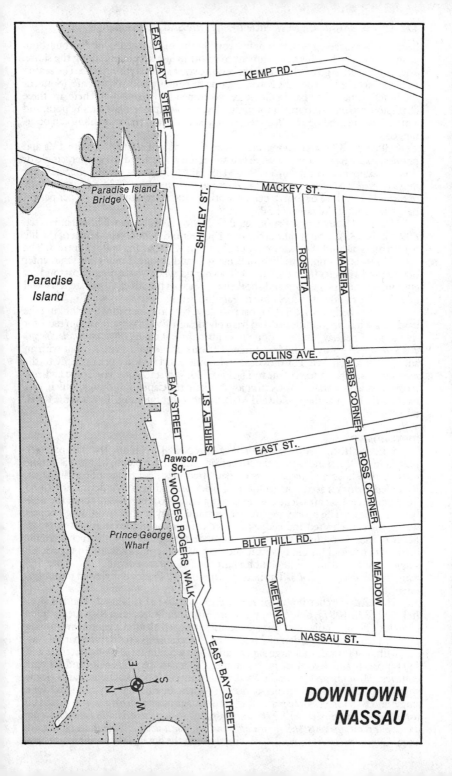

DOWNTOWN NASSAU

bayfront. Nevertheless, whether or not you like this place may depend on your room assignment. The hotel is a monument to resort living, spread out along the shore. You won't need to go off the premises, because you have everything here. The dining facilities include Blackbeard's Forge, Bayside Restaurant, and Wharf Café. (Some of the hotel's dining and bar facilities are recommended separately.) There are three championship tennis courts lit for night play, an Olympic-size swimming pool, and a private white-sand beach. Deep-sea fishing, skin diving, and snorkeling can be arranged.

All of the 325 large rooms are air-conditioned and contain satellite TVs and phones; many have ocean views. Seven suites are also offered. In winter, single or double occupancy costs from $129 to $189 daily, with suites renting for $229. *For single or double occupancy in summer, rates range from $84 to $134 daily, with suites costing $174.* A third or fourth person sharing a room pays another $35 per person daily, year round. All rates are EP.

The Pilot House, East Bay Street, P.O. Box N-4941, Nassau, The Bahamas (tel. 809/393-3930), is built on the site of a 150-year-old pilot house. Much of the life here centers around the swimming-pool garden with banana and palm trees. The Pilot House is a 5-minute walk from Paradise Island Bridge, 2 miles from the center of town and 15 miles from the airport. The marina, where you can rent boats and get equipment for scuba diving and snorkeling, is across the street. A private ferry will take you free to downtown Nassau or Paradise Beach.

The 120 bedrooms, for the most part, have balconies or patios overlooking the garden. Each is air-conditioned and has a phone and TV. In winter, a room rents for $95 to $115 per day, single or double occupancy. *In summer, single or double charges are $70 to $90 per day.* Children under 12 years of age who share a room with an adult are accepted free. For breakfast and dinner, add $24 per person daily to the rates quoted. Many guests come to The Pilot House just to dine. The Three Ladies is recommended separately. You can enjoy drinks in the Captain's Lounge, which has a nautical decor, or at the Windward Mark in the tower building. To reach the hotel, take bus no. 17.

Inexpensive

El Greco Hotel, West Bay Street, P.O. Box N-4187, Nassau, The Bahamas (tel. 809/325-1121), stands across the street from Lighthouse Beach, within a 5-minute walk of the shops and restaurants of Bay Street. Its design has a Spanish flavor. Rounded archways accent its façade, and black-painted iron chandeliers are found inside the reception area. The owners direct a staff who seem to care about the well-being of guests. The rooms are clustered around a tiny central swimming pool set within the vine-covered and hedge-trimmed confines of an Iberian-style courtyard. Many of the 26 accommodations have separate sitting rooms, while each has a tile bath, air conditioning, and furniture such as you might find in Spain. In winter, EP singles cost $75 daily, while doubles rent for $85. *In summer, EP singles cost $55 daily, and doubles go for $65.* The hotel restaurant, Del Prado, is reviewed in the dining section.

The Little Orchard, Village Road, P.O. Box N-1514, Nassau, The Bahamas (tel. 809/323-1297), only 500 yards from Montagu Beach, is an apartment/hotel complex offering individual cottage facilities grouped around a central swimming pool in a semitropical garden of 2 acres. The cottages are in a residential part of Nassau, within 800 yards of a large supermarket and a 5-minute drive from tennis and squash courts and several island restaurants. There are 16 efficiencies and 12 pink cottages. All units are air-conditioned, with fully equipped kitchens, baths (some with balconies), and daily maid service. In winter, an EP efficiency costs $67 for a single and $78 for a double per day, while a cottage costs $86 for a single and $100 for a double. *In summer, an EP efficiency costs $51 for a single and $58 for a double per day, while a cottage costs $68 for a single and $80 for a double.* Taxes and service are extra. Guests can take bus no. 17, which stops near the hotel, if they want to go shopping in downtown Nassau (the bus service also runs to Paradise Island). Later, economy-minded vacationers share stories at the convivial Tree Frog Bar, on the premises.

New Olympia Hotel, West Bay Street, P.O. Box N-984, Nassau, The Bahamas (tel. 809/322-4971), is a three-story hostelry whose blue-and-white façade reflects the national colors of Greece, a bow to their heritage by owners Kate Kiriaze and her brother, John Constantakis, although they were born in The Bahamas. Their hotel is across from the community beach in the heart of Nassau, just a short walk from West Beach and the shopping along Bay Street. The pleasantly decorated, sunny rooms, 50 in all, are accessible via long hallways. The oceanside accommodations have private balconies and views of the water. Each room contains two beds, air conditioning, a private bath, color TV, and a phone. Many have recently refurbished with wallpaper and paint. In winter, EP singles and doubles range from $80 daily. *In summer, the EP charge for singles and doubles is from $70 daily.* After a refreshing dip in the ocean, you can head for the garden patio or Sonny's Pizzeria & Sports Pub, outfitted with antique decorations from Europe and Asia. Menu offerings have been expanded. The pub is definitely the hotel's social center, offering cold drinks and satellite TV. A lobbyside drugstore and boutique make shopping for sundries easy. Services include babysitting, room service, and laundry.

Ocean Spray Hotel, West Bay Street, P.O. Box N-3035, Nassau, The Bahamas (tel. 809/322-8032), is a modestly modern 30-room corner hotel, a short stroll from the shopping district and across the street from the beach. Bedrooms are conservative, with twin beds, air conditioning, private baths, phones, and wall-to-wall carpeting. Best known for its restaurant-bar Europe, which serves good imported wines and continental, Bahamian, German, and American specialties, the hotel has an informal atmosphere. In winter, EP singles rent for $73 daily, with doubles costing $85. *Prices are lowered in summer to $66.80 daily for a single and $80 for a double,* EP. Ocean Spray offers guests both beach and town, a winning combination in Nassau.

Parthenon Hotel, West Bay Street, P.O. Box N-4930, Nassau, The Bahamas (tel. 809/322-2643, or toll free 800/327-0787 in the U.S., toll free 800/432-5594 in Florida), is a small hotel only 3 minutes from Bay Street and the beaches. Although modern, it's styled in the old Bahamian way with continuous covered balconies overlooking a well-tended garden. The 18 rooms are simple, with basic, restrained decor, air conditioning, TVs, phones, and private baths. In winter, singles or doubles are $52 daily, rising to $58 in a triple. *In summer, singles or doubles cost $42 daily, with triples renting for $48.* Rates quoted are on the EP. Fishing, golfing, tennis, and water sports can be arranged.

WHERE TO DINE

I'll recommend a range of places offering good food in downtown Nassau, where you'll find hotel restaurants serving American and Continental specialties, as well as a number of Bahamian restaurants where you can enjoy crab fat and dumplings, peas 'n' rice, cracked conch (also conch chowder, conch fritters, and conch salad), grouper (in every way known), and red snapper in anchovy sauce. Since most meat is imported frozen, it's generally better to rely on the tasty local fresh fish and seafood.

Note that all prices quoted are per person. Most restaurants add a 15% service charge.

Very Expensive

Graycliff, West Hill Street (tel. 809/322-2796), is the elegant and aristocratic dining choice of Nassau (see my hotel recommendations). In an antiques-filled colonial mansion, opposite Government House, Graycliff was once the home of the Earl and Countess Dudley of Staffordshire. Its present owner, Enrico Garzaroli, has hired an exciting young Bahamian chef, Phillip Bethel, who produces a Continental cuisine of culinary excellence, served at opulently set tables in a setting of charm and grace, surrounded by lush gardens.

The menu opens with caviar and gourmet terrines, including foie gras with truffles and a pâté of hare with pine kernels, perhaps young wild Abaco boar pâté with walnuts. The soups and pastas are outstanding, including chilled cream of cucumber and fettuccine Enrico (made with a mixture of white truffles if you're willing to pay extra). The chef is a master at the charcoal grill and spit, as my recently sampled spit-roasted duckling flambé with apple brandy showed. Also offered are such classic main courses as roast rack of lamb with herbs, and chateaubriand with a perfectly made béarnaise sauce. The seafood pasta is another favorite order. The fish selection in general is outstanding, including grilled spiny lobster, grouper in a cream–and–Dijon mustard sauce, and Dover sole à la ciboulette. All main dishes are cooked *à la minute*.

If you've survived all that, you'll find a masterful array of Italian desserts, including soufflés, a chilled zabaglione, and/or a selection from the master pastry chef. Expect to spend at least $75 for dinner, plus wine and service. The wine is the best in all The Bahamas, with more than 1,000 selections, some often stunning vintages priced at thousands of dollars. The collection of Cuban cigars here—almost 90 types—is considered the most varied in the world. Before dinner, try the charming balcony bar. Lunch is served Monday through Friday from noon to 3pm; dinner, nightly from 7 to 10pm. Reservations are essential, and men should wear jackets.

Expensive

Buena Vista, Delancy and Meeting Streets (tel. 809/322-2811), lying one block west of Government House, is a 200-year-old colonial mansion set on 5 acres of tropical foliage, a dining choice of traditional elegance and fine eating. The house has had a long and colorful history and was once owned by a Presbyterian minister. Perhaps Rhett Butler types stayed here during the Civil War, loading schooners to run through the North's blockade. Today, it's a favorite of the local banking and business community. When the weather's right, which is most of the time, tables are set out on the garden patio, surrounded by flowers and palms.

The cooking is Continental, with a wide variety of local seafood, and in addition to haute cuisine, under the direction of host Stan Bocus, the restaurant turns out a number of nouvelle cuisine dishes. A menu of daily specialties is featured, including a set dinner for $39; otherwise, you can order from the regular à la carte menu costing from $45 per person, which features a number of main dishes for two, such as roast rack of lamb in the style of Provence. The chef also prepares excellent beef and veal dishes. Many guests like to begin their meal with the daily pasta; cream of garlic soup rates as a novelty dish. Desserts include cherries jubilee or orange crêpes au Grand Marnier. Service is deft and efficient, but also polite. Buena Vista is open for dinner only, nightly from 7 to 10pm, and it's necessary to make reservations. The restaurant is closed on Sunday from May to mid-December. Delancy Street is opposite the cathedral close of St. Francis Xavier, only a short distance from Bay Street.

The aura of the Mediterranean has been re-created in Nassau at **Del Prado Restaurant,** West Bay Street (tel. 809/325-0324), set within the El Greco Hotel, just west of the center of town. Amid a contemporary decor accented with stained-glass windows, fine bone china, and candlelight, you can enjoy well-prepared and well-presented meals. Menu items include a local seafood coquille, pâté, escargots, beef Wellington, chateaubriand, shrimp, steak, local fish and chicken, with an array of well-flavored sauces. Try the medallions of veal à l'orange. Meals cost from $50 per person at dinnertime, and less formal meals at lunchtime cost from $20 per person. Reservations are suggested, and jackets are preferred for men. Lunch and dinner are served daily from 11am to 3pm and from 5 to 11pm, respectively. This is considered one of the better restaurants of Nassau.

Sun and . . . , Lake View Road, off Shirley Street (tel. 809/323-1205), is one of the oldest restaurants in Nassau, lying near Fort Montagu. Everybody has dined here—from Sir Winston Churchill to the Gabors, even Queen Elizabeth and Prince Philip. The place became a bit of a local legend when it was run by Pete Gardner, a former Battle of Britain "ace" who'd originally come to Nassau when he was an aide to the then governor, Lord Ranfurly. To get to the restaurant, you pass over a drawbridge between two pools, going into a Spanish-style courtyard of a fine old Bahamian home, complete with fountains. You can order drinks in the patio bar, followed by dinner either inside or al fresco around the rock pool. The pool, incidentally, is the oldest private swimming pool in Nassau. As a historical note, the rock removed from it was used to build the house.

You might begin with conch chowder. Reflecting both a Stateside and a Continental cuisine, main dishes are likely to include braised duckling in lemon sauce, sweetbreads and kidneys in mustard sauce, spiny Caribbean lobster with a corn and pimiento sauce, or roast grouper with scallop mousse and a light lobster sauce. The dessert specialty is a coconut soufflé. The restaurant shuts down every year from the first of August until the first of October; otherwise, it is open Tuesday through Sunday from 6:30 to 9:30pm. You should make a reservation. Your tab will run around $50 or more.

Moderate

Blackbeard's Forge, British Colonial Beach Resort, 1 Bay St. (tel. 809/322-3301), is a far cry from the rough-and-ready pirate days in Nassau, with its rich red velvet, good food, and courteous service. But nautical touches such as old prints and maps and the huge bay window shaped like the stein of a sailing vessel do remind diners of the days when Nassau was a haven for buccaneers. Each of the wood and chrome tables has a box-shaped vent above to catch the smoke from its individual grill. It is primarily a beef and seafood restaurant. You can feast on Bahamian conch chowder or onion soup, followed by sirloin steak, jumbo shrimp kebab, lobster tail, grouper filets, surf and turf, or breast of chicken, topped off by coconut-cream layer cake or walnut cake. Expect to pay from $25. Blackbeard's is open nightly from 6 to 11pm. Reservations are advised.

Cellar and Garden Patio, 11 Charlotte St. (tel. 809/322-8877), lies half a block from Bay Street in the downtown section, near the Straw Market and Rawson Square. It makes for a pleasant dining choice, not only because of its good food but because its garden patio setting creates an oasis of greenery. Midday meals are served from a countertop in the outermost room, near the entrance. In an ambience midway between a Mediterranean cellar and an English pub, you can lunch on specials, salads, and sandwiches. During dinner the setting moves to the lattice-rimmed courtyard, where glass-topped tables are set under cascading vines. Many diners, however, prefer the formal dining room in an old cottage at the far end of the courtyard. When it was built, it was a simple clapboard outbuilding with a large fireplace at one end. Today the napery, candlelight, and well-prepared food make the rustic setting even more charming. Since only eight tables can be served here without cramping, dinner reservations are important.

Specialties include chicken gumbo Cajun style, steamed filet of grouper in a piquant sauce, shrimp Créole (or shrimp jambalaya), filet of pork in a lemon sauce flavored with coriander, steak-and-mushroom pie cooked in Guinness, and lamb cutlets in an orange-and-ginger sauce. Several main dishes have the vegetarian in mind. There is always a homemade soup of the day, and the chef also prepares delectable appetizers (and not just conch fritters). Lunch costs $12 per person and is served daily from 11am to 4pm. Dinner, priced from $25, is served Monday through Saturday from 6 to 10pm. The owners hire live steel-drum bands to perform nightly.

Europe, Ocean Spray Hotel, West Bay Street (tel. 809/322-8032), offers the best German specialties in Nassau, along with a sampling of Continental dishes. Attached to a moderately priced hotel already recommended, the Europe restaurant is appropriately named. It is attracting more and more German visitors who are "discovering" The Bahamas, but it also draws a good patronage among locals as well as North Americans. If you're driving, you'll find parking in the rear of the restaurant.

You might begin with such fare as a hearty soup, perhaps lima bean and sausage. You can then go on to bratwurst, a Wiener Schnitzel, perhaps peppersteak cognac. Sauerbraten is an eternal favorite, and the chef also prepares two kinds of fondue, both bourguignonne and cheese. Everybody's favorite dessert is German chocolate cake. Lunches cost from $12, with dinners priced from $25. Hours are 10am to 10pm Monday through Saturday.

Green Shutters Restaurant, 48 Parliament St. (tel. 809/325-5702), is about as close as Nassau comes to having an authentic English country pub, which features five imported British beers and serves steak-and-kidney pie. After being gutted by fire in 1971, this charming 190-year-old colonial house was completely restored. The place is large, and you can dine either in the pub section with the regulars or in the mahogany-paneled restaurant. The menu is varied, offering the best from The Bahamas, with fresh seafood complemented by traditional British fare: bangers and mash, shepherd's pie, and "chip butty." For dinner, roast prime rib with Yorkshire pudding and fresh Key lime pie for dessert are winners. Some Bahamian specialties such as grouper and conch salad are also featured. Vichyssoise, called "tater soup" here, and escargots with fresh spinach salad may also tempt you. The sandwiches at lunch are particularly good and well stuffed, including the triple-decker club. Courage beer is on tap, and the bartender also offers fresh-frozen sugar apple-banana daiquiris. Count on spending $15 for lunch and $30 for dinner. Lunch is served daily from 11:30am to 4pm and dinner daily from 6 to 10:30pm. The place has live music five nights a week.

Mai Tai Chinese-Polynesian Restaurant, Waterloo Lodge, East Bay Street (tel. 809/326-5088), near Fort Montagu, is a family run establishment hailed as the leading Asian eating place in Nassau. Its setting is the former mansion of Sir Stafford Sands, once the Bahamian tourist minister. Today, Peter Wong and his family provide diners with Polynesian, Szechuan, and Cantonese dishes, with some Hawaiian influences evident. Before settling down to lunch or dinner in this old Bahamian mansion, try one of the exotic drinks the place offers to complement the Asian theme: Volcanic Flame (served with flaming rum), Lover's Paradise, or perhaps a Fog Cutter.

Appetizers may vary from a pupu platter with ingredients heated over a flaming brazier to tidbits served on wooden platters. In the Polynesian mood? You might choose chow samsee, deviled Bahamian lobster, Mandarin orange duck, or sizzling Mai Tai steak. Szechuan dishes include, among many others, hot shredded spiced beef, kung pao chicken ding, and such chef's specials as chu ka fook (happy family) and lemon chicken. Cantonese selections are lengthy, with chicken almond ding and moo goo gai pan competing for my preference with the sweet-and-sour chicken or pork. The list of excellent Chinese-Polynesian dishes makes it hard to decide what to select, but of course you can go with a party and follow tradition by having everybody order something different so you get to taste a lot of delectable dishes. Also the place has take-out service. Lunch costs from $15. A complete dinner is likely to cost from $30 per person, and you get a lot of good food and polite service for that. Mai Tai is open daily for lunch from 11:30am to 3pm and for dinner from 5:30 to 11pm.

Roselawn Café, Bank Lane, off Bay Street (tel. 809/325-1018), operated by the previously recommended Buena Vista restaurant, is one of the most delightful places for dining in downtown Nassau. You'll forget the bargain-seeking cruise-ship crowds as you wander into its private courtyard. At this old Bahamian house you can select a table inside or one on the patio, in a setting of potted plants and statues. I go here mainly for the superb homemade pastas, including creamy lasagne and spaghetti cooked al dente. They even have a pizza oven, turning out familiar favorites, including a house special made with olives and anchovies. There is a selection of antipasti, and also an array of fresh Bahamian seafood, including spiny lobster. The chef also prepares an excellent minestrone, which might be a fine beginning to your meal. Desserts are luscious as well. In the evening, there is live entertainment. Lunches cost about $10; dinners from $25. The restaurant is open daily for lunch from 11:30am to 2:30pm and for dinner from 6:30 to 10pm. Look for the daily specials. The place is also open from 10pm to 6am for drinks and late supper, such as pizzas and pastas.

The Three Ladies, Pilot House Hotel, East Bay Street (tel. 809/322-8431), was named after a trio of experts on Bahamian cookery. It is separated from the inner-courtyard pool of this hotel by low lattice balustrades and awnings. This is al fresco dining, and there is a large floral mural against the wall. The restaurant offers American, Continental, and Bahamian dishes. Among the latter offerings are steamed Andros conch, native curried lamb, barbecued short ribs, and fish chowder Eleuthera style. The setting, which draws the boating crowd, is especially pleasant in the evening. Meals cost from $25. Daily hours are noon to 2:30pm for lunch and 7 to 10pm for dinner. The place lies one block east of Paradise Island Bridge.

Inexpensive

Bahamian Kitchen, Trinity Place, off Market Street (tel. 809/325-0702), next to Trinity Church, is one of the best places for good Bahamian cookery at modest prices. Specialties include lobster Bahamian style, fried red snapper, conch salad, stewed fish, steamed mutton, okra soup, and pea soup and dumplings. Most dishes are served with peas 'n' rice. For dessert, the guava duff is my preference, but I'm also tempted by the coconut pie, the rum cake, and the banana pudding. Breakfast is an event here, including such old-fashioned Bahamian fare as stewed fish and corned beef and grits, all served with johnnycake. Of course, you can order ham and eggs as well. There is a takeout service. The place, open daily from 8am to 11pm, is honest, decent, and upright. Breakfasts cost from $6, lunches from $12, and dinners from $18.

Bayside Buffet Restaurant, British Colonial Beach Resort, 1 Bay St., (tel. 809/322-7479), is worth visiting almost as much for its view as for its good and reasonably priced buffets. The tall, 100-foot-long windows front the entrance to Nassau's harbor, allowing a panoramic view of cruise ships, yachts, and other boats around Prince George Wharf. Lunch and dinner feature such selections as prime rib, steamed shrimp, ham, turkey, roast pork loin, and fish. There are homemade pasta salads and crabmeat salad, as well as salads of greens, fresh vegetables, and other ingredients. In fact, the salad bar is arguably the best in town. Breakfast costs from $6. Lunch is offered for $10.95 and dinner for $16.95 and up. You can have breakfast daily from 7 to 11:30am, with other meals served daily until 11pm without interruption.

If you don't want to choose from the buffet, you might like to have lunch or dinner à la carte at the Wharf Café, next to the Bayside's buffet area. Omelets, seafood salad, and desserts are offered. A meal here costs around $12. The Wharf Cafe is open daily from 7am to 11pm.

Choosy Foods, Market Street (tel. 809/326-5232), is housed in a colonial-style building one block from the Straw Market. The floor space is divided between a health-food store and a "natural foods" restaurant. You can browse through the inventory of books, herbal teas, and macrobiotic supplies after enjoying a wholesome meal that might include vegetable soup, quiche, freshly squeezed juice, and vegetarian specials. The lobster lasagne is a gourmet treat you may not want to miss. There's also a salad bar and an array of deli-style sandwiches. Of course, conch is the featured salad, although a full range of others can be ordered as well. Only regular beer, non-alcoholic beer, and wine are served. A full meal costs from $14. Lunch is served from 11am to 5pm and dinner from 5 to 9:30pm, Monday through Saturday.

Coco's Café, Marlborough Street (tel. 809/323-8778), stands across from the British Colonial Beach Resort. A casual, informal café, decorated in a modern art deco style with neon, it is a good all-around daily choice for either breakfast, lunch, or dinner. You might begin by perusing the drink menu, including every concoction from Bahama Mama to Goombay Smash. The menu is quite extensive, including hot and cold sandwiches, along with such prepared dishes as crab thermidor or cracked conch. You might order that old budgeteer's favorite, grouper fingers, or perhaps a seafood lasagne. There is also a long list of burgers, or perhaps you'd prefer a generous Caesar salad. Cheesecake comes with a choice of toppings, or else you might opt for one of the rich, moist cakes, perhaps chocolate or carrot. Meals cost from $12 and up. At breakfast, you could come here for that typically Bahamian favorite, boiled fish and grits, should you desire. But the kitchen will also prepare eggs any way you want them, along with pancakes and French toast. Meals cost from $12. Breakfast is served from 7:30 to 11am, lunch from 11:30am to 5pm, and dinner from 5 to 11pm.

18 Parliament Street, 18 Parliament St. (tel. 809/322-2836), is set in the palm-studded tropical garden of Nassau's oldest operating hotel, the Parliament. Previously called the Parliament Terrace Café, it made its address its name to avoid confusion with other similarly named establishments in Nassau. Casually dressed diners go here for Bahamian seafood specialties and native entertainment in the evening. Bahamian calypsos are heard here, making the Parliament one of the few places left in Nassau where you can hear this type of music. It's run by the husband-and-wife team of Graham and Anne Bruce. Their chef is "Pappy" Sam Smith, who knows how to produce an onion soup that is said to have come from Farouk, former king of Egypt.

Appetizers include conch salad or snails in garlic butter. The fish dishes are excellent, especially the house special, grouper Florentine. Try also cracked conch or conch curry. The dessert special is Graham's own English trifle. Dinners cost from $20. The regular luncheon buffet, costing $10, usually lets you choose a hot dish with vegetables and rice as well as make a trip to the salad bar. The café is open daily from 7:30 to 10am, 11:30am to 4pm, and 6 to 10pm. Closed Sunday at lunch. There is, as well, a large tropical drink menu, featuring frozen fruit daiquiris. With a view of the Supreme Court Building, the café stands in downtown Nassau.

Oriental Express Restaurant, on Bay Street opposite the Straw Market (tel. 809/326-7127), one level below the street, is a budget Chinese eatery. Cantonese and Szechuan food is served cafeteria style, with large helpings, in a dining room decorated with Asian fittings and a mirrored ceiling that lends an airy feel. A meal of standard Chinese dishes—which might include the likes of sweet-and-sour ribs, pork, shrimp, or chicken; barbecued ribs; or pineapple chicken or beef—costs from $15. The restaurant is open Monday through Saturday from 11:30am to 9pm.

Palm Restaurant, Bay Street (tel. 809/323-7444). At first glance you might think this place is just a coffeeshop, but the menu reveals a varied selection. Decorated like a tropical version of a Stateside cafeteria, it has ceiling fans, fern-patterned wallpaper, and waitress service. It's a sure bet as a place where you can get an early dinner or even a midafternoon snack after browsing in the shops that line the sidewalks on either side. Conchburgers are an unusual adaptation of the familiar favorite shellfish, or you can order Bahamian fried chicken, barbecued spareribs, black-bean soup, several veal dishes, crab thermidor, or an array of salads and sandwiches. For dessert, you can select from an array of ice-cream flavors, including rum raisin, guava, and soursop. Full meals range from around $18, although lighter orders will cost less. The location is opposite John Bull. Hours are 7:30am to 9:30pm Monday through Saturday.

Poop Deck, Nassau Yacht Haven Marina, East Bay Street (tel. 809/322-8175), is a favorite with the yachting set, who find a perch on the second-floor open-air terrace, overlooking the harbor. Across from the Pilot House, the deck not only opens onto the yachts in the harbor, but fronts Paradise Island as well. The outside tables are reserved for lunch and dinner service, and there's an inside bar as well if you're dropping in only for a drink. At lunch, you can order conch chowder, followed by beefburgers. In the evening, native grouper fingers are served with peas 'n' rice, or you might prefer Rosie's special chicken or Bahamian broiled crayfish. Stuffed deviled crab is another specialty, and the chef does a homemade lasagne with crisp garlic bread. Your check should come to $12 at lunch, $25 at dinner. The bar opens at 11:30am. Food is served all day, seven days a week. Lunch is from noon to 5pm, dinner from 5 to 10:30pm.

Tony Roma's, Saunder's Beach, West Bay Street (tel. 809/325-6502), on the main road between Nassau and Cable Beach, at Saunders Beach, is a favorite place on New Providence for rib-sticking portions and good value. The stone-trimmed modern building offers views of Saunders Beach from the tables of its open-air veranda. Inside, the decor includes exposed paneling, spindle-backed captain's chairs, and ceiling fans.

The establishment advertises itself as "the place for ribs," and if you order them, you'll discover that they are a good choice for the house specialty. Barbecued in a special sauce, they come in small (lunchtime) or large orders. They can be accompanied by barbecued chicken as part of the same platter. Juicy sandwiches made from barbecued beef or London broil, about the best hamburgers on the island, Bahamian conch chowder, chef's or green salad, and pan-fried grouper are also offered. Every weekday there's a daily special, such as Eleuthera chicken curry, roast turkey with giblet gravy, or Exuma steamed conch. I always begin my meal with an order of the succulent onion rings, which are served in a steaming loaf to be eaten with a spicy sauce. Beer on tap can accompany any meal, and there is also an array of tropical drinks, such as the Bananaroma Float. Open daily from 11am to midnight (until 2am on Friday and Saturday), the restaurant charges from $20 for full meals.

---

4. Where to Stay & Dine on Cable Beach

Cable Beach is regarded by many as the ultimate island resort area, with broad stretches of beachfront, a wide array of activity and entertainment, and hotel facilities that offer an ideal blend of modern convenience with tropical charm. The range is from a deluxe penthouse suite to a simple housekeeping unit in an apartment hotel.

Sports facilities abound on both land and water. For example, the tennis facility at the Cable Beach Hotel offers 10 courts, 5 of them lit, plus a stadium for tournament and exhibition play. Adjacent is an indoor complex featuring 3 courts each for squash and racquetball, while an 18-hole championship golf course is just across the street.

Along the beachfront, craft and equipment are available for all manner of water sports, often including private instruction. Sailing and waterskiing are the traditional activities, but windsurfing and parasailing are the rage with contemporary travelers.

The shoreline west of the city of Nassau was named for the telegraph cable laid in 1892 from Jupiter, Florida, to The Bahamas, making it possible for the first time to send messages directly to the United States and England.

For many years horse racing was the main attraction at Cable Beach. The 104-acre Hobby Horse Hall Race Course was mentioned in newspaper accounts as early as 1809. Racing continued throughout the 19th century, carried on mainly by officers of the British West India Regiment stationed in Nassau. After a hiatus during World War I, horse racing resumed in 1933, marking the beginning of an annual season that continued until the track closed in 1975.

Much of Cable Beach was once devoted to the cultivation of pineapples for the J. S. Johnson Company, which exported to the United States. In the 1920s, according to the historian Michael Craton, the area "became dotted with the stucco palaces of American nouveaux riches."

HOTELS OF CABLE BEACH

After World War II, Nassau's first luxury beach resorts were built at Cable Beach. The 213-room Emerald Beach Hotel, opened in 1954, was the first to feature air conditioning. The 145-room Balmoral Beach Hotel was built in 1946 as a private club and opened as a resort in 1967. The 410-room Nassau Beach Hotel was built in the late '60s by the Crothers family of Canada and acquired in 1969 by Trusthouse Forte. The 400-room Ambassador Beach Hotel, built by Sonesta Hotels, opened in 1971.

In 1974 the government bought the Emerald Beach, Balmoral Beach, and Ambassador Beach hotels for a total of $20 million, and the Hotel Corporation of The Bahamas was set up to run them.

Of all these hotels, the Balmoral was a special case. It was created by the British developer Sir Oliver Simmonds, who began work on its construction almost immediately following the close of World War II. For years he'd been aware that the wealthy, the powerful—world leaders, royalty, and the most famous stage, screen, opera, ballet, and concert stars—were constantly searching for closed little corners of the world where they could find peace and privacy, along with the best accommodations available.

Simmonds spread the word that his Balmoral Beach Club was so ultraexclusive that it would operate as a private club and would be absolutely restricted only to members and their approved guests. As a result, Simmonds found himself besieged with requests for memberships and reservations from all corners of the world. The Balmoral became an immediate success worldwide. After 16 years of this, Simmonds decided on semiretirement and leased the property to the Hotel Corporation of America. Beginning in 1962 and for 22 years thereafter, the Balmoral underwent constant changes in physical structure and in management.

When the Beatles were being mobbed from New York City to Hong Kong and could find no place where they could escape from their fame, they were accepted by the Balmoral. The lads from Liverpool were awed by the fact that they could walk the byways of the compound, sun at the poolside, walk through the dining room, and roam the beaches of Balmoral Island seemingly unrecognized.

The Duke and Duchess of Windsor frequently journeyed to The Bahamas, where the former monarch of England and governor-general of The Bahamas enjoyed the blessings of being just another Balmoral guest. Another frequent visitor was Richard Nixon, who also appreciated the anonymity afforded by the hotel. He used to arrive unexpectedly, sometimes by boat. The Gabors visited to become simple, unadored, and unadorned—but only for so long.

Changes in management continued until 1974 when Simmonds resumed control of the property, but only long enough to sell it outright to the Hotel Corporation of The Bahamas. In 1984 the corporation decided on a major multimillion-dollar restoration of the historic property, and Wyndham Hotels, a subsidiary of the Trammell Crow Hotel Company, was named to operate and manage the property.

One of the first steps was to change the name from the Balmoral Beach Club to the Royal Bahamian and begin a $7-million remodeling program to restore the resort to its niche among luxury retreats. The transformation was completed, and the resort reopened in December 1984. In the previous year, the 700-room Cable Beach Hotel had opened, making Cable Beach a glittering beachfront strip in its new incarnation. It has now been taken over by the French-owned Le Meridien. Its latest and most dazzling property is Carnival's Crystal Palace Resort & Casino.

All of these hotels are reviewed below. To reach any of the establishments, take bus no. 10 from Nassau.

Expensive

Carnival's Crystal Palace Resort & Casino, Cable Beach, West Bay Street, P.O. Box N-8306, Nassau, The Bahamas (tel. 809 / 327-6200, or toll free 800 / 453-5301 in the U.S.), is the largest, most intriguingly ostentatious, most shamelessly

---

What the Symbols Mean

AP (American plan): Includes three meals a day (sometimes called full board or full pension).

BP (Bermuda plan): Popularized first in Bermuda, this option includes a full American breakfast (sometimes called an English breakfast).

CP (Continental plan): A Continental breakfast (that is, bread, jam, and coffee) is included in the room rate.

EP (European plan): This rate is always cheapest, as it offers only the room— no meals.

MAP (modified American plan): Sometimes called half board or half pension, this room rate includes breakfast and dinner (or lunch if you prefer).

---

spectacular, and most strenuously promoted hotel in the Bahamian-Caribbean basin, incorporating 1.5 million square feet of floor space and endlessly rythmic rows of balconies painted in shades of eggplant, pink, lilac, and mauve. Set on its own beachfront, near a concrete and teakwood re-creation of a beached clipper ship (deliberately designed as a changing room), the hotel was the creation of Joe Farcus, known previously for his innovative work on Carnival's superliners.

The Crystal Palace incorporates into one sprawling compound a series of high-rise towers carrying names like Blue Marlin, Flamingo, Lignum Vitae, and Yellow Elder; a futuristic central core; and a cluster of gardens and beachfront gazebos—all interconnected with arcades, underground passages, and minipavilions. The complex contains more than 1,550 bedrooms and suites; 14 specialty restaurants; six bars, a high-tech disco, a cabaret theater (the Palace Theater, recommended separately in the nightlife section of this chapter), and a casino; a series of swimming pools (one of which contains a 100-foot water slide); a complete array of water-sports facilities; 18 different tennis courts; a nearby 18-hole golf course; and a health club with sauna, massage facilities, and exercise machines. Most spectacular among the accommodations is a high-tech showplace suite (with a voice-controlled robot named Ursula in attendance who will do everything from serving drinks to reproducing the sound of thunder and lightning), which rents for $25,000 a night. The regular rooms are spacious, but nowhere near as opulent as the public rooms. They are modern, well furnished, and comfortable.

In winter, single or double rooms range from $175 to $265 per day, with all but the most spectacular of the suites costing $330 to $3,000. *In summer, single or double occupancy ranges from $110 to $205 per day, with suites priced at between $330 and $3,000.* A third occupant of any double room pays a supplement of $35 in any season. MAP can be arranged throughout the year for an additional $40 per person per day. Service and taxes are extra. This resort, perhaps more than any other in The Bahamas, is eminently capable of providing transportation on its own airline (Carnival Airlines) from dozens of cities throughout North America. In its eagerness to fill its vast number of rooms, cost-effective packages are sometimes offered.

The previously mentioned 14 restaurants run as wide a culinary gamut as you'll find within a single establishment anywhere. The most expensive and formal is the Sole Mare, serving sophisticated Italian food. Some of the other choices include a Chinese restaurant, between two and four (depending on the way you define them) seafood restaurants, a restaurant featuring a series of buffets, a pizza restaurant, a poolside grill, a New York City–inspired deli, a European restaurant called Le Grille, and a brightly informal area that advertizes itself as the only authentic Mexican restaurant in The Bahamas.

Le Meridien Royal Bahamian Hotel, West Bay Street, P.O. Box N-10422, Nassau, The Bahamas (tel. 809/327-6400, or toll free 800/543-4300 in the U.S.), is an elegant and lavishly refurbished hotel acquired in the 1980s by the French-based Meridien hotel chain. Built as a private club in 1946 to shelter the rich and famous from prying eyes and outsiders, it became a hotel in 1967, the Balmoral Beach. The establishment still exudes a kind of timeless colonial charm. A sweeping canopy shelters guests on their way from the driveway to the entrance portico, where smartly tailored female concierges welcome newcomers with offers of assistance. Many old British customs are observed here, including the serving of afternoon tea in one of the tastefully conservative public rooms. Each of these has been furnished with Chippendale reproductions, brass chandeliers, marble and carpeted floors, comfortable French settees, and, along the curved walls of one of the rose-colored salons, about a dozen bandy-legged desks for letter writing.

The central core of the property, known as the Manor House, has a courtyard where a stork fountain spits water at what might remind you of the façade of a Corinthian temple. The 145 bedrooms within the Manor House are not the only lodging option for guests, since the resort also contains 21 suites within outlying villas. Some of these suites have Jacuzzis and private pools, and some of the bathrooms are as spacious as many big-city apartments. The bedrooms have cove moldings, formal English furniture, satellite TVs, air conditioning, and baths loaded with such amenities as bathrobes, perfumed soaps, and cosmetics. Those rooms that face the ocean offer small curved terraces with ornate iron railings and views of an offshore sand spit still named Balmoral Island. In winter, EP single or double occupancy ranges from $205 to $300 daily, with villa suites priced at $380 to $500. *In summer, EP single or double rooms range from $135 to $220 daily, with suites priced at $350 to $400.*

The establishment's premier restaurant, the Café de Paris, is recommended separately. The hotel has one of the most appealing bars in the Bahamas, the Balmoral Bar, where you can listen to the evening pianist. Waiters serve your drinks as you're seated in low-slung French armchairs, near lamps with porcelain bases shaped like English retrievers and Irish setters.

There's a complete spa facility on the premises, equipped with masseurs and masseuses, exercise machines, and health programs. The establishment also has a complete array of water and racquet sports, access to golf facilities, and a complimentary shuttlebus that transports hotel guests to the casino and nightlife options of the nearby Crystal Palace complex. There's a long stretch of sandy beach, as well as an hourglass-shaped pool.

Nassau Beach Resort Club, West Bay Street, P.O. Box N-7756 Nassau, The Bahamas (tel. 809/327-7711, or toll free 800/225-5843 in the U.S.). Part of its allure has been overshadowed by the almost irresistible glitz of the glossy new superhotels nearby, but to a crowd of loyal fans its allure is still strong. The club was built about 30 years ago (long before many of its neighbors), with three separate wings in a dignified gray-and-white twin-towered design with Neo-Georgian detailing and tile and marble-covered floors. In the 1980s its new owners, the London-based Trusthouse Forte properties, invested $8.5 million in its restoration. Today the place has been enhanced by a series of Bahamian accessories that include ceiling paddle fans and upholstered wicker furniture, landscaping, and lots of space in the public areas.

Within the hotel is an assemblage of recreational facilities called the Palm Lounge, where complimentary coffee and tea, a pool table, daily newspapers, a handful of game tables, a library, and video tapes of Hollywood movies are available free to hotel guests looking for diversions from the nearby beach. Free, too, are nightly cocktails. There are also charming restaurants, one of which—Pineapple Place—is reviewed separately.

The resort opens onto a 3,000-foot white-sand beach and has a tennis complex of six all-weather courts lit for night play, with a resident pro for lessons. There are also an unsupervised health club on the premises with weight and exercise machines, a children's clubhouse with facilities for child-watching supervised by full-time counselors, and an array of water sports (the nonmechanized versions of which are free to hotel guests). The hotel is home to an annual windsurfing competition—the Bahamas International Windsurfing Regatta—offering the most generous prizes of any such event in the North Atlantic.

Each of the accommodations contains a marble-sheathed bath and dressing area, and has a color TV and a hairdryer. In winter, EP single or double rooms range from $115 to $200 daily, with suites priced at $300 to $650. *In summer, EP single or double rooms range from $95 to $155 daily, with suites priced at $250 to $500.* Taxes and service charges are extra.

Wyndham Ambassador Beach Hotel, West Bay Street, P.O. Box N-3026, Nassau, The Bahamas (tel. 809/327-8231, or toll free 800/822-4200 in the U.S., 800/631-4200 in Canada), is a resort and convention hotel, which, although owned by the Commonwealth of The Bahamas, is operated and staffed by the Wyndham Hotel Corp. of Dallas, Texas. The inner courtyard formed by the hotel's U-shaped design embraces a leafy collection of palms, a freshwater swimming pool, and a sugar-white stretch of fine-sand beach. The property combines both modern and colonial style in an informally attractive collection of restaurants, bars, and public rooms, which are upholstered and sheathed in decorator colors of dusty rose, peach, and mauve, whose tones are highlighted with paneling painted either in white enamel or in natural-grain finishes. On the premises are the Palm Court and a game room with wide-screen satellite TV. A full array of water sports can be arranged, as well as day or night tennis, squash, and racquetball. Parking is free, and both babysitting and room service are available.

The attractively furnished modern rooms contain TVs, phones, and air conditioning. Winter rates for single or double rooms range from $140 to $170 per day, plus service and taxes. *In summer, single or double units cost $95 to $125 per day.* A third person can share an accommodation for $35 extra per day year round. MAP can be arranged for an additional $40 per person per day year round.

Housekeeping Units

Cable Beach Manor, West Bay Street, P.O. Box N-8333, Nassau, The Bahamas (tel. 809/327-7785), is on an excellent sandy beach in the Cable Beach area 5 miles west of Nassau. It caters to those seeking self-sufficient accommodations without a lot of fanfare or glitz. A tastefully designed group of 34 carnation-pink–and–white apartments, where guests have all the comforts of home, it's built like a Santa Barbara hacienda, with long encircling covered verandas that overlook a swimming pool and gardens. Under tall palms and umbrella trees are shady spots with adjoining sunbathing areas. There's a public lounge with books, a TV, and free video movies on the premises. The location is about 15 minutes from the airport, the same distance into downtown Nassau. Around the corner are a supermarket, a liquor store, and a bus stop.

Each accommodation is decorated in Nordic modern, all elements harmoniously brought together in matching color tones. In winter, EP studio apartments cost $110 to $130 for single occupancy and $120 to $140 for double occupancy per day, while one-bedroom apartments, double occupancy, cost $150 to $170. *In summer, EP studio apartments cost $65 to $75 for single occupancy and $70 to $80 for double occupancy per day, while one-bedroom apartments, double occupancy, rent for $90 to $105.* Service and taxes are extra. Daily maid service is included (and paid for with a supplemental service charge at the end of your stay).

Casuarinas of Cable Beach, West Bay Street, P.O. Box N-4016, Nassau, The Bahamas (tel. 809/327-7921, or toll free 800/327-3012 in the U.S.), is a well-managed Bahamian-owned hotel that grew over many years until it now occupies land on both sides of the main road connecting Nassau with Cable Beach. This family-run apartment-hotel complex is the creation of Nettie Symonette, an enterprising woman who was the former general manager of the old Balmoral Beach Hotel before acquiring her own property. In her former post she became the first native-born Bahamian general manager of a major hotel. Over the years she has welcomed a varied array of international guests, including Senator Bob Graham of Florida and Stevie Wonder.

Contained within clusters of brown-and-white buildings set amid casuarina trees on the western edge of the Cable Beach complex, the establishment contains two swimming pools, a tennis court, two restaurants (see my dining recommendations), and a lobby/piano lounge. It also has an outdoor roadside café set within a garden. You'll be offered a choice of accommodations. The less expensive rooms are clustered around their own swimming pool across the road from the beach. The more expensive rooms lie closer to the beach, also around their own swimming pool. Ms. Symonette rents out a total of 90 units. In winter, EP single or double rooms cost $85 to $105 daily, triples $110 to $119, and quads $180. *In summer, EP singles or doubles cost $65 to $85 daily, triples $89 to $100, and quads $135.*

WHERE TO DINE

That long stretch of beachfront property, Cable Beach, or the Bahamian Riviera, now competes successfully with Paradise Island in top-quality restaurants, many of which are found in the deluxe and first-class hotels.

We'll pick up our forks for a survey of the best of Cable Beach restaurants in several price ranges. All prices quoted are per person.

Very Expensive

Riviera Restaurant, The Riviera Tower, Crystal Palace Resort & Casino, West Bay Street (tel. 809/327-6200). Considered one of the three most upscale restaurants within the enormous Crystal Palace Resort, it lies one floor above the lobby of the cement-sided building that was originally built as the Cable Beach Hotel. Decorated in a theme some diners describe as colonial New England–inspired, with tones of Newport blue and a big-windowed view of the beach and the sea, the Riviera serves an array of seafood specialties such as Maryland crab cakes, blackened grouper with a passion-fruit beurre-blanc sauce, smoked Scandinavian salmon, tuna steak sautéed in a mustard sauce, several different preparations of lobster, and a filet of dolphin fish cooked with jalapeño oil and fresh herbs and served with a vanilla sauce. Desserts are sumptuous, including Bahamian guava duff, and might be followed with a Jamaican, Bahamian, Mexican, or calypso coffee, each liberally laced with the appropriate liqueur. The restaurant charges around $70 per person for full meals, which are served only at dinner, Thursday through Tuesday from 5:30 to 11pm. Reservations and jackets and ties for men (and equivalent attire for women) are necessary.

Expensive

Androsia Seafood Restaurant, Henrea Carlette Hotel, Cable Beach, West Bay Street (tel. 809/327-7805), is housed in an unpretentious apartment hotel but sets one of the finest tables on the island, featuring fresh seafood cooked to order, among other dishes. At a location west of the Cable Beach Hotel, Siegfried von Hamm maintains both the cuisine and the ambience; he has elegantly fed everybody, including Sean Connery and Michael Caine. The decor of his restaurant is inviting, with light fabrics, artwork, and captain's chairs and banquettes upholstered in red. A nautical effect is achieved with such artifacts as fishnets, harpoons from old whaling vessels, and fenders from long-gone ships. Broiled local lobster is one of his most popular dishes or you can order it thermidor style. Nassau-style grouper is perhaps the most ordinary dish, but you can also ask for a seafood platter and such international fare as a perfectly flavored coq au vin. Filet mignon is another well-chosen dish. After one of the daily dessert specials, you can finish with one of Hamm's "coffee adventures." A meal costs $40 and up. Only dinner is served, Monday through Saturday from 6pm to midnight.

Café de Paris, Le Meridien Royal Bahamian Hotel, West Bay Street (tel. 809/ 327-6400), offers a tastefully Europeanized setting and cuisine for clients seeking respite from the casino glitter of nearby Cable Beach's Crystal Palace complex. Contained within the inner courtyard of the previously recommended Meridien Royal Bahamian Hotel, it contains a soothing French decor of fan-topped windows, Louis XVI–style armchairs, views of a manicured garden, and such accessories as crisp napery and glistening silverware. Menu specialties might include such French and Bahamian dishes as a gâteau of conch and scallops with saffron sauce, filets of Dover sole with a mousse of smoked fish, a mosaic of grouper with fines herbs, and a bisque of wild mushrooms laced with sherry. Desserts are delicious, highly caloric, and predictably French. Only dinner is served—nightly from 5:30 to 10:30pm—for a perperson price of between $45 and $50. Reservations are not essential, but it's recommended to dress well.

Pineapple Place, Nassau Beach Resort Club, West Bay Street (tel. 809/327-7711). Nestled amid the sheltering wings of this previously recommended hotel, the restaurant has a design that evokes a Bahamian plantation house in the early 19th century. The views from its interior encompass a sheltered garden-style courtyard with formal plantings and a cedar-shingled gazebo. The backs of the wicker chairs are inspired by the shape of a pineapple, while ornamental pineapple-shaped finials adorn the tops of the decorative walls near the entryways.

A buffet breakfast is served daily here from 8 to 10:30am, costing $10 per person. At lunch, from noon to 5pm, a menu of salads, sandwiches, and locally caught fish costs from $15 per person. Dinner by candlelight is a festive and gracious event at $45 per person. Two seatings are held every night of the week except Thursday, one from 6:30 to 7pm and another from 8:30 to 9pm. Dishes are likely to include escargots, smoked duckling salad, snail soup with herb butter, oven-roasted rack of lamb, breast of duckling, prime rib of beef, filet mignon, and Dover sole meunière. For dessert, try the Key lime mousse or the cherries jubilee. Reservations in advance are suggested at dinner.

Sole Mare, Carnival's Crystal Palace Resort & Casino, West Bay Street (tel. 809/327-6200), is the most extravagantly upscale restaurant, as well as the culinary showcase, within the previously recommended Crystal Palace megaresort, where 13 other restaurants compete fiercely for its business. It is set on the third floor of the resort's Casino Tower, within a stylishly up-to-date decor that features the "carnival colors" of lilac, mauve, and pink. A view of the sea complements the elegant menu items, all inspired by the best and most sophisticated traditions of Italy.

For your meal you might choose among spinach salad; apple-scented lobster bisque laced with cream and cognac; an array of pastas; veal sweetbreads sautéed in butter with capers and sliced olives; deep-fried baby squid served with a Sicilian eggplant relish; salmon tartare; veal sautéed with endive, white wine, and capers; grilled tuna or beefsteak; a filet of whatever fresh fish is available that day; and at least three different varieties of freshly made dessert soufflés served with vanilla sauce. Meals cost from $80 per person, and are served only at dinnertime, Wednesday through Monday from 6 to 11pm. Jackets and ties for men and advance reservations are required.

Moderate

Round House Restaurant, Casuarinas of Cable Beach, Western Road (tel. 809/327-8153), Nettie Symonette's restaurant, is reached by an entrance leading through foliage into a room with muted lighting and soft-grained paneling. It's a family affair, serving some of the best Bahamian cuisine on the island. The waiter will bring you a generous drink from the alcove bar if you wish, after which you can enjoy a choice of steak, seafood, or other specialties. These might include New York strip, Eleuthera chicken, and shrimp Créole, plus lobster and conch prepared in various ways. The health-conscious will order from the "fit for life" menu. For dessert, try Nettie's guava duff. Full dinners cost from $30 per person, and regular hours are 6 to 9:30pm Wednesday through Monday.

---

5. Where to Stay & Dine in Southwestern New Providence

There are two other spots on the island that must be mentioned. They fulfill the highest expectations of what a Bahamian visit should provide in accommodations and dining.

What the Symbols Mean

AP (American plan): Includes three meals a day (sometimes called full board or full pension).

BP (Bermuda plan): Popularized first in Bermuda, this option includes a full American breakfast (sometimes called an English breakfast).

CP (Continental plan): A Continental breakfast (that is, bread, jam, and coffee) is included in the room rate.

EP (European plan): This rate is always cheapest, as it offers only the room—no meals.

MAP (modified American plan): Sometimes called half board or half pension, this room rate includes breakfast and dinner (or lunch if you prefer).

WHERE TO STAY

Remotely situated on the southwestern shore of New Providence, **Divi Bahamas Beach Resort & Country Club,** SW Bay Road, P.O. Box N-8191, Nassau, The Bahamas (tel. 809/326-4391, or toll free 800/367-3484 in the U.S.), is a delightfully secluded resort that covers more than 180 rolling acres, which include a 1,500-foot white-sand beach and an 18-hole golf course. Like other Divi Resorts, this complex offers a casual yet sophisticated "barefoot elegance," with personalized attention to your needs.

In addition to the PGA-rated golf course, the resort also has two freshwater swimming pools (one of which lies very close to the beach) and a full water-sports facility that includes a five-star Peter Hughes PADI-registered scuba-diving operation. Four lit tennis courts, volleyball facilities on the beach, and illuminated shuffleboard courts complete the recreational pleasure picture.

The resort's 260 air-conditioned guestrooms are equally divided between older but still very comfortable units set inland within a garden around a swimming pool, and newer units on the sands of the beach. Regardless of the location, each accommodation contains a phone, either one king-size bed or two double beds, a safe-deposit box, and a complete bath. The newer units contain color TVs with VCRs, and all but a handful have private terraces or balconies. The older, inland rooms rent for substantially less than their oceanfront counterparts. In winter, EP single or double occupancy costs $165 per day in the older units and $235 in the newer beachfront units. *In summer, EP single or double occupancy costs $120 per day in the older units and $175 in the newer units.* In any season, service and taxes cost extra.

You can dine in the hotel's premier eatery, the Papagayo Italian restaurant; enjoy the handful of bars scattered throughout the property; and travel to the casinos of Cable Beach or to the shops of downtown Nassau—either on a public bus or on one of the hotel's shuttlebuses. These make frequent east-west runs across the island several times a day for a round-trip fee of $5 per passenger.

WHERE TO DINE

Traveller's Restaurant, West Bay Street, near Gambier (tel. 809/327-7633), has long been a Bahamian culinary tradition. It's the best bet for dining if you're heading out to West Bay Street in the exclusive Lyford Cay area. Set in a grove of sea-grape and palm trees, the place is completely down to earth, serving routine Bahamian fare. But that hasn't stopped the world, including many celebrities, from beating a path to its door. Mick Jagger once came here every day for a week before anyone figured out who he was. Other famous visitors have included Julio Iglesias, Donald Sutherland, Sidney Poitier, and Diana Ross.

You can dine outside on wooden tables placed under a portico or else on the terrace. If it's rainy (highly unlikely), you can go inside the tavern with its small bar and decor of local paintings and seashell art. Many diners bring their swimsuits and use the white-sand beach across from the restaurant; others arrive in their own boats. In this casual laid-back atmosphere, you can feast on grouper fingers, barbecue ribs, steamed (or curried) conch, or minced crawfish, finishing perhaps with bread pudding. Whatever is being served that day is hand lettered on a blackboard. Count on spending from $25 per person for a big meal. Daily hours are noon to 10pm, and nobody makes a reservation. You just show up at this stucco building, which lies about 9 miles west of the center of Nassau.

---

6. Attractions

IN & AROUND NASSAU

Most of Nassau can be covered on foot, beginning at **Rawson Square** in the center, where the stalls of the Straw Market are found. I also enjoy the **native market** on the waterfront, a short walk through the Straw Market. Here is where Bahamian fishermen (including two hardy women on my last visit) unload a variety of produce and fish—crates of mangoes, oranges, tomatoes, and limes, plus lots of crimson-lipped conch.

Facing Rawson Square is a colonial-style structure, housing Parliament, the Law Courts (where wigged judges dispense standards of British justice), and the Senate. In the center is a statue of Victoria as a young queen.

At the top of George Street, **Government House** is the most imposing building of New Providence. It's the residence of the governor-general of The Bahamas. The Duke and Duchess of Windsor lived here during the war years, when he was governor. At the main entrance stands a much photographed 12-foot statue of Columbus, who landed at San Salvador (in The Bahamas) in 1492. Every visitor in town likes to attend the **Changing of the Guard ceremony** on alternate Saturdays at 10am.

At Elizabeth Avenue, turn right (away from the water) and walk uphill to the **Queen's Staircase,** 65 steps leading to Fort Fincastle. These steps, hand-hewn by slaves, were carved out of solid limestone in the 18th century to allow troops stationed at the fort to escape in case of danger.

Reached by climbing the Queen's Staircase, **Fort Fincastle** was constructed in 1793 by Lord Dunmore. Here you can take an elevator ride to the top and walk on the observation floor (a 126-foot-high water tower and lighthouse), enjoying a view of the harbor. The tower is the highest point on New Providence. Admission cost is 50¢ for adults and children, and the tower is open Monday through Saturday from 9am to 4pm.

Another fort, **Fort Charlotte,** off West Bay Street on Chippendale Road (tel. 809/322-7500), begun in 1787 and built with plenty of dungeons, is worth a trip. The largest of Nassau's three major defenses, it used to command the western harbor. Named after King George III's consort, it was built by Governor Lord Dunmore, who was also the last royal governor of New York and Virginia. Its 42 cannons never fired a shot, at least not at an invader (Lord Dunmore was fond of building unnecessary forts). Within the complex are underground passages and a waxworks, which can be viewed on free tours Monday through Saturday from 8:30am to 4pm.

Another fort to visit, **Fort Montagu,** Eastern Road, was built in 1741 and stands guard at the eastern entrance to the harbor of Nassau. It's the oldest fort on the island. The Americans captured it in 1776 during the War of Independence. There are no regular hours, and no admission is charged.

Another historic mossy ruin, **Blackbeard's Tower,** stands 5 miles east of Fort Montagu, on Yamacraw Hill Road. These crumbling remains of a watchtower are said to have been used by the infamous pirate Edward Teach in the 17th century. It can be visited at any time during the day, with no admission charge.

The **Botanical Gardens,** Chippendale Road (tel. 809/323-5975), lie on 16 acres of grounds. More than 600 species of tropical flora are found here, and the curator will answer your questions. The gardens are open Monday through Friday from 8am to 4:30pm, on Saturday and Sunday from 9am to 4pm, charging adults $1 for admission and children 50¢.

Ardastra Gardens

In almost 5 acres of lush tropical planting, about a mile west of downtown Nassau and almost in the shadow of Fort Charlotte, are the Ardastra Gardens, Chippendale Road (tel. 809/323-5806), where the main attraction is the parading flock of pink flamingos. The Caribbean flamingo, national bird of The Bahamas, had almost disappeared in the early 1940s but was brought back to significant numbers through efforts of the National Trust, and they now flourish in the rookery on Great Inagua. The flock of these exotic tropical feathered creatures at the Ardastra Gardens has been trained to march in drill formation, responding to the drillmaster's oral orders with long-legged precision and discipline.

Other exotic wildlife to be seen at the gardens are boa constrictors (very tame), kinkajous (honey bears) from Central and South America, green-wing macaws, peacocks and peahens, blue-and-gold macaws, and Capuchin monkeys, together with iguanas, raccoons, hutias (a ratlike animal indigenous to the islands), ringtail lemurs, red-ruff lemurs, margays, brown-headed tamarins (monkeys), and a crocodile. There are also numerous waterfowl to be seen in Swan Lake, including black swans from Australia and several species of wild ducks.

You can get a good look at the flora of the gardens by walking along the signposted paths, as many of the more interesting and exotic trees bear plaques with their names.

The Marching Flamingoes perform Monday through Saturday at 11am, 2pm, and 4pm. Guided tours of the gardens and the aviary are given Monday through Saturday at 10:15am and 3:15pm. The gardens are open daily from 9am to 5pm, charging $7.50 for adults and $3.75 for children.

Coral World

On Silver Cay just off West Bay Street, **Coral World Bahamas** (tel. 809/328-1036) is a marine park with a network of aquariums, landscaped park areas, lounges, a gift shop, and a restaurant, but the outstanding feature is the Underwater Observation Tower. Coral World is directly off the main harbor entrance to Nassau on Silver Cay between downtown Nassau and Cable Beach. Visitors take a tram over a bridge to the cay.

At the Underwater Observatory, you descend a spiral staircase to a depth of 20 feet below the surface of the water, where you can view tropical fish in their natural habitat, coral reefs, and abundant sea life, seen through 24 large clear windows. The tower rises 100 feet above the water, with two viewing decks plus a bar where you can have a drink while enjoying a panoramic view of Nassau, Cable Beach, and Paradise Island. Among the marine attractions are a reef tank, a shark tank, a turtle pool, and a stingray pool, plus 24 aquariums under one roof as well as tidal pools.

Admission is $14 for adults, $10 for children under 12 years of age. Coral World is open daily from 9am to 6pm.

Organized Tours

There's a lot to see in Nassau, and tours have been arranged to suit your tastes in seeing the colorful historic city as well as the outlying sights of interest.

ON FOOT Free Goombay Guided Walking Tours are arranged by the Ministry of Tourism as a gesture of welcome to newcomers. They leave from the Tourist Information Booth on Rawson Square at 10am and again at 2pm; there are no tours on Thursday and on Sunday afternoon. Tours last for about 45 minutes and include descriptions of some of the city's most venerable buildings, with commentaries on the history, customs, and traditions of Nassau. The briskly informal tours require no advance reservations and few advance preparations.

BY BUS Majestic Tours, Hillside Manor, P.O. Box N-1401, Cumberland, The Bahamas (tel. 809/322-2606), offers a number of trips, both night and day, to many points of interest.

A 2-hour city and country tour leaves daily at 2:30pm, going to all points of interest in Nassau, including the forts, the Queen's Staircase, the water tower, the Straw Market (passing but not entering it), and other sights. The tour costs $13 per person.

An extended city and country tour, also leaving daily at 2:30pm, includes the Ardastra Gardens on its route, the charge being $22 per person, half for children.

A combination tour, departing Tuesday, Wednesday, and Thursday at 10am, is just that—a combination of all the sights you see on the first tour listed above, plus the Botanical Gardens and lunch, at a cost of $27 per person, half for children.

Majestic has a native nightclub tour every night except Saturday and Sunday. They take you to one of Nassau's leading nightclubs to see an exotic floor show consisting of limbo, fire-dancing, and other entertainment. Transportation to and from your hotel is included in the prices. The tour without dinner goes for $22 per person; with dinner included, $50 per person, half for children.

For information about these tours, as well as for reservations and tickets, many hotels have a Majestic Tours Hospitality Desk in the lobby, and others can supply you with brochures and information as to where to sign up. Ask at the hotel activities desk.

SATELLITE ISLANDS & CAYS

A short boat trip will take you to several small islands lying off the north coast of New Providence. One of these, **Blue Lagoon Island,** just 3 miles north of the Narrows at the eastern end of Paradise Island, has seven beaches. Nassau Cruises Ltd. (see "Boat Trips" under "Sports & Recreation," below) will take you there to see the pirate's stone watchtower, to relax in a hammock under swaying palms, to party and dance at a pavilion, or just to stroll along narrow pathways edging the sea.

Discovery Island, renamed in honor of the 1992 Quincentennial of Columbus' discovery of The Bahamas, used to be known as Balmoral Island. For it was the private stomping ground of the now defunct Balmoral Club. But all that changed long ago at this island, which is visible offshore from the hotels strung along Cable Beach. It is a haven for picnickers and sun worshippers, most of whom consider it a blissful eyrie remote from the civilized world. The island is ringed by a superb beach, with a network of paths connected to the dock. There's even a lookout for sundowners, as well as a bar and barbecue along with toilets and changing rooms. Shuttle boats going from the water-sports kiosk at the Cable Beach Hotel take you to the casuarina-dotted sands of Discovery Island. Recreational facilities include windsurfing, parasailing, snorkeling, waterskiing, and volleyball. The small sandy cay requires a 5- to 10-minute boat ride to reach it, a round-trip ticket costing $10 for adults and children. Boats depart daily every half hour on the half hour from 9:30am to 4pm. For more information, call the Crystal Palace at 809/327-6000.

Athol Island and **Rose Island** are slivers of land poking up out of the sea northeast of the Prince George waterfront docks of Nassau. Shelling is one of the lures of these little islands. Do-it-yourself skippers can make the trip in motorboats.

You don't have to go to sea to reach **Potters Cay.** It's to be found under the Paradise Island Bridge, linked by causeway to Nassau, so you can walk to it. The attraction here is a fish-and-vegetable market. If you want to, you can sample some raw conch fresh from its shell.

---

7. Where to Shop

You can find an astonishing variety of bargains in Nassau—Swiss watches, Japanese cameras, French perfumes, Irish crystal and linens, and British china, usually at prices below those charged in stores in the United States. Goods imported from Europe and elsewhere are subject to Bahamian duty, but are often 30% to 40% lower in price than at home. The principal shopping area is a stretch of the main street of town, **Bay Street,** and its side streets downtown, as well as the shops in the arcades of hotels.

Bahamian shops offer so many bargains you may be tempted beyond what you are allowed to take home duty free (see "Information, Entry Requirements, Customs & Money" in Chapter VII), but sometimes you'll find the prices lower than back home even if you have to pay duty. And many times, especially for such articles as cashmere items, liquor, and the goods mentioned above, the quality will be better too.

Don't try to bargain with the salespeople in Nassau stores as you would at the Straw Market (see "Markets," below). The price asked in the shops is the price you must pay, but you won't be pressed to make a purchase. The salespeople here are courteous and helpful in most cases.

You're likely to find yourself mingling with passengers from the cruise ships docked in the harbor, but there always seems to be a laid-back feeling, perhaps nurtured by the beaming sun.

Store hours are 9am to 5pm Monday through Saturday at most shops in Nassau. The Nassau Shop closes at noon on Thursday, and a few other places lock their doors at noon on Friday. No stores are open on Sunday, although the Straw Market does business seven days a week. You can have purchases mailed to wherever from many stores.

In lieu of street numbers along Bay Street (true in most cases), look for signs advertising the various stores instead.

The stores along Bay Street and its tributaries are often in buildings that were constructed in colonial days, and some of them are family-run concerns that have been in business for generations. The merchants are often referred to as the "Bay Street Boys," an appellation given them when their word was pretty much law in civic and government affairs of the town. Independence has made changes in that rule of iron, but many of the store owners still take a keen interest in the present and future of The Bahamas.

A sample of some of the leading Nassau stores follows, and there are many more that you may discover for yourself as you go window shopping.

NASSAU SHOPPING A TO Z

Art

Spectrum, Charbay Plaza, Charlotte Street North, between Bay Street and Woodes Rogers Walk, P.O. Box N-10796 (tel. 809/325-7492), has an elegant yet affordable display of fine art. Original oil paintings, pastels, watercolors, and prints of Bahamian landscapes, seascapes, and people are to be found here.

Brass & Copper

Brass and Leather Shop, P.O. Box N-1688, with two shops on Charlotte Street, between Bay and Shirley Streets (tel. 809/322-3806), offers English brass and copper reproductions, Land luggage, briefcases and attachés, and personal accessories. Shop No. 2 has handbags, belts, scarves, and small leather goods from such famous Italian designers as Bottega Veneta, Braccialini, Desmo Fendi, and others.

Cigars

Pipe of Peace, Bay Street, between Charlotte and Parliament Streets (tel. 809/325-2022), is called the "world's most complete tobacconist," and here you can buy Cuban and Jamaican cigars. The Cuban cigars can't be brought back to the United States, however. For the smoker, the collection is amazing. The shop is really a gift center, selling such name-brand watches as Seiko and Girard-Perregaux, along with cameras, stereos, Dunhill and other lighters, and calculators from such makers as Sharp and Casio.

Coins & Stamps

Bahamas Post Office Philatelic Bureau, in the General Post Office at the top of Parliament Street on East Hill Street, P.O. Box N-8302 (tel. 809/322-3344), has beautiful Bahamian stamps. Destined to become collector's items is a series of stamps, printed in lithography, and issued to commemorate the discovery of the New World. Called "Discovery stamps," they were first released on February 24, 1988. In all, there are four stamps, the first of a number of issues culminating in 1992. One stamp depicts Ferdinand and Isabella, another shows Columbus before the Talavera Committee (convened to examine his claims).

Coin of the Realm, Charlotte Street, just off Bay Street, P.O. Box N-4845 (tel. 809/322-4497), is a family run concern managed by W. Philip Brown. The shop lies in a lovely building more than two centuries old that was hewn out of solid limestone. The building has been designated as a historic site in Nassau. But that's not why it's visited by the public. It offers not only fine jewelry, but mint and used Bahamian and British postage stamps, as well as rare and not-so-rare Bahamian silver and gold coins. It also sells old and modern paper currency of The Bahamas. Bahama pennies, the ones minted in 1806 and 1807, are now rare and expensive items.

Crystal & China

Bernard's China & Gifts Ltd., Bay Street and 5th Terrace, P.O. Box N-4817, Centreville (tel. 809/322-2841), has a wide selection of Wedgwood, Coalport, Royal Copenhagen, Royal Crown Derby, Royal Worcester, and Crown Staffordshire china; Baccarat, Lalique, Daum, and Schott Zwiesel crystal; and Ernest Borel and Seiko watches. You can also find jewelry and gift items here.

Treasure Traders, Bay Street, P.O. Box N-635 (tel. 809/322-8521), offers the biggest selection of gifts made of crystal and china in The Bahamas. All the big names in China are here, including Royal Doulton and Royal Copenhagen. Counters contain crystal by Waterford, Lalique, Orrefors, and Daum. There are a multitude of designs, and the store sells not only traditional designs but also modern sculpted glass.

Department Stores

The Nassau Shop, 284 Bay Street, between Parliament Square and the British Colonial Beach Resort, P.O. Box N-3946 (tel. 809/322-8405), is one of the largest department stores in The Bahamas, with lots of good buys if you shop and pick carefully. French perfume is a good value here, including Hermès. Piaget watches are for sale, as are Shetland pullovers and cardigans, for both men and women.

Emeralds

Greenfire Emeralds Ltd., Bay Street, west of Parliament Street (tel. 809/326-6564), has a rare collection of pure, deep-green stones from Colombia, which produces gems of high quality. You can purchase emeralds and have them set in jewelry of your choice, or select from the shop's array of rings, earrings, and pendants.

Fabrics

National Hand Prints, corner of Mackey and Shirley Streets, P.O. Box SS-6416 (tel. 809/393-1974), welcomes visitors to its display room and workshop to watch fabrics being screen-printed and processed. You can buy goods by the yard or made up into ready-to-wear items for men, women, and children, including shirts, shorts, dresses, skirts, and tops. Placemats, tea towels, wall hangings, aprons, and pillow covers make good gifts to take home.

Fashion

Ambrosine, Marlborough Street, between West and Nassau Streets, near the British Colonial Beach Resort (tel. 809/322-4205), is the leading boutique of Nassau, occupying an attractive white gable-roofed building that contains a selection of outstanding European designs for both men and women, from formal to beachwear.

Cole's of Nassau, Parliament Street, near Bay Street (tel. 809/322-8393), is a household word in The Bahamas. Marion Cole established it in 1956, and it's now co-owned by her daughter, Diane Cole Morley. The boutique offers the most extensive selection of designer fashions in Nassau. Women can be outfitted from top to bottom in everything from sleepwear to formal gowns, from sportswear (including swimwear) to lingerie and hosiery. Cole's also sells sterling-silver and costume jewelry. A second shop is at The Mall at Marathon, Marathon and Robinson Roads (tel. 809/393-3542).

Jewelry

John Bull, Bay Street, one block east of Rawson Square, P.O. Box N-3737 (tel. 809/322-3328), acclaimed for its excellence, carries the world's most renowned selection of watches (Cartier and Rolex), jewelry, cameras (Nikon), and accessories. Founded in 1929, the firm recently renovated the Bay Street store, adding to it a wide selection of perfumes and cosmetics (Chanel and Yves Saint Laurent) and a designer boutique featuring accessories from Nina Ricci, Gucci, and many others. For convenience, John Bull also has branches on Paradise Island. Another store under the same ownership is **Old Nassau,** Bay Street (tel. 809/322-2057), one block east of John Bull.

Little Switzerland, Bay Street, P.O. Box N-3218 (tel. 809/322-8324), offers a wide variety of jewelry, watches, china, perfume, crystal, and leather in top brands. For many years this store has sold to Bahamians and visitors world-famous Swiss

NEW PROVIDENCE ISLAND

-N→

East End Point

Salt Cay

Paradise Island

Montague Bay

Nassau

Foxhill Village

North Cay

Cable Beach

Lake Killarney

Carmichael Village

Love Beach

Gambier

Nassau International Airport

Old Fort

Mt. Pleasant

Adelaide

Coral Harbour

Clifton Point

Clifton

watches including Ebel, Rado, Omega, Baume & Mercier, Tag-Heuer, Audemars Piguet, Bertolucci, and Gucci, plus such scents as Oscar de la Renta, Dior, Chloë, and Giorgio. Figurines from Royal Doulton and Lladró, Bing & Grondahl, as well as crystal by Schott Zwiesel and, of course, Waterford, will please your eye.

The Treasure Box, Bay Street, on the corner of Market Street and in the Sunley Shopping Mall (tel. 809/322-1662), offers "gifts from the sea"—that is, conch-shell and coral jewelry, including earrings, necklaces, and pillboxes.

Leather

Gucci, Saffrey Square, Bay Street, opposite Rawson Square (tel. 809/325-0561), offers a wide selection of designer handbags, wallets, small leather goods (and accessories), luggage, briefcases, gift items, scarves, ties, designer casual wear and evening wear for men and women, beach towels, umbrellas, shoes and sandals, all by Gucci of Italy. Also featured are Gucci watches and perfume—all at savings over most U.S. prices.

Leather Masters, Parliament Street (tel. 809/322-7596), carries a collection of internationally known leather bags and accessories by "i Santi," Lavin, Ted Lapidus, and Etienne Aigner among others. There is also a handsome range of leath-er wallets and small gift items by Royce and Hugo Bosca, along with pens, cigarette lighters, and watches, even perfumes. You'll also find luggage by Gonari of Colombia at this store. Another branch is at Carnival's Riviera Towers at Cable Beach (tel. 809/327-6770).

Linens

The Linen Shop, Bay Street, P.O. Box N-1013 (tel. 809/322-4266), carries such select items as exquisite bed linen, Irish handkerchiefs, hand-embroidered women's blouses, tablecloths, and infant wear, as well as Japanese designer kimonos and children's pajamas.

Maps (Antique)

Balmain Antiques, Bay Street, on the second floor two doors east of Charlotte Street, P.O. Box N-9562 (tel. 809/323-7421). Its merits become visible after you probe and search the contents of its voluminous but hidden inventories. There's probably no other store in The Bahamas with as wide and varied an assortment of 19th-century etchings, engravings, and maps, many of them antique and all of them reasonable in price. Jonathan Ramsey, the owner, scours Britain for stock. It's usual-ly best to discuss your interests with Mr. Ramsey before you begin your hunt, so he can direct you to the proper drawers.

Markets

The **Nassau International Bazaar** consists of some 30 shops selling interna-tional goods in a new arcade, pleasant for strolling and browsing at leisure. The $1.8-million complex sells goods from around the globe, including items from South America, Spain, Mexico, and Greece. The bazaar runs from Bay Street down to the waterfront (near the Prince George Wharf, where cruise liners berth and un-load passengers who go on shopping sprees). At the bazaar, alleyways have been cob-bled and storefronts are garreted, evoking the villages of old Europe.

Prince George Plaza, Bay Street, P.O. Box N-871 (tel. 809/325-7774 for in-formation), is the latest venture of George and Cally Papageorge, who developed the just-previewed Nassau International Bazaar. Their new shopping plaza, which is popular with cruise-ship passengers, has a Mediterranean feeling, perhaps as befits their Greek background. Many fine shops selling such quality merchandise as Gucci are found here. Not only that, but you can patronize an open-air rooftop restaurant overlooking Bay Street and another fast-food place offering not only hamburgers but also shish kebabs.

The **Straw Market** in Straw Market Plaza on Bay Street, is a must visit. Here you can watch the Bahamian craftswomen weave and pleat straw hats, handbags, dolls, placemats, and other items, including straw shopping bags for you to carry your purchases in. You can buy items ready-made or order special articles, perhaps bearing your initials, and you can have fun bargaining to get the stated prices reduced.

Perfumes

The Perfume Shop, corner of Bay and Frederick Streets, in the heart of Nassau, easy walking from the cruise ships, P.O. Box N-431 (tel. 809/322-2375), offers good savings on world-famous perfumes. Please yourself or someone important to you with a flacon of Eternity, Giorgio, Poison, Joy, Shalimar, or Chanel. Those are just a few of the heavenly scents for women. For men, there are Drakkar Noir, Polo, and Obsession. In **Beauty Spot** the shop carries a full line of Lancôme, Estée Lauder, Biotherm, Clinique, and Elizabeth Arden cosmetics.

Scottish Products

The Scottish Shop, Charlotte Street, just off Bay Street, in The Perfume Shop, P.O. Box N-422 (tel. 809/322-4720), lives up to its name, offering an array of merchandise from Scotland, including tartan material, kilts for women and children, Shetland wool, lambswool and cashmere sweaters and cardigans, Celtic and clan jewelry, Perthshire paperweights, Edinburgh crystal, Buchan thistle pottery, and much more. You'll also find English-made Kangol hats, heraldic plaques, and Peggy Nisbet dolls.

---

8. Sports & Recreation

One of the great sports centers of the world, Nassau (as well as the islands that surround it) is for swimming and sunning, snorkeling, scuba diving, boating, waterskiing, and deep-sea fishing, as well as for tennis and golf.

At last count, there were 32 different sports being actively pursued in The Bahamas. You can learn more about any of them by calling the **Bahamas Sports and Aviation Information Center** (tel. 305/442-4867, or toll free 800/32-SPORT) from anywhere in the continental United States. Call Monday through Friday from 9am to 5pm, EST. Or write the center at 255 Alhambra Circle, Suite 425, Coral Gables, FL 33134. Although you might have to ring several times before you're eventually connected, it's staffed by congenial (but overworked) experts who can answer questions about Bahamian-related activities, which range from skeet shooting to motorbiking. They also give briefings to pilots of private aircraft about flying conditions in The Bahamas, including the locations of airports, conditions of landing strips, and a general overall briefing. They will send a flight-planning chart if you request it. They do not, however, give weather reports.

BEACHES

On New Providence Island, the hotels at Cable Beach have their own stretches of sand, as do the hotels on Paradise Island. Of course, everyone wants to head for the famed and spectacular **Paradise Beach,** especially those occupants of downtown Nassau hotels. The beach can be reached by boat from the Prince George Wharf, costing $3 per person for a round-trip ticket. However, you must pay a separate $3 for admission to the beach, but this fee includes the use of a shower and locker. An extra $10 deposit is required for the safe return of towels. If you're traveling with children under 12, you pay $1 admission for each of them. It's also possible to drive to the beach across the Paradise Island Bridge for a toll of $2, 25¢ to walk.

To reach **Saunders Beach,** where many of the local people go on weekends, take Bay Street West toward Coral World. This beach lies across from Fort Charlotte.

On the north shore, past the Cable Beach Hotel properties, is **Caves Beach,** some 7 miles west of Nassau. It stands near Rock Point, right before the turnoff along Blake Road that leads to the airport.

Continuing west along West Bay Street you reach **Love Beach,** across from Sea Gardens, a good stretch of sand lying east of Northwest Point.

BOAT TRIPS

Cruises from the harbors around New Providence Island are offered by a number of operators, with trips ranging from daytime voyages for diving, picnicking, sunning, and swimming to sunset and night cruises mainly for leisure activity.

Wild Harp Cruises, P.O. Box 1914 (tel. 809/393-5545 days, 809/324-2359 nights), operates trips aboard the 56-foot, two-masted schooner *Wild Harp* to deserted Rose Island, where you can swim, snorkel, or just relax in the sun on the sand. Lunch, plus snorkeling gear, is included in the $40 per-person price. A sunset dinner cruise, which costs $40 per person, includes a full-course Bahamian dinner, with complimentary Wild Harp punch and a glass of wine, all accompanied by music and a fun crew. Morning departures are at 10am from The Bahamas Agricultural Corporation Dock, off Bay Street, in downtown Nassau. The dinner cruise departs at 5pm. On either cruise, the boat stops at 10:15am or 5:15pm at the Loews Harbour Dock on Paradise Island to take on more passengers. If you make arrangements in advance, the *Wild Harp* staff will arrange to have you picked up in a minivan at your hotel in time to reach one of the two departure points.

Nautilus Ltd., P.O. Box N-7061 (tel. 809/325-2871), is the place to arrange for various boat trips. The 97-foot *Nautilus,* a glass-bottom showboat, leaves from the New Mermaid Marina, at the corner of Bay and Deveaux Streets, daily at 1:30 and 3:30pm, with trips costing $20 for adults and $10 for children under 11. The vessel takes passengers to the *Mahoney* shipwreck and over the teeming reefs offshore. Each cruise lasts 1 hour and 45 minutes. Morning departures aren't recommended, as they are almost always fully booked by cruise-ship passengers who are in Nassau just for the day.

Majestic Tours Ltd., Hillside Manor, P.O. Box N-1401 (tel. 809/322-2606), will book 3-hour cruises on two of the biggest catamarans in the Atlantic, offering you views of the water, sun, sand, and outlying reefs. *Yellow Bird* is suitable for up to 250 passengers, and *Tropic Bird* carries up to 170 passengers. They depart from either Prince George's Dock or Woodes Rogers Walk near the British Colonial Beach Resort, depending on the day of the week. Ask for the departure point when you make your reservation. There's a 9:45am departure Tuesday through Saturday and a 1pm departure on Saturday followed by a 2pm departure on Sunday. The cruises include a 1-hour stop on a relatively isolated portion of Paradise Island's Cabbage Beach. The cost is $20 per adult, with children under 12 paying $10 on either cruise.

Nassau Cruises Ltd., P.O. Box N-8209 (tel. 809/326-3577), offers dinner cruises on the *Calypso I* and *Calypso II,* leaving Paradise Island at 8pm and returning at 11pm. Tickets, costing $40 per person, include a steak-and-grouper dinner and a glass of wine. The dinner cruises take place on Monday, Wednesday, and Saturday, and reservations are required. Daytime trips are also offered, *Calypso I* going to secluded Blue Lagoon Island and *Calypso II* taking passengers to Blue Lagoon West, where a party pavilion is the center of the fun. A complete buffet lunch is included, and complimentary snorkeling is available. The 6-hour daily cruise costs $40 per person.

El Galleon II/El Buccanero II, P.O. Box N-4941 (tel. 809/393-7772), which bears a double name, docks behind Victor's Department Store off Bay Street. Suitable for up to 300 passengers, this is a 93-foot replica of an 18th-century Spanish galleon. Daytime cruises depart at 10:30am, returning to the dock at 4pm daily except Monday and Wednesday. This tour includes a buffet lunch, free snorkeling equipment, unlimited punch, and at least 3 hours on an offshore cay called Discovery Island. The cost is $40. Nighttime cruises last from 7:30 to 10:30pm every

Monday, Thursday, Friday, and Saturday at a cost of $40 per person. Included in the price is a buffet dinner, along with unlimited punch. Reservations are recommended.

FITNESS CLUBS

Among the best health spas in the country is the one operated at **Le Meridien Royal Bahamian Hotel,** Cable Beach, West Bay Street (tel. 809/327-6400), which is open to both hotel guests and visitors. It has state-of-the-art equipment, including Universal exercise machines, a sauna and steamroom, whirlpool baths, Scandinavian-type massages, mud baths, an outdoor freshwater swimming pool, and an aerobics workout room, among other features.

SPECIFIC SPORTS

Deep-Sea Fishing

Many sportsmen come to Nassau just to fish, and they know the seasons for it. May through September are the best months for the oceanic bonita and the blackfin tuna; June and July, for blue marlin; and November through May, for the amberjack found in reefy areas. The list seems endless. This is, of course, a costly sport. Arrangements can be made at big hotels.

Golf

Some of the best golfing in The Bahamas is found in Nassau. The **Cable Beach/Crystal Palace Golf Course,** Cable Beach, West Bay Street, P.O. Box N-4914 (tel. 809/327-6200), has a spectacular 18-hole, 7,040-yard, par-72 championship golf course. Greens fees for 18 holes are $20 in summer, $25 in winter. Electric golf carts rent for $25 for 18 holes, and golf clubs rent for $10 for 18 holes.

Divi Bahamas Beach Resort & Country Club, SW Bay Road, P.O. Box N-8191 (tel. 809/362-4391), is one of the finest golf courses in The Bahamas, a 30-minute drive from Nassau on the southwest edge of the island. The course has palm-fringed greens and fairways. Overlooking the ocean, the 6,706-yard beauty has some first-rate holes with a backdrop of trees, shrubs, ravines, and undulating hills. The 18-hole, USPGA-sanctioned course, has a par of 72. Players are charged $37.50 for greens fees, the price including a golf cart. It's best to phone ahead in case there's a golf tournament scheduled for the day you had planned to play.

Horseback Riding

At Coral Harbour, on the southwest shore, **Happy Trails Stables,** P.O. Box N-7992 (tel. 809/362-1820), offers a 1-hour horseback trail ride for $30 per person. This includes free transportation to and from your hotel. The weight limit for riders is 185 pounds.

Parasailing

This increasingly popular sport, which allows you to zoom up to 200 feet in the air, parachute style, is offered at **Sea Sports,** Nassau Beach Resort Club, Cable Beach, West Bay Street, P.O. Box CB-11818 (tel. 809/327-7711). Parasailing costs $30 for 7 minutes or $45 for 12 minutes.

Tennis

Courts are available at most hotels. Guests usually play free or for a nominal fee, while visitors are charged from $5 per hour at hotels and clubs. Call for open hours. **Carnival's Crystal Palace Resort & Casino** (tel. 809/327-6200) has eight courts; **Carnival's Riviera Towers** (tel. 809/327-6000) has five clay and five all-weather courts; **Nassau Beach Resort** (tel. 809/327-7711) has nine Flexipave night-lit courts; **Nassau Squash and Racquet Club** (tel. 809/322-3882) has eight

Har-Tru courts; **British Colonial Beach Resort** (tel. 809/322-3301) has three hard-surface lit courts; and **Divi Bahamas Beach Resort & Country Club** (tel. 809/326-4391) has four night-lit asphalt courts.

Underwater Sports & Walks

You'll find good service at **Peter Hughes Dive South Ocean,** Divi Bahamas Beach Resort & Country Club, SW Bay Road, P.O. Box N-8191 (tel. 809/326-4391). It is a five-star training facility, the largest and most complete diving facility on New Providence. The Resort Course begins in the pool, then heads out for a one-tank shallow dive in water 30 feet deep. All gear is included, and the center accepts children 12 and up. The cost is $70 for the course, including one hour in the pool. A one-tank dive for already certified divers costs $35, including weight belts and tanks. If all equipment is included, the price goes up to $53. The shop is open from 8:30am to 5:30pm daily.

Runway, much publicized in skin-diving magazines, is one popular dive site in the neighborhood. Big stingrays come up to feed and to be cleaned by a host of smaller fish who remove parasites from their bodies. Divers explore the "James Bond wreck," a 90-foot freighter called the *Tears of Allah,* which was sunk for the filming of a 1969 Bond movie. Soft coral and feeding fish now glide through the steel infrastructure of a mockup Vulcan fighter plane, also used in the film. Weather permitting, you can go 8 miles southwest of the Divi Bahamas Beach Resort & Country Club Hotel to Razorback Reef and Playground Reef, which teem with marine life, including thousands of fish and eels. A two-tank dive, including a wall dive and also a shallow dive, costs $50 if you have your own gear or $68 if you need equipment.

Bahama Divers, Pilot House Hotel, East Bay Street, P.O. Box N-5004 (tel. 809/393-5644). The true value of this dive operation becomes obvious at one of the many dive sites that its instructors know about. Some of the packages include a half day of snorkeling to offshore reefs, costing $20 per person, and a half-day scuba trip with preliminary pool instruction for beginners, costing $50. Half-day excursions for experienced divers to offshore coral reefs with a depth of 25 feet go for $35, and half-day scuba trips for certified divers to deeper outlying reefs, drop-offs, and blue holes cost $50 and offer two tanks as part of the experience. Participants in this establishment's excursions receive free transportation from their hotel to the boats.

Stuart Cove's Nassau Undersea Adventures, Lyford Cay, P.O. Box CB-11697 (tel. 809/362-4171, or toll free 800/468-9776 in the United States), is about 10 minutes from top dive sites such as the coral reefs, wrecks, and an underwater airplane structure used in filming such James Bond thrillers as *Never Say Never Again, Thunderball,* and *For Your Eyes Only.* There are also the Porpoise Pen Reefs, named for *Flipper,* and steep sea walls on the diving agenda. An introductory scuba program costs $77, with morning two-tank dives priced at $60, and one-tank dives (morning, afternoon, or night) going for $40. All prices for boat dives include tanks, weights, and belts. An open-water certification course starts at $350. Escorted boat snorkeling trips cost $25.

An educational and exciting experience is offered by the **Hartleys,** P.O. Box SS-5244 (tel. 809/393-7569), who take you out from Nassau Yacht Haven aboard the yacht *Pied Piper.* On the 3½-hour cruise, you're submerged for about 20 minutes, making a shallow-water descent to a point where you walk along the ocean bottom through a "garden" of tropical fish, sponges, and other undersea life. You'll be guided through the underwater world wearing a helmet that allows you to breathe with ease and to see. Entire families can make this walk, costing $35 per person in groups of five. You don't even have to be able to swim to make this safe adventure.

Windsurfing

Your best bet for this sport is **Sea Sports,** Nassau Beach Resort Club, Cable Beach, West Bay Street, P.O. Box CB-11818 (tel. 809/327-7711). Windsurfing equipment rents for $20 for the first hour and $15 for each additional hour. If you rent a board for 4 hours, the total cost is $40. Lessons cost from $45 for 1 hour of instruction.

9. Evening Entertainment

Gone are the days of such famous native nightclubs as The Yellow Bird and The Big Bamboo, where tuxedo-clad gentlemen with their elegantly gowned ladies drank and danced the night away. Life is much more democratic now. You still get dancing, along with limbo and calypso, but for most visitors, the major attraction is gambling.

CASINOS

The dazzling new casino of The Bahamas is **Carnival's Crystal Palace Casino,** Cable Beach, West Bay Street, P.O. Box N-8360 (tel. 809/327-6459), part of Carnival's Crystal Palace Resort & Casino on the Bahamian Riviera. It's a joint undertaking of Carnival Cruise Lines and the Continental Companies of Miami (the resort was already reviewed). The casino complex is a spectacular addition to the island's night life, and it is open daily from 9am to 4am, charging no admission. In hues of purple, pink, and mauve, the 30,000-square-foot casino is filled with flashing lights. The gaming room features 750 slot machines in true Las Vegas style, along with 51 blackjack tables, seven craps tables, nine roulette wheels, a baccarat table, and one big six. An oval-shaped casino bar extends onto the gambling floor, and the Casino Lounge, with its bar and bandstand (offering live entertainment), overlooks the gaming floor.

DISCOS

Near the casino, and accessible only from there, is an all-black two-story disco, the **Fanta-Z,** where a marble dance floor and tiers of laserlike lights perched above a wraparound balcony create what might be the most technologically intriguing disco in Nassau. In its center is an expandable mobilized sculpture that looks like a spiral staircase accented with spotlights, especially designed for the display of the club's unusual lighting system. A big-windowed view of the sea brings the open spaces of the Atlantic into the dazzlingly electrified interior. Open nightly from 9pm to 4am, it charges an entrance fee of $20, plus $4 for a mixed drink, and reserves the right to refuse admittance to anyone in jeans or shorts.

There's nonstop dancing until the wee hours at **Club Waterloo,** East Bay Street (tel. 809/398-1108), housed in a former Nassau mansion. It is one of the most frequented clubs in town and is open Monday through Saturday from 11am to 4am, so you can drop in almost anytime. However, live music is offered only Wednesday through Saturday nights. During the day, people take their beer around the pool or in the satellite lounge, with most drinks costing from $3. The club has an ever-changing array of activities (who knows what it will be when you go?). There might be an Oldies Night or even a pool party (bring your swimsuit). It stands next to the Mai Tai Restaurant.

The Ritz, Bay and Deveaux Streets (no phone). Rising from the ashes of its earlier incarnation as a long-standing club named Confetti, this popular spot offers both live and recorded dance music within a half-indoor, half-outdoor setting close to the sea and convenient to the center of town. Open Tuesday through Sunday from 9pm to 3am, it usually charges a $10 entrance fee (and $4 for a gin and tonic), except whenever the managers declare "ladies' night," at which time women are admitted for half price. The place can be fun, and is especially popular with night owls in their 20s.

STAGE SHOWS

Near Carnival's Crystal Palace Casino with a separate entrance all its own, is the 800-seat **Palace Theater,** which is considered one of the major nightlife attractions of The Bahamas. With simulated palm trees on each side and lots of glitter, it provides an appropriate setting for the Las Vegas–inspired extravaganzas of "sophisticated adult entertainment" that are presented on its stage. Dinner within the theater which is a fixed-price affair with an international menu, is served in a single seating every night except Monday at 7pm. The meal, plus a follow-up view of the show, costs $40 per person. Many guests, however, prefer to dine in one of the resort's 13 other restaurants, arriving either before or after their meal to see the tastefully evocative flesh, feather, and glitter shows. With two drinks included, the show without dinner costs $28. Reservations in advance are recommended, especially on Tuesday and Saturday nights, when many of the seats might be filled with cruise-ship passengers. Shows begin at 8:30pm and again at 10:45pm. There is no show on Monday.

Peanuts Taylor's Drumbeat Club, West Bay Street, P.O. Box N-1435 (tel. 809/322-4233). Known as the "King of Drums," Peanuts Taylor is locally famous. His Afro-Bahamian review has been seen by thousands of visitors, all of whom are invited to bring their cameras. Peanuts usually provides the rhythms for the limbo artists, the dancers of the African fire ritual, and the array of male and female vocalists and comedians. If you precede the show with dinner, the combined tab will be $30 per person. Visitors who prefer just to see the show pay between $10 and $15, which includes between one and two drinks, depending on the night of the performance. After you've soaked up the allowance of drinks included in the entrance price, most drinks—a gin and tonic, for example—will cost from $4. Monday, Wednesday, Thursday, and Friday show times are at 8:30 and 10:30pm; on Tuesday and Saturday, the shows begin at 8:45 and 10:45pm. There is no performance on Sunday.

THE BAR SCENE

A good rendezvous is the **Palm Patio Bar** of the British Colonial Beach Resort, 1 Bay St. (tel. 809/322-3301). Many scenes from the James Bond movie *Never Say Never Again* were shot here and on the grounds. It opens every day at 6pm, staying open until 2am. There is live music every Friday, Saturday, and Sunday from 8:30pm to 1am. At those times, there is a two-drink minimum. Drinks are less expensive before 8:30pm. Gin and tonic, for example, costs $3 before 8:30 and $4 thereafter.

Out Island Bar, Nassau Beach Resort Club (tel. 809/327-7711), is nostalgically named after the former label of today's so-called Family Islands. Although set in a modern hotel, it often plays music heard on the island for many years. It's open daily from 7pm to 2am. A band plays Wednesday through Sunday. Drinks cost from $3.50, half price during happy hour, 5 to 7pm.

LOCAL NIGHTCLUBS

At some point in Nassau, you'll hear the islanders say it's time to "go over the hill." That's a reference to the **local clubs** that lie in the native quarter beyond Bay Street. Roughly, the border is on a parallel with Gregory Arch, stretching some 2 miles inland. From downtown Nassau, "over the hill" leads to Grant's Town, where freed slaves settled in 1838. Most of Nassau's native population lives there today in houses often shaded by lacy casuarinas and royal poincianas. If you'd like to check it out, chances are someone at your hotel will inform you of the latest hot spot. The area, however, is considered dangerous at night and might be best avoided for all but the extremely adventurous.

PARADISE ISLAND

The choicest real estate in The Bahamas was once known as Hog Island, serving as the farm for Nassau. Purchased for $294 by William Sayle in the 17th century, in 1960 it was to become the fiefdom of the A&P grocery chain heir, Huntington Hartford, although he eventually sold out his interests. After paying out $11 million, he decided to rename it Paradise.

With dreams of Versailles, he spent many more millions of dollars, turning the 4-mile-long sliver of land, just 600 feet off the north shore of Nassau, into a resort. In front of the Ocean Club, a 14th-century cloister built by Augustinian monks in France was reassembled in The Bahamas stone by stone. The A&P heir purchased the cloister from the estate of William Randolph Hearst at San Simeon in California. Regrettably, when the newspaper czar originally purchased the cloister, it had been dismantled in France for shipment to America. The parts were not numbered. Arriving unlabeled on Paradise Island, the cloister baffled the experts until artist and sculptor Jean Castre-Manne set about to reassemble it piece by piece. It took him two years, and what you see today, presumably, bears some similarity to the original. The gardens, extending over the rise to Nassau Harbour, are filled with tropical flowers and classic statuary. No admission is charged to visit them.

Celebrated for its white-sand beach, the island also has beautiful foliage, including brilliant red hibiscus and a grove of casuarina trees sweeping down to form a tropical arcade. It has become one of the favorite vacation areas in the western hemisphere.

The Paradise Island Resort & Casino, which is comprised of the Britannia Towers, the Paradise Towers, the Paradise Club, and the Paradise Island Casino (my recommendations coming up), all operate under one facility. Extending over several acres, it is considered the world's most complete island resort and casino. There's nothing in Europe, not even on the Riviera, and certainly nothing in the Caribbean, to match it.

1. History

Little is known of the early history of "Hog Island," although the Lucayan Indians knew it, as proven by the discovery of their relics here. In the 1700s the island was a favorite watering hole for pirates, many of whom made Nassau their home port, going out to prey on ships in the trade routes of the Atlantic and scurrying back to the comparative safety of Bahamian waters. It isn't known if Edward Teach (popularly called "Blackbeard") came here, but this and New Providence Island were for a long time a haven for freebooters, especially those of British origin.

During the American Civil War, Confederate munitions and medical supplies were sometimes stored here, hidden away from Yankee spies infiltrating the hierarchy of Nassau—supplies awaiting shipment to the South by blockade-runners. Later, bootleggers stashed alcoholic beverages on what is now Paradise Island—liquor to be delivered at night across the Gulf Stream to Florida during the Prohibition era.

Long a retreat for millionaires, In the 1980s, the island experienced a massive building boom, and its old Bahamian charm is now gone forever, as high-rises, condos, and second homes of the wintering wealthy, plus casino gambling, take over.

How did this extravaganza begin (forgetting the Indians, the pirates, and the rum-runners)?

Before it developed worldwide publicity in the 1960s, Hog Island was the home of a couple of multimillionaires. One was Joseph Lynch, who has become part of the vocabulary of the stockbroker's world, as he was a partner in the brokerage firm of Merrill, Lynch, Pierce, Fenner, and Smith. He lived on the island in the 1930s.

Shortly, he was followed by Dr. Axel Wenner-Gren, a Swedish industrialist and real estate tycoon (now deceased). Wenner-Gren became friends with the Duke and Duchess of Windsor, when the former king was the wartime governor of The Bahamas. The duke found much poverty and unemployment in the islands, and he persuaded Wenner-Gren to construct a canal system and make other improvements on Hog Island to provide employment to many Bahamians, some of whom had not had a full-time job since Prohibition days. A horde of Bahamian men constructed a rock-bottom lake on Hog Island at a cost of $50,000. Each of the hard-working laborers was paid a dollar a week for his efforts.

Dr. Wenner-Gren sold his share of Hog Island to A&P heir Huntington Hartford, and it was with that purchase that the little strip of land began to make world headlines. Hartford not only bought Wenner-Gren's huge portion of the island, he also purchased more property from other individual owners who had constructed houses there. Realizing that the name Hog Island wouldn't be likely to attract the jet set, Hartford, seeking a complete switch of imagery, renamed it Paradise Island.

Dr. Wenner-Gren's guesthouse, which was on the shore of the artificial Paradise Lake, was eventually turned into the Café Martinique (which we'll visit when we explore the restaurants of Paradise Island). The Ocean Club, which had been Dr. Wenner-Gren's winter home, was converted into Hartford's winter retreat.

In 1966 Hartford, disenchanted because the Bahamian government would not grant him gambling-casino rights, sold Paradise Island to Paradise Island Ltd., a Bahamian-franchised firm owned by Mary Carter, the famed Florida-based paint company. It was under this organization that Paradise Island really started to grow. The company purchased the Ocean Club and the Café Martinique, and by 1969 it had opened the Britannia Beach Hotel.

Billionaire recluse Howard Hughes for a while retreated to Paradise Island, occupying suites at the Britannia Towers and earning more fame for what was increasingly becoming a favorite haven for winter vacationers, cutting heavily into the Caribbean business. More and more hotels and cheaper package deals began to change the image of Paradise Island. It was no longer the exclusive retreat of the wintering wealthy, and it was connected by a bridge to Nassau.

It became so popular that its owners went out of the paint business (selling the name "Mary Carter," of course), going whole hog, so to speak, into the Hog/Paradise Island resort industry. The company then became known as Resorts International, Inc., which runs the choice real estate to this day.

By 1980 Resorts International had opened a 352-room addition to what was then the Britannia Beach Hotel and Casino. In 1982 it also took over operation of the Paradise Island Hotel, and the two were incorporated into the Paradise Island Resort & Casino, which combination makes it the most complete offshore resort/casino in the world. By 1984 it had purchased the 100-room Paradise Beach Inn, which lies on 9 acres of the west end of the island and opens onto Paradise Beach. The inn was renamed Paradise Paradise (see "Where to Stay," below). In a $900-million deal in 1988, television impresario Merv Griffin concluded a real estate deal with tycoon Donald Trump and became the owner of Resorts International's properties.

To prevent guests from getting bored with "just going to the beach," most of the big hotels here have activity-packed calendars, especially for that occasional windy, rainy day that comes in winter. Hordes of Americans can be seen taking group lessons such as how to play backgammon or how to cook local style. They are even taught how to mix such tropical drinks as a Goombay Smash or a Yellow Bird. There are also lessons in how to play whist and tennis, even to dance Bahamian style.

At some point during the day everyone likes to stop by and watch Brit and Tanya, pet performing dolphins who swim in a private tank at the Paradise Island Resort. There are two free shows daily, at noon and at 4pm. Cameras are out en masse when the dolphins perform. Hotel waiters are fond of pointing out that the dolphin offered on the menu is "quite a different kettle of fish" from Brit and Tanya (who are really mammals, not fish). In other words, Flipper isn't being served for dinner.

Resorts International now owns the Ocean Club and the Paradise Paradise, as well as the Paradise Island Resort & Casino, which includes the Britannia Towers, Paradise Towers, Paradise Island Golf Club, Café Martinique, the Boathouse Restaurant, and Le Cabaret Theatre. The company also operates the Paradise Island Casino. All of these properties will be described in detail.

2. Getting There & Getting Around

GETTING THERE

With the inauguration of the **Paradise Island International Airport** in 1989 (tel. 809/363-2845), a 3,000-foot runway allows passengers to land directly on the island. This eliminates the Customs delays at Nassau International Airport, as well as the expensive 30-minute taxi ride. A U.S. Customs office at Paradise Island clears passengers disembarking from international connections, mainly from Florida, which lies 50 miles to the west.

If you'd like to fly directly to Paradise Island, avoiding the Nassau International Airport, review the section "Flying to the Family Islands Directly from Florida" in Chapter VII. Airlines making this run include **Paradise Island Airlines** (tel. toll free 800/432-8807 in the U.S.), with flights from Palm Beach, Fort Lauderdale, and Miami, and **Chalk's International Airline** (with the same U.S. toll-free number as Paradise Island Airlines: 800/432-8807), with service from Miami.

GETTING AROUND

The most popular way to reach Paradise Island from Nassau is to drive or walk across the $2-million **toll bridge** to "P.I.," as it is called by its wealthy residents. A car costs $2 going over (nothing on the return), and you can walk across for just 25¢.

If you arrive at the Nassau International Airport, there is no airline bus waiting to take you to Paradise Island unless you're on a package deal that includes transfers. If so, then your hotel may have made arrangements to have you met and your luggage transferred.

Unless you're renting a car, you'll need to take a **taxi.** Taxis in Nassau are metered. It will usually cost you $20 to go by cab from the airport to your hotel on Paradise Island. The driver will also ask you to pay the bridge toll. Luggage is carried at the cost of 50¢ per piece.

If you want to leave Paradise Island and tour New Providence by taxi, you can make arrangements. Taxis wait at the entrances to all the major hotels. The going hourly rate is about $12 to $20, depending on the size of the vehicle.

If you're without a car and don't want to take a taxi or walk, you can go to Nassau by a **ferry service.** If you're already on Paradise Island, you may want to take a shopping stroll along Bay Street. If so, the ferry to Nassau leaves from behind the Café Martinique (recommended below) across from the Britannia Towers. It runs every half hour, the 10-minute ride costing $2 round trip. Quicker and easier than a taxi, the ferry deposits you right at Bay Street. Service daily is from 9:30am to 4:15pm.

Water taxis also operate daily from 8:30am to 6pm at 20-minute intervals between Paradise Island and Prince George Wharf in Nassau. A round-trip fare is $3 per person.

You can also go by **jitney** from Nassau to Paradise Island at a cost of 50¢ to $1 per ride. The small buses operate every half hour, daily from 8am to 1am. They make regular stops at all hotels on Paradise Island. After 6pm they stop only at the entrance to the casino. Some hotels on Paradise Island run their own jitney service.

If you are a guest of one of the properties of Paradise Island Resort & Casino, you can take a complimentary tour of the island, leaving daily at 10 and 11am and at 2pm. There is no tour on Tuesday, however.

A free bus service is offered daily to Rawson Square in Nassau for Paradise Island Resort & Casino guests. The bus departs from the Paradise Towers. Tickets can be obtained from the bell captain's desk.

---

3. Where to Stay

You're faced with your most spectacular choice of lodgings in all The Bahamas here, and they come in a wide range of prices, from the deluxe and exclusive Ocean Club to the more moderately priced Paradise Paradise. You can stay at an expensive Club Med or a very modestly priced (and rather incongruously located) Yoga Retreat (see "Alternative/Adventure Travel" in Chapter VII). As a final alternative, some condo developments will rent you space when their owners aren't in residence.

If you're contemplating a visit during the busy winter season, always nail down a reservation far in advance.

EXPENSIVE

Ocean Club, Ocean Club Drive, P.O. Box N-4777, Paradise Island, The Bahamas (tel. 809/363-3000, or toll free 800/321-3000 in the U.S.), run by Resorts International, is the most discreetly prestigious address on Paradise Island. Guests can revel in the casino and nightlife activities of the other parts of the resort a short

What the Symbols Mean

AP (American plan): Includes three meals a day (sometimes called full board or full pension).

BP (Bermuda plan): Popularized first in Bermuda, this option includes a full American breakfast (sometimes called an English breakfast).

CP (Continental plan): A Continental breakfast (that is, bread, jam, and coffee) is included in the room rate.

EP (European plan): This rate is always cheapest, as it offers only the room— no meals.

MAP (modified American plan): Sometimes called half board or half pension, this room rate includes breakfast and dinner (or lunch if you prefer).

distance away, knowing the option always exists for a quiet retreat back to the seclusion of this exclusive, small-scale hotel. This is one of the best-developed tennis resorts in The Bahamas and includes nine well-maintained courts and a full-time tennis pro within sight of a lattice-covered colonial-style clubhouse. The appointments of the accommodations are plushly comfortable, imbued with a kind of stately contemporary dignity, having air conditioning, satellite TVs, refrigerators, spacious tile baths, and tasteful colors and fabrics. In winter, single or twin rooms range from $195 to $494 daily. *In summer, twins or singles rent for $190 to $235 daily.*

Despite the plushness of the 71 bedrooms, the real heart and soul of the resort lies in the surrounding gardens and landscapes, which were designed by the island's former owner, Huntington Hartford, mentioned earlier. During his residency here, all of Paradise Island was almost a private fiefdom for this affluent landowner and his glamorous houseguests. The ornamentation includes formal panoramic gardens whose focal point is a reconstructed French cloister set on 35 acres of manicured lawns. Today the rhythmically graceful 12th-century carvings are visible at the crest of a hill, across a stretch of terraced waterfalls, fountains, a stone gazebo, and rose gardens in a vista that is one of the sights of The Bahamas. The bigger-than-life statues that dot the vine-covered niches on either side of this landscaped extravaganza include quirky reflections of Hartford's taste—FDR and Dr. Livingstone, the Scottish missionary and explorer in Africa, as well as reclining Renaissance nudes and depictions of Hercules. If you're visiting these gardens, you should begin your promenade at the large swimming pool whose waters feed the series of reflecting pools stretching out toward the cloister.

The beach that lies adjacent to the colonial-style sweep of the hotel is a white stretch of sand, arguably the best beach in the Nassau/Paradise Island area. The walkways to the accommodations run down the verandas, which ring one of the garden courtyards on the island. At night the Courtyard Terrace (see "Where to Dine," below) is filled with light from a pair of illuminated fountains. The repeat business at this posh resort runs to a high 65%. Services include a concierge, babysitting, and a complimentary shuttle to the casino and golf course.

A bastion of the good life, the **Paradise Island Resort & Casino,** P.O. Box N-4777, Paradise Island, The Bahamas (tel. 809/363-3000; 305/891-3888 in Dade County, Florida; 305/462-8555 in Broward County, Florida; or toll free 800/321-3000 in the U.S.), is the patriarch of Paradise Island hotels, still giving the newcomer hotels stiff competition. This resort is very much a self-contained world of its own, filled with so many entertainment and dining facilities that many visitors are not even tempted to leave the compound. Run by former television-talk-show host Merv Griffin, who has pumped more than $40 million of improvements into it since his takeover in 1988, this radically reorganized Resorts International property is the unquestioned focal point of Paradise Island. Set atop a sandy, pine-dotted strip of land between 3 miles of beachfront and the calm waters of a saltwater lagoon, it is comprised of a trio of architectural elements built during different eras and today interconnected by a series of passageways, arcades, and gardens. Their focal point is the Paradise Island Casino (see "Evening Entertainment," below), on either side of which rise the Britannia Towers and the Paradise Towers.

Accommodations in both towers are eminently comfortable and conservatively stylish, although rooms in the Britannia Towers are slightly larger, more recently renovated, and more expensive. The most expensive rooms are on the concierge floor of the Britannia Towers, where a staff of uniformed concierges check guests in within a special reception area and provide enhanced service and amenities. Regardless of its location within the hotel, each accommodation contains a refrigerator, color TV with satellite and U.S. network programming, a balcony with water view, air conditioning, and 24-hour room service. Each accommodation contains either two queen-size beds or one king-size bed and dozens of amenities. In winter, single or double occupancy ranges from $185 to $375 per night, with suites priced from $570. *In summer, single or double rooms range from $140 to $245 per night, with suites priced from $360.*

In addition to the 12 gourmet and specialty restaurants, a dozen bars and lounges, and a full array of discos and nightlife possibilities, there are 12 tennis courts illuminated for night play, a health club and sauna, a jogging path, an array of shops, all water sports, a menagerie of trained porpoises, and an 18-hole golf course —the Paradise Island Golf Club, located on the north end of the island. (Many of these facilities are covered in subsequent sections of this chapter.)

Sheraton Grand Hotel, Casino Drive, P.O. Box SS-6307, Paradise Island, The Bahamas (tel. 809/326-2011, or toll free 800/325-3535 in the U.S.), is dramatically opulent. Its strikingly angled 14-story exterior incorporates spacious balconies and sweeping water views from each of the 360 plushly furnished bedrooms. The architects chose to build this palace on an uncluttered 3-mile stretch of beach so that guests leaving the shelter of the poolside terrace could settle almost immediately onto one of the waterside chaises longues. The Grand is within walking distance of the casino, restaurants, and nightlife facilities of the Resorts International properties.

If you arrive by car, the smartly uniformed doorman will take charge of your vehicle, giving you a receipt that you'll later use to reclaim it. Welcoming drinks are served while you relax on comfortable chairs near the waterfall of the soaring reception area, as sunlight glitters off the surface of the plant-rimmed lagoon in the wood-trimmed lobby. The hotel is big enough that its frequent conventions hardly make a ripple in the smooth tenor of operations carried out by the staff. A full array of restaurant and entertainment facilities is on the premises. The premier restaurant of the Grand is the Rôtisserie, serving a haute cuisine nightly from 6:30 to 10:30pm. Other dining choices include the multilevel Verandah Restaurant and its adjoining terrace, where you can order breakfast, lunch, and dinner within view of the sea. Sunbathers in need of a poolside drink will be served at their chaises longues by waiters, and burgers as well as lobster or chicken salads are available all day at the Grand Bar and Grille. After dark, the most elegant disco on Paradise Island, Le Paon (see "Evening Entertainment," below), offers a computerized sound system where 57 speakers focus the music onto the dance floor, leaving the banquettes free for conversation.

All the accommodations here are deluxe, decorated in tastefully mixed pastels. In the Sheraton Towers, the 12th and 14th floors are really grand. There, Continental breakfast is served in a panoramic private breakfast room, complete with silver tureens and fine porcelain. You can also have five-o'clock tea in this room, where fresh conch salad and delicately flavored soups are dispensed by a concierge.

Regardless of the category, each of the rooms of this hotel also has air conditioning, a minibar, satellite color TV with broadcasts of U.S. programs, and direct-dial phone. In winter, single or double occupancy costs from $199 to $275, *falling in summer to $120 to $175.* A range of wintertime packages is offered for stays of more than three nights, many covering use of the hotel's sports facilities—an almost bewildering array, including four tennis courts and a fleet of boats for various water pursuits. Babysitting, room service, and valet services are available.

Club Méditerranée, P.O. Box N-7137, Paradise Island, The Bahamas (tel. 809/326-2640, or toll free 800/CLUB-MED in the U.S.), is made up of two wings of three-story pastel bungalows curving above the 3-mile beach. In between stands a Georgian-style mansion housing the intimate restaurant (both indoor and outdoor dining), the midnight disco, and the beach bar. Behind the mansion, guests frolic in a large swimming pool. A walk through the garden brings members to harborside and the main restaurant. Adjoining is an open-air theater/dance floor/bar complex. The village occupies 21 acres. In winter, tours from New York include round-trip airfares, transfers, seven nights' accommodation, three full meals a day (including unlimited free wine at lunch and dinner), all sports activities and facilities, (including equipment and qualified instruction), picnics, glass-bottom-boat rides, and live entertainment nightly.

Accommodations are twin-bedded rooms, small but comfortably furnished with rattan furniture, each with a private bath.

In winter, the highest prices are charged at Christmas and New Year's, when the weekly land arrangement can be $1,100 to $1,350 per person; Otherwise, the winter price hovers around the $1,080 mark. *In summer, the per-person rate is about $900 a week, land arrangements only.* Special holiday-package rates are also quoted, including Fourth of July weekend jaunts and Thanksgiving trips. Everybody here seems to play tennis—there are 20 courts, 8 of which are lit at night.

Bay View Village, P.O. Box SS-6308, Paradise Island, The Bahamas (tel. 809/363-2555, or toll free 800/321-3000 in the U.S.), is a handsomely landscaped condominium complex. Its verdant and flowery surroundings occupy the full-time efforts of six gardeners. There are reputedly more than 20 kinds of hibiscus and many varieties of bougainvillea, which screen accommodations from one another. Although it is near the geographic center of Paradise Island, it's only a short walk to either the sands of Cabbage Beach or the harbor. Three pools are scattered around the premises, along with a tennis court.

Each of the 30 units provides a suitable setup for visitors who prefer independent living. Each of the accommodations is air-conditioned and has its own kitchen, TV, and patio or balcony, plus daily maid service. The villas and townhouses have dishwashers, and some have views of the harbor. A full-time maid or personal cook can be arranged on request. The units come in a wide variety of sizes and can hold up to six occupants. Rates are slightly less for weekly rentals, but otherwise, winter tariffs range from $155 daily for two persons to $405 for up to six. *In summer, the range is from $100 daily for two occupants to $250 for six persons.* A minimarket and two coin-operated laundry rooms are on the property. The nightlife, casino, and sports facilities of the Paradise Island Resort & Casino are only a few minutes away.

MODERATE

Paradise Paradise, P.O. Box SS-6259, Paradise Island, The Bahamas (tel. 809/363-3000, or toll free 800/321-3000 in the U.S.), is a pleasantly unpretentious hotel run by Resorts International. It's a rambling, veranda-lined building set on sandy soil within an encircling copse of pines. Half the accommodations offer direct access to the beach, which lies on the far side of a stand of trees. In many ways, being here is like living in a forest. The hotel restaurant is a short distance away, in a teepee-shaped building directly on the beach. The hotel also offers free transportation by shuttlebus to the casino and its adjacent bars and restaurants. All of the 100 rooms have been redecorated, with carpeting, draperies, and accessories, to the tune of $1 million. Rooms have air conditioning, TVs, minibars, and phones. In winter, single or double occupancy ranges from $155 to $235 daily. *In summer, single or double occupancy costs $115 to $170 daily.* Included free are a variety of water sports: sailing, snorkeling, windsurfing, and waterskiing. Guests are not locked into any meal plan, although many of them opt to arrange one of the resort's dine-around plans.

Pirate's Cove Holiday Inn, P.O. Box SS-6214, Paradise Island, The Bahamas (tel. 809/363-2101, or toll free 800/HOLIDAY in the U.S.). Many guests of this large (566-room) hotel consider the pool their favorite splash area in The Bahamas. It stretches sinuously around the cabaña-style bar on an island in its center. Guests who prefer not to undress can reach it via a footbridge here and there, but many guests swim over for their afternoon cocktails. The hotel rises 18 floors in a massive rectangle above a forest of pine trees a few steps from a wide stretch of Pirate's Cove Beach. The comfortable accommodations usually have views of the sea and are decorated in pastel shades of what the staff calls "Goombay colors." In winter, singles rent for $125 to $185 per day, with doubles costing from $135 to $195. *In summer, tariffs are reduced to $88 to $125 per day, with doubles paying $98 to $134.* MAP can be arranged for another $39 per person per day year round.

There are several restaurants here from which to choose, including Matilda's poolside snackbar, where the best cheeseburgers in the area are served with cold beer and tropical drinks. Then there's the garden-style Calico Jack's, where lunches and breakfasts are breezy. Dinner is a gourmet affair at the wood-paneled Paradise Grill, which offers seafood and beef specialties. This is a complete holiday resort, having tennis courts with a full-time pro; all water sports, including parasailing; crab races; and other organized games and contests; plus weekly buffets and poolside parties. The lobby is often the site for daytime lectures on subjects that might include local crafts, tips on buying mother-of-pearl, and ornamental napkin folding. Later in the day, the spacious lobby resounds to the playing of a musical group that provides dance tunes every night until 1am.

Club Land' Or, Paradise Drive, P.O. Box SS-6429, Paradise Island, The Bahamas (tel. 809/363-2400, or toll free 800/446-3850 in the U.S., 800/552-2839 in Virginia), lies across the saltwater canal from the Paradise Island Resort & Casino. A series of self-sufficient apartments are in white concrete buildings set in a landscaped garden dotted with shrubs and reflecting pools. Although the club isn't located on the bay, the beach is a short drive away, and there's a small freshwater swimming pool as well as a promenade beside the canal for guests interested in sniffing the salt air. If you wish to visit the casino, you must drive along winding pine-hedged roads to get there. The reception area, containing plants and a fountain, is below the staircase leading up to the Oasis lounge and the Blue Lagoon Restaurant. This place is for guests interested in a maximum of independence, their own cooking facilities, and something approaching apartment living with dining and bar amenities in easy reach. The management hosts some of the most energetic activities programs on the island, sometimes broadcasting the daily agenda over a public address system.

Each of the 70 accommodations includes a separate bedroom, a patio or balcony, a fully equipped kitchenette, and a living room. Depending on the view (garden or water), apartments rent for $205 to $225 per day for two people in winter, *$145 to $170 in summer.* For reservations and information, get in touch with the club's executive offices: P.O. Box 100, Ladysmith, VA 22501 (tel. 804/346-8200, or toll-free numbers given above).

4. Where to Dine

RESORTS INTERNATIONAL DINING PLANS

Available only to guests of Resorts International Paradise Island hotels are two dining plans that provide interesting culinary experiences. A minimum of two days' residence is required for either of the plans, which are not tied in solely to the hotel where you stay.

For $35 per person per day, the **Paradise Dining Plan** provides for breakfasts and dinners at eight of the specialty restaurants in the Resorts International complex: the Grill Room, Coyaba, Spices, the Terrace Grill, Café Casino, Seagrapes, Paradise Pavilion, and Le Cabaret Theatre. For $59 per person per day, you can sign up for the **Gourmet Dining Plan,** featuring full breakfasts and a complete choice of dinner menus at all of Resorts International's gourmet and specialty restaurants, including those mentioned above as well as the Café Martinique, the Gulfstream Restaurant, the Courtyard Terrace at the Ocean Club, the Bahamian Club, and the Boat House.

Paradise Island also has several other restaurants. It even has a few (very few) budget restaurants (see below). Most of the restaurants described here are clustered along the famous Bird Cage Walk at the Paradise Island Casino. Next door to each other, these restaurants tempt you with their international cuisine. All prices quoted are per person.

RESTAURANTS OF PARADISE ISLAND

Expensive

Bahamian Club, Bird Cage Walk, Britannia Towers (tel. 809/363-3000), was a well-established restaurant and gambling club in Nassau until the developers of Paradise Island offered its management a new home in Bird Cage Walk. Today it's known both for its Caesar salads and its prime ribs and thick steaks. The Georgian colonial-style dining room offers spacious vistas over dark-grained half columns, white walls, tall mirrors, leather-back chairs, and dozens of candles. The prime rib is served from a trolley with a carver, to be sure you are satisfied, and it's accompanied by Yorkshire pudding and fresh horseradish. Other Continental specialties include veal Cordon Bleu, calves' liver lyonnaise, duckling à l'orange with wild rice, tournedos Rossini, steak tartare, and a limited selection of Bahamian seafood, such as lobster and grouper. There are some excellent appetizers, such as snow crab claws and fettuccine verde with lobster, shrimps, and scallops. For dessert, try the cherries jubilee or the peach flambé. Full meals cost from $60. Dinner only is served and seatings are Wednesday through Monday at 6:30 and 9pm. Music and dancing accompany the dinner hours. Jackets are required for men.

Café Martinique, Paradise Island Resort & Casino (tel. 809/363-3000), across from the Britannia Towers, is one of the choicest restaurants in The Bahamas, serving everything from beef Wellington to cherries jubilee, at a cost that is likely to zoom to more than $60 per person. James Bond, in front of millions of moviegoers, dined here in *Thunderball,* from a perch overlooking the Paradise Lagoon. Patrons select tables either inside or outdoors under a starry sky. The best French and Continental food on Paradise Island is served here, backed up by a well-stocked cellar. When you sit down, enjoying the fin-de-siècle decor, you are presented almost immediately with a list of dessert soufflés. The chef is justifiably proud of these delicacies, but because of the time and preparation involved, they can't be ordered at the last minute (unless you're prepared to wait); therefore many people order the dessert first, especially the soufflé Grand Marnier and the soufflé au chocolat.

Then it's on to a dazzling menu, with an appealing list of hors d'oeuvres likely to include everything from escargots bourguignonne to foie gras with truffles. For those to whom money is no object, the kitchen will produce beluga caviar served with a glass of Stolichnaya vodka. There's even conch chowder on the menu (how did it get there?). Fish dishes are limited, but select, including fresh Bahamian grouper with fennel and Noilly Pratt sauce or sautéed with sliced almonds, and Bahamian lobster with spices served in its shell (or broiled with melted butter). For a main course, you might like the grenadin de veau au Calvados, which is prepared perfectly here, or chateaubriand with béarnaise sauce, or perhaps a rack of lamb roasted with herbs in the style of Provence. Café Bahamien would be a nice finish to just a repast. The French-style decor suggests the Moulin Rouge of Paris. Diners once glided in here by boat, but nowadays they cross the bridge. Reservations are absolutely imperative. Dinner only is served and seatings are nightly at 7 or 9:30pm. Jackets are required for men.

The café also serves a deluxe Sunday brunch from 11:30am to 2:30pm, costing $25 per person. Enticing arrays of fresh fruits, salads, cold meats, smoked fish, and cheeses are laid out, along with hot dishes and a dessert selection. A complimentary glass of champagne or a mimosa is served with the brunch. Reservations are vital in winter but always preferred.

Courtyard Terrace, Ocean Club, Ocean Club Drive (tel. 809/363-3000), is located at the island's most exclusive hotel. When the moon is right, an evening meal here can be the closest thing to paradise on the island. You dine amid palms and flowering shrubs in a flagstone courtyard surrounded with colonial verandas flanked by symmetrical fountains whose waters spurt upward in circular patterns. A musical group on one of the upper verandas sends music wafting down onto the patio below. This isn't the most glittering dining room on the island, but in many ways it is the most sophisticated. Much will depend on the weather, but regardless of climate, men are requested to wear jackets and ties, and women should bring some kind of evening wrap in case it becomes chilly. Continental and Bahamian menu specials include beefsteak tartare, prime sirloin, lobster quiche, chateaubriand, blackened dolphin (the fish, not the mammal), Nassau grouper, shrimp provençale, roast rack of lamb, and calves' liver lyonnaise. Reservations for either of the two nightly sittings are requested at either 7 or 9pm. Dinner only is served. Full meals cost from $60.

Grill Room, Paradise Island Resort & Casino, Paradise Towers, (tel. 809/363-3000), is a spacious and comfortable restaurant that carries a sense of European elegance. Its dignified decor is brightened with patterns of bird of paradise juxtaposed to the palms and the uniformed staff. The establishment is known for its well-prepared steaks, which can be flambéed at your table or charcoal-broiled, as can be fish specialties, depending on your order. Filet mignon with sauce choron, strip sirloin Café de Paris, brochette of chicken with peanut sauce, and well-seasoned beef brochettes with Oriental rice are just a few of the meat dishes. There are also many Bahamian seafood specialties, such as fresh Bimini swordfish with pistachio butter and lime-flavored butter, surf and turf on a skewer, tuna marinated in soy and ginger, and, of course, lobster, grouper, and snapper. Long Island duckling capped with kiwi fruit and Grand Marnier sauce is a particular favorite. Full dinners, costing from $50 each, are served Tuesday through Sunday from 6:30 to 11pm. Dinner only is served. Reservations are advised.

Gulfstream Restaurant, Paradise Island Resort & Casino (tel. 809/363-3000), is separated from the main lobby of the Paradise Towers by a trio of etched-glass panels depicting three of the nine muses. Once you're inside, a formally dressed waiter will usher you to a seat near walls of exposed stone whose angles are softened with masses of plants, flowers, and candles. This is a seafood restaurant, but if you prefer steak, chicken, or veal, these are also on the menu. Specialties include such appetizers as fresh cherrystone clams, smoked salmon, fresh conch salad, and stone crab claws with mustard sauce. Soups are lobster bisque and conch chowder (prepared either traditionally or in a local adaptation of creamy New England clam chowder). For a main course, you might enjoy Bahamian lobster, shrimp curry Bombay, red snapper, Nassau-style grouper, or paella. Full meals cost from $45 per person. Dinner only is served nightly at two seatings, one at 6:30pm for early birds and another at the more fashionable hour of 9pm. You dine to piano music.

Rôtisserie, Sheraton Grand Hotel (tel. 809/326-2011), the premier restaurant of this deluxe hotel, is deliberately understated, with oversize rattan chairs and exposed stone. Here you will enjoy what might be the thickest cuts of steak and prime rib in The Bahamas. From behind a glass window, a team of uniformed chefs prepares the grills to your specifications. You can also order such beef dishes as blackened Cajun steak or a filet mignon. Should you want seafood, they'll tempt you with Bahamian grouper or perhaps swordfish steak. They'll also prepare several international dishes, including honey-glazed duck. Meals cost around $50 per person. Dining is Wednesday through Monday from 6:30 to 10pm, when a strolling guitarist is featured. Only dinner is served. Jackets are required.

Villa d'Este, Bird Cage Walk, Britannia Towers (tel. 809/363-3000), is Nassau's most elegant Italian restaurant, with classic dishes of the repertoire of Rome, Florence, and Venice prepared with skill and served with flair. Italian murals decorate the walls. The restaurant takes its name from the world-famed hotel on Lake Como. Its viands are outstanding, and the word gets around. Freshly made fettuccine Alfredo, prepared here nigh to perfection, can be served as a first course or as a main dish. A good-tasting Florentine version of minestrone is also served. Main dishes include several most acceptable chicken and veal dishes, including deviled chicken and scaloppine alla parmigiana. Desserts feature a selection of pastries from the trolley. You are likely to spend around $45 or more for a meal. It's necessary to reserve a table. Only dinner is served, nightly from 6:30 to 11pm.

Moderate

Blue Lagoon, Club Land' Or, Paradise Drive (tel. 809/326-2400), is a pleasant environment lying across the lagoon from the Paradise Island Resort & Casino. It's located two floors above the reception of the Club Land' Or, and you can stop on the way up in the Oasis bar for an aperitif. In the restaurant, with a view of the harbor and Paradise Lake, the music of an island combo will complement your meal —served by candlelight as well as the light coming through the stained-glass ceiling dome. The decor is unabashedly nautical, with polished railings and lots of full-grain hardwood. Seafood is the specialty. Menu items are stone crab claws in cocktail sauce, Nassau conch salad, Caesar salad for two, broiled grouper amandine, seafood brochette, grouper (stuffed with chopped shrimp, lobster, and scallops and covered with mornay sauce), almond-fried shrimp, shrimp sautéed in mushroom and garlic butter and served with Créole rice, and other dishes. Meat specialties include steak au poivre with brandy sauce, duck à l'orange, and chicken chasseur. Dessert might include crêpes Suzette for two or a Tía María parfait. A la carte dinners come to around $35 and are served nightly from 5 to 10pm. Only dinner is served.

Boat House, Paradise Island Resort & Casino (tel. 809/363-3000), is located next to the Paradise Lagoon near the Café Martinique. A group of friends might find this the most appealing restaurant on the island, especially if they don't feel like dressing up. Behind its nautical façade, the richly polished leather and hardwood, as well as the warm color scheme, contribute to a clubhouse ambience that you would expect to find at a marina on one of the most remote Family Islands. You cook your own dinner on the charcoal grill that's the focal point of each group of diners. Suspended above each table is a rectangular copper hood with a powerful suction fan to whisk the smoke away from the conversation and good food. The ambience can be fun, especially if you enjoy participating in the preparation of a meal. The bartender serves generous drinks to accompany the top-quality meats, which are the house specialty.

The menu is limited to a choice of four main courses, each of which is priced as part of a full meal at from $40 per person. Choices, as you'd expect, include a wellmarbleized New York sirloin, prime filet mignon, sea and steer (filet mignon with half a Bahamian lobster tail), or gulf shrimp kebab marinated in a special sauce. Each main course is accompanied with Bahamian conch chowder to which a generous splash of sherry is added at your table. Also offered are a crisp Boat House salad and a baked potato or rice. Cheesecake, raisin fudge, and coffee are also included as part of the meal. Reservations are suggested. The restaurant is open only for dinner, seven days a week in winter, closed Sunday in summer. Seatings are at 6:30 and 9pm.

Coyaba, Bird Cage Walk, Britannia Towers (tel. 809/363-3000), offers an Asian setting and features Szechuan, Cantonese, and Polynesian specialties in a casual and relaxed atmosphere. Many people come here just for a drink, but if you want to eat, you'll be faced with an appetizing choice of first courses—curried conch Coyaba (conch, duck liver, barbecued pork, and scallions in a curry sauce), say, or a two-person pupu bowl (a flaming hibachi on your table with baby back ribs, eggrolls, chicken wings, shrimp tempura, and wontons with an array of succulent spices). These could be followed by three kinds of Chinese soups, ginger or curried salads, or a full range of Chinese main courses. These include twice-barbecued pork (there's an intermediate wok-steaming between the barbecue stages for added tenderness), deboned Polynesian duck, Coyaba duck imperial (cooked with 12 spices for a full 3 hours), eight treasures of Buddha (eight vegetables cooked quickly in a wok), spicy Paradise chicken, Szechuan shrimp, and a selection of dishes for the less adventuresome. Full meals cost $40 and can be accompanied by tea or one of several deceptively potent tropical drinks. Open nightly only, from 6:30 to 11pm.

Spices, Britannia Towers (tel. 809/363-3000). Since the design of this garden restaurant includes both natural pine and forest-green walls, the look is a lot like the effect you'd get in a tree house. The impression is heightened by the tables clustered together on raised platforms under a skylight admitting the sunshine. The appetizing specialties served here include Out Island conch salad, Jamaican pepperpot soup, Bahamian gumbo, and peppery shrimp. Other dishes are likely to include spareribs, roast chicken, and curried lamb with mango chutney and shredded coconut. For dessert, you can order guava duff with a brandy sauce. The restaurant is open Friday through Wednesday for breakfast from 8 to 11am, and for dinner from 6:30 to 10pm. Breakfast costs from $12, with dinners averaging $25.

Inexpensive

Café Casino, Paradise Island Casino (tel. 809/363-3000). If you want a late-night snack or a break from the activity of the gaming tables, you have only to walk to the far end of the casino to find this rattan-decorated coffeeshop. Its menu includes pizza and well-stuffed sandwiches—corned beef, pastrami, and Reubens—as well as many kinds of salad. Soup-and-sandwich meals cost around $8, although full dinners, which might include lasagne bolognese, deep-fried grouper fingers, or beef brochette with rice, cost from $20. Dinner only is served nightly from 6 to 11pm, although you can always get a snack or sandwich until the casino closes at 3am, at 4am on Saturday and Sunday.

Paradise Pavilion, Paradise Paradise Hotel (tel. 809/363-3000), with its beachfront location and barbecue specialties, is a good choice for those who want a casual ambience with ocean views, good value, and good food. The restaurant is in an indoor/outdoor thatch-roofed pavilion directly on the beach. The menu includes steaks, barbecued chicken, Bahamian lobster tails, succulent ribs, and a variety of appetizers, soups, salads, and desserts. You might try the Paradise mudpie or Key lime pie. Meals cost from $15. You can enjoy a sundowner before dinner if you arrive early at the pavilion, where service is nightly from 6 to 10pm.

Seagrapes Restaurant, Paradise Towers (tel. 809/363-3000), off the lobby, is a pleasantly decorated tropical restaurant serving breakfast daily from 7 to 11am, a buffet lunch from 12:30 to 3pm, and a fixed-price buffet dinner, costing $20, from 6 to 10:30pm. Access to the salad bar is $10 per person, plus service, and some patrons consider this to be a full meal. Each day a different specialty is served, such as barbecued ribs, shrimp Créole, beef Stroganoff, and desserts like apple pie and pineapple upside-down cake.

Swank's Pizza Restaurant, Paradise Island Shopping Centre (tel. 809/363-2765), lies at the beginning of the driveway leading to the casino and its nearby hotels. This restaurant is the most conspicuous building in the brick-walled shopping center that surrounds it. Open daily from 8am to 2am, it offers simple breakfasts costing $6, as well as a variety of pizzas, including a Bahamian one with conch, from $8. Spaghetti and meatballs and lasagne each cost $9. Salads, such as conch or chicken, are available, as is cheesecake for dessert. The place is informal, and no one minds if you want only a snack.

---

5. Where to Shop

For really serious shopping, you'll want to cross over the Paradise Island Bridge into Nassau (see the preceding chapter). However, many of Nassau's major stores, as previewed below, also have shopping outlets on Paradise Island. There are also a number of fashionable boutiques in the major hotels, which come and go with the seasons.

For chic women's clothing in both Bahamian and foreign styling, **Mademoiselle** is an excellent place to shop. You can find branches of this charming store at the Britannia Towers (tel. 809/363-3000), at the Holiday Inn (tel. 809/326-3154); and at Paradise Village (tel. 809/326-3102). There's yet another branch at the Paradise Towers (tel. 809/363-3000). This place specializes in women's sportswear up to size 14. Designs are usually in brightly colored cottons. For this category of clothing, it's a good choice.

John Bull, known for its Bay Street store and as a pioneer seller of watches throughout The Bahamas, has two branches on Paradise Island at the Paradise Island Resort & Casino (tel. 809/363-3000) and the Paradise Island Shopping Centre (tel. 809/323-7114), selling watches, cameras, jewelry, and designer accessories.

For a rich collection of emeralds and jewelry from Colombia, as well as other precious and semiprecious stones and pearls from around the world, you can't go wrong by shopping at **Greenfire Emeralds Ltd.,** also agents for Seiko watches. They have a store at the Paradise Towers (tel. 809/363-3000).

The riches of **Solomon's Mines** are offered to shoppers at the Britannia Towers (tel. 809/326-3667). Here you'll find good buys in crystal, porcelain figurines, china, perfumes, and gifts—something to suit almost everybody.

Original designs in coral and natural pearls are spread out before you at **Jewels of the Sea** (tel. 809/326-3420) at the Holiday Inn. You can also buy gold jewelry set with gemstones at this boutique beside the water.

---

6. Sports & Recreation

Visitors interested in something more than lazing on the beaches have only to ask hotel personnel to lay on the necessary arrangements. Guests at the Paradise Island Resort & Casino (tel. 809/363-3000), for example, can have a surprising catalog of diversions without so much as leaving the hotel property. They can splash in private pools (one with a swim-up bar), play tennis, Ping-Pong, and shuffleboard, ride the waves, snorkel, and boat from the beach nearby.

Anyone in search of more ambitious water sports can sign up through the hotel for powerboat sightseeing, or catamaran sailing. Experienced crews also run guests 4 or 5 miles out to reefs, where they strap on snorkel masks or scuba gear.

Sports anglers can fish for grouper, dolphin, red snapper, crabs, even lobster close to shore. Farther out, in first-class fishing boats fitted with outriggers and fighting chairs, they troll for billfish or the giant marlin that Hemingway used to pursue regularly in The Bahamas.

BEACHES

For comments about the beach at Paradise Island, refer to "Beaches" under "Sports & Recreation" in the preceding chapter on Nassau.

HEALTH CLUBS & BEAUTY SALONS

If you miss your hometown gym or just want to test the newest kinds of exercise equipment, head for the **Britannia Towers Health Spa** (tel. 809/363-3000, ext. 6536), where you can use Universal machines, as well as a sauna and Jacuzzi. There are massage facilities available, although an advance appointment is necessary for this service.

If you're mainly interested in a facial, sauna, or massage, the female staff can take care of you at the **Paradise Island Health Studio,** Paradise Towers (tel. 809/326-2431, ext. 4070). Appointments are necessary.

SPECIFIC SPORTS

Golf

The superb **Paradise Island Golf Club** (tel. 809/326-3925) basks in the sunshine at the north end of the island. This 18-hole championship course, designed by Dick Wilson, has a fully stocked pro shop. In summer, greens fees are $40 for 18 holes or $20 for 9 holes; in winter, fees are $45 for 18 holes and $25 for 9 holes. An electric cart will cost you $40 for 18 holes. Golfers, who have included Jack Nicklaus, Gary Player, and other stars, face the challenge of shooting a ball through the twirling blades of a small windmill, through a waterpipe, over or around a lion's den, and other such obstacles. The 14th hole of the 6,771-yard par-72 course has the world's largest sand trap: the entire left side over the hole is white-sand beach.

Parasailing

For a sport combining the gliding power of a seagull with the aquatic skill of an osprey, try parasailing. It's sometimes the highlight of a vacation here—for daredevils. After donning waterskis, you're connected to a powerboat that circles around in the shallow offshore waters, where a modified parachute takes you aloft.

Paradise Para-Sail, operating from the Britannia Towers (tel. 809/363-3000, ext. 6123), can arrange a sail for you. A 6- to 8-minute ride costs $25 per person.

Tennis

Many visitors come to Paradise Island just for tennis, which can be played day or night on the nine Har-Tru courts near the **Ocean Club** (tel. 809/363-2501). Guests booked into the cabañas and villas of the club can practically roll out of bed onto the courts. Although beginners and intermediate players are welcome, the courts are often filled with first-class competitors. Two major tennis championships a year are played at the Ocean Club courts, drawing players from the world's top 20.

Other hotels with courts are: **Britannia Towers** (tel. 809/363-3000), with nine hard-surface courts; **Holiday Inn** (tel. 809/326-2101), with four night-lit asphalt courts; **Harbour Cove Hotel** (tel. 809/326-2561), with two night-lit asphalt courts and lessons and equipment to rent; the **Sheraton Grand Hotel** (tel. 809/

326-2011), with four night-lit Har-Tru courts, and lessons available. Nonguests usually are charged $2 during the day, $3 per hour for night play. Guests play free.

---

7. Evening Entertainment

Among all the islands of The Bahamas, nightlife reaches its zenith on Paradise Island. There is no other spot with the diversity of attractions, especially after dark, that this self-contained playground can offer. A few of the choices are covered below.

A CASINO & THEATER

All roads on the island eventually lead to the focal point of the nightlife: the extravagantly decorated **Paradise Island Casino** (tel. 809/326-3000), run by Resorts International. It's a pleasure palace in the truest sense of the term. No visit to Nassau would be complete without a promenade through the Bird Cage Walk, where assorted restaurants, bars, and cabaret facilities make this one of the single most visited attractions anywhere outside the United States. For sheer gloss, glitter, and show-biz-oriented extravagance, this 30,000-square-foot casino, with adjacent attractions, is *the* place to go.

The gaming tables provide the main attraction in the sanctum sanctorum of the enormous room, where Doric columns and a kind of modernized British colonial classicism vie with batteries of lights, a mirrored ceiling, and a color scheme of pastel greens and corals. The $50,000 chandelier under the dome of the entrance vestibule is fashioned from clusters of palm leaves crafted from brass, whose motif is repeated in the wall sconces throughout the inner rooms. Some 1,000 whirring and clanging slot machines operate 24 hours a day.

From 10am until early the following morning, the 60 blackjack tables, the 10 roulette wheels, and the 12 tables for craps, three for baccarat, and one for Big Six are seriously busy with the exchange of large sums of money.

The boutiques that line the corridors leading to the adjacent hotels offer additional temptations. If you've ever lusted for the flashing glint of a Colombian emerald, a discreetly luxurious Swiss watch, or a complete set of silver dinnerware, you'll find these and other posh articles in the shops near the casino.

The old, and best, days of vaudeville, coupled with battalions of attractive male and female dancers, are extravagantly brought back in the $2-million production that is presented between one and three times a night Monday through Saturday in the red-and-gold **Cabaret Theatre** of the Paradise Island Casino (tel. 809/326-3000). Visitors usually purchase tickets in advance at the booth adjacent to the casino. The lineup before curtain call sends spectators in well-organized waves into curved seating areas where they sit elbow to elbow with their neighbors.

The show employs an army of magicians, acrobats, jugglers, and comedians, as well as five complete theater sets, one with a skating rink. There's also a trio of "felines": a lion, a panther, and a tiger. Certainly not the least of all, a carefully choreographed set of routines is performed, sometimes with a trapeze, by a bevy of showgirls culled from auditions in New York, Las Vegas, Atlantic City, and, of course, The Bahamas. Each long-legged beauty is clad in what representatives of the hotel describe as $4,000 worth of feathers and $5,000 worth of body jewelry. There's even a black-light dance where only the costumes seem to fly through the air.

The cost for the cocktail show is $29, which includes two drinks. If you opt for the establishment's dinner-and-show package, the cost will be $45 per person. Dinner is served between 5:30 and 7pm, depending on that night's schedule. Most guests, however, opt for a meal at one of the resort's other restaurants, and then head for the show afterward. Shows are presented three times a night on Tuesday and Saturday (at 7:15, 9:30, and 11:30pm), two times a night on Wednesday and Friday (at 9 and 11pm), and once a night on Monday and Thursday (at 9:30pm). No shows are presented, and no dinner is served on Sunday.

A COMEDY CLUB

Jokers Wild Comedy Club, Paradise Island Resort & Casino (tel. 809/326-3000), was launched by owner Merv Griffin as the only comedy club in The Bahamas. The club features stand-up comedians from the U.S. circuit. There's a $10 cover charge. The club is closed Sunday and Monday, but is open Tuesday through Friday for shows at 9:30pm. On Saturday, there are two shows: at 8:30 and 10:30pm. Call for a reservation.

DISCOS

Le Paon (The Peacock), in the Sheraton Grand Hotel (tel. 809/326-2011), is a spacious, multilevel disco in the back of the hotel's main lobby. It's decorated in a graceful series of illuminated curved lines and surfaces, and painted in night shades of purple and black. If you're with a group of friends, you may want to establish your nighttime headquarters in the conspicuously isolated circular banquette in the middle of the floor, close to the dancing area. The bar is long, providing views of the ocean. Happy hour is from 5 to 9pm, and regular disco takes over from then until the club closes at 2am. There's a two-drink minimum, costing around $10 per person. The place is closed on Monday and Tuesday.

Club Pastiche, Paradise Island Casino (tel. 809/363-3000). If you want to dance close to the confines of the casino, you can head for this darkly intimate disco where the sound is broadcast over 116 speakers. The sounds and lights are among the best on the island, although if you just want a drink, the soft illumination in the bar area is a lot like that in a tropical jungle at twilight. The club is separated from the blackjack tables of the casino by a low balustrade. Disco music begins at 10pm. There's no cover charge, but on Friday, Saturday, and Sunday night, there's a two-drink minimum of $12; other nights, the two-drink minimum is $10. The club is open from 8pm to 4am every night of the week.

Tradewinds Lounge, Paradise Towers (tel. 809/363-3000). Crowded, noisy, and deliberately underlit, this is one of the busiest nightclubs on Paradise Island. It's said to have one of the best-engineered sound systems. Hosts of candles turn the pulsating crowd into an intriguing mass of moving shadows. On Tuesday, Friday, Saturday, and Sunday, it is open from 8:30pm to 3am. On those nights, there is a show from 9 to 11pm. On Wednesday, hours are from 7:30pm to 3am, with a show that lasts from 8:30 to 10pm. On Monday and Thursday, there are no shows and the club usually closes at midnight. A series of live bands alternate with disco—live music usually begins after 9pm. After that time, two drinks are included in the Friday- and Saturday-night cover of $10 per person.

THE BAR SCENE

There are so many different nightspots at the Paradise Island Resort that a visit to each of them could occupy an entire evening for anyone who wanted to "discover" the perfect tropical libation. Drinks in each of these places usually cost $4 each.

One of the best vantage points for a view of both the entrance of the casino and the pedestrian traffic on the Bird Cage Walk is the intimately cozy **Gallery Bar** in Paradise Towers. Set up within a view of a bronze statue of a laughing child, it offers seating in low-slung, comfortable chairs and an English-club atmosphere perfect for watching yet not becoming too intimately involved with the action. Hours are from 11am to 4pm daily.

If you're looking for a taste of Polynesia, head for the bar in the **Coyaba Restaurant,** recommended in the restaurant section, off the casino's arcade, where fruited cocktails exude a hint of the Pacific.

Daytime drinkers can swim and enjoy a drink at the **swim-up bar** in the pool of the Britannia Towers, before moving on to the **View Bar,** whose scope encompasses the floor of the casino. Also here are a thatched hut beside the pool, which dispenses waterside drinks, and the **Beach Bar.**

   Buccaneer Lounge, Harbour Cove Hotel (tel. 809/326-2561), is a good bet for a convivial crowd, jazzy music, and two-fisted drinks. The lounge is open from 9:30pm to 1am every night except Monday and Wednesday. A cover charge of $10 includes two drinks. Live calypso bands usually alternate with disco music.

GRAND BAHAMA (FREEPORT/LUCAYA)

On Grand Bahama Island, Freeport/Lucaya was once just a dream, some lonely coral and pine stands that almost overnight turned into one of the world's major resorts. The resort was the dream of Wallace Groves, a Virginia-born financier who saw the prospects of developing the island into a miniature Miami Beach/Las Vegas extravaganza. Today, with El Casino, the International Bazaar, high-rise hotels, golf courses, marinas, and a bevy of Continental restaurants, that dream has been realized.

Originally, Freeport was developed as an industrial free zone in 1956. Groves wanted to attract international financiers who could appreciate the fact that Grand Bahama was less than 80 miles from Florida and only 3 hours by air from New York. The package was comfortably lined with tax incentives and Customs exemptions. Billionaire financier D. K. Ludwig built a deep-water harbor to accommodate freight and passenger vessels.

The Lucaya district was born eight years later, as a resort center along the coast. It has evolved into a comfortable blend of residential and tourist facilities. As the two communities grew, their identities became almost indistinguishable. But elements of their original purposes still exist. Today, Freeport is the downtown attracting visitors with its commerce and industry and its own resorts, while Lucaya is called the garden city, pleasing residents and vacationers alike with its fine sandy beaches.

A major sports center, Freeport/Lucaya has six championship golf courses on the island, plus a nine-hole executive layout. Because of the plentiful supply of fresh water, the greens and fairways are in top condition year round, but the asset that golfers prize most is the fact that there's seldom a wait for starting time. Water sports —skiing, skin diving, swimming, fishing, sailing—abound. With some 40 tennis courts on the island, there's plenty of opportunity to hit the ball. There are also riding stables and jogging tracks.

Grand Bahama Island is the northernmost and fourth-largest land mass in The Bahamas. Lying 76 miles east of Palm Beach, it is 73 miles long and 4 to 8 miles wide. Nearly everything here is new, including the people. Before the boomtown development, the population numbered only 4,000 souls, some of whom made their living working in a lumber camp that had been in existence since 1929. Historically, not much had happened since Ponce de León is believed to have landed here searching for the Fountain of Youth.

In West End, a town 25 miles to the east of Freeport, are skeleton warehouses and half-sunk piers, all reminders of that village's heyday in bootlegging times. Because of its proximity to the Florida coast, in the 1920s the fishing village was a reservoir for liquor to be smuggled into the United States by rum-runners.

---

1. Getting There & Getting Around

For a general discussion of traveling to The Bahamas, refer to Chapter VI.

GETTING THERE

A number of airlines fly to Freeport from points within the continental United States. Flights between Florida and Freeport can be connected with flights from throughout the United States. Frequent flights between Freeport and the United States are scheduled by **Bahamasair** (tel. 800/222-4262). **Air Canada** (tel. 800/776-3000) provides the Canadian link.

Cruise Links to Grand Bahama

Because of its proximity to the Florida coastline, Freeport is popular with cruise ships that depart and return from the U.S. mainland on the same day. The most visible of these short-term cruises are run by **Crown Cruise Lines,** P.O. Box 3000, Boca Raton, FL. 33431 (tel. toll free 800/841-7447), which offers them every Monday, Tuesday, Thursday, and Saturday, departing from the port of West Palm Beach at 9am and returning there by midnight the same day.

Passengers can stay on Grand Bahama for a few days or make the most of 3 hours ashore in Freeport (just enough time for some shopping, a margarita, and a visit to the casino) before cruising back to Florida. At presstime, the cost for this cruise ranges from $64 to $89 per person, plus $18 in port taxes for each visitor. The cost includes three meals, a shipboard cabaret show and video movies, an on-board swimming pool, and live calypso entertainment. If you want to rent a cabin for the course of the day (for midafternoon naps or whatever), you can arrange for one for an additional charge ranging between $25 and $100, depending on size and location. Other on-board facilities include a casino, bingo games, and skeet shooting, all of which you pay for separately.

The ship used by Crown Lines is the *Viking Princess,* built in Helsinki in 1964 and fully refurbished in 1988. For those passengers wishing to use the *Princess* as a relaxed means of starting and ending a short vacation on Grand Bahama, Crown Cruise Lines can arrange discounted hotel accommodations in Freeport.

Other cruise lines offering three- or seven-day tours of The Bahamas and Caribbean often make stops at Grand Bahama. Among the largest of these companies is **Carnival Cruise Lines** (tel. toll free 800/327-7373) and **Norwegian Cruise Lines** (tel. toll free 800/327-7030), both of which offer large ships and lots of on-board activities.

GETTING AROUND

Taxis

The government sets the taxi rates, and the cabs are metered (or should be). A trip from the airport to one of the hotels in Freeport or Lucaya costs about $10. (No buses connect the airport with the hotels.) The cost is $1.20 for the first quarter mile, plus 20¢ for each additional mile. You can call for a taxi, although most of them wait at the major hotels to pick up passengers. Two taxi companies are **Austin and Sons,** Queens Highway (tel. 809/352-5700), and **Freeport Taxi Company,** Old Airport Road (tel. 809/352-6666).

Buses

There is a public bus service from the International Bazaar to downtown Freeport and from the Pub on The Mall to the Lucaya area. The typical fare is 75¢. A private company, **Franco's People Express,** runs a twice-daily service from the International Bazaar and the Holiday Inn to West End, costing $8 round trip. Check with the tourist office (see "Information" under "Fast Facts," below) for changing bus schedules.

Local Air Services

You can charter a plane for flying around Grand Bahama or to other islands at **Taino Air Service** at the Freeport International Airport, P.O. Box F-4006, Freeport, The Bahamas (tel. 809/352-8885). An airborne excursion over the lagoons, golf courses, and outlying reefs of Grand Bahama, suitable for one to five people, costs $255 per hour. The only regularly scheduled flights are from Freeport to the Abacos and Bimini. One-way passage to Marsh Harbour on Great Abaco is $53, and flights leave daily except Tuesday and Thursday. Passage to Bimini is daily except Tuesday and Thursday, and the cost is $42 one way. A chartered plane from Freeport to Nassau, a five seater, costs $385.

Car Rentals

Your need for a car will be less intense on Grand Bahama than in Nassau because of the self-contained nature of many of the island's major hotels. Still, if you want to explore, and drive yourself, you can try **Avis** (tel. toll free 800/331-2112), **Hertz** (tel. toll free 800/654-3001), or **National** (tel. toll free 800/328-4567), each of which maintains offices within small bungalows outside the exit of the Freeport International Airport.

Traveler's Alert: Rental Cars

Regarding Budget Rent-a-Car, know that a Bahamas-based car-rental company has, without authorization, copied Budget's name and trademark orange-and-black logo, and plastered them on billboards around Grand Bahama. There is no affiliation between this company and the car-rental giant based in Chicago. Despite many lawsuits, however, the local company is protected under Bahamian law. This has caused much confusion for prospective renters and much consternation from Budget in Chicago. Know in advance that if you decide to rent from the company calling itself Budget in Freeport, your rental will not be subject to the insurance-policy safeguards or the maintenance standards of the highly reputable U.S.-based Budget Rent-a-Car.

Avis, Hertz, and National each charge a daily or weekly rate, with unlimited mileage included. The arithmetic usually works out that the per-day rate is reduced for rentals of a week or more. You get the cheapest tariff by reserving a car several days in advance. At presstime, Avis and National offered the least expensive winter charges, a manual-transmission Suzuki Fronte without air conditioning costing around $295 per week with unlimited mileage. Among cars with air conditioning (which you might appreciate in the summer months), an air-conditioned Suzuki Forza at Avis or National rents for around $336 per week with unlimited mileage.

Regardless of the company you select, take the collision damage waiver, which, depending on the company, is priced between $9.50 and $12 a day. That may seem expensive, but unless you have it you'll be liable for up to the full value of damages in case of an accident.

Bicycles & Motorscooters

Bicycles and motorscooters are good means of transport here. Try **Curtis Enterprises Ltd.,** P.O. Box F-2511, Queens Highway (tel. 809/352-7035). A two-seater scooter requires a $100 deposit and rents from $30 per half day, whereas a one-seater requires a $50 deposit and costs $20 per half day. Bicycles require a $50 deposit and cost $12 per half day, but only $15 for a full day (9am to 5pm). Gas is provided and there's no charge for mileage. The rental agency also supplies helmets for drivers and passengers, which are required by law. The operator of the vehicle must also have a valid driver's license. The establishment is open daily from 9am to 5pm.

---

2. Fast Facts: Grand Bahama (Freeport/Lucaya)

Much factual information regarding Freeport/Lucaya is also applicable to the rest of The Bahamas and appears in "Fast Facts: The Bahamas" in Chapter VII. The data presented here should help you on matters pertaining specifically to the Grand Bahama area.

AMERICAN EXPRESS: The local representative is **Mundytours,** Block 4 Regent Centre, Suite 20, Freeport (tel. 352-4444). Hours are 9am to 5pm Monday through Friday.

AREA CODE: The area code for Grand Bahama is **809,** which can be dialed directly from North America.

BANKS: As in New Providence, the banking hours on Grand Bahama are 9:30am to 3pm Monday through Thursday, until 5pm on Friday. There is no weekend service. A number of U.S., Canadian, and British banks maintain branches in Freeport and Eight Mile Rock. Among them is **Gulf Union Bank** (formerly Chase Manhattan), located on The Mall at Pioneer's Way, P.O. Box F-876 (tel. 352-9792). You'll find the main branch of **Barclays Bank International Ltd.** on The Mall at Pioneer's Way, P.O. Box F-2404 (tel. 352-8391).

BOOKSTORES: One of the biggest selection of books lies within the **Freeport Book Centre,** 14 West Mall (tel. 352-3759).

BUSINESS HOURS: See "Fast Facts" in Chapter VII.

CAR RENTALS: See "Getting Around" earlier in this chapter.

CLIMATE: See "When to Go" in Chapter VII.

CURRENCY: See "Information, Entry Requirements, Customs & Money" in Chapter VII.

CURRENCY EXCHANGE: Americans need not bother to exchange their dollars into Bahamian dollars, as the currencies are on par. However, Canadians will need to convert their dollars or Britishers their pounds, which can be done at local banks or sometimes at a hotel. Hotels, however, offer the least favorable rates.

DENTIST: A reliable dentist is **Dr. Larry Bain,** Sun Alliance Building, Freeport (tel. 352-8494).

DOCTOR: For the fastest and best services, use a member of the staff at the **Rand Memorial Hospital** (see "Hospitals," below).

DRUGS: The strict drug laws of The Bahamas were cited under "Fast Facts" in Chapter VII, but the warning bears repeating. The authorities do not smile on visitors possessing or selling marijuana or other narcotics, and offenders are speedily and severely punished. A normal lapse of three days between arrest and sentencing can be expected. Penalties are harsh.

DRUGSTORES: For prescriptions and other pharmaceutical needs, go to L.M.R. Mini Mall, where you'll find **L.M.R. Prescription Drugs** (tel. 352-7327), next door to Burger King. Hours are 8:30am to 6pm; closed Sunday.

EMBASSIES/CONSULATES: See "Fast Facts" in Chapter VII.

EMERGENCIES: In case of an emergency, here are some phone numbers you may find helpful. For **police,** call **911;** for **fire,** call **352-8888; for an ambulance,** call **352-2689** or **352-6735;** and for **Air-Sea Rescue,** call **352-2628** or **911.**

EYEGLASSES: The island's biggest and most famous specialist in eyeglasses and contact lenses is the **Optique Shoppe,** 7 Regent Centre, P.O. Box F-3040, downtown Freeport (tel. 352-9073).

HAIRDRESSERS/BARBERS: One of the best places for beauty and grooming services is the **Modalena Beauty Salon,** Princess Tower, The Mall at West Sunrise Highway (tel. 352-2829). Open Monday through Saturday from 9am to 5pm, and on Sunday from 10am to 2pm, it prefers that clients call ahead for an appointment. One of the most popular barbershops on Grand Bahama lies off the patio of the **Princess Country Club** in Freeport (tel. 352-6721).

HOLIDAYS: See "When to Go" in Chapter VII.

HOSPITAL: If you have a medical emergency, get in touch with **Rand Memorial Hospital,** East Atlantic Drive, P.O. Box F-71 (tel. 352-6735; emergency, 352-

2639). This is a government-operated 78-bed hospital, with departments of medicine, surgery, obstetrics and gynecology, pediatrics, and an emergency ward. It also has an outpatient clinic and clinical laboratories.

INFORMATION: Assistance and information are available at the **Ministry of Tourism** at the International Bazaar, P.O. Box F-251 (tel. 352-8044).

LAUNDRY/DRY CLEANING: Freeport's hotels almost universally provide both laundry and dry cleaning services, usually for a slight surcharge over what it would cost had you physically carried your clothes to the dry cleaners yourself. If you want to spare yourself the extra charges, and perhaps get a glimpse of workaday island life, you can take your dry cleaning to **Jiffie Cleaners,** West Mall at Pioneer's Way (tel. 352-7079). Across the street (also at West Mall at Pioneer's Way) is the **D.P.S. Laundromat** (no phone), which by anyone's guess is the most popular do-it-yourself Laundromat in town.

LIBRARY: Grand Bahama's library is the **Sir Charles Hayward Library,** The Mall (tel. 353-7048), which allows temporary visitors to browse through its books and periodicals.

LOST PROPERTY: There is no office for this. You must call the police station and report your loss.

LUGGAGE STORAGE/LOCKERS: There are no facilities for this.

NEWSPAPERS/MAGAZINES: The *Freeport News* is an afternoon daily newspaper published in Freeport Monday through Saturday except holidays. The two dailies published in Nassau, the *Tribune* and the *Nassau Guardian,* are also available here, as are some New York and Miami papers, especially the *Miami Herald,* usually on the date of publication. The cost of these is increased by air-freight charges. American news magazines, such as *Time* and *Newsweek,* are flown in on the day of publication.

PHOTOGRAPHIC NEEDS: Virtually every major hotel in Grand Bahama offers kiosks for the sale and processing of film. If your hotel doesn't have such a service, head for the shopping arcade within the Bahamas Princess Resort and Casino. Otherwise, there are several within the International Bazaar. Most of these establishments can develop and process your film within about an hour.

POLICE: **Freeport Police Headquarters** are located at the International Building, 2nd Floor, McKenzie St., Freeport, Grand Bahamas (tel. 809/352-8352). In an emergency, dial **911.**

POST OFFICE: The main post office is on Explorers Way in Freeport (tel. 352-9371). Airmail is delivered daily; surface mail, weekly. Open Monday through Friday from 9am to 5pm on Saturday from 9am to 1pm.

RADIO/TV: See "Fast Facts" in Chapter VII.

RELIGIOUS SERVICES: Grand Bahama has a large number of houses of worship. Of the major faiths, the following are established in Freeport/Lucaya: **Angli-**

can: Christ the King, East Atlantic Drive and Pioneer's Way, P.O. Box F-87 (tel. 809/352-5402). **Baptist:** First Baptist Church, Columbus Drive and Nansen Avenue (tel. 809/352-9224); St. John's Native Baptist, Ponce de León and Coral Road (tel. 809/352-2276). **Lutheran:** Our Saviour Lutheran Church, East Sunrise Hwy. (tel. 809/373-3500). **Methodist:** St. Paul's Methodist Church, East Sunrise Hwy. and Beachway Drive (tel. 809/373-1888). **Presbyterian:** Lucaya Presbyterian Kirk, West Beach Road and Kirkwood Place, Lucaya (tel. 809/373-2568). **Roman Catholic:** Mary Star of the Sea, East Sunrise Hwy. and West Beach Road (tel. 809/373-3300).

REST ROOMS: These are generally inadequate. Visitors often have to rely on the facilities available at hotels, restaurants, cafés, and other commercial establishments, although usage in some of these places is restricted to customers. There are also some at the airport.

SAFETY: Safeguard your valuables and take all the discretionary moves on Grand Bahama you would when traveling anywhere. Avoid walking—or jogging—along lonely roads. There are no particular "danger zones," but stay alert.

SHOE REPAIR: Many visitors and residents of Freeport seem to wear the kind of shoes that never need repair (sneakers, throwaway sandals), but if you lose a heel or need a repair to one of your shoes, head for **Simmon's Shoe Repair,** 4 Sunrise Shopping Centre (tel. 373-1714).

TAXES: There is no city tax other than the 4% national tax already mentioned, which is imposed on hotel rates. There is also a 4% to 6% "resort levy." All visitors leaving Freeport also pay a $7 **departure tax.**

TAXIS: See "Getting Around" earlier in this chapter.

TELEGRAMS/TELEXES/FAXES: Nearly all major hotels send telexes and faxes, but if yours is too small to offer such services, go to the main post office (see above). To send a telegram, head for or call the Freeport branch of the **Bahamas Telecommunications Company,** West Mall at Pioneer's Way (tel. 809/352-6220). Telegrams can be charged to a valid credit card.

TRANSIT INFORMATION: To call for **airport information,** dial 352-4020; to summon a **taxi,** call 352-6666; for **bus schedules,** call the Ministry of Tourism at 352-8044.

WEATHER: Grand Bahama, in the north of The Bahamas, has temperatures in winter that vary from about 60° to 75° Fahrenheit daily. Summer variations range from 78°F to the high 80s.

USEFUL TELEPHONE NUMBERS: In Freeport/Lucaya, phone **352-8111** for **time of day, 352-6675** for **weather information.**

YELLOW PAGES: All the phone numbers for The Bahamas are condensed in one book, revised annually. Freeport/Lucaya has an extensive listing of goods and services in the Yellow Pages at the back of the book.

3. Where to Stay

Your choice is between hotels in the Freeport area, near the Princess Casino and the International Bazaar, or else at Lucaya, closer to the beach. Always inquire about package plans when making reservations, as some very moderate ones are offered periodically, especially to excursionists coming over from Florida. Sometimes the cost of the room is thrown in for practically nothing. The hotel managements of the major resorts apparently think that once they get you on the premises, money can be made off you in the bars, nightclubs, and restaurants.

Don't expect to find any cheap guesthouses in Freeport, as you will in Nassau. However, some of the smaller hotels at the bottom of my list are so reasonable in price they charge "guesthouse prices."

Remember: In most cases, a 4% room tax, a "resort levy" of 4% to 6%, and a 15% service charge will be added to your final bill. Be prepared.

What the Symbols Mean

AP (American plan): Includes three meals a day (sometimes called full board or full pension).

BP (Bermuda plan): Popularized first in Bermuda, this option includes a full American breakfast (sometimes called an English breakfast).

CP (Continental plan): A Continental breakfast (that is, bread, jam, and coffee) is included in the room rate.

EP (European plan): This rate is always cheapest, as it offers only the room— no meals.

MAP (modified American plan): Sometimes called half board or half pension, this room rate includes breakfast and dinner (or lunch if you prefer).

IN FREEPORT

Expensive

Bahamas Princess Resort and Casino, The Mall at West Sunrise Highway, P.O. Box F-2623, Freeport, Grand Bahama, The Bahamas—queen of Freeport's resort hotels—is a multimillion-dollar resort/golf/convention complex set into 2,500 acres of tropical grounds. There are in fact two "Princesses," the Princess Country Club (tel. 809/352-6721) and the Princess Tower (tel. 809/352-9661). Combined, they offer a total of 965 rooms, which, with no contest, make it the largest resort in the Freeport/Lucaya area. Ten minutes from the airport, near the International Bazaar, the resort also takes in the casino and includes two 18-hole championship golf courses, 12 tennis courts, two pools, a Jacuzzi, a beach club, and a full complement of restaurants (some of which will be recommended separately), cocktail lounges and bars, plus a disco.

First, the PRINCESS COUNTRY CLUB. The hotel's design is not unlike an enormous wagon wheel, with a Disneyland-style minimountain at its core, surrounded by an extravagant swimming pool with cascading waterfalls. There's an arched bridge allowing guests to pass over the water between the rocks. The hotel is so spread out that guests often complain jokingly that they need ground transport to reach their bedrooms, a total of 565. Nine wings radiate from the pool, sheltering buildings that are only two or three stories high (some are sold as time-share units with kitchenettes). Accommodations come in several classifications. However, even the standard rooms are well equipped, with two comfortable double beds, dressing areas, tile baths, and color TV sets. Both the Country Club and the Tower also rent out a number of lavishly furnished—and expensive—suites, such as the "royal suite," the "presidential suite," and get this, "the monarch suite."

The Country Club rents singles or doubles in winter for $135 daily, *the price lowered in summer to $100 per day, also single or double.* The Princess Tower charges $165 daily in winter, single or double, *or $130 per day in summer. Suites in either the Country Club or Tower range from $200 per day in summer* or $240 per day in winter. MAP can be arranged in any season for $42 per person, plus a 15% service charge. There is no charge for children under 12 years old when sharing a room with their parents; however, the management limits that to two children.

Daytime dress is casual. In the evening, men are requested to wear jackets in the Rib Room—the most deluxe establishment at the Country Club—but there are several other more informal dining spots. There is also dining at Guanahani's, which offers smoked ribs and other dishes in a setting overlooking the waterfall. Both of these serve dinner only. Guests can also order three meals a day, and that means breakfast too, in The Patio, which also has a view over the pool. John B offers lunch, dinner, and late-night snacks, such as hamburgers and quiche. It has an open-air setting.

The PRINCESS TOWER, lying across the Mall from its larger sister, is smaller, containing 400 luxuriously furnished units, large and airy bedrooms, adjoining the Princess Casino and the International Bazaar. Moorish in theme, the tower rises 10 floors, standing on 7½ acres of landscaped grounds. The Arabic motif, set by the Moorish-style tower, with turrets, arches, and a white dome, is continued through the octagon-shaped lobby, with its Portuguese hand-painted emerald-green and royal-blue glazed ceramic tile floor, plus a colonnade of white Arabesque arches. Guest rooms are designed in both "tropical and traditional," as they say here, each containing two double beds, cable TV, and individual climate control.

Swimming is in fresh water in an Olympic-size pool, and there is a mile-long sandy beach at the nearby Princess Beach Club. A full program of water sports is available, including arrangements for deep-sea fishing. Three professional-caliber tennis courts are lit for night play, and there are two 18-hole golf courses nearby.

At the Princess Tower you're faced with a choice of different restaurants. Two of the best, Morgan's Bluff and La Trattoria, are recommended separately. You can select either the Lemon Peel or the outdoor veranda, La Terraza, which in season has a breakfast buffet spread out. The Lemon Peel opens at noon for lunch and continues to serve dinner until 11pm. The Princess Tower also shelters one of the most popular discos on the island, the Sultan's Tent.

For reservations and information, phone Princess Hotels International toll free at 800/223-1818; in New York State, toll free at 800/442-8418; in New York City, 212/715-7000; in Ontario and Québec, toll free at 800/268-7140; and in other Canadian provinces, toll free at 800/268-7176.

Xanadu Beach and Marina Resort, Sunken Treasure Drive, P.O. Box F-2438, Freeport, Grand Bahama, The Bahamas (tel. 809/352-6782, or toll free 800/333-3333 in the U.S.). Originally built as condominiums, and later inhabited by the reclusive millionaire Howard Hughes, this symmetrical tower reopened in 1986 after months of costly renovations. It sits amid a complicated series of marinas and peninsulas, a few steps from a wide sandy beach. The hotel, just 10 minutes from the international airport, was inspired by the line from Coleridge: "In Xanadu did Kubla Khan a stately pleasure dome decree." In 1969, when it opened, it was an exclusive private club and you were likely to see Sammy Davis, Jr., and Frank Sinatra walking through the lobby. No one saw Mr. Hughes, but he was safely tucked away in the penthouse.

Carefully balanced with evenly spaced rows of carved balconies, the hotel combines the kind of pyramid-shaped roof you'd expect on a Tibetan monastery with a certain kind of modern theatricality. Tennis courts, an oval swimming pool, and easily booked water sports are on the premises. A golf course is nearby. Rooms are attractively and comfortably furnished, among the finest at the resort. Each has a phone, TV, and air conditioning. The hotel rents 186 accommodations, including 47 one-bedroom suites. In winter, EP single or double occupancy ranges from $124 to $154 daily, with suites priced from $184 to $205. *In summer, EP single or double occupancy costs $97 to $127 daily, with suites for two priced from $157 to $177.* The premier restaurant of the hotel is Escoffier, serving dinner only (a Continental cuisine). The hotel also offers the Casuarina Café and Bar, the Port of Call (a pool-deck bar), and the Ocean Front Bar and Grill.

Moderate

Caravel Beach Resort, 8 Port-of-Call Dr., Bahama Terrace, Freeport, Grand Bahama, The Bahamas (tel. 809/352-6390). Built in the 1960s and renovated in 1987, this miniresort stands across a canal from the famous Xanadu hotel, directly on the beach. Set within its own garden, it contains 12 two-bedroom apartments, each designed in a two-story townhouse style, with its own kitchenette, color TV, air conditioning, and one and a half baths. In winter, EP singles or doubles cost from $90 to $100, triples $120, and quads $130 daily. *In summer, EP singles or doubles cost $80, triples $90, and quads $100 daily.* Deep-sea fishing, golf, and tennis are available nearby. On the premises is the Windsurfer Restaurant with an interconnected bar.

Inexpensive

Castaways Resort, International Bazaar, P.O. Box F-2629, Freeport, Grand Bahama, The Bahamas (tel. 809/352-6682, or toll free 800/327-0787 in the U.S.), is a long hotel with Caribbean styling at the International Bazaar and Princess Casino. The hotel has pagoda roofing and an indoor and outdoor Caribbean garden lobby, and is surrounded by well-kept gardens. There is a swimming-pool area with a wide terrace. Accommodations, decorated in cool greens or blues and whites, have air conditioning, single king-size beds or two double beds, cable TVs, and phones. Winter tariffs (either single or double) are $70 to $96 per day on the EP. *In summer, one or two guests pay $58 to $73 per day in a room on the EP.* In the lobby you'll find a gift shop, a clothing shop that carries both men's and women's apparel, a game room, and tour desks. The Flamingo Restaurant is also on the premises, featuring Bahamian and American specialties. There is a pool bar that serves sandwiches and cool drinks. A disco, Yellow Bird, stays open until 6am. The manager's cocktail party, a complimentary feature, is held on Monday. A laundry room is located on the second floor, and there are babysitting services. There is continuous free transportation to Xanadu Beach, 5 minutes away. Free parking is available.

Freeport Inn, The Mall, P.O. Box 200, Freeport, Grand Bahama, The Bahamas (tel. 809/352-6648, or toll free 800/327-0787 in the U.S.), is composed of a cluster of buildings built Bahamian style with white balustraded covered balconies. In all, 170 well-furnished and air-conditioned rooms overlook a large swimming pool area with its extensive sun terrace and poolside snackbar. Most rooms contain two double beds, many have dressing areas, and some have kitchenettes. With service charge included, EP singles cost $80, doubles $88, triples $98, and quads $108 daily in winter. *In summer, EP single or double rooms cost $59, triples $69, and quads $79 daily.* Children under 12 sharing a room with their parents stay free. There is courtesy transportation to the beach, 10 minutes away. The inn is 1 mile from El Casino and the International Bazaar.

Lakeview Manor Club, West Sunrise Highway, P.O. Box F-2699, Freeport, Grand Bahama, The Bahamas (tel. 809/352-9789), was originally built as private apartments and today is classified as a time-sharing project. Offering 23 luxurious one-bedroom and studio apartments, the club overlooks the fifth hole of the PGA approved Ruby Golf Course. It stands away from the beach, but is ideal for golfers or for anyone to whom a sea view isn't important. The hotel maintains a five-times-per-day shuttlebus taking guests to the dining, drinking, and shopping facilities of the International Bazaar. There is no bar or restaurant on the premises. However, the resort features tennis courts, a swimming pool, free use of bicycles, reduced greens fees, and other extras. Each unit has well-chosen furniture, a private balcony, a kitchen, phone, TV, and air conditioning. This place offers bargain headquarters for those seeking tranquility. Rates, on the EP, are the same throughout the year: $75 per night or $450 weekly for two persons in a studio apartment, $100 per night or $600 weekly for two in a one-bedroom apartment. The hotel is closed for one week each November. Laundry facilities are available.

Sun Club Resort, Settlers Way, P.O. Box F-1808, Freeport, Grand Bahama, The Bahamas (tel. 809/352-3462, or toll free 800/327-0787 in the U.S.). Clean, well maintained, and relatively economical, this small-scale resort sits at the edge of a busy traffic intersection. White, with shutters, it hides its best section in the rear of the building. There, behind a vine-covered entrance arbor, is a quiet enclave of greenery, encompassing a tennis court, a pool, and a clubhouse with a bar. The establishment contains only 48 rooms and is often completely booked. Each room, decorated in strong colors and with simple furniture, has a kitchenette, air conditioning, a TV hookup, and a private bath. In winter, daily EP single or double occupancy costs $70, triples $80, and quads $90, plus taxes and service. *In summer, daily single or double occupancy on the EP costs $49, triples $59, and quads $69, plus taxes and service.* A complimentary bus takes residents every hour to the beach, providing service throughout most of the day.

IN LUCAYA

Expensive

Lucayan Beach Resort & Casino, Royal Palm Way, P.O. Box F-336, Lucaya, Grand Bahama, The Bahamas (tel. 809/373-7777, or toll free 800/772-1227 in the U.S.). Set on a spit of land midway between the open sea and a protected inlet, this is the latest incarnation of a well-known hotel that originally opened in the mid-1960s. Often heavily booked in winter, it has one of the island's two casinos within its walls, a collection of popular restaurants, a cabaret act, a sweeping expanse of beachfront, a pool, and a host of water-related activities. There are also tennis, golf, and an array of boutiques. The hotel's gourmet restaurant, Les Oursins, and the cabaret are reviewed separately.

The 247 accommodations are contained in two wings that stretch toward either edge of a curved garden filled with tropical trees and crotons. Each room has air conditioning, a veranda, satellite-transmitted color TV, a phone, and all the comforts you'd expect from a major international hotel. In winter, units cost $150 to $180 daily for a single or double room. *In summer, single or double rooms rent for $130 to $155 daily.* MAP can be arranged in any season for another $35 per person daily. The hotel's much less expensive partner establishment, the Lucayan Marina Hotel, is reviewed separately.

Moderate

Atlantik Beach Hotel, Royal Palm Way, P.O. Box F-531, Lucaya, Grand Bahama, The Bahamas (tel. 809/373-1444, or toll free 800/622-6770 in the U.S.), a Swiss International Hotel, is better than ever, following a $5-million renovation.

Combining European flair with tropical style, the 175-unit high-rise opens onto a palm-shaded beach near the Holiday Inn, 6 miles from Freeport. The hotel owns the Lucaya Park Golf and Country Club, a par-72, 18-hole course, and is well equipped for other sports as well, including boating, deep-sea fishing, and tennis. It has a large rectangular pool for those who don't want to go to the adjoining beach. Special features of the hotel include a shopping arcade, with a Swiss chocolate and pastry shop and an espresso bar where some visitors like to take their breakfast. There are several places to dine, including the Butterfly Brasserie coffeeshop, where most guests enjoy breakfast, and there is gourmet fare in the second-floor Spanish Main. The Yellow Elder Bar/Lounge, also on the second floor, was named for the Bahamian national flower. The hotel offers regular shuttlebus service to their nearby golf course, free access to the tennis courts at the neighboring Holiday Inn, and free evening entertainment. In winter, singles range from $96 to $115, doubles from $120 to $130, with suites beginning at $150 per night. *In summer, singles range from $80 to $100, doubles from $90 to $110, with suites beginning at $125 per night.*

Holiday Inn, Royal Palm Way, P.O. Box F-2496, Lucaya, Grand Bahama, The Bahamas (tel. 809/373-1333, or toll free 800/HOLIDAY in the U.S.), is a large first-class hotel with few surprises, but it is a resort hotel that's far superior to many of its chain members. It is directly on Lucaya Beach, with an entrance portico that seems to envelop arriving visitors in a well-designed sweep of soaring concrete. There is a swimming pool ringed with palm trees, as well as four all-weather tennis courts, which cost $3 per hour. Live entertainment is featured nightly in the lounge. Each of the 505 rooms has its own bath, TV, air conditioning, and phone. In winter, single rooms range from $108 to $128 per day, and doubles cost $114 to $142. *These tariffs drop to $71 to $105 daily for a single in summer, $80 to $115 for a double.* Year round, for breakfast and dinner, add another $38 per person daily to the prices quoted. Children are specially catered to here. If they are under 12, there is no charge for them when sharing a room with an adult. Room service is available here for guests wishing to dine in their rooms on many of the specialties offered in the restaurants. There is an emphasis on sports programs, including golf and water sports. Deep-sea fishing trips can be arranged.

Inexpensive

Coral Beach, Royal Palm Way, P.O. Box F-2468, Lucaya, Grand Bahama, The Bahamas (tel. 809/373-2468). Built in 1965 as an upscale collection of privately owned condominiums, this peacefully isolated property sits amid well-maintained gardens and groves of casuarinas in a residential neighborhood. Only 10 apartments and rooms are rented to vacationers. All units have air conditioning, TVs, and private baths, but no phones. Some contain verandas, but not all have kitchenettes. Studio units with verandas and kitchenettes cost $78 daily for a single and $93 for a double in winter, with studio units without kitchens or porches going for $63 daily for a single and $78 for a double. *In summer, studio units with verandas and kitchenettes rent for $63 daily for a single and $72 for a double, whereas units without kitchenettes and porches cost $52 daily for a single and $67 for a double.* The private community aura of the place makes it a high-quality hideaway for the discerning. On the premises is a sandy and well-maintained beach, as well as a swimming pool. Even if you're not staying there, the public can visit **Chicago's** (tel. 809/373-6600), featuring U.S. prime beef, or **Juliat Lin's Chinese Restaurant** (tel. 809/373-8061), which is open for lunch and dinner from noon to 9:30pm, serving an array of Mandarin and Szechuan food.

Lucayan Marina Hotel, Midshipman Road, P.O. Box F-336, Lucaya, Grand Bahama, The Bahamas (tel. 809/373-8888 or toll free at 800/772-1227 in the U.S.), stands on Lucayan Bay, across from the already previewed Lucayan Beach Resort & Casino. The Marina is a separate hotel unit comprised of 18 villa-type buildings with 142 guest rooms as well as slips for 150 boats, a swimming pool, a whirlpool spa, and laundry facilities. A water taxi provides free shuttle service between both hotels at every half hour. Complimentary minibus service between Lucaya and the Shopping Bazaar at Freeport is also available. Guests staying at either the Lucayan Beach Resort & Casino or the Lucayan Marina Hotel have reciprocal privileges of all facilities at both properties. In winter, singles or doubles cost $70 daily, with triples priced at $90. *In summer, well-furnished single or double units rent for only $60 a day, with triples costing $80.* MAP can be arranged for another $35 per person daily. The main dining facility is Hemingway's After Deck Restaurant & Bar, featuring Bahamian specialties and a selection of American and Italian dishes. There is also a bar offering wine and drinks in a casual setting, with a hand-hewn wood bar as its focal point.

Silver Sands Sea Lodge, Royal Palm Way, P.O. Box F-2385, Lucaya, Grand Bahama, The Bahamas (tel. 809/373-5700), 7 miles from the Freeport International Airport, consists of three buildings clustered around two swimming pools. Set 100 yards from a white-sand beach are 144 modern studio apartments, plus 20 one-bedroom first-class suites, all with a view of the ocean, pool area, marina, or garden. All the spacious units are air-conditioned, and contain TVs, phones, private baths, balconies, fully equipped kitchens, and bars. There is full maid service. In winter, singles or doubles range from $85 to $105 daily, while one-bedroom suites cost from $110 to $120, depending on which floor the accommodation occupies, plus tax and maid service. *Expect discounts of about 20% in summertime.* Although swimming and snorkeling are possible from the nearby beach, most serious watersports enthusiasts head for the facilities at the Holiday Inn, ¾ of a mile to the east. The lodge, however, has two hard-surface tennis courts (free to guests; $3 per hour to nonresidents, plus a $10 deposit for equipment), two paddleball courts, and two shuffleboard courts. The poolside snackbar, La Conch, is open for breakfast, lunch, and sunset drinks. The lodge's main restaurant, La Phoenix (reviewed separately), is one of the best in the Freeport/Lucaya area.

---

4. Where to Dine

In The Bahamas, Freeport/Lucaya is second only to Nassau and Paradise Island in the nature and scope of its international restaurants. Many are centered around the big resort hotels, but there are a few local joints as well. My choices follow.

All prices quoted are per person.

FREEPORT

Expensive

Crown Room, Princess Casino, The Mall at West Sunrise Highway (tel. 809/352-6721), is for those who prefer casino dining. Offering an international menu, it looks like a chic dining room on an art deco ocean liner, with pink-marble accents, brass-trimmed walls, and rose-colored mirrors. The armchairs are Eastlake inspired, and the chandeliers are clusters of etched-glass leaves gathered into illuminated sheaves. You have to walk through a section of the casino to reach this restaurant. Eight hot and cold hors d'oeuvres, ranging from liver pâté to shrimp deJonge, from oysters to fresh wild mushrooms, are featured. Soups include conch bisque, onion, matzoh ball, and vichyssoise. Among the 14 fish and meat main dishes are lobster, grouper, jumbo shrimps, fettuccine, duckling, rack of lamb, filet mignon, roast prime rib of beef, medallions of veal, and chicken. Desserts range from crêpes Casino to selections from the pastry trolley. The restaurant, which has a candlelit setting, can seat 100. Dinners, costing from $40, are served Tuesday through Sunday from 6:30pm to midnight. Reservations are recommended.

Guanahani's Restaurant, Princess Country Club, The Mall at West Sunrise Highway (tel. 809/352-6721), is an attractive place that's easy to find, as it lies within the circular poolside arcade of this previously recommended hotel. To enter, you cross over a small drawbridge before passing through louvered doors. The decor is country-style tropical, with massive brass chandeliers, lots of exposed wood, and bentwood chairs. The restaurant is named after the designation the Arawak Indians gave to San Salvador, the island on which Columbus supposedly first landed in the New World. The establishment prepares island roasts and barbecues by marinating top-quality meats and then roasting them for hours in specially constructed barbecue ovens. The house specialty is hickory-smoked ribs. Other choices include scampi, sirloin steak, beef brisket, fried conch with red sauce and fresh limes, and a Bahamian lobster and fish pot. Full meals cost $35 and are served only at dinner, Sunday through Friday from 5:30pm to 10:30pm.

Among the gourmet dining rooms in the big hotels, the **Rib Room** at the Princess Country Club, The Mall at West Sunrise Highway (tel. 809/352-6721), serves dinner only, nightly from 6 to 11pm. At this seafood and beef specialty restaurant, you'll be delighted with the traditional British-pub decor and service. You can choose from broiled Bahamian lobster, native grouper, succulent shrimp, steak au poivre, steak Diane, or rack of lamb for two. Blue-ribbon prime rib of beef with Yorkshire pudding is also served. Your meal might begin with one of a goodly selection of "soups from the kettle," including vichyssoise, French onion, conch chowder, and lobster bisque. The final bill comes to around $35 per person. There is an excellent wine list to complement your meal. Reservations are necessary, as patrons at the hotel can quickly fill up the limited number of seats, and jackets are required for men.

Ruby Swiss Restaurant, West Sunrise Highway at West Atlantic Avenue (tel. 809/352-8507). Airy, open, and imaginative, this Swiss-owned restaurant occupies a building capped with a quintet of steeply pointed roofs. The design creates an unexpected spaciousness that is appreciated by the professional organizations that arrange to meet here. Inside are two bars (one, rescued from a Victorian building, is an antique), an inviting dining room, and a less formal eating area for snacks and drinks. There are three different menus listing the food items offered every day during the establishment's long service hours. Lunch, served daily from 11am to 5pm, includes pâté maison, seafood or Caesar salads, burgers, and Reuben or club sandwiches. The cost ranges from $12 to $20. Dinner, served daily from 6 to 10:30pm, costs $35 to $45 and might include lobster cocktail, seafood platter, scampi with garlic, catch of the day, Créole-style shrimp, filet Stroganoff, fondue bourguignonne, or filet Richelieu with hollandaise sauce. Viennese strudel is a dessert specialty. Late-night snacks, often served to diners taking a break from the gambling casino, are offered daily from 11pm to 5am. Items such as omelets, scrambled eggs, sandwiches, conch chowder, and burgers cost from $6.

Moderate

Mai-Tai, Princess Country Club's Emerald Clubhouse (tel. 809/352-7637). The stone-trimmed entrance to this Chinese and Polynesian restaurant is flanked by a pair of Easter Island–type heads. This sets the tone for the decor of this isolated restaurant, which lies near a golf course about a half mile from the casino. In fact, golfers from the nearby links, as well as members of the local business community, may drop in for a midday meal.

The interior contains hanging buoys, palm-frond ceilings, and big windows through which the iron grill can be observed during the preparation of your dinner. Meals are served daily at lunch and dinner, and include both Polynesian and Szechuan specialties. Flaming appetizers feature a pupu platter, fried wontons, Mai-Tai sardar beef (barbecued beef on bamboo sticks), lobster chicken ball, deviled native lobster, Szechuan shrimp with green peas, and tempura shrimps and vegetables. There are also dishes from the Cantonese repertoire, as well as American dishes and a wide range of sandwiches at lunchtime. Full dinners begin at $30, with light lunches costing from $15. The house drink, of course, is the mai tai, although the Maui Maui sour is also popular, as is the Volcanic Flame, which someone will ignite before it arrives at your table. Open Tuesday through Saturday from 11am to 10pm, on Sunday from 5:30 to 10pm.

Marcella's, Kipling Lane, The Mall at West Sunrise Highway (tel. 809/352-5085), has been serving traditional Italian food since 1963. Decorated somewhat like a New York trattoria, with a bar and TV screen, it serves Monday through Friday from 11:45am to 2:30pm and 5:45 to 10:30pm. On Saturday and Sunday it is open only from 5:45 to 11pm. The menu is large, with all the classic Italian dishes, including a fisherman's risotto, chicken cacciatore, saltimbocca, Venetian liver, and scaloppine marsala. You can, in addition, order a zuppa di pesce (fisherman's soup) or calamari (squid) fritti. Full meals are reasonably priced at $25 per person. Reservations are necessary.

Morgan's Bluff, Princess Tower, The Mall at West Sunrise Highway (tel. 809/352-9661). Near the reception desk of the previously recommended Princess Tower, this seafood restaurant looks a bit like a high-tech version of a pirate's lair. Painted an enticing shade of coral, and accented with a duet of huge tropical murals, it serves full meals for $25. It's open only for dinner, from 6 to 11pm, offering such seafood specialties as lobster thermidor, a captain's platter of mixed seafood, cracked conch, Bahamian lobster tail, lobster bisque, seafood crêpes, and clams Benedict. Closed Wednesday.

La Phoenix, Silver Sands Sea Lodge, Royal Palm Way (tel. 809/373-5700). Amusing, witty, and nautically inspired, this highly recommendable restaurant sits above the reception area of a previously endorsed hotel. Diners climb a broad flight of exterior stairs to reach it. An eclectic decor of driftwood paneling, Bahamian paintings, plants, and intimate table groupings provides for fun evenings. A huge iron chandelier, hanging in the center of it all, almost fills the room. The restaurant serves dinner only, every night of the week. From 6:30 to 11pm, à la carte dinners range from $20 to $28. Specialties include fresh grouper Phoenix style, seafood stew, seafood kebab, cracked conch, fresh lobster kebab, sirloin kebab, and chicken Kiev, climaxed by either Nassau or Irish coffee. Reservations are a good idea.

La Trattoria, Princess Tower, The Mall at West Sunrise Highway (tel. 809/352-9661). The focused spotlights aimed at the open parasols near the entrance imitate the Mediterranean sunlight glaring down a café terrace you might find in Capri. A few steps later, you find yourself among the stucco arches of what looks a lot like a thick-walled cellar. Interesting photographs depicting the workaday poses of some of Italy's least pretentious citizens line the walls. The restaurant is open Friday through Wednesday from 5:30 to 10:30pm. Budgeteers are encouraged to dine before 6:30pm, when a fixed-price bargain is offered for $15, plus service. After 6:30pm regular à la carte meals are served for about $28 per person, including five versions of pizza and nine kinds of pastas such as fettuccine Alfredo and spaghetti carbonara. You can follow any of these with a Caesar salad, saltimbocca, and veal milanese, finished off with either a cappuccino or espresso.

Inexpensive

The Pub on the Mall, Ranfurly Circus, P.O. Box F-395, across the street from the International Bazaar (tel. 809/352-5110), gives you several types of rooms in which to eat, including an Italian restaurant. The pub and two other rooms have a British flavor. In the pub at lunchtime, you can order an English-style shepherd's pie or fish and chips. The Baron's Hall Grill Room, decorated in a medieval fashion, serves a well-selected menu that includes certified Angus beef, fish, and fowl. Prime rib is a specialty of the house. English imported draft beer is served, and the chef does some Bahamian specialties. The Prince of Wales Lounge is a place where both locals and tourists eat lunch and dinner. Silvano's Italian Restaurant offers Italian dishes and fresh pasta, serving dinner Tuesday through Sunday from 5:30 to 11pm. The Prince of Wales lounge is open seven days a week from 11:30am to 4am, and the Baron's Hall Grill Room serves Monday through Saturday from 5:30 to 11pm. All the rooms are fully air-conditioned. Lunch begins at around $8 if you're eating light, but expect to pay from $20 for dinner.

Sir Winston Churchill, East Mall, next to the Straw Market and the International Bazaar (tel. 809/352-8866), is a pub and restaurant offering not only a beer garden out back, but meals, a happy hour, even entertainment. Short-time visitors to Freeport have been known to adopt it quickly as their local watering spot. From 11am to 2am, the pub swings with activity. At lunch you can order the open hot sandwiches or pizzas, followed by homemade apple pie. The Chartwell Room in back of the pub features a complete menu, including cracked conch, fish platters, T-bone steaks, and prime rib of beef. Lunch can cost as little as $12 or less, and dinner averages around $25 per person. Some readers have found it better for drinking than dining.

THE INTERNATIONAL BAZAAR

Within this shopping complex, you can travel to many lands by sampling their various cuisines.

Moderate

Café Valencia, International Bazaar (tel. 809/352-8717), is sheltered under a tile-roofed building. On several occasions I have come here to sample the paella, but the chef prepares an array of other specialties as well, including Spanish, Italian, Bahamian, and American dishes. You might begin with a chowder or onion soup or a lobster salad if you're visiting for lunch, which costs $15 to $20. Dinner, at $25 to $30, features such pasta dishes as lasagne and fettuccine. You might also like the Bahamian grouper cutlet or the yellowtail. The stuffed lobster is also good, as is the stuffed chicken breast. For regular dining, the Valencia is open Monday through Saturday from 11am to 11pm, on Sunday from 5 to 11pm. A late-night menu is in effect from 11:30pm to 4am. Dinner reservations are suggested.

Japanese Steak House, International Bazaar (tel. 809/352-9521), offers a touch of Asia in the tropics. Kimono-clad waitresses serve a complete hibachi steak and chicken dinner. The house specialties are sukiyaki steak and tappanyaki steak. The restaurant's most expensive dish—and a favorite—is hibachi-grilled New York strip steak and a lobster tail. Occidental drinks, such as Playgirl, are served. You can, in addition, ask for sake or plum wine. Most dinners include soup, salad, and five different vegetables as well as rice. Dinners, costing from $25 to $30, are served Monday through Saturday until 10:30pm. However, if you want to save money, go for dinner from 5 to 8:30pm, when an early bird special is presented, costing only $14.95. Lunch is also served, Monday through Saturday from 11:30am to 2:30pm. Representing one of the best noontime bargains in town, it costs only $8.59 and gives you unlimited access to a buffet arrangement of vegetables and salads. Main dishes, brought to your table, include Japanese peppersteak, teriyaki pork loin, tempura don (that is, tempura shrimp and vegetables), and Japanese-style fried rice.

Café Michel, International Bazaar (tel. 809/352-2191), is an open-air place with an adjoining popular bar where guests prefer a café table placed under an umbrella. Breakfast is served from 9am to 11:30am and lunch from 11:30am to 5pm. Dinner, prepared by European chefs, is served from 6 to 9pm. Lunch, costing from $15, always features a plat du jour, along with such standard favorites as prime rib, fresh broiled grouper, broiled lobster, and seafood platter. At dinner, costing $25 and up, Continental specialties predominate. The café is closed on Sunday.

Inexpensive

Bavarian Beer Garden, International Bazaar (tel. 809/352-5050), is a hearty choice for food and drink anytime daily from 10:30am to 9pm. Try for an outside table located beneath the Moorish-style arches of the bazaar. Happy hour is from 5 to 7pm, when mixed drinks cost only $1. You get such German fare here as knockwurst, bauernwurst, sauerkraut, and snacks, along with bottled German beer or

Budweiser on tap. Bahamian and American dishes are also featured, including lobster salad and conch (fritters, chowder, salad). Meals cost from $10 to $15.

China Temple, International Bazaar (tel. 809/352-5610), offers Chinese food Monday through Saturday from 10:30am to 10:30pm. A restaurant that also prepares takeout orders, the China Temple has outside café tables, or you can retreat inside. It's the bargain dining spot of the Bazaar, offering lunchtime specialties from $6.50. It's the typically classic Chinese "chop suey menu," with all the standard items such as sweet-and-sour fish. A three-course set dinner costs $13.75.

LUCAYA

Expensive

Les Oursins (Sea Urchins), Lucayan Beach Resort & Casino, Royal Palm Way (tel. 809/373-7777), lies a few steps from the entrance to the busy Lucayan Casino. It is the most elegant—and most expensive—restaurant in the previously recommended hotel. Its minimalist decor includes a collection of gray and white tables, some of which are set on daises, and framed silk scarves in brilliant tones of aquamarine and rose. A uniformed staff caters to your needs during full dinners, served Sunday through Thursday from 6 to 11pm, on Friday and Saturday from 6pm to midnight; closed Tuesday in summer. Full meals cost from $50 and include an array of Continental dishes, perhaps a creamy lobster bisque with dumplings, fresh goose liver terrine with black truffles, many different preparations of lobster, bay scallops with garlic and provençal-herbs, and several beef, veal, and chicken dishes. Dessert might be a baked Alaska or a Sachertorte. Reservations are suggested.

The **Stoned Crab,** at Taino Beach, Lucaya (tel. 809/373-1442), is a popular dining nook on Grand Bahama, great if you don't mind the cab fare from downtown Freeport to its waterside perch. A pleasant oceanfront restaurant right on the beach, the restaurant vaguely evokes an alpine chalet, the type built in France. Guests can dine inside or on the beach patio. Reservations are necessary, as this place fills up at night, not only with visitors, but also with local residents who know of the large portions and the fine seafood.

To get you going, try the conch chowder. The snow crab claws are sweet and delicate. You might also like the stone crab claws. In honor of its namesake, the restaurant specializes in a number of other crab dishes, including crab Andrew and a crab-and-avocado cocktail. Dolphin (the fish, not the mammal) is regularly featured, as is the game fish wahoo. Fresh, not frozen, fish are used whenever possible. Accompaniments include a salad bowl, as well as home-baked raisin bread. You might like to cap your meal with Irish coffee. That meal could easily top the $35 mark. You might also order a carafe of the house wine; the restaurant has a very nice burgundy bottled under its own label in France. The bartender's special is a "Stoned Crab" drink based on various liqueurs, fruit juices, and rum. At night, taxis are usually lined up outside to drive you off to the Princess Casino. The restaurant serves dinner only, nightly from 5 to 11:30pm.

Moderate

Britannia Pub, King's Road on Bell Channel (tel. 809/373-5919), a mock-Tudor structure, is one of Grand Bahama's most convivial bars. Men gather at the bar to watch sports on TV, and English beer is available on draft. The pub is also a restaurant, serving both Bahamian and a Greek cuisine. Meals, costing from $25, might include lobster tails, the invariable "catch of the day," grouper meunière, or cracked conch. The chef will also prepare barbecued ribs or Greek shish kebab. You might begin with stuffed crab served as an appetizer, or a Greek salad. There are also a few beef dishes. Daily hours are 11am to 5pm.

Captain's Charthouse Restaurant, P.O. Box 449, East Sunrise Highway and Beach Drive ("five minutes from anywhere"; tel. 809/373-3900), is open seven days a week. In a relaxed, treetop-level dining room, guests can select from an international menu that features such specialties as prime rib of beef, teriyaki steak, chateaubriand for two, lobster thermidor, the catch of the day, surf and turf, Bahamian lobster, grouper filet, and other seafood selections, along with the chef's homemade bread and "do-it-yourself" salad bar. You can also have a Caesar salad for two, prepared at your table. Portions are large, but if you still have an appetite you can choose from a list of homemade desserts, including a coconut tart and Key lime pie. The tab is likely to be around $25. A happy hour is held in the Mates Lounge from 5 to 7pm, offering complimentary hors d'oeuvres. An early bird special meal from 5 to 6:30pm costs from $7.95. Dinner is from 5 to 11pm, and entertainment is also presented nightly. The atmosphere is nautical, vaguely Polynesian, and the service is deft. Courtesy transportation to and from your hotel is offered.

Lucayan Lobster & Steak House, Midshipman Road (tel. 809/373-5101), near the Britannia Pub, is large and popular, drawing a lot of local residents as well as visitors. The prices are right, with meals costing from $20, and the food is hearty, familiar fare, well cooked and pleasantly served. It's a surf-and-turf kind of place, except, as an unusual variation, it mixes cracked conch and lobster tail on one order. Conch chowder is the usual opener, together with a lobster or conch salad, followed by the catch of the day. That might be Bahamian baked grouper. The chef also does good prime rib, and you might like a side order of onion rings. Early-bird specials, costing from $11, are offered from 4 to 6:30pm. The restaurant is open daily from 4pm until midnight. Diners often precede their meal with a libation near the front entrance (the bartender makes a powerful drink).

PORT LUCAYA

Expensive

Luciano's, Port Lucaya (tel. 809/373-9100), brings Continental chic and refined cuisine to Port Lucaya. It is, in fact, the finest and most sophisticated Italian restaurant on Grand Bahama. Although it is found upstairs from a Pizza Hut, all thoughts of mass-market fast food are abandoned as you enter its rarefied precincts, decorated in a monochromatic gray-and-pink color scheme. You can go early and enjoy an apértif in the little bar inside or else on the wooden deck overlooking the marina.

Food is freshly prepared from high-quality ingredients and beautifully served. You might begin with oysters Rockefeller or smoked salmon, then go on to one of the soups, perhaps a thick, rich fish soup made of mussels, fish, and lobster. One of the soups is based on the chef's culinary inspiration for that day. Fish and shellfish are regularly featured, and imaginatively prepared in such dishes as filet of merou Bercy poached in a white wine and cream sauce or bay scallops simmered in a delicate sauce made with shallots and parsley. Steak Diane is one of Luciano's classics, or else the chef will prepare a rack of baby lamb in the style of Provence. Veal Luciano's is the finest milk-fed veal sautéed with shrimp and plump pieces of lobster. Meals cost from $50, and there is also an impressive wine list. The restaurant is open for dinner only Monday through Saturday from 6 to 11pm. Reservations are required.

Moderate

Big Buddha, Port Lucaya (tel. 809/373-8499), is a Japanese restaurant overlooking the yachts in the harbor along the waterfront of this shopping complex. Decorated in a restrained style, it offers both inside and outside dining. You might visit the sushi bar, or select from an à la carte menu. Several versions of tempura are offered, but you may prefer the salmon teriyaki or the broiled snapper. Lobster fried rice is another favorite, and the chef also offers prime rib of beef. Its hours are daily from 11am to 3pm for lunch and 5 to 10:30pm for dinner. However, no lunch is served on Sunday. Specials are offered daily from 5 to 7:30pm, when light meals costing from about $15 are available. A full dinner will run about $25 later in the evening.

Fatman's Nephew, Port Lucaya (tel. 809/373-8520), serves some of the best Bahamian regional cuisine in the Lucaya area. It lies on the second floor above Pusser's Co. Store & Pub, overlooking the marina at Port Lucaya. Guests can enjoy drinks or meals inside a well-decorated main dining room; but if the weather is right (and it is most of the time), diners prefer to eat on a large deck where they can survey the action in the harbor. As you climb the steps, you'll see "today's catch" posted on blackboard menus. Dishes are likely to include the game fish, wahoo, and Cajun blackened fish. If you don't want fish, you can order such selections as curried chicken. I suggest you begin your meal with either a freshly made conch salad or conch chowder. For those who want something simpler, the chef prepares the usual array of tuna fish sandwiches and hamburgers at lunch. Service is Monday through Saturday from noon to 11pm, on Sunday from 5pm to midnight. Reservations are rarely needed. Lunch costs around $12, with dinners starting at $25.

Pusser's Co. Store & Pub, Port Lucaya (tel. 809/373-8450), is the most popular place to hang out at this shopping and dining complex in the Lucaya area, offering Continental, Bahamian, and English pub fare. While a robot piano player hammers out golden oldies, you can dine indoors in air-conditioned comfort among memorabilia or else outside at a table overlooking the yachts in the marina. You are served at pinewood tables while seated on reproductions of antique pine chairs, amid plank floors covered with sawdust. There's an open grill turning out your favorite foods, and plenty of stained glass, polished brass, and pub artifacts.

For lunch most guests select either a New York–style sandwich, such as a Reuben or hot pastrami, or else an English pie, ranging from shepherd's to fisherman's. You can also order fish and chips. Dinners are more elaborate, including a wide list of appetizers that ranges from potato skins with Bahamian seasonings to lobster bisque. English pies include steak and ale, along with chicken asparagus. For the main course, you can order the catch of the day, calves' liver, double-cut lamb chops, or center-cut pork chops. For dessert, try either Pusser's pecan pie or Key lime pie. The restaurant is open daily from 10am to midnight. Lunches cost from $12, and dinners cost from $25, maybe less.

HUNTERS VILLAGE

Inexpensive
Freddie's Native Restaurant, Hunters Village (tel. 809/352-3250), an unpretentious, well-scrubbed, and welcoming local restaurant, offers an unusual alternative to the many foreign-owned restaurants filling the more commercial neighborhoods of the casino districts. It sits on a flat sandy plot of land in Hunters Village, said to be the site of one of the Grand Bahama's oldest settlements. From the outside it's little more than a painted concrete house; inside, carefully installed pinewood planks add warmth. The owners prepare an excellent Bahamian cuisine. Dinner features such dishes as lobster salad, conch salad, cracked conch, grouper, pork chops, shrimp, seafood platters, steak, and several different preparations of chicken. There is a wine list. Full meals are served Monday through Saturday. Lunch, from 11am to 3pm, costs $8. Dinner, from 5 to 11pm, is priced at $18 to $20.

5. Attractions

Except for the coral rock and pines, there isn't much on Grand Bahama that's very old, unless you count some of the Lucayan Indian artifacts. However, the ef-

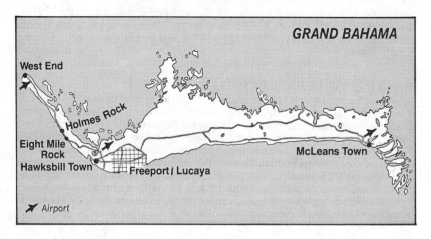

forts toward beautification have paid off in interesting botanical gardens and parks where you can see tropical plants in their glory in the right seasons. Also, plant preservation has become important here.

GARDEN OF THE GROVES

The prime attraction of the island is this garden, reached along Seahorse Road (tel. 809/352-4045). It honors the founder, Wallace Groves, and his wife, Georgette. It's an 11-acre botanical garden 7 miles east of the International Bazaar. This scenic preserve of waterfalls and flowering shrubs has some 10,000 trees. Tropical birds flock here, making this a lure for birdwatchers and ornithologists. There are free-form lakes, footbridges, ornamental borders, lawns, and flowers. A small chapel, open to visitors, looks down on the garden from a hill. The nondenominational chapel is a miniature of an old church that once served the now-defunct community of Pine Ridge, where Wallace and Georgette Groves pioneered the lumber industry on Grand Bahama Island. The **Grand Bahama Museum** (tel. 809/352-4045) traces the history of Grand Bahama for four centuries, up to the development since 1955. There are displays of Arawak (Lucayan) Indian sites. Admission to the museum is $2 for adults, $1 for children under 15, while there is no charge to visit the garden, which is open Tuesday through Sunday from 9am to 5pm.

LUCAYA NATIONAL PARK

This 40-acre park consists of unspoiled growths of mangrove, pine, and palm trees, plus one of the loveliest, most secluded beaches on Grand Bahama. To reach it, drive east along Midshipman Road, passing Sharp Rock Point and Gold Rock, about 12 miles from Lucaya. The long, wide, dune-covered stretch of sandy beach is found by following a wooden path winding through the trees. As you wander through the park, you'll cross Gold Rock Creek, fed by a spring from what is said to be the world's largest underground freshwater cavern system. Two of the caves can be seen, exposed when a portion of ground collapsed. The pools there are composed of 6 feet of fresh water atop a heavier layer of salt water. Spiral wooden steps have been built down to the pools. There are 36,000 passages in the cavern system, some of which may have been opened to scuba diving by the time of your visit.

The freshwater springs once lured Lucayan Indians, those Arawak-connected tribes who lived on the island and depended on fishing for their livelihood. They would come inland to get fresh water for their habitats on the beach. Lucayan bones and artifacts, such as pottery, have been found in the caves as well as on the beaches. Information about the park is available from the National Trust, South Riding Holdings, P.O. Box 2530 (tel. 809/348-3475). The park is always open, charging no admission.

RAND MEMORIAL NATURE CENTRE

Another attraction for nature lovers is the 100-acre site of this nature center, on East Settlers Way (tel. 809/352-5438), about 5 minutes from downtown Freeport. Charging visitors $2, it offers a naturalist-guided nature walk at 10:30am and 2 and 3pm Monday through Friday, and at 2 and 3pm on Sunday. The center is closed on Saturday. The gates open half an hour before the nature walks begin. Children under 8 years of age are not admitted. Named after James Rand, founder of Remington Rand and one of the pioneer developers of the island, the memorial is the only Bahamian nature center, a site of unspoiled forest and trails where 5,000 birds have banded together, including rare olive-capped warblers and striped-headed tanagers, as well as West Indian flamingos.

HYDROFLORA GARDEN

On East Beach at Sunrise Highway, an artificially created botanical wonder is the Hydroflora Garden (tel. 809/352-6052), where you can see 154 specimens of plants that grow in The Bahamas. A special section is devoted to bush medicine, widely practiced by Bahamians (who have been using herbs and other plants to cure everything from sunburn to insomnia since the Lucayan Indians were here centuries ago). Admission is $1 for adults, 50¢ for children; guided tours cost $2 per person. The garden is open Monday through Sunday from 9 to 5:30pm.

ORGANIZED TOURS

Several informative tours of Grand Bahama are offered. One company is **Executive Tours,** P.O. Box 2509, Freeport (tel. 809/352-8858). Tours depart Monday through Saturday at 10am lasting 3 hours. Included are visits to the Garden of the Groves, drives past residential sections, visits to open fish and vegetable markets, a view of one of the West End's distilleries, and a drive by the late Count Basie's home, terminating at the International Bazaar for shopping. The cost is $25 per adult, $12 for children under 12.

---

6. Where to Shop

There's no place in The Bahamas for shopping quite like the International Bazaar, where the goods of the world come together for you to browse among. In the 93 fascinating shops, you're bound to find something that is both a discovery and a bargain. Here are displayed African handcrafts, French perfumes, Chinese jade, British china, Spanish silver and leather, Swiss watches, Irish linens, and Colombian emeralds—and that's just for starters. The price tags on goods you find here will probably be from 10% to 40% below those on the same merchandise at home.

At the Straw Market are items with a special Bahamian touch—colorful baskets, hats, handbags, and placemats—all of which make good gifts and souvenirs of your trip. The Straw Market is beside the International Bazaar.

Keep your eyes open as you stroll through downtown Freeport or explore the smaller settlements of the island. You'll often find special items at bargain prices.

Shopping hours in Freeport/Lucaya are 9:30am to 3pm Monday through Thursday, 9:30am to 5pm on Friday. Many shops are closed on Saturday and Sunday. However, in the International Bazaar hours vary widely. Most places there are open Monday through Saturday, closing only on Sunday. Some begin business daily at 9:30am, others not opening until 10am. Closing time ranges from 5:30 to 6pm.

THE INTERNATIONAL BAZAAR

One of the world's most unusual shopping marts, the International Bazaar covers 10 acres in the heart of Freeport. The location is at the corner of East Mall Drive and East Sunrise Highway. There is a major bus stop at the entrance of the complex. Unfortunately, buses aren't numbered; however, buses marked International Bazaar will take you right to the gateway. Built at a cost of more than $4 million, it was designed by Charles Perrin, a Hollywood special-effects artist. Visitors walk through the much-photographed Torii Gate, a Japanese symbol of welcome, into a miniature world's fair setting. Continental cafés and dozens of shops loaded with merchandise await visitors. The bazaar blends architecture and cultures from some 25 countries. The place was re-created with worn cobblestones, narrow alleys, and authentically reproduced architecture.

On a street patterned after the Ginza in Tokyo, just inside the entrance to the bazaar, is the Asian section. A rich collection of merchandise from the Far East is here for your scrutiny and purchase, including cameras, handmade teak furniture, fine silken goods, and even places where you can have clothing custom made. If browsing among the jade figurines and kimonos makes you think of Japanese food, drop in at the Japanese Steak House, previously recommended, for sushi or other delicacies.

To the left you'll find the Left Bank of Paris, or a reasonable facsimile, with sidewalk cafés where you can enjoy a café au lait and perhaps a pastry under shade trees.

In the Continental Pavillion, there are offerings of leather goods, jewelry, lingerie, and gifts at shops with names such as Love Boutique.

A narrow alley leads you from the French section to East India, where shops sell such exotic goods as taxi horns and silk saris. Moving on from the India House, past Kon Tiki, you arrive in Africa, where you can purchase carvings or a colorful dashiki, the loose-fitting African robe worn from Cape Horn to the Mediterranean.

For a taste of Latin America and Iberia, make your way to the Spanish section, where serapes and piñatas hang from the cast-iron railings. Imports are displayed along the cobblestoned walks. Besides browsing through the shops, you may enjoy stopping in Hispanic restaurants such as Café Valencia.

Many items sold in the shops here are said to be about 40% less costly than if you bought them in the United States, but don't count on that. You can have purchases sent anywhere you wish (you'll pay the charges, of course). In case a shop is not able to fill your order from the warehouse stock, many of them will have your purchase sent to you directly from the manufacturer, especially in the case of European makers.

A sampling of various shops follows.

Art

Flovin Gallery, Arcade (tel. 809/352-7564), sells original Bahamian and international art, frames, lithographs, posters, and sculptures. It also offers handmade Bahamian straw dolls, pottery, and other gift items. Another branch is at Port Lucaya (see below).

Garden Gallery, Arcade (tel. 809/352-9755), features paintings and prints by local Bahamian and international artists. It also sells Bahamian craft souvenirs. All art, incidentally, is duty free.

Asian Items

Far East Traders, Chinese Section (tel. 809/352-6425), sells linens, exotic gifts, decorative ornaments, silk coats, hand-embroidered dresses and blouses, coral jewelry, and freshwater pearls.

Boutiques

Gemini II, Arcade (tel. 809/352-2377), is known for the funny and irreverent. It offers a European-inspired collection of female accessories, including women's suits, sweaters, and purses.

London Pacesetter Boutique, Arcade (tel. 809/352-2929), sells stylish sportswear, Pringle and Braemar cashmere sweaters, Gottex swimwear, and assorted European fashions. London Pacesetter Boutique also has a shop in Regent Center (tel. 809/352-2844).

Penny Lane, Arcade (tel. 809/352-3654), is one of the best women's boutiques. Its staff offers a good selection of casual wear, swimwear, cocktail dresses, and accessories.

Bric-a-Brac

The Old Curiosity Shop, Arcade (tel. 809/352-8008), specializes in antique English bric-a-brac, including original and reproduction items: Victorian dinner rings and cameos, antique engagement rings, lithographs, old and new silver and porcelain, and brass candlesticks and trivets.

Crystal & China

Island Galleria, Arcade (tel. 809/352-8194). China by Wedgwood, Rosenthal, and Aynsley, and crystal by Waterford, are the major lure of this store. Bahamian paintings are in the art gallery in the back room.

Midnight Sun, Arcade (tel. 809/352-9510), is the best bet for exquisite crystal and china. Its high-quality dinnerware from several well-known manufacturers is displayed in twin boutiques. It offers Baccarat, Hummel, Royal Worcester, and Daum, among others.

Emeralds

Colombian Emeralds International, South American Section (tel. 809/352-5464), sells emeralds, of course, as well as gold and silver jewelry, prestige watches from Japan and Switzerland. In the Jewelry Factory, local craftspeople set gemstones in jewelry while explaining the process. The shop is also the authorized agent for Ebel, Omega, Seiko, Citizen, Tissot, Heuer, Audemars, Piguet, and other well-known watches.

Footwear

Gemini I, Scandia Section (tel. 809/352-4809), is a shoe boutique with a wide range of designer shoes, leather bags, and costume jewelry.

La Sandale, French Section (tel. 809/352-5380), is known for its collection of fine women's footwear. It also sells Michel Herbelin and Courrèges watches.

Jewelry

Casa Simpatica, Spanish Section (tel. 809/352-6425), sells gold, silver, and gemstone jewelry. Discounts range as much as 40% and beyond. Semiprecious beads and coral items are made in The Bahamas. There is also a large selection of Japanese watches.

Ginza, Far East Section (tel. 809/352-7515), specializes in 14-karat and 18-karat gold chains. It also sells Mikimoto pearls, bracelets, and rings, some with gemstones. Its watches include those from Baume & Mercier, Pulsar, Seiko, Rolex, and Raymond Weil. It also has a Cartier leather collection. Top-brand cameras are also on display.

Sea Treasures, Spanish Section (tel. 809/352-2911), sells jewelry inspired by the sea and handcrafted on the island. Prices go from $25 to $3,000. The staff will show you 14K gold necklaces and bracelets, along with diamonds, topazes, pearls, and both pink and black coral. Jewelry made in The Bahamas is duty free when brought back to the United States.

Perfumes & Fragrances

Casablanca Perfumes, Moroccan Section (tel. 809/352-5380), offers a wide range of perfumes (the latest from Paris). It also sells Lancôme cosmetics. Skin-care products are another feature of this shop.

Fragrance of The Bahamas, at the rear of the International Bazaar (tel. 809/352-9391), is housed in a model of an 1800 mansion, through which visitors are invited on a guided tour. There they can see the mixing of fragrant oils. There's even a "mixology" department where you can create your own fragrance, with several oils from which to select. The shop's well-known products include Island Promises, Goombay, Paradise, Pink Pearl (which has conch pearls in the bottle), and Sand (which has actual beach sand within it). They also carry Penhaligon fragrances from England.

Parfum de Paris, French Section (tel. 809/352-8164), features practically all existing French perfumes and colognes. Discounts are often granted with prices up to 40% less than in the United States. (There's another branch at the Holiday Inn.)

Stamps & Coins

Bahamas Coin and Stamp Ltd., Arcade (tel. 809/352-8989), sells stamps, coins, commemorative medallions, and uncirculated coin sets. It has Bahamian and Grenadian stamps, along with $100 gold coins, British half-sovereigns, and gold jewelry.

Sweaters

The Sweater Shop, Indian Section (tel. 809/352-7863), fulfills most sweater needs. It features men's and women's sweaters in lambswool, cashmere, and cotton from such diverse countries as Scotland and Italy. Cotton sweaters, made in Italy, were especially created for The Bahamas market.

Tobacco Items

Pipe of Peace, International Section (tel. 809/352-7704), displays pipes, tobacco, cigars, cigarettes, lighters, watches, figurines, cameras, jewelry, and souvenirs.

PORT LUCAYA MARKETPLACE

The first of its kind in The Bahamas, Port Lucaya on Sea Horse Road was named after the original settlers of Grand Bahama. This is a shopping and dining complex set on 6 acres near the Lucayan Beach Resort & Casino, Holiday Inn, and Atlantik Beach Hotel. Free entertainment, such as steel drum bands, strolling musicians, jugglers, mimes, and magicians, adds to a festival atmosphere. The architecture and pastel colors of the buildings were influenced by the design of traditional island homes, but the marketplace was modeled along the lines of Miami Bayside or Faneuil Hall in Boston.

The complex rose on the site of a former Bahamian straw market, but the good ladies and their straw products are back in full force after being temporarily dislodged.

Full advantage is taken of the waterfront location. Many of the restaurants and shops overlook a 50-slip marina, home of a "fantasy" pirate ship featuring lunch and dinner/dancing cruises. Glass-bottom boats, deep-sea fishing boats, catamarans, and a variety of charter vessels are also based at the Port Lucaya Marina. Dockage at the marina is available to visitors coming to shop or dine by boat.

A boardwalk along the water makes it easy to watch the frolicking dolphins and join in other activities at the Underwater Explorers Society (UNEXSO). (For more information about the popular programs offered by UNEXSO, see "Sports & Recreation," below.)

Merchandise in the shops of Port Lucaya ranges from linens to leather and lingerie to jeweled watches to wind chimes. Traditional and contemporary fashions are featured for men, women, and children. Shoppers will also discover perfumes, Colombian emeralds, imported china and crystal, hand-embroidered items, as well as an international selection of liquors.

However, one is exceptional. It's **Pusser's Co. Store & Pub,** Port Lucaya (tel. 809/373-8450), which in addition to its pub and restaurant (described earlier) is also part nautical museum, part general store. It's a shopping adventure, with Pusser's own line of travel and sports clothing in classical design, along with fine ship models, antiques, and other nauticalia. You'll also find unusual gift items, flags, and pennants, along with ceramic rum flagons, decanters, and hip flasks.

Coconits by Androsia, Port Lucaya (tel. 809/373-8387), is the Port Lucaya outlet of this famous batik house of the Andros Islands. Its designs and colors capture "the spirit of The Bahamas." Fabrics are handmade on the island of Andros, and the store sells quality resortwear and fabric of 100% cotton knit. One line offers airbrushed cotton knits in simple skirts, tops, and jackets for women.

Flovin Gallery II, Port Lucaya (tel. 809/373-8388), is a branch of the art gallery at the International Bazaar, selling a collection of oil paintings (both Bahamian and international), along with lithographs, posters, and sculptures. It also features a number of gift items.

OTHER SHOPPING SELECTIONS

Bahamian Things, P.O. Box F-2103, 15B Poplar Crescent, Pestco Building (tel. 809/352-9550), offers Bahamian-made products—jewelry, perfume, clothing, arts and crafts, and Androsia fabrics. With the unusual selection of items here, you have a chance to "take home a little bit of our islands" that is different.

7. Sports & Recreation

A wide variety of sports activities abounds on Grand Bahama Island. Miles of white-sand beaches, some of the finest golf courses anywhere in the islands, and lighted tennis courts are easily accessible. The blue-green waters are also enticing for swimmers.

Other sports popular with visitors are fishing, scuba diving, snorkeling, and horseback riding.

BEACHES

It is estimated that Grand Bahama has some 60 miles of beaches. The heaviest concentration is in the Lucaya area, site of the major resort hotels. Most of these resorts have their own beaches, with a fairly active program of water sports that tends to grow sluggish in summer. **Xanadu Beach,** at the Xanadu Beach and Marina Resort in the Freeport area, is one of Grand Bahama's premier beaches with its mile of white sand. These resort beaches tend to be the most crowded in winter. However, there are also beaches on the way to Grand Bahama.

Other island beaches include **Taino Beach,** site of the Stoned Crab restaurant, lying to the east of Freeport, plus **Smith's Point** and **Fortune Beach.** Another good beach, about a 20-minute ride east of Lucaya, is **Gold Rock Beach,** a favorite picnic spot with the locals, especially on weekends.

BOAT CRUISES

Any tour agent can arrange for you to go out on the *Mermaid Kitty,* which is supposed to be the world's largest twin-diesel-engine glass-bottom boat. You'll get an excellent view of the beautiful underwater marine life that lives off the coast of Grand Bahama. Departures are from the Lucayan Bay Hotel at 10:30am and 12:30 and 2:30pm, lasting 1½ hours. The tour costs $12 for adults, $5 for children. For information or reservations, contact International Travel & Tours, P.O. Box F-850 (tel. 809/352-9311).

THE DOLPHIN EXPERIENCE

A group of bottle-nosed dolphins are involved in a unique dolphin/human familiarization program at the **Underwater Explorers Society (UNEXSO)** (tel. 809/373-1250), next to Port Lucaya. As part of the program, swimmers and snorkelers are invited to get into the water and interact with the dolphins for about 20 minutes, following a brief informational program about these fascinating animals. Swim sessions are conducted in the safe, calm water of the dolphin enclosure. The animals are also released daily to swim with snorkelers and scuba divers in the open ocean. *This is the only destination in the world where divers and snorkelers may interact with dolphins in the open ocean on a scheduled basis.* The informational program, which includes close-up observation of the dolphins, costs $10; the swim session is $49; snorkeling with the dolphins in the open ocean is $59; and diving with the dolphins in the open ocean is $95. There are several sessions daily. All Dolphin Experience sessions are videotaped, with copies available to participants for $35. Because of the popularity of the program, advance reservations are essential. In the United States call 305/359-2730, or toll free 800/992-DIVE.

FITNESS CENTERS

For complete fitness services, try the **Princess Fitness Centre,** Princess Country Club, Bahamas Princess Resort and Casino, The Mall at West Sunrise Highway (tel. 809/352-6721, ext. 4606). This health club, which you can join even if you're not a guest of the hotel, is open daily from 10am to 7pm, offering sauna, facials, massages, and use of an exercise room with bodybuilding equipment. Aerobics and dance classes are available at the Bahamas Dance Theatre of the hotel (tel. 809/352-6721, ext. 4656). Aerobics classes are at 10am and 6pm Monday through Friday. Ballet is taught at 4pm Monday through Friday and at 11am (for children 4 to 6 years) on Saturday. Jazz is offered Monday through Friday at 5pm, with tap on Saturday at noon. Classes last one hour.

SPECIFIC SPORTS

Golf

This island boasts more golf links than any other of The Bahamas or any island in the Caribbean. In a week here, you can play on a different course almost every day, taking two days off for rest and relaxation on a white-sand beach. Most courses are tight, with heavily wooded areas demanding precision golfing. The courses are within 7 miles of one another, and you'll find no traffic and no waiting to play. Here is a rundown of the major courses in Freeport/Lucaya, plus the one at West End:

Lucayan Park Golf & Country Club, Lucaya Beach, P.O. Box F-333 (tel. 809/373-1066). This is the best-kept and most manicured course on Grand Bahama. Greens are fast, and there are a couple of par 5s more than 500 yards long. It totals 6,824 yards from the blue tees and 6,488 from the whites. Par is 72. Greens fees are $27 for 18 holes. Electric carts cost $26.

Fortune Hills Golf and Country Club, Richmond Park, Lucaya, P.O. Box F-2619 (tel. 809/373-4500). Designed as an 18-hole course, the back 9 were never completed. You can replay the front 9 for 18 holes and a total of 6,916 yards from the blue tees. Par is 72. The club caters to members, many of whom are expatriate executives working for Freeport industry, but the course is open to the public. Greens fees are $9 for 9 holes, $16 for 18. Electric carts cost $16 and $24 for 9 and 18 holes, respectively. The nearest hotels are the Atlantik Beach, Holiday Inn, and Lucayan Beach. The location is 5 miles east of Freeport.

Princess Ruby Course, West Sunrise Highway, P.O. Box F-207, (tel. 809/352-6721). This is one of two courses owned and operated by the Bahama Princess Resort and Casino. The championship course was designed by Joe Lee, and it was the former site of the Hoerman Cup Caribbean Championship. Fees are $18 if you are a Princess guest, $25 if you are staying elsewhere. Carts are $36 for 18 holes. It's a total of 6,750 yards if played from the championship blue tees.

Under the same management, the **Princess Emerald Course,** The Mall South, was designed by Dick Wilson. It was the site of the Bahamas National Open some years back. The course has plenty of trees along the fairways as well as an abundance of water hazards and bunkers. The toughest hole is the ninth, a par 5 with 545 yards from the blue tees to the hole. Fees are the same as at the Princess Ruby.

All courses in Grand Bahama are open to the public year round, and clubs can be rented from all pro shops on the island.

Horseback Riding

Get back in the saddle again at **Pinetree Stables,** Beachway Drive, P.O. Box F-2915, Freeport (tel. 809/373-3600), offering trail rides to the beach Tuesday through Sunday at 9am, 11am, and 2pm. The cost is $25 per person for a ride lasting 1½ hours. Lessons in dressage and jumping are available for $30 for 45 minutes of instruction.

Parasailing

When the weather is rough, which it often is in winter, no one goes parasailing, of course. But during some of the year this is a popular sport. **Sands Watersports** (no phone) offers this activity. Their kiosk is found midway between the Holiday Inn and the Atlantik Beach Hotel along Royal Palm Way. The cost is $30 for a ride lasting 3 to 5 minutes. The tour desk at either the Holiday Inn (tel. 809/373-1333) or at the Atlantik (tel. 809/373-1444) will provide information.

Snorkeling & Scuba

The **Underwater Explorers Society (UNEXSO),** P.O. Box F-2433, Lucaya Beach (tel. 809/373-1244), is one of the premier facilities for diving and snorkeling throughout The Bahamas and Caribbean. *Skin Diver* magazine has called UNEXSO "one of the most modern dive resorts in the world." There are three dive trips daily, including reef trips, wreck dives, and night dives. Also, this is the only facility in the world where divers can dive with dolphins in the open ocean on a scheduled basis (see "The Dolphin Experience," above). Also, a popular 3-hour learn-to-dive course is offered every day. Over UNEXSO's 25-year history, more than 50,000 people have completed this course, from 12-year-old children to adults in their 60s. For $79, students learn the basics in UNEXSO's training pools. Then, the following morning, they dive the beautiful shallow reef with their instructor. For experienced divers, a guided reef dive is $29, a three-dive package is $75, and a seven-day pass (up to three dives per day) is $295. A snorkeling trip to the reef costs $15, all equipment included, and a half-hour snorkeling lesson is $10. Snorkeling with the dolphins costs $95. Many dives are videotaped, and copies are available to participants for $35. In the United States call 305/359-2730, or toll free 800/992-DIVE. Advance reservations recommended.

Paradise Watersports, Xanadu Beach, P.O. Box F-3529 (tel. 809/352-

2887), at the Xanadu Beach and Marina Resort, offers snorkeling trips. You cruise to a coral reef on a 28-foot pontoon boat for $15 per person, with snorkeling gear costing $9 per hour. Sunfish are rented for $15 per half hour. Perhaps you're more the paddleboat type. They rent for $7 for a half hour, $10 per hour. Waterskiing, hydrosliding, and ski biscuit rides are priced at $15 for a 15-minute ride. Windsurfing, at $15 per hour, and other water activities are available.

The buoyant and enthusiastic owners, Toronto-born Colleen Lewis and Bahamas-born Larry Lewis, also offer parasailing at $25 for a 7-minute ride. Their sunset cruise, at $20 per person, includes live dance music, unlimited Bahama Mamas (the drink, that is), and cheese and crackers. A glass-bottom boat ride costs $12 for adults and $6 for children under 12 for a cruise lasting 1½ hours.

Sportfishing

In the waters off Grand Bahama you can fish for barracuda, snapper, grouper, yellowtail, wahoo, and kingfish, along with other denizens of the deep.

Check with **Running Mon Marina,** Bahama Terrace, P.O. Box F-2663 (tel. 809/352-2663). A half day's deep-sea fishing costs $300, a full day going for $600, and it takes six people to make up the party.

Reef Tours, Ltd., Port Lucaya, P.O. Box F-2609 (tel. 809/373-5880), offers the least expensive way to go deep-sea fishing around Grand Bahama Island. Adults pay $50 if they fish, $25 if they only go along to watch. Departures for the half-day excursion are at 8:30am and 1pm seven days a week. Included in the cost are bait, tackle, and ice.

Tennis

This game is widely available on Grand Bahama Island.

The **Bahamas Princess Resort and Casino,** The Mall at West Sunrise Highway, almost has the monopoly. At its Princess Country Club (tel. 809/352-6721), there are six hard-surface courts. Guests and nonguests are charged $5 per hour. Lessons are also available. At the Princess Tower (tel. 809/352-9661), there are three clay and three hard-surface courts, all of which are lit for night play. The charge for both guests and nonguests is $5 ($10 at night).

Holiday Inn, Royal Palm Way (tel. 809/373-1333), has four hard-surface courts, costing $5 per hour for guests and nonguests alike. There is no night play.

At the **Lucayan Beach Hotel,** Royal Palm Way (tel. 809/373-6545), there are four hard courts (not illuminated). Free for guests, these courts cost nonresidents $5 per hour.

Windsurfing

Courses are offered at the **Atlantik Beach Hotel,** Royal Palm Way (tel. 809/373-1444), for beginners, advanced, and freestyle. Each course is 8 hours and costs $150. Windsurfing boards and equipment rent for $15 per hour or $40 per day.

---

8. Evening Entertainment

Grand Bahama has Las Vegas–type show revues, casino action, dance clubs, and native entertainment such as steel bands. Many of the resort hotels stage their own entertainment at night; if yours does not, you can go to one that does, as hotel shows are open to the general public.

LOCAL CULTURAL ENTERTAINMENT

The **Freeport Players' Guild,** Regency Theatre (tel. 809/352-5165), is a non-profit repertory company. It offers about four plays during its September to June season.

Grand Bahama Players (tel. 809/373-2299), a local amateur group, also uses the Regency Theatre for its productions, which consist of works by Bahamian, West Indian, and North American playwrights. Sometimes performances are staged at the International Bazaar. Call for information.

All performances of both of these groups are advertised in the local papers.

CASINOS

Most of the nightlife in Freeport/Lucaya centers around the glittering **Princess Casino,** The Mall at West Sunrise Highway (tel. 809/352-7811), the giant Moroccan-style palace that's one of the largest casinos in The Bahamas and the Caribbean. Under this Moorish-domed place, visitors play games of chance and attend Las Vegas–type floor shows. They can also dine in the gourmet restaurant, the Crown Room (recommended under "Where to Dine" in this chapter). The casino is open daily from 9am to 3:30am.

The **Lucayan Beach Casino,** Lucayan Beach Resort, Royal Palm Way (tel. 809/373-7777), is the center of casino action at Lucaya Beach, daily from 9am to 3am. It is as large as its competitor, about 20,000 square feet, offering 550 super slots. Its happy hour, lasting daily from 11am to 7pm, is considered the longest in The Bahamas. Novices can take free gaming lessons daily from 11am to 7pm.

CABARET

If you're staying at Lucaya, you'll want to attend the **Showcase Theatre,** in the Lucayan Beach Resort, Royal Palm Way (tel. 809/373-7777). The decor is predictably cabaret-oriented, with endless rows of parallel tables. But what makes the place unique is the high quality and professionalism of its Las Vegas–type shows. The revues are among the best in The Bahamas. Shows change all the time, sometimes lasting no more than two weeks. One of the most popular and long-running was entitled "The Red Hot Black & Blues." Count on spending from $19.95 per person, a price that includes two drinks, but that could go higher, depending on the show offered. Performances are Monday through Saturday at 8:30 and 10:30pm. Because of the popularity of the room, reservations are needed.

Many guests come to the Bahamas Princess Resort and Casino, The Mall at West Sunrise Highway, to attend the **Casino Royale Showroom** (tel. 809/352-6721), which presents two shows nightly, the first at 8:30 and the second at 10:45pm (there are no shows on Monday). Shows come and go, but there are usually Las Vegas–type revues. Expect more than a dozen performers who cavort in goombay-inspired colors with lots of glitter and a smattering of toplessness. With two drinks included, entrance to the show costs $25, and advance reservations are a good idea.

THEME NIGHTS

Holiday Inn, Royal Palm Way (tel. 809/373-1333), has theme nights, which are very popular in Lucaya. Although these are planned mainly for guests staying at the hotel, they are also open to outsiders (including local residents), provided they've made reservations and there is enough space. On Tuesday night there's a Bahamian Luau, with a live Bahamian show from 6:30 to 9pm. Adults pay $23. For that, you get a buffet spread with fresh salads, desserts, and such main courses as sweet-and-sour pork, chicken, roast beef, shrimp chow mein, and barbecued spareribs. Although the Bahamian Luau is by far the hotel's most popular and enduring theme night, other buffets with different themes (including an occasional Italian one) are offered during periods of peak occupancy.

DANCE CLUBS

Sultan's Tent, Bahamas Princess Resort and Casino, The Mall at West Sunrise Highway (tel. 809/352-6721), features an Arabian Nights theme. You can dance here to the latest international records (there are no floor shows, but there are live bands). The cover charge of $12 per person includes your first two drinks. The place is open every night from 9pm to 3am.

Panache Disco, Holiday Inn, Royal Palm Way (tel. 809/373-1333), can fill up with 200 frenzied patrons. The management has totally rebuilt the disco and decorated it in red-wine colors. A good sound system enables guests to hold conversations while still listening to the disco beat. A live band performs Wednesday through Sunday from 9pm to 3am, and the $10 door charge (paid only by nonresidents of the hotel) covers the cost of your first two drinks.

THE CLUB & MUSIC SCENE

Yellow Bird Show Club, Castaways Resort, International Bazaar (tel. 809/352-6682), in the rear of Howard Johnson's Restaurant, offers an evening of Bahamian entertainment, with steel drums, the limbo, conga drums telling stories, the fire dance, and glass-eating. The show even presents its highly stylized version of the Caribbean Queen of Calypso. The charge of $18 covers two drinks and the tip. Doors open at 9pm, with show time at 10:30pm except Tuesday. You can disco here after the show.

Skipper's Lounge, Princess Country Club, The Mall at West Sunrise Highway (tel. 809/352-6721), is a good bet if you want tamer fare. There is no cover and no minimum, and drinks are priced from $3.50. In the east lobby of the hotel, a five-piece combo plays good jazz and you get a "little soft shoe." Live music is provided Friday through Wednesday from 9pm to 2am.

---

9. Day Trip: West End

One of your most refreshing days on Grand Bahama can be spent by escaping from the plush hotels and casinos of Freeport/Lucaya and heading to West End, 28 miles from Freeport. At this old fishing village you'll get glimpses of how things used to be before the development of Freeport and before package-tour groups started arriving on Grand Bahama.

To reach West End, you head north along Queen's Highway, going through Eight Mile Rock and on to the northernmost point of the island. West End has several good restaurants, so you can plan to make a day (or a night) of it.

A lot of the old buildings of the village now stand dilapidated, but a nostalgic air prevails. Many old-timers remember a better day (at least for them economically), when boats were busy and the docks buzzed with activity day and night. This was during the era from about 1919 to 1933, when Prohibition reigned in the United States—but not with great success. West End was so close to the U.S. mainland that rum-running became a lucrative business, with booze flowing out of West End to be slipped into Florida at night so that the flappers and their beaux of the Roaring '20s would not go thirsty in the speakeasies. Al Capone is reputed to have been a frequent visitor.

Villages along the way to West End have colorful names, such as Hawksbill Creek. For a preview of some local life, try to visit the fish market along the harbor here. You'll pass some thriving harbor areas too, but the vessels you see will be oil tankers, not rum-runners.

Eight Mile Rock is a hamlet of mostly ramshackle houses that stretch along both sides of the road for—you guessed it—8 miles. The names of other little hamlets may also intrigue you, places like Bootle Bay, for instance.

At West End, you come to an abrupt stop. Then it's time to visit the weathered old Star Club (see below). If you stick around till night, you're likely to hear some calypso music nearby.

Harry's American Bar (see below) is the place for a sundowner. You can enjoy a meal either there or at the nearby Buccaneer Club before heading back to Freeport/Lucaya to catch the last show at the casino.

•

WHERE TO DINE IN WEST END

Moderate

Buccaneer Club, Deadman's Reef (tel. 809/348-3794), is a tropical version of a German beer garden. Most of the inspiration for the whimsical decor came from Switzerland-born Heinz Fischbacher, who, with his Bahamian wife, Kitty, added as much lighthearted Teutonic flavor as you'll find west of the Rhine. The compound is ringed with stone walls, within which are palm-dotted terraces where foot-stomping alpine music provides lots of fun for the yachting crowd you'll see here. The collection of inner rooms contains mismatched crystal chandeliers, pine trim, oddly shaped pieces of weathered driftwood, and a beerhall ambience that's unique in The Bahamas.

Three times weekly, the Fischbachers have beach parties, which cost $30 per person. The price includes transportation from hotels, an hourlong open bar, a table-groaning buffet, a beer-drinking contest, a spaghetti-eating contest, crab races, limbo dancing, and lively games of musical chairs. The establishment is open Tuesday through Sunday. Only dinner is served, from 5 to 10pm.

Many people head for **Pier One,** Freeport Harbour (tel. 809/352-6674). Because of its location close to the waterway used by the cruise ships that arrive daily from Florida, this is the first Bahamian restaurant many arriving passengers see. Covered with gray-tinged cedar shingles, it rises on stilts above a rocky shoreline a few steps from the water's edge. A wooden footbridge leads into a plank-covered interior loaded with nautical artifacts. Don't overlook the high-ceilinged bar as a place for a round of drinks before your meal. Sunset watchers come here. There are several dining rooms, the most desirable of which overlooks schools of fish.

Lunch is Monday through Saturday from 11am to 4pm, costing from $15. The bill of fare includes a delectable version of a cream-based clam chowder, lobster soup, fresh oysters, fresh conch salad, spaghetti with seafood, the fresh fish of the day, and pan-fried grouper. Dinner is daily from 4 to 10pm, costing from $30 per person. Specialties include baked stuffed flounder, red snapper filet with Pernod, coconut-flavored shrimp, shrimp curry, and filet of lemon shark with green Madagascar peppercorns and pineapple. Meat dishes include roast prime rib and sirloin. For dessert, you might try Black Forest cake, Italian rum cake, or Key lime pie. Reservations are suggested for dinner.

Inexpensive

Harry's American Bar, Deadman's Reef (tel. 809/348-6263), is an isolated rendezvous point on a side lane leading off the only road into West End. You pass beneath a pair of stone columns marking the entrance and come to a compound dotted with shrubs and trees. On a good day, the seafront terrace, with its frond-covered sun umbrellas and sea-grape trees, can be one of the most relaxing places on the island.

Kitty Fischbacher, who is also the part owner of the previously recommended Buccaneer Club (see above), runs the place. Only lunch is served, and it's offered daily except Monday, Wednesday, and Friday from 10am to 5pm. After dark, the party moves to the nearby Buccaneer Club. Lunches, costing from $12, include soup, salads, sandwiches, and cheeseburgers. The house special drink is called Harry's Hurricane, made with coconut- and banana-flavored rums, Bacardi, and fruit juices.

The **Star Club,** Bayshore Road, P.O. Box F-1726 (tel. 809/346-6207). When it was built in the 1940s, this was the first hotel on Grand Bahama. Today it contains the only 24-hour-a-day bar and snackbar on the island, which sometimes encourages people from the casino to motor out here after a night at the tables. At one time the Star was painted white and had accommodations. Today it's only a restaurant, bar, and pool hall with a jukebox and slightly tattered Naugahyde furniture. You'll probably be able to strike up a conversation with Austin Henry Grant, Jr., a former Bahamian senator who owns the place. Mr. Grant knew many of the famous guests who stayed here incognito in the 1940s, when West End enjoyed a cachet that it has since lost to the burgeoning center, Freeport/Lucaya. His wife, Anne Grant, is likely to be here as well.

A full range of drinks is available as well as simple meals. Menu items include Bahamian chicken in the bag, hamburgers, cheeseburgers, fish and chips, and "fresh sexy" conch prepared as chowder, fritters, or salads. Drinks cost $2.50, while informal meals go for $12.

XI

BIMINI, THE BERRY ISLANDS & ANDROS

1. BIMINI
2. THE BERRY ISLANDS
3. ANDROS

In this chapter we begin to travel through the Family Islands to a very different world from that found in the major tourist meccas of Nassau, Cable Beach, Paradise Island, and Freeport/Lucaya, which we have considered so far.

To begin our exploration, we have an unusual blend of Bimini, the Berry Islands, and Andros. Bimini is famous and overrun with tourists, particularly in summer, but visitors practically have the Berry Islands to themselves. These islands to the north and west of Nassau might be called the "westerly islands," as they, along with Grand Bahama, lie at the northwestern fringe of The Bahamas. As such, they are the closest islands to the Florida coastline.

Of all these islands, Andros in many ways is the most fascinating. Actually a series of islands, it looks like a mosaic when you fly over it because of all the bodies of water that divide the island. It is laced with creeks and densely forested inlands, once said to have been inhabited by mysterious creatures. It is also considered the bonefishing capital of the world. Two of its major attractions are offshore: the Tongue of the Ocean, 1,000 fathoms deep and 142 miles long, and the Great Barrier Reef, the second-largest underwater coral reef in the world. But more about these later.

First, after takeoff in Miami, our plane will wing its way to Bimini, where our trip will begin.

1. Bimini

Bimini is known as the big-game fishing capital of the world, and fishing is excellent throughout the year in flats, on the reefs, and in the streams. Ponce de León didn't find the legendary Fountain of Youth on Bimini, but Ernest Hemingway came to write and fish and publicize Bimini around the world in his *Islands in the Stream*, in which he described the artistic self-discipline of a "good painter," Thomas Hudson, on the lush island, once the rum-running capital of the world. He also wrote much of *To Have and Have Not* on Bimini.

Fifty miles east of Miami, Bimini consists of a number of islands, islets, and cays, including North and South Bimini, the targets of most visitors. You'll most often encounter the word "Bimini," but it might be more proper to say the "Biminis." That's because North Bimini and South Bimini are two distinct islands, separated by a narrow ocean passage. There is ferry service between the islands. Tourist facilities are on North Bimini, mostly in Alice Town, its major settlement.

Guided by native fishermen, visitors can go bonefishing or deep-sea fishing. Divers find the reefs laced with conch, lobster, coral, and many tropical fish. Sightseers are allowed to visit the Lerner Marine Laboratory for Marine Research on North Bimini. It was founded by Michael Lerner, an outstanding fisherman.

It's also traditional to pay a visit to the former haunt of the late, controversial congressman Adam Clayton Powell, at the End of the World Bar in Alice Town (see "Evening Entertainment," below).

Off North Bimini, in 30 feet of water, are some large hewn-stone formations. Many people believe them to be from the lost continent of Atlantis.

Bimini's location off the Florida coastline is at a point where the Gulf Stream meets the Bahama Banks. That has made Bimini a favorite cruising ground for America's yachting set, who follow the channel between North and South Bimini into a spacious, sheltered harbor where they can stock up on food, drink, fuel, and supplies at well-equipped marinas.

Hook-shaped North Bimini is 7½ miles long. Combined with South Bimini, it makes up a land mass of only 9 square miles. That's why Alice Town looks so crowded, everything squeezed together. Another reason is that a large part of Bimini is privately owned, and in spite of pressure from the Bahamian government, the landholders have not sold their acreage yet—so Bimini can't "spread out" until they do.

At Alice Town, the land is so narrow that you can walk "from sea to shining sea" in just a short time. Most of Bimini's population of some 1,600 people live in Alice Town. Other hamlets include Bailey Town and Porgy Bay.

South Florida visitors flock to Bimini in the summer months; winter, especially the season from mid-December to mid-March, is quieter. In that sense, Bimini is different from the other islands in The Bahamas. Winter months in the rest of the Family Islands, including Nassau, Paradise Island, and Freeport/Lucaya, are the high season.

Fishermen, as mentioned, and divers are attracted to Bimini, and have been for years. But in recent years Bimini is attracting more and more visitors who don't care about sports at all. The reason for this is that many Americans, especially from the Middle West and the Great Lakes states, drive to Florida. Great numbers of these visitors have never set foot outside the United States. Therefore a "foreign country" lying just 50 miles off the coastline of Florida, a "short takeoff and land" flight away, becomes a potent lure.

If you're not a fisherman or scuba diver, one of the most interesting experiences in Bimini is to cruise the cays that begin south of South Bimini. Each has its own special interest, beginning with Turtle Rocks and stretching to South Cat Cay (the latter which is uninhabited). Along the way you'll pass Holm Cay, Gun Cay, and North Cat Cay.

If you go to Bimini, you'll hear a lot of people mention **Cat Cay,** and you may want to go there. You can't stay overnight on the island, which lies 8 miles off South Bimini, unless you are a member of **Cat Cay Yacht Club,** with headquarters at 2,000 South Dixie Highway, Suite 205A, Miami, FL 33133 (tel. 305/858-6856). The initiation fee is $7,500. This is a privately owned island, attracting titans of industry and such famous families as the Goulds. It is for the exclusive use of Cat Cay Club members and their guests, who enjoy a magnificent golf course, a large marina, white-sand beaches, and club facilities such as restaurants and bars. Many wealthy Americans maintain homes on the island, which has a private airstrip (Chalk's International flies into the cay from Fort Lauderdale and Miami).

Don't confuse Cat Cay with Cat Island, far to the south (see Chapter XV).

THE MYTHS OF BIMINI

Bimini has long been shrouded in myths, none greater than the one that claims that the lost continent of Atlantis lies off the shores of North Bimini. This legend grew because of the weirdly shaped rock formations that lie submerged in about 30 feet of water near the shoreline. Pilots flying over North Bimini have reported what they envision as a "lost highway" under the sea. This myth continues, and many scuba divers are attracted to North Bimini to explore these rocks.

Ponce de León came to South Bimini looking for that legendary Fountain of Youth. He never found it, but people still come to South Bimini today in search of it. Near the turn of the century it was reported that a religious sect came here to "take the waters." Supposedly there was a bubbling fountain, or at least a spring, in those days.

If you arrive in South Bimini and seem interested enough, a local guide (for a fee) will be only too happy to show you "the exact spot" where the Fountain of Youth once bubbled.

Long before Ponce de León came this way, much less Hemingway, Arawak Indians had settlements on Bimini. It is also reported that the Seminoles came over from Florida to form settlements as well.

GETTING THERE

By Air

Although it lies closer to the Florida coastline than any of the other Bahamian islands, many Americans fly to Bimini, often by chartering a small aircraft or by flying their own plane. The island's only airstrip is at the southern tip of South Bimini, a time-consuming transfer and ferryboat ride away from Alice Town on North Bimini, site of most of the archipelago's hotels and yacht facilities.

The best way to avoid this transfer is with a small airline previously recommended in Chapter VII, "Planning a Trip to The Bahamas," **Chalk's International Airlines,** 1550 SW 43rd St., Fort Lauderdale, FL 33315 (tel. toll free 800/432-8807 in North America, 800/327-2521 in Florida—this is also the number for Paradise Island Airlines). Chalks has a fleet of 17-passenger amphibious aircraft that land in the waters near Alice Town three times a day. Flights depart from the calm waters near Watson Island Terminal, near downtown Miami.

Because the seaplane is likely to be crowded—in both summer and winter—the people at the Chalk's check-in desk ask that you always show up with a confirmed reservation, and get there at least an hour before departure, even though the flight is short.

There is a baggage allowance of only 30 pounds per passenger. But don't worry: there's no place in Bimini where you'll need to dress up. However, if you're carrying heavy travel or fishing gear, you'll be hit with overweight charges (the price is 45¢ per pound). In addition, Chalk's doesn't allow any hand luggage on board. Every piece of your luggage must be checked and weighed in.

Unfortunately, at certain peak periods the plane is fully booked and the passengers have a lot of excess luggage. In that event, your luggage may not accompany you on the flight, but should be on the next plane leaving Miami.

After you've checked in, don't fret about gate or seat numbers (this is a very small operation). After all those regulations and the trouble of getting there, you're airborne for only between 20 and 30 minutes before landing in the waters near Alice Town.

Flights depart from Watson Island three times a day, at 7:45am, 10am, and 3:15pm. The fare is $62.50 each way.

Another airline flying between the Florida mainland and Bimini is **Aero Coach**

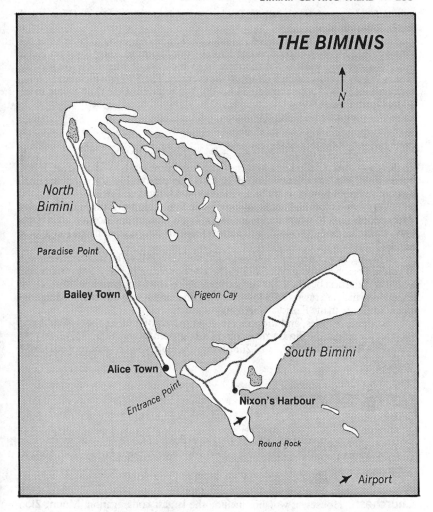

THE BIMINIS

N

North
Bimini

Paradise Point

Bailey Town •

Pigeon Cay

South Bimini

Alice Town •

Entrance Point

Nixon's Harbour •

Round Rock

✈ Airport

Aviation International, Inc., P.O. Box 21604, Fort Lauderdale, FL 33335 (tel. 305/359-1600, or toll free 800/327-0010). It offers one daily flight, departing around 4:20pm, from Miami for Bimini, and a different flight departing four days a week from Fort Lauderdale for Bimini, also around 4:20pm. The one-way fare is $72 from either city, with some discounts granted for round-trip reservations arranged and paid for more than a week in advance.

By Boat

In olden days, long before anyone ever heard of Chalk's International Airlines, the traditional way of going from Nassau to Bimini was by a slow-moving boat. That sea trip still exists. You can go by sea on the M/V *Bimini Mack,* leaving from Potter's Cay Dock in Nassau, stopping at Cat Cay and Bimini. The vessel leaves Nassau weekly on Thursday at 4pm, returning to Nassau weekly on Monday. For details of sailing (subject to change), call the Dockmaster at Potter's Cay Dock in Nassau (tel. 809/393-1064).

SeaEscape, 1080 Port Blvd., Miami, FL 33132 (tel. 305/379-0000, or toll free 800/432-0900), also offers day cruises from Miami to Alice Town on North Bimini. Cruises depart in the morning from the Port of Miami on Wednesday, Thursday, and Friday, with a return in the evening. The $90 fare includes a buffet, entertainment, and access to a small casino. You're given some time ashore to explore North Bimini.

GETTING AROUND

Most people, if they've taken my advice and traveled lightly to Bimini, can walk to their hotel from the point where the Chalk's seaplane lands in Alice Town. If not, then a small minibus will transport them for $3 per person. If you arrive at the small airport on South Bimini, it is a $5 taxi and ferry ride to Alice Town.

Very few visitors need a car on Bimini—in fact, there are no car-rental agencies. Most people walk to where they want to go. The walk is up and down King's Highway, which has no sidewalks. It's so narrow that two automobiles have a tough time squeezing by.

This highway, lined with low-rise buildings, splits Alice Town in North Bimini. If you're a beachcombing type, stick to the side bordering the Gulf Stream. It's here you'll find the best beaches. The harborside at Alice Town contains a handful of inns (many of which are reviewed below), along with marinas and docks unloading supplies. You'll see many Floridians arriving on yachts.

Scooters, bicycles, and mopeds are other means of getting about. You'll find bicycles for rent at the **Big Game Fishing Club and Hotel** (tel. 809/347-2391). At **Sawyer's Rentals** (tel. 809/347-2555), near the club, you can rent mopeds for $8 per hour.

FAST FACTS: BIMINI

Banks: For necessary transactions, the **Royal Bank of Canada** has a branch office in Alice Town (tel. 809/347-2031), open Monday through Friday from 9am to 1pm.

Churches: Houses of worship include the largest congregation, **Mount Zion Baptist,** P.O. Box 645 (tel. 809/347-2056), and the **Anglican Church Rectory,** P.O. Box 666 (tel. 809/347-2268).

Clothing: Don't bother with a coat and tie in Bimini. This place is *casual.* No one requires that you wear a jacket; however, if you're going to Bimini in the winter months, you'd better take along a windbreaker for those occasional chilly nights. At night such hotels as the Bimini Big Game Fishing Club & Hotel will not accept dinner guests in bathing suits or without shoes. The most comfortable clothes for relaxing you've got in your wardrobe would fit in just fine in Bimini.

Customs & Immigration: The Chalk's plane from Miami stops right near the Alice Town office of Customs and Immigration (tel. 809/347-2100) for The Bahamas. For many visiting mainlanders, Bimini will be their gateway to The Bahamas. The small size of this building is a proper introduction to the way things are done in the Family Islands. Outside of Nassau and Freeport, everybody thinks small here. There's only one Immigration officer, plus another Customs official.

In Miami you will have been handed a Bahamian Immigration Card, which you should have filled out. You must carry proof of your citizenship. For U.S. visitors, that most ideally would be a passport, but a voter registration card or a birth certificate will also do. The matter two require photo ID. Regrettably, many passengers cross over from Miami with only a driver's license, hoping that it will be sufficient proof of citizenship. *A driver's license will not be accepted by Immigration.*

The officer will ask the nature of your visit, the hotel at which you plan to stay, and the duration of your trip. Customs may or may not examine your baggage, and will ask if all items carried by you are for other than "personal or sporting" uses.

Drugs: The rum-runners of the Prohibition Era have now given way to a more deadly criminal: the smuggler of illegal drugs into the United States from The Bahamas. Because of its proximity to the U.S. mainland, Bimini, as is no secret to anyone, is now a major dropoff point for drugs, many of which have found their way here from Colombia, South America. If not intercepted by the U.S. Coast Guard, those drugs will find their way to the Florida mainland and eventually to the rest of the United States.

As I pointed out in the introduction to The Bahamas, buying and/or selling illegal drugs such as cocaine and marijuana in The Bahamas is an extremely risky business. You may be approached several times by pushers in Bimini, but make sure you don't get "pushed" into jail. If caught with any illegal drugs in Bimini, or elsewhere in The Bahamas, you will be apprehended and will face immediate imprisonment.

Incidentally, all sorts of undercover agents, particularly U.S. narcotics agents, are likely to be found on Bimini, often bearded and blending well into the social landscape.

Emergencies: To call the **police** or report a **fire,** dial **919.**

Laundry: Chances are, you won't need any dry cleaning done on Bimini, but you may need some laundry done. Most of the housekeeping staffs of the major hotels, for a fee, will be glad to do your laundry for you.

Mail: If you're sending mail back to the U.S., I suggest you skip the Bahamian postal service entirely and drop your letter off at Chalk's Airlines special basket. You can use U.S. postage stamps, and your mail will reach its mainland target far quicker than by the usual route.

Medical Care: There are a doctor, nurses, and a dentist on the island, as well as the **North Bimini Medical Clinic** (tel. 809/347-2210). However, for a medical emergency, patients are usually airlifted to either Miami or Nassau. Helicopters can land in the well-lit baseball field in North Bimini.

WHERE TO STAY

Accommodations in Bimini are extremely limited, and it's almost impossible to get a room during one of the big fishing tournaments unless you've reserved way in advance. Inns are cozy and simple, many often family owned and operated (chances are, your innkeeper's name will be Brown). No one puts on airs here: the dress code, even in the evening, is very simple and relaxed. From where you're staying in Alice Town, it's usually easy to walk to another hotel for dinner or drinks.

What the Symbols Mean

AP (American plan): Includes three meals a day (sometimes called full board or full pension).

BP (Bermuda plan): Popularized first in Bermuda, this option includes a full American breakfast (sometimes called an English breakfast).

CP (Continental plan): A Continental breakfast (that is, bread, jam, and coffee) is included in the room rate.

EP (European plan): This rate is always cheapest, as it offers only the room— no meals.

MAP (modified American plan): Sometimes called half board or half pension, this room rate includes breakfast and dinner (or lunch if you prefer).

Moderate

Bimini Big Game Fishing Club & Hotel, King's Highway, P.O. Box 609, Alice Town, Bimini, The Bahamas, or P.O. Box 523238, Miami, FL 33152 (tel. 809/347-2391, 305/447-7480 in Miami, or toll free 800/327-4149 in the U.S.), run by the Bacardi rum people, is the premier place for accommodations in Bimini. Filled with fishermen and the yachting crowd, the hotel is the largest place to stay on the island. It's a self-contained world with 35 well-furnished guest rooms in the main building, surrounded by 12 cottages and four luxurious penthouse apartments, the latter often housing VIPs. The general manager, Michael Kaboth, is the most experienced hotelier on the island, and he will see to your requests and help you ease your adjustment to Bimini, especially if you want to know about fishing in all its many forms. Established in 1946, the hotel places most of its accommodations in its central structure, where each unit is large and equipped with two beds. Everything is clean and comfortable, and the rooms are air-conditioned and have TVs. These accommodations have patios or porches opening onto a marina and the club's swimming pool. You can usually spot wet fishing clothes drying out in the hot Bimini sun. Guests can also play tennis.

Many of the sporting guests here prefer one of the ground-floor cottages instead. They are even more spacious than the standard bedrooms and have tiny kitchenettes with refrigerators—but they are not to be used for cooking, which is strictly forbidden. If you want to charcoal-broil your catch of the day, you will have to use one of the outdoor grills. Year-round EP rates for rooms are $134 to $144 daily for a single or double; an extra person pays $20. In one of the cottages, the EP charge for singles or doubles is $169 daily, rising to $295 in a penthouse.

A freshwater swimming pool is set aside for guests so that it won't be overrun with "day trippers." Even if you didn't arrive by yacht, you may want to stroll over to the dockmaster's office and look at those who did. Here is where incoming yachts must clear Bahamian Customs and Immigration. There is a 60-slip marina. The hotel is also the best place to go for food on the island, and it's an entertainment hub as well (see below). The best anglers at the big-game fishing tournaments stay here. Then it's next to impossible to get a room without reservations long in advance.

Bimini's Blue Water Resort Ltd., King's Highway, P.O. Box 601, Alice Town, Bimini, The Bahamas (tel. 809/347-2166). Blue Water is essentially a resort complex for sports fishermen and is one of the finest in The Bahamas, with complete dockside services. It has as its main building a white frame waterfront Bahamian guesthouse, the Anchorage, where Michael Lerner, the noted fisherman, used to live. It's at the top of the hill, with a dining room and bar from which you can look out onto the ocean. Its regular bedrooms contain double beds, air conditioning, TVs, wood-paneled walls, and white furniture with some sea-blue touches. Picture-window doors lead to private balconies. A swimming pool, buried in a tropical garden, with an adjoining refreshment bar, is also available. Across the highway are 12 more units opening onto the water, and encircling the upper and lower floors are covered latticework verandas, providing a comfortable area for watching sunsets. The Marlin Cottage, although much altered, was one of Hemingway's retreats in the 1930s. In honor of his memory, the hotel sponsors the Hemingway Billfish Tournament every March.

Rates, on the EP, are the same all year. A suite at the Anchorage costs $205 per day, and a single or double room goes for $90. The three-bedroom, three-bath Marlin Cottage, with large living room and two porches, rents for $285 per day.

Inexpensive

Brown's Hotel, King's Highway, P.O. Box 601, Alice Town, Bimini, The Bahamas (tel. 809/347-2227). Here you encounter the Brown name again. The hotel is run by Neville Brown, son of Harcourt Brown, who spawned a whole generation of Bimini innkeepers. A half block from the Chalk's Airline ramp, Brown's Hotel is a simple motel unit built right along the harbor, with 20 rooms and two apartments, each air-conditioned and containing a private bath. Accommodations are plain, but you can get good value for your money here: $55 for a double, $40 for a single. These EP rates are in effect year round. It's a favorite of economy-minded Bimini visitors, but it doesn't accept credit cards. There is a 22-slip marina, and fishing boats are for rent. Bahamian specialties are offered in the dining room, and there's talk of the "catch of the day" in the bar.

The Compleat Angler Hotel, King's Highway, P.O. Box 601, Alice Town, Bimini, The Bahamas (tel. 809/347-2122); or c/o Chalk's International Airlines, Watson Island, Miami, FL 33132, for reservations. Right on the main street, King's Highway, in the heart of Alice Town, the hotel was built in the '30s, when big-game fishing was at its peak. The building is designed like an old country house, employing Bahamian timber. The wood on the face of the building is from rum barrels used during the time of Prohibition. Pictures on the walls depict its history. Ernest Hemingway made the hotel his headquarters on and off from 1935 to 1937, and the room in which he stayed and wrote is still available to guests. He worked on *To Have and Have Not* here. At the bar, Ossie Brown, bartender, host, and manager, will be helpful.

This very small hotel has only 12 bedrooms. The lone single room rents for $70 a day year round; doubles cost $70 to $80. Each unit is air-conditioned, but there are no phones or TVs. Dress is casual in a relaxed and informal atmosphere. You can swim, dine, shop, or fish right at your doorstep, and fishing charters can be booked at the hotel.

Weech's Bimini Dock and Bay View Rooms, Kings Highway, P.O. Box 613, Alice Town, Bimini, The Bahamas (tel. 809/347-2028), has five double rooms, costing $50 per day on the EP all year for double occupancy, as well as an efficiency apartment accommodating five to six persons and costing $100 daily year round. Dockage is also offered.

WHERE TO DINE

Come to Bimini to feast on conch and the famous homemade Bimini bread. Outside the hotels (and even in the hotels) restaurants are simple, with a natural and to-be-expected emphasis on fresh seafood (often caught by the guests themselves). Of course, choice steaks and chops are flown in as well. Conch salad and conch fritters are everywhere.

All prices quoted are per person.

Expensive

Bimini's Seafood Haven, Bimini Big Game Fishing Club & Hotel, King's Highway, Alice Town (tel. 809/347-2391), is "the other" restaurant at the club (see below). It is less expensive and almost equally popular. Conch is a Bahamian delicacy, and you can taste it at lunch in conch fritters, conch salad, or conch chowder— even cracked conch, which is breaded like veal cutlet milanese. You can also order grouper fingers or barbecued back ribs, along with a selection of hamburgers and sandwiches. Check out the daily special. At night the temptation is wider, beginning with, for example, smoked game fish or a Bahamian gumbo, a spicy, chunky soup with conch, salt beef, and fresh vegetables. You can also order crab and callaloo (greens and crabmeat). At the salad bar you can make your own combinations with assorted dressings. From the Gulf Stream comes grilled wahoo or dolphin steak broiled to perfection and served with an herb butter. You can also order native lobster broiled just right or "smothered grouper," which is a Bahamian classic. If not fish, then Bimini roast chicken with a banana stuffing and cognac sauce is tempting, as are the finest American lamb chops, which will be grilled for you. Lunches, costing from $10, are served from 11:30am to 4:30pm. Dinners cost from $25 and are served nightly from 7 to 10:30pm.

Fisherman's Wharf, Bimini Big Game Fishing Club & Hotel, King's Highway, Alice Town (tel. 809/347-2391), consistently serves the finest food on the island in its curved dining room, which opens onto the pool. Both breakfast and dinner are offered here. Dining includes many island specialties such as crisp homemade Bimini bread and freshly caught kingfish, along with broiled local lobster and grouper meunière. Instead of french fries, why not go Bahamian and order peas 'n' rice with your meal? You can also make a selection from the buffet salad bar, and if you're tired of fish, the kitchen will usually serve you a steak, roast prime rib of beef, lamb chops, or stuffed Cornish game hen. Meals cost from $30. The restaurant is open daily. Breakfast is served from 7:30 to 11am, dinner from 7 to 10:30pm (there is no lunch). Before dinner, you can come and have a drink in the most sophisticated bar in Bimini. You don't have to dress up for dinner, but wear something! Sport clothes are fine, but not bathing attire.

Red Lion Pub, King's Highway, Alice Town (tel. 809/347-2259). This centrally located restaurant is far larger and more substantial than its simple russet-colored façade would imply. The dining room is in a large extension of the original pub, overlooking the marina in back. Its creative force lies in the person of Bimini-born Dolores Saunders, who worked as an employee of the place for 20 years before buying it in 1982. Many guests never venture beyond the cozy enclaves of the pub, whose bar fills the room nearest the front entrance. Above the cash register hangs a photograph of Stephanie Saunders, Dolores's daughter, who won the title of Miss Bimini in 1977. The well-prepared meals include the local fish of the day, cracked conch, barbecued ribs, baked grouper in foil, followed by either Key lime pie or banana cream pie. Tuesday through Sunday, lunch is served from 11:30am to 2:30pm, dinner from 6 to 11pm; the pub is open from 5pm to 1am. Meals cost from $25 each.

Moderate

Anchorage Dining Room, King's Highway, Alice Town (tel. 809/347-2166), run by Bimini's Blue Water Ltd., overlooks the harbor of Alice Town. At night, if you're seeking atmosphere "at the top of the hill," it has the jump on every other establishment. You can see the ocean through picture windows. Have a before-dinner drink in the bar. The modern, paneled room is filled with captain's chairs and Formica tables. You can visit the place for all three meals a day if that is your desire. You might begin with conch chowder, then follow with one of the tempting seafood dishes, including spiny broiled lobster or perhaps a chewy cracked conch. They also do fried Bahamian chicken and a New York sirloin. Lunch costs from $12 and dinner from $20. Open daily, the Anchorage serves breakfast from 7 to 11am, lunch from noon to 4pm, and dinner from 6 to 10pm.

Budget

Pricilla's Epicurean Delights, King's Highway, Alice Town (no phone). Its very grand name and its flavorful cuisine were invented by island entrepreneur Priscilla Bain. There's only one Formica-topped table inside for dining, so most visitors call to Ms. Bain through a windowless opening that looks out over the street in front of the Bimini Big Game Fishing Club & Hotel. Many of the yacht owners from the nearby marinas make it a point to enjoy at least one take-away meal prepared here. Most of it is prepared early in the morning at another location, then heated up in the simple cottage that houses Epicurean Delights. Only the conch fritters, said to be the best on the island, are deep-fried to order. Selling for $3 a dozen, they are the main dish of many a meal served on some of the ultraexpensive yachts moored nearby. You can order a complete platter of chicken or pork chops, beef stew, fried fish, or meatloaf for around $6, and any of these can be accompanied with pigeon peas 'n' rice, potato bread, macaroni salad, or potato salad. Cold beer is also available. Every day, food is dispensed from 11:30am to 6:30pm.

ATTRACTIONS

At the southern tip of North Bimini, **Alice Town** is all that many visitors ever see of the island. The hotel center of Bimini, it can be thoroughly explored in an hour or two.

Nothing is spic and span in Alice Town. First-timers are warned not to judge The Bahamas by Bimini. A yachting guide poses a question: "Would you judge the rest of America if you visited only Miami?"

If you're traversing the island, you may want to stop off at the Bimini **Straw Market,** speak with some of the Bahamians, and perhaps pick up a souvenir or take home one of their crafts.

King's Highway runs through the town and continues north. It's lined with houses, painted in such colors as gold, lime, buttercup yellow, and pink—pastels gleaming in the bright sunshine.

At some point you may notice the ruins of Bimini's first hotel, the Bimini Bay Rod and Gun Club. Built in the early 1920s, it did a flourishing business with 165 rooms and a casino until a hurricane later in that decade wiped it out. It was never rebuilt.

If you're on the trail of Papa Hemingway, you may want to visit **The Compleat Angler,** King's Highway, P.O. Box 601, Bimini, The Bahamas (tel. 809/347-2122), where there is a museum of Hemingway memorabilia. The collection of prints and writings describes the times he spent in Bimini, mainly from 1935 to 1937. The prints are posted in the sitting room downstairs. In case you didn't read it, Hemingway devoted nearly a third of his novel *Islands in the Stream* to Bimini; Cuba was one of the other islands. Much of this memorabilia makes interesting browsing. For example, in a page from *My Brother, Ernest Hemingway,* Leicester wrote of a fight he had with Ernest at the Bimini dock. After the fight, Leicester wrote, "Ernest was worried about what he had done. Back in his room at the Compleat Angler, he showered and found that he had ripped off the tops of two toenails on the dock." There is a wide variety of books by Hemingway in the library collection.

If you want to cross over to **South Bimini,** still, like Ponce de León, hopelessly looking for that Fountain of Youth, you can take a ferry, costing $3 and leaving every 20 minutes from Government Dock. The ferry ride takes about 10 minutes or so.

Once you land at South Bimini, you can rent a taxi to see the island's limited attractions for about $15. There's not a lot to see, but you are likely to hear some "tall tales" worth the cab fare.

One of the chief points of interest can be reached only by boat. It's the *Sapona,* which was built by Henry Ford during World War I. This huge concrete ship lies between South Bimini and Cat Cay. It was once a private club and a rum-runner's storehouse in the Roaring '20s. The 1929 hurricane blew it ashore, and in World War II, U.S. Navy pilots used it as a practice bomb range. Now spearfishermen are attracted to the ruins, looking for the giant grouper. The dive operations on Bimini include it in their repertoire.

WHERE TO SHOP

You might go to the **Bimini Big Game Fishing Club & Hotel,** King's Highway, Alice Town (tel. 809/347-2391), where you will find two shops on the grounds. The first is the Butler and Sands Liquor Store, which has some of the best liquor buys in town. At the other, Bubbles of Bimini, you can pick up jewelry, watches, and other gift items at tariffs often 20% to 30% (or even more) lower than Stateside prices. If you're a souvenir collector, ask at the front office (a one-room structure that's also the lobby) for T-shirts, sunglasses, coffee mugs, and Big Game Club hats.

SPORTS & RECREATION

There are fishermen and scuba divers who go nowhere but Bimini, reserving their favorite rooms in local inns every year. Otherwise, except for snorkeling, the people of Bimini don't "muck about" with many other water sports.

Snorkeling & Scuba

This has become an increasingly popular sport in the last 20 years. Visitors can snorkel above a wonderworld of black coral gardens and reefs, or go scuba diving, exploring the wrecks and the blue holes, plus a mystery formation on the bottom of the sea that many people claim is part of the lost continent of Atlantis. A cliff extends 2,000 feet down in Bimini waters—known for a breathtaking dropoff at the rim of the Continental Shelf, an underwater mountain. A major attraction for snorkelers and divers, not to mention fish, is the *Sapona,* lying hard aground in 15 feet of water ever since it was blown there by a hurricane in 1929. In the heyday of the roaring '20s, it was a ship that was a private club and speakeasy. This rum-runner plied the Bimini coast, often with visitors to the Bimini Bay Rod and Gun Club, who were attracted to its casino.

The people to see are Bill and Nowdla Keefe at their **Bimini Undersea Adventures,** King's Highway, Alice Town, Bimini, The Bahamas (tel. 809/347-2089). Full-day snorkeling trips cost $25. Scuba rates are $35 for a one-tank dive, $50 for a two-tank dive, and $60 for a three-tank dive. All-inclusive dive packages are also available. For further information or reservations, the Keefes can be reached through P.O. Box 21766, Fort Lauderdale, FL 33335 (tel. 305/763-2188, or toll free 800/327-8150).

Sportfishing

Bimini is called the "Big Game Fishing Capital of the World," and Ernest Hemingway, above all others, has given fame to the sport practiced here. But Zane Grey came this way too, as did Howard Hughes. Richard Nixon used to fish and then relax docked here aboard the posh cruiser of his friend, Miamian Bebe Rebozo. In the trail of Hemingway, fishermen today still flock to fish in the Gulf Stream and the Bahama Banks.

Of course, everyone's after the "big one," and a lot of world records have been set in this area: marlin, sailfish, swordfish, wahoo, grouper, and tuna. Fishing folk can spincast for panfish, and can boat snapper, yellowtail, and kingfish. Many experts consider stalking the shallow flats for bonefish, long a pursuit of baseball great Ted Williams, to be the toughest challenge in the sport.

Five charter boats are available in Bimini for big-game and little-game fishing, with some center console boats rented for both bottom and reef angling. At least eight bonefishing guides are available, and experienced fishermen who have made repeated visits to Bimini know the particular skills of each of these men who take you for a half or full day of "fishing in the flats," as bonefishing is termed. Most skiffs hold two anglers, and part of the fun in hiring a local guide is to hear their fish stories and other island lore. If they tell you that 16-pound bonefish have turned up, don't think it's invented. Such catches have been documented.

Reef and bottom fishing are easier than bonefishing, and can be more productive of results. There are numerous species of snapper and grouper to be found, as well as amberjack. This is the simplest and least expensive boat fishing, as you need only a local guide, a little boat, tackle, and a lot of bait. Sometimes you can negotiate to go out bottom fishing with a Bahamian, but chances are he'll ask you to pay for the boat fuel for his trouble. That night, back at your Bimini inn, the cook will serve you the red snapper or grouper you caught that day. (At least you'll know it's fresh.)

Most hotel owners will tell you to bring your own fishing gear to Bimini. A couple of small shops sell some items, but you'd better bring major equipment with you. Bait, of course, can be purchased locally.

At the **Bimini Big Game Fishing Club & Hotel,** King's Highway, P.O. Box 699, Alice Town (tel. 809/347-2391), you can charter a 41-foot Hatteras at $600 for a full day, $350 for a half day of fishing. A Bertram, either 31 feet or 28 feet, will cost $400 for a full day, $275 for a half.

Bimini Blue Water Ltd., King's Highway, P.O. Box 627, Alice Town (tel. 809/347-2166), offers for charter a 28-foot Bertram with tackle and crew for $450 or $350 for a full or half day, respectively.

Brown's Marina, King's Highway, P.O. Box 601, Alice Town (tel. 809/347-2227), has full marina facilities, including a restaurant and bar. Here you can charter boats for deep-sea fishing and reef and shark fishing, costing $350 for a full day or $225 for a half day.

Tennis

The **Bimini Big Game Fishing Club & Hotel,** King's Highway, Alice Town (tel. 809/347-2391), has hard-surface courts, which are complimentary to hotel guests and members. The courts are lit for night play, and you can purchase balls at the club.

EVENING ENTERTAINMENT

You can dance to a Goombay beat or try to find some disco music. Most people have a leisurely dinner, drink a lot in one of the local taverns, and go back to their hotel rooms by midnight so they can get up early to continue their pursuit of the elusive "big one" the next morning on some fishing boat. Every bar in Alice Town is likely to claim that it was "Papa's favorite." He did hit quite a few of them, in fact. Most drinks cost $3.50, and there's rarely a cover charge anywhere unless some special entertainment is being offered.

One of the almost mandatory requirements, to firmly establish you on Bimini soil, is to have a drink at the **End of the World Bar,** King's Highway, Alice Town (tel. 809/347-2370). When you get there, you may think you're in the wrong place. The place may be famous, but it isn't the Ritz. It's just a waterfront shack with sawdust on the floor. It was the late congressman from Harlem, Adam Clayton Powell, who put this bar on the map. Between stints in Washington battling Congress and preaching at the Abyssinian Baptist Church in Harlem, the controversial congressman might be found sitting at a table in this bar. The world knew where to find him. (One man who had pressing business with Powell couldn't get an appointment with him in Washington. He found it easier to fly to Bimini, where he found Powell very approachable.) Regardless of what his fellow congressmen thought of Powell, he was a hero locally, and many people of Bimini still remember him. For example, Brown's Hotel to this day still has plaques honoring Powell for his contributions to big-game fishing. Maybe this place doesn't attract the media attention it did in Powell's heyday, when the press swarmed all over the bar, but it's still going strong as a local favorite, and everybody takes a felt marker and signs his or her name. It's open daily from 11am to 3am.

If you're a fisherman (or woman), or accompanying a fishing aficionado, chances are you'll head for the **Harbour Lounge** of the Bimini Big Game Fishing Club & Hotel, King's Highway, Alice Town (tel. 809/347-2391), for your sundowner. In some cases, that "sundowning" can last until midnight. If you're a first-time visitor, ask for Mr. Cooper's locally celebrated rum punch. Made with Bacardi rums, it's *the* drink to order here. The outside bar is romantically called "Rum Keg," and beginning at lunchtime it's open throughout the day and evening. Adjacent to the main dining room, the major bar opens at 6pm. When are closing hours? Management says the bars are open "until . . ."

The favorite watering hole for every visiting Hemingway buff is **The Compleat Angler Hotel,** King's Highway, Alice Town (tel. 809/347-2122). Ossie Brown, the bartender (he's also the manager), is said to make the best planter's punch in The Bahamas. He challenges anyone to make a better one. "I guarantee it can only be equaled," he says. Nightly entertainment by a calypso band turns this place into a real island hot spot, featuring Goombay drinks from 9pm to 1am. If you've booked a room here, remember that it's only for night owls. The place, as mentioned, is filled with Hemingway memorabilia, and it's open daily from 11am "until . . ."

---

2. The Berry Islands

A dangling chain of cays and islets on the eastern edge of the Great Bahama Bank, the unspoiled and serene Berry Islands begin 35 miles northeast of New Providence (Nassau), 150 miles east of Miami. This 30-island archipelago is known to sailors, fishermen, yachtsmen, Jack Nicklaus, and a Rockefeller or two, as well as the beachcombers who explore its uninhabited reaches.

As a center of fishing, the Berry Islands are second only to Bimini. At Chub Cay you can charter boats for fishing trips or just plain cruising. At the tip of the Tongue of the Ocean, called TOTO, world-record-setting big-game fish are found, plus endless bonefish flats. Scuba diving is arranged for visitors on the semiprivate island of Chub Cay, and a 250-yard driving range attracts golf buffs. There is a fine sheltered marina for yachts of any size.

In the "Berries" you can find your own tropical paradise islet, enjoying, totally unmolested and sans wardrobe, the white-sand beaches against a palm-fringed shore and a backdrop of green foliage.

Some of the best shell collecting in The Bahamas is found on the beaches of the Berry Islands and in their shallow-water flats.

The main islands are, beginning in the north, Great Stirrup Cay, Cistern Cay, Great Harbour Cay, Anderson Cay, Haines Cay, Hoffmans Cay, Bonds Cay, Sandy Cay, Whale Cay, and Chub Cay. (As of this writing, Great Harbour Cay and Chub Cay are the only places within the Berry Islands where accommodations can be recommended.)

The largest island within the Berry Islands is Great Harbour Cay, which sprawls over 3,800 acres of sand, rock, and scrub. The development here received a great deal of publicity when Douglas Fairbanks, Jr., was connected with its board. It became a multimillion-dollar resort for jet-setters who occupied waterfront town houses and villas overlooking the golf course or marina. There are 7½ miles of almost solitary beachfront. Once Cary Grant, Brigitte Bardot, and other stars romped on this beach.

During the reign of William IV, that spit of land known as Great Stirrup Cay figured in Bahamian history. The king ordered the building of Williamstown (named after himself, of course). It was to be a resettlement post for homeless slaves.

A Custom House was erected, the ruins of which remain today. Obviously, the former slaves sought greener cays, or whatever, elsewhere, because the settlement was later abandoned.

Bond's Cay, a bird sanctuary in the south, and tiny Frazer's Hog Cay (stock is raised here) are both privately owned. An English company used to operate a coconut and sisal plantation on Whale Cay, also near the southern tip.

Sponge fishermen and their families inhabit some of the islands. One of the very small cays, lying north of Frazer's Hog Cay and Whale Cay, has, in my opinion, the most unappetizing name in the Bahamian archipelago: Cockroach Cay.

GETTING THERE

The deluxe way to go is on your own private plane, which will land at one of several private airstrips. The emphasis, as you'll find in the Berry Islands, is on the word "private." That's how many of the landowners would like to keep it. After all, they "discovered" the Berry Islands as a retreat from civilization. However, as the world tourist march continues, the Berry Islands are increasingly gaining attention from visitors.

Chub Cay and Great Harbour Cay are both official points of entry for The Bahamas if you're flying from a foreign territory such as the United States. You can fly to either the Chub Cay Airport or the Great Harbour Cay airstrip. **Trans Island Airways** (tel. 809/327-8329) offers two flights a day from Nassau to Great Harbour Cay. **Stanair** (tel. 407/386-5748) also operates a charter service from Palm Beach to Great Iarbour Cay. To reach Chub Cay, you can fly on charters arranged by the **Chub Cay Club** (tel. 305/445-7830 in Florida, or toll free 800/662-8555). It has flights from both Fort Lauderdale and Miami.

If you're contemplating the **mailboat** sea-voyage route, the M/V *Champion II* leaves Potter's Cay Dock in Nassau weekly on Thursday, heading for the Berry Islands. Inquire at the Potter's Cay Dock for an up-to-the-minute report (contact the Dockmaster at 809/393-1064).

FAST FACTS: THE BERRY ISLANDS

Medical Care: The **Great Harbour Cay Medical Clinic** is at Bullock's Harbour on Great Harbour Cay (tel. 809/322-2400).

Police: The **Police Station** is also at Bullock's Harbour, Great Harbour Cay (tel. 809/322-2344).

GREAT HARBOUR CAY

The largest concentration of people—an estimated 500 residents—live on the most populated island of the Berry chain, Great Harbour Cay. Its main settlement is Bullock's Harbour, which might be called the "capital of the Berry Islands." The cay is about 1½ miles wide and some 8 miles long. There isn't much in town: a grocery store and some local restaurants. Most visitors arrive to stay at the Great Harbour Cay Resort (see below), outside of town. Fishermen are especially fond of the place.

Reached from Miami in about an hour, 150 miles to the west, or in half a day by power boat, Great Harbour Cay lies between Grand Bahama Island and New Providence (Nassau), and is 60 miles northwest of Nassau. Unlike most islands in The Bahamas, the island isn't flat but contains rolling hills.

Deep-sea fishing possibilities abound here, including billfish, dolphin, king mackerel, and wahoo. Light-tackle bottom fishing is also good, netting yellowtail snapper, barracuda, and trigger fish, as well as plenty of grouper. Bonefishing here is considered among the best in the world.

The Great Harbour Cay marina is called "world class," with some 80 slips and all the amenities. Some of Florida's fanciest yachts pull in here. When you tire of fishing, there are 8 miles of white-sand beaches. There is also a nine-hole golf course, designed by Joe Lee, plus four clay tennis courts.

Where to Stay & Dine

What the Symbols Mean

AP (American plan): Includes three meals a day (sometimes called full board or full pension).

BP (Bermuda plan): Popularized first in Bermuda, this option includes a full American breakfast (sometimes called an English breakfast).

CP (Continental plan): A Continental breakfast (that is, bread, jam, and coffee) is included in the room rate.

EP (European plan): This rate is always cheapest, as it offers only the room— no meals.

MAP (modified American plan): Sometimes called half board or half pension, this room rate includes breakfast and dinner (or lunch if you prefer).

Great Harbour Cay, P.O. Box N-918, Nassau, The Bahamas (tel. 809/322-4782). It rents eight luxurious villas and eight town houses. The three-level waterfront townhouses overlook the marina, each with its own private dock, topped off with a garage and patio. Townhouses have a light, airy feeling, with some 1,600 square feet of air-conditioned living space. Each has two bedrooms and 2½ baths, and is suitable for up to six people. Fully equipped kitchens are featured. Villas, covered in cedar shakes, have ceramic-tile floors and a Mediterranean-type decor. They can be rented in various configurations—from studio apartments to three-bedroom units. Daily maid service is available by request. On a year-round basis, townhouses for two rent for $150 daily, or $200 for three; and beach villas begin at $70 daily for a one-bedroom studio, going up to $250 for a two-bedroom suite. Weekly and monthly rates are also available.

Dining facilities include the Beach Club, serving breakfast and lunch; Basil's Bar and Restaurant at the end of the marina, serving three meals a day; and the Tamboo Club, at the west end of the marina—open Tuesday through Saturday for drinks and dinner only.

CHUB CAY

The southernmost cay in the Berry Island chain, Chub Cay, one of the best diving resorts in The Bahamas, is an exclusive retreat attracting members, although the general public is accepted as well. It was once a strictly private facility, however. When the island was originally purchased, there were no native inhabitants. Fifty-five Bahamians were brought in, and housing had to be provided for them. The island is really a tranquil little sandspit.

There is a liquor store on the island, but you can also bring in 1 quart of liquor from a duty-free shop before you board the plane. Remember to arrive light: the plane allows approximately 50 pounds of baggage, and that's it!

The water temperature around Chub Cay averages 80° to 85° Fahrenheit year round at all depths. There is only a small tide change, and there is no swell or current noticeable.

Many divers have waxed enthusiastic over the dive spots of the Berry Islands, including Chub Wall and Mamma Rhoda Rock, as well as the caverns, reefs, caves, and tunnels. It's important to remember that it is forbidden by Bahamian authorities to bring back coral as souvenirs. It violates local ecological laws to take anything from the sea for purposes other than obtaining food. The government wants to preserve the natural beauty of the reefs of the Berry Islands. But you're allowed to look all you want.

Where to Stay & Dine

The only place to stay is **Chub Cay Club** (for reservations, write Chub Cay Club, P.O. Box 661067, Miami Springs, FL 33266; tel. 305/445-7830. There is no mail delivery to Chub Cay through The Bahamas.) This is one of the finest fishing resorts in the world. Adjacent to the marina and just a step away from the dining room and lounge, the 15 Yacht Club rooms for nonmembers are tastefully decorated and have TV, and air conditioning. The rooms overlook a freshwater swimming pool and cost $85 per day year round. MAP is another $35 daily. About 80 slips within the marina welcome the yachts of nonmembers, the rest being devoted to the exclusive use of certain long-standing associates of the club. There is a Laundromat. The club has the Flying Bridge Restaurant; the food is excellent, especially the well-prepared Bahamian lobster, along with good steaks from the States.

Sports & Recreation

The **Chub Cay Club** works in association with an on-the-premises scuba facility, one of six branches of the internationally recognized Neal Watson Undersea Adventures chain. Since the majority of clients at Chub Cay are interested in either fishing or diving, most reservations for the hotel are arranged as part of dive packages, which are sold directly by Undersea Adventures rather than by the hotel itself. The organization offers a pair of large mono-hulled dive boats, all the necessary equipment, and a team of experienced PADI-registered instructors who know firsthand the amazing variety of dive spots already referred to within this chapter. The resort welcomes beginners, and experienced divers can earn PDIC registration, which is required for anyone interested in becoming a registered scuba instructor. The facility includes a full-service underwater photography program, with strobe and camera rentals available.

Arrangements for bonefishing are usually made on location once clients reach Chub Cay. It is said that one of the several reasons why fishing is so good in the Berry Islands is because bait fish are swept up by the underwater currents of TOTO (Tongue of the Ocean). Their hungry pursuers include dolphins, mako sharks, barracudas, wahoos, and the 300-pound blue marlins described by Hemingway in *Islands in the Stream.* Unknown to these big fish, yet another hunter—man—is waiting.

For more information about fishing at Chub Cay, and for reservations and package discounts (which can, depending on your wishes, include accommodations at the Chub Cay Club, meals, and prearranged scuba), contact **Neal Watson's Undersea Adventures,** 700 SW 34th St., Suite 2, Fort Lauderdale, FL 33315 (tel. 305/359-0065, or toll free 800/327-8150).

3. Andros

The largest island in The Bahamas, Andros is also one of the largest unexplored tracts of land in the Western Hemisphere. Mostly flat, its 2,300 square miles are riddled with lakes and creeks, and most of the local population, who still indulge in fire dances and go on wild boar hunts on occasion, live along the shore.

One of the most mysterious islands in The Bahamas, Andros is 100 miles long and 40 miles wide. Its interior is a dense, tropical forest, really rugged bush and mangrove country. The marshy and relatively uninhabited west coast is called "The Mud," and the east coast is paralleled for 120 miles by the second-largest underwater barrier reef in the world. The reef drops to over a mile into The Tongue of the Ocean, or TOTO. On the eastern shore, this "tongue" is 142 miles long and 1,000 fathoms deep.

Lying 170 miles southeast of Miami and 30 miles west of Nassau, Andros, although spoken of as if it were one island, is actually divided into three main land areas: North Andros, Middle Andros, and South Andros. Ferries, operated free by the Bahamian government, ply back and forth over the waters separating Mangrove Cay from South Andros. At the end of the road in North Andros, private arrangements can be made to have a boatman take you over to Mangrove Cay. In spite of its size, Andros is very thinly populated, its local residents numbering around 5,000, although the tourist population swells it a bit. The temperature range here averages from 72° to 81° Fahrenheit.

The Spaniards, who came this way in the 16th century looking for Indian slaves, called the island La Isla del Espíritu Santo or the "Island of the Holy Spirit," but the name didn't catch on, although it came from the belief that the Holy Spirit dwells over water, with which Andros is abundantly supplied. It constantly ships the precious liquid to water-scarce New Providence (Nassau) in barges.

The name used for the island today is believed by some experts to have come from Sir Edmund Andros, a British commander.

You won't find the western side of Andros much written about in yachting guides, as it is almost unapproachable by boat because of the tricky shoals. The east coast, however, is studded with little villages, and hotels have been built here that range from simple guest cottages to dive resorts to fishing camps. "Creeks" (I'd call them rivers) intersect the island at its midpoint. Called "bights," in the main they have three channels. Their width ranges from 5 to 25 miles, and they are dotted with tiny cays and islets. There are miles of unspoiled beach along the eastern shore.

Few people draw comparisons between overly developed Paradise Island and underdeveloped Andros. However, their tourism industry has a common ancestor, Dr. Axel Wenner-Gren, the Swedish industrialist introduced in Chapter IX on Paradise Island. In addition to investing in what was then Hog Island (renamed Paradise Island by Huntington Hartford), Dr. Wenner-Gren also built the Andros Yacht Club, to the south of Fresh Creek on Andros. That now defunct club began to attract the island's first tourists following World War II.

The fishing at Andros is famous, establishing records for blue marlin caught offshore. Skindivers report that the coral reefs are among the most beautiful in the world.

A word of warning: If you visit Andros, be sure to take along plenty of mosquito repellent.

THE MYTHS OF ANDROS

One of the myths of the island is that aborigines live in the interior. These were thought to be a lost tribe of Arawak Indians—remnants of the archipelago's original inhabitants, who were exterminated by the Spanish centuries ago. However, low-flying planes, looking for evidence of human settlements, have not turned up any indication to support this far-fetched assertion. But who can dispute that chickcharnies (red-eyed Bahamian elves with three toes, feathers, and beards) live on the island? The demise of Neville Chamberlain's ill-fated sisal plantation was blamed on these mischievous devils.

The chickcharnie once struck terror into the hearts of superstitious islanders. They were supposed to live in the depths of the Androsian wilderness, making their nests in the tops of two intertwined palm trees. Tales are told of how many a woodsman in the old days endured hardship and misery because he thoughtlessly felled the trees that served as stilts for a chickcharnie nest. Like the leprechauns of Ireland, the chickcharnies belong solely to Andros. They are the Bahamian version of the elves, goblins, fairies, and duppies of other lands. Children may be threatened with them if they fail to behave, and business or domestic calamity is immediately attributed to their malevolent activities.

The origin of the legend is shrouded in mystery. One story has it that the tales began in the late 19th century when a Nassau hunting enthusiast who wanted to protect his duck-hunting grounds in Andros invented the malicious elves to frighten off unwanted interlopers. Another has it that the myth was brought to The Bahamas by bands of Seminoles fleeing Florida in the early 1880s to escape the depredations of white settlers. Some of the Seminoles settled on the northern tip of Andros. But the most probable explanation is one that traces the chickcharnie to a once-living creature—an extinct 3-foot-high flightless barn owl (*Tyto pollens*)—which used to inhabit The Bahamas and West Indies.

According to the Bahamas National Trust, the local conservation authority, such a bird, "screeching, hissing and clacking its bills in characteristic barn owl fashion, hopping onto its victims or pouncing on them from low tree limbs, would have been a memorable sight. And a frightening one."

The species may have survived here into historical times, and Andros, being the largest Bahamian land mass, was probably able to sustain *Tyto pollens* longer than the smaller islands, where the necessary prey species died off as the land area shrank during the present interglacial period. It is probable that the early settlers on Andros encountered such beasts, and it's probable, too, that *Tyto pollens* was the inspiration for the chickcharnie, a poor substitute for the real thing.

Nevertheless, the tales are still told in Andros, and there is no doubt that the chickcharnie will live on as a fascinating component of The Bahamas' diverse cultural legacy.

GETTING THERE

When you arrive somewhere in The Bahamas, you say, "Ya reach!"

By Air

Reaching Andros is not that difficult. **Bahamasair** (tel. toll free 800/222-4262 in the U.S.) has flights to the airports at Andros Town and San Andros twice daily. Four weekly flights land at Congo Town on South Andros. It is only a 15-minute flight from Nassau to, say, Andros Town. There is also a small airstrip on Mangrove Cay. Flight schedules are subject to change.

If you're going to Small Hope Bay Lodge, there is a 1-hour flight service from Fort Lauderdale to Andros Town.

Warning: Make sure you know where you're going in Andros. For example, if you land in South Andros and you've been booked in a hotel at Nicholl's Town, you'll find connections nearly impossible at times (both ferryboats and a rough haul across a bad highway).

By Boat

Many mocals, along with a few adventurous visitors, use the mailboats as a means of reaching Andros, the trip taking 5 to 7 hours across some beautiful waters.

North Andros is serviced by the M/V *Lisa J. II,* a mailboat departing from Potter's Cay Dock in Nassau, heading for Morgan's Bluff, Mastic Point, and Nicholl's Town. It departs Nassau on Wednesday, returning to Nassau on Tuesday.

To reach Central Andros, you have to take the M/V *Andros Express,* departing from Market Wharf in Nassau. The boat goes to Fresh Creek, Bering Point, Blanket Sound, and Stafford Creek, leaving Nassau on Wednesday. It returns to Nassau on Sunday.

For details about sailing and costs, contact the Dockmaster at Potter's Cay Dock in Nassau (tel. 809/393-1064).

GETTING AROUND

Transportation can be a big problem on Andros. If you have to go somewhere, it's best to use one of the local taxi drivers.

What *cars* there are to rent are in North Andros. These are few and far between, owing to the high costs of shipping cars to Andros. The weather also takes a great toll on the cars that are brought in, so no car-rental agencies are represented. Your best bet is to ask at your hotel to see what's available. Once you've arrived on the island, expect to spend at least $60 or more per day for a car. It's not really recommended that you drive on Andros, because roads are mainly unpaved, in bad condition, and gasoline stations are few and far between. However, if you'd like to give a car a try, call **Bereth Rent-A-Car,** Fresh Creek (tel. 809/368-2102), or **Basil Martin,** Mastic Point (tel. 809/329-3169).

If you'd like to attempt the roads of Andros on a **scooter or bicycle,** call Andros Beach Hotel & Villas, at Nicholl's Town on North Andros (tel. 809/329-2582), or **Small Hope Bay Lodge,** Fresh Creek (tel. 809/368-2014), and see if one is available for rent.

There are no guided tours as such on Andros. This is do-it-yourself country. If you'd like to see North Andros by car, it's best to try to put together a party at your hotel, at least four or five to share the costs. If you don't know any of your fellow guests, perhaps the hotel manager will ask around for you or advise you. The reason is simple: a half-day tour is likely to cost in the neighborhood of $180, perhaps more if you have a lot of stopovers. The party will help you share not only the ride, but the huge expense.

On South Andros and Mangrove Cay there will be less to see. You can do the job in 1½ hours by taxi. Again, it's best to share. Prices always have to be negotiated locally.

From the Airport

Taxi drivers—what few there are—know when the planes from Nassau are going to land, and they drive out to the airports, hoping to drum up some business. If two couples, or whatever combination, are heading in the same direction, taxis are most often shared. Figure on a rate of at least $1.50 a mile, maybe more. A typical fare from Andros Town Airport to Small Hope Bay Lodge is about $15.

FAST FACTS: ANDROS

Banks: These are rare creatures on Andros. There is one, the **Canadian Imperial Bank of Commerce** (tel. 809/368-2071), in Fresh Creek. It is open Wednesday from 10:30am to 2:30pm.

Churches: Protestant denominations are represented on the island. If you want to attend, ask at your hotel where the nearest place of worship is. Outsiders are usually warmly welcomed and received in local congregations.

Clothing: Dress is casual, but don't come to Andros expecting to catch up on your dry cleaning. If you need shirts and blouses washed and ironed, ask at your hotel. Even if they don't have a service themselves, they usually know someone in the community who "takes in wash," so to speak.

Hair Care: Women should be prepared to do their own hair, unless someone at a hotel tells them about a local woman "who's studying to be a beautician." Men can get a haircut—and that's it.

Mail: The island has no big post office as such, although there is a post-handling

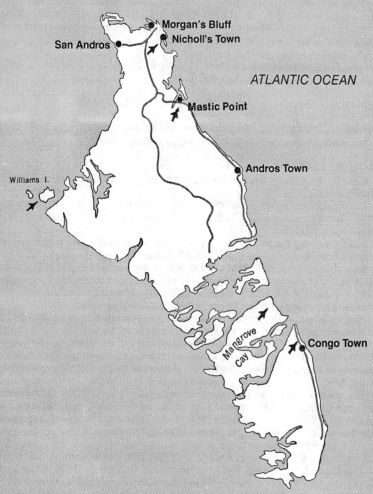

ANDROS

N

Morgan's Bluff

Nicholl's Town

San Andros

ATLANTIC OCEAN

Mastic Point

Andros Town

Williams I.

Mangrove Cay

Congo Town

✈ Airport

office in the Commissioner's Office in Nicholl's Town on North Andros (tel. 809/329-2278). Hotel desks will sell you Bahamian stamps. Make sure you mark cards and letters airmail; otherwise, you'll return home before they do, as they're put on a "slow boat to China," in this case the mailboat to Nassau. Each little hamlet in Andros has a store that serves as the post office, just as it was in America of long ago.

Medical Care: Government-run clinics are at Mastic Point (tel. 809/329-3055) and at Lowe Sound (tel. 809/329-2055), all on North Andros. On Central Andros, there is a health center at Fresh Creek (tel. 809/368-2038), with a doctor and a nurse. Bring along whatever drugs (legal ones) or medicines you'll need while visiting Andros. Local supplies are very limited.

Police: Call the **police** on North Andros at **919,** on Central Andros at **368-2626,** and on South Andros at **329-4620.**

Telephone: Service is available only at the front desks of hotels.

Traveler's Checks: Your hotel probably will be able to cash traveler's checks for you, but if not, there is one bank on Andros (see "Banks," above).

WHERE TO STAY

Chances are, your hotel will be in North Andros, in either Andros Town or Nicholl's Town.

North Andros is the most developed of the three main Andros islands. **Nicholl's Town** is a colorful old settlement with some 600 people and several places serving local foods.

Most visitors come to Nicholl's Town to buy supplies at a shopping complex. The major hotel is the Andros Beach Hotel & Villas.

Directly to the south is **Mastic Point,** which was founded in 1781. If you ask around, you'll be shown to a couple of concrete-sided dives that offer spareribs and Goombay music. To the north of Nicholl's Town is **Morgan's Bluff,** a Sir Henry Morgan (a pirate later knighted by the British monarch) namesake.

Andros Town, with its abandoned docks, is another hamlet, lying about a 29-mile drive south of Nicholl's Town. Here the major hotel is Small Hope Bay Lodge. On the opposite side of the water is **Coakley Town.** If you're driving, before you get to Andros Town you may want to stop and spend some restful hours on the beach at the hamlet of **Staniard Creek,** another old settlement on Andros. There's a South Seas aura here.

The major reason most visitors come to Andros Town is either to stay at the already-mentioned Small Hope Bay Lodge or to avail themselves of its facilities. The biggest retail industry, Androsia, is in the area too. The scuba diving—minutes away on the barrier reef—is what lures the world to this tiny place. Many people come here just for the shelling.

Continuing south, **Central Andros** is smaller than either North or South Andros. It's also the least built-up. The island is studded with hundreds upon hundreds of palm trees. Queen's Highway runs along the eastern coastline, but the only thing about this road that's regal is its name. In some 4½ miles you can practically travel the island. Talk about sleepy—this place drowses, and for that very reason many people come here to get away from it all. They don't find much in the way of accommodations. There are a few guesthouses a half mile from the Mangrove Cay Airport. Boating, fishing, scuba diving, and snorkeling are the popular sports practiced here.

Another hamlet (don't blink as you pass through or you'll miss it) is **Moxey Town,** where you'll see the fishermen unloading conch.

Finally, **South Andros** takes in the wonderfully named **Congo Town,** location of Emerald Palms by the Sea Hotel. The pace here is that of an escargot on a marathon. The Queen's Highway, lined in part with pink-and-white conch shells, runs on for about 25 miles or so. The island, as yet undiscovered, has some of the best beaches in The Bahamas, and you can enjoy them almost by yourself.

Cargill Creek

Cargill Creek Lodge, Cargill Creek (tel. 809/329-5129, or toll free 800/628-1447 in the U.S.). The newest and best-accessorized hotel on Andros, this is the creative statement of Stanley Bain, a local resident who made his fortune as a contractor and developer in Nassau before returning to his hometown to build his own hotel. It opened in 1990 on a 7-acre tract, most of which is devoted to the cultivation of fruit trees. The hotel consists of a complex of white stucco buildings with marine-blue trim set directly on the beachfront.

Each of the 11 bedrooms and three outlying cottages contains satellite-reception TV, air conditioning, and a bathroom, and each is outfitted in Florida-tropical furniture in colors of green, yellow, and white. The cottages contain small kitchenettes, two full bathrooms, two bedrooms, a sitting room, and all the amenities of the regular single or double rooms. Throughout the year, with three daily meals (AP) included, singles cost $140, doubles cost $220, and cottages cost $440, an expense usually borne by four occupants.

Meals are served in a pleasantly airy restaurant, trimmed with Andros Island cedar, set close to a waterfront pier. A lounge/game room does a healthy percentage of its business with the local community. Fishing trips on boats, which range in length from 16 to 36 feet, can be arranged, either on site or as part of a fishing/hotel package prearranged in advance. For reservations and information on fishing, diving, or land-only rates, contact **Angler Adventures,** P.O. Box 872, Old Lyme, Connecticut 06371 (tel. 203/434-9624, or toll free 800/628-1447).

Andros Town & Fresh Creek

Small Hope Bay Lodge (tel. 809/368-2014, or toll free 800/223-6961 in the U.S.; write c/o P.O. Box 21667, Fort Lauderdale, FL 33335), at Fresh Creek, one of the most important underwater centers in The Bahamas, is an intimate and cozy cottage colony on the beach, engulfed by tall coconut palms. Canadian-born Richard Birch created the resort, which now is the oldest dive operation on the island. Its name, Small Hope, shouldn't deter you from a vacation here. It comes from a prediction (so far, accurate) from Henry Morgan, the pirate, who claimed there was "small hope" of anyone finding the treasure he's buried on Andros. There is a spacious living and dining room, as opposed to a "lobby." Here guests congregate for conversational get-togethers and to share meals. Andros Town airport is a 10-minute, $12 taxi ride from the lodge. The beach is at the doorstep, and if you want to get a tan all over, you'll be shown a private terrace surrounded by a thatched palm fence. With 20 cabins, a "full house" means only 40 guests at the lodge. Cabins are of coral rock and Andros pine, decorated with batik Androsia fabrics. Honeymooners like to order breakfast served on their waterbed.

The hotel operates on the all-inclusive plan, including three meals a day. Year-round charges for one night are $130 per person daily based on double occupancy. For guest groups of three or more, the resort has a limited number of family cottages, featuring two separate rooms connected by a single bath. Single travelers have a choice of staying in a family cottage with private accommodations (which is the same as per-person double occupancy) or staying in a regular cottage with private bath, to which $50 per person is added nightly.

The bar is an old boat, dubbed *Panacea.* The food is wholesome, plentiful, and good—conch chowder, lobster, hot johnnycake. The chef will even cook your catch for you. Lunch is a buffet; dinner, a choice of seafood and meat every night. Children dine in the game room. A picnic lunch can be prepared for those who request it. Drinks are offered on a rambling patio built out over the sea where conch fritters are served at evening bar time. Nightlife is spontaneous—that is, dancing in the lounge or on the patio; underwater movies and slides are shown. Or you can play the club's guitar yourself. Definitely don't wear a tie at dinner—the owners have been known to snip it off if you do.

When you're making a reservation, inquire about special dive packages. This is the lodge's specialty (see "Sports & Recreation," below). The owners have been diving for three decades, and they have sufficient equipment, divers, boats, and flexibility to give guests any diving they want, whether it be shallow or deep. The lodge closes from Labor Day to mid-November.

Landmark Hotel & Restaurant, Andros Town, Andros, The Bahamas (tel. 809/368-2082), offers 15 of the most comfortable rooms in Andros Town. Each is sheathed in glowing planks of pinewood, complete with carefully crafted cove moldings, modern windows, big closets, a private bath, balcony, color TV, phone, and air conditioning. All of the finish work on the property was executed by the former owner, Wendall (Skinny) Moxie, who took an entrepreneurial pride in his property. Each of the rooms costs from $60 per night, single or double occupancy, in winter; *prices are reduced to $45, single or double, in summer.* All rates are for the EP. Calabash Bay Beach is within a 5-minute walk of the hotel, and guests rarely lack for companionship because of the lively bar and restaurant (Carmetta's) on the premises. The house drink, the Andros Special, is memorable. Full meals are served throughout every day without interruption, with lunches priced at around $10 and dinners at around $17 each. This is one of the most popular nightlife spots on the island. Some of its patrons are nightclubbing students from Andros Island's branch of the Marine Biology Studies Center.

Chickcharnie Hotel, Fresh Creek, Andros Town, Andros, The Bahamas (tel. 809/368-2025), is charmingly named after those Bahamian elves with three toes, feathers, and beards, all mischievous red-eyed devils. The location is 3 miles east of the Andros Town Airport. A simple concrete structure, the hotel attracts fishermen and an occasional business traveler. It offers 10 rooms, 4 with air conditioning, private baths, and TVs with satellite hookups. These rent year round for $60 daily, either EP single or double occupancy. The other rooms have sinks with hot and cold running water, access to a bathroom off the hallway, and ceiling fans. They rent for $40 daily, either EP single or double.

Island-born brothers Henry and Charles Gay, the owners, maintain a grocery store on the ground floor of the building. A few steps away, in the hotel's Spartan dining room, meals are served every day of the week. Breakfast and lunch are offered from 9am to 2pm, while dinner is served from 7 to 10pm. Fish, chicken, lobster, or conch dinners cost from $12 to $18 per person.

Nicholl's Town

Andros Beach Hotel, Nicholl's Town, Andros, The Bahamas (tel. 809/329-2582, or toll free 800/327-8150 in the U.S. except in Florida), is a pleasantly informal establishment with a stylish low-rise façade where the 14 air-conditioned accommodations lie beneath coconut palms at the edge of a beach. Many visitors choose only to remain in the sun-dappled shade by the sugar-white beach. The resort is very sports oriented, catering to the needs of visitors who want to go scuba diving. The hotel has its own pool and dock. Occasional live entertainment is provided after Bahamian dinners in the oceanfront dining room or on the garden-style terrace. Each unit of the hotel has a private patio, two double beds, and a private bath. Rates for the accommodations stay the same throughout the year: single or double rooms cost $85 per day, and cottages range from $100 for two.

Lowe Sound

Kevin's Guest House, Lowe Sound, Nicholl's Town, Andros, The Bahamas (tel. 809/329-2517). Built in 1986, and connected by the same management to Big Josh Seafood Restaurant and Lounge a few steps away, this is one of the most recently built hotels on the island. The hotel was established by a legendary, now-deceased bonefisherman and guide, Joshua Bootle (the hotel is named after one of Bootle's sons), and still attracts a clientele of Stateside fishing enthusiasts. The hotel contains only half a dozen windowless rooms, each simply furnished (including a queen-size bed), but with air conditioning and satellite-connected TV. In winter or summer, EP single or double rooms cost from $65 a day.

Behring Point

Nottages Cottages, Fresh Creek, Behring Point, Andros, The Bahamas (tel. 809/329-5293). Set on a knoll above the waterway separating North Andros and Mangrove Cay, this clean and stylish guesthouse (owned by Daisy Nottage) is fronted with a garden of croton and hibiscus. A favorite with bonefishermen, it has as its social center a blue-and-white dining room where West Bahamian food is served to guests and visiting nonresidents. You can stay in one of the well-furnished motel-like rooms whose glass windows face the sea, or in an outlying cottage equipped with a kitchenette. Year-round rates based on double occupancy are from $90 per person, including all meals. Four people can rent the cottage from $150 daily without meals.

Charlie's Haven, Behring Point, Andros, The Bahamas (tel. 809/329-5261), lies about 25 miles from Andros Town Airport near what are said to be some of the best bonefishing banks in the world. This is a remote outpost for fishermen who like the rustic but comfortable hospitality. Many anglers who check in here have tried other fishing spots throughout The Bahamas, ultimately finding this place and returning again and again. It is the very isolation and rather rawboned qualities that appeal to many patrons, most of whom are men, although families of fishermen sometimes come too. As you can imagine, many tall tales of fish that got away are swapped over the informal meals served here. There's occasionally live entertainment following the evening meal, as well as a separate bar area.

The unpainted concrete building sits on the edge of the sound separating North Andros from Mangrove Cay. There are only seven bedrooms, all with air conditioning, ceiling fans, simple white walls, a minimum of furniture, and plenty of space to store fishing rods and tackle. With all meals included, EP singles rent from $80 daily, and doubles go for $110 throughout the year.

Many people come here exclusively for the fishing, which can be arranged with Charles Smith, patriarch of the family that owns the hotel and one of the region's most respected bonefishing guides. Mr. Smith's many sons, some or all of whom you're likely to meet here, include Benry, Andy, and Prescott.

South Andros

Emerald Palms By-the-Sea, Driggs Hill, P.O. Box 800, South Andros, The Bahamas (tel. 809/329-4661, or toll free 800/825-5099 in the U.S.). Staying here is a lot like staying at a beachside ranch. The hotel has only 20 accommodations, which are set on 5 miles of beachfront on an island containing 10,000 palm trees. The hotel is informally casual—a place to get away from urban life for a sojourn on a white-sand beach. No one minds if you wear jeans or a bikini all day long. Guests are treated like members of the family.

Scattered over the palm-studded property are a freshwater swimming pool, a tennis court, and shuffleboard. The cocktail lounge offers live musical entertainment, and there's sometimes a live local show. The dining room features Bahamian seafood, including broiled lobster and grouper prepared in the local style. Outdoor steak barbecues and seafood buffets are sometimes held. The air-conditioned rooms are large, with minibars and TVs but no phones, and are situated directly on the sands of the beach. Year-round rates for single or double accommodations are $135 to $155. MAP (half board) is another $38 per person daily. South Bight marina is 1½ miles away, serving as a yacht anchorage for anyone who wants to arrive by boat. The hotel is 2 miles from the Congo Town Airport, and you can rent a car or bicycles if you wish.

WHERE TO DINE

Andros follows the rest of The Bahamas in its cuisine. Conch, in all its many variations, is the staple of most diets, along with heaping peas 'n' rice and johnny-cake, pig souse, or chicken souse.

The best places to dine are at the major hotels, including those previously recommended: the **Chickcharnie Hotel,** Fresh Creek, near Andros Town (tel. 809/328-3025); and if you're in South Andros, **Emerald Palms By-the-Sea,** outside Congo Town (tel. 809/329-4661). Most guests book into these hotels on the modified American plan, which frees them to shop around for lunch. At any of these hotels a dinner will run around $20 to $30 per person.

If you're touring the island during the day, you'll find some local spots that serve food. If business has been slow at some of these little places, you might find nothing on the stove. You take your chance.

Cargill Creek

If you're heading south, you might want to know about one of the most charming restaurants in the region, the **Green View Restaurant,** Cargill Creek (tel. 809/329-5097). Set within a pleasant and cozy pink-sided house, ringed with a garden beside the main highway, this establishment is inextricably tied to the personalities of its owners, Elizabeth ("Liz") and Alton Bain. The cuisine reflects the national origins (Canada and The Bahamas, respectively) of its owners, and includes both North American and Bahamian dishes concocted from seafood, cracked conch, grouper cutlets, crayfish, and chicken. Full meals cost from $9 to $14 each, depending on what you order. Meals are served daily any time you want them between 9am and 9:30pm, but require an advance telephone call. Your menu will be prearranged, and your arrival will probably be celebrated with a jug of the house special drink (a mixture of gin, sweetened condensed milk, and fresh coconut water) set beside your waiting table.

Nicholl's Town

If you're heading north, try to make it to Nicholl's Town in time for lunch. There, **Picaroon Restaurant,** Stanley and Burnside Streets (tel. 809/329-2607), is the most welcoming restaurant in town. Contained in a low-slung building a few steps from the beach, it's the undisputed domain of one of Andros's wisest and best-recommended chefs, Mrs. Eva Henfield. You order your meals at a rectangular bar near the entrance, then proceed into an airy dining room with multipatterned curtains, a pseudo-vaulted ceiling, and windows on three sides. There really isn't much of a printed menu—only the dishes Mrs. Henfield has ingredients for at the moment. My most recent meal consisted of an overflowing platter of chicken and barbecued ribs, a mound of coleslaw, bread, butter, and Hawaiian punch. All this, plus a preliminary bowl of vegetable soup, cost $12 per person. The establishment is open Monday through Saturday from 7am to 9pm.

Mrs. Henfield also rents out a quartet of well-scrubbed and decent rooms in her private home about four blocks away. Each has a table fan, a shared bath, and access to a communal kitchen for the preparation of meals. Single or double occupancy throughout the year costs $40 per person. For information about the rooms, call Mrs. Henfield.

Dorothy's Palm Tree Restaurant, Swamp Street (tel. 809/329-2373), also in Nicholl's Town, is an alternative choice. Amid a simple modern decor of tiles and exposed wood, you can enjoy the ambience created by the owners, Joniah Walkes and his wife, Dorothy. Your meal is likely to include such dishes as bean soup, steamed conch, steamed pork chops, the catch of the day, peas 'n' rice, and coleslaw. Breakfast here costs from $5; lunch or dinner, from $10 per person. The establishment is open Monday through Saturday from 8am to 10pm, on Sunday from 8am to 6pm.

If you're on the trail of the bonefishermen who hand out at Lowe Sound you'll find good local dishes at a very typical place, the **Big Josh Seafood Restaurant and Lounge** (tel. 809/329-2517). The restaurant was established years ago by Joshua Bootle, a legendary (now deceased) bonefishing guide. The restaurant that bears his name is managed today by his charming widow, Malvese, who still does most of the cooking herself. Hours are from 7am to 11pm daily.

ATTRACTIONS

Andros is vastly unexplored—and with good reason. Getting around takes some doing. Roads—what roads there are—are badly maintained and potholed, except for the main arteries. Sometimes you're a long way between villages or settlements, and if your car breaks down, all you can do is stop and wait, hoping someone will come along and give you a ride to the next settlement, where (you pray) there will be a skilled mechanic. If you're striking out on an exploration, make sure you have a full tank, as service stations are not plentiful.

All of Andros certainly can't be explored by car, although there is a dream that as Andros develops, it will be linked by a road and causeways stretching some 100 miles or more. Most of the driving and exploring is confined to North Andros, and there only along the eastern sector, going by Nicholl's Town, Morgan's Bluff, and San Andros.

If you're driving in Central Andros or South Andros, motorists must stay on the rough Queen's Highway. The road in the south is paved and better than the one in Central Andros, which should be traveled only in an emergency or by a local.

Divers from all over the world come to explore the **Andros barrier reef,** running parallel to the eastern shore of the island. After Australia's Great Barrier Reef, this is the largest in the world, but unlike the one in Australia, some 200 miles off the coast, the barrier reef of Andros is easily accessible, beginning a few hundred yards offshore.

One side of the reef is a peaceful haven for snorkelers and scuba divers, who report that the fish are tame (often a grouper will eat from your hand, but don't try it with a moray eel). The water here is from 9 to 15 feet deep. On the other side of the reef it's a different story. The water plunges to a depth of a full mile into the awesome TOTO (Tongue of the Ocean). One diver reported that, as an adventure, diving in the ocean's "tongue" was tantamount to a flight to the moon.

Much marine life thrives on the reef, and it attracts nature lovers from all over the world. The weirdly shaped coral formations alone are worth the trip. This is a living, breathing garden of the sea, and its caves are often called "cathedral-like."

For many years the U.S. Navy has conducted research at a station on the edge of TOTO. The research center is at Andros Town. It is devoted to oceanographic, underwater weapons, and antisubmarine research. Called AUTEC (Atlantic Undersea Testing and Evaluation Centre), this is a joint U.S. and British undertaking.

When this station first opened, Androsians predicted that the naval researchers would turn up "Lusca." Like the Loch Ness monster, Lusca had been reported as having been sighted by dozens of locals. The sea serpent was accused of sucking both sailors and their vessels into the dangerous **"blue holes"** around the island's coastline. No one has captured Lusca yet, but the blue holes do exist, including the most famous—made so by Jacques Cousteau—Uncle Charlie's Blue Hole, which is mysterious and fathomless. The other blue holes are almost as incredible. Essentially, these are narrow circular pits that plunge straight down as much as 200 feet through rock and coral into murky, difficult-to-explore depths. Most of them begin under the level of the sea, although others appear unexpectedly (and dangerously) in the center of the island, usually with warning signs placed around the perimeter.

One of these holes, called Benjamin's Blue Hole, is named after its discoverer, George Benjamin. In 1967 he found stalactites and stalagmites 1,200 feet below sea level. What was remarkable about this discovery is that stalactites and stalagmites are not created underwater. This has led to much speculation that The Bahamas are actually mountaintops, all that remains of a mysterious continent (Atlantis?) that sank beneath the sea in dim, unrecorded times. Although Cousteau came this way to make a film, making the blue holes of Andros internationally famous, most of them, like most of the surface of the island itself, remain unexplored.

Tour boats leaving from Small Hope Bay Lodge (see below) will take you to these holes.

Near Small Hope Bay at Andros Town you can visit the workshop where **Androsia batik** is made (that same Androsia batik sold in the shops of Nassau, Freeport, Lucaya, and Paradise Island). This well-known Bahamian batik is also seen now at fashionable resorts around the world. Androsia's artisans create their designs using hot wax on fine cotton and silk fabrics. The fabrics are then made into island-style wear, including blouses, skirts, caftans, dresses, shirts, scarves, bags, and accessories. All hand-painted and hand-signed, the resortwear comes in dazzling reds, blues, purples, greens, and earth browns. Androsia, of course, takes its name from Andros. You can visit the factory, P.O. Box A-931, Andros Town, Andros, The Bahamas (tel. 809/368-2020), Monday through Saturday from 8:30am to 4pm.

Morgan's Bluff lures men and women hoping to strike it rich. Sir Henry Morgan, the pirate, is supposed to have buried a vast treasure here, which remains undiscovered to this day. Many have searched for it, however, using the most scientific methods.

Typical of discoveries that continue to make Andros mysterious is **Red Bay Village,** where inhabitants were found in recent times living as a tribe. Their leader was "the chief," and old rituals were religiously followed. The passage of time had made little difference to these people. Now the world comes to their door, and changes are inevitable, although the people still follow their longtime customs. The village, it is believed, was settled sometime in the 1840s by Seminoles and blacks fleeing slavery in Florida. Their location is a small community lying off the northwestern coast of Andros. A causeway now connects them to the mainland, and sightseers can visit. Red Bay Village can be reached by road from Nicholl's Town and San Andros. You should be polite and ask permission before indiscriminately photographing these people.

Birdwatchers are attracted to Andros by its varied **bird population.** In the dense forests, in trees such as lignum vitae, mahogany, madeira, "horseflesh," and pine, lives a huge feathered population: many parrots, doves, and marsh hens. (Ever hear a whistling duck?)

Botanists are also attracted here, because of the **wildflowers** of Andros. It is said that some 40 to 50 species of wild orchids thrive here, some that are found nowhere else. New discoveries are also being made, as more and more botanists seek out the rich growth of Andros.

One custom in Andros sounds like the Tennessee Williams drama *Suddenly Last Summer.* This is the catching of **land crabs,** which must leave their safe and protected terrestrial burrows to march relentlessly to the sea to lay their eggs. This annual ritual occurs between May and September. However, many of these hapless crabs will never have offspring. Both visitors and Androsians walk along the beach with baskets, catching the crustaceans as they march to the sea. Later, they clean them, stuff them, and bake them for dinner.

SPORTS & RECREATION

Golfers and tennis pros should go elsewhere, but those who want some of the best bonefishing and scuba diving in The Bahamas flock to Andros. I'll survey where to find the best of local sports for those who want to abandon the beach for a while.

Fishing

As widely touted, Andros is called the "Bonefish Capital of the World." The actual capital is Lowe Sound Settlement, a tiny hamlet with only one road. It lies 4 miles north of Nicholl's Town. Fishermen go here to hire bonefish guides.

Regardless of what area you're staying in—North Andros, Central Andros, or South Andros—someone at your hotel can arrange for you to go fishing.

One of the best places is **Charlie's Haven,** Behring Point (tel. 809/329-5261), already recommended as a rustic hotel. Bonefishing trips are arranged for $100 for a half day, $180 for a full day. Deep-sea fishing is also available.

Fishing is also arranged at **Small Hope Bay Lodge** (tel. 809/368-2014) at Andros Town. A guide will take you to where there is superb bonefishing, and tackle and bait are provided.

Scuba & Snorkeling

As mentioned several times, scuba divers and snorkelers are attracted to Andros because of the barrier reef, which lies on the eastern shore along the Tongue of the Ocean. Blue holes, coral gardens, drop-offs, wall and reef diving, and wrecks make it even more enticing. The best dive operations are previewed below.

Small Hope Bay Lodge, P.O. Box N-1131, Nassau (tel. 809/368-2014, 305/359-8240 in Florida, or toll free 800/223-6961 in the U.S.), at Fresh Creek, Andros Town, lies a short distance from the barrier reef, with its still-unexplored caves and ledges. A staff of trained dive instructors at the lodge caters to levels of expertise from beginners to experienced divers (the staff having various credentials, including certification from many of the world's professional diving organizations). Snorkeling expeditions can be arranged as well as scuba outings, and the staff even claims to be able to teach novices to dive even if they can't swim, beginning with the steps off the establishment's docks. The visibility of the water exceeds 100 feet on most days, with temperatures ranging from 72° to 84° Fahrenheit.

Without hotel accommodations, half-day excursions to the reef, with snorkeling gear included, cost $10; with scuba gear, $30. Scuba instruction is free. Night dives cost $35 per person and require a minimum of six participants. To stay at the hotel here for five nights and six days, all inclusive (meals, tips, taxes, airport transfers, and the like), costs $600 per person. All guests are allowed access to the beachside hot whirlpool as well as to all facilities of the hotel, such as free use of Sunfish, Windsurfers, and bicycles.

Andros Beach Hotel & Villas, Nicholl's Town (tel. 809/329-2582), takes advantage of the proximity to the Andros Barrier Reef, offering a complete dive package with a full array of options for interested participants. Simple rentals of the equipment you need can be arranged if you're qualified, although many guests prefer the complete package, with transportation included. A handful of experienced instructors and guides will show you sections of the barrier reef and the Tongue of the Ocean.

When not included in the price of a package, single-tank dives cost $35, two-tank dives go for $50, and three-tankers cost $65. Half-day snorkeling trips cost $25 per person. The price per package, which includes hotel accommodations, varies with the number of days a visitor wants to spend. The cost includes round-trip airfare from Fort Lauderdale or Nassau, land transfers, three meals a day, taxes, tips, and double occupancy. A three-day, two-night package, which include seven dives, costs $470. A similar package, covering eight days, seven nights, and 22 dives, goes for $1,045. Single occupancy on any package requires an additional $30 per day.

For additional information, write to **Andros Undersea Adventures,** P.O. Box 21766, Fort Lauderdale, FL 33335. In Florida, call 305/359-0065. Outside of Florida, call 800/327-8150 toll free in the United States and Canada.

XII

THE ABACO ISLANDS

1. WALKER'S CAY
2. GREEN TURTLE CAY (NEW PLYMOUTH)
3. TREASURE CAY
4. MARSH HARBOUR
5. GREAT GUANA CAY
6. MAN-O-WAR CAY
7. ELBOW CAY (HOPE TOWN)
8. LITTLE HARBOUR

The northernmost of the Bahamas—called the "top of The Bahamas"—the Abacos form a boomerang-shaped miniarchipelago 130 miles long, consisting of both Great Abaco and Little Abaco as well as a sprinkling of cays (pronounced "keys").

Ponce de León landed here in 1513, looking for the Fountain of Youth. Visitors, many of them retired Americans, still arrive searching—if not for eternal youth, at least for a pleasant way of life that has disappeared from much of the world.

Fishermen find some of the finest offshore fishing in The Bahamas, and yachtsmen call this the "world's most beautiful cruising grounds" (an appellation also used to describe the Exumas—I'll give them a tie). In the interior are wild boar, and, I am told, wild ponies, although I've never seen the latter.

The location, at least of the Abaco airports, is 200 miles east of Miami and 75 miles north of Nassau.

The Abacos are the leading and most visited attraction in The Bahamas, after Nassau, Paradise Island, and Freeport/Lucaya. The weather is about 10° Fahrenheit warmer than in southern Florida, but if you visit in January or February, don't expect every day will be beach weather. Remember, Miami and Fort Lauderdale, even Key West, can get chilly at times. When winter squalls hit, temperatures can drop to the high 40s in severe cases. Spring in the Abacos, however, is one of the most glorious and balmy seasons in all the islands. In summer it gets very hot around noon, but if you do as the islanders do and find a shady spot, the trade winds will cool you off.

Once the waters around the Abacos swarmed with Robert Louis Stevenson–type pirates and treasure ships. It is estimated that 500 to 600 Spanish galleons—many treasure-laden—went to their watery graves in and around the Abaco reefs. To this day, an occasional old silver coin or a doubloon is found along the beaches, particularly after a storm.

Many of the Bahamians who live in the Abacos are descendants of Loyalists who left New England or the Carolinas during the American Revolution. An Elizabethan accent still exists in their speech. They founded towns like New Plymouth and Hope

Town, which are reminiscent of New England fishing villages. Many of these early settlers were shipbuilders, and they naturally brought that skill with them. To this day many Abaconians claim that the finest island boats are those built with Abaco pine by the Man-O-War Cay artisans. This is still the boatbuilding center of The Bahamas, and it is also rather grandly acclaimed as "the finest sailing capital" in the world.

Other early settlers were farmers who, when they found that they could not make a living in that line—the soil wasn't fertile enough—turned to wrecking (the business of salvaging ships that were wrecked or foundered on the reefs). Since there wasn't a lighthouse in the Abacos until 1836, many vessels crashed on the shoals and rocks, and salvagers legally claimed the cargoes, at the same time saving the lives of crews and passengers when possible. However, this enterprise became so profitable that some unscrupulous wreckers deliberately misled ships to their doom and became rich from the spoils.

Most of the pockets of "Tories"—descendants of the British Loyalists—still live on Elbow Cay, Green Turtle Cay, and Man-O-War Cay. From a sightseeing point of view, these are the main islands of the Abacos to visit, having more interest, in my opinion, than the Abaco "mainland." The first-timer will likely head for Treasure Cay, Marsh Harbour, even Walker's Cay or Green Turtle Cay, but repeat visitors learn more esoteric destinations.

TOURISM

Regular tourists now visit the Abacos because of the first-rate resorts. However, for many years it was a preferred cruising ground for the yachting set, who like to sail in what they call "the Sea of Abaco," perhaps the finest cruising waters not only in The Bahamas but also in the Caribbean. Yachting people know of such quaintly named places as Little Pigeon Cay, Tea Table Cay, and Umbrella Cay.

As for accommodations, you can expect special resorts that offer a combination of tropical rusticity and sporting elegance. These are places where oceangoing yachts anchor and celebrities, even U.S. presidents (retired), escape. You may encounter an industrialist on the tennis court, a foreign head of state by the pool, a movie star by the bar, or a princess strolling along the beach. Or you may beachcomb for hours encountering no one at all.

You have a choice of first-class resorts, cottage colonies for self-sufficient types, and a scattering of guesthouses.

Fishing, swimming, and boating—especially boating—are the top sports on the Abacos. There are also diving, golf, and tennis. If you're a boating type, the favorite pastime is to rent a small boat, pack a picnic (or have it done for you), and head for one of the cays just big enough for two.

Excellent marine facilities, with guides, charter parties, and boat rentals are available on Great Guana Cay, Green Turtle Cay, Hope Town, Marsh Harbour, Treasure Cay, and Walker's Cay. Sunfish, Sailfish, Hobie Cats, and Morgan bareboats are available. In fact, Marsh Harbour is the bareboat charter center of the northern Bahamas.

Anglers from all over the world come to test their skill against the blue marlin, kingfish, dolphin, yellowfin tuna, sailfish, wahoo, amberjack, and grouper. Fishing tournaments abound at Walker's Cay. There are plenty of Boston Whalers for bottom fishing and Makos for reef fishing and trolling. Many cruisers for deep-sea fishing can be rented.

Scuba divers can dive to the depths with UNEXSO (Underwater Explorers Society) and discover the Abacos' caverns, inland "blue holes," coral reefs and gardens, along with marine preserves and wrecks. Night dives are featured. Top-rated dive centers can be found at Marsh Harbour, Hope Town, Treasure Cay, and Walker's Cay, all offering NAUI/PADI instructors and a full line of equipment sales, rentals, and air-fills.

GETTING THERE

By Air

Three airports service the Abacos: Marsh Harbour (the major one), Treasure Cay, and Walker's Cay. The official points of entry are Marsh Harbour, Treasure Cay, Walker's Cay, and Green Turtle Cay (New Plymouth). Green Turtle Cay doesn't have an airstrip, but many people of the yachting set clear Customs and Immigration there.

Many visitors arrive from Nassau or Miami on **Bahamasair** (tel. toll free 800/222-4262). Flight schedules change frequently in The Bahamas, but you can usually get a daily flight out of Nassau, going first to Marsh Harbour, then on to Treasure Cay. If you're in Miami, you can usually get a morning flight to Marsh Harbour. There is also service from Miami on to Treasure Cay.

Aero Coach (tel. toll free 800/327-0010) flies to Marsh Harbour and Treasure Cay from Miami and Fort Lauderdale.

American Eagle (tel. toll free 800/433-7300) flies from Miami nonstop to the Abacos, touching down at both Marsh Harbour and at Treasure Cay.

Walker's Cay Airline (tel. toll free 800/327-3714) flies in from Fort Lauderdale to Walker's Cay. This is the resort's own airline, which flies to the private airstrip at Walker's Cay.

USAir (tel. toll free 800/251-5720) has one flight daily from Fort Lauderdale to Treasure Cay, and also flies in on direct flights from Orlando.

By Cruise Line

Premier Cruise Line, P.O. Box 573, Cape Canaveral, FL 32920 (tel. 809/327-7113), sails its *Majestic* on three- and four-day jaunts to the Abacos. Departures are from Port Canaveral in Florida on Monday and Friday. Cruise-ship passengers get to explore Green Turtle Cay, Great Guana Cay, Man-O-War Cay, and Treasure Cay, which are the sightseeing highlights of the Abacos.

By Mailboat

The mailboat M/V *Deborah I K II* leaves from Potter's Cay Dock in Nassau, going to Cherokee Sound, Green Turtle Cay, Hope Town, and Marsh Harbour. It departs on Wednesday, and the trip to the Abacos takes 7 hours. The return is on Monday.

In addition, the M/V *Champion II* also heads out from Potter's Cay Dock in Nassau on Thursday, calling first at Sandy Point, then Moore's Island and Bullock's Harbour before returning to Nassau on Saturday. For details of sailings and costs, passengers should get in touch with the Dockmaster at Potter's Cay Dock in Nassau (tel. 809/393-1064).

GETTING AROUND

Unmetered **taxis,** often shared with other passengers, meet all arriving planes. They will take you to your hotel if it's on the Abaco "mainland"; otherwise, they will deposit you at a dock where you can hop aboard a water taxi to one of the neighboring offshore islands like Green Turtle Cay or Elbow Cay. Most visitors use a combination taxi and water taxi ride to reach the most popular hotels. From Marsh Harbour Airport to Hope Town on Elbow Cay costs about $10 for the transfer. From the Treasure Cay Airport to Green Turtle Cay, there is a transportation charge of about $12.

It's also possible to make arrangements for a **taxi tour** of Great Abaco or Little Abaco. These, however, are expensive. You don't really see that much either. It's much better to go sightseeing in one of the Loyalist settlements, such as New Plymouth. That you can do on foot.

If you want to risk the Abacos' potholed roads, you can rent a car, usually for $60 a day. Try **H & L Car Rentals,** Don MacKay Boulevard, P.O. Box 490, Marsh

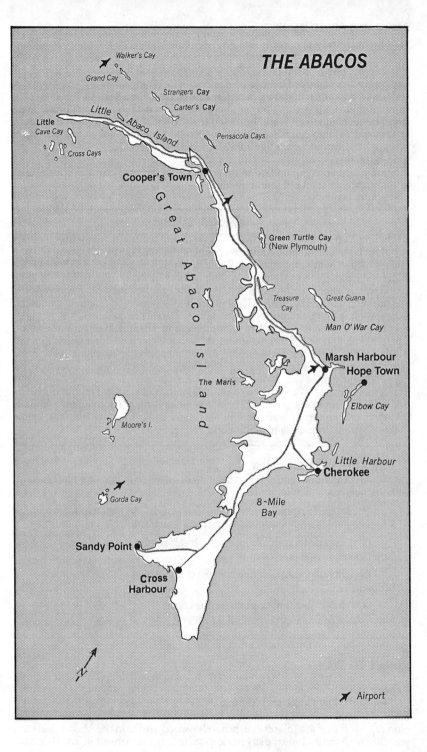

Harbour (tel. 809/367-2840), which is open Monday through Saturday from 7am to 6pm.

Mostly, you'll probably use **Albury's Ferry Service** (tel. 809/367-2306). Its departures from Marsh Harbour coincide with incoming and outgoing flights. It provides ferry connections to Elbow Cay (Hope Town) and Man-O-War Cay, a 20-minute trip to each destination. The round-trip fare is $12 if you return the same day. The boats run from Hope Town and from Man-O-War Cay to Marsh Harbour at 8am and 1:30pm daily, making the run from Marsh Harbour to the two island ports at 10:30am and 4pm. For car-ferry service to Green Turtle Cay, refer to the writeup on that cay below.

We'll begin our exploration of the Abacos with the northernmost point, Walker's Cay, then descend in a southerly route.

---

1. Walker's Cay

This is the northernmost and outermost of the Abaco chain of islands, and one of the smallest, lying at the edge of the Bahama Bank. The cay produces its own fresh water and electricity. Coral reefs surrounding this island drop off to depths of some 1,000 feet. It's known around the world as one of the best deep-sea fishing resorts, and has been featured on the ABC-TV network's "American Sportsman" on several occasions. It is usually mentioned as being the "Top of The Bahamas."

Ponce de León is said to have stopped here in 1513 looking for fresh water. That was just six days before he discovered Florida. From the 17th century, this was a place known to pirates, who stored their booty here. It became a bastion for blockade-runners during the American Civil War, and later it was a hideout for rum-runners in the days of U.S. Prohibition.

To service those who want to reach the island, Walker's Cay Hotel and Marina operates its own plane service, part of Walker's Cay Airline (tel. toll free 800/327-3714), operating out of Walker's Cay Jet Center in Fort Lauderdale. The airline makes 45-minute flights daily to the island.

What the Symbols Mean

    AP (American plan): Includes three meals a day (sometimes called full board or full pension).

    BP (Bermuda plan): Popularized first in Bermuda, this option includes a full American breakfast (sometimes called an English breakfast).

    CP (Continental plan): A Continental breakfast (that is, bread, jam, and coffee) is included in the room rate.

    EP (European plan): This rate is always cheapest, as it offers only the room—no meals.

    MAP (modified American plan): Sometimes called half board or half pension, this room rate includes breakfast and dinner (or lunch if you prefer).

WHERE TO STAY

Expensive

Walker's Cay Hotel and Marina, Walker's Cay, Abaco, The Bahamas (tel. 305/359-1400 in Fort Lauderdale, or toll free 800/327-3714, 800/432-2092 in Florida), has the largest full-service, privately owned marina in the Abacos, and each year runs what has become the largest deep-sea fishing tournament in The Bahamas.

The hotel has 71 air-conditioned and attractively furnished villas and bedrooms, each with a view of the ocean from its own private terrace. For either a single or a double, EP rates range from $160 to $191 daily. The "in season," incidentally, is from mid-March to May 31. *In the off-season, from June 1 through the middle of February, rates drop to $110 to $145 per day, either single or double occupancy.* Of course, the villas and ocean-view suites are more expensive. For breakfast and dinner, add another $29.50 per person daily. If you're planning a winter visit, ask a travel agent (or else call directly) to see if the resort will still be offering its "Discover Us Package." Its most recent one (good through the winter until the end of February) included three days and two nights, with round-trip airfare from Fort Lauderdale or West Palm Beach, for $349 per person.

The food is good, with an assortment of American and Bahamian specialties. The chef bakes his own bread and pastries, and there is also an excellent wine selection. Bahamian lobster and conch fritters are invariably featured, along with fresh fish. The Deep Jigger lounge evokes the early Bahamas of Hemingway, and the Marlin Room and dining terrace overlook the sea. In season, guests can dance to disco music in the Lobster Trap Lounge, at Marina North Dock. There are two all-weather tennis courts, and the resort offers every kind of water sport from scuba to ski, along with freshwater and saltwater swimming. Some of the finest offshore fishing in The Bahamas is just 5 minutes from the 75-slip marina (many world records have been set here).

To write for a reservation, address your letter to Walker's Cay Hotel and Marina, 700 SW 34th St., Fort Lauderdale, FL 33315

---

2. Green Turtle Cay (New Plymouth)

Three miles off the east coast of Great Abaco, Green Turtle Cay is the jewel of the archipelago, a little island with an uneven coastline, deep bays, sounds, and good beaches, one of the best stretching for 3,600 feet. There are green forests, gentle hills, and secluded inlets. The island is 3½ miles long and half a mile across, and lies some 170 miles due east of Palm Beach, Florida.

Water depths seldom exceed 15 to 20 feet inside the string of cays that trace the outer edge of the Bahama Bank. It is the reefs outside the cays that provide the abundance of underwater flora and fauna that delight snorkelers and fishermen. The coral gardens that make up an inner and an outer reef teem with colorful sea life, and shelling on the beaches and offshore sandbars is considered among the finest in The Bahamas.

If you have a boat, you can explore such deserted islands as Fiddle Cay to the north and No Name Cay and Pelican Cay to the south of Green Turtle Cay.

New Plymouth, at the southern tip of the cay, is an 18th-century settlement that has the flavor of a New England sailing port back in the days when such towns were filled with boatbuilders and fishermen. Much of the masonry of the original town was made from lime produced from conch shells, broken up, burned, and sifted for cement. Records say that the alkali content was so high that it would burn the hands of the masons who used it.

Clapboard houses with gingerbread trim line the narrow streets of the little town, which once had a population of 1,800 people, now shrunk to 400. Green Turtle Cay became known for the skill of its shipbuilders, although the industry, like many others in the area, failed when total emancipation of the slaves came in The Bahamas in 1838. Today the streets lie somnolent in the sun most of the time, except when a festival is under way or when people are going to church on Sunday.

Parliament is the village's main street, and you can walk its entire length in only 10 minutes, perhaps acknowledged only by the clucking of a few hens. Many of the houses have front porches, usually occupied in the evening, as people take the breezes and watch their small world go by. The people here are friendly but not out-going, having lived for generations far from the madding crowd.

THE PEOPLE

The settlers of New Plymouth were Loyalists who found their way here from other parts of the Abacos shortly before the end of the 18th century, with some "new" blood thrown in when émigrés from Eleuthera moved to Marsh Harbour and other Abaconian settlements. The people today are mostly named Curry, Lowe, Russell, Roberts, and especially Sawyer. Because they all came from the same rootstock—English, Welsh, and Scottish—and because of a long history of inter-marriage, many of the faces are amazingly similar: deeply tanned, often freckled skin, blue eyes, and red or blond hair. Most of them, even in these sun-worshipping days, wear broad-brimmed hats to protect themselves from the sun.

One morning I spent an hour with a lifelong resident. The next morning en-countering what I took to be the same man on the ferryboat, I resumed our conver-sation, only to learn I was talking to a different man entirely. "No relation," he said, until chided by a woman passenger, which elicited from him, "Well, I think my mother's cousin did marry . . ."

The insularity of these people has also caused their speech patterns to retain many facets of those their forebears brought from the mother country, with even a smattering of Cockney to flavor it. Many drop their initial letter *h*, using it instead at the beginning of words that start with vowels. You may hear someone ordering "'am" and with it some "heggs." Also, the letter *v* is often pronounced as *w*, and vice versa.

Many of the inhabitants of New Plymouth today are engaged in turtling, lob-stering, shark fishing, and sponging. New Plymouth is a "sister city" to Key West, Florida, and if you have ever visited there, you'll see startling similarities between the American people of "conch" descent and the Abaconians, even to their wrecking history, fishing industries, and appearance.

A big event in the day-to-day life of the people of New Plymouth is the arrival at the Government Dock of the mailboat from Nassau. People gather there also when-ever the ferryboat is arriving or leaving, just to keep tabs on what's going on.

There is no auto traffic in New Plymouth except for a few service vehicles—but who needs a car? You can walk all the way around the village in a fairly brief stroll.

GETTING THERE

Most guests fly to Treasure Cay Airport, where a taxi will take them to the ferry dock for departures to Green Turtle Cay (New Plymouth).

At the dock, you may have to wait a while for the ferry (which has no phone), or else have one called for you. It's about a 10-minute ride to Green Turtle Cay from the dock. The ferry will take you to the Green Turtle Club, if you're staying there, or to New Plymouth. This land and sea transfer costs $10 per person.

FAST FACTS: GREEN TURTLE CAY (NEW PLYMOUTH)

Crime: There's no crime in New Plymouth, unless you import it yourself. There is a little jail made of stone, which makes visitors chuckle: the doors have fallen off. No one can remember when, if ever, it held a prisoner.

Banks: Service is limited. **Barclay's Bank PLC** operates a branch (tel. 809/365-4144), open only from 10am to 1pm every Thursday.

Churches: The people of New Plymouth, for the most part, are deeply religious. With such a small population, they manage to support five churches. The Anglican church is the oldest, dating from 1786.

Medical Care: If you need medical attention on Green Turtle Cay, there is a clinic (tel. 809/365-4222), run by a nurse.

Post Office: Green Turtle Cay's post office (tel. 809/365-4242) is entered through a pink door. It has the only public telephone on the island.

Shopping: In New Plymouth, there are several gift shops, and well-stocked grocery stores feature freshly baked Bahamian bread.

WHERE TO STAY

Expensive

The Green Turtle Club, Green Turtle Cay, Abaco, The Bahamas (tel. 809/365-4271), is where such celebrities as Christopher Reeve, Tanya Tucker, Kenny Rogers, and former President Jimmy Carter have gone for a retreat from the pressures of daily life. The resort was built on a half-moon-shaped beach off which yachts of all sizes ride at anchor. The flag-festooned bar is the social center of the resort, which was originally built as a boathouse. Today its ambience is very much that of a clubhouse, lodge, and country club, capped with heavy rafters and flanked on one side by a panoramic veranda and on the other by a pine-covered dining room.

The Green Turtle Yacht Club has its base here. It's associated with the Birdham Yacht Club, one of the oldest in England, and with the Palm Beach Yacht Club. Members have their own villas right on the water, often with private docks, although temporary guests will be lodged in exceptionally spacious bungalows set on the side of the hill. There are no locked doors on this tree-dotted estate. Also, the only telephone is the one in the main office, where the polite staff can organize a full array of sporting as well as sightseeing excursions.

There's an unmistakably British note here—both in the evening meals which begin with before-dinner cocktails beside a roaring fire in the bar (in chilly weather only, of course), and in the courteous staff, who offer assistance yet don't intrude on anyone's tranquility. Some guests choose to walk the several miles into New Plymouth as part of their daily exercise regimes, although if you prefer a boat ride, someone from the hotel will arrange for you to go on one of the several daily trips. The waters around the resort are shallow enough that landlubbers can spot schools of fish and sometimes even a green turtle paddling along above the sandbanks. Nature has blessed the resort with enough visual splendor to more than make up for its relative isolation. There's a swimming pool dug into one of the flower-dotted hillsides in case swimmers don't want to bathe in the turquoise waters off the hotel's beach.

Single or double occupancy of regular rooms cost from $140 daily in winter, *the tariffs lowered to $110 in summer.* Poolside suites for two cost $160 daily in winter, *dropping to $125 in summer.* To rent a villa in winter, two persons pay $260 daily, *but only $185 in summer.* At Christmas, prices go up slightly. Each additional adult in a room pays $20 per day, and children up to age 12 share free. Year round, MAP is an additional $31 for adults, $21.50 for children. To get to the resort, which is closed from the end of August to mid-November, most guests arrive at the Treasure Cay Airport, then take a taxi (there are usually plenty there) to the ferry dock. From there, a water taxi will take you to the club.

Moderate

Bluff House Club & Marina, Green Turtle Cay, Abaco, The Bahamas (tel. 809/365-4247, or toll free 800/327-0787 in the U.S.), is managed by an English-born brother-and-sister team, Martin Havill and Barbara Bartley. Bluff House, featured in the Fletcher Knebel novel *Night of Camp David,* has 12 acres fronting on the Abaco

Sea on the one side and the harbor of White Sound on the other. It is a 5-minute boat ride from the village of New Plymouth, and a boat takes guests to the village three mornings a week for sightseeing and shopping and also for a Saturday-night dance.

The main building has paneled and glass walls, slow-whirling tropical fans, wicker furnishings, and polished wooden floors. The dining room (the Club House) has a pitched, beamed ceiling. A wide wooden deck surrounds the swimming pool, sheltered by palms and with a panoramic view of the surrounding waters and the sunsets. Breakfast and dinner (including complimentary wine) are served in the main Club House, where cocktails and fresh hors d'oeuvres are offered before a candlelit dinner that features local conch, grouper, snapper, and lobster (the latter in dozens of dishes), as well as other specialties such as roast duck à l'orange, sweet-and-sour chicken, and of course, the chef's special—blackened grouper—as depicted in *Gourmet* magazine. The Beach Club, which opens every day throughout the year at 11:30am, serves luncheons featuring Bahamian cracked conch, fresh grouper, conch fritters, and conch chowder (as well as hamburgers and other American favorites).

The 30-unit hotel offers beach or hillside villas and suites as well as hotel rooms, plus complete seclusion and views. Favored units are spacious "tree houses" with private porches and balconies. Inside, the decor has floral bedcovers and tropical furniture. In winter, single or double occupancy costs $85 daily in a hotel room, $100 in a split-level suite, and $135 in a one-bedroom villa. Treehouses for four adults are $220. *Off low-season rates exist for only part of the summer:* Certain holiday weeks, such as Memorial Day, July 4, and Labor Day, are considered high season. However, for *the rest of the off-season, rates are reduced by at least $10 daily.* MAP can be arranged for another $32 per person daily. The resort is open year round.

There are many facilities, including a marina, boats for rent, and a tennis court. Rackets and balls as well as snorkeling equipment are available without charge to guests. Babysitting can usually be arranged, and there is a gift shop/boutique.

Reef-fishing, deep-sea-fishing, and bonefishing guides can be arranged, as well as a snorkeling/fishing picnic during which your guide will take you diving for conch, spearing native lobster, or fishing for grouper and yellowtail. Your catch will be used for a shore lunch.

New Plymouth Inn, New Plymouth, Abaco, Green Turtle Cay, The Bahamas (tel. 809/365-4161, or 305/665-5309 in Florida), is a restored New England–Bahamian-style inn, which stands next door to the former home of Neville Chamberlain, the prime minister of Great Britain on the eve of World War II. It has colonial charm, a Loyalist history, cloistral gardens, and a patio pool, and it's in the heart of New Plymouth village. It was one of the few buildings in town to survive the 1932 hurricane. The inn is run by Wally Davies, an expert diver and swimmer. He has turned New Plymouth Inn into a charming oasis, refurbishing the 150-year-old building with taste and care.

The inn has wide, open verandas, intricate cut-out wooden trim, and an indoor A-frame dining room. The comfortable hammock on the front porch is constantly fought over. The light and airy rooms are kept spotlessly clean, and each has a private bath and shower. Many of the same guests have come back every year since the inn opened in 1974. Year-round rates, with breakfast and dinner included, are $120 daily for a double, $80 for a single. The inn is closed in September and October.

Out on the veranda, you can smell night-blooming jasmine mixing with fresh baked island bread. Island candlelit dinners of fresh native lobster, snapper, conch, and vintage wines are served. Also roasts, steaks, chops, and imported beer in frosty steins are part of the menu. The bar and lounge, which overlook the garden's small freshwater swimming pool, are the social center of the establishment. If you plan to dine at the Captain's Table, as the restaurant is called, you'll have to make a reservation. Former President Richard Nixon has dined here. Breakfast is daily 8 to 9am, lunch from noon to 1pm, and dinner at 7:30pm sharp. The Sunday brunch, from 11:30am to 1pm, is the most popular on the island, costing only $8 per person.

Cottage Rentals

Sea Star Beach Cottages, P.O. Box 282, Gilliam Bay, Green Turtle Cay, Abaco, The Bahamas (tel. 809/365-4178), is a 14-unit bungalow colony set on 19 acres, with Black Sound on one side and Gilliam Bay Beach on the ocean side. A variety of tropical trees and flowers abound in the colony—coconut palm, citrus, banana, hibiscus, bougainvillea, gumbo-limbo, and casuarina.

Life at Sea Star is simple—you get up at dawn, walk right down to the beach for your morning swim, then go back to a breakfast of homemade bread and tropical fruit. All cottages are on the ocean side (best swimming there), and come completely equipped for housekeeping. They are frame buildings, basic, with few frills. Each cottage has a bath or shower, a weekly supply of linens, stove, refrigerator, and, important, 24-hour electricity. The cottages are only half a mile by footpath to New Plymouth. They cost from $100 per day for two guests on EP. Boat rentals are available.

Deck House, White Sound, Green Turtle Cay, Abaco, The Bahamas (no phone), lies on the leeward side of the island at the entrance to White Sound. Rented weekly as a complex, it can house up to six people; in other words, it houses three couples "with privacy." It consists of two bedrooms and two baths, plus a small guesthouse for two with bath. There is a living room, plus a kitchen. Linens and all utensils are provided. Out back is a sundeck. Owners A. V. and Dorothy Lang prefer bookings from Saturday noon to Saturday noon. Incidentally, a maid comes in Saturday to put things in order. The charge for four guests is $750 weekly year round. If two more guests join the party, the charge is only $250 extra for the week. As an added bonus, the Langs include a 30-horsepower Malibu, a Butterfly, and the use of a Sunfish at no additional charge. For information and more details, write or call Mrs. Lang at 535 Hickory Hill Lane, Cincinnati, OH 45215 (tel. 513/821-9471).

WHERE TO DINE

Inexpensive

The hotels previously recommended have the best food on the island. But if for a change of pace you'd like to escape for either lunch or dinner, I recommend the following small dining rooms in New Plymouth.

Laura's Kitchen, Parliament Street (tel. 809/365-4287), is set on the main street of town, across from the Albert Lowe Museum. This family owned operation occupies a well-converted white-sided Bahamian cottage. Owner Laura Sawyer serves breakfast, lunch, and dinner within a decor that might best be described as pleasant, cozy, and homey. Open seven days a week, the restaurant serves food from 8am to 2pm and 5:30 to 9pm. Chicken is the specialty, and meals cost from $12 each.

Plymouth Rock Restaurant, Parliament Street (tel. 809/365-4234). It's difficult not to see this Bahamian lunch-only restaurant and liquor store, because it lies on the main street of town at Long Dock. Its cozy air-conditioned dining room is accentuated by lots of local chatter. The Bethell family offers homemade pies and cakes from a 100-year-old glass display case. Bahamian conch chowder and homemade soups are regular fare, while daily-changing main courses might feature lobster, conch, grouper, or beef. You can accompany your food with beer, wine, or mixed drinks—try a Goombay Smash or their own Calypso Cooler. Lunch starts at $8 per person. Hours are 9am to 3pm Monday through Saturday. The restaurant closes for the last two weeks of August.

Rooster's Rest Pub and Restaurant, Gilliam's Bay Road (tel. 809/365-4066), serves good Bahamian food, including lobster, conch, and fresh fish. The establishment lies just beyond the edge of town, at the far side of a hill that conceals it from most sections of Parliament Street. Lunch costs from $9 per person, and dinner from $16 for a complete meal. The restaurant is open Monday through Saturday from 11:30am to 2:30pm for lunch and 7:30 to 10pm for dinner. It's wise to call for dinner reservations. It's closed from mid-September to mid-October.

Sea View Restaurant, Crown Street (tel. 809/365-4345). Shortly after her marriage to locally born Alphonso, Betty McIntosh set up this restaurant in a green cinderblock building not far from the sea. Today she serves Bahamian meals to loyal clients, some of whom return every day. The establishment is spacious, airy, unashamedly simple, and easy to find because about a dozen signs posted all over town point to it. Lunch menus include conch fritters, conch chowder, conch burgers, conch snacks (actually a platter of cracked conch), and tuna sandwiches. At dinner, conch chowder, peas 'n' rice, and potato salad or coleslaw are served as part of the full meal. Main dishes, listed on a blackboard, include fish, chicken, Bahamian lobster, and pork chops. There's a well-stocked bar if you want to stop by just for a drink. Lunches cost from $6 and dinners from $18 per person. The restaurant is open Monday through Saturday from 10am to 10pm year round. Dinner reservations are preferred.

ATTRACTIONS

New Plymouth celebrated its bicentennial in 1984 by opening a **Memorial Sculpture Garden** in the center of town across from the New Plymouth Inn. A monument honors American Loyalists and also some of their notable descendants, including Albert Lowe, a pioneer boatbuilder and historian. The garden is designed in the pattern of the Union Jack.

No visitor to New Plymouth should miss seeing the **Albert Lowe Museum,** Parliament Street (tel. 809/365-4095), where the one-block King Street up from the dock comes to a dead end. This museum, more than anything else I've seen in The Bahamas, gives a view of the rawboned and sometimes difficult history of the Family Islands. You could easily spend a couple of hours reading the fine print of the dozens of photographs that show the hardship and the valor of citizens who changed industries as often as the economic circumstances of their era dictated.

There's a garden in the back of the beautifully restored Loyalist home, where Ivy Roberts, the caretaker, will give you a guided tour of the stone kitchen, which occupants of the house used as a shelter when a hurricane devastated much of New Plymouth in 1932. Inside the house a narrow stairway leads to a trio of bedrooms that reveal simplicity as the keynote of 18th-century life on Green Turtle Cay.

A plaque in the memorabilia-packed parlor of the house proudly declares: "The museum is dedicated to those Loyalists who crossed the Gulf Stream to settle among the islands of The Bahamas, particularly those who settled on or near the islands of Abaco, and their descendants." Amid Victorian settees, irreplaceable photographs, and island artifacts, you'll see a number of handsome ship models, the work of Albert Lowe, for whom the museum was named.

Also displayed are paintings by Alton Lowe, son of the former boatbuilder. Alton Lowe, in fact, founded the museum. Cherub-faced and red-haired, Alton, who now resides in Miami most of the time, has for some time been one of the best-known painters in The Bahamas. His works hang in collections all over the world. The Bahamian government asked him to paint a landscape, which it then presented to Prince Charles and Princess Diana as a wedding present. Many of Alton Lowe's paintings have been used as the background for Bahamian postage stamps, blowups of which are displayed in the museum. Whoever guides you on your tour might open the basement of the house for you as well, here you'll see some of Alton Lowe's work, as well as that of other local painters, for sale. The entrance fee for this unusual museum is $3. Hours are flexible, usually from 9:30 to 11:30am and 1 to 3pm Monday through Saturday.

SPORTS & RECREATION

Some critics have hailed the yearly **Regatta Week** as the "premier annual yachting event in the Abacos." Every year, it's held sometime between Independence Day in the United States and Independence Day in The Bahamas (July 4 and July 10). The events include sailboats and their crews from around the world, who compete in races that are divided into many categories. Some of the corporate sponsors in past years have been Shell Oil of The Bahamas, Barclays Bank, and the Green Turtle Club, which usually accommodates many of the participants.

Another event that draws visitors is the **Green Turtle Club Fishing Tournament,** held sometime in May. In 1984 the winner hooked a 500-pound blue marlin that was so heavy the competing participants from other boats generously came aboard the winning craft to bring the fish in.

The previously recommended Bluff House Club & Marina (tel. 809/365-4247) is the place to go for **scuba** facilities. The hotel also has access to a 29-foot "sportsfish" boat, with all equipment included. **Bonefishing** is on a smaller boat. Each trip takes about 4 hours, and the schedule depends completely on the tide. Bonefish are said to be, pound for pound, the strongest, most "fighting" fish in The Bahamas.

If you want to go **deep-sea fishing,** the people to see are the Sawyer family, two brothers and a father. Referrals are usually made through the Green Turtle Club, or else you can call directly at 809/365-4173. Prices are to be negotiated.

The Green Turtle Club (tel. 809/365-4271) has one **tennis** court, charging guests $5 per hour. At Bluff House (tel. 809/365-4247), guests play free; others are charged $5 per hour.

EVENING ENTERTAINMENT

Everybody goes to **Miss Emily's Blue Bee Bar,** Victoria Street (tel. 809/365-5811), and it's likely to have the liveliest party in the Family Islands going on in its unpretentious confines any time of the day or night. Despite its simplicity, this family-run bar is one of the most famous places east of Miami. When I was last there, an energetic party was developing just before lunch, as a yachtswoman from West Virginia was rehearsing the frug she'd learned in college, to the enthusiastic applause of her comrades. This and more are likely to be part of the scene at this hallowed bar, where the walls and furniture are virtually indestructible. The walls near the bar area are covered with the business cards of the clientele, who have included Glen Campbell, Jimmy Buffet, and the late Lillian Carter.

The Goombay Smash, the specialty here, has been called "Abaco's answer to atomic fission," and its recipe includes secret proportions of coconut rum, "dirty" rum, apricot brandy, and pineapple juice. The world's record for drinking these concoctions is set at 23, but the valiant toper had to be carried out in a wheelbarrow. Jerry Hulse once wrote: "Miss Emily, bless her, gives her customers the impression they've discovered El Morocco, or maybe another Copacabana. It's neither of those, of course. The Blue Bee is really rather tacky, but with loads of atmosphere."

The owner (she's really Mrs. Emily Cooper) is filled with humor and anecdotes. Failing health makes it impossible for her always to be on duty at the bar, but she has taught her daughter, Violet Smith, how to make the secret recipe, which seems to please customers. Although Miss Emily has a fine soprano voice, her singing is confined to St. Peter's Anglican Church. Tips at the bar go into Miss Emily's cigar pot for St. Peter's, one of the church's best sources of revenue. The bar is open every day (except Sunday) at 10am, remaining open till late. No food is served here other than the sugar content of the tasty, habit-forming drinks, each of which costs $3.50.

An out-of-the-way nightspot, **Rooster's Rest Pub and Restaurant,** Gilliam's Bay Road (tel. 809/365-4066), recommended separately as a restaurant, attracts a crowd including both yachting people and locals, who gather here every Friday and Saturday night. "The Gully Roosters" perform on weekends, "the best time to go," according to New Plymouth residents. Beer costs $3 per bottle. The place is open daily from 10:30am to 10pm on quiet nights, later when there's activity. Not visible from most of Parliament Street, the pub-restaurant is at the far side of a hill beyond the edge of town.

3. Treasure Cay

Treasure Cay, called Lovel's Island in records as far back as the 1780s, was once separated from the Abaco mainland by Carleton Creek. Over the years, however, landfill operations have joined the two, although Treasure Cay retains the name. It now contains one of the most popular and elaborate resorts in the Family Islands. On the east coast of Great Abaco, it boasts not only 3½ miles of private sandy beach but also one of the finest marinas in the Commonwealth, with complete docking and charter facilities.

In the publicity advertising this cay, a story has been printed about a German submarine commander, Paul Schmidt, who in World War II emerged from the sea to enjoy a little bit of Bahamian air before going back to Europe. Apparently he was so taken with the place that he vowed to return one day when the war was over and build a retirement home here. In 1968 he fulfilled that long-ago commitment to himself.

Much of today's Treasure Cay owes its look to Capt. Leonard Thompson, a former Royal Canadian Air Force pilot from Marsh Harbour, and Dumas Milner, once the biggest Chevrolet dealer in the United States. In 1962 the two launched a development here, digging 7 miles of canals through the mangroves.

Before the opening of the tourist complex, the cay was virtually unsettled. So the resort has become the "city," providing its thousands of visitors with all the supplies they need, including medical goods, grocery store items (liquor, naturally), and even bank services. The real estate office peddles the condos, and the builders predict that they will one day reach a capacity of 5,000 guests. What is hoped is that many visitors will like Treasure Cay so much that they'll buy into it.

CARLETON

The first settlement in the Abacos was a village that no longer exists—Carleton —to the north and a little east of Treasure Cay (then called Lovel's Island). It was separated from the cay by Carleton Creek, a rivulet that flowed to join the sea. The little town was abandoned some 200 years ago and largely forgotten until 1979, when the site of the settlement was discovered and artifacts were found by archeological excavation. In a bicentennial ceremony in 1983, a point of land near the site was designated **Carleton Point,** and a bronze plaque was placed there describing Carleton's brief history.

Loyalist refugees, fleeing the United States in 1783 following the formation of the new country and the withdrawal of British troops from the former colonies, migrated to The Bahamas, some settling in the Abacos, which were uninhabited at the time. Their aim was grandiose—they thought they could establish a colony that would be prosperous enough to replace British commerce with Virginia, Boston, New York, and Baltimore, and that would become a new agricultural/mercantile empire within the protection and privileged access provided by the British Crown.

Carleton, named for Sir Guy Carleton, who had been British commander-in-chief in New York, did not fulfill the dreams of the colonists. They staked out claims to land, but they learned, as had other settlers in other parts of The Bahamas, that this was not farming country. They built ships, but could not produce cargoes for them. The town initially had a population of 600 people, but civil strife and a devastating hurricane added to their woes, and soon some two-thirds of the settlers moved 18 miles to the southeast to found Marsh Harbour. Others moved to Cocoa Plum Creek and elsewhere, and some left The Bahamas. By 1800 Carleton had ceased to exist.

The Loyalists remaining in the Abacos were joined by migrants from Harbour Island on Eleuthera, who taught them to fish and even how to farm the rough acreage, and this union formed the nucleus from which today's Abaconians descend.

WHERE TO STAY & DINE

Moderate

Treasure Cay Beach Hotel, P.O. Box TC-4183, Abaco, The Bahamas (tel. 809/367-2847, or toll free 800/327-1584 in the U.S., 800/432-8257 in Florida). The foundation for this sun-drenched resort was laid in 1962. Today the area enjoys an ambience more like a country club than a hotel, and the yachting crowd gathers here for sundowners at the Tipsy Seagull lounge. The resort is one of the most publicized, advertised, and frequented in the Family Islands. It has its share of celebrities too, beginning with George C. Scott, who filmed the movie *The Day of the Dolphin* here.

Visitors who prefer to come by boat to Treasure Cay will be able to dock at one of the 150 berths at the marina, which can accommodate vessels up to 100 feet long. They can even plug their TV sets into the cable-TV hookup. The resort has a golf course (see below), tennis courts, and a beautiful stretch of white-sand beach. Fronting the swimming pool is the main dining facility, the Abaco Room, where you're offered a tempting menu with such choices as fresh grouper, snapper, spicy conch salad, and Bahamian lobster. Huge poolside buffets are set up several nights a week. In addition, the glass-enclosed Spinnaker Restaurant overlooking the marina offers good food and a piano bar on its upper level.

The various time-share buildings scattered around this resort are attractively planned with an abundance of tropical planting and a *House and Garden* look. Interiors are handsomely styled, often in tropical bamboo and rattan. The accommodations in the 96-room Harbor House with private porches or terraces built along the Marina, include large air-conditioned hotel rooms and suites. In winter, EP rates are $100 daily for a single and $125 for a double. *In summer, tariffs are $100 per room, single or double.* For reservations and information, write to Treasure Cay Beach Hotel, 2301 S. Federal Hwy., Fort Lauderdale, FL 33316 (tel. 305/525-7711).

SPORTS & RECREATION

Full-service facilities for a variety of water sports are offered at the Treasure Cay Marina (tel. 809/367-2570). **Fishing boats** with experienced skippers will guide anglers to tuna, marlin, wahoo, dolphin, barracuda, grouper, yellowtail, and snapper. Treasure Cay's own bonefish flats are just a short cruise from the marina. A full day of bonefishing costs $175, a half day $120; a sportfishing boat goes for $300 for a half day, $600 for a full day.

In addition, sailboat, Hobie Cat, and windsurfing board rentals can be arranged, as well as rental of snorkeling gear and bicycles. The marina has showers, fish-cleaning facilities, 24-hour weekday laundry service, and water and electricity hookups.

The **Treasure Cay Golf Club,** P.O. Box TC-4183 (tel. 809/367-2590), offers 6,985 yards of fairways and was designed by Dick Wilson. Greens fees are $26.25 for 18 holes and $15.25 for 9 holes.

---

4. Marsh Harbour

The largest town in the Abacos, Marsh Harbour on Great Abaco is the third largest in The Bahamas. The first settlers were a group of Loyalists who were among those who tried to start a town called Carleton near Treasure Cay (see above). The Abaconians who live here are usually shy but gracious.

Marsh Harbour is also a shipbuilding center, but tourism accounts for most of its revenues. The commercial center of the Abacos, the town has a shopping center and various other facilities not found in many Family Island settlements. You'll even spot the green turrets of a "castle" here, which was designed and constructed by Evans Cottrell, who wrote *Out Island Doctor.*

The shoreline provides one of the finest anchorages in the Family Islands, which is probably what lured the first settlers here 200 years ago. There are good water-taxi connections, making this a center for exploring some of the offshore cays, including Man-O-War and Elbow Cay. Its international airport serves not only the resorts at Marsh Harbour but those at Elbow Key (Hope Town).

I prefer to treat Marsh Harbour more as a refueling depot than a sightseeing attraction, as there are far more colorful towns in the Abacos and the offshore cays. However, because of its location—roughly in the center of the island—you may want to use it as a base, since it has a number of good inns. Several places will rent you a bike if you want to pedal around the town, getting to know it.

FAST FACTS: MARSH HARBOUR

Banks: If you're going to be in the Abacos for an extended vacation, Marsh Harbour can serve your banking needs in an emergency. Some cays have banks that operate only 3 hours a week. In Marsh Harbour, try **Barclays Bank,** on Don MacKay Boulevard (tel. 809/367-2152).

Car Rentals: In Marsh Harbour, there's **Veronica's Car Rental,** P.O. Box 463 (tel. 809/367-2725). It charges $90 per day for Jeeps, $60 per day for other cars.

Drugstore: For your pharmaceutical needs, go to **Lowe's Pharmacy,** Lowe's Shopping Centre, P.O. Box 503 (tel. 809/367-2667).

Hair Care: Women or men who want to get their hair done should drive up to Treasure Cay. There, they will be taken care of at the **Looking Glass Beauty Salon** (tel. 809/367-2570).

Immigration: The office of Bahamas Immigration is at the airport (tel. 809/367-2675).

Medical Care: The best medical clinic in the Abacos is in Marsh Harbour, the **Great Abaco Clinic,** Steede Bonnet Road (tel. 809/365-2510).

Police: To call the police, dial **367-2560.**

Post Office: Marsh Harbour's post office (tel. 809/367-2571) is on Don MacKay Boulevard.

Shopping: If you'd like to shop for gifts or souvenirs, about the best place is the **Loyalist Shoppe,** Don MacKay Boulevard, P.O. Box 445 (tel. 809/367-2701), which has leather goods from England and Italy, pottery, crystal, bone china, periodicals, cosmetics, souvenirs, cameras, and nautical gift items.

WHERE TO STAY

Expensive

Abaco Towns by the Sea, P.O. Box 486, Marsh Harbour, Abaco, The Bahamas (tel. 809/367-2221), is a pleasant 64-unit time-share resort complex set on sandy soil on a rolling terrain of rises and valleys. There's a small crescent of beach looking out over the Sea of Abaco, as well as a free-form swimming pool, tennis

---

What the Symbols Mean

AP (American plan): Includes three meals a day (sometimes called full board or full pension).

BP (Bermuda plan): Popularized first in Bermuda, this option includes a full American breakfast (sometimes called an English breakfast).

CP (Continental plan): A Continental breakfast (that is, bread, jam, and coffee) is included in the room rate.

EP (European plan): This rate is always cheapest, as it offers only the room—no meals.

MAP (modified American plan): Sometimes called half board or half pension, this room rate includes breakfast and dinner (or lunch if you prefer).

---

courts, and a cluster of white stucco villas grouped in a flowering landscape. You'll be able to identify bougainvillea, coconut, hibiscus, and banana trees scattered over a property that is considered deluxe for the area.

Each of the accommodations contains two bedrooms, a living room, a kitchen, two baths, ceiling fans, and air conditioning. Year-round EP rates for rental of any of these units costs $150 a day, for between one and six occupants, with slight discounts offered for rentals of a week or more. Visitors have the opportunity to purchase time shares or to rent for a single sojourn. There's a snackbar on the premises, as well as other restaurants; each is under a different management, and all are within walking distance. You can rent a bicycle from a nearby rental agency to pedal into town.

Great Abaco Beach Resort, P.O. Box 511, Marsh Harbour, Abaco, The Bahamas (tel. 809/367-2158, or toll free 800/468-4799 in the U.S.; 305/359-2720 in Florida), was created by a former pilot who served with Canadian forces in World War II. It is now run by Peter Sweeting and Jack Albury. You can rent one of six air-conditioned villas, with two bedrooms, two baths, a kitchen, and both a living and a dining area. Other units are a series of 20 air-conditioned and spacious bedrooms, each with a terrace overlooking a private beach. The rooms are decorated in a tropical motif. In winter, EP single or double occupancy costs $165 a day, with luxury villas suitable for four costing $250 to $375. *In summer, EP single or double rooms rent for $95, with villas for up to four persons costing $200 to $300.* The hotel has a beach bar and a restaurant, Harbour Lights, which serves both Bahamian and American food. The hotel lies 4 miles from the Marsh Harbour airport. You take a taxi from the airport to the hotel, where cars and bicycles can be rented. Special events with native music are often on the bill of fare.

Inexpensive

At the southeastern corner of the harbor, **Conch Inn Resort & Marina,** P.O. Box 434, Marsh Harbour, Abaco, The Bahamas (tel. 809/367-2800), is a small hotel, painted yellow, angled to allow each of its nine bedrooms a view of the harbor from its own private terrace. Etched into the neighboring harborfront is a 60-slip marina where visiting yachtspeople like to tie in for fuel, ice, fresh water, and use of the Laundromat. Many guests of this hotel are repeat visitors sailing Florida-based yachts or are scuba aficionados. Each room contains air conditioning, a private bathroom, and a color scheme of green and white. EP rates are the same throughout the year, $75 for single or double occupancy, with each additional person paying a supplement of $10, to a maximum of four occupants per room.

Affiliated with this hotel is the Conch Crawl Bar and its adjoining restaurant, the Sunset Patio (set directly on the water's edge), which is open for breakfast, lunch, and dinner. On the premises is an open-air swimming pool, and a branch of the Dive Abaco scuba facility, with a separate phone for information and reservations (tel. 809/367-2787). The location is 3 miles north of the Marsh Harbour airport.

Bungalow Rentals

The Lofty Fig Villas, P.O. Box 437, Marsh Harbour, Abaco, The Bahamas (tel. 809/367-2681), is a bungalow colony across from the Conch Inn Resort & Marina, overlooking the harbor. Built in 1970, it is spread around a free-form swimming pool, which is the social center. White lounge chairs are set on a wide sun terrace, and flowering tropical trees and shrubbery surround the pool and bungalows. There are a poolside gazebo and barbecue. Each of the six air-conditioned bungalows is fully furnished for housekeeping and contains one full double and one single bed. Interiors are smartly decorated, with colors of the sea contrasted with bone-white walls and furniture. Each unit contains its own fully equipped kitchen, with a pass-through window to the large, screened-in patio. Maid service is provided Monday through Saturday. All year, villas are rented on the EP either as doubles or singles and cost $80 per day, with an additional person paying a supplement of $10 per day. Management requires a minimum rental of at least two nights, and many clients rent for a full week, in which event a slight discount is granted.

It's just a 7-minute walk to a pair of supermarkets, and 3 miles to the airport.

WHERE TO DINE

There are more than half a dozen local restaurants serving both American and Bahamian dishes in and around Marsh Harbour. If you've been in The Bahamas for very long, the fare will be familiar to you: conch chowder, conch salad, conch fritters, along with grouper and Bahamian lobster. But, first, you have a Goombay Smash for your sundowner (everybody, seemingly, makes his or her own version).

Moderate

Mangoes Restaurant, Front Street, Marsh Harbour (tel. 809/367-2366). It's probably the best restaurant, and certainly one of the most popular, on the island, attracting both yachting types and residents from throughout the Abacos. Set near the harborfront, it is also one of the town's most distinctive buildings: fronted by either a gazebo or a pagoda (depending on your interpretation), it also boasts a cedar-topped bar and a cathedral ceiling that soars above a deck jutting out above the waters of the harbor.

Within the pink-and-white dining room you can order such appetizers as mozzarella sticks, or order from an array of fritters, chowders, and pizzas. Main dishes at lunchtime include a pasta special of the day, a daily platter of the season, salads, sandwiches, and grilled and blackened filets of dolphin or grouper. Main evening courses include grilled steaks, swordfish, chicken tropicana, baby back ribs, and roasted rack of lamb. Lunch costs from $7 to $12; dinner costs from $16 to $24. The restaurant is open daily for food orders from 11:30am to 9pm, although its bar (which even after the dining room closes makes available a list of appetizers that some diners assemble to create full meals) is open from 11:30am to midnight. Annual closing is every autumn for between six to eight weeks, depending on renovation schedules.

Marsh Harbour Marina & Restaurant, Pelican Shores, P.O. Box 518, Marsh Harbour (tel. 809/367-2700), lies across the harbor from the main concentration of buildings at Marsh Harbour, so getting here involves a taxi ride. This place is the drinking arena of local residents and boat owners who like its welcoming spirit. It has a garden with trees, shrubs, and flowers, and a building right on the water, with a restaurant area on the ground level and a bar upstairs. The bar has a yellow-and-white canvas roof and breezy views over the harbor. Dinners cost from $25 per person in the Jib Room and are served daily from 7 to 10pm. Bahamian and American dishes are featured, including a seafood platter, New York strip steak, and broiled lobster. Most nights a special is featured, such as barbecued baby back ribs. Throughout the day you can order snacks such as hot dogs and hamburgers. Hours are daily from 11am to 10pm for meals. Live music is often featured.

Ask about the reef and beach snorkeling tours offered daily at about $30 per head.

Wally's, East Bay Street, Marsh Harbour (tel. 809/367-2074), competes with Mangoes as one of the island's most popular luncheon stopovers. It occupies a well-maintained pink colonial villa behind a lawn dotted with begonias across the street from the water. There's an outdoor terrace covered with terra-cotta tiles, a boutique, and an indoor bar and dining area filled with Haitian paintings. The special drinks are daiquiris, Bahama Mamas, and Goombay Smashes, which most visitors accompany with conchburgers, beefburgers, grouper Nantua style, a selection of sandwiches, and such homemade desserts as guava-filled chocolate cake. Lunch is served Monday through Saturday from 11:30am to 3pm, costing from $12 per person. The bar, however, stays open until 5:30pm. The only dinner served is on Monday, promptly at 7pm. It costs from $25 per person, requires an advance reservation, and is anticipated by local residents as a kind of weekly ritual of fine dining. The food is both Bahamian and international. The owner, Wally Smith, personally greets each visitor at the door.

Inexpensive

Many locals will direct you to **Cynthia's Kitchen,** P.O. Box 580 (tel. 809/367-2268), right in the center of Marsh Harbour. Local dishes, and good ones, are served in this simple, basic place. Cracked conch and conch chowder are traditionally featured, and you might get Bahamian lobster on occasion, perhaps grouper, even a burger. You can also order a seafood platter, in which the emphasis is on the local catches. Cynthia also does curried goat or chicken, and peas 'n' rice. You can finish off with coconut-and-pineapple pie. Meals here cost $15 and up each, although you can have a much less expensive breakfast. Breakfast, lunch, and dinner are served daily from 8:30am to 10pm.

Mother Merle's Fishnet, P.O. Box 476, Dundas Town (tel. 809/367-2770). More substantial, and far more elaborate than you might have suspected, this restaurant sits about 1½ miles from the main marinas and harbors of Marsh Harbour. Dundas Town was created as a settlement by the government in the postwar years. Mother Merle for many years has been known as one of the best local cooks. Behind an unpretentious façade is a pair of raftered rooms dimly lit with flickering candles. You can drink in the This Is It lounge before heading in for dinner. The menu includes barbecued chicken, cracked conch, grouper, fresh lobster, conch chowder, and game fish when it's available. Hot johnnycake accompanies most meals, or peas 'n' rice with hot sauce. For dessert, try one of her Key lime pies or her coconut ice cream. Dinner is served Thursday through Tuesday from 6 to 11pm and costs from $18 per person. Reservations are recommended.

SPORTS & RECREATION

All the hotelkeepers at Marsh Harbour can help fix you up with the right people to take care of your sporting requirements. For variety, you can also take the ferry over to Hope Town and avail yourself of the facilities offered there.

Boat Charters

If you've got a good track record as a sailor, even of small boats, you can charter a yacht here big enough for the entire family, with just yourself as skipper to sail to all those places you've heard about. **Sunsail,** based in Marsh Harbour, is the operator of the largest charter fleet in The Bahamas. A bareboat charter is likely to cost you less than a comparable land-based vacation in the Family Islands or in Florida. Of course, you can cook your own meals in the fully equipped galley, one on every boat, complete with icebox (on larger boats, refrigerator and deep-freeze). You can barbecue your steak and fish on a hibachi fixed to the stern rail. You can go where you like, subject to instructions to keep out of shoal waters and staying, with one exception, within the line of the outer cays. Most of the time you cruise in waters 6 to 18 feet deep, the bottom clearly visible.

When you board your boat, you'll find it cleaned, fueled, watered, provisioned, inspected, and ready to sail. Sunsail will give you and your crew a complete familiarization briefing on everything on board from bow to stern—anchors, rigging, sails, engine, radio, lights, navigational aids, galley, stove, cooking equipment, marine toilets, shower, storage spaces, and the outboard dinghy towed astern of every boat. Before you actually sail, they'll give you a chart briefing, warning you of the few dangerous areas, how to "read" the water, and how best to make the Whale Cay ocean passage that takes you to the northern section of Abaco Sound.

Bareboat charters are usually in the range of $980 to $4,550 per week, depending on the vessel. For more information, or reservations, write Sunsail, 2 Prospect Park, 3347 NW 55th St., Fort Lauderdale, FL 33309 (tel. toll free 800/327-2276 in the U.S. and Canada, 305/484-5246 in Florida).

Tennis

Two hard-surface courts are available at the **Great Abaco Beach Hotel,** P.O. Box 419 (tel. 809/367-2158). Nonguests pay $5 per hour.

Water Sports

If you're interested in water sports, your best bet is to go to the **Conch Inn Resort & Marina,** Marsh Harbour (tel. 809/367-2800), a previously recommended hotel. There you can rent jet skis at $35 per hour, Hobie Cats at $20 per hour, and aquabikes at $10 per hour. They have other offerings as well.

Scuba and skin diving are offered by **Dive Abaco,** P.O. Box 555 (tel. 809/367-2014), among unspoiled undersea gardens and blue holes. You can rent equipment and take the Resort Course in scuba diving, costing $65 for a one-tank dive, $80 for two tanks. The tank and weights are included in the prices for the dives. Snorkeling trips cost $30. Dive Abaco trips are offered daily, weather permitting, at 9:30am and 2:30pm.

---

5. Great Guana Cay

Longest of the Abaco cays, Great Guana, on the east side of the chain, stretches 7 miles from tip to tip, lying between Green Turtle Cay and Man-O-War Cay. The cay has a 7-mile-long beach, which some consider unsurpassed in The Bahamas. The reef fishing is superb, and bonefish are plentiful in the shallow bays.

The settlement stretches along the beach at the head of the palm-fringed Kidd's Cove, named after the pirate; and the ruins of an old sisal mill near the western end of the island make for an interesting detour. The island has about 150 residents, most of them descendants of Loyalists who left Virginia and the Carolinas to settle in this remote place, often called the "last spot of land before Africa."

As in similar settlements in New Plymouth and Man-O-War Cay, their houses resemble old New England. Over the years the traditional pursuits of the islanders have been boatbuilding and carpentry. They are also farmers and fishermen. It won't take you long to explore the village, because it has only two small stores, a one-room schoolhouse, and an Anglican church—and that's about it.

Instead of automobiles, small boats are used for getting around the island. On the cay, small boats are available to charter for a half day or a full day (or a month, for that matter). For example, a 23-foot sailboat, fully equipped for living and cruising, is available for charter, and deep-sea fishing trips can be arranged.

Albury's Ferry Service, Marsh Harbour (tel. 809/367-3147), runs a charter service to the island, a one-way ride costing $60 for one to five passengers.

WHERE TO STAY & DINE

Moderate
Guana Beach Resort, P.O. Box 455, Marsh Harbour (tel. 809/367-2207), is the only hotel on the island. It is a remotely located resort of 15 comfortably furnished units, ideal for boat owners and escapists. Year-round rates (EP) are from $105 daily for a single or double. The resort has a marina, as well as a good Bahamian dining room and bar if you're over only for the day. Conchburgers with cold beer are often served for lunch, although some guests prefer a picnic packed for them. You'll find no tennis courts and no golf course, but informal local entertainment is often arranged. Babysitting can also be arranged, and laundry facilities are available.

---

6. Man-O-War Cay

Visiting here is like going back in time. Man-O-War Cay shares a cultural link with New Plymouth on Green Turtle Cay, but perhaps the people here have not advanced quite so far into later 20th-century life-styles. The island has some lovely beaches, and many visitors come here to enjoy them—but it's best to leave your more daring swimwear for other shores and look in the back of your closet for some old conservative thing.

Some find the people here puritanical in outlook. They are deeply religious, and there is no crime—unless you bring it with you. Also, you'll find no Miss Emily's Blue Bee Bar here, as you will in New Plymouth. Alcoholic beverages aren't sold, although you can bring your own supply.

Like New Plymouth, Man-O-War is a Loyalist village, with indications of a New England background. The pastel clapboard houses, built by ships' carpenters and trimmed in gingerbread, are set off by freshly painted white picket fences intertwined with bougainvillea.

The people here are basically shy, but they do welcome outsiders to their remote, isolated island. They are proud of their heritage, and many, especially the old-timers, have known plenty of hard times. They are similar to (and related to many of) the "conchs" of Key West, a tough, insular people who have exhibited a proud independence of spirit for many years.

If you look through the tiny listing for this cay in the phone book, you'll see that the name Albury predominates. In this famed boatbuilding capital of The Bahamas, Albury long ago became synonymous with that business. You can still see descendants of the early Alburys at work at a boatyard on the harbor. Albury shipbuilders still make Man-O-War runabouts, so often seen sailing in the waters of The Bahamas.

Tourism has really only begun on Man-O-War Cay. Because of the lack of hotels, many visitors come over just for the day, often in groups from Marsh Harbour.

Television has come to the island, and many of the older folk will tell you it's changed their lives, but they won't necessarily say whether that's to the good or bad.

GETTING THERE

By Ferry
To reach Man-O-War Cay, you must cross the water from Marsh Harbour. **Albury's Ferry Service** (tel. 809/367-3147 in Marsh Harbour, or 809/365-6010 in Man-O-War) leaves from a dock near the Great Abaco Beach Resort there. The round-trip fare is $10 for adults and $5 for children, and the ride takes about 45 minutes. Except for a few service vehicles, the island is free of cars. But if you want to

explore—and don't want to walk—ask around and see if one of the locals will rent you a golf cart.

WHERE TO DINE

Inexpensive

Bite Site, Man-O-War Cay (tel. 809/365-6052). Other than two solitary chairs backed up against display racks, there's no place to sit in this tiny establishment. That doesn't prevent it from enjoying one of the most devoted clienteles on the island, many of whom buy take-out food for consumption at wooden picnic tables near the wharves in front. It sits behind a sea-green–and–white clapcoard house at the edge of the marina. You order food at the countertop from an employee who might have spent her morning baking a tempting array of pastries.

The place is known far and wide for its milkshakes (ever had rum raisin?), which at $2.50 will appease your craving for ice cream for months. You can also order hamburgers, cheeseburgers, conchburgers, black-eyed peas, and such baked goods as coconut pie, pumpkin pie, apple pie, and doughnuts. A hamburger costs $3; a steaming mug of conch chowder, $3. Every Monday, Tuesday, and Thursday the place is open from 9am to 4:30pm, with an additional opening from 8:30 to 9pm for ice cream sales. Every Wednesday, Friday, and Saturday it's open without interruption from 9am to 9pm. It's always closed on Sunday.

WHERE TO SHOP

Joe's Studio (tel. 809/365-6082). Its inventory of island-related odds and ends makes this an appealing stopover. Favorite items for sale here are the half-rib models of local sailing dinghies crafted from mahogany and mounted in half profile on a board. They're a substantial but durable souvenir of your visit. Other items include original watercolors, handcrafted woodwork from native woods, and nautical souvenirs and gifts.

Perhaps the most unusual store and studio on the island is **Uncle Norman Albury's Sail Loft** (no phone). It occupies a century-old clapboard house that members of the Albury family have painted a soothing shade of avocado green. Part of the floor space is devoted to the manufacture (and the other half to the display) of an inventory of brightly colored canvas garments and accessories. The cloth that is universally used—8-ounce cotton duck—once served as sailcloth for the community's boats. When synthetic sails came into vogue, four generations of Albury women put the cloth and their talents to use. Don't stop without chatting with the Albury matrons, who say they got into the business "because we wanted to be bag ladies."

---

7. Elbow Cay (Hope Town)

Elbow Cay, noted for the many lovely beaches that attract hundreds of visitors to its shores, is connected by a regular 20-minute, $10-round-trip ferry or water-taxi service to Great Abaco at Marsh Harbour. The cay's largest settlement is Hope Town, a little village with a candy-striped 120-foot lighthouse, the most photographed attraction in the Family Islands. The kerosene-powered light is still in service.

You can climb to the top of the lighthouse for a sweeping view of the surrounding land and water. From the time construction on this beacon first began in 1838, it came under a great deal of harassment from the Abaco wreckers, who lived on salvaged cargo from wrecked and foundered ships. Seeing an end to their means of livelihood, they did much to sabotage the light in the early days.

Hope Town, often called a "time-warp" hamlet, like other offshore cays of the Abacos, was settled by Loyalists who left the new United States and came to The Bahamas to remain subjects of the British Crown, spreading out from the now long-vanished settlement of Carleton near Treasure Cay. The town will evoke thoughts of old Cape Cod or, closer to home, of New Plymouth on Green Turtle Cay. Like them, it has clapboard saltbox cottages weathered to a silver gray or painted in pastel colors, with white picket fences setting them off. The buildings may remind you of New England, but this palm-fringed island has a definite South Seas flavor.

Over the years Hope Town has attracted many famous visitors, some of whom, such as Dr. George Gallup, the pollster, liked it so much that they built "homes away from home" here.

The island is almost free of vehicular traffic. In exploring Hope Town, you can take one of two roads: "Up Along" or "Down Along," the latter running along the water.

Malone seems to be the most popular name here. The founding mother of the town back circa 1783 (perhaps 1775) was Wyannie Malone, who came here as a widow with four children. Her descendants are still a big part of the population of 500 full-time residents. A **museum** on Queen's Highway (no phone), is dedicated to Wyannie's memory, containing exhibits tracing the rich history of the cay. It's generally open from 10am to noon but you can't be sure. Donations are welcome.

FAST FACTS: ELBOW CAY (HOPE TOWN)

Pharmacy: Try the **Clear View Drug Store** (tel. 809/365-6217).

Post Office: There is a local post office (tel. 809/365-6214), but expect mail sent from here to take a long time reaching its destination. The location is at the head of the upper public dock.

WHERE TO STAY

Moderate

By anyone's standards, the **Abaco Inn,** Hope Town, Elbow Cay, Abaco, The Bahamas (tel. 809/366-0133, or toll free 800/366-0133 in the U.S.), is the area's most sophisticated and desirable resort. It nestles on a ridge of sandy soil on the narrowest section of Elbow Cay, about 1½ miles south of Hope Town. As you stand on the ridge, you'll find yourself on a strategically important land bridge between the crashing surf of the jagged eastern coast and the sheltered waters of White Sound and the Sea of Abaco to the west. The establishment's clusters of shingle-sided buildings were once part of a private club, the Fin & Tonic. But informal "barefoot elegance" and welcoming enthusiasm now prevail. The resort's social center is in a modern and rambling clubhouse that looks a lot like a beach house in Northern California. There's an open fireplace set into a stone wall, heavy beams, pinewood paneling, comfortable sofas, and the most appealing bar on the island. Its modernity is relieved by an antique airplane propeller.

The 10 accommodations are scattered between the palms and sea grapes of the sandy terrain. Each has a hammock placed conveniently nearby for quiet afternoons of reading or sleeping. Each has a ceiling fan and private bath, along with a comfortably unpretentious decor of white wooden walls and conservative furniture. When you tire of your cabin with its carefully maintained privacy, you can dream of faraway places from a perch in the cedar-capped gazebo, which sits between the saltwater pool and the rocky tidal flats of the Atlantic.

In winter, rooms cost $119 daily for a single and $125 for a double. *Summer singles cost $89 daily; doubles $95.* Year round, MAP can be arranged for another $29 per person daily. The inn is closed from early September to mid-November.

Villa Rentals

The Villas of Hope Town, Hope Town, Abaco, The Bahamas (tel. 809/367-2004), offers privacy and convenience in air-conditioned villas set on 10 acres of forest running from the sea to the harbor. Each waterfront villa sleeps six, with two master bedrooms—each with a full bath, queen-size beds, and a private deck—plus two single daybeds in the living room. Kitchens are fully equipped, and the island-style homes also have ceiling fans and are accented with French windows and doors, Spanish roof tiles, exposed ceiling beams, and a large wooden deck. For eight days and seven nights on the EP, the cost year round is $950 per week for two to four persons; an extra person pays another $50 per week. Chris and Peggy Thompson do everything from overseeing housekeeping to arranging rental boats, guided fishing trips, picnics, island-hopping excursions, and scuba and snorkeling trips.

WHERE TO DINE

Moderate

The best food is served at the **Abaco Inn,** Elbow Cay (tel. 809/367-2666). It's in the clubhouse of the previously recommended hotel, within view of the crashing surf of the Atlantic and a weathered gazebo looking out to sea. The chef prepares such lunch dishes as conch chowder, lobster salad, pasta primavera, and salads with delectable homemade dressings laced with tarragon and other herbs. There is a changing dinner menu of seafood and meats, each expertly seasoned and well prepared. Typical meals are likely to begin with seafood bisque or vichyssoise, followed by broiled lobster, grilled tuna with béarnaise sauce, broiled red snapper with a light salsa sauce, or grouper sautéed with butter and lime. The Key lime pie or coconut pie is delectable. Lunch is offered daily from noon to 2pm, costing $10 per person. Dinner is served in a single seating at 7:30pm every evening, costing $20 to $24 per person. The place is closed from early September to mid-November. The inn will send a minivan to collect you from other parts of the island if you phone in advance.

Harbour's Edge, Hope Town (tel. 809/366-0087). One of the town's most popular restaurants is set on piers above the water, in a clapboard house next to the post office. A bar is found near the entrance, with an adjacent waterside deck for watching the passage of boats. There's also a tile-floored dining room, where the crackle of VHF radio is always audible. Boat owners and local residents reserve tables on the short-wave radio, Channel 16. The lunch bill of fare includes conch fritters, conch chowder, hamburgers, sandwiches, and conch platters. Dinners include plain yet well-prepared food such as pan-fried pork chops, char-grilled grouper, New York strip steak, and fried chicken. The place is open Wednesday through Monday. Lunch, costing $12, is served from 11:30 to 2pm. Dinners cost from $28 each and are served from 6:30 to 8:30pm. The restaurant is closed from mid-September to mid-October.

WHERE TO SHOP

Of course, no one comes to Hope Town just to shop, but once you're here you might want to buy a souvenir or gift at **Native Touches,** Hope Town (no phone). Several of the items sold here are handcrafted.

Ebb Tide Gift Shop, Hope Town (no phone), is the best-stocked gift shop in town. It's found in a white clapboard house with yellow trim, one block from the harbor. Inside, an employee sells Androsia batiks, jewelry, T-shirts, fabric by the yard, engravings, maps, baby-size quilts, and suntan lotion.

Also, at **Kemp's Straw Market,** Hope Town, you can find some gift items made by local residents.

SPORTS & RECREATION

The best dive operation is **Dave Gale's Island Marine,** Parrot Cay (tel. 809/366-0282). Gale, a NAUI instructor, takes guests to coral reefs and wrecks, among other attractions. One dive site includes the *Adirondack,* a Civil War gunboat that is covered by 10 to 25 feet of water. It sank on the barrier reef in the summer of 1862. Scuba-diving trips are arranged for two to five people, costing $35 per diver for a half-day trip. Snorkeling, at $25 per person for half a day, includes free use of equipment. A 15-foot Boston Whaler (40 horsepower) rents for $55 per day; a 17-footer (70 horsepower) goes for $65 per day. If you prefer, you can rent a 19-foot Aquasport (115 horsepower) for $75 per day.

Boat excursions, costing from $20 to $50 per person, will take you to the boatbuilding settlement on Man-O-War Cay, to sculptor Randolph Johnston's bronze foundry in Little Harbour (see below), to the abandoned remains of Wilson City, and to many uninhabited cays and deserted beaches where you can go shelling, beachcombing, exploring, and picnicking. Charter boats are available for bonefishing, reef fishing, and deep-sea fishing. Bonefish, grouper, snapper, wahoo, yellowtail, dolphin, kingfish, and others are abundant in the local waters, and resident Bahamian guides can show you where they are. Or you may prefer to rent a boat and try your own skill.

Boat rentals are offered by **Sea Horse Marine,** Boat Harbour Resort (tel. 809/366-0023), on the waterfront of Hope Town Harbour. Eighteen-foot Boston Whalers can be had for $85 per day for one to two days. The 22-footers rent for $110 for one to two days. You can also rent bicycles here for $2 per day.

---

8. Little Harbour

In the Abaco gift and souvenir shops you'll see a remarkable book, *Artist on His Island,* detailing the true-life adventures of Randolph and Margot Johnston, who lived a Swiss Family Robinson–type adventure with their three sons. Arriving on this southerly point of the Abacos aboard their old Bahamian schooner, the *Langosta,* they lived in one of the natural caves on the island until they eventually erected a thatched dwelling for themselves.

That was some time ago—in 1951. Now the Johnstons have achieved international fame as artists and sculptors while still living on their own Little Harbour island, a cay shaped like a circle, with a white-sand beach running along most of it.

If you ask at your hotel in Marsh Harbour, chances are that an arrangement can be made for you to visit the island, which is serviced by Albury's Ferry. This is the southernmost stop of the ferry line. Since the island is private property, you are asked to treat it as if it's someone's home you're visiting—as indeed it is.

On the island is a foundry in which Mr. Johnston, using an old "lost-wax" method, casts his bronze sculptures, many of which are in prestigious galleries today. Mrs. Johnston creates porcelain figurines of island life—birds, fish, boats, and fishermen. She also works in glazed metals. They welcome visitors at their studio daily from 10 to 11am and 2 to 3pm. It's also possible to purchase their art, which comes in a wide price range.

XIII

ELEUTHERA, HARBOUR ISLAND & SPANISH WELLS

1. ROCK SOUND
2. WINDERMERE ISLAND
3. TARPUM BAY
4. GOVERNOR'S HARBOUR
5. PALMETTO POINT
6. HATCHET BAY
7. GREGORY TOWN
8. THE CURRENT
9. HARBOUR ISLAND
10. SPANISH WELLS

The most developed of the Family Islands, sickle-shaped Eleuthera was settled in 1648, the first permanent settlement in The Bahamas. It is considered the seat of the first true democracy in the Western Hemisphere. In search of religious freedom, the Eleutherian Adventurers came here from Bermuda, finding and colonizing the long, narrow island that still carries their name (Greek for freedom). The locals call it "Cigatoo."

What these adventurers found was an island 100 miles long and a bowshot wide (an average of 2 miles), lying on the eastern flank of The Bahamas. There, after a long journey from the Iberian Peninsula, Atlantic rollers crash ashore. These rollers wash up on an island of white- and pink-sand beaches edged by casuarina trees, high, rolling green hills, sea-to-sea views, dramatic cliffs, sheltered coves, old villages of pastel-washed cottages, and exclusive resorts built around excellent harbors.

Eleuthera begins 70 miles east of Nassau, and can be reached by a 30-minute air flight. It encompasses about 200 square miles. The island is known for its ocean holes that swirl salt water into land-locked rock formations.

The population today is estimated at 10,000, a medley of farmers, shopkeepers, and fishermen, and many of course engaged in tourism serving the 20 or so resorts. Eleuthera has come a long way since it was first described by its mid-17th-century

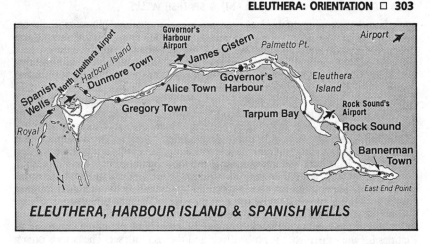

ELEUTHERA, HARBOUR ISLAND & SPANISH WELLS

colonists as "Ye barren rock." Roads run along the coastline today, but if you engage in any extensive touring, you'll find some of them adequately paved while many others are devastating to cars.

Long before the first English colonists arrived, Eleuthera was inhabited by Lucayan Indians. However, around the mid-16th century Spaniards came this way, capturing the peaceable people and shipping them out to the Caribbean as slaves.

Pirates plied the waters off Eleuthera and its adjacent islands, but after the removal of the Lucayans there were no inhabitants here for a century, until Captain William Sayle led the Eleutherian Adventurers here from Bermuda to start a new life. The founding party consisted of about 70 people. They had a rough time of it. Dangerous reefs on the north coast of the island caused their ship and cargo to be lost. Trapped, they had to live off the land as best they could, initially inhabiting a cave (for a description, see "The Current," below).

They were not adept at earning a living in this new environment, and many of them nearly starved, but they nevertheless drew up their own constitution, promising justice for all. Help came from Virginia colonists, who, despite being short of supplies themselves, sent food to the little band of adventurers.

Life on Eleuthera proved too much for many of the founding party, however. Many, including Captain Sayle, later returned to Bermuda. But reinforcements were on the way, both from Bermuda and from England, some bringing slaves with them. A permanent settlement had been founded. Freed slaves also came to this island and established settlements. The next wave of settlers were fleeing Loyalists leaving the new United States in order to continue living under the British Crown. These settled principally in two offshore cays, Harbour Island and Spanish Wells.

Eleuthera is considered the "birthplace of The Bahamas," a sort of Bahamian Plymouth Rock.

TOURISM

The island once had a flourishing farm industry, especially in pineapples, although tomatoes and oranges were also exported. Several dairy and poultry farms were also started. One major plantation still exists today—run by the government. After many eventual failures in various industries, most of the people of Eleuthera are turning to tourism as their major hope for the future.

Eleuthera rivals the Abacos in its lure for the foreign visitor. Along with the Abacos, it has the largest concentration of resort hotels outside of Nassau/Paradise Island and Freeport/Lucaya. Some of the more famous resorts, such as Cotton Bay

Beach and Windermere Island, charge superexpensive prices. However, for those willing to book a no-frills type of accommodation, I've included several self-sufficient housekeeping cottages and some low-cost guesthouses. In some of these places you'll have plumbing that "sometimes has a problem," and furnishings that may have seen better days (or never had a better day when new). But the warmth and hospitality of the local people often make up for inconveniences likely to be encountered. At any rate, these places provide the only low-cost way of vacationing here.

Of the 10 destinations recommended in this chapter, Harbour Island gets my vote as the number-one choice. Here you'll find a wide range of accommodations. Dunmore Town on Harbour Island was the original capital of The Bahamas, and is the island's oldest and most charming settlement. Many visitors who have traveled all over The Bahamas consider Harbour Island the most beautiful in the archipelago.

Spanish Wells is another small island just off the north end of Eleuthera. Spanish galleons put sailors ashore to fill the ships' casks with fresh water after long sea voyages—hence the present-day name of the island. The men of Spanish Wells are said to be the best seamen in The Bahamas.

Fishing and diving in the waters around Eleuthera are top-notch. There are facilities for the fishermen, the scuba diver, and the yachting set. The islands offer a wide choice of coral gardens, reefs, drop-offs, wrecks, and drift dives. As divers know, wrecks often form the best dive sites. Eleuthera has several, including a submerged freight train wrecked during a storm off North Eleuthera while being barged to Cuba.

Fishermen come to Eleuthera for bottom, bone-, and deep-sea fishing, testing their skill against the dolphin, the wahoo, the blue or white marlin, the Allison tuna, and the amberjack. Charter boats are available at Powell Point, Rock Sound, Spanish Wells, and Harbour Island.

Sunfish, sailboats, and Boston Whalers for reef fishing can also be rented.

GETTING THERE

Eleuthera has three main airports. North Eleuthera Airport, obviously, serves the north along with two major offshore cays, Harbour Island and Spanish Wells. Governor's Harbour Airport serves the center of the island, and Rock Sound International Airport handles traffic to South Eleuthera. Make sure, when booking a flight, that you arrive at the right airport. Otherwise, your experience might resemble that of one visitor who flew into Rock Sound Airport, only to face a $100 ride and a water-taxi trip before reaching his final destination of Harbour Island in the north.

By Air

Bahamasair (tel. 800/222-4262) offers daily flights between Nassau and the three airports, North Eleuthera, Governor's Harbour, and Rock Sound. Bahamasair also flies in from Miami daily.

In addition, several commuter airlines, with regularly scheduled service, fly from the Florida mainland with either nonstop or one-stop service. Many private flights use the North Eleuthera Airport, with its 4,500-foot paved runway. It is an official Bahamian port of entry, and a Customs and Immigration official is on hand.

Aero Coach (tel. 800/327-0010) serves all three of Eleuthera's airports from its bases in Miami, Fort Lauderdale, and West Palm Beach.

American Eagle (tel. 800/433-7300) flies twice daily from Miami to Eleuthera's Governor's Harbour.

USAir (tel. 800/428-4322) operates what might be the most popular way of reaching two of Eleuthera's airports directly from the mainland of Florida. Flights depart every day from Fort Lauderdale, flying nonstop to North Eleuthera, then continuing on after a brief unloading of passengers and baggage to Governor's Harbour. Every Saturday, two flights instead of one are offered, following basically the same itinerary. Fort Lauderdale, by the way, is considered one of the airline's busier destinations, with direct or nonstop flights winging in from throughout North America, including daily service from Los Angeles.

By Mailboat

Several mailboats from Nassau, leaving from Potter's Cay Dock, visit Eleuthera, but their schedules are subject to change because of weather conditions. For more details of sailings, consult the Dockmaster at Potter's Cay Dock in Nassau (tel. 809/393-1064).

The M/V *Current Pride* goes from Nassau to Current Island, serving Lower and Upper Bogue. It departs Nassau at 7am Thursday, returning on Tuesday.

The M/V *Bahamas Daybreak II* leaves Nassau, heading for North Eleuthera, Spanish Wells, and Harbour Island. Departures are on Thursday at 6am from Nassau, with a return on Monday.

The M/V *Harley and Charley* leaves Nassau on Friday (returning on Sunday), heading for Central Eleuthera: Hatchet Bay and Governor's Harbour. The same vessel goes from Nassau to South Eleuthera: Davis Harbour and Rock Sound. It leaves Nassau on Monday, returning on Thursday.

---

1. Rock Sound

In South Eleuthera, Rock Sound is a small, tree-shaded village, the principal center of the island and its most exclusive enclave. To the south of Tarpum Bay, it opens onto Exuma Sound. The town is at least two centuries old, and it has many old-fashioned homes with picket fences out front. Once it was notorious for the wreckers who lured ships ashore with false beacons. In those days it was known as "Wreck Sound."

The largest settlement in Eleuthera, Rock Sound is serviced by an airport. It is also the commercial heart of the southern area, with a modern shopping center. Many residents who live in South Eleuthera come here to stock up on supplies.

Arthur Vining Davis, the Florida millionaire, and Juan Trippe, developer of Pan American Airlines, did much to publicize Rock Sound. A lot of famous people have visited here, including the Mountbattens, and more recently the Prince and Princess of Wales, as well as titans of industry and an occasional movie star.

The Ocean Hole to the east is about 1¼ miles from the heart of the town. This is a saltwater lake that eventually links to the sea. You can walk right down to the edge of the water. This is one of the most attractive spots on Eleuthera. The "hole" is said to be bottomless. Many tropical fish can be seen here; they seem to like to be photographed—but only if you feed them first.

FAST FACTS: ROCK SOUND

A few pointers may help you enjoy your visit to Rock Sound even more than you may expect.

Car Rentals: Ask at your hotel for what's available. No national car-rental agencies operate here. **Dingle Motor Service,** King's Highway (tel. 809/334-2031), might rent you a vehicle.

Church: Rock Sound has an Anglican church, near the water.

Medical Care: A doctor and four resident nurses form the staff of the **Rock Sound Medical Clinic** (tel. 809/334-2226).

Police: Telephone **334-2244** to call the police.

Shopping: If you're looking for gifts and souvenirs, try **Goombay Gifts,** Market Place King, P.O. Box 21 (tel. 809/334-2191). Buy liquor at **Sturrup's Liquor Store,** Queen's Highway, Market Place (tel. 809/334-2219).

What the Symbols Mean

AP (American plan): Includes three meals a day (sometimes called full board or full pension).

BP (Bermuda plan): Popularized first in Bermuda, this option includes a full American breakfast (sometimes called an English breakfast).

CP (Continental plan): A Continental breakfast (that is, bread, jam, and coffee) is included in the room rate.

EP (European plan): This rate is always cheapest, as it offers only the room—no meals.

MAP (modified American plan): Sometimes called half board or half pension, this room rate includes breakfast and dinner (or lunch if you prefer).

WHERE TO STAY

Expensive

One of the most prestigious and luxurious beach, golf, and tennis resorts in The Bahamas is **Cotton Bay Club,** Powell Point, P.O. Box 28, Rock Sound, Eleuthera, The Bahamas (tel. 809/334-6101, or toll free 800/334-3523 in the U.S.). Once a private club built by Juan Trippe (founder of Pan Am), Cotton Bay, while still having memberships, has been open to nonmembers since 1975. Lying 12 miles from the Rock Sound Airport, the oceanside resort is on a 2-mile stretch of pink-sand beach, and also has acres of landscaped grounds. It advertises itself as "Where Who's Who in America Goes Barefoot in The Bahamas." All public rooms have been newly redecorated with elegant tropical decor. The main cocktail lounge is built with a peaked circular roof and has furnishings of rattan. Drinks are served in the comfortable Founders Lounge, or al fresco on the palm-fringed terrace overlooking the sea. Dinner at Cotton Bay is served outside on the pool terrace, weather permitting. Menus are American and Continental cuisine, spiced with Bahamian specialties.

Life is quiet and leisurely at this aristocrat of Bahamian resorts. Of the 77 units, most overlook the ocean. Rooms are comfortable and tropically stylish—all newly redecorated with air conditioning, ceiling fans, and refrigerators. All rates are quoted on the MAP (half board). In winter, they range from $255 to $305 daily for a single, from $300 to $350 for a double. *In summer, singles on the MAP pay $165 to $185 daily, with doubles charged $205 to $225.*

The resort contains a Robert Trent Jones–designed 18-hole championship golf course, with oceanfront holes, and four championship tennis courts. Deep-sea fishing and bonefishing trips are available at nearby Davis Harbour Marina.

Inexpensive

Edwina's Place, P.O. Box 30, Rock Sound, Eleuthera, The Bahamas (tel. 809/334-2094), is Bahamian-owned—"Edwina Burrows' place"—just a mile south of Rock Sound Airport. Its utter simplicity is balanced by enthusiastic hospitality of the good-natured Mrs. Burrows. Set directly on the water, her nine rooms are clean and furnished plainly. There is a restaurant on the premises (see below). All village facilities are within walking distance of the motel, and if you want to go farther afield, Mrs. Burrows says that if you'll put some gas in her old car, "you can take off," but you'll be charged for the privilege. Most of the guests live in their swimsuits, so the dress is decidedly casual. Year-round rates are $40 daily for a single, rising to $50 for a double, including breakfast. Tennis, snorkeling, scuba diving, deep-sea fishing, and boating can be arranged by the management.

WHERE TO DINE

Expensive

Many guests staying at other hotels enjoy the food served at **Cotton Bay Club,** Powell Point, Rock Sound (tel. 809/334-6101), one of the most prestigious hotels in The Bahamas. If you call for a reservation (not always necessary), the maître d' will be happy to welcome you. Cotton Bay's chilled hearts of palm soup is famous at lunch. Dinner, a relatively formal affair (jackets requested for men), is served by the pool and near a screen of palms and bougainvillea on an open terrace; in iffy weather, dinner is served in a curved modern dining room stretching toward the sea. The menu includes a changing array of specialties such as sautéed grouper filet, veal Oscar, duck à l'orange, and lobster medallions with mango sauce, followed by such desserts as fresh lemon pie or chocolate-and-walnut pie. The big nights to come here are Wednesday, for the buffet (when it becomes "just Bahamian"), and Saturday, for the barbecue ("How do you like your steak?"). Breakfast is served daily from 7:30 to 10am, costing $8 per person. Lunch is served daily from 12:30 to 2:30pm and averages from about $15 per person. Dinner is served nightly from 7:30 to 9:30pm, costing from $45 per person without drinks.

Inexpensive

At **Edwina's Place,** a mile south of Rock Sound Airport (tel. 809/334-2094), you "haven't tasted anything yet till you've tried my conch fritters or my conch chowder." That's Edwina Burrows talking, the hospitable owner of this simple little roadside restaurant and adjoining motel (see above). One diner noted, "I get the best food in Eleuthera here." A hardworking, devout Christian woman, Mrs. Burrows will prepare you cracked conch or perhaps a baked fish based on the catch of the day. She takes time with her vegetables too. I've enjoyed her five-bean salad, and her stuffed tomatoes are delicious. "Whenever possible, I use vegetables right from my own little cabbage patch," she confides. Prices for a main course include appetizers. You can also drop in for breakfast starting at 7am. Each person should figure on spending $12 with tip for lunch, which can be simple fare, such as fish sandwiches. Top off the meal with Mrs. Burrows' coconut pie, or try her rum cake or guava duff. You'll probably spend about $18 for dinner, everything included. Try to go for dinner before 8pm.

SPORTS & RECREATION

Golf

Cotton Bay Club, Powell Point, Rock Sound (tel. 809/334-6101), has an 18-hole, par-72 golf course—one of the most famous in The Bahamas—that was designed by Robert Trent Jones. Its 7,068 yards are almost completely surrounded by the ocean. Greens fees are $30 for 18 holes. A caddy costs $20 for 18 holes, and electric carts rent for $25 for 18 holes. There are a lounge, a bar, and a snackbar in the clubhouse, along with showers and lockers. The clubhouse also has a complete pro shop. The course, which meanders through the resort and lies some 10 miles from Rock Sound, is open daily from 8am to 5:30pm.

Fishing

At **Cotton Bay Club,** Powell Point, Rock Sound (tel. 809/334-6101), guests can make arrangements for deep-sea-fishing excursions at the resort's main office. With all equipment included, a half-day trip costs $250, and a full-day voyage is $450. Bonefishing, with a guide, can be arranged at the resort as well.

Tennis •

Cotton Bay Club, Powell Point, Rock Sound (tel. 809/334-6101), has four Har-Tru surfaced courts that are restricted to guests of the club.

---

2. Windermere Island

Windermere is a very tiny island, connected by a bridge to "mainland" Eleuthera. It is midway between the settlements of Governor's Harbour and Rock Sound.

This island couldn't be more discreet. "We like to keep it quiet around here," one of the staff at the famed Windermere Island Club recently told me. But, regrettably for this deluxe and snobbish citadel, that isn't always possible. When Prince Charles first took his Princess Di here, she was photographed in her swimming suit, even though pregnant, and the picture gained wide notoriety, much to the horror of the club.

Prince Charles himself had first heard of the club long ago, through his great-uncle, Earl Mountbatten of Burma, who was assassinated in 1979 while sailing off Ireland. He was one of the island's more frequent visitors and one of its major enthusiasts.

Aristocrats on both sides of the Atlantic, not only the Mountbattens but the Astors and the Biddles, have flocked to this club, along with an occasional visiting head of state and tycoons of industry.

The club reportedly has some 700 members, and, naturally, these guests are given preference when it comes to renting a room. But the general public is invited as well—that is, those who can afford it. It's one of the most expensive retreats in The Bahamas.

Even if you can't afford its hotel tariffs, you may want to consider dining there. Of course, you must make a reservation and show up in your finery (that is, jackets and ties for men and, preferably, long gowns for women).

The island has its own charm, especially Savannah Sound, which has lovely sheltered beaches and facilities for waterskiing, sailboating, snorkeling, and skin-diving. There are also excellent beaches for shelling. Frequent picnics are arranged at West Beach on Savannah Sound, and there is good bonefishing, with some catches more than 10 pounds.

GETTING THERE

By Air Taxi

An air-taxi service operates from Miami's Opa-Locka Airport to Rock Sound International Airport on Eleuthera, just minutes away from Windermere. Escorted transfers to Opa-Locka Airport for the approximately 1-hour flight are provided from Miami International Airport, eliminating any delay in the journey to Eleuthera. The aircraft may also be chartered from Fort Lauderdale and West Palm Beach.

The turbo-propelled, twin-engine aircraft seats passengers in comfort within an executive-level interior. The fare for a one-way flight, carrying five passengers, is $380, which can be added to the bill at the club.

For more information and reservations for both the air taxi and Windermere Island Club, contact Orient-Express Hotels Reservation Center (tel. 212/839-0222 in New York, toll free 800/237-1236 nationwide, and toll free 800/451-2253 in Canada).

WHERE TO STAY

Expensive

The ideal place for persons seeking a tranquil haven is **Windermere Island Club,** P.O. Box 25, Rock Sound, Eleuthera, The Bahamas (tel. 809/332-6003, or toll free 800/237-1236 in the U.S., 800/451-2253 in Canada; for New York City, 212/839-0222). Operated by the prestigious chain that runs the Venice Simplon–Orient Express, this gracious and isolated resort is for those who crave unspoiled seclusion. It occupies the sun-flooded southern end of Windermere Island, a snake-shaped formation lying off the eastern coast of Eleuthera. Accommodations sit in a large garden of soft fir trees and palms, directly on one of the most beautiful beaches in The Bahamas.

Capped with a wooden replica of a pineapple—the symbol of hospitality—the central building is octagonal, with a second-floor sitting room whose pine beams soar into a single point high above the modern white furniture. A beautiful swimming pool, shaped like an angular interpretation of a pineapple, opens onto a protected terrace. Tall coconut trees, illuminated at night, sway at the edge of the sunbathing area, the white garden chairs of which serve double duty for fair-weather breakfasts and buffet lunches. Windermere Island Club is equipped with six all-weather tennis courts. Twice weekly an Eleutheran band plays for dancing. The main living room of the club is overscale and airy, with ring-around 360° windows and a paperback library. The resort's dining facilities are reviewed separately.

The club has 21 rooms, 10 suites, and 10 apartments, each with a private patio or balcony overlooking the sea. Both suites and guest rooms are on the beach, overlooking the Atlantic, its rolling surf, and its sunrises. Each suite contains a living room, bedroom, dressing room, kitchenette, and veranda. There are beachfront private apartments, each with two bedrooms, two baths, a full kitchen, a large living room, and a veranda. (These are available all year; however, the club is closed from June to November.) There are also a dozen two- to five-bedroom privately owned homes available for rent year round. Most accommodations, regardless of their size, have private verandas ringed with neo-Victorian gingerbread, plus wooden ceilings covered with planks of picket cedar.

In the guest rooms, winter prices are $175 daily for a single and $330 for a double, with one-bedroom suites renting for $445 single and $490 double, all MAP (half-board) tariffs. The hotel quotes *EP shoulder season rates (that is, spring and fall) of $125 daily for a single or double, with one-bedroom suites, either single or double occupancy, going for $230.*

WHERE TO DINE

Expensive

Even if you're staying elsewhere, you can visit the glamorous dining room of **Windermere Island Club,** Rock Sound (tel. 809/332-6003). Lunch is a fixed-price buffet laden with a smörgåsbord of warm and cold dishes, elegantly prepared and served by a polite and impeccably uniformed staff. It costs $15 per person and is offered daily from 12:30 to 2pm. Sunday brunch, from noon to 2pm, goes for $20 per person, plus service. On Tuesday and Saturday, its location moves to West Beach, where a barbecue buffet is presented from 7:30 to 8:30pm. It requires an advance reservation and proper attire. Fixed-price meals cost from $35 per person, not including drinks, and are supervised by Rodney Pinder, one of the most capable maître d's in The Bahamas. Don't overlook the possibility of a before-dinner drink in the nearby bar. No meals are served in September and October, when the hotel shuts down. Jackets are required for men after 6pm.

SPORTS & RECREATION

Guests can enjoy a number of activities from bonefishing to windsurfing. The Dockmaster at West Beach is well qualified to guide and advise about bonefishing, or perhaps you'd like to go deep-sea fishing for white marlin, dolphin, grouper, wahoo, Allison tuna, and amberjack, just a few of the big fish found in these waters.

Scuba diving and snorkeling are also available; equipment for club guests and members is issued from the shed adjacent to the tennis pro's shop. The resort's glass-bottom dinghy is also available free for use by guests. Sunfish and Windsurfers, available from the Dockmaster at West Beach, can be used by guests. Windermere Island Club has its own speedboat, based at the Dockmaster's office. It can be used to go waterskiing.

West Beach, a good place for sunning and swimming (great for children), is about a 10-minute walk from the hotel, although the club bus will transport you there and back if necessary. Beer and soft drinks are available. The beach is on Savannah Sound, the body of calm, protected water separating Windermere from the main island of Eleuthera.

Six all-weather tennis courts are near the main Windermere complex.

---

3. Tarpum Bay

If you're looking for an inexpensive holiday on high-priced Eleuthera, forget Windermere Island or Cotton Bay and head here. A waterfront village, some 9 miles north of the superexpensive citadels of fine living at Rock Sound, it has a number of guesthouses that take in economy-minded tourists. This tiny settlement with its many pastel-washed houses is a favorite of artists who have established a small colony here.

It was once flourishing as a pineapple export center. That's when many of the present clapboard homes with their gingerbread trim were constructed. Nowadays an air of nostalgia pervades this old community. It's also good for fishing.

Honors as the community's artistic patriarch are given to a Scottish-Irish sculptor and painter who since 1957 has occupied an oceanfront house on the northern edge of the hamlet. Bearded, psychic, and gracious, Peter MacMillan-Hughes, at his **MacMillan-Hughes Gallery and Castle** (tel. 809/334-4091), has sold paintings to an impressive array of patrons, one of whom was Lord Mountbatten. Mr. MacMillan-Hughes imagines himself a Neptune among the mermaids in Bahamian waters. Eccentric, yes, but fascinating. His pen-and-ink tinted maps, drawings of birds, and hand-lettered poems and histories are displayed in many prominent homes. Some of the canvases glow with the reflected light of Bahamian moonscapes and are sought after by art dealers from as far away as London. Often clad in purple ("a difficult color to paint with, but very high in spiritual power"), he built with his own hands the tower of the limestone castle that rises from the center of town, a short walk from his studio. Soft-spoken, talented, and accessible, Mr. MacMillan-Hughes might in his own person be the single most interesting tourist attraction at Tarpum Bay. Visitors are welcome to show up at his door.

One of the local clubs has a fascinating name: Dark End of the Street Club. The location is about 7 miles from Rock Sound Airport.

WHERE TO STAY

Inexpensive

Cartwright's Ocean View Cottages, Tarpum Bay, Eleuthera, The Bahamas (tel. 809/334-4215), is a cluster of two- and three-bedroom cottages right by the sea, with fishing, snorkeling, and swimming at your door. This is one of the few places where you can sit on your patio and watch the sunset. The five cottages are fully furnished, with bedding, towels, utensils, stove, refrigerator, and pots and pans. Maid service is also provided. Year round, a large three-bedroom cottage suitable for six people on the EP goes for $160 per day. In winter, the EP rate for the other cottages is $100 a day for a single, $80 for a double, and $95 for a room for four persons. *In summer, the EP charge is $60 a day for a single, $65 for a double, and $95 for a room for four guests.* The establishment is within walking distance of local stores and restaurants. The owners, Iris and Hervis Cartwright, are helpful. Hervis operates an informal taxi business and will meet you at Rock Sound Airport, 7 miles away.

Hilton's Haven Motel and Restaurant, Tarpum Bay, Eleuthera, The Bahamas (tel. 809/334-4231), with 10 rooms, is in a modern Bahamian two-story structure with covered verandas. Comfortably furnished apartments, each with its private sun patio and bath, are rented. The units come with either air conditioning or ceiling fans. What makes this place special is Mary Hilton herself, everybody's "Bahama Mama." In fact, as a professional nurse, she has delivered some 2,000 of Eleuthera's finest citizens. Her brother is T. Langton Hilton, solicitor-general of the Commonwealth until his retirement in 1980. "Hilton is our God-given name," she says. "We never met Conrad." She invites you to "come and stay long enough to get to know us." If you arrive hot and thirsty, she'll tell the woman who works for her, "Go and get me a fresh lime off the tree. We'll make these people something cold to drink." To provide a retirement income for herself, she started Hilton's Haven "when it was just a pond. I had it filled in and started to build."

The main tavern-style dining room, with a library in the corner, provides well-cooked food; the cuisine puts its emphasis on freshly caught fish. You can order grouper cutlets with peas 'n' rice, steamed conch, and an occasional lobster. There is also a well-stocked bar. Lunches, costing from $8 each, are served from 12:30 to 2:30pm, and dinners, from $15 each, are offered from 6:30 to 8pm.

Mainly retired, Mrs. Hilton is still a registered nurse, and medical facilities are always available. If you're handicapped in any way, you've come to the right place. She'll take good care of you. Life is casual and informal at Hilton's, and you can have privacy and relaxation. In winter, singles on the EP pay from $45, and doubles cost from $50 per day. *In summer, singles on the EP pay only $40, and a double goes for $45.*

---

4. Governor's Harbour

After passing through Tarpum Bay, the next destination is Governor's Harbour, which, at some 300 years old, is the island's oldest settlement. This is believed to have been the landing place of the Eleutherian Adventurers. It's the largest settlement in Eleuthera after Rock Sound, lying about midway along the 100-mile island, wrapped around a curving bay. It has an airport where Bahamasair comes in on both morning and evening flights from Nassau.

The town today has a population of about 750, with some bloodlines going back to the original settlers, the Eleutherian Adventurers, and to the Loyalists who followed some 135 years later. Many old homes—waiting for "discovery"—can still be seen, showing the wear and tear of decades. A quiet nostalgia prevails amid such vegetation as bougainvillea and casuarina trees.

Leaving Queen's Highway, you can take a small bridge to Cupid's Cay (I don't know how it got that romantic name). The bridge is thought to be about a century and a half old, although there don't seem to be any records as to its construction. As you're exploring, you'll come upon one of the most interesting buildings in the area, an old Anglican church with its tombstone-studded graveyard.

The long-ago opening of the Club Med brought renewed vitality to the once-sleepy village. Tourism has unquestionably altered sleepy Governor's Harbour.

FAST FACTS: GOVERNOR'S HARBOUR

If you're staying outside the town in one of the housekeeping colonies, you may find much-needed services and supplies in Governor's Harbour or at nearby Palmetto Point.

Bank: Governor's Harbour has a branch of **Barclays Bank International,** Queen's Highway, P.O. Box 22 (tel. 809/332-2300). It is open Monday through Friday from 9am to noon.

Car Rental: If you need a car, try **Asa-Rent-a-Car Service,** Palmetto Shores, P.O. Box 131 (tel. 809/332-2305). The cost is $60 for one day.

Hair Care: Women can get their hair done at **Ann's Beauty Salon,** South Palmetto Point, P.O. Box 35 (tel. 809/332-2342). She also offers manicures and pedicures.

Medical Care: On Queen's Highway are both the government clinic (tel. 809/332-2001) and the dentist's office (tel. 809/332-2704).

Police: To telephone the police, call **332-2111.**

Post Office: Governor's Harbour has a post office on Haynes Avenue (tel. 809/332-2060).

Taxis: If you need a cab, call **Cecil Cooper Taxi Service,** Palmetto Point, P.O. Box 101 (tel. 809/332-2575).

Shopping: For gifts or souvenirs, try **Norma's Gift Shop,** Haynes Avenue (tel. 809/332-2002), which sells batik dresses, blouses, skirts, beachwear, swimwear, and men's siirts, as well as jewelry. Some of the clothing is handmade on the premises.

Nearby is yet another place to shop, **Brenda's Gift Store,** Haynes Avenue (tel. 809/332-2089). This two-room store occupies a clapboard-sided building a few steps away from the only traffic light in Eleuthera. Inside is a large inventory of T-shirts, sundresses, bathing suits, and such Bahamian souvenirs as conch jewelry.

WHERE TO STAY

Inexpensive

Cigatoo Inn, Haynes Avenue, P.O. Box 86, Governor's Harbour, Eleuthera, The Bahamas (tel. 809/332-2343), set on a hillside, is a motel-like cluster built around a small swimming pool with a terrace. Cigatoo, which is the Arawak name of Eleuthera, is one of the best and most reasonably priced inns (both for accommodations and food) in the Governor's Harbour area. You enter between two rows of Christmas palms to reach the hotel. Set on grounds planted with such tropical foliage as hibiscus, the inn rents 28 streamlined, functional air-conditioned bedrooms, all with double beds, private baths, and patios overlooking the distant sea or

What the Symbols Mean

AP (American plan): Includes three meals a day (sometimes called full board or full pension).

BP (Bermuda plan): Popularized first in Bermuda, this option includes a full American breakfast (sometimes called an English breakfast).

CP (Continental plan): A Continental breakfast (that is, bread, jam, and coffee) is included in the room rate.

EP (European plan): This rate is always cheapest, as it offers only the room— no meals.

MAP (modified American plan): Sometimes called half board or half pension, this room rate includes breakfast and dinner (or lunch if you prefer).

the hotel's pool. Each unit also has a TV. The beach is about a 5-minute walk away, and there is a tennis court.

The most expensive accommodations are the oceanview units, and the least expensive are the standard rooms with patio views. Depending on your room assignment, winter prices range from $58 to $116 daily for a single and $70 to $116 for a double. *Summer rates range from $48 to $90 daily for a single, going up to $55 to $90 in a double.* The hotel's restaurant, one of the best in the area, serves a combination of Bahamian and American dishes, costing from $18. If you're exploring Governor's Harbour for the day, you can drop in seven days a week from 11:30am to 2pm and 7 to 9pm for a good-tasting meal. The inn also has a bar serving such drinks as piña coladas and Goombay Smashes. Local entertainment is often provided.

Wykee's World Resort, Queen's Highway, P.O. Box 176, Governor's Harbour, Eleuthera, The Bahamas (tel. 809/332-2701), run by Chuck and Lee Weiche, is a snug and cozy retreat on a private estate. Lying 3 miles north of Governor's Harbour, the resort was once owned by a former prime minister of The Bahamas, Sir Roland Symonette. It is set in a landscape of coconut palms and tropical plants. Six well-equipped stone-built villas, each one different, are rented all year, with names such as Bougainvillea House or Jasmine House. The least expensive is the Allamanda House, with one bedroom, one bath, a kitchen, a living/dining room, and a screened-in porch. Some villas offer views of the ocean; all have ceiling fans. One or two guests on the EP pay $90 per night in winter, *falling to $70 in summer.* The two-bedroom Oleander House, which will sleep four, costs $150 per night in winter on the EP, *falling to $120 in summer.* Families may want to consider the four-bedroom Coconut Palm House, ideal for eight guests, which costs $200 per night in winter, falling to $160 in summer. Minimum rental is one week unless other arrangements are made. The estate has a saltwater pool, and beaches are on the Atlantic Ocean. No more than 30 guests at one time are ever at the hotel. Such sports as snorkeling, fishing, windsurfing, and tennis can be arranged.

An All-Inclusive Resort

Along the uncluttered beach of fine sand and toughened vegetation, **Club Méditerranée,** French Leaves, P.O. Box 80, Governor's Harbour, Eleuthera, The Bahamas (tel. 212/750-1687 in New York City, or toll free 800/CLUB-MED), is housed in a cluster of pastel-colored twin-bedded bungalows built in two- and three-story colonies. There's heavy emphasis here on social life for families with children. Activities include day-long picnics, nightly entertainment, disco, organized games in the resort's centerpiece free-form swimming pool (set within a garden), and taped classical music concerts after sunset.

Each room contains air conditioning, furniture crafted from Philippine mahogany, a private bathroom, and (in a deliberate policy change from the more trusting and liberal-minded 1960s and 1970s) door locks. Although up to two children can be housed with their parents in any room, accommodations for adults are based on double occupancy only. Three full meals a day, including free unlimited wine at lunch and dinner, plus most water sports and evening entertainment, are included in the rates, which in winter range from $970 to $1,030 per week per adult, from $580 to $610 per child aged 6 to 11, and from $485 to $675 for each infant aged 2 to 5. *In summer, autumn, and most of springtime, adults pay $800 per week, children aged 6 to 11 pay $480 per week, and infants aged 2 to 5 pay $400 per week. During certain promotional periods in late spring and during the autumn, children under 12 can stay free, with meals included, when sharing a room with their parents. (No more than one child per adult couple is allowed during these promotions.)* These tariffs are all-inclusive, except for drinks consumed at hours other than mealtimes; there are several bars scattered throughout the property. The club is the most heavily booked by French groups in midsummer, with greater percentages of English-speaking North American clients in wintertime.

The club's scuba program is not geared to experienced divers—only to beginners. Those just taking up the sport go through a series of four lessons before their first deep dive in the nearby harbor. All equipment and instruction are provided. At its underwater photo lab, the club provides cameras and you provide the film; same-day processing is available for an extra charge. Waterskiing, snorkeling, sailing, bicycling, tennis (eight courts, two lit for night play), picnics, aerobics, and jogging on the pale pink sands of the beach are ways most members spend their days. Children frequently get caught up in the club's Circus School, where a team of instructors teach fundamentals of tightrope walking, low-level trapeze work, trampolining, greasepaint makeup, and costuming. At the end of their stay, children (along with any willing adults) perform as clowns and comic animals in the club's weekly circus performance.

WHERE TO DINE

In and around Governor's Harbour and Palmetto Point are found some of the best local restaurants in the Family Islands of The Bahamas. They include those described below.

All prices quoted are per person.

INEXPENSIVE

Kohinoor, Queen's Highway (tel. 809/332-2668), lies 3½ miles north of Governor's Harbour and 3 miles south of Governor's Harbour Airport. It occupies a veranda-fronted modern building north of town. Guests can also eat in the big-windowed dining room. You get Bahamian and international fare here, including crayfish, cracked conch, red snapper, and broiled grouper, along with pasta dishes. Lunches cost from $8, with dinners going for around $25. The restaurant is open daily from 11am to 10pm. Anne and Clyde Bethel occasionally present entertainment on Sunday afternoon.

La Rastic Restaurant, Queen's Highway, on the road to Palmetto Point (tel. 809/332-2164), is owned by Rodney Pinder, the polite maître d' at the exclusive Windermere Island Club. His wife, Sharon Pinder, runs the place. In the back is his mother-in-law, Vangie Culmer, one of the best native cooks in Eleuthera. Opened in 1985, this is a pleasant place for either a light meal or a full dinner. The fare includes such hearty dishes as barbecued chicken or spareribs, and boiled or stewed fish. You might begin with conch chowder, then go on to a grilled T-bone steak or broiled lobster tail. Finish off your meal with one of the good-tasting rich pastries, perhaps lemon pie. Lunches cost from $8, dinners run $20 and up, and service is Monday through Saturday from 8:30am to 9pm, on Sunday from 9am to 9pm.

Ronnie's Sunset Inn Restaurant and Bar, Queen's Highway (tel. 809/332-2232). Airy, very clean, and flooded with sunlight, this popular bar/restaurant is one of the best known on the island. Since it was established in 1985 by Mark Thompson, wedding receptions have been held on its patio, and hundreds of workers have left their lunchboxes to be filled in the tile kitchen. Don't overlook the possibility of a drink in the lower-level Sloop Bar, where nautical implements line the intimate spaces. If you're looking for a skillfully seasoned meal, the street-level dining rooms serve them with style beneath a raftered ceiling with picture windows opening onto the sea. You can order stewed fish, omelets, johnnycakes, sheep's-tongue souse, fresh conch salad, conch chowder, crayfish salad, pork chops, or grouper cutlet. Dinners are more elaborate, and typical fare includes pork chops, cracked conch, strip steak, chicken dishes, and changing daily specials. The chef prepares breakfast and lunch from 8am to 2pm. Lunches cost $8 and up, and they're served Monday through Saturday. Dinner costs from $25 per person and is served Monday through Saturday from 6 to 10pm. The bar closes at 2am.

5. Palmetto Point

On the east side of Queen's Highway, south of Governor's Harbour, North Palmetto Point is a charming little workaday hamlet where visitors rarely venture (although you can get a meal there). Far from the much-traveled tourist routes, little hamlets like this are laid-back and suited for the visitor who is seeking an escapist retreat.

Also south of Governor's Harbour, on the western coast of Eleuthera, lies the beach-fronting South Palmetto Point, which has some inexpensive housekeeping units for those interested.

WHERE TO STAY

Inexpensive

The creation of a local builder, **Palmetto Shores Vacation Villas,** P.O. Box 131, Governor's Harbour, Eleuthera, The Bahamas (tel. 809/332-2305), is a good choice for a housekeeping holiday. Asa Bethel rents 12 air-conditioned waterside vacation villas, suitable for two to six guests. Units are built in Bahamian style, with wraparound balconies. Best of all, they open directly onto your private beach. Furnishings are simple but reasonably comfortable, maid service is included, and the villas lie within walking distance of local shops and tennis courts. Some units contain TVs. In winter, a villa with one bed, a living room, and kitchen costs one or two people on the EP a total of $80 daily. A three-bedroom villa, suitable for up to six guests, rents for $190 per day. *In summer, one or two people on the EP are housed in the one-bedroom villa for $70 per day, the cost going up to $100 to $180 in a three-bedroom villa for four guests.* Deep-sea fishing and waterskiing are available. Free Sunflower sailboats are also provided. You can rent a flipper, mask, and snorkel. For reservations, call Asa Bethel.

WHERE TO DINE

Inexpensive

Even if you have a kitchen in your bungalow, at some point you'll want to head for a meal at **Mate & Jenny's,** South Palmetto Point (tel. 809/332-2504), a simple, concrete building right off Queen's Highway. It's a pizza restaurant (known for its conch pizza), with a jukebox and pool table along with a dartboard. It's also one of the most popular gathering places on the island. The Bethel family will also prepare pan-fried grouper, cracked conch, or whatever. Light meals, including snacks and sandwiches, are regularly featured; however, full-course meals, costing from $16 each, require a reservation. The place is open Wednesday through Saturday from noon to 3pm and from 6:30 until the last customer leaves. On Sunday, only dinner is served, beginning at 6:30pm.

If you're an adventurer, and in the vicinity of North Palmetto Point, a good place to remember is **Muriel's Home Made Bread, Restaurant, and Grocery,** North Palmetto Point (tel. 809/332-2583). Eleuthera-born Murial Cooper's operation is open Monday through Saturday from 9am to 10pm. She operates a bakery, a take-out food emporium, and a grocery store. Her establishment is contained in a simple house half filled with the canned goods of her grocery. Her rich and moist pineapple or coconut cake is some of the best you'll find in the Family Islands. A limited cooked-food menu includes full dinners. Your choice includes chicken with chips, cracked conch with chips, conch chowder, and conch fritters. A dining room, decorated with family memorabilia, is available for clients who want to consume their food on location. If you want a meal more elaborate than the ones cited, you'll have to stop by in the morning to announce your arrival time and menu preference. Dinners cost from $10 each.

6. Hatchet Bay

North of Governor's Harbour, Hatchet Bay was once known for its plantation that raised prize Angus cattle. But that operation now produces poultry and dairy products. The unused chicken parts are thrown to devouring fish at "Shark Hole."

Hatchet Bay Harbour is one of the finest in The Bahamas, a favorite port of call for hundreds of private yachts and charter boats. Full docking facilities and moorings are available. The area is known for its high, rolling green hills, sea-to-sea views, pink- and white-sand beaches, and excellent fishing on both shores.

The location of Hatchet Bay is 25 miles north of Governor's Harbour. This is a relatively undiscovered part of Eleuthera, and you may want to veer off Queen's Highway and take one of the side roads, which have such names as Lazy Road and Smile Lane.

WHERE TO STAY

Moderate

Two miles south of Alice Town, the **Rainbow Inn,** P.O. Box 53, Governor's Harbour, Eleuthera, The Bahamas (tel. 809/332-2690, or toll free 800/327-0787 in the U.S.), is an isolated collection of cedar-sided bungalows, each designed in the shape of an octagon. The bar/restaurant has a high beamed ceiling, stone trim, and the kind of thick-topped bar where guests down a brace of daiquiris or piña coladas. Each of the tables in the adjacent dining room was crafted of wood salvaged from some kind of wrecked boat. The menu for the evening meal is posted near the bar every day, costing from $12 to $24 per person. The restaurant is one of the most popular on the long island, featuring live native music and one of the most extensive menus on Eleuthera. Local Bahamian food includes fish, conch chowder, fried conch, fresh fish, and Bahamian lobster, and international dishes feature French onion soup, escargots, steaks, and seafood Newburg, followed by Key lime pie for dessert.

There are 12 simple but comfortable accommodations. Each is air-conditioned and has a private bath, minibar, lots of exposed wood, and a ceiling fan. Most of the units also contain kitchenettes but no stoves. In winter, a studio apartment with a kitchen costs $70 daily for a single, $85 for a double. A one-bedroom apartment with kitchen, suitable for one to four people, is priced at $110 daily. A two-bedroom apartment for up to seven goes for $130. *In summer, studio apartments with kitchen cost $60 daily for a single, $70 for a double. One-bedroom apartments with kitchens rent* *for $98 for one to four people, and two-bedroom apartments, suitable for between one and seven guests, are $110 per day.* For MAP in any season, add $22 per person. The hotel is closed from September 15 to November 15. There's a sandy beach a few steps away, plus a tennis court. Free tennis balls and rackets are provided, along with snorkeling gear and bikes. Free guided tours of the Hatchet Bay Caves are offered. Rental cars are available at the inn.

WHERE TO DINE

Inexpensive

At the hamlet of James Cistern, **Lucky's Wagon Wheel** (tel. 809/332-2131) is noted for its Bahamian food. You might choose chicken, grouper, or conch for your main dinner dish, served with peas 'n' rice, potato salad, and vegetables or coleslaw. The charge for these dinners is from $10 per person. If you prefer the lobster, steak, or beef menu, costing from $20 per person, you get the same side dishes as with the regular dinner, but with the addition of tossed salad. Fresh Bahamian bread and conch chowder are also available. Lunches, served daily from noon to 2pm, when a smaller selection is offered, cost from $8.

On Sunday night, the owner occasionally offers entertainment. From 7pm, join the party, sipping a tropical drink such as a Goombay Smash, rum punch, piña colada, or fruit punch. The staff will also serve beer, wine, or soda. The place is open for dinner seven days a week from 7pm until midnight or later.

---

7. Gregory Town

On the ribbon of road that continues north for 5 miles, Gregory Town stands in the center of Eleuthera against a backdrop of hills, which breaks the usual flat monotony of the landscape. A village of clapboard cottages, it was once famed for growing pineapples. It still grows them, but not as it used to. However, the local people make a good rum out of the fruit. You can visit the Gregory Town Plantation and Distillery, where pineapple rum is still produced. You're allowed to sample it, and surely you'll want to take a bottle home with you.

WHERE TO STAY

Moderate

The Cove, Queen's Highway, P.O. Box 2007, Gregory Town, Eleuthera, The Bahamas (tel. 809/332-0142). For reservations, contact William Gardiner Corp., P.O. Box 281, Riverdale, New Jersey 07457 (tel. 800/552-5960). Opening onto its own private beach, 1½ miles north of Gregory Town and 2 miles south of Glass Windows, this is an up-and-coming resort acquired by George and Ann Mullin, who operate it in cooperation with Bahamian-born Harcourt Cambridge. From a vandalized and rundown resort they acquired in the 1970s, formerly named the Arawak Cove Club, they have re-created a new resort.

Set on 28 acres partially planted with pineapple, the resort cluster consists of 32 cement-sided units, comfortably furnished and reasonably spacious, decorated with pastel fabrics and colors and rattan furniture. Each also has a private bath and porch. In winter, with service and taxes included, singles cost $100, doubles $118 per day. *In summer, singles cost $90, doubles $110 per day.* Year round, MAP costs an additional $30 per person per day. Children under 12 stay free if sharing a room with their parents. The resort, which closes the last two weeks of every September, contains many different paths leading along coral coves and clifftops, offering beautiful views of the nearby coastline.

WHERE TO DINE

Inexpensive

You'll receive a warm welcome at **The Cove,** Queen's Highway, (tel. 809/332-0142), lying a mile and a half north of Gregory Town. In a large, spacious dining room, decorated in a tropical style, you'll enjoy a daily changing menu of Bahamian and American dishes. You might begin with the inevitable conch chowder, then go on to such fare as a rib-eye steak, grilled grouper, or baked chicken. Occasionally the menu also offers baked ham. The owners and managers invite you to come early and enjoy watching the sunset from their patio, which surrounds a swimming pool. They don't promise, but hold out the possibility of your seeing the famous "green flash" written about by Ernest Hemingway. They also offer occasional entertainment. Lunch is from noon to 2:30pm daily, costing from $10 per person, and dinner is served from 6 to 9:30pm for $22.

Budget

While in Gregory Town, you can follow your nose. A tantalizing aroma of freshly baked goods draws you toward **Thompson's Bakery** at Green Hill (tel. 809/332-0053). There, on a tiny hill in a pint-size building with a wooden sign, Daisy Thompson has been turning out what are considered the best baked goods in Eleuthera, and she's been at it for almost a quarter of a century. Not only do the locals come to her for their doughnuts, dinner rolls, and buns, but visitors flock here as well, buying her coconut tarts and pies (all with frothy toppings). She also makes exotic guava and sapodilla cakes. Gregory Town is noted for its fresh, sweet pineapples, and Daisy makes one of the best pineapple tarts I've ever had. So drop off and pick up a bag of goodies to take with you. She also sells medium-size pizzas for $5 each. The bakery is open Monday through Saturday from 8:30am to 6pm. You can return for dinner to enjoy Bahamian and American cuisine. You might begin with conch chowder, then follow with crawfish lasagne, ending your meal with one of Daisy's delectable desserts. Dinner is served nightly from 7 to 9pm, and costs from $10 to $16 per person.

ATTRACTIONS

Dedicated surfers have come here from as far away as California and even Australia to test their skills on the "second-best wave in the world." (The best is in Hawaiian waters.)

An increasingly popular activity here is spelunking (exploring and studying caves). South of the town on the way to Hatchet Bay are several caverns worth visiting, the largest of which is called simply **The Cave.** It has a big fig tree out front, which the people of Gregory Town claim was planted long ago by area pirates who wanted to conceal this cave where they had hidden treasure.

Local guides (you have to ask around in Gregory Town or Hatchet Bay) will take explorers through this cave. The bats living inside are considered harmless, even though you know they must resent the intrusion of tourists with their flashlights. At one point the drop is so steep—about 12 feet—that you have to use a ladder to climb down. Eventually you reach a cavern studded with stalactites and stalagmites. At this point the reason you hired a guide will become obvious, as you're faced with a maze of passageways leading off through the rocky underground recesses. The cave comes to an abrupt end at the edge of a cliff, where the thundering sea is some 90 feet below.

After leaving Gregory Town and driving north, you come to the famed **Glass Windows,** chief sight of Eleuthera. This is the narrowest point of Eleuthera. Once a natural rock arch bridged the land, but it is gone, replaced by an artificially constructed bridge. As you drive across it, you can see the contrast between the deep blue of the ocean and the emerald green of the shoal waters of the sound. The rocks rise to a height of 70 feet. Often, as ships in the Atlantic are being tossed about, the crew has looked across the narrow point to see a ship resting quietly on the other side. Hence the name Glass Windows.

---

8. The Current

At a settlement called The Current, in North Eleuthera, some houses are built on low piles. The inhabitants are believed to have descended from a tribe of Native Americans. A narrow strait separates the village from Current Island, where most of the men make their living from the sea and the women spend their days pleating straw goods.

The **Boiling Hole** is in a shallow bank in front of the Current Club. It boils at changing tides.

This is a small community where the people often welcome visitors. There are no crowds and no artificial attractions. Everything focuses on the sea, which is a source of pleasure for the visiting tourists but a way to sustain life for the local people.

From The Current, you can explore some interesting sights in North Eleuthera, including **Preacher's Cave.** This is where the Eleutherian Adventurers found shelter in the mid-17th century when they were shipwrecked with no provisions. However, if you want to be driven there, know that your taxi driver may balk. The road is treacherous on his expensive tires. If you do reach it, you'll find a cave that has been compared to an amphitheater. The very devout Eleutherian Adventurers held religious services inside this cave, which are penetrated by holes in the roof, allowing light to intrude. The cave is not too far from the airport, in a northeasterly direction.

WHERE TO STAY

Inexpensive

A good place for families is **Sandcastle Cottages,** The Current, Eleuthera, The Bahamas (tel. 809/333-0264), a two-unit housekeeping-cottage complex set amid coconut palms at the edge of the sea. The private beach is furnished with chaises longues and wooden parasols, the sun barriers of which consist of matted blankets of woven palm fronds. The white sands are perfect for building (what else?) sandcastles, although many guests choose simply to gaze into the azure depths of the expansive waters, which come close to the accommodations. The beach is safe for children: you can wade long distances before reaching the deep water. Many families choose this place for its relaxed seclusion. In winter, the two-bedroom cottage for four is $60 a night, and the one-bedroom cottage for two rents for $45 on the EP. *In summer, a two-bedroom cottage, suitable for four persons, costs $50 a night on the EP, and the one-bedroom cottage for two goes for only $40.* An extra person is charged $5 a night year round. There's a village store where you can purchase supplies to use in your built-in kitchen.

---

9. Harbour Island

One of the oldest settlements in The Bahamas, founded before the United States was a nation, Harbour Island lies off the northern end of Eleuthera, some 200 miles from Miami. It is 3 miles long and ½ a mile wide.

Affectionately called "Briland," Harbour Island is studded with good resorts and is famous for its spectacular pink-sand beach, which runs the whole length of the island on its eastern side. The beach is protected from the ocean breakers by an outlying coral reef, which makes for some of the safest bathing in The Bahamas. Except for unseasonably cold days, you can swim and enjoy water sports year round. The climate averages 72° Fahrenheit in winter, 77° in spring and fall, and 82° in summer. Occasionally they have cool evenings with a low of around 65° from November to February.

For years most of the breadwinners of Harbour Island were engaged in farming and boatbuilding, along with fishing and sponge diving. Farming is still done today on the main body of Eleuthera on land given to the Brilanders by Andrew Devereaux, a colonel in the British army back in 1783. The Civil War in the United States brought an economic boom, with the Brilanders prospering on running the blockade the Union had placed on shipping to and from the Confederate states.

By 1880 Dunmore Town had become the second most important town of The Bahamas. It not only was a port of entry, but also had a major shipyard turning out vessels as large as four-masted schooners, as well as a trio of sugar mills—and it produced rum. It eventually fell on bad days, but with the coming of Prohibition to the United States, another boom era came to Dunmore Town. There was a market for its rum on the U.S. mainland, and rum-running became a major source of income.

The Brilanders suffered a great financial setback with the repeal of the Prohibition amendment, and then came the Great Depression and World War II, neither event helping matters much for Harbour Island. Finally, tourism has again brought prosperity.

GETTING THERE & GETTING AROUND

By phone, Harbour Island is only 1½ hours from Fort Lauderdale or Miami and a 30-minute flight from Nassau. To get here, you take a flight to the North Eleuthera airstrip, from which it's a 1-mile ride to the ferry dock, costing $2 per person. The final lap is the 2-mile ferry ride direct to Harbour Island, at a cost of $3 per person. Most people don't need transportation on the island. They walk to where they're going or else take a golf cart.

If you consider a **vehicle** a necessity even on such a small island, you can rent a golf cart or a Moke at Johnson's, P.O. Box 64 (tel. 809/333-2376). Mokes (a cross between a Jeep and a golf cart) cost $40 per day. It's wise to reserve well in advance.

FAST FACTS: HARBOUR ISLAND

Hospital: The **Harbour Island Medical Clinic,** at Dunmore Town (tel. 809/333-2227), handles routine medical problems.

Police: The **police** can be called at **333-2111.**

WHERE TO STAY

Every major inn or resort on Harbour Island has its own following. Many are quite good, and each has unique qualities. But as the saying goes, that's why they print menus.

Expensive

Dunmore Beach Club, P.O. Box 122, Harbour Island, The Bahamas (tel. 809/333-2200), is an elegant oasis, a colony of cottages placed in a tropical setting of trees and shrubbery on well-manicured grounds. The 12 Bahamian-style air-conditioned bungalows are an attractive combination of traditional furnishings and tropical accessories. The club leans toward the old-world style of innkeeping and takes only 28 guests. Year round, two people can stay here for about $275 daily, including three meals a day. The single AP charge is $200 a night.

Excellent Bahamian and international meals are served in a dining room with a high-pitched, beamed ceiling; shutter doors, windows with views, modern oil paintings on the walls, and pots of tropical plants add to the charm. Breakfast is served in a garden terrace under pine trees with a clear view of the beach. Dinner is served at one sitting at 8pm, when men are required to wear coats and ties in winter. Nonresidents can call for reservations, paying $40 per person. The club is open November to July.

Pink Sands, P.O. Box 87, Harbour Island, The Bahamas (tel. 809/333-2030, or toll free 800/729-3524 in the U.S.), is an elite retreat on an 18-acre beachfront estate, functioning somewhat like a private club but open to the general public. By now, it's become a Harbour Island legend, having been founded by Allen Malcolm, a Connecticut Yankee. In 1988 he sold the resort to, among others, Wally and Robbie Bregman, formerly of the Cormorant Club in St. Croix. They appointed New York–born Duncan and Joanie Burns as their on-site managers. Lots of paint and modern touches have given Pink Sands a new look as it launches itself into the 1990s. Much of the old crowd is long, long gone, but new friends are made every year.

The innovative team wants to keep the best of the old but also initiate changes. Rooms are let on a full AP basis, but as an added extra, afternoon tea and all the drinks you can consume before 5pm are included as well. Morning croissants and coffee are delivered to your door in a woven basket each morning before the formal breakfast service. The social center of the resort lies between a pair of fireplaces (one stone and traditional, the other a witch's cap iron fireplace in the center of the dining room, with smoke funneled up through a pipe in the ceiling).

The resort offers 42 bedrooms within 34 coral and stucco cottages, each of which contains one, two, or three bedrooms. The large and airy accommodations have tropical furnishings, as well as dressing rooms, baths, private patios, and refrigerators. In winter, singles on AP (full board) range from $225 to $275, with doubles costing $275 to $325. *In summer, AP rates range from $150 to $200 daily for a single, with doubles costing $200 to $250.*

Access to the grounds is restricted during the day but open to the public after 5pm (see my dining recommendation, below). Touches of whimsy at Pink Sands combine with touches of elegance. As you lie on the beach, you can raise a flag attached to the top of a pole, which will signal a beachfront waiter to come and take your order.

The clientele at Pink Sands has been described as "socially secure." The centerpiece of the beachfront is a deck cantilevered over sands, capped with parasols and beach tables. The colony has its own fleet of several types of small sailboats and boats with outboard motors for exploring. Scuba diving, snorkeling, and waterskiing are available. The resort places a big emphasis on tennis, and there are three professional courts available.

For reservations and information, contact Flagship Hotels and Resorts, 43 Kensico Dr., Mount Kisco, NY 10549 (tel. 914/241-8771).

Moderate

Coral Sands, P.O. Box 23, Harbour Island, The Bahamas (tel. 809/333-2350, or toll free 800/468-2799 in the U.S.), is the beachfront lair of two remarkable people, Brett and Sharon King. Theirs is a self-contained, all-purpose resort built on 14 hilly and tree-covered acres overlooking a beach of pink sand and lying within walking distance of the center of Dunmore Town, across from Pink Sands, another leading resort.

Brett King had an adventurous life before coming to Harbour Island. A wartime flyer and veteran of 134 combat missions in Europe and Africa, and winner of many medals for his bravery and daring, he later became an actor. He worked with such stars as Bette Davis, John Wayne, and Robert Mitchum and dated, among others, Elizabeth Taylor. He came to Harbour Island to complete plans for the resort, which had been envisioned by his father before his death. Brett stayed and the rest of the story is now part of Harbour Island lore.

Since their opening in 1968, the world has come to their door. Sharon functions as a gracious hostess, running between phone calls and welcoming guests as if to her own private party, which at times it becomes. California born and bred (a self-styled "Valley girl"), Sharon is known for her style and vivacity. She's also very active in the community of Harbour Island.

Guests have a choice of 33 rooms, each refurbished in a Caribbean motif. Many prefer the two-room, two-bath cottage with kitchen (set back from the beach), which rents for $175 for two persons daily in winter, *falling to $125 in fall and spring*. In the main building, you can rent a single for $125 daily in winter, with a double going for $140. However, *off-season rates fall to $90 daily for a single and $100 for a double, a remarkable bargain*. The suites, which have oceanview patios, sleep a total of four persons and are ideal for families. In winter, two persons can occupy one of these suites for $175 daily, *the off-season cost dropping to $125*. Year round, MAP is available for another $33 per person daily. The hotel is closed from U.S. Labor Day to mid-November.

The food is one of the reasons for staying here. It's like good home cooking, with a selection of American, Bahamian, and international dishes. For example, if you take lunch at the Beach Bar Sun Deck, order a bowl (not a cup) of some of the best-tasting conch chowder in the islands, served with a slice!of freshly made coconut bread. You might follow with a toasted lobster sandwich that other hotels have imitated it's so good. Dinner might be preceded by one of the potent rum drinks in the Yellow Bird Bar. The meal might begin with conch fritters and go on to a fresh Bahamian fish such as grouper, prepared in a number of ways. Outsiders who call for a reservation can order dinner from 7 to 8pm at a cost of $28 per person. Entertainment is often provided in the nightclub in the park, where you can dance under the stars.

The resort is very sports oriented, offering a tournament-class tennis court, which can be lit for night play. All water sports, including boats and gear, can be arranged, as well as sailboats, rowboats, surf riders, and snorkeling equipment. The Kings provide beach umbrellas and chaises longues among other equipment, and will have their staff pack a picnic lunch should you desire to explore some uninhabited islands nearby.

Fronting on both beach and harbor, **Romora Bay Club,** P.O. Box 146, Harbour Island, The Bahamas (tel. 809/333-2325, or toll free 800/327-8286 in the U.S.), owned by Bill and Nancy Steigleder, is an intimate resort of 38 well-furnished bedrooms, 9 of which are suites. Created from a former private estate, the T-shaped main house is the center of social activities. The club stands in a decades-old semi-tropical garden with tall, bearing coconut palms, filmy pine trees, and beds of flowering shrubbery.

The air-conditioned accommodations assure more privacy than most, and only yards away is a harbor where you can swim in vodka-clear waters. Each unit is comfortably furnished, containing a private bath and a private patio or balcony. Rooms are classified as standard, superior, and deluxe, each carrying a different price tag. In winter, singles cost $116 to $130 daily, with doubles renting for $148 to $175. *In summer, singles range from $65 to $90 per day, with doubles paying $85 to $140.* For MAP (breakfast and dinner), add $30 per person daily. Year round, a third person sharing a room is charged another $20; children under 10 stay free.

Buffet luncheons are served at the waterfront patio and bar. Home cooking is a feature, with Continental, Bahamian, and American cuisine served. The homemade breads and pastries are superb. All flights are met at the airport by taxis for the 1-mile drive to the ferry dock. There's a 2-mile ferry ride direct to the club's private dock. Picnic trips, including an "X-rated one for honeymooners," is offered to a nearby uninhabited island. Couples are shown some low bushes just right for hanging up their bathing suits. They tell the captain when they'll be ready to be picked up, and after that they're strictly on their own. The club is closed from mid-September until the first of November.

For reservations write or call the Romora Bay Club, P.O. Box 7026, Boca Raton, FL 33431 (tel. 305/427-4830 in Florida).

Runaway Hill Club, P.O. Box 31, Harbour Island, The Bahamas (tel. 809/ 333-2150), is a small, intimate hotel overlooking the pink sands of Briland's beach. The resort, built in 1947 as a private home, was later sold to two sisters from New Zealand who ran it as a small inn. After they sold the property, the hotel remained closed for several years. In 1983 a group of Brilanders renovated the property and opened it to the public. The hotel has 7 acres of beachfront and a huge lawn, separated from Colebrook Street by a wall. The mansion's original English colonial dormers are still prominent, as are the four stately palms set into the circular area in the center of the driveway. In winter, a crackling fire is sometimes built in the hearth near the entrance.

Each bedroom is different, giving the impression of lodging in a private home, as this used to be. There are eight accommodations in the two buildings that the hotel occupies. Winter rates are $195 daily for single rooms, $145 for doubles. *Tariffs in summer are $100 daily for singles, $120 for doubles.* Year round, MAP is $35 additional per person per day. The club is usually closed in September and October.

Dinners are served on the breeze-filled rear porch looking over the freshwater swimming pool, which is set into a steep hillside and surrounded by plants, midway between the main building and the pink sweep of the sandy beach. The dining room accepts paying nonresidents who want to drop in for dinner. Fishing trips and water sports can be arranged at the front desk. Roger and Carol Becht are the capable managers here.

Valentine's Yacht Club & Inn, P.O. Box 1, Harbour Island, The Bahamas (tel. 809/333-2142, or toll free 800/491-1010 in the U.S.), is a low-slung, rustic-modern, and comfortable place near the sea and a marina complex. You register in the wood-paneled main building. In back, in view of the dining room, there's a swimming pool where first-time divers may have just finished their introductory lessons. There's also a hot tub/Jacuzzi. Simple accommodations sit bungalow style, each with its own private veranda, in a somewhat hilly flowering garden. In winter, singles cost $110 to $130 daily, depending on the location, and doubles go for $120 to $140. For MAP, add $32 per person. *In summer, MAP charges are $100 to $120 daily for a single, $110 to $130 for a double.* The place is closed in September and October.

The Bahamian cuisine served in the restaurant is usually preceded by drinks in the comfortably intimate wood- and brass-trimmed bar. Dinner is served by candlelight at tables where artificial gold coins sparkle beneath laminated surfaces and hanging ships' lanterns—each an antique—cast an intimate glow. Either before or after dinner, you might enjoy one or two of the bartender's almost hallucinogenic Goombay Smashes. The bar area often provides live entertainment, becoming one of the social centers of town.

If you plan to arrive by yacht, you'll be in good company, since the likes of Barbara Mandrell and Mick Jagger have also moored their vessels here. It's a full-service marina with everything you could need for your yacht, including a "yacht-sitting" service, which makes this dock one of the focal points of the marine activities on Harbour Island. For more information on the Dive Shop, which offers everything a scuba or snorkeling aficionado could want, See "Sports & Recreation," below.

WHERE TO DINE

Expensive
Pink Sands, (tel. 809/333-2030), is closed to the public until 5pm but is open thereafter to those who call for a dinner reservation. You can go by early and have a predinner drink, enjoying the physical plant and the amenities of the largest of the

hotels on this New England–like island. You might have, for example, "grouper paradise" (with crabmeat, asparagus, and a dill-flavored mousseline sauce) or else seafood lasagne. The chef likes to emphasize creative Caribbean specialties, so the menu is forever changing. Bahamian and international dishes are featured, and fresh produce is used whenever possible. Service is polite, even a bit formal. In all, it's a low-key but elegant choice for dining. For residents of the hotel, dinner is included in the daily AP rates. However, nonresidents can order a fixed-price meal for $45 per person, served nightly from 7:30 to 9pm.

Moderate

Known for its well-prepared American and Bahamian food, **Runaway Hill Club** (tel. 809/333-2150) has a dining room that enjoys a sweeping view over the sandy slope stretching down the beach. Inside, in a green-and-white decor accented with polished wood and nautical accessories, you can enjoy evening meals. The restaurant is contained in a hotel, previously recommended, but outside guests are welcome for the single-service meal. The kitchen prepares such specialties as marinated London broil, suprême of chicken piccata, spaghetti with conch, crabmeat soup with scotch, spicy lobster bisque, and many versions of local fish. Dessert might be a local favorite, French chocolate pie with a meringue crust and walnuts. There is one dinner seating, nightly at 8pm. Meals cost from $35 per person, plus service and drinks. Reservations are recommended. The restaurant is closed in September and October.

Valentine's Yacht Club & Inn (tel. 809/333-2142). Don't even think of a meal here without stopping first for a drink in the warmly masculine bar beforehand. Surrounded with nautical accessories and burnished paneling, you can while away the predinner hours with denizens of the island's boating crowd. The fare in the dining room includes steamed pork chops, steak or grouper cutlets, asparagus soup (or some other freshly made soup), baked stuffed grouper, and roast leg of lamb. Breakfast runs from $8, and it's served daily from 8:30 to 9:30am. Lunch, at $10, is from noon to 2pm, and a set dinner, at $28, is served promptly every night at 7:30pm (prices are per person). When the main bar closes at 9, you can walk out to the more raucous bar on the marina (known as the Reach Bar), which remains open till 11 on most nights. Both the restaurant and the hotel are closed from early September to mid-November.

Inexpensive

Angela's Starfish Restaurant (tel. 809/333-2253) is one of the simplest and also one of the most popular eating places in Harbour Island. Residents as well as visitors literally plan their Sunday around an evening meal here, although it's equally crowded on other nights. Run by Bahamians, Angela and Vincent Johnson, the house sits on a hill above the channel in a residential section somewhat removed from the center of town. Angela can often be seen in the kitchen baking. The kitchen is a turquoise-colored house where the dishes are prepared for service in the dining area.

Cracked conch and an array of seafood are specialties, and chicken pot pie and pork chops are frequently ordered. You can dine on the palm-dotted lawn with its simple tables and folding chairs, although for chilly weather there's an unpretentious dining room inside near the cramped kitchen. Some of the best local food is offered here. It can get quite festive at night, after the candles are lit and the crowd becomes jovial. You should call ahead for a reservation. Full dinners, served on tables where conch shells are usually the centerpiece, cost $20 per person. Lunch costs from $10, breakfast from $6. The establishment is open daily without a break, beginning at 9am. The last dinner order is taken at 8:30pm.

ATTRACTIONS

Harbour Island's historic old **Dunmore Town,** with its pastel clapboard houses, often with whitewashed picket fences, was once the capital of The Bahamas.

It's one of the oldest settlements in the archipelago, and even today remains one of the most colorful villages in the Family Islands. It evokes thoughts of waterfront vacation spots in the Carolinas.

Titus Hole, a cave with an open mouth that looks out onto the sheltered harbor, is said to have been the first jail on Harbour Island. Also worth seeing is the **Loyalists Cottage,** dating back to 1790. Vestiges of colonial architecture can be seen in other old houses that were built during the latter part of the 19th century.

The town was settled by English religious dissidents who came here in the 17th century. They were joined about 135 years later by Loyalists coming from the new United States, where they had become unpopular during the American Revolution for their support of British sovereignty. Dunmore Town was named for Lord Dunmore, an 18th-century royal governor of The Bahamas.

SPORTS & RECREATION

The two main sporting centers are the Romora Bay Club and Valentine's Yacht Club, the activities of which are reviewed below.

Romora Bay Club (tel. 809/333-2325) is fully geared for a wide array of water sports. The sandy bottom of the sheltered bathing precincts off the hotel (reviewed above) serves as the learning area for the introductory scuba lessons. An introductory lesson followed by a half-day dive trip costs $35, with equipment included. Guided scuba trips cost $30 per tank in daytime, $35 for night dives. Call to agree on departure time.

Those who prefer snorkeling can join a half-day expedition for $15 per person. Experienced divers can rent any piece of scuba equipment they need. Bill Steigleder, the owner of the hotel, is an experienced diver. He is assisted by two PADI instructors. The Romora Bay Club offers dive packages that make combined MAP, housing, and diving less expensive.

Valentine's Dive Center, P.O. Box 1 (tel. 809/333-2309), has a full range of dive activities. The dive center is in a wooden building near the entrance to Valentine's marina. Free lessons in snorkeling and scuba diving for beginners are given daily at 9:30am. Snorkeling from a boat costs $20 for a half-day tour. A full certification course for scuba is taught for $350. Single-tank dives, daily at 9:30am and 1:30pm, cost $30, and night dives (four divers minimum) cost $45 per person. Underwater cameras, with film included, rent for $15 for a half day, $25 for a full day.

In addition to the dive operation, Valentine's will rent boats to qualified sailors. Daysailers cost $25 per hour, $75 for half a day. If you're not that ambitious, perhaps you'd like a Hobie Cat for $15 per hour. Windsurfers cost $10 per hour.

The diving in this part of The Bahamas is considered among the most diversified in the region, with visibility in midsummer reaching as much as 200 feet on good days. The guides at Valentine's, including New York–born divemaster Bob Beregowitz, are proud to point out the wreck of the *Carnarvon* (also spelled *Caernarvon* and pronounced in endlessly different variations by the locals). A 197-foot steel freighter, it sank in 1917 and is considered today one of the highlights of the region. Nearby are the badly rusted chassis of a half-dozen railway boxcars reportedly captured by Confederate soldiers from the Union Army during the Civil War and sold to the owner of a sugar plantation in Cuba. Hit by a hurricane during their southbound transit, the barge containing them was sunk, scattering the boxcars along the sea bottom. Today, only the wheelbases remain visible above the reef fish and kelp that have made the site their home.

The most spectacular pastime of all, however, judged among the 10 top dive sites in the world and visited by scuba enthusiasts from as far away as Europe, is the Current Cut Dive. Considered one of the fastest (9 knots) drift dives in the world, it involves the descent of a diver into the fast-moving current racing between the rock walls that define the underwater chasm between Eleuthera and Current Island. Swept up in the underwater currents with schools of stingrays, mako sharks, and reef fish, divers are propelled along a half mile of underwater distance in less than 10 minutes. The dive is defined as one of the highlights of a diver's career.

EVENING ENTERTAINMENT

Don't come here expecting much nightlife. However, various resorts schedule live entertainment on different evenings, and there are a few local clubs that come and go. Just ask around to find out what's happening. Most of the resorts are an easy walk from one another.

One of the most pleasant spots on the island for a drink, the **Pink Sands Lounge,** Bay Street (tel. 809/333-2031), is a place reminiscent of New England but with a tropical twist. The lounge is directly opposite Government Dock. The expansive veranda in front is likely to be filled with chatting locals who socialize here during parades and regattas, although Sunday afternoon is also a popular meeting time. The roughly finished interior shows the thick posts and beams of the old house. Seated in one of the bentwood or rattan chairs scattered throughout the pair of inside rooms, you can enjoy a tropical drink or a two-fisted pick-me-up. Drinks average around $3.50. The bar is usually open daily from 11am to 9pm.

---

10. Spanish Wells

Called a "quiet corner of The Bahamas," Spanish Wells is a colorful cluster of houses on St. George's Cay, half a mile off the coast of northwest Eleuthera. It is characterized by its sparkling bays and white beaches, sleepy lagoons, and a fine fishing and skin-diving colony.

The Eleutherian Adventurers were the first people to inhabit St. George's Cay after the Spanish had exterminated the original residents, the Arawak (Lucayan) Indians. However, it was prominent on the charts of Spanish navigators as the final landfall for galleons heading home from the New World laden with plunder. The Spaniards early on sank a well here from which to replenish their potable water before setting off across the Atlantic. Hence the name "Spanish Wells." Ponce de León noted this stopover, where he was able to get water, if not the youth-giving liquid for which he was searchiog.

After the American Revolution, Loyalists joined the descendants of the Eleutherian Adventurers in Spanish Wells. Some of these, particularly those from southern plantations in America, did not stay long on St. George's Cay, however, as the Spanish Wellsians were adamantly opposed to slavery. Since slaves had been brought by the new wave of immigrants hoping to start island plantations, they were forced to move on to other parts of The Bahamas with their black bondsmen. The people of Spanish Wells still have strong religious beliefs, and there's a bounty of churches on the island.

The towheaded, blue-eyed people of this little town number fewer than 1,500 souls, a white enclave in a predominantly black country. More than half the people on the island are named Pinder. As the saying goes, "We was Pinders before we married, and we're Pinders now." The names Albury, Higgs, Sawyer, and Sweeting are also prominent. The islanders' patois blends old English with the accents of others who have settled on the island over the centuries. For years they have been known as good seamen and spongers, and some of them are farmers. Because of the infertile soil on St. George's Cay, however, they have to do their planting on "mainland" Eleuthera.

Over the centuries the Spanish Wellsians have tried their hand at many economic ventures, from growing cotton and pineapples for export to shipbuilding, lumbering, and fishing. Of these, fishing and some agriculture have been lasting moneymakers, joined today by tourism. Many have grown rich on harvesting crawfish.

You can walk or bicycle through the village, looking at the houses, some more than 200 years old, which have New England saltbox styling but bright tropical coloring. You can see handmade quilts in many colors, following patterns handed down from generations of English ancestors. No one locks doors here or removes ignition keys from cars.

There are those who suggest that the island doesn't offer much to do, but this is disputed by those who just want to snorkel, scuba dive, fish, sunbathe, read, or watch the sun set. You'll also have a choice of tennis, sailing, volleyball, shuffleboard, or windsurfing.

GETTING THERE

By Ferry

To reach the island, you can fly to the airstrip on North Eleuthera, from which taxis will deliver you to the ferry dock. Regardless of the time of day you arrive, a ferryboat will either be waiting for passengers or about to arrive with a load of them. A memorable skipper of one of them is Caleb Sawyer, who runs a well-maintained speedboat, the *Moldie Crab* (tel. 809/333-4254). The boat runs between Gene's Bay in North Eleuthera to the main pier at Spanish Wells. The ferries depart whenever passengers show up. The cost ranges between $10 and $12 per person round trip.

WHERE TO STAY

Moderate

The premier resort of the island is the **Spanish Wells Beach Resort,** P.O. Box 31, Spanish Wells, The Bahamas (tel. 809/333-4371). Set on flat, sandy ground, a 5-minute walk from the most congested part of the town, it occupies the edge of a good beach, which throughout most of the day permits walking in waist-deep water for long distances without reaching a drop-off—a fact that makes its 800 feet of beachfront ideal for children. During the life of the resort, it has submitted to many different managements and name changes, yet seems to endure almost timelessly as a permanent staple on the island.

Set beside a grove of palm trees, its 21 comfortable prefabricated bedrooms and seven tiny cottages were built during the early 1960s. Perhaps to give visitors a taste of the fishing expeditions that help to keep the community here alive, each of the simply furnished cottages is named after a local reef or fishing site, including Ignamally's Rock, Ridley's Head, and Pierce's Rock. Each unit contains a wall of sliding glass that opens onto a view of the beach and the sea, air conditioning, a private bath, and a TV hookup. In winter, depending on the accommodation, singles range from $85 to $125, doubles from $100 to $132, triples from $112 to $140, and quads from $120 to $150 per day. *In summer, singles cost from $68 to $105, doubles from $80 to $117, triples from $92 to $129, and quads from $104 to $140 per day.* Taxes and service are extra, children under 12 sharing a room with their parents stay free, and MAP can be arranged in any season for $30 per day for adults and $16 per day for children under 12.

Spanish Wells Yacht Haven, P.O. Box 27, Spanish Wells, The Bahamas (tel. 809/333-4255), is one of the newest and most modern marinas in the islands. It is now owned by the Nassau Yacht Haven, which also rents apartments and rooms for the boating crowd or any other visitors to Spanish Wells. As for the marine facilities, they include a self-service laundry, hot and cold showers, an ice machine, a saltwater swimming pool, and a lounge and restaurant. You can also get Exxon marine fuels and lubricants. Should you not happen to have a yacht to service, you'll find a quintet of rentable rooms. Each of them has servicable furniture, a satellite-reception TV, a private bath, and air conditioning. Two of them contain small kitchenettes. In winter, occupancy for between one and four persons on the EP ranges from $85 to $105 per day. *In summer, occupancy for between one and four persons on the EP costs from $75 to $95 per day.* Tax is extra.

WHERE TO DINE

Moderate

The most gracious restaurant on an island not overloaded with choices is **Spanish Wells Beach Resort** (tel. 809/333-4371), housed in the social center of this previously recommended hotel beneath a sloping ceiling of varnished pine. The place is air-conditioned, and spinning ceiling fans stir the air as you relax on comfortable chairs. Service is polite. An old wood-sided skiff is transformed into a decorative accent at one end of the room. The bill of fare is likely to include locally caught lobster, breaded or pan-fried grouper, cracked conch, pork chops, steak, and a selection of international dishes. The restaurant is open daily from 7:30 to 10am for breakfast, from noon to 2pm for lunch, and from 6:30 to 9pm for dinner. Breakfast costs from $8, lunch from $14, and dinner from $20 (prices are per person).

Spanish Wells Yacht Haven (tel. 809/333-4255) is owned by the Nassau Yacht Haven. Its facilities and rooms have been previously recommended, but it's also one of the finest places to dine on the island. Visitors mingle with a yachting crowd from around the world in the lounge and restaurant which is decorated with a few nautical artifacts overlooking the marina. Naturally, the emphasis is on seafood here, including lobster "right out of the water and into the pot." You can order such Bahamian fish as grouper, prepared several different ways. Conch is prepared in a number of ways as well, including a tasty chowder. A meal costs from $15 to $25 per person at dinner and from $12 at lunchtime. Service is Tuesday through Sunday from 8 to 10am for breakfast, from noon to 2pm for lunch, and from 6:30 to 9:30pm for dinner.

Walton's Langosta (tel. 809/333-4147), set on the port and painted a vivid shade of ultrapurple, is the first building most visitors see as they approach by ferryboat. The establishment's orange Formica countertops and horseshoe-shaped bar seem designed to spotlight one of the town's most vocal and colorful citizens, Walton Pinder. Many of the establishment's fish and lobster selections are caught by Mr. Pinder, and are flavorfully prepared in a well-scrubbed kitchen that guests are welcome to inspect personally.

The very fresh conch salad, marinated in salad lemon and vinegar, is a specialty. Other dishes include red snapper, chicken, several different preparations of lobster, grouper cutlets, fish sandwiches (including one made with conch), and the inevitable conch chowder. Full meals are served daily from 9am to 4pm. After a 2-hour break, dinner service lasts from 6 to 10pm. Per-person tabs for breakfast cost from $6; lunch, from $8; and a full dinner, from $20.

Inexpensive

Roddy's Place (tel. 809/333-4219) stands along the waterfront on the way to Spanish Wells Yacht Haven. It is known for its home cooking and Bahamian foods. It is also a social center of the town, with its game machines and pool tables. Painted in vivid Caribbean colors, it offers the usual array of sandwiches and hamburgers. But you can also order some good local dishes (not available every day), including a fresh lobster salad. Cracked conch is invariably offered, as is conch chowder. A crayfish salad might be on the menu, or a barbecued or baked chicken. Lunches cost from $9 per person, with dinners priced at $15 and up. The restaurant is open daily from 9am to 10pm.

SPORTS & RECREATION

Although it offers an array of water-related activities, the main preoccupation of the **Spanish Wells Dive Center,** Spanish Wells Beach Resort (tel. 809/333-4371), is diving. It maintains a duet of flattopped boats that make expeditions to some of the most beautiful reefs in the region. Its headquarters and information center are in this previously recommended resort. However, its boats moor on the opposite side of the island in a channel between Spanish Wells and Russell Island. For beginners, a Resort Course with an introductory lecture costs $75. A two-tank dive goes for $50, and NAUI certification costs from $350.

If you're interested in above-water activities, the center offers beach picnics from a flat-topped boat that goes to an array of sandy islands. Perhaps the most alluring of all, an X-rated picnic called Adam and Eve is arranged on special request. The Dive Center provides transportation to an uninhabited island, a hammock, a picnic lunch, and then privacy. Guests are requested not to divulge the location to anyone (so future picnics can continue in uninterrupted solitude). The cost of the picnic is $45 per couple.

EVENING ENTERTAINMENT

The Cave Bar, The Harbour Club (tel. 809/333-4339). Firmly entrenched as one of the town's most popular bars, ideal for swapping fishing stories and beers with the locals, it's located on the ground floor of a two-story cement-sided building within a 5-minute walk of the center of town, facing the harbor. Its almost total lack of windows and its thick walls give the place its name. There's a jukebox blasting out oldies, with pool tables available to help while away the time. The preferred libation is beer, but a piña colada or Goombay Smash costs around $4. Drinks are served daily from noon to midnight.

THE EXUMA ISLANDS

A spiny, sandy chain of islands, the Exumas, which begin just 35 miles southeast of Nassau, stretch more than 100 miles from Beacon Cay in the north to Hog Cay and Sandy Cay in the south. These islands have not been developed like the Abacos and Eleuthera, but they have much to offer, with gin-clear waters on the west around the Great Bahama Bank and the 5,000-foot-deep Exuma Sound on the east, plus uninhabited cays ideal for picnics, rolling hills, ruins of once-great plantations, and coral formations of great beauty. Although it's crossed by the Tropic of Cancer, the island has average temperatures ranging from the mid-70s to the mid-80s.

On most maps this chain is designated as the "Exuma Cays," but only two of the main islands—Great Exuma and Little Exuma—bear the name. A single-lane bridge connects those two cays, where the major communities are concentrated.

The Exumas, scattered over an ocean area of 90 square miles, are favorites with sailors and yachtsmen, considered some of the finest cruising grounds in both The Bahamas and the Caribbean. The annual regatta in April in Elizabeth Harbour has attracted such notables as Prince Philip and ex-King Constantine of Greece. The Exumas are often referred to by yachting people as "where you go when you die if you've been good."

HISTORY

The history of the Exumas, whatever it was, is not much documented before the latter part of the 18th century. It is assumed that the island chain was inhabited by Lucayan Indians, at least until the Spaniards wiped them out. Columbus didn't set foot on this chain of islands. However, from the northern tip of Long Island, he is believed to have seen Little Exuma, naming whatever was in the area "Yumey." At least, that's how the island chain appears on a 1500 map of the New World.

By the late 17th century Great Exuma had become a major producer of salt, and permanent settlers began to arrive. The sailing vessels of the salt merchants were constantly harassed by pirates, but some families from Nassau must have looked on this as the lesser of two evils. On New Providence they were subjected to the terrorism inflicted by both the pirates and the Spanish, and in the latter part of the 17th century and the first of the 18th they fled to the relative peace of the Exumas (they still do!).

Some Loyalist families, fleeing the newly established United States of America after British defeat, came to the Exuma Cays in 1783, but nothing like the number that came to settle in Harbour Island, New Plymouth, and Spanish Wells.

In the 18th century cotton and salt were "king" on the Exumas. English plantation owners brought in many slaves to work the fields, and many of today's Exumians are direct descendants of those early bond servants, who were mostly of African origin. The "king" did not stay long on the throne. Insects went for the cotton, and salt lands such as those of the Turks and Caicos Islands proved much too competitive for those of the Exumas, so these pursuits were eventually abandoned.

Most of the white owners went back to where they came from, but the slaves, having no such option, stayed on, subsisting by working the land abandoned by their former owners and taking the names of those owners as their own. A look through the George Town directory turns up such names as Bethel, Ferguson, and especially Rolle, the same as those of the long-gone whites.

At one time Lord John Rolle held much of the Exumas under a grant from the British Crown, giving him hundreds of acres. He is reported to have owned nearly 400 slaves who worked this acreage, but Lord Rolle never set foot on his potentially rich plantation. Stories vary as to what happened to the slaves—whether they were, as some claim, freed by Lord Rolle and given the land by him, or whether, upon being released from bondage by the United Kingdom Emancipation Act in 1834, they just took over the land, with or without Rolle's approval. Whichever, descendants of those same slaves are important Exumians today.

The Exumas Today

These are among the friendliest islands in The Bahamas, the people warmhearted and not (yet) spoiled by tourism. They seem genuinely delighted to receive and welcome visitors to their shores. They grow a lot of their own food, including cassava, onions, cabbages, and pigeon peas on the acres their ancestors worked as slaves. Many fruits grow on the cays, including guavas, mangoes, and avocadoes. You can watch these fruits being loaded at Government Wharf in George Town for shipment to Nassau. The sponge industry is being revived locally, as the product of the sea is found in shallow waters and creeks to the south side of the Exumas.

This is considered one of the prettiest island chains in The Bahamas. Some even liken its beauty to that of Polynesia. In the Exumas, shades of jade, aquamarine, and amethyst in deeper waters turn to transparent opal near sandy shores: the water and the land appear almost inseparable. Sailors and their crews like to stake out their own private beaches and tropical hideaways, and several vacation retreats have been built by wealthy Europeans, Canadians, and Americans.

Most of my resort recommendations are in and around pretty, pink George Town, on Great Exuma, the capital of the Exumas. A community of some 900 residents, it was once considered a possible site for the capital of The Bahamas because of its excellent Elizabeth Harbour (see below).

The action in the Exumas is, naturally, mainly water oriented, with fishing, scuba-diving, snorkeling, and boating activities leading the list. However, you can also play tennis, windsurf, waterski—whatever.

The cruising grounds around the Exumas are perhaps the finest to be found in the Western Hemisphere, if not in the world, for both sail- and powerboats. If you don't come in your own craft, you can rent one here, from a simple little Daysailer to a fishing runabout, with or without a guide.

Snorkeling and scuba-diving opportunities draw aficionados from around the world to the Exuma National Land and Sea Park, a vast underwater preserve, and to the exotic limestone and coral reefs, blue holes, drop-offs, caves, and night dives. Dive centers in George Town and Staniel Cay provide air fills and diving equipment.

Fishing is top-grade here, the "flats" on the west side of Great Exuma being famous for bonefishing. You can find (if you're lucky) blue marlin on both sides of Exuma Sound, as well as sailfish, wahoo, and white marlin, plus numerous others.

A LAND & SEA PARK

Under the protection of The Bahamas National Trust, **Exuma National Land and Sea Park** begins at Conch Cut in the south and extends northward to Wax Cay Cut, encompassing Halls Pond Cay, Warderick Wells, Shroud Cay, Hawksbill Cay, Cistern Cay, and Bell Island, as well as numerous other small, uninhabited islands. It lies to the northwest of Staniel Cay. The park is some 22 miles long, and much of it is a sea garden with reefs, some only 3 to 10 feet beneath the water's surface. The park is reached only by chartered boat, and is very expensive to visit.

This is an area of natural beauty that can be enjoyed by beachcombers, skin divers, and the yachting crowd, but it's unlawful to remove any plant, marine, or bird life, except for specific limited catches of certain fish. The park's rules differ from the fishing regulations for the rest of The Bahamas, permitting catches of six spiny lobster (in season), 12 conchs, one hogfish, one rockfish, one grouper, and one muttonfish. Catches must be made by hand, with hook and line, or with a Hawaiian sling. Apply to the park warden, who lives in the area, for information.

Many birdwatchers visit the park, looking for the red-legged thrush, the nighthawk, even the long-tailed "Tropic Bird," plus many, many more winged creatures.

This was once the home of the Bahamian iguana, which is now found only on Allan's Cays, a tiny island group just north of Highborne Cay. The government is taking belated steps to protect this creature, which is found nowhere else in the world. If a person kills or captures an iguana, the penalty on conviction is a fine of as much as $300 and/or imprisonment for a term as long as six months.

GETTING THERE

By Air

The most popular way to visit the Exumas is to fly there aboard **Bahamasair** (tel. toll free 800/222-4262) with daily service from Nassau.

Exuma has some private airstrips, but its major commercial airport—the new Exuma International Airport—is 10 miles from George Town, the capital. (For flights to the private airstrip at Staniel Cay, refer to Section 4 of this chapter.)

Aero Coach (tel. toll free 800/432-5034) offers flights between George Town and the Florida gateways of Miami and Fort Lauderdale. For tickets and reservation information, call 305/359-1600 in Fort Lauderdale. The number to call in the Exumas is 809/336-2186.

By Mailboat

Several mailboats leave from Potter's Cay Dock in Nassau, stopping at various points along the Exumas.

The M/V *Grand Master* goes from Nassau to George Town. Departures are on Tuesday at 1pm. It returns to Nassau on Saturday.

Since hours and sailing schedules are subject to change because of various weather conditions, it's best to check with the Dockmaster at Potter's Cay Dock in Nassau (tel. 809/393-1064).

GETTING AROUND

After your arrival at the airport in George Town, chances are you'll meet Kermit Rolle. He's known by everybody. You can stop in at his **Kermit Airport Lounge,** P.O. Box 29078 (tel. 809/336-2002), which is just across from the airport terminal building. Having the same name as Lord Rolle, Kermit knows just as much about the Exumas as anyone else (maybe more). You learn that Kermit runs things up in Rolleville (more about this later). You'll be lucky if Kermit is free, and you can negotiate a deal with him to take you in his car for a tour of the Exumas. He's filled with local lore.

If your hotel is in George Town, it will cost about $21.50 to get there in a taxi from the airport. Rides often are shared. The island has only a few taxis. Most of them wait at the airport. Hotels can usually get you a taxi if you need to go somewhere and don't have a car. There are no taxi-service telephone numbers to call, other than that of the Kermit Airport Lounge.

It's also possible to rent a car during your stay. Try **Exuma Transport,** P.O. Box 29019, George Town (tel. 809/336-2101). They have cars to rent for $60 per day or $300 per week. A $200 deposit is required.

At the same place, you can ask about renting a scooter for $25 a day. Some adventurous visitors make use of them on the islands' roads. But, be warned, there have been accidents because of the potholed and dangerous conditions of many of the roads on the island chain.

A TRAVELER'S ADVISORY: NORMAN'S CAY

Throughout the Exumas, you'll see islands with "No Trespassing" signs posted. In some cases this is meant with a vengeance. In the early 1980s, at least on one island, you could have been killed if you had gone ashore!

On a long-ago summer day, the boat containing my party sailed by Cistern Cay. Back then, we were told that Robert Vesco owned part of that island. "He likes to keep it *very, very private* here," our guide cautioned, heading for friendlier shores. (Vesco, of course, is the financier much wanted by the U.S. government.) Even though the fugitive is long gone, people around here still like to keep it quiet.

Perhaps the most bizarre Out Islands episode in all The Bahamas centers around Norman's Cay, one of the northernmost islands in the Exumas, 44 nautical miles southeast of New Providence Island. At one time when I stayed at the former hotel there, Norman's Cay Club, this was a South Seas island–type outpost. Reportedly it was once the retirement home of the pirate, Norman.

This was always a very special cay. It isn't flat, since parts rise to 50 feet above sea level. It is heavily wooded with lignum vitae, royal poinciana, palmetto, tamarind, and casuarina, and it used to be considered a birdwatcher's paradise. Snorkeling and scuba diving on the coral heads were among the best in the Exumas, with vertical drop-offs, black-coral forests, spectacular cuts, and wrecks. The location is adjacent to the Exuma National Land and Sea Park.

In the old days you might have run into Ted Kennedy, Walter Cronkite, or William F. Buckley, Jr., enjoying the pleasures of Norman's Cay. The remote outpost enjoyed great popularity with a Harvard/Boston clique.

However, in the 1980s the situation changed drastically when a German-Colombian, Carlos Lehder (pronounced Leader) Rivas (his mother's name), purchased most of the island. The story of his purchase of Norman's Cay was mentioned in the 1985 *Newsweek* article "Empire of Evil," documenting the horrors of cocaine smuggling. A short time after Lehder's purchase of the property, the Colombian flag was flying over Norman's Cay, and many of the wintering wealthy fled in horror from the island when they returned to find their homes broken into and "trashed."

Norman's Cay, experts have stated, became the major distribution point for drug export to the U.S. Millions of dollars worth of cocaine was flown from Colombia and deposited in hangars at Norman's Cay before being smuggled into the United States. It is estimated that some 30 pilots crashed attempting to fly in their illegal cargoes. You can still see the wreckage of a C-46 that went down in the bay.

When an undersecretary of state arrived from Washington and landed on the island, he was ordered off at gunpoint by a Colombian commando. He left, but when he returned to the U.S. capital, he launched a major protest. Apparently, strong, hard pressure was applied by the U.S. government on the Bahamian government to "clean up the act" at Norman's Cay.

Lehder fled Norman's Cay for further adventures in Colombia, where he was captured and extradited to the United States (he was later tried, convicted, and imprisoned). The Bahamian police now have the island under surveillance.

Norman's Cay may one day realize its tourist potential again, but it is still in private hands and is strictly off-limits, unless you've been personally invited to visit by one of the owners. If you arrive in a boating party, you should seek special permission before going ashore.

FAST FACTS: THE EXUMA ISLANDS

Much factual information regarding George Town and the Exumas is also applicable to the rest of The Bahamas and appears under the "Fast Facts: The Bahamas" in Chapter VII. The information here is aimed at helping you on matters more specifically pertinent to this area.

Banks: In George Town, a branch of the **Bank of Nova Scotia,** Queen's Highway, P.O. Box 29014 (tel. 809/336-2651), is open Monday through Thursday from 9am to 3pm, on Friday from 9am to 1pm and 3 to 5pm.

Churches: If you're a Protestant churchgoer, you'll be warmly welcomed at **St. John's Baptist Church,** Queen's Highway, P.O. Box 29012, George Town (tel. 809/336-2682).

Customs: The Bahamian Customs office (tel. 809/336-2071) is at the George Town Airport.

Docking: If you come to the Exumas aboard your own boat, **Exuma Docking Services,** P.O. Box 29019, George Town (tel. 809/336-2578), has slips for 40 boats, with water and electricity hookups. There's a restaurant on the premises, and you can replenish your liquor stock from the store here. Also they have a Laundromat, fuel dock, land-based fuel pumps, and a store selling supplies for boats and people.

Dry Cleaning: To get dry cleaning done, go to **Exuma Cleaners,** Queen's Highway, P.O. Box 29096, George Town (tel. 809/336-2038).

Hair Care: For attention to your hair, try **Exuma Beauty and Barber Fashion,** Queen's Highway, George Town (tel. 809/336-2682).

Medical Care: The government-operated medical clinic in George Town can be reached by phone (tel. 809/336-2-88).

Police: To call the police in George Town, dial **336-2666,** but only for an emergency or special services.

---

1. George Town

The Tropic of Cancer runs directly through George Town, the capital and principal settlement of the Exumas, located on the island of Great Exuma. Some 900 people live in this tranquil seaport village, opening onto a 15-mile-long harbor. George Town, part in the tropics and part in the temperate zone, is a favorite port of

THE EXUMAS

N

Great Exuma Island

Rolleville
Steventon
The Bluff
Mosstown
George Town
Rolle Town
Williamstown
Richmond Hill

Stocking I.
Little Exuma Island
Hog Cay

Airport

call for the yachting crowd. Its one road runs parallel to the shoreline of the harbor. Flights from Nassau, Miami, and Fort Lauderdale come into nearby George Town Airport.

Sometimes the streets of George Town are nearly deserted, except when the mailboat from Nassau arrives at Government Wharf, bringing everybody out. If you've rented a housekeeping unit on the Exumas, you can come here to buy fresh fish when the fishermen come in with their catch.

If you need to stock up on supplies, George Town is the place, as it has more stores and services than any other place in the Exumas. There are dive centers, marinas, and markets, as well as a doctor and a clinic.

George Town doesn't have street names, but it is so small that everything is easy to find.

What the Symbols Mean

AP (American plan): Includes three meals a day (sometimes called full board or full pension).

BP (Bermuda plan): Popularized first in Bermuda, this option includes a full American breakfast (sometimes called an English breakfast).

CP (Continental plan): A Continental breakfast (that is, bread, jam, and coffee) is included in the room rate.

EP (European plan): This rate is always cheapest, as it offers only the room— no meals.

MAP (modified American plan): Sometimes called half board or half pension, this room rate includes breakfast and dinner (or lunch if you prefer).

WHERE TO STAY

Moderate

In the heart of George Town, **Peace and Plenty,** P.O. Box 29055, George Town, Great Exuma, The Bahamas (tel. 809/336-2551, or toll free 800/525-2210 in the U.S.), is an attractive and historic waterside inn. Once it was a sponge warehouse and later the home of a prominent family before it was converted into a hotel in the late 1940s, making it the oldest in the Exumas. It was named for a vessel that brought Loyalists from the Carolinas to the Exumas. The hotel is run by the most famous manager in the Exumas, Charles Pflueger, who once worked for Pan American Airlines. He managed the hotel in the late 1960s and early 1970s and has now returned. Since his arrival, Peace and Plenty has become the finest "ship" in town. The two-story pink-and-white hotel has dormers and balconies. There are 35 units, all tastefully furnished and air-conditioned. In winter, singles or doubles peak at $95 to $125 per day. *In summer, charges are $72 to $94 for singles or doubles.* All rates are on the EP.

The grounds are planted with palms, crotons, and bougainvillea. Peace and Plenty fronts on Elizabeth Harbour, which makes it a favorite of the visiting yachting set. The hotel faces Stocking Island and maintains a private beach club there, offering food and bar service as well as miles of sandy dunes. A free boat makes the run to Stocking Island for hotel guests. There is a small free-form freshwater pool on the patio of the hotel; drinks are served here. They are served also in two cocktail lounges. One of these lounges was built in the original kitchen of an old slave market; it's filled with nautical gear, including lanterns, rudders, and anchors. Food consists of Continental, Bahamian, and American specialties. Dining is both indoor and outdoor. Calypso music is played on the terrace.

Scuba equipment is available for rent, and an instructor not only takes out diving and snorkeling parties but also arranges deep-sea fishing trips. Bonefishing is especially popular in the area. Rental cars, motorcycles, and boats can be arranged.

You can also stay at the hotel's annex, called **Peace & Plenty Inn,** a mile west of George Town. It contains 16 first-class and well-furnished double rooms that open onto 300 feet of white-sand beach, with a bar, restaurant, swimming pool, and dinghy dock. The air-conditioned bedrooms have tile floors as well as balconies overlooking Bonefish Bay and Elizabeth Harbour. Rates in winter are $118 per day for one or two persons on the EP, *lowered in summer to $94.*

Flamingo Bay Hotel & Villas, February Point, P.O. Box 29090, George Town, Great Exuma, The Bahamas (tel. 809/336-2661), is the scaled-down, very comfortable remnants of a massive time-share project that did not survive the real estate crunch of the late 1980s. Surrounded on three sides by a saltwater cove, amid 1,300 acres of virgin scrub a short distance east of George Town, the development at press-time offered 21 rentable accommodations, 7 of which were villas with kitchens. Overlooking Elizabeth Harbour, the development is the creation of Canadian investor and publisher Robert Hart.

Most social activities happen within the pale-pink walls of the main house, a pocket of posh decorated somewhat like a private home, with a mixture of modern and antique furniture and jewel-toned Caribbean colors. There are six rentable accommodations upstairs. In winter, two-bedroom villas and luxury suites, suitable for between one and four occupants, cost $175 per day, while one-bedroom villas and luxury bedrooms cost $95 for single or double occupancy. *In summer, the wintertime price of each accommodation is reduced by $20 per day.* All rates are for the EP. The resort contains a tennis court, a private 30-foot dock, and a beach. Nearby entrepreneurs offer such water sports as scuba diving and the rental of sailboats. At presstime, the resort's restaurant was closed, although plans were in effect to re-establish it sometime during the life of this edition.

Inexpensive

Pieces of Eight Hotel, Queen's Highway, P.O. Box 29049, George Town, Great Exuma, The Bahamas (tel. 809/336-2600), set a half mile northwest of the town, on a hill overlooking Stocking Island and Elizabeth Harbour, is built around a pool and deck. Each of the 33 rooms has an individual balcony and bright tropical-inspired decor renovated in the early 1990s. Daily rates in winter are $90 for a single and $104 for a double. *In summer, they are $76 per day for a single and $92 for a double.* Included in the cost are tax, free use of the hotel's bicycles, and breakfast. On the premises is the Pieces of Eight Restaurant and the Pirate's Den bar, recommended separately.

Two Turtles Inn, P.O. Box 29051, George Town, Great Exuma, The Bahamas (tel. 809/336-2545). Set opposite the village green, midway between the town's harborfront and a saltwater estuary known as Victoria Pond, this pleasant 14-room hotel is as popular for its drinking and dining facilities (see separate recommendation) as for its accommodations. Originally built of stone and stained planking in the early 1960s, these are arranged around a courtyard, the centerpiece of which is the enormous Norfolk Pine that is the envy of gardeners throughout the island. Each room has air conditioning, a ceiling fan, and a private bath. In winter, EP single or double rooms cost $78 per day; *in summer, they go for $68.* Beach enthusiasts and water-sports aficionados head for the facilities of Peace and Plenty, a short walk away. Although the Two Turtles does not specifically offer them itself, tennis, sailing, boating, snorkeling, and scuba diving can all be arranged through other nearby hotels.

Regatta Point, P.O. Box 2906, George Town, Great Exuma, The Bahamas (tel. 809/336-2206, or toll free 800/327-0787 in the U.S.), lies on a small cay just across the causeway from George Town. The cay used to be known as Kidd Cay, named after the notorious pirate. Overlooking Elizabeth Harbour, the present complex consists of five efficiency apartments. This little colony hums with action at the time of the Family Island Regatta. Your hostess, Nancy Bottomley, does much to ease your adjustment into the slow-paced life of the Exumas. An American, she discovered this palm-grove cay—really bush country—in 1963, opening the little colony of efficiencies in 1965. She even had to build the causeway herself. Each of the pleasantly furnished units has its own kitchen. The daily EP rate for one or two people is $96 in winter, *lowered to $70 in summer.* There is a two-bedroom apartment available, suitable for up to four people, which costs $128 per day in winter, *the price dropping to $88 per day in summer.*

There is a little beach for the use of guests, and Mrs. Bottomley will help with arrangements for water sports and outings. One guest liked the place so much he stayed for seven years. Trade winds keep the place fairly cool. Those guests who don't want to cook for themselves can take dinner out in George Town. They have a choice of the already-recommended hotels in town or else at one of the local restaurants. Grocery stores are fairly well stocked if you want to do it yourself, however. The hotel staff will direct you to their whereabouts.

WHERE TO DINE

In general, the best places to take meals in George Town are the main hotels, reviewed above, although there are exceptions.

All prices quoted are per person.

Moderate

Peace and Plenty Hotel (tel. 809/336-2551), has one of the finest island dining rooms, where there is good home cooking and enough of it so that no one leaves unsatisfied. Who knows who might be seated at the next table? In days of yore, it might have been King Constantine of Greece, maybe Jack Nicklaus. Your host, Charles Pflueger, welcomes guests. The cuisine includes both French and Italian dishes, along with Bahamian seafood and standard American fare. You might begin with escargots or one of the salads made with hearts of palm or hearts of artichoke, then follow with Scottish salmon or fresh crab. You sit under ceiling fans, looking out over the harbor, at a table right off the hotel's Yellow Bird Lounge. Windows on three sides and candlelight make it particularly nice in the evening.

But you can also visit for lunch. You have a selection of such dishes as homemade soups, followed by, perhaps, a conchburger, a chef's salad, or deep-fried grouper. For breakfast you're given a selection of such dishes as French toast or scrambled eggs and sausage. But if you want to go truly Bahamian, you'll order the breakfast of boiled fish and grits. Breakfast costs $6 and is served daily from 7:30 to 10:30am; lunch costs $8 and is served daily from noon to 2:30pm; and dinner costs from $15 to $30 and is served daily from 6:30 to 9:30pm. Guests must sign up by 5pm for dinner.

Pieces of Eight Restaurant, Queen's Highway (tel. 809/336-2600), on the ground floor of this previously recommended hotel, brings exotic Chinese flavors to wake up the taste buds of a town somewhat jaded by a diet of all-Bahamian food. Overlooking a swimming pool, it contains a half-moon-shaped bar, the Pirate's Den, and a pleasant dining room where the menu includes such dishes as wonton soup, shrimp tempura, Exuma pineapple chicken, sweet-and-sour grouper, and tempting versions of fried rice, the most interesting of which is prepared with fresh Bahamian lobster. A specialty of the house is lobster Cantonese, served with a black-bean–and –garlic sauce. Lunch is served daily from noon to 3pm and costs from $9; dinner is daily from 6:30 to 9pm and costs from $19.

Sam's Place, P.O. Box 29019 (tel. 809/336-2579). If Bogie were alive today, he'd surely head for this second-floor restaurant and bar overlooking the harbor in George Town. It opened in 1987 and is one of the best restaurants in Great Exuma, popular with the yachting set. The decor has been called "Bahamian laid-back." Sam Gray, the owner, offers breakfasts, catching the early boating crowd. Lunches are likely to include everything from freshly made fish chowder to spaghetti with meat sauce. You'll also be able to order an array of sandwiches throughout the day. The dinner menu changes daily, but you're likely to find such main courses as Exuma lobster tail, roast lamb, Bahamian steamed chicken, and pan-fried grouper. Of course, you can always get native conch salad. At dinner the talk here is one of everybody's dream—that of owning a private utopia, one of those uninhabited cays still remaining in the Exuma chain. Breakfasts and lunches cost from $6; dinners cost from $20. The restaurant is open from 7am to 10pm.

Two Turtles Inn (tel. 809/336-2545), contained within the previously recommended hotel, is one of the most popular drinking and dining establishments in George Town. Set within a dining room composed of local stone and Tudor-inspired black-and-white detailing, it has an aviation motif ("We didn't want to just drape a lot of fish nets everywhere and call it nautical"), which includes aircraft memorabilia and an antique airplane propeller proudly displayed above the bar. Both Bahamian and American food is served. English-born manager Valerie Noyes (an aviatrix herself) offers meals likely to include cracked conch, strip steak, or pan-fried grouper. Lunches cost from $8.50 and are served daily from noon to 3pm. Dinners cost from $20 and are served Saturday through Thursday from 5:30 to 9pm; a special barbecue menu is offered every Friday night from 6 to 10pm.

ATTRACTIONS

There isn't much to see here in the way of architecture except the confectionary pink-and-white **Government Building,** which was "inspired" by the Government House architecture in Nassau. Under an old ficus tree in the center of town there's a straw market where you can talk to the friendly Exumian women and perhaps purchase some of their handcrafts.

George Town has a colorful history, despite the fact that it appears so sleepy today (there's so little traffic, there is no need for a traffic light). Pirates used its deep-water harbor in the 17th century, and then what was called the "plantation aristocracy," mainly from Virginia and the Carolinas, settled here in the 18th century. In the next 100 years **Elizabeth Harbour,** the focal point of the town, became a refitting base for British men-of-war vessels, and the U.S. Navy used the port again during World War II.

The greatest attraction is not George Town but **Stocking Island,** which lies in Elizabeth Harbour. It faces the town across the bay, less than a mile away. This is a long, thin barrier island with some of the finest white-sand beaches in The Bahamas. Snorkelers and scuba divers come here to explore the blue holes, and it is also ringed with undersea caves and coral gardens. Boat trips leave from Elizabeth Harbour heading for Stocking Island at 10am and 1pm daily. The cost is $5 per person one way. However, guests of Peace and Plenty are transported free.

Mystery Cave is a famous dive site, tunneling for more than 400 feet under the hilly, 7-mile-long island with its palm-studded beaches.

If you'd like to go shelling, walk the beach that runs along the Atlantic side. You can order sandwiches and drinks at the beach club on the island, which is run by Peace and Plenty (see below). Stocking Island used to be a private enclave for guests at Peace and Plenty, but now it is used by all visitors. They reach the island on high-speed Boston Whaler runabouts (ask at your hotel desk for departure times). The boats leave from Government Wharf in George Town.

Lake Victoria covers about 2 acres in the heart of George Town. Landlocked, it has a narrow exit to the harbor and functions as a diving and boating headquarters.

One of the offshore sights in Elizabeth Harbour is **Crab Cay,** which can be reached by boat. This is believed to have been a rest camp for British seamen in the 18th century.

SPORTS & RECREATION

If you'd like to go scuba diving, the people to see are the **Exuma Divers,** P.O. Box 290110 (tel. 809/336-2710). The dive center is behind the Peace and Plenty boutique, right off Queen's Highway. Experienced divers are taken on night dives. Divers can explore blue holes and Mystery Cave under Stocking Island, as well as the coral gardens. Snorkeling trips with rental equipment cost $19 per person. If you want to go fishing, deep-sea trips are also offered. Call to negotiate prices and times.

Minns Watersports, P.O. Box 29020 (tel. 809/336-2604), opposite Government Building in George Town, is the best place for boat rentals. You can rent a MWS boat and spend the day snorkeling, sailing, or just beachcombing. You can even take a picnic lunch along. Outboard-motor boats include a 15-foot Boston Whaler. You can also rent windsurfers along, with snorkeling equipment such as mask and fins. Office hours are 9am to 5pm Monday through Friday; 9am to noon on Saturday; and 9 to 10am on Sunday. Prices are negotiable.

Many men come to the Exumas just to go bonefishing. The best arrangements can be made at **Peace and Plenty,** P.O. Box 29055 (tel. 809/336-2551), from which you can go out for a half day.

Family Island Regatta

In April, the Family Island Regatta draws a yachting crowd from all over the world to Elizabeth Harbour. It's a rollicking week of fun, song, and serious racing when the island sloops go all out to win. It's said that some determined skippers bring along extra crewmen to serve as live ballast on windward tacks, then drop them over the side to lighten the ship for the downwind run to the finish. Command post for the regatta is the Flamingo Bay Club. The event, a tradition since 1954, comes at the end of the crayfish season. The George Town regatta is considered the most popular of all the traditional sloop races held in the archipelago.

WHERE TO SHOP

Unless you're one of the islanders who resides permanently in Great Exuma, chances are you won't visit George Town just to shop. However, there are a few places where you can purchase souvenirs and gifts.

The Sandpiper, P.O. Box 29020 (tel. 809/336-2609), stands across from Peace and Plenty next to Minns Watersports. Its main draw is its original serigraphs by Diane Minns, but it also offers a good selection of Bahamian arts and crafts, along with such items as Bahamian straw baskets (or other handcrafted works), sponges, ceramics, silkscreen fabrics, Seiko cameras, and post cards.

Peace and Plenty Boutique, P.O. Box 29055, (tel. 809/336-2551), stands next to the Sandpiper and across the street from this previously recommended inn, which owns it. Its main draw is its selection of Androsia batiks for women. Androsia cloth is also sold by the "yard" (a yard measures 43 inches wide). You can also find the usual practical items such as film and suntan oil.

Perhaps the most popular store in town is **Exuma Liquor and Gifts,** Queen's Highway (tel. 809/336-2101), which sells liquor, wine, and some souvenirs.

DAY TRIPS

Queen's Highway, which is still referred to as the "slave route," runs across Great Exuma, and you may want to travel it, in either a taxi or a rented car, to take in the sights in and around George Town.

Two villages, Rolleville and Rolle Town, each named after Lord Rolle, are still inhabited by descendants of his freed slaves. It is claimed that his will left them the land. This land is not sold but is passed along from one generation to the next.

Rolleville is to the north of George Town. As you travel along the highway, you'll see ruins of plantations. This land is called "generation estates," and the major ones are Steventon, Mount Thompson, and Ramsey. You pass such settlements as Mosstown (which has working farms), Ramsey, The Forest, Farmer's Hill, and Roker's Point. Steventon is the next settlement before you reach Rolleville.

At Rolleville, the traditional luncheon stopover is at **Kermit's Hilltop Restaurant & Tavern,** P.O. Box 29078 (tel. 809/336-6038). I've already introduced

Kermit Rolle in the "Getting Around" section. He not only has a taxi service, but operates a lounge across from the terminal building of the Exuma International Airport. This is one of the most popular places in the Exumas, and it serves fresh fish like conch and grouper. Occasionally it will offer Bahamian lobster. The place is situated so that you'll have a good view. Sometimes a local group will come in and entertain on weekends. You should call in advance to let Kermit know you're coming. As for hours, he simply promises "good food all day." That usually means from 10am to 10pm Monday through Saturday, from noon to 10pm on Sunday. Meals cost from $15 each. Many locals come here just to play the game machines.

Rolleville is the largest of the plantation estates. It is about 28 miles. There are several beautiful beaches along the way, especially the one at Tarr Bay and Jimmie Hill.

On the way back, if you didn't have lunch at Kermit's place in Rolleville, you might stop in at **Central Highway Inn** (no phone), a roadside tavern run by Iva Bowe (Bowe, along with Rolle, is one of the most popular names on the island). The location is along Queen's Highway some 6½ miles northwest of George Town. Mrs. Bowe is known locally for her cracked conch. The conch is marinated in lime, pounded to make it tender, and then fried with her own special seasonings. Her food is good Bahamian cookery, and meals cost from $12 each. Hours are from 10am to 10pm daily.

Some visitors may also want to head south of George Town, passing Flamingo Bay and **Pirate's Point.** In the 18th century Captain Kidd is said to have anchored at Kidd Cay (you can stay here at the Regatta Point, recommended previously).

Flamingo Bay, the site of a hotel and villa development, begins just half a mile from George Town. It's a favorite rendezvous of the yachting set and bonefishermen.

On the road to Little Exuma, you come to the hamlet of **Rolle Town,** which is another of the generation estates that was once, like Rolleville in the north, owned by Lord Rolle and is filled with what are called his "descendants" today. A sleepy town, Rolle Town has some houses about a century old. In an abandoned field, where goats frolic, you can visit the Rolle Town Tombs, burial ground of the McKay family, who died young. Captain Alexander McKay, a Scot, came to Great Exuma in 1789, having been granted 400 acres for a plantation. His wife joined him in 1791, and they had an infant child. However, tragedy struck, and Anne McKay died in 1792, as did her child. She was only 26. Perhaps grief stricken, her husband died the following year. Their story is one of the romantic legends of the island.

The village claims a famous daughter, Esther Rolle, the actress. Her parents were born here, but they came to the United States before she was born.

The road goes on to Little Exuma, coming up.

ORGANIZED TOURS

Christine Rolle (there's that name again) is the one to show you Great and Little Exuma with her **Island Tours,** P.O. Box 29055, George Town (tel. 809/336-4016). She offers two jaunts, each costing $12 and leaving daily at 10am and 2pm. The first takes you north along Queen's Highway all the way to Barraterre, including native dishes for lunch, and the second takes you from George Town to Little Exuma, calling on the Shark Woman (see below), also with lunch at a local restaurant. If something ails you, Christine Rolle has a cure "from the bush," and she'll explain the medicinal properties of local plants and herbs.

2. Little Exuma

This is a faraway retreat, the southernmost of the Exuma Cays. It has a subtropical climate, despite being actually in the tropics, and beaches of white sand. In some places, sea life is visible from about 60 feet down in the gin-clear waters. The island, about 12 square miles in area, is connected to Great Exuma by a 200-yard-long bridge. It's about a 10-mile trip from the George Town Airport.

WHERE TO DINE

Inexpensive

The "hot spot" of the island is **Gordy's Palace,** (no phone), at Gray's Ville. It's certainly no palace, and if you drop in here on a sleepy afternoon you might think only the weather is hot. You might, in fact, interrupt a poker game. Nevertheless, things get lively around here, especially on Friday and Saturday disco nights. The place is popular mainly with locals, although it gets an occasional visit from a member of the U.S. military stationed in the area. You get typical island fare here, including grouper fingers, conch fritters, or cracked conch, served in modest surorundings. You can also visit just to drink and soak up the laid-back Little Exuma atmosphere. Beer costs $2.50. A meal costs $12 and up. The restaurant is open daily, serving food from 9am to 10:30pm.

ATTRACTIONS

Less than a mile offshore is **Pigeon Cay,** which is uninhabited. Visitors often come here for the day and are later picked up by a boat that takes them back to Little Exuma. You can go snorkeling and visit the remains of a wreck, some 200 years old, right offshore in about 6 feet of water.

On one of the highest hills of Little Exuma are the remains of an old pirate fort. Several cannons are located near it, but documentation is lacking as to when it was built or by whom. Pirates didn't leave too much data lying around.

Coming from Great Exuma, the first community you reach on Little Exuma is called **Ferry,** so named because the two islands were linked by a ferry service before the bridge was put in. See if you can visit a private chapel of an Irish family, the Fitzgeralds, erected generations ago.

When you come onto Little Exuma, you might ask a local to direct you to the cottage of Gloria Patience, the "most unforgettable character of the Exumas." Her house, called Tara, lies on the left side of the road after you come over the bridge. She is famous and much publicized as the **Shark Woman.** Now in her 70s, she earns her living collecting sharks' teeth, which she sells to jewelers. Called the "Annie Oakley of the Family Islands," this barefoot septuagenarian has some tall fish stories to tell, and she's told them to such people as Peter Benchley, author of *Jaws.* She's also appeared on television with Jacques Cousteau. She discounts some modern theories that sharks are kindly souls with a bad press. Take it from the woman who's bagged at least 1,800 of them single-handedly: "They're vicious." The biggest deadly choppers, she claims, are found in the jaws of the female hammerhead. She sells the flesh of her prey to restaurants, although she says she doesn't eat shark meat herself. Her home is like a museum, and you can come here on a shopping expedition, not only for shark teeth, but for all the flea-market stuff and more valuable pieces she's collected over the years. She's a remarkable woman, living in a house split by the Tropic of Cancer.

Along the way, you can take in **Pretty Molly Bay,** site of the now-shuttered Sand Dollar Beach Club. Pretty Molly was a slave who committed suicide by walking into the water one night. The natives claim that her ghost can still be seen stalking the beach every night.

Many visitors come to Little Exuma to visit the **Hermitage,** a plantation constructed by Loyalist settlers. It is the last surviving home of the many that once stood in the Exumas. It was originally built by the Kendall family, who came to Little Exuma in 1784, establishing their plantation at **Williamstown** and, with their slaves, setting about growing cotton. However, they encountered so many difficulties in having the cotton shipped to Nassau that in 1806 they advertised the plantation for sale. The ad promised "970 acres more or less," along with "160 hands" (referring to the slaves). Chances are you'll be approached by a local guide who, for a fee, will show you around. Ask to be shown several old tombs in the area.

Also at Williamstown (look for the marker on the seaside), you can visit the remains of the **Great Salt Pond.**

Finally, the explorer who has to "see everything" can sometimes get a local to take him or her over to **Hog Cay,** the end of the line for the Exumas. This is really just a spit of land, and there are no glorious beaches here. As such, it's visited mainly by those who like to add obscure islets to their chain of exploration.

Hog Cay is in private hands, and it is farmed. The owner seems friendly to visitors. His house lies in the center of the island. There is also an old lookout tower with a 5-foot cannon at its base. At one time this stood guard for ships coming and going into Elizabeth Harbour.

---

3. Barraterre

For years linked to the world only by boat connections, Barraterre during the 1980s became connected to "mainland" Great Exuma by a road link. The area is now open for development, but no one here expects that to happen soon. The place is no more than a sleepy hamlet, and everybody seemingly is named McKenzie. As you're heading north, instead of continuing to "end of the line" Rolleville, turn left in the direction of Stuart Manor. You pass through Alexander and keep going until you reach the end of another road, and there lies little Barraterre, asleep in the sun. For the boating crowd, it is the gateway to the Brigantine Cays, which stretch like a necklace to the northwest.

Here you'll see how the "life of the cays" is lived, with the biggest event being the arrival of the mailboat, which is a vital link to the outside world. No one, not even one of the McKenzies, is absolutely certain how the place got its name. Perhaps it came from the French, *bar terre,* or land obstruction.

The Barraterrians live in a hilly community, with vividly painted houses (many in decay).

WHERE TO DINE

Inexpensive

Virtually your only choice is a happy one. **Fisherman's Inn** (tel. 809/336-5017) is the social center of town, presided over by Mr. and Mrs. Norman Lloyd. The place has a large dance floor, where reggae and calypso music often fills the night, and a pool table. It is especially active during those homecoming parties when Barraterrians return, often in August, from either Nassau or the United States with their newfound ways. Everybody seems to have a good time, and the kitchen promises that "fish eaters make better lovers." Conch is the specialty here, and you can order it in fritters, cracked, or scorched, even steamed. You can also ask for grouper fingers and fried chicken. No one will look askance if you want only a hot dog. Meals cost from $18 per person. The place is open daily from 8am "until the last person leaves."

---

4. Staniel Cay

Staniel Cay lies at the southern end of the little Pipe Creek archipelago 80 miles southeast of Nassau, which is part of the Exuma Cays. This is an 8-mile chain of uninhabited islets, sandy beaches, coral reefs, and bonefish flats. There are many places for snug anchorages, making this a favorite yachting stopover in the mid-Exumas. Staniel Cay, known for years as "Stanyard," has no golf course or tennis courts, but it's the perfect island for "The Great Escape." It was described by one yachting visitor as lying "in a sea of virtual wilderness."

An annual bonefishing festival is sponsored here on July 10, during the celebration of Bahamian Independence Day.

There are about 100 Bahamians living on this island, and there's a local straw market where you can buy handcrafts, hats, and handbags. The little cay was settled in the mid-18th century. Its oldest building is a 200-year-old shell.

Just off Staniel Cay is the *Thunderball* grotto, where some sections of the famous James Bond movie were filmed. Divers can explore this grotto, but removal of anything but yourself is forbidden, as it is under the protection of the Bahamas National Trust. At low water, it's possible to swim in; a blow hole in the roof illuminates the cave. Tropical fish can be seen in their natural habitat. Another James Bond flick, *Never Say Never Again,* was also partially filmed at this grotto, as, more recently, was *Splash*.

GETTING THERE

Before the coming of the airplane, it took days to reach the island from Miami or Nassau, but now it has a 3,000-foot paved airstrip. Some of the vacation homes on Staniel Cay today are owned by pilots. A telecommunications center links the island with both The Bahamas and the U.S.

The easiest way to get here is on a flight departing from Fort Lauderdale International Airport. **TransMar International** flies in (call toll free at 800/327-3011). In Florida, information or brochures can be obtained by writing TransMar International, 4250 SW 11th Terrace, Fort Lauderdale, FL 33315 (tel. 305/467-6850).

WHERE TO STAY

Expensive

What might be the oldest continually operated yacht facilities in the Exumas is also a getaway haven with a handful of rentable rooms. The **Staniel Cay Yacht Club,** Staniel Cay, The Exumas, The Bahamas (tel. 809/355-2024, or 809/255-2011 in the U.S.), was originally established in 1959 by its present owner, Bob Chamberlain. Although it contains only six accommodations, its docking and fueling facilities—as well as its bar and restaurant—are so sought after that it's one of the most famous such establishments in The Bahamas. (In fact, because of its strategic location, many yachts and sailboats headed for George Town are almost obligated to stop in for supplies because of the configuration of the nearby archipelagos.)

With a complete marina facility, it can accommodate between 12 and 15 boats at its docks at any time, although other visiting yachts sometimes bob at anchor in the calm waters nearby. Its social center is its pierside restaurant and clubhouse, whose palm-thatched ceiling is decorated with the burgees (insignia flags) and inscribed T-shirts of almost every other yacht club in the North Atlantic. As you might expect from such an isolated place, hours are flexible. It remains open throughout the day, providing service whenever someone happens to show up for solid or liquid refreshments.

Accommodations range from a landlocked houseboat to a quintet of cottages ringed with casuarina trees. Most rooms are sold AP (all meals included), which in this case also includes the free use of a 14- or 16-foot motorized skiff for fishing expeditions. Single occupancy, with AP (all meals) included, costs $165 per day; double occupancy, $180. Taxes and service are extra, and rates are the same year round.

Inexpensive

Happy People Marina, Staniel Cay, The Exumas, The Bahamas (tel. 809/355-2008), near the Staniel Cay Yacht Club, is operated by an Exumian, Kenneth Rolle (one of the many descendants of slaves who once belonged to Lord Rolle). His mother was the famous Ma Blanche, who had a mailboat named for her. He offers motel-like rooms on the water, as well as a restaurant and bar, a swimming pool, and a private beach. There are dockage facilities, but no ability to fuel or service the majority of the island's visiting yachts, the!better-equipped of which usually head for the previously recommended Staniel Cay Yacht Club. The prevailing atmosphere is casual. A dozen waterfront bedrooms rent year round for $75 daily for a single or double.

Meals and drinks are served in a separate building closer to the center of town, within a 3-minute walk of the marina. Known as the Royal Entertainer Lounge, it sometimes welcomes local bands and serves meals according to a flexible schedule. Lunches cost from around $12 per person, dinners around $18.

SPORTS & RECREATION

Want to go boating? The **Staniel Cay Yacht Club** (tel. 809/355-2011) has Boston Whalers and small sailboats for rent. Scuba gear is also available.

The **Happy People Marina** (tel. 809/355-2008) also arranges sportfishing trips with local guides.

Snorkeling trips can be arranged through both the yacht club and the marina.

---

5. Sampson Cay

In the heart of what has been called the "most beautiful cruising waters in the world," Sampson Cay is tiny and has a certain charm. It lies directly northwest of Staniel Cay and just to the southeast of the Exuma National Land and Sea Park. It has a full-service marina and some accommodations (see below), as well as a small dive operation. Along with Staniel Cay, Sampson Cay has the only marina in the Central Exumas. To fly to it, you must go to Staniel Cay, unless you arrive on your own boat, as do most visitors. Local guides take out sportfishermen for the day, and this can be arranged at the club. Sampson Cay lies 67 nautical miles southeast of Nassau, and is considered one of the safest anchorages in the Exumas and a natural "hurricane hole." The cay lies near the end of Pipe Creek, which has been called a "tropical Shangri-La."

WHERE TO STAY

Inexpensive

A trio of accommodations are available on the premises of another of the island's marina facilities, **Sampson's Cay Colony,** Sampson Cay, The Exumas, The Bahamas (tel. 809/355-2034). Your host is Mrs. Rosie Mitchell, whose husband, Marcus, is well known in these parts for his marine salvage company, which rescues yachts foundering on nearby rocks and reefs.

Each of the establishment's three air-conditioned units has a tiny kitchenette (with a hot plate, sink, and refrigerator, but no oven) and a bathroom. The most noteworthy of the accommodations is contained within a stone-sided, two-story tower—probably the most prominent building on the island. Single or double occupancy costs between $90 and $100 a day throughout the year, depending on the accommodation.

Guests are quickly absorbed in the community's main pastime, which involves running the grocery store and commissary, the fuel and dockage facilities of the marina, and the bar and restaurant favored by visiting yachtspeople. Its nautically decorated clubhouse serves drinks and sandwiches any time of the day to anyone who shows up, but reservations are required before 4pm for the single-seating dinner, which is served every night between 7:30 and 8pm. A fixed-price meal costs $19 per person. (Reservations can be made via ship-to-shore radio on Channel 16 VHF.)

On the premises, a pair of 13-foot Boston Whalers can be rented for $45 per half day.

THE SOUTHERN BAHAMAS

1. CAT ISLAND
2. SAN SALVADOR/RUM CAY
3. LONG ISLAND
4. ACKLINS ISLAND & CROOKED ISLAND
5. MAYAGUANA ISLAND
6. GREAT INAGUA
7. RAGGED ISLAND & JUMENTO CAYS

This cluster of islands on the southern fringe of The Bahamas might be called the "undeveloped islands." That they are—in fact, some of them are proud to proclaim that "we are as we were when Columbus first landed here."

But their history hasn't been that uneventful. In the 18th century Loyalists from the Carolinas and Virginia came here, settling into many of the islands and bringing in slave labor. For about 20 years they had thriving cotton plantations until a blight struck and killed the industry. A second, and perhaps more devasting "blight" from the planters' point of view was the freeing of the slaves in 1834. The Loyalists moved on to more fertile ground, in many cases leaving behind the emancipated blacks, who were left with only the name of their former master. Many people in the southern Bahamas have had to eke out a living as best they can.

With some notable exceptions, such as on Rum Cay and Long Island, tourism developers have stayed clear of these islands, although their potential is enormous, as most of them have excellent beaches, good fishing, and fine dive sites.

If you consider visiting any of these islands, be forewarned that transportation will be a major problem. Also, except for two or three resorts, accommodations are severely limited. For these and other reasons, people who have yachts have been the primary visitors up to now.

Many changes may be in the wind for the southern Bahamas. But if you want to see things the "way they used to be," as they say in those Jamaica ads, go not to Jamaica but to Mayaguana Island. That's *really* how things used to be in The Bahamas.

1. Cat Island

The sixth-largest island in The Bahamas, fishhook-shaped Cat Island is some 48 miles long and 1 to 4 miles wide, comprising some 150 square miles of land area about 130 miles southeast of Nassau and 325 miles southeast of Miami. This is not —repeat *not*—Cat *Cay*. The cay is a little private island near Bimini. The location of Cat Island—named after the pirate Arthur Catt—is near the Tropic of Cancer, between Eleuthera and Long Island. Its climate is one of the finest in The Bahamas, with temperatures in the high 60s during the short winters, rising to the mid-80s in summer, and with trade winds making the place more comfortable. Some 2,000 residents call it home.

With its virgin beaches, Cat Island is considered one of the most beautiful islands in The Bahamas, and it is visited by so few people it could be called "undiscovered." Even though it has remained relatively unknown to mainstream tourism, many local historians claim that it was Cat Island that first saw Columbus. The great explorer himself was believed by some to have been first welcomed here by the peaceful Arawak Indians.

Cat Island remains mysterious to some even now. It's known as a stronghold of such romantic practices as *obeah* (West Indian witchcraft) and of miraculously healing bush medicines. Its history has been colorful. Regardless of whether or not Columbus stopped off here, the island has seen a parade of adventurers, slaves, buccaneers, farmers, and visionaries of many nationalities.

GETTING THERE

By Air

A commercial flight on **Bahamasair** (tel. 800/222-4262 in the U.S.) leaves Nassau for Arthurs Town on Tuesday and Saturday, but that could change so check locally.

By Mailboat

Cat Island is also serviced by mailboat. The M/V *North Cat Island Special* (tel. 809/393-1064) leaves Potter's Cay Dock in Nassau, heading for Bennett's Harbour and Arthurs Town weekly. It leaves on Tuesday and returns to Nassau on Thursday. Another vessel, M/V *Maxine* (tel. 809/393-1064), departs Potter's Cay in Nassau on Tuesday, going to Old and New Bight, with a return on Saturday.

GETTING AROUND

There is no taxi service available on Cat Island. Hotel owners, if notified of your arrival time, will have someone drive to the airport to pick you up. You can, however, rent a car from **Russell Brothers,** Bridge Inn, New Bight (tel. 809/354-5013), to go exploring on your own.

A straight asphalt road (in terrible shape) leads from the north to the south of the island. Along the way you can select your own beach, and chances are you'll have complete privacy. These beaches also offer an array of water sports, and visitors can go swimming or snorkeling at several places. The island's north side is considered wild, untamed shoreline. Diving lessons are possible for the novice, and the experienced will find boating and diving among the reasons to go to Cat Island.

An airport near The Bight, the most beautiful village on the island, is open, and Bahamasair flies to **Arthurs Town** in the north, the major town and the boyhood home of the actor Sidney Poitier. (He has many relatives still living on the island, including one or two amazing look-alikes I recently spotted.)

WHERE TO STAY & DINE

Moderate

On Fernandez Bay, **Fernandez Bay Village,** Cat Island, The Bahamas (no local phone), is a place where you can enjoy the same water and sun activities as at big

What the Symbols Mean

AP (American plan): Includes three meals a day (sometimes called full board or full pension).

BP (Bermuda plan): Popularized first in Bermuda, this option includes a full American breakfast (sometimes called an English breakfast).

CP (Continental plan): A Continental breakfast (that is, bread, jam, and coffee) is included in the room rate.

EP (European plan): This rate is always cheapest, as it offers only the room—no meals.

MAP (modified American plan): Sometimes called half board or half pension, this room rate includes breakfast and dinner (or lunch if you prefer).

resorts but without the hassle of crowds and constant coming and going. It has been in the Armbrister family since it was originally established on a plantation in 1870. It's a place where rusticity and seclusion are part of the charm, and yet, if you wish, you can get acquainted with other guests with like interests (or even watch video movies). Right on the beautiful white-sand beach of the bay, nestled among the casuarina trees, are seven full housekeeping villas, each sleeping up to six people, as well as two double-occupancy cottages, built of stone, driftwood, and glass. Full maid service is provided. Because of the lack of nearby dining facilities, most clients opt for accommodations with MAP, which in this case means either breakfast or lunch ("because so many people don't even eat breakfast") and dinner. Double occupancy in all of the units costs between $155 and $180, MAP included; single occupancy, MAP included, costs $135. Prices are the same throughout the year. There's a surcharge of $3 per person per day for electricity. Fernandez Bay Village often has visiting yachtspeople who moor in the waters offshore (there are no marina facilities), taking advantage of the resort's general store and the fresh supplies to be found there. Nearby is Smith's Bay, one of the best storm shelters in the region, where even the government mailboats take refuge during hurricanes.

The resort contains a beachfront bar plus a much-appreciated ice machine. Its restaurant is considered one of the best in the Family Islands, largely because of the ample amounts of fresh meat and produce flown in several times a week by Tony Armbrister, the owner's son, who with his wife, Pam, is managing director of the resort.

There is free use of Zuma sailboats and bicycles, and snorkeling and waterskiing are also on the agenda. Rental vans are available for $15 per hour for drives into the hills. You can picnic on deserted beaches around the island, then dine on authentic island cuisine at the resort's restaurant, after which on many nights a blazing bonfire near the water is the focal point for guests to listen to island music.

For reservations and information, write to Fernandez Bay Village, 5260 SW 6th St., Plantation, FL 33318 (tel. 305/792-1905). The resort will supply air transportation from Nassau on request (usually within the private plane owned and operated by the manager himself). Flights land at the nearby New Bight Airport.

Inexpensive

Bridge Inn, The Bight, Cat Island, The Bahamas (tel. 809/354-5013, or 305/634-1014 in Florida), is managed by Allan Russell, who is ably assisted by a group of family members. The inn offers babysitting services so that parents can play tennis or go diving, windsurfing, jogging, bicycling, fishing, or just sightseeing with the knowledge that their youngsters are being carefully tended and are having fun too. Year round, guests pay $70 daily for EP double occupancy, $60 for EP single occupancy. The 12 bedrooms have minibars and TVs but no air conditioning. There are packages for longer stays. Room service is available, and there are a full bar and a restaurant serving Bahamian and international cuisine. Local jam sessions ("rake and scrape") are easily arranged for your entertainment. As manager Russell points out, you'll learn that life can be "no problem, mon, on Cat Island."

Hotel Greenwood Inn, Port Howe, Cat Island, The Bahamas (tel. 809/359-3068), is a group of modern buildings on the ocean side with a private sandy beach. There are 16 spacious oceanview double rooms, all equipped with full baths and showers and their own terraces. The hotel is open all year. There is an all-purpose bar and a dining room. The staff meets each Bahamasair flight when it arrives. Make time for some comfortable chats with fellow guests before jumping into the swimming pool. Tariffs year round are $65 per day for a single, $115 for a double, including two meals a day. Children 4 to 12 sharing a room with their parents pay only half the rate. The inn has a 40-foot motorboat for diving excursions. Its Tabaluga Diving Base has complete equipment for 20 divers at a time.

ATTRACTIONS

There's an interesting **Arawak Indian cave** at Columbus Point on the southern tip of the island. In addition, you can see the ruins of many once-flourishing plantations. Some old stone mounds are nearly 200 years old. Early planters, many of them Loyalists, marked their plantation boundaries with these mounds. These include the **Deveaux Mansion,** built by Colonel Andrew Deveaux of the fledgling U.S. Navy, who recaptured Nassau from the Spanish in 1783. Its heyday was during the island's short-lived cotton boom. Yet another mansion, **Armbrister Plantation,** lies in ruins near Port Howe.

You can hike along the natural paths through native villages, past exotic plants. Finally, you reach the peak of **Mount Alvernia,** the highest point in The Bahamas at 206 feet above sea level, and are rewarded with a splendid view. The mount is capped by the Hermitage, a religious retreat built entirely by hand by the late Father Jerome, the former "father confessor" of the island, who was once a muleskinner in Canada. Curiously, the building was scaled to fit his short stature (he was a very, very short man). An Anglican who switched, this Roman Catholic "hermit priest" became a legend on Cat Island. He died in 1956 at the age of 80, but his memory is kept very much alive here and he's known even among young people born long after his death.

The boating activities reach their peak at the **Annual Three-Day Regatta,** usually conducted at the end of July. That's when Cat Island receives its biggest collection of visitors, and its inns prove inadequate to receive them.

---

2. San Salvador/Rum Cay

This may be where the New World began. Christopher Columbus, it has for some years been believed, made his first footprints in the Western Hemisphere here, although this is still strongly disputed. The easternmost island in the Bahamian archipelago, San Salvador lies 200 miles east-southeast of Nassau. It is some 60 square miles in asea, much of which is occupied by water. There are said to be 28 land-locked lakes on the island, the largest of which is 12 miles long and serves as the principal route of transportation for most of the island's 1,200 population. A 40-mile road circles the perimeter of San Salvador.

The tiny island keeps a lonely vigil in the Atlantic. The Dixon Hill Lighthouse at South West Point can be seen for 90 miles. The last lighthouse of its type in The

Bahamas, it rises about 165 feet; the light is a hand-operated beacon fueled by kerosene. It was built in the 1850s. The highest point on the island is Mount Kerr at 138 feet.

HISTORY

Back in 1492 a small group of peaceful Lucayan (Arawak) Indians went about their business of living on a little island they called Guanahani, which they and their forebears had called home for at least 500 years. It is this island that is believed to have been the first landfall for Columbus and his fleet, who were looking for a route to the riches of the East. It is said that the discoverer knelt and prayed—and claimed the land for Spain.

Unfortunately, the event was not so propitious for the reportedly handsome, near-naked Indians. Columbus later wrote to Queen Isabella about what ideal captives they would make—perfect servants, in other words. It wasn't long before the Spanish conquistadors cleared the island—as well as most of The Bahamas—of Lucayans, sending them into slavery and early death in the mines of Hispaniola (Haiti) to feed the Spanish lust for gold from the New World.

No lasting marker was placed by Columbus on the sandy, sun-drenched island he had found, resulting in much study and discussion during the last century or so as to just where he really did land. Some said that it was on one of the cays of the Turks and Caicos Islands, others claimed that it was on Cat Island.

During the days of the buccaneers, an Englishman and pirate captain, George Watling, took over the island as his own and built a mansion to serve as his safe haven (see the description of Watling's Castle, below). This was in the 17th century, and the island was listed on maps for about 250 years as Watling's (or Watling) Island.

In 1926 the Bahamian legislature formally changed the name of the island to San Salvador, feeling that enough evidence had been brought forth to support the belief that this was the site of the landing of Columbus. Finally, in 1983 artifacts of European origin (beads, buckles, and metal spikes) were found on this island together with a shard of Spanish pottery, plus Arawak pottery and beads. It is unlikely that the actual date of these artifacts can be pinned down, although they are probably from about 1490 to 1560. However, the beads and buckles fit the description of goods recorded in Columbus's log as having been traded by his crewmen for Indian objects.

It was in 1986 that *National Geographic* magazine published a meticulously researched article by its senior associate editor, Joseph Judge, with a companion piece by former chief of the magazine's foreign editorial staff, Luis Marden, setting forth the belief that Samana Cay, some 65 miles to the southeast of the present San Salvador, was Guanahani, where Columbus first landed in the New World and whose name he declared to be San Salvador. The question may never be absolutely resolved, but there will doubtless be years and years of controversy about it.

GETTING THERE

This can be a real problem, made all the more so by the scarcity of accommodations on San Salvador and by the long time you'll have to wait before being able to get off the island. Nevertheless, history buffs still flock here every year.

By Air

Bahamasair (tel. toll free 800/222-4262) has direct weekly flights, on Tuesday and Saturday, to San Salvador (check flight schedules).

By Mailboat

In addition, a mailboat, the **M/V Maxine,** leaves Potter's Cay Dock in Nassau, heading to Cat Island, Rum Cay, and San Salvador. It departs Nassau weekly on Tuesday, returning there on Saturday. For details about sailing, contact the Dockmaster at Potter's Cay Dock in Nassau (tel. 809/393-1064).

GETTING AROUND

Taxis meet arriving planes and will take you to **Riding Rock Inn** (see below), where you can rent a car for $65 a day to explore the island on your own. You can also rent motor bikes at $30 a day (but don't expect good road conditions) or bicycles at $5 a day. These are the most popular means of transport for visitors. Pedaling energetically, you can traverse all of San Salvador in about an hour.

FAST FACTS: SAN SALVADOR/RUM CAY

Hospital: The **San Salvador Medical Clinic** (tel. 207) services the island's residents, but serious cases are flown to Nassau.

Police: To call the police, dial **218**. (Phones are rare on the island, but the front desk at Riding Rock Inn will place calls for you.)

WHERE TO STAY & DINE

Moderate

San Salvador's only resort is the **Riding Rock Inn,** Cockburn Town, San Salvador, The Bahamas (tel. 809/322-2631, or toll free 800/272-1492 in the U.S.), which is almost exclusively (95%) patronized by divers and underwater enthusiasts. Containing a total of 24 accommodations (which face either a pool or the open sea), the resort specializes in weeklong packages that include three dives a day, all meals, and accommodations in single or double rooms. Packages begin and end on Saturday and, if a client pays a $250 supplement, can include specially chartered round-trip air transportation from Nassau. Although most of this resort's clients are already experienced and certified divers, beginners can arrange a $75 Resort Course for the first day of their visit, and afterward participate in most of the community's daily dives. (Full PADI certification can also be arranged for another supplement of $350.)

Accommodations contain private baths, simple tropics-inspired furnishings, and ceiling fans. In winter, the weeklong dive package costs $1,200 for AP single occupancy and $950 per person for double occupancy. *In summer, the same package costs $1,000 for single occupancy and $800 per person for double occupancy.* An island tour is included in the package, but after that, most clients find that the best way to navigate is by bicycle (the hotel rents them, plus scooters). On the premises are a restaurant and a bar whose seating area juts above the water on a pier.

ATTRACTIONS

If a preponderance of monuments is anything to go by, this is the San Salvador found and named by the historic explorer. Three of them are on land, and they certainly can't all mark the spot where Columbus first came ashore, but Long Bay, marked by the **Cross Monument,** is deemed the most likely spot. The *Chicago Herald* installed a monument to the explorer in the 1890s, but it is not probable—indeed, it's almost impossible—that any landing was made at that site. It opens onto reefs along the eastern shore, surely a dangerous place for a landing.

The **Olympic Games Memorial** to Columbus—3 miles south of Cockburn Town, as is the Cross Monument—was erected in 1968 to commemorate the games in Mexico. At the time, runners carrying an Olympic torch circled the island before coming to rest at the monument and lighting the torch there, which was then taken to Mexico on a warship for the games. A fourth marker is underwater, supposedly where Columbus dropped anchor.

Watling's Castle, also known as Sandy Point Estate, has substantial ruins that are about 85 feet above sea level and some 2½ miles from the "Great Lake," on the southwestern tip of the island. Local "experts" will tell you all about the castle and its history. Only problem is, each "expert" I've listened to—three in all, at different times—has had a conflicting story about the place. Ask around and perhaps you'll get yet another version. One of the most common legends involves a famous pirate who made his living either by salvaging the wreckage from foundered ships or by attacking them for their spoils.

In the early part of the 19th century some Loyalist families moved from the newly established United States to this island, hoping to get rich from farmland tended by slave labor. That dream ended when the United Kingdom Emancipation Act of 1834 freed the slaves. The plantation owners, having been compensated for their bond servants' value, moved on, but the former slaves stayed behind.

A relic of those times, **Farquharson's Plantation,** is the best-known ruin on the island. People locally call it "Blackbeard's Castle," but it's a remnant of slavery days, not of the time of pirates. You can see the foundation of a great house, a kitchen, and what is believed to have been a punishment cell.

San Salvador is one of the most unspoiled of the Bahamian Family Islands—not that much has changed since Columbus landed. It has wooded hills, lakes, and white-sand beaches. Its people are hospitable. Some still practice obeah and bush medicine.

The island's capital, **Cockburn** (pronounced Coburn) **Town,** is a harbor village that also has an airstrip. It takes its name from George Cockburn, who is said to have been the first royal governor of The Bahamas who cared enough about this remote island to visit it. That was back in 1823.

Look for the town's giant, landmark almond tree. Whatever is happening at San Salvador generally takes place here, especially the Columbus Day parade held every October 12. The island will probably be in for a tremendous influx of visitors when the 500th anniversary of the landing of Columbus is celebrated in 1992.

The **New World Museum** in Cockburn Town has relics dating back to Indian times, but you'll have to ask until you find someone with a key if you want to go inside.

Among the settlements on San Salvador are Sugar Loaf, Pigeon Creek, Old Place, Holiday Track, and Fortune Hill. United Estates, the one with the largest population, is a village in the northwest corner near the Dixon Hill Lighthouse. The U.S. Coast Guard has a station at the northern tip of the island.

Bonefishermen are attracted to Pigeon Creek, and some record catches have been chalked up there. San Salvador is mainly visited by the boating set who can live aboard their craft, but if you're visiting for the day, you'll find one or two local cafés. They all serve seafood.

SPORTS & RECREATION

Associated with the Riding Rock Inn (see above), **Guanahani Company** (tel. 809/322-2631) offers dive packages, as well as snorkeling trips, fishing trips, and boating trips. One-, two-, and three-dive trips cost from $30, $45, and $65, respectively.

Riding Rock Inn also has a tennis court where guests can play free.

DAY TRIPS: RUM CAY

"Rum Cay?" you ask. "Where on earth is Rum Cay?" (That's pronounced *key,* of course.) Even many Bahamians have never heard of it. Midway between San Salvador and Long Island, this is a cay that time forgot.

That wasn't always so. The very name conjures up images of swashbucklers and rum-runners, and it was doubtless at least a port of call for those doughty seafarers, as it was for ships taking on supplies of salt, fresh water, and food before crossing the Atlantic or going south to Latin America. The cay's name is supposed to have derived from the wrecking of a rum-laden sailing ship upon its shores.

Like many other Bahamian islands, this one for a while attracted Loyalists fleeing the former 13 colonies of Great Britain on the North American mainland. They were drawn here by the hope of establishing themselves as farmers and plantation overlords, but even those brave and homeless immigrants abandoned the island as unproductive.

Salt mines were the mainstay of the island's economy before they were wiped out by hurricanes at the turn of the century. After that, most of the inhabitants migrated to Nassau, so that by the 1970s the population of Rum Cay stood at "80 souls."

The well-known underwater cinematographer Stan Waterman visited here and described Rum Cay as the "unspoiled diving jewel of The Bahamas." For that reason, a diving club was opened here in 1983 but it closed, regrettably, in 1990.

Port Nelson, the island's capital, is where most of the Rum Cay's present 100 inhabitants live.

There have been statements in some printed matter that Rum Cay was the island where Columbus landed next after finding and naming San Salvador. He dubbed that second island Santa María de la Concepción. However, many students of history and navigation believe that the second stop was at the island today called Conception, which lies in a northwesterly direction from Rum Cay and about the same distance northeast of Long Island. You'll have to go there in a private boat.

Both of these views as to the second island on which Columbus landed are disputed by Joseph Judge in the 1986 *National Geographic* article (see under "San Salvador," above). He holds that, based on modern computer science and knowledge of the ocean bottom and currents, the island the discoverer named Santa María de la Concepción has to be Crooked Island.

Conception is not inhabited, and it is under the protection of The Bahamas National Trust, which preserves it as a sea and land park. It's a sanctuary for migratory birds. The most esoteric of divers find excellent dive sites here, and the rapidly diminishing green turtle uses its beaches as egg-laying sites. Park rules are strict about littering or removing animal or plant life.

With the demise of the Rum Cay Club, tourist traffic to the island came to a halt except for the odd yachting party or two. But with the increased interest in tourism, in the wake of the 1992 Columbus celebrations, perhaps the area will gain renewed interest.

3. Long Island

Having nothing to do with that 100-mile land mass at the southern tip of New York State, the Long Island of The Bahamas was the third island to which Columbus presumably sailed during his first voyage of discovery, a point on which many historians seem to agree. The Lucayan (Arawak) Indians who lived there at the time (having come from South America via Cuba) called their island Yuma, but Columbus renamed it Fernandina, in honor of King Ferdinand, and claimed it for Spain.

Loyalist plantation owners came here in the 18th century from the Carolinas and Virginia, bringing with them their slaves and their allegiance to the British Crown. There was a brief cotton boom, but when the slaves were freed in 1834, the owners abandoned the plantations and left the island. Inhabited by the former slaves, Long Island slumbered for years, until its rediscovery in the 1960s by German resort developers.

The Tropic of Cancer runs through this long, thin sliver of land, 400 square miles in area, lying 150 miles south of Nassau. It stretches for some 60 miles running from north to south, and averages 1½ miles wide. It's only 3 miles wide at its broadest point.

Only recently emerging as a minor tourist resort, Long Island is characterized by high cliffs in the north, wide and shallow sand beaches, historic plantation ruins, Indian caves, and Spanish churches. It is also the site of the saltworks of the Diamond Crystal Company. The island's present population is some 3,500 people. Offshore are famed diving sites, such as the Arawak "green" hole, a "bottomless" blue hole of suunning magnitude.

GETTING THERE

By Air

There are two airstrips here, connected by a bad road. The Stella Maris strip is in the north, and the other, called Deadman's Cay, is in the south, north of Clarence Town. **Bahamasair** (tel. toll free 800/222-4262 in the U.S.) wings in four times a week from Nassau, connecting the two airports. Flights are on Saturday, Sunday, Monday, and Thursday.

By Mailboat

Mailboats service Clarence Town weekly, with service to Deadman's Cay and Stella Maris once a week or every other week. The boats leave from Potter's Cay Dock in Nassau. The M/V *Nay Dean* sails from Nassau on Monday, returning on Friday, and makes stops at the Exumas as well as other cays and Long Island. For information on sailing, days and times, and costs, get in touch with the Dockmaster at Potter's Cay Dock, Nassau (tel. 809/393-1064).

GETTING AROUND

The **Stella Maris Resort Club** (tel. 809/336-2106) can make arrangements to have you picked up at the airport upon arrival and can also arrange to rent you a car.

FAST FACTS: LONG ISLAND

Police: The police at Clarence Town can be called at **231.**

WHERE TO STAY & DINE

Moderate

On the Atlantic, overlooking the coastline, the **Stella Maris Inn,** P.O. Box 105, Long Island, The Bahamas (tel. 809/336-2106, or toll free 800/426-0466 in the U.S.; 305/467-0466 for the Florida booking office), has 60 rooms. Courtesy transportation is provided to a 3-mile beach reserve. Accommodations vary widely—rooms, studios, apartments, and cottages consisting of one to three bedrooms. Rentals are all in individual buildings, including cottages and bungalows, set around the clubhouse and a trio of hotel pools.

Each accommodation has its own air conditioning, walk-in closets, and fully equipped bath. Some bungalows are 100 feet from the water; others are directly on its edge. Winter EP rates are from $96 daily for a double, from $76 for a single. A one-bedroom cottage for two rents for $116 daily, and a two-bedroom cottage for two costs $180. *In summer, the rates drop to $80 daily for double occupancy, from $60* *for single occupancy. A one-bedroom cottage for two rents for $100 daily, and a two-bedroom villa for two costs $160.* The inn serves a Bahamian cuisine, as well as Continental specialties. Dress here is informal.

The inn provides rum punch parties, cave parties, barbecue dinners, Saturday dinners, and dancing. There are two hard-surface tennis courts, and water sports are excellent here. Divers and snorkelers have a wide choice of coral head, reef, and drop-off diving, along the protected west coast of this island and at the north and all along the east coast, around Conception Island and Rum Cay. Bottom and reef fishing are also offered; there are three good bonefish bays close by. Other sports include waterskiing. Windsurfing boards and 12-foot Scorpion and Sunfish sailboats are free to hotel guests.

Inexpensive

Located at Salt Pond, 12 miles south of Stella Maris, **Thompson Bay Inn,** Main Road, Thompson Bay, P.O. Box 30123, Stella Maris, Long Island, The Bahamas (tel. the Deadman's Cay operator), is a modest eight-room inn. Rising two floors, it was constructed of stone. Other than the Stella Maris Inn, it is the most popular gathering place on the island, with its bar, lounge, dance hall, and restaurant serving such Bahamian dishes as conch, grouper, and peas 'n' rice. Dinners cost $12 each. Rooms are simply furnished, and the inn's four baths are shared. Rooms have TVs but no phones or air conditioning. Year round, EP singles rent for $40 daily, doubles going for $50.

ATTRACTIONS

Most of the inhabitants live at the unattractively named **Deadman's Cay.** Except for Burnt Ground, other settlements have colorful and somewhat more pleasant names: Roses, Newfound Harbour, Indian Head Point, and at the northern tip of the island, Cape Santa Maria, generally believed to be the place where Columbus landed and from which he looked on the Exumas (islands that he did not visit). My favorite place name, however, is Hard Bargain. No one seems to know how this hamlet came to be called that. Hard Bargain, now a shrimp-breeding farm, lies 10 miles south of Clarence Town.

Try to visit **Clarence Town** in the south, 10 miles below Deadman's Cay, along the eastern coastline. It was here that the stubby little priest, Father Jerome, who became known as the "father confessor" of the islands, built two churches before his death in 1956—one, **St. Paul's,** an Anglican house of worship and the other, **St. Peter's,** a Roman Catholic church. The "hermit" of Cat Island, where you can visit his Hermitage, was interested in Gothic architecture, and he must also have been of a somewhat ecumenical bent, having started his ministry as an Anglican but embracing Roman Catholicism along the way.

The days when local plantation owners figured their wealth in black slaves and white cotton are recalled in some of the ruins you can visit. The remains of **Dunmore's Plantation** at Deadman's Cay stand on a hill with the sea on three sides. There are six gateposts (four outer and two inner ones), as well as a house with two fireplaces and wall drawings of ships. At the base of the ruins is evidence that a millwheel was once used. It was part of the estate of Lord Dunmore, for whom Dunmore Town on Harbour Island was named.

At the village of Grays stand **Gray's Plantation** ruins, where you'll see the remnants of at least three houses, one with two chimneys. One is very large, and the other seems to have been a one-story structure with a cellar.

Adderley's Plantation, off Cape Santa Maria, originally occupied all the land now known as Stella Maris. The ruins of this cotton plantation's buildings consist of three structures that are partially intact but roofless.

Two underground sites that can be visited are **Dunmore's Caves** at Deadman's Cay, and **Deadman's Cay Cave,** also at Deadman's Cay. You'll need to hire a local guide if you wish to visit these attractions. Dunmore's Caves are believed to have been inhabited by Lucayans and later to have served as a hideaway for buccaneers. The cave at Deadman's Cay, one of two that lead to the ocean, has never been fully explored. There are two Indian drawings on the cavern wall in the one you can visit. It also has stalagmites and stalactites.

Long Island Regatta

In June, the sailors of Long Island participate in the big event of the year, the **Long Island Regatta.** They've been gathering since 1967 at Salt Pond for this annual event, which lasts for four days. In addition to the highly competitive sailboat races, Long Island takes on a festive air with calypso music and reggae and lots of drinking and partying. Many expatriate Long Islanders come home at this time, usually from Nassau, New York, or Miami, to enjoy not only the regatta but rake and scrape music (accordion playing).

4. Acklins Island & Crooked Island

These little tropical islands far to the southeast of Nassau comprise an undiscovered Bahamian frontier outpost. Columbus came this way looking for gold. Much later Crooked Island, Acklins Island, and their surrounding cays were retreats of pirates who attacked vessels in the Crooked Island Passage, the narrow waterway separating the two islands, through which Columbus sailed. Today a well-known landmark, the **Crooked Island Passage Light,** built in 1876, guides ships to a safe voyage through the slot. A barrier reef begins near the lighthouse, stretching down off Acklins Island for about 25 miles to the southeast.

These are neighboring islands, which, although separate, are usually mentioned as a unit because of their proximity to one another. The northern one, Crooked Island, is 70 square miles in area, lying 223 miles from Nassau. Acklins Island, to the south, occupies 120 square miles and is 260 miles from the Bahamian capital, which is to the northwest.

In his controversial article in *National Geographic* in 1986, Joseph Judge identifies Crooked Island as the site of Columbus's second island landing, the one he named Santa María de la Concepción.

It is estimated that by the end of the 18th century there were more than three dozen working plantations on these islands, begun by Loyalists fleeing mainland North America in the wake of the Revolutionary War. At the peak plantation period, there could have been as many as 1,200 slaves laboring in the cotton fields (which were later wiped out by a blight).

GETTING THERE & GETTING AROUND

There is a government-owned ferry service connecting the two islands, operating daily from 9am to 4pm. It links Lovely Bay on Acklins Island with Browns on Crooked Island. The one-way fare is $4. Both these islands have magnificent white-sand beaches, and good fishing and scuba diving are possible. Both islands are inhabited mainly by fishermen and farmers.

An airport lies at Colonel Hill on Crooked Island, and there is another airstrip at Spring Point, Acklins Island. If you arrive on one island and intend to go to the other, you can use the ferry, mentioned just above.

Bahamasair (tel. toll free 800/222-4262 in the U.S.), has two flights a week from Nassau, on Tuesday and Saturday, to Crooked Island and Acklins Island, with returns to Nassau scheduled on the same day.

There is also **mailboat** service aboard the M/V *Windward Express.* It leaves Potter's Cay Dock in Nassau, heading for Acklins Island, Crooked Island, Long Cay, and Mayaguana Island each week. Check on days of sailing and costs with the Dockmaster at Potter's Cay Dock in Nassau (tel. 809/393-1064).

Once you arrive at Crooked Island, there is a **taxi** service available, but because of the lack of telephones, it's wise to advise your hotel of your arrival, and they will probably send a van to meet you.

FAST FACTS: ACKLINS ISLAND & CROOKED ISLAND

Banking: If you're coming to these islands, take care of all your banking needs before you arrive, as there is no banking service on either Crooked Island or Acklins Island.

Hospitals: There are two government-operated clinics. Phones are few on the island, but your hotel desk can reach one of these clinics by going through the operator. The clinic on Acklins Island is at Spring Point and Chesters Bay, and the one on Crooked Island is at Landrail Point.

Police: The police station on Crooked Island can be reached at **336-2197.**

WHERE TO STAY & DINE

Moderate
Pittstown Point Landing, Landrail Point, Crooked Island, The Bahamas (tel. 809/336-2507). For reservations and information, call Sporty's Pilot Shop, Sporty's Drive, Batavia, OH 45103 (tel. 513/732-2593, ext. 300). It lies in a position so isolated, at the extreme northwestern tip of Crooked Island, 2½ miles north of the nearest hamlet of Landrail Point (population 60 souls), that it's easy to forget the world outside. Its position on a sandy peninsula jutting seaward benefits from unending ocean views and easy proximity to some of the most weirdly historic sites in The Bahamas. These include the Marine Farms Fortress, located within a 5-minute paddle across a saltwater pond.

The resort is owned by a consortium of aviators connected with one of the largest aviation supply houses (Sporty's Pilot Shop) in North America. The resort has its own 2,300-foot hard-surface landing strip, and a series of clean and orderly villas, each ringed with vegetation and each containing four accommodations. The resort's 14 bedrooms, because of the trade winds blowing in constantly, contain no air conditioning, only large paddle-shaped ceiling fans, as well as private bathrooms. The entire resort shares only one telephone, which is reserved for calls of great urgency. In winter, singles rent for $95, doubles for $100, EP. *In summer, prices are reduced to $65 single or $70 double, EP.*

Meals are served within a stone-walled building that was originally erected late in the 1600s as a barracks for the British West Indies Naval Squadron, and later served as the post office for the region. Offering sea views, it serves seafood and a menu composed of North American and Bahamian specialties.

Inexpensive
Lying right on the waterfront, **T & S Guest House,** Cabbage Hill, Crooked Island, The Bahamas (tel. 809/133-62096), stands a 10-minute walk from the airport. E. A. Thompson, the manager, will welcome you and offer island hospitality in one of his 10 bedrooms, which rent year round for $40 for an EP single, rising to $55 for an EP double. Children under 11 can stay free with their parents. Facilities include TV and laundry, and Mr. Thompson will explain local life, including how to spend the day on the best beach, 2 miles away. You can prepare your own meals in some of the units, or else enjoy good Bahamian seafood, simply cooked, at the inn itself. Boating and skin diving can also be arranged. If you fall in love with the place, you can also ask about building lots that are available on the beachfront strip.

ATTRACTIONS

Crooked Island opens onto the Windward Passage, the dividing point between the Caribbean Sea and The Bahamas. Whatever else he may have named it, it is said that when Columbus landed at what is now **Pittstown Point,** he called it Fragrant Island because of the aroma of its many herbs. One scent was cascarilla bark, used in a native liqueur, which is exported. For the best view of the island, go to Colonel Hill, if you didn't land at the Crooked Island Airport (also known as the Colonel Hill Airport) when you arrived.

Guarding the north end of this island is the **Marine Farms Fortress,** an abandoned British fortification that saw action in the War of 1812. It looks out over Crooked Island Passage and can be visited (ask your hotel to make arrangements for you).

Also on the island is **Hope Great House,** with its orchards and gardens, dating from the time of George V of England.

Other sights include **French Wells Bay,** a swampy delta leading to an extensive mangrove swamp rich in bird life, and the **Bird Rock Lighthouse,** built a century ago.

Fortune Island, south of Albert Town, lies off the coast of Crooked Island. Based on the research done for the article in *National Geographic* mentioned above, Fortune Island (sometimes confusingly called Long Cay) is the one Columbus chose to name Isabella, in honor of the queen who funded his expedition. Once it had a thriving salt and sponge industry, now long gone. Albert Town, classified as a ghost town, officially isn't. There are some hardy souls still living there. **Fortune Hill** on Fortune Island is the local landmark, visible from 12 miles away at sea. This small island got its name from the custom of hundreds of Bahamians who went there in the two decades before World War I. They'd wait to be picked up by oceangoing freighters, which would take them as laborers to Central America—hence, they came here to "seek their fortune."

At the southern end of Acklins Island lies **Castle Island,** a low and sandy bit of land where today an 1867 lighthouse stands. Pirates used it as a hideaway, sailing forth to attack ships in the nearby passage.

Acklins Island has many interestingly named hamlets—Rocky Point, Binnacle Hill, Salina Point, Delectable Bay, Golden Grove, Goodwill, Hard Hill, Snug Corner, and Lovely Bay. Some Crooked Island sites have more ominous names, such as Gun Point, Cripple Hill, and Landrail Point.

5. Mayaguana Island

"Sleepy Mayaguana" it might be called. It seems to float adrift in the tropical sun, at the remote extremities of the southeastern "edge" of The Bahamas. It occupies 110 square miles and has a population of about 500. It's a long, long way from the powers at Nassau, who rarely visit here.

Standing in the Windward Passage, Mayaguana is just northwest of the Turks and Caicos Islands, coming up in Part Three. It's separated from the British Crown Colony by the Caicos Passage. Around the time of the American Civil War, inhabitants of Turks Island began to settle in Mayaguana, which before then had dozed undisturbed for centuries.

Acklins Island and Crooked Island, just visited, lie across the Mayaguana Passage. Mayaguana is only 6 miles across at its widest point, and about 24 miles long. It has most enticing beaches, but you'll rarely see a tourist on them, except sometimes an occasional German. A few tourism developers have flown in to check out the island, but so far no activity has come about.

Mayaguana has hardwood forests, and because of its remote location, the United States has opened a missile-tracking station here.

Its southern location makes it ideal in winter, and if you seek it out as a place to retreat from cold weather, no one will ever think of looking for you here. Summers are scorchingly hot, however.

GETTING THERE

By Air
Getting to Mayaguana presents a problem. **Bahamasair** (tel. toll free 800/222-4262 in the U.S.) flies in here to a little airstrip, but only the most adventurous of travelers seek the place out. A plane wings in from Nassau only on Tuesday, Thursday, and Saturday.

By Mailboat
From Nassau, the **M/V Windward Express,** going also to Crooked Island, Acklins Island, and Fortune Island (Long Cay), makes a stop at Mayaguana. For information on the days and times of departure from Nassau and return, check with the Dockmaster at Potter's Cay Dock in Nassau (tel. 809/393-1064).

WHERE TO STAY & DINE
If you should find yourself on the island, ask to be shown to a little café and guesthouse belonging to **Doris and Cap Brown** (no phone) at Abraham's Bay. They'll feed you some locally caught seafood and, *maybe,* put you up for the night. They're at Abraham's Bay, the biggest and most populated place on the island.

---

6. Great Inagua

The most southerly and third-largest island of The Bahamas, Great Inagua, some 40 miles long and 20 miles wide, is a flat land that is home to 1,150 people. It lies 325 miles southeast of Nassau. Henri Christophe, the self-proclaimed Haitian king, is supposed to have had a summer palace built for himself here in the very early part of the 19th century, but no traces seem to be in evidence today. This island is much closer to Haiti than it is to the Bahamian capital.

In 1687, long before the coming of Christophe, a Captain Phipps discovered 26 tons of Spanish treasure from sunken galleons off these shores.

This is the site not only of the Morton Salt Crystal Factory, here since 1800, but also of one of the largest nesting grounds for flamingos in the Western Hemisphere. The National Trust of The Bahamas protects the area around **Lake Windsor,** where the birds breed and the population is said to number 50,000. Besides the pink flamingo, the Bahamian national bird, you can also see roseate spoonbills and other birdlife here.

Flamingos used to inhabit all of The Bahamas, but the bird is nearly extinct in many places, and the reserve can only be visited with a guide. Before going to Great Inagua, serious birdwatchers should get in touch with the Trust Office in Nassau, P.O. Box N-4105 (tel. 809/322-8333).

Green turtles are raised here too, at **Union Park.** They are then released into the ocean to make their way as best they can; they, too, are an endangered species. The vast windward island, almost within sight of Cuba, is also inhabited by wild hogs, horses, and donkeys.

The settlement of **Matthew Town** is the chief hamlet of the island, but it's not of any great sightseeing interest. Other sites have interesting names, such as Doghead Point, Lantern Head, Conch Shell Point, and Mutton Fish Point, with Devil's Point making one wonder what happened there to give rise to the name. There's an 1870 lighthouse at Matthew Town.

Little Inagua has no population. It's just a little speck of land off the northeast coast of Great Inagua, about 30 square miles in area. It has much birdlife, including West Indian tree ducks, and wild goats and donkeys live there.

GETTING THERE & GETTING AROUND

Bahamasair (tel. toll free 800/222-4262 in the U.S.) flies to Matthew Town Airport from Nassau on Tuesday and Saturday.

You can also go by **mailboat,** the M/V *Windward Express,* making weekly trips from Nassau to Matthew Town (schedule varies). Call the Dockmaster's office (tel. 809/393-1064) at Potter's Cay in Nassau for details.

Taxis meet incoming flights from Nassau. Both hotels on Great Inagua are at Matthew Town on the southwest coast, each lying about a mile from the airport.

FAST FACTS: GREAT INAGUA

Hospital: The **Inagua Hospital** can be called at 4249.

Police: The police can be reached at **4263.**

Telephones: There is no area code; all calls must be placed through the operator. Tell him or her the name of the town and the number.

WHERE TO STAY

Inexpensive

Ford's Inagua Inn, Matthew Town, Inagua, The Bahamas (tel. 4277), is built of concrete blocks, lying about a mile from the airport and hosting birdwatchers every year. Leon Ford is proud of his island and likes to share it with you. He opens (usually) the last week in July, closing the first week in April. In summer and winter, he charges $45 per day for one of his five simply furnished rooms, for either a single or double on the EP. You can get good Bahamian seafood from his kitchen.

Of the guesthouses on this remote island, I prefer **Main House,** Matthew Town, Inagua, The Bahamas (tel. Matthew Town 4267). Owned by Morton Bahamas Ltd., the salt people, this place is for the willing recluse or the devotee of flamingos, which abound on the island. Only four bedrooms are rented, and the furnishings are modest. Two of the rooms have private baths, but each is air-conditioned. The rates, in effect all year, are $25 per day for a single room, $40 per day for a double, and $55 for a triple, all these tariffs on the EP (no meals). The dining room is simply furnished, and the cook prepares good meals with an emphasis on locally caught fish. Life is casual and decidedly informal.

---

7. Ragged Island & Jumento Cays

This, the most remote territory recommended in this guidebook, might come under the classification of "far-away places with strange-sounding names." The area is visited by very few tourists, except for a few stray people who come in on yachts.

The thing that's truly memorable here is the sunset, which daily, except in the rare times when clouds obscure the sky and the horizon, bursts forth in some of the most spectacular golds, purples, reds, and oranges, sometimes with a green flash, to be seen in The Bahamas, reflected in the gin-clear waters.

This island group, a miniarchipelago, begins with Jumento Cays off the west point of Long Island, running in a half-moon shape for some 100 miles down to Ragged Island, with Little Ragged Island as the southernmost bit of land at the bottom of the crescent. They comprise the southeastern limit of the Great Bahama Bank.

Ragged Island and its string of uninhabited cays could be called the backwater of The Bahamas, since most of them are so tiny and so unimportant they don't often appear on maps. However, visitors who return from this area talk of the remarkable beauty of the little pieces of land and coral.

Sailing in this area in bad weather is considered dangerous because of the unrelenting winds. Otherwise, the cays would probably be better known among the boating crowd. In summer it's usually a good place to cruise the waters.

Like nearly all the islands considered in this chapter, Ragged Island knew greater prosperity when hundreds of inhabitants worked its salt flats. Today Duncan Town, the little hamlet still standing on the island, evokes a far-away memory. Some of its people are hardworking and weather-beaten, and many have a difficult time making a living. Nassau seems to have forgotten this outpost of the nation.

Some of the little cays, from Jumento Cay around the semicircle toward Ragged Island, have names such as No Bush Cay, Dead Cay, Sisters, Nurse Cay, Double-Breasted Cay, and Hog Cay. There's a Raccoon Cay, as well as a Raccoon Cut. A light tower stands on Flamingo Cay.

Visitors are so rare that anybody's arrival is treated as an event, and the townspeople are eager to help in any way they can. There's a 3,000-foot paved airstrip here, but it's only accessible for private planes to land on, so it's not much used.

A **mailboat,** the M/V *Captain Moxey,* leaves Potter's Cay Dock in Nassau on Thursday en route to Ragged Island. It returns on Sunday. For details about costs and sailing, contact the Dockmaster at Potter's Cay Dock, Nassau (tel. 809/393-1064).

Regrettably, there are no hotel facilities for tourists.

PART THREE

TURKS & CAICOS ISLANDS

TURKS & CAICOS ISLANDS

A recent discovery of sun-seeking vacationers, the Turks and Caicos Islands (or "Turks and Who?" as they're often called) have long been called the "forgotten islands," but there is now talk of a "second Bahamas" in the making. Although they are actually a part of the Bahamian archipelago, they are under a separate government and are tucked away to the east of the southernmost islands of The Bahamas. They are directly north of Haiti and the Dominican Republic, at the crossroads of the Caribbean and the Americas. This obscure outpost is technically not the Caribbean but on the fringe of the Atlantic. *Le Figaro* once quoted a developer, and I concur, that "these islands will be the only place left where the jet set, tired of Florida and The Bahamas, will be able to take refuge. They already are!"

The Turks take their name from a local cactus with a scarlet blossom, which resembles the Turkish fez. The word *caicos* is probably derived from the word *cayos,* Spanish for cays or small islands.

The Caicos Passage separates these islands from The Bahamas, some 30 miles away. The Turks Islands are separated from the Caicos Islands by a 22-mile deep-water channel. The entire land mass of both these island groups consists of only 193 square miles. With a population of 7,000 citizens—mostly black or mulatto—who live on six islands and cays, everybody could have about a mile of private beach.

Of the Turks Islands, Grand Turk and Salt Cay are regularly inhabited. Northwest of the Turks, the Caicos group includes six principal islands, of which South Caicos and North Caicos are the most important. Coming into the limelight is Providenciales, a little island just west and north of North Caicos, which is rapidly being "discovered" and developed for tourism.

Grand Turk and Salt Cay (which constitute the Turks Islands) and Cockburn Harbour (South Caicos) are ports of entry.

Many of the islanders today work in the salt-raking industry; others are engaged in the export of lobsters (crayfish) and conch, as well as conch shells.

The mean temperature in these islands is 82° Fahrenheit, dropping to 77° at night, but the cooling breezes of the prevailing trade winds prevent the climate from being oppressive, a fact that vacationers are learning and taking advantage of. Perhaps the first VIP to recognize the attractions of these islands for a holiday retreat was Haiti's self-proclaimed king, Henri Christophe, who is rumored to have made excursions to South Caicos in the early 19th century.

The Turks and Caicos Islands are a coral-reef paradise, shut off from the world, free of pollution and crowds. Even with increasing development as a tourist mecca under way, the beauty and tranquility of this little island chain are sure to be still in existence for the foreseeable future.

The inns of the Turks and Caicos Islands, except those on Providenciales, are small and personally run, very casual, and island entertainment is most often impromptu. The islands have no TV, no daily papers, but there is a radio station. Most visitors are interested in skin diving and scuba diving, fishing, sailing, and boating. Divers still dream of finding that legendary chest of gold hidden in the coral reefs or underwater caverns.

Note: These islands are recommended only to those readers who dare to venture off the beaten track.

HISTORY

The Arawak Indians first settled the Turks and Caicos Islands, and in time Ponce de León sighted the little chain in 1512, although there are those who believe that Columbus landed here, not at San Salvador (Watling Island) or Samana Cay in The Bahamas. It was not far to the south, in the waters off the north coast of Hispaniola (the part that is now Haiti), that the *Santa María,* the flagship of the discovery fleet of Columbus, sank on Christmas night, 1492.

This claim of the Columbus landfall has grown increasingly probable in recent years, and has received the endorsement of eminent Caribbean historians. Symposiums have been held on the subject, at which supporting data have been presented. The claim is that Grand Turk was the site of the first landfall of Columbus, on October 12, 1492, and that he set foot on the island's western shores later that same day. He was, supposedly, greeted by the natives, the Arawaks, who called the island Guanahani.

Pirates marauding on the Spanish Main learned of the hidden coves of the Turks and Caicos Islands, from which they ventured out to plunder Spanish galleons sailing out of Cuba and Haiti. This nest of cutthroats was called "Brothers of the Coast," multiracial pirates. The most famous of these was Rackam the Red, an Englishman.

After the Arawaks were removed to their doom in the mines of Hispaniola, the islands had no permanent inhabitants until 1678. In that year the Bermudians, who had built ships and were searching for goods to trade with the American colonies, established the salt-raking industry. The Spanish drove the Bermudians away in 1710, but they soon returned and thereafter repelled attacks by both Spain and France. Their ranks were augmented during and after the American Revolution by Loyalists fleeing America, bringing with them the slaves who had worked their plantations, adding to the island population of bond servants of African ancestry.

Bermuda finally lost out in 1799, when representation in the Bahamian assembly was given to the little island neighbors to the southeast. This attachment to The Bahamas ended in 1848. The people of the Turks and Caicos Islands petitioned to withdraw from the assembly that met in Nassau. They said the Bahamian government had paid no attention to them except to send collectors of the salt tax, and that they saw the mailboat only four times each year.

The islands were allowed to break their ties with their northern relatives and to have their own president and council, supervised as a separate colony by the governor of Jamaica. After a quarter of a century, however, they were annexed by Jamaica as a dependency. It was not until 1962, when Jamaica became independent, that the little group of islands became a separate British Crown Colony.

The Turks and Caicos Islands are mainly self-governing today, having a governor selected by Queen Elizabeth, who is her representative in island affairs and appoints the chief minister. He or she, in turn, appoints minor ministers.

GETTING THERE

By Air

Miami is the only U.S. gateway for flights into the Turks and Caicos Islands, and from Miami, **Pan Am** (tel. toll free 800/221-1111) is the only carrier flying from the U.S. mainland. So many flights wing into Miami from all parts of the world, however, that most connections are usually relatively convenient. To Providenciales (also known as Provo) the most frequently visited of the nation's islands, Pan Am flies nonstop from Miami every day except Tuesday, returning to Miami after a brief unloading and loading of passengers. Flight time between Miami and Provo is 1 hour 40 minutes. Pan Am departs for Grand Turk from Miami every Friday and Sunday, arriving nonstop after about 1 hour 50 minutes.

Cayman Airways (tel. toll free 800/422-9626) flies nonstop to Providenciales from Miami every Tuesday, Friday, and Sunday. On Tuesday only, the flight continues on to Grand Turk. The total flight time from Miami is about 90 minutes.

Bahamasair (tel. toll free 800/222-4262) flies between Nassau and South Caicos every Thursday.

GETTING AROUND

This can be a problem. There is almost no ferry service among the islands, and car-rental agencies are few and far between (most visitors don't use this means of transport, but see below). Each of the islands has taxi drivers with just-adequate vehicles.

Taxis are found at the three airports—on Providenciales, South Caicos, and Grand Turk. They'll quote you a fixed price to and from the various hotels. They'll also deposit you on an isolated beach and return at a predetermined time to pick you up. Don't be surprised if your ride is shared (the government is trying to save fuel). Ask your hotel to make arrangements for you.

If you wish to visit the outlying islands, and if you don't own or rent your own boat, you can travel by **Turk and Caicos National Airlines** (TCNA) (tel. 809/946-2082), the interisland plane service that has frequent flights to the **Out Islands** of Turks and Caicos (not to be confused with the Family Islands of The Bahamas). Some flights take only 3 minutes. The local airline is ideal for island hopping, as it provides a twice-daily scheduled air-taxi service to all the inhabited islands as well as charter services. However, make sure you've nailed down a reservation at the airport.

Car Rentals

Because of the island's large size and the far-flung nature of its hotel and restaurant locations, you might find a car on Providenciales useful. There are some local outfits, but advance reservations with them, and easy settlement of any possible dispute in the event of an accident, can be very difficult. The only U.S.-based car-rental agency with a franchise in the Turks and Caicos Islands is on Providenciales itself, as represented by **Budget Rent-a-Car,** Butterfield Square, near the airport (tel. 809/946-4079, or tel. toll free 800/527-0700 in the U.S.). An air-conditioned Mitsubishi Precis with automatic transmission rents for $234 per week, with unlimited mileage. This contract requires a 24-hour advance booking from the North American mainland, and also requires that drivers be at least 25 years of age or older. Collision damage insurance costs $10 a day, but even if it's purchased, the holder of such a policy is still liable for the first $350 worth of repair costs to the vehicle. (If you don't buy the policy, you'll be liable for up to the full value of repair costs to the car if you damage it.) A slightly bigger vehicle, a Mitsubishi Mirage, also with air conditioning and automatic transmission, costs $264 per week. The local government will collect a $10 tax for each rental contract, regardless of the number of days you keep the car.

For information once you arrive on Providenciales, Budget's phone number is 809/946-4079. Because the company's main office lies in the commercial center of the island, a short drive from the airport, a representative will come to meet your flight at the airport if you notify them in advance of your arrival.

Note: In the British tradition, *cars throughout the country drive on the left.*

FAST FACTS: TURKS & CAICOS

American Express: American Express is not represented anywhere on the Turks and Caicos Islands.

Area Code: The area code for the Turks and Caicos Islands is **809,** which can be dialed directly from the North American mainland.

Banks: For cashing of travelers checks and other banking services, head for **Barclay's Bank** (tel. 809/946-4246) or for the **Bank of Nova Scotia** (tel. 809/946-4750), both within the Butterfield Mall on Providenciales. On Grand Turk, both **Barclay's Bank** (tel. 809/946-2831) and the **Bank of Nova Scotia** (tel. 809/946-2831) are located on Front Street.

Business Hours: Banking hours are 8:30am to 2:30pm Monday through Thursday and 8:30am to 5pm on Friday. Most business offices are open Monday through Friday from 8:30am to 4 or 4:30pm.

Churches: The islanders are deeply religious, and details of church services are available from your hotel.

Clothing: Generally, dress on these islands is informal. Light cotton clothing is the most comfortable. Jackets or ties are not required in the evening for men in bars or dining rooms. A light sweater is advisable for breezy evenings.

Crime: Although crime is minimal in the islands, petty theft does take place, so protect your valuables, money, and cameras. Don't leave luggage or parcels in an unattended car. Beaches are vulnerable to thievery, so don't take chances.

Currency: The U.S. dollar is the coin of the realm here.

Customs: On arriving, you may bring in 1 quart of liquor, 200 cigarettes, 50 cigars, or 8 ounces of tobacco duty free. There is no restriction on cameras, film, sports equipment, or personal items provided they aren't for resale. *Absolutely no spearguns are allowed,* and the importation of firearms without a permit is also prohibited. Illegal drugs imported bring heavy fines and lengthy terms of imprisonqment.

Each U.S. citizen is eligible for a $400 duty-free exemption if he or she has been out of the country for at least 48 hours and if a period of 41 days has elapsed since that privilege was last exercised. This allowance may include 1 quart of liquor. In addition, you can mail home a number of unsolicited gifts to friends and relatives amounting to $50 or less per day and not to include more than 4 ounces of liquor or 1 ounce of perfume.

Documents for Entry: U.S. and Canadian citizens must have a birth certificate, plus a photo ID, to enter the country. The latter could be an official driver's license with a photograph or a voter's registration card with a photograph, plus a return or ongoing ticket. Of course, valid passports are always acceptable. Passports and visas are required for all aliens except nationals of certain countries, which include the United Kingdom, Commonwealth countries of the Caribbean, the Republic of Ireland, and specific European countries. Visas for the Turks and Caicos Islands may be obtained from the British High Commission or various consulate offices in the United States.

Driving Rules: *Driving is on the left,* in the British tradition.

Drugstores: On Grand Turk, go to the **Government Clinic,** Grand Turk Hospital, Hospital Road (tel. 809/946-2333). In Providenciales, go to the **Providenciales Health Medical Center,** Leeward Highway and Airport Road (tel. 809/946-4201). Actually, it's best to arrive on the islands with whatever prescribed medication you think you will need.

Electricity: The electric current on the islands is 120 volts, 60 cycles, AC.

Emergencies: Most emergencies are handled by the police on the various islands (see "Police," below).

Etiquette: Beach wear is best left for the beach. When entering a restaurant or bar, the locals prefer you to cover up a bit, although the islands are decidedly informal. It is customary to greet people you encounter walking along the roads.

Food: The specialties are whelk soup, conch chowder and fritters, lobster, and special types of fresh fish.

Holidays: Actual dates of some of these observances may vary from year to year. If the date of a particular celebration falls on Saturday or Sunday, the actual observance may not take place until the following Monday. Holidays include New Year's Day, Commonwealth Day (March 11), Good Friday, Easter, Easter Monday, Birthday of Her Majesty the Queen (June 15), Emancipation Day (August 1), Columbus Day (October 14), International Human Rights Day (October 24), Christmas Day, and Boxing Day (December 26).

Information: The **Turks & Caicos Sales and Information Office,** Front Street, Cockburn Town, Grand Turk, B.W.I. (tel. 809/946-2321, or toll free 800/441-4419 in the U.S.), is open Monday through Thursday from 8am to 4:30pm, on Friday from 8am to 4pm. The U.S. public relations and marketing representative for the Turks and Caicos Tourist Board, **Medhurst & Associates,** is located at 271 Main St., Northport, NY 11768 (tel. 516/261-9600).

Language: The official language is English.

Medical Care: Should you become ill, the islands are served by three medical practitioners and a qualified nursing staff. There is a 20-bed hospital on Grand Turk, **Grand Turk Hospital,** Hospital Road (tel. 809/946-2333), with X-ray facilities, an operating theater, and a pathology laboratory. In Providenciales, there is the **Providenciales Health Medical Center,** Leeward Highway and Airport Road (tel. 809/946-4201). There are clinics on South Caicos, Middle Caicos, and North Caicos. All the islands are served by one dentist, who can be reached at the Providenciales Health Center. Anyone critically ill is transferred to Grand Turk for hospital treatment or evacuated to Nassau, Miami, or Jamaica for specialist treatment. Should you become ill, your hotel will locate the nearest medical facility.

Police: In Grand Turk, call **946-2299;** in Providenciales, **946-4259;** and in South Caicos, **946-3299.**

Post Office: The General Post Office is on Grand Turk (tel. 809/946-2300), and there are suboffices on South Caicos, Salt Cay, Providenciales, Bottle Creek, and Middle Caicos. They are open Monday through Thursday from 8am to 4:30pm, on Friday from 7am to 1:30pm.

Shopping: You can purchase native straw and shell work, sponges, and rare conch pearls here and there on the islands.

Stamps: Collectors consider Turks and Caicos stamps as valuable, and there is a philatelic bureau that operates separately from the post office to take care of the demand. It is the **Turks & Caicos Islands Philatelic Bureau,** P.O. Box 121, Grand Turk, Turks Islands, B.W.I.

Taxes: There is a departure tax of $10, payable when you leave the islands. Also, the government collects a 7% occupancy tax, applicable to all hotels, guesthouses, and restaurants in the 40-island chain.

Telecommunications: It's not too difficult to keep in touch with the outside world—if you really want to. **Cable & Wireless Ltd.** provides a modern diversified international service via submarine cable and an earth station. There are automatic exchanges on Grand Turk, South Caicos, and Providenciales. Incoming direct dialing is available from the United States, the United Kingdom, and most countries in the world. Outgoing direct dialing is being introduced. The Telex service is fully automatic, operating 24 hours a day. The international-operator telephone service is available 24 hours a day and the telegraph service from 8am to 5pm Monday through Friday from the company's main office on Front Street, Cockburn Town, Grand Turk (tel. 809/946-2222).

Time: The islands have the same time as Miami, Florida; that is, they are in the Eastern Time Zone.

Tipping: Hotels usually add 10% automatically to handle service. If individual staff members perform various services for you, it is customary to tip them something extra. In restaurants, 10% to 15% is appropriate unless service has already been added. If in doubt, ask. Taxi drivers like at least a 10% tip.

Water: Remember that water is precious on the islands. Try to conserve it. Hotels provide safe drinking water. Don't drink from the tap and avoid ice in your drinks that was made from tap water. Don't even use tap water to brush your teeth.

Weather: The islands receive approximately 21 inches of rainfall annually. The

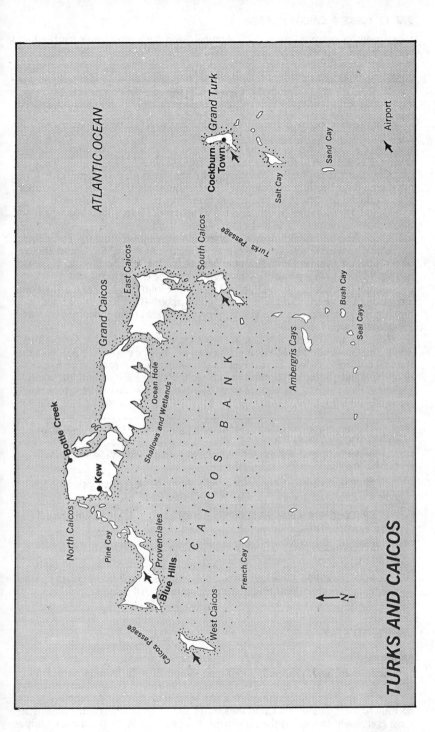

TURKS AND CAICOS

ATLANTIC OCEAN

Grand Turk
Cockburn Town

Salt Cay

Sand Cay

Airport

South Caicos

Turks Passage

East Caicos

Grand Caicos

Bush Cay

Ocean Hole

Seal Cays

Ambergris Cays

Shallows and Wetlands

Bottle Creek

Kew

North Caicos

CAICOS BANK

Pine Cay

Provenciales

Blue Hills

French Cay

West Caicos

Caicos Passage

N

mean monthly temperature is 80° Fahrenheit, and the winter water temperature ranges from 72° to 80°.

---

1. Grand Turk

The most important of the island chain, Grand Turk (Cockburn Town), with its Government House, is the capital of the Turks and Caicos Islands. Cockburn (pronounced Coburn) Town is also the financial and business hub. The largest concentration of population in the colony, 3,500 people, is here.

Cockburn Town might remind you of New Plymouth on Green Turtle Cay, but there's more bustle here because of the larger number of inhabitants. The harbor road is called Front Street, as is the one in Hamilton, the capital of Bermuda.

Grand Turk is rather barren, and it's windswept. There is little vegetation, so don't come here expecting to find a lush tropical island.

Once this was the teeming headquarters of a thriving salt industry. Today there are those who want to restore the economy of the colony by making Grand Turk an offshore banking center like the Cayman Islands, but that may be difficult. There are many problems to face with both Great Britain and the U.S. government.

Grand Turk was in the limelight in 1962, when John Glenn, the first American astronaut to orbit the earth, alit in the ocean about 40 miles offshore and was brought in by helicopter to the U.S. Air Force Base here, to be welcomed by Vice-President Lyndon Johnson.

Chances are, if you come here for your vacation, you'll land at Grand Turk. You'll find **Governor's Beach** near—you guessed it—the governor's residence on the west coast of the island. It's the best for swimming. If you are going on to another of the islands, at least, take time to tour the town's historic section, particularly Duke and Front Streets. Here, three-story houses built of wood and limestone stand along the waterfront.

What the Symbols Mean

AP (American plan): Includes three meals a day (sometimes called full board or full pension).

BP (Bermuda plan): Popularized first in Bermuda, this option includes a full American breakfast (sometimes called an English breakfast).

CP (Continental plan): A Continental breakfast (that is, bread, jam, and coffee) is included in the room rate.

EP (European plan): This rate is always cheapest, as it offers only the room— no meals.

MAP (modified American plan): Sometimes called half board or half pension, this room rate includes breakfast and dinner (or lunch if you prefer).

WHERE TO STAY

Moderate

Guanahani Beach Hotel, Pillory Beach, Grand Turk, Turks and Caicos, B.W.I. (tel. 809/946-2135). Composed of a handful of hip-roofed, colonial-inspired villas set directly on the sands of one of the finest beaches on the island (supposedly, according to local lore, where Columbus made one of his landfalls), this hotel is almost exclusively devoted to the enjoyment of the sun, the sand, and the sea. Only a decorative wooden railing separates its sandy grounds from the unobstructed ocean views. Concrete walkways connect each of the 14 accommodations to the hotel's pair of bars, its square-sided swimming pool, and its restaurant, where lunches cost from $8 and dinners from $18 each.

Each room has a private balcony, cable TV, air conditioning, a phone, and a collection of simple furniture appropriate to the accommodation's beachside location. Dutch-born manager Peter van Allan charges $90 per day for an EP single and $100 for a double in winter, plus 17% tax and service. *In summer, the daily EP rate for a single is $70, and for a double it's $75, plus the tax and service charge.* The hotel lies a 10-minute walk north of Cockburn Town.

Island Reef, P.O. Box 10, Grand Turk, Turks and Caicos, B.W.I. (tel. 809/ 946-2055, or toll free 800/328-2288 in the U.S.), lies on a stretch of beachfront on the eastern coast. As you negotiate the steep access road that winds down to it, a sweeping view of the sea seems to surround the property in an azure frame. Pleasantly isolated, this is the investment created by Texas-based entrepreneurs Tom and Shirley Strasburger, who also own the country's home-based airline, TCNA. Stretched end to end along the beachfront, and interconnected with a sunny boardwalk, the 19 air-conditioned oceanview accommodations contain fully equipped kitchenettes and are designed like comfortably furnished studio apartments. Each was prefabricated in the United States, then constructed on the site the Strasburgers selected. There is maid service. Single or double occupancy in winter costs from $75 to $85 daily in a studio apartment, from $95 to $105 in a one-bedroom apartment, and $135 in a two-bedroom apartment. *In summer, prices are reduced by $10 per room category.* MAP can be arranged in any season for an extra $25 per person per day. Taxes and service charges are extra.

At presstime, an attractive dive package was offered for $500 per person for seven nights' accommodation, double occupancy, with 10 tank dives included. The hotel has its own on-the-premises dive operators, named Off the Walls Divers (see the separate writeup under "Sports & Recreation"). Guests can use a small freshwater pool and play on a tennis court. Food is served in a cabaña-style restaurant, the thatch roof of which is supported by vertical beams.

Hotel Kittina, Duke Street, P.O. Box 42, Grand Turk, Turks and Caicos, B.W.I. (tel. 809/946-2232, or toll free 800/548-8462 in the U.S.; 305/667-0966 in Coconut Grove, FL), is a 43-unit inn, the owners of which, Tina and Kitt Fenimore, are credited with giving tourism on Grand Turk its initial boost. Their hotel straddles two sides of the main street leading through the center of town. The older section is a low-slung building covered with trailing vines and bougainvillea. It contains a bar and restaurant. The Sandpiper Restaurant is one of the best known on the island, offering a combination of American and local dishes with an emphasis on freshly caught seafood such as lobster and red snapper. The conch chowder is invariably good. Watch for special buffets.

Across the street rise the modern two-story townhouses containing the newer accommodations. Each of these has a ceiling crafted from varnished pine, carpeting, a kitchen, a veranda with a view of the sea, air conditioning, a phone, and ceiling fans. The units on the upper floors benefit from high ceilings and more space. These rooms have sheltered everyone from Mariel Hemingway to Princess Alexandra. Year-round EP rates are $65 daily for a single, rising to $85 to $140 for a double.

You can snorkel or swim near the white sands of the hotel's beach. If you're sailing, be sure to ask one of the Fenimore's sons for instructions on the best places to moor your sailboat.

Salt Raker Inn, Duke Street, P.O. Box 1, Grand Turk, Turks and Caicos, B.W.I. (tel. 809/946-2260). Consciously informal, it occupies a clapboard house that was originally built in 1810 by a Bermudian shipwright. Its English-colonial style is visible in its front veranda, where guests can rock in chairs overlooking the ocean and a garden filled with bougainvillea. The main house, set close to the road paralleling the sea, contains a wide front hallway, a guest library, the establishment's office, and the three best accommodations. Each of the rooms has a private bath and a ceiling

fan, and some offer air conditioning as well. The two large upstairs suites have verandas overlooking the sea. The downstairs accommodation has a large screened porch.
Several other units are in two motel units spread end to end on either side of the
garden. The owners charge year-round EP rates of $35 to $115 daily for a double,
$35 to $85 for a single, depending on the accommodation and size, plus 17% service and taxes.

Meals at the Salt Raker are simple but well prepared and served beneath a metal
canopy in the rear garden. Full dinners cost from $20, and include such specialties as
an award-winning version of local junkanoo-style (spicy) barbecued spareribs, three
different preparations of grouper, lobster, and steak. Lunches cost from $8. Food is
served continuously every day from 7am to 9pm, with diners lingering at tables till
several hours later.

Inexpensive

Turks Head Inn, P.O. Box 58, Grand Turk, Turks and Caicos, B.W.I. (tel. 809/
946-2466), is an adaptation of a century-old building constructed by a Bermudian
shipwright. It is the principality's oldest and busiest pub. Typically, there is a two-
level covered veranda with an orange cut-out balustrade. The inn, now owned by
French-born Xavier Tonneau (affectionately known as "Froggie" to his friends), is
placed in an old garden with towering trees and a shady terrace with outdoor tables.
A thatch-roofed addition shelters outdoor diners. An indoor dining room, raffish
and tropical, enjoys popularity with divers, writers, local eccentrics, and the occasional contessa who happens to be barefooting her way through the islands. The
well-flavored food is served informally, in copious portions. Specialties are recited
by a waitress and, depending on the mood of the chef, might include baked grouper,
steak, lobster, or steak and lobster on the same platter. Full dinners cost from $24
each, lunches from $12, and breakfasts from $6. The restaurant is open every day
from 7am for breakfast, from noon for lunch, and from 7pm for dinner. The bar is
open continuously during those hours, doing business throughout the day until the
last client has been tucked away for the night, usually sometime after midnight.

In addition to the restaurant, the inn maintains four rentable bedrooms, two
with access to an open second-floor veranda and two with access to the enclosed veranda overlooking the back. Each has a private bathroom, ceiling fan, an old-
fashioned kind of spaciousness, and simple furnishings. All contain double beds,
two of which are four-posters. With a full cooked breakfast included, singles cost
$65, doubles $80, throughout the year.

WHERE TO DINE

Moderate

Papillon's Rendez-Vous, Duke Street (tel. 809/946-2088). Of all the independent restaurants on Grand Turk, this one takes its cuisine the most seriously,
producing the most successful combinations of flavors on the island. Contained
within a 50-year-old West Indian house ringed with a garden and set almost directly
on the water, it's sheltered from the road that runs out of town by a screen of
pinewood lattices and flowering vines. Run by a team of entrepreneurs from French-
speaking Canada (Suzanne and Hélène), the place offers a charming bar outfitted
with a scattering of antiques. Menu items are likely to include a combination of
French, North American, and West Indian dishes prepared from lobster, escargots,
rib-eye steak, baked snapper, pepper steak, and the fresh catch of the day. Only dinner is served, with meals costing from $23 each. Hours are 7 to 10pm Tuesday
through Saturday, with the bar remaining open until 1am. Because of the restaurant's popularity, advance reservations are a good idea. The place is closed for two or
three weeks every autumn, usually in September.

The Pepper Pot, Front Street (tel. 809/946-2083). Guests are served on battered plastic tables amid crêpe-paper streamers and the kind of decor that might have adorned a 1930s dance at a junior high school prom. Despite its drawbacks, diners retain a happy memory of this place. It's the domain of a hardworking member of the island's Anglican church, Philistina Louise ("Peanuts") Butterfield. Born in North Caicos, she has attracted an ardent array of fans. Her conch fritters, carefully frozen and packaged, accompany diners back to the U.S., where they've been served at receptions on Fifth Avenue.

To dine here, you must phone in the evening of the day before your arrival. Any taxi driver in town will conduct you to the clean but simple cement-sided house and pick you up at a prearranged time at the end of your meal. The menu depends on whatever Peanuts produced that day. It's likely to be lobster with all the fixings. Full meals cost from $25 per person and are served only at dinner at a time mutually agreed upon.

SPORTS & RECREATION

On Duke Street, **Omega Diving Services,** P.O. Box 67, Grand Turk (tel. 809/946-2232, or toll free 800/255-1966 in the U.S.), occupies a clapboard West Indian house a few steps from the reception area of the Kittina Hotel, with which it is associated. The safety-conscious divemasters and instructors offer a morning two-tank dive for $55 and a one-tank afternoon dive for $30. Full PADI open-water certification, with all equipment and boat fees included, goes for $350, requiring between five and seven days. Most divers combine underwater excursions with hotel packages at the previously recommended Kittina Hotel. Accommodations arranged in this way are usually less expensive.

Off the Wall Divers, Island Reef Hotel, P.O. Box 10, Grand Turk, Turks and Caicos, B.W.I. (tel. 809/946-2055, or toll free 800/328-2288 in the U.S.), offers single dives, PADI registration, and dive packages that include accommodations in the hotel that contains it, the Island Reef.

A Resort Course for beginning divers sells for $100, PADI certification for open-water diving costs $350, and a two-tank dive is $55.

---

2. Salt Cay

Just 9 miles south of Grand Turk, this sparsely settled cay is named for its salt ponds, a once-flourishing industry that may be revived. In its day it was known for this "white gold," and some 100 vessels a year sailed from here and Grand Turk with their heavily laden cargoes bound for the United States. It is estimated that during the American Revolution more than 20 Bermudian privateers were running salt on a regular schedule from the Turks Islands past British blockades to Washington's battered armies. Salt was the chief preservative of meat for the colonial army.

In 1951 the government took control of the 300-year-old industry, and in 20 years managed to completely destroy it through bureaucratic mismanagement. Salt Cay fell into a long slumber and has only been revived in 1990 with the arrival of chic guests visiting the Windmills Plantation (see below).

The cay has a land mass of 3½ square miles, with a beautiful beach bordering the north coast.

You can walk down to the salinas and see the windmills that once powered the salt business, and you can stroll past the 150-year-old "White House," built by a Bermudian salt raker. In addition, you can visit the ruins of an old whaling station and learn how fearless seamen caught whales in the early 19th century. It's also possible to drop in at the local school, where the children are likely to greet you with island calypso songs.

Essentially, Salt Cay is peaceful, quiet, and colorful—the perfect relaxation spot to get away from it all.

GETTING THERE

For most of their lives, the residents were dependent on their small sailboats for communication with the outside world, and the island is still often reached by private boat. With the opening of a 3,000-foot landing strip, lying 575 miles southwest of Miami, the island is connected to the wider world once again. For information about the 5-minute flight from Grand Turk, call **Turks and Caicos National Airlines** (tel. 809/946-2606) for departure times.

WHERE TO STAY

Expensive

The Windmills Plantation at Salt Cay, Turks and Caicos, B.W.I. (tel. 809/946-6962, or toll free 800/822-7715 in the U.S.). Set in the midst of 17 acres of scrubland beside a white-sand beach on the north side of the island, the hotel was entirely built by local artisans using centuries-old building techniques. Each of the dozen or so buildings within the compound has been designed in a whimsically derivative colonial style that differs from that of its neighbor. These styles, best defined as "Caribbean vernacular," include plantation-inspired influences from the French, English, Dutch, and Spanish colonies of 200 years ago. Their design by architect/owner Guy Lovelace was the culmination of years of research by a man who—until recently—made a career of designing other people's Caribbean resort hotels. The Windmills Plantation is the highly creative result of a dream come true. Its centerpiece is a trio of dramatically proportioned swimming pools, which include a 50-foot lap pool and a "fun pool" only 4 feet deep centered around a mermaid-shaped fountain.

Each of the resort's eight accommodations contains a tasteful selection of antique reproductions (mostly handmade in the Dominican Republic or in Haiti), a veranda, a cathedral ceiling with a ceiling fan, a private bath, and a white-with-splashes-of-tropical-color decor. Four of the accommodations are considered suites, and two of these have their own plunge pools. Throughout the year, with AP and all drinks included (the hotel maintains a constantly open bar for its clients), single occupancy ranges from $315 to $425, double occupancy from $415 to $525. Tax (but not service) is extra.

Meals are not for the finicky, but might provide interesting culinary diversions with dishes that are sometimes concocted from whatever fresh catch of the day is available. They are heavily seasoned and curried in the island manner, using age-old recipes, and served in ample portions.

For reservations and information, contact the establishment's Florida address, Windmills Plantation at Salt Cay, 440 32nd St., West Palm Beach, FL 33407 (tel. toll free 800/822-7715).

Inexpensive

One of the friendliest little oases you're likely to encounter between Bermuda and Venezuela, **Mount Pleasant Guest House,** Salt Cay, Turks and Caicos, B.W.I. (tel. 809/946-6927, or toll free 800/441-4419 in the U.S.), owned by Bryan and Emily Sheedy, is a remote outpost offering four simple accommodations. Year round, tariffs are $85 daily for a double, $65 for a single, on the full-board plan: tax and service are extra. Laundry and baby-sitting can be arranged.

The chef's skill with the local cuisine, particularly native dishes and seafood, is known all over the island. Guests can meet at the Gazebo Bar and on the breezy patio to get acquainted.

The water here is crystal clear, with coral heads running close to the excellent beach, which makes it ideal for snorkeling and diving. There is a full PADI scuba-diving facility on the premises, with complete equipment and rentals. Divers can dive the famous walls of Grand Turk, Salt Cay, and Great Sand Cay.

3. North Caicos

North Caicos is the most northern of the major islands in the archipelago. This 41-square-mile island is strictly for people who want to get away from it all. If you're seeking deserted soft white-sand beaches and crystal-clear water, then this is the place. No one dresses up here, so leave your jacket and tie at home. It contains miles and miles of uncrowded sandy beaches and is surrounded by a sea teeming with fish —an ideal place for scuba divers and snorkelers. Experienced guides can take you fishing for snapper, barracuda, or bonefish. Beach picnics, boating excursions, and fish cookouts on deserted cays are easily arranged. You can snorkel on a barrier reef or tour the island by taxi. Ask to be taken to **Flamingo Pond,** lying south of Whitby. This is a nesting place for these elegant pink birds. You'll also be shown the ruins of old plantations and such tiny hamlets as Sandy Point and Kew.

A resort in the making, North Caicos is slated for development.

GETTING THERE & GETTING AROUND

The local airline, **Turks and Caicos National Airlines** (tel. 809/946-2606), runs connecting flights to the island's terminal. If you disembark at Providenciales, the airline takes only 6 minutes to fly you to North Caicos.

The best way to see the island is to have your hotel arrange a **taxi** tour at the rate of about $20 per hour.

For a day's adventure, you can take a **car-ferry** over to Middle Caicos.

WHERE TO STAY

Moderate

Ocean Beach Hotel, Whitby Settlement, North Caicos, Turks and Caicos, B.W.I. (tel. 809/946-7113, or toll free 800/223-6510 in the U.S.), sits on a fine beach, a 6-mile taxi ride from the airport and 1 mile from the center of Whitby. Family owned and operated, its accommodations lie within a U-shaped motel-like building composed of cedarwood and local stone. There are 10 comfortable units, with private baths; permutations of these units can create up to 16 accommodations. Year-round EP rates are $89 to $140 daily for a single and $100 to $170 for a double. From November to April, the place is in full hotel operation; from May to October, units are self-contained and the restaurant and bar are closed. Car rentals!can be arranged.

All correspondence should be sent to Karen L. Preikschat, Station B, P.O. Box 1152, Burlington, Ontario, Canada L7P 3S9 (tel. 416/336-2876).

Pelican Beach Hotel, North Caicos, Turks and Caicos, B.W.I. (tel. 809/946-7112, or toll free 800/441-4419 in the U.S.), is the culmination of a dream of Clifford Gardiner, a native of North Caicos who has always believed in its future possibilities. He operated Gardiner Flying Service, but he always wanted to get into the hotel business, so in 1975 he opened this modern eight-room facility. Bedrooms are furnished in a simple, functional modern style. In 1984 Mr. Gardiner won acclaim from the then chief minister, who came here to voice praise to the hotelier for his "blood, sweat, and tears" in getting the hotel launched. In winter, rooms cost $110 daily for a single, $150 for a double, on MAP. *In summer, MAP is $75 daily for a single, $100 for a double.* The hotel also offers skin-diving and snorkeling trips. You can snorkel for a full day, with lunch included, for $40.

Prospect of Whitby Hotel, Whitby Settlement, c/o Kew Post Office, North Caicos, Turks and Caicos Islands, B.W.I. (tel. 809/946-7119, or toll free 800/441-4419 in the U.S.). Originally established in 1974, and recently reopened after a long slumber, this beachside hotel was named after one of the most historic Thames-side pubs of London, the Prospect of Whitby. Repaired and renovated, and working hard to regain a niche in the touristic marketplace, the hotel is surrounded by vegetation considered verdant for the Turks and Caicos Islands, and is near the white sands of a highly desirable beach. Each of the half-dozen buildings that compose this complex is painted a soft pink. At presstime there were plans for the construction of a yacht-fueling depot and a more complete marina facility, although the establishment's bar and restaurant are already popular with yachtspeople who moor their sailing craft off the expansive north coast beach on which the hotel sits.

All of the 28 units contain air conditioning, a scattering of art, ceiling fans, comfortable furnishings, and views of the sea. In winter, EP singles cost $100 per day, doubles $120, and suites $150. *In summer, EP singles cost $80 per day, doubles $100, and suites $130.*

The hotel's Belgian-born managers imbue the cuisine with a European flair, and they help to arrange excursions to nearby cays. Many different water sports activities, including scuba diving, windsurfing, snorkeling, and sailing, can be organized by the staff.

4. Middle Caicos

Called Grand Caicos by some islanders, Middle Caicos is the largest island in the archipelago, consisting of 48 square miles. It is 15 miles long. Middle Caicos is the least developed of the main islands of Turks and Caicos. Towering limestone cliffs protruding into the sea along the north coast and scalloped with secluded beaches, give Middle Caicos the most dramatic coastline of the islands. Conch Bar, on the north side of the island, offers cathedral-size limestone **caves** once used by the Lucayan Indians, as attested by artifacts found within. In the 1880s these caves were the site of a thriving guano export industry. With their clear underground salt lakes, the caves have been called a "natural museum" of stalagmites and stalactites. Nearby wild cotton plants derive from the 18th century, when Loyalists from the southern colonies in the new United States came to try their hand at establishing plantations.

Middle Caicos men were some of the most expert boatbuilders in the island nation, making their vessels from pine from the middle island's pine groves. The boats were used by fishermen working the waters around many of the cays, and gathering conchs for shipment to Haiti.

Most visitors come to Middle Caicos on a private-boat tour just for a one-day visit to the caves. Ask at your hotel in North Caicos if any boats will be going during your stay. If you're staying on Providenciales, you can often arrange to go on a day tour of the caves offered by **Executive Tours** (call the staff at 809/946-4524 about possible offerings).

Accommodations on Middle Caicos can be found only in private homes, if you want to stay over. The only way to find them is to "ask around."

5. South Caicos

Some of the finest diving and snorkeling in The Bahamas, as well as in this Crown Colony, are found on South Caicos, an 8½-mile island with numerous secluded coves and spectacular coral reefs. **Long Beach** is a beachcomber's paradise. One visitor wrote, "This is like escaping to another era." There are always locals available to take you sailing, boating, or fishing for a small fee. Bonefishing here is the best in the country.

Some 600 miles southeast of Miami and 22 miles east of Grand Turk, South

Caicos can be reached by Turks and Caicos National Airlines (tel. 809/946-2606). There is a 6,500-foot paved and lit jetport, where passengers disembark as they head for **Cockburn Harbour,** considered the best natural harbor of the island nation. It is the site of the annual **Commonwealth Regatta** in May. Although the island may appear nearly deserted, there are 1,400 permanent residents and what one local described as "about 65 vehicles and a few wild horses and donkeys in the bush." Some of the residents use their cars as taxis and meet visitors at the airport. Because of its lack of suitable accommodations, the island is most often visited by boaters on a day trip.

---

6. Providenciales

Affectionately known as Provo, this 38-square-mile island has white-sand beaches that stretch for 12 miles along the northeast coast. It is also an island of peaceful rolling hills, clear water, a natural deep harbor, flowering cactus, and a barrier reef attracting swimmers, divers, and boaters. The roads may not be paved, but you'll still find some stores and two full-service banks. The island is served by an airport capable of handling wide-body jets and has good marina and diving facilities.

Provo is the most built-up island in the Turks and Caicos chain, a development that began with the opening of the Club Med–"Turkoise" (see below) at the cost of $23 million. Once known mainly to a group of millionaires headed by Dick Du Pont, Provo has now developed a broader base of tourism.

It was first discovered by the rich back in the 1960s, but word just had to get out, and now the bulldozers are there in full force. Throughout most of the 1970s it was known as a "pedigreed playground." Other celebrities have arrived more recently, including Dick Clark, "American Bandstand" idol, who liked the place so much he bought property.

To reach the island, see "Getting There," at the beginning of this chapter.

What the Symbols Mean

AP (American plan): Includes three meals a day (sometimes called full board or full pension).

BP (Bermuda plan): Popularized first in Bermuda, this option includes a full American breakfast (sometimes called an English breakfast).

CP (Continental plan): A Continental breakfast (that is, bread, jam, and coffee) is included in the room rate.

EP (European plan): This rate is always cheapest, as it offers only the room—no meals.

MAP (modified American plan): Sometimes called half board or half pension, this room rate includes breakfast and dinner (or lunch if you prefer).

WHERE TO STAY

Expensive

Ramada Turquoise Reef Resort, Grace Bay, Providenciales, Turks and Caicos, B.W.I. (tel. 809/946-5555, or toll free 800/228-9898 in the U.S.). Set on 15 acres of flat sandy land, with a 900-foot beachfront along the island's northeastern coast, this is one of the newest resorts on the island, built with touches of style and offering fairly priced accommodations that seem even better during its seasonal promotions.

Managed (but not owned) by Ramada Resorts, it is the first of the island's properties to contain a casino, and offers probably more glitter and flash than any of its competitors. The resort has been designed with prominent balconies in a modern hip-roofed compound, the buildings of which are symmetrically arranged around a landscaped garden and central swimming pool.

The resort's most upscale restaurant, the Portofino, features grilled seafood and steaks, with an emphasis on Mediterranean cuisine. Less formal dining is available at the Conch Corner Pool Bar and Grill, or at the Coral Terrace Restaurant and Lounge, where meals are served from a stone buffet table. Out on the beach, Buddy's Beach Bar serves daytime drinks. On the premises is a health club with exercise machines and a Jacuzzi, a swimming pool, two tennis courts, a disco adjacent to the previously mentioned casino, several souvenir shops, and a well-stocked watersports facility.

Each of the resort's 228 bedrooms contains clay-tile floors, wicker furniture, ceiling fans, and air conditioning, with splashes of color partly provided by framed illustrations. In winter, single or double occupancy costs from $170 to $205 daily, with suites beginning at $290. *In summer, single or double occupancy ranges from $105 to $140 daily, with suites beginning at $220.* Taxes and service are extra, and MAP can be arranged in any season for $50 per person.

Club Med–"Turkoise," Grace Bay, Providenciales, Turks and Caicos, B.W.I. (tel. 809/946-4491, or toll free 800/CLUBMED in the U.S.), lies on a 70-acre tract of land, 10 miles from the airport. This link in the Club Med chain was erected near a bleached-white sweep of sand for a total cost of $27 million. An irrigation system keeps the arid landscape green. Whether or not you like communal-style vacations, Club Med makes holiday-making easy. This particular branch opened in 1984, and it was conceived as the "most upscale" of all the club villages in the Western Hemisphere. Unlike certain other Club Meds, this particular branch does not particularly go out of its way to entertain children with a barrage of special programs —that is, it is not designated as a Club Med "Family Village."

The village-style cluster of two- and three-story accommodations are painted a pastel pink and capped with cedar shingles imported from Sweden. All meals and most sports are included in the weekly package rates. Drinks are paid for with beads from a necklace. Scuba diving is included on a space-available basis. Other group activities, part of the package, include windsurfing, sailing, waterskiing, and arts and crafts. There are two Jacuzzis on the property, along with nine tennis courts, four of which are lit for night play. A disco keeps residents active if they wish, from 11:30pm to at least 3am nightly.

The resort contains 600 beds, each twin size. Meals are shared at long tables, where the house wine is served in pitchers. Club Med prices its vacations by the week on a per-person basis. In winter, the charge for a seven-night all-inclusive stay runs from $950 to $1,400, with the exception of Christmas and New Year's, when the price rises to $1,600 per person per week. *Between May and early December, the cost is $950 per person per week, all inclusive.* These tariffs include services within the resort, but the cost of transfers is paid by Club Med only for those clients who opt for airfare as part of their land package arrangements. First-time visitors pay a $30 initiation fee to Club Med. After that, there's an annual membership fee of $50 per year.

Moderate

Erebus Inn, Turtle Cove, Providenciales, Turks and Caicos, B.W.I. (tel. 809/946-4240), a 30-unit resort, occupies a hillside above Turtle Cove on the northern shore of the island. Its 10 studio apartments face the marina at the bottom of the hill. Additional accommodations are in a long and narrow stone-sided annex whose breeze-filled central hallway evokes an enlarged version of an old Bahamian house. Ringing both sections of the hotel are dry-weather plants such as cactus and carefully watered vines such as bougainvillea. In the older section, lying closer to the seacost, guests pay year-round rates of $75 daily for an EP single, $96 for a double, and $100 for two in a poolside room. Newer rooms, higher up on the hillside, cost $140 to $170 daily for two people, depending on the view. The establishment is closed every year from the end of August until the beginning of October.

The social center is the big-windowed Spinnaker Bar, the perimeter of which offers a view of the marina and the gulf. There is also an open-air terrace ringed with walls of chiseled stone. The inn has a French restaurant, serving what many consider to be the best cuisine on the island. Facilities include two pools (one saltwater), two tennis courts, and a health club.

Island Princess Hotel, The Bight, Providenciales, Turks and Caicos, B.W.I. (tel. 809/946-4260). In 1979 an enterprising American engineer returned after years of building roads and dams in Iran to an island he vaguely remembered from a brief stopover many years before. Today the well-designed domain of Cal Piper includes 80 pleasant rooms, a popular bar, and a sunny dining room with a view of the sea. The hotel sits on some of the best beachfront on Provo. Built of local stone and designed in a zigzagging labyrinth of two-story annexes, the property contains acreage devoted only to gardens, plus a water-sports kiosk where visitors can rent sailboats and snorkeling equipment, or depart with divemasters on scuba expeditions. The hotel has amply proportioned sheets of glass, which are angled for the best views of the sea and the sands of the beach.

It offers an open-handed welcome, often to Canadian tour groups. Each of its 80 comfortable bedrooms has a ceiling fan, a patio or balcony, wall-to-wall carpeting, a private bath, and big windows. All year, EP singles cost $70 to $100 daily; doubles go for $80 to $100. Reasonably priced dive packages are available, allowing divers to take advantage of the hotel's location at the edge of "The Walls," which drops 6,000 feet into unchartered waters a short distance offshore. Meals are served in an airy dining room. The chef prepares concoctions of island seafood and international specialties. If you catch a conch or lobster during your explorations in the water, it can be prepared for your dinner.

Le Deck Beachclub and Hotel, P.O. Box 144, Grace Bay, Providenciales, Turks and Caicos, B.W.I. (tel. 809/946-5547). Set a few steps from the very white sands of the island's eastern beaches, one of the newest hotels on Provo (it opened in 1989) contains 23 accommodations, each of which has a cable-connected TV, air conditioning, a ceiling fan, a private bathroom, a phone, a minibar, and a comfortable decor of beach-inspired furniture and Caribbean colors. With a full breakfast included, winter rates, single or double occupancy, cost $135 per day for a standard room and $200 for a small suite. *In summer, single or double occupancy costs $110 per day for a standard room, $175 for a small suite.* Rental of a villalike condominium, which sits a short distance from the rest of the hotel, costs $260 in any season. Taxes and service charges are extra.

Arranged in a U-shape around a deck that serves as a social center (and gives the establishment its name), the hotel is painted pink and contains on its premises a curve-sided freshwater swimming pool, a wood-trimmed clubhouse-bar-restaurant with big windows and sea views, and a full array of water-sports options.

Mariner Inn, Sapodilla Point, Providenciales, Turks and Caicos, B.W.I. (tel. 809/946-4488). Uncluttered simplicity is the byword of!this informal hotel, the principal decor of which is derived from the sweeping sea vistas around it. It stands 3 miles from the airport. The only object interrupting the panorama is a Shell Oil unloading dock, a concrete-and-steel giant jutting into the sea at the bottom of the slope supporting the hotel. Even the dock, however, has a form of isolated grandeur about it. The owners have worked hard to turn the locale into an oasis of flowering plants. These grow around the bases of the villas containing the accommodations. The social center is the sundeck, where palms and parasols protect the planking of the boardwalks that give residents access to it.

Accommodations are basic, unfussy places, with ceiling fans, bathrooms, and modern lines. Prices in winter are $90 to $95 daily for a single or double and $105 for a triple. *In summer, singles or doubles cost from $65 daily, with triples renting at $75.*

However, if the season is slow, this place might be closed for several months at a time. Always check before heading there.

Ocean Club at Grace Bay, P.O. Box 240, Grace Bay, Providenciales, Turks and Caicos, B.W.I. (tel. 809/946-5880, or toll free 800/223-6510 in the U.S.), is a recently inaugurated condominium complex set on a splendid beach. Each of its units contains a fully equipped modern kitchen, a screened-in balcony with sea view, a clothes washer and dryer, cable TV, and between one and three tastefully furnished bedrooms. Appropriate for travelers who want to prepare their own meals, the resort at presstime offered only a glimpse of what it would be like after completion, since only 10 of an eventual 70 units had been completed. Year-round daily rates for EP single or double occupancy range from $105 to $150 for studio apartments and one-bedroom apartments. Occupancy of a two-bedroom apartment costs $260 to $300 for between two and four occupants, and occupancy of a three-bedroom apartment costs $335 to $395 for between three and six occupants.

WHERE TO DINE

Moderate

Sheltered by a low-slung hip roof and lined with louvered shutters, **Banana Boat Restaurant,** Turtle Cove Marina (tel. 809/946-4312), is the most popular independent restaurant on the island. It was established in 1981. Since then there's hardly been a yachtsperson on Providenciales who hasn't enjoyed at least one of the establishment's island meals and potent drinks. Menu items include a blend of local dishes coupled with foods such as baked chicken with dressing, New York strip steak, cracked conch, lobster or tuna salad, and a cracked conch sandwich. Half-pound burgers are always a favorite. A choice perch is on the timber-and-plank veranda jutting on piers above the waters of Turtle Cove. A full meal costs from $18 per person, unless your bar tab makes it higher. The establishment welcomes newcomers every Monday through Saturday from 11am to midnight. On Sunday, a $10 barbecue special of ribs, chicken, coleslaw, potato salad, and dessert is served from 11am to 10pm.

Inexpensive

Henry's Roadrunner Restaurant, Blue Hills (tel. 809/946-4216). Intensely local and unpretentious, this island restaurant occupies a blue-sided cottage in a ramshackle but respectable neighborhood called Blue Hills. At any hour it's open you're likely to find two dozen or so of owner Henry Williams's friends playing cards, watching a blaring TV, and drinking away the heat. Established in 1975, it's a center of the island's black community. The fish served is often caught by Henry himself, and it's usually the freshest on the island: red snapper, grouper, lobster, and conch. A breakfast costs from $6; a fixed-price lunch, $8; and a dinner, $15. The restaurant is open daily from 8am until "late at night."

ATTRACTIONS

The national treasure of Provo is a famous Atlantic bottle-nosed dolphin, **JoJo,** who has lived and played around these waters since 1983. What makes this wild dolphin unusual is that he chose to leave his pod and seek out the company of people. He cavorts and plays with the children of the residents of The Bight, on the northern shore of Provo, giving them rides out to the reef and back. Very few incidents of dolphins having chosen such a lifestyle have been recorded.

Provo is the seat of the Society for the Protection of Reefs and Islands from Degradation and Exploitation (PRIDE). In fact, **Chalk Sound,** a land-locked lagoon west of Five Cays Settlement, has been turned into a public park. The hamlet of Five Cays itself boasts a small harbor and a modern airport.

On an isolated section of the island, in a region surrounded by scrub and sand, is **Caicos Conch Farm** (call Marco Travel at 809/946-4393 for an appointment to visit it). This establishment is a pioneer in the commercially viable production of conch. Tours are offered of its breeding basins every Tuesday and Thursday at 3:30pm. For tours of the hatchery and laboratory, along with a visit to the gift shop, adults pay $6; children, $3. There's an annex for the enhanced production of algae as well. Rare conch pearls, shell jewelry, and conch T-shirts are for sale.

SPORTS & RECREATION

On Providenciales, **Provo Turtle Divers Ltd.,** Turtle Cove (tel. 809/946-4232, or toll free 800/328-5285 in the U.S.), with headquarters directly in front of Erebus Inn on the water, is a dive operation offering a personalized service. Dive experts have considered Provo "one of the finest sites for diving in the world," as a barrier reef runs the full length of the island's 17-mile north coast. At Northwest Point there is a vertical drop-off to 6,000 feet.

There are scuba tanks for rent, plus ample backpacks and weight belts. Snorkel equipment is also available, plus 12 full sets of diving gear. A single dive costs $40. A PADI open-water certification course is $400. Provo Turtle is a PADI training facility, with full instruction and Resort Courses.

Dive Provo, P.O. Box 350, Grace Bay, Ramada Turquoise Reef Resort (tel. 809/946-5555), has one of the best scuba programs on the island, its Grace Bay dive boat leaving the Ramada Pier daily at 9am. It also offers PADI open-water certification courses, along with snorkeling trips, glass-bottom boat rides, equipment rental, windsurfer or sailboat instruction, and sailing excursions. A two-tank scuba dive costs $55, with a PADI certification course going for $350. Snorkeling trips go for $30, and Windsurfers or sailboats can be rented for $20 per hour.

---

7. Pine Cay

This exclusive territory, a private island in the West Indies, is owned and managed by members of the Meridian Club, who rightly praise its 2-mile talcum-powder beach, which is among the finest in all the islands.

Pine Cay is one of a chain of islets connecting Providenciales and North Caicos. Two miles long and 800 acres in land area, it is a small residential community with a large area set aside for a park. It has its own 3,900-foot airstrip with scheduled local air service, as well as dock and harbor facilities. No cars are allowed, and transportation is by golf cart or bicycle. There is just enough fresh water, and the cay has its own generating plant.

Once a private club, Pine Cay still has members but they now join the public guests for swimming, sunning, and shelling along the 2½-mile white-sand beach. Snorkeling and diving are possible in an unspoiled barrier reef. Explorers look for Arawak Indian and British colonial remains. There is also a wide range of birds and plants.

The islands' possibilities were recognized by Ferdinand Czernin, son of the last prime minister of the Austro-Hungarian Empire. It is said he was looking for an "intellectual Walden Pond" when he discovered this unspoiled, pristine retreat. The count died before his dream could be realized, but his widow, Helen Czernin, carried on. Her efforts, and those of others, led to the creation of The Meridian Club (see below).

GETTING THERE

To reach it, you fly to Miami and then take a Pan Am (tel. 800/221-1111) flight lasting 1½ hours to Providenciales. There, an air taxi can be arranged to meet you for the 10-minute flight to Pine Cay.

WHERE TO STAY & DINE

Very Expensive

The Meridian Club, Pine Cay, Turks and Caicos, B.W.I. (tel. toll free 800/331-9154), is an environmentally sensitive resort that includes a main clubhouse that faces the beach and a freshwater pool. The club, often patronized by members of the Social Register, has a delightful dining room, a comfortable library, and an intimate bar with a panoramic terrace for sunset cocktails. A dozen accommodations are offered, with bed- and sitting-room areas, dressing rooms, outdoor showers, and terraces facing the beach. In winter, double occupancy on AP (full board) is from $400 to $500 daily, whereas *off-season AP rates are $350 daily.* For single occupancy, deduct $60 per person daily year round.

The Meridian Club has one dining room and two bars, one of which is poolside. The open-air dining room offers full American breakfasts, buffet-style lunches served poolside, and dinners by candlelight. The food is a Caribbean/Continental cuisine, the high standard of which is complemented by the extensive use of local produce, especially lobster, conch, and snapper. Guests can enjoy poolside barbecues and a band once or twice weekly. The club has one tennis court, a large freshwater swimming pool, and a variety of nature trails. There are activities planned daily, such as offshore snorkeling trips or boat trips to neighboring islands. Boats, snorkeling gear, tennis rackets and balls, and fishing tackle are available, as are fishing guides and experienced boatmen.

For reservations and information, contact The Meridian Club, c/o Resorts Management, Inc., 201½ East 29th St., New York, NY 10016 (see the toll-free number above).

APPENDIX A

METRIC WEIGHTS AND MEASURES

In Bermuda & The Bahamas, you will run into the metric system, and if you are prepared for it, you can avoid confusion. Here's a quick run-down on equivalences:

LENGTH

1 millimeter = 0.04 inches (*or* less than ¹⁄₁₆ inch)
1 centimeter = 0.39 inches (*or* just under ½ inch)
1 meter   = 1.09 yards (*or* about 39 inches)
1 kilometer = 0.62 mile (*or* about ⅔ mile)

To convert kilometers to miles, take the number of kilometers and multiply by .62 (for example, 25km × .62 = 15.5 miles).

To convert miles to kilometers, take the number of miles and multiply by 1.61 (for example, 50 miles × 1.61 = 80.5 km).

CAPACITY

1 liter = 33.92 ounces
        = 1.06 quarts
        = 0.26 gallons

To convert liters to gallons, take the number of liters and multiply by .26 (for example, 50 l × .26 = 13 gal).

To convert gallons to liters, take the number of gallons and multiply by 3.79 (for example, 10 gal × 3.79 = 37.9 l).

WEIGHT

1 gram   = 0.04 ounce (*or* about a paperclip's weight)
1 kilogram = 2.2 pounds

To convert kilograms to pounds, take the number of kilos and multiply by 2.2 (for example, 75kg × 2.2 = 165 lbs).

To convert pounds to kilograms, take the number of pounds and multiply by .45 (for example, 90 lb × .45 = 40.5kg).

AREA

1 hectare (100m²) = 2.47 acres

To convert hectares to acres, take the number of hectares and multiply by 2.47 (for example, 20ha × 2.47 = 49.4 acres).

To convert acres to hectares, take the number of acres and multiply by .41 (for example, 40 acres × .41 = 16.4 ha).

TEMPERATURE

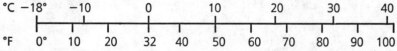

To convert degrees C to degrees F, multiply degrees C by 9, divide by 5, then add 32 (for example 9/5 × 20°C + 32 = 68°F).

To convert degrees F to degrees C, subtract 32 from degrees F, then multiply by 5, and divide by 9 (for example, 85°F − 32 × 5/9 = 29°C).

INDEX

GENERAL INFORMATION

Bermuda

The Bahamas

Turks & Caicos Islands

DESTINATIONS

Bermuda

The Bahamas

Turks & Caicos Islands

NOW, SAVE MONEY ON ALL YOUR TRAVELS!
Join Frommer's™ Dollarwise® Travel Club

Saving money while traveling is never a simple matter, which is why the **Dollarwise Travel Club** was formed 31 years ago. Developed in response to requests from Frommer's Travel Guide readers, the Club provides cost-cutting travel strategies, up-to-date travel information, and a sense of community for value-conscious travelers from all over the world.

In keeping with the money-saving concept, the annual membership fee is low —$20 for U.S. residents or $25 for residents of Canada, Mexico, and other countries—and is immediately exceeded by the value of your benefits, which include:

1. Any TWO books listed on the following pages.
2. Plus any ONE Frommer's City Guide.
3. A subscription to our quarterly newspaper, *The Dollarwise Traveler*.
4. A membership card that entitles you to purchase through the Club all Frommer's publications for 33% to 40% off their retail price.

The eight-page **Dollarwise Traveler** tells you about the latest developments in good-value travel worldwide and includes the following columns: **Hospitality Exchange** (for those offering and seeking hospitality in cities all over the world); **Share-a-Trip** (for those looking for travel companions to share costs); and **Readers Ask . . . Readers Reply** (for those with travel questions that other members can answer).

Aside from the Frommer's Guides and the Gault Millau Guides, you can also choose from our Special Editions. These include such titles as **California with Kids** (a compendium of the best of California's accommodations, restaurants, and sightseeing attractions appropriate for those traveling with toddlers through teens); **Candy Apple: New York with Kids** (a spirited guide to the Big Apple by a savvy New York grandmother that's perfect for both visitors and residents); **Caribbean Hideaways** (the 100 most romantic places to stay in the Islands, all rated on ambience, food, sports opportunities, and price); **Honeymoon Destinations** (a guide to planning and choosing just the right destination from hundreds of possibilities in the U.S., Mexico, and the Caribbean); **Marilyn Wood's Wonderful Weekends** (a selection of the best mini-vacations within a 200-mile radius of New York City, including descriptions of country inns and other accommodations, restaurants, picnic spots, sights, and activities); and **Paris Rendez-Vous** (a delightful guide to the best places to meet in Paris whether for power breakfasts or dancing till dawn).

To join this Club, simply send the appropriate membership fee with your name and address to: Frommer's Dollarwise Travel Club, 15 Columbus Circle, New York, NY 10023. Remember to specify which single city guide and which two other guides you wish to receive in your initial package of member's benefits. Or tear out the next page, check off your choices, and send the page to us with your membership fee.

FROMMER BOOKS
PRENTICE HALL PRESS
15 COLUMBUS CIRCLE
NEW YORK, NY 10023
212/373-8125

Date_____

Friends: Please send me the books checked below.

FROMMER'S™ GUIDES

(Guides to sightseeing and tourist accommodations and facilities from budget to deluxe, with emphasis on the medium-priced.)

☐ Alaska	$14.95	☐ Germany	$14.95
☐ Australia	$14.95	☐ Italy	$14.95
☐ Austria & Hungary	$14.95	☐ Japan & Hong Kong	$14.95
☐ Belgium, Holland & Luxembourg	$14.95	☐ Mid-Atlantic States	$14.95
☐ Bermuda & The Bahamas	$14.95	☐ New England	$14.95
☐ Brazil	$14.95	☐ New Mexico	$13.95
☐ Canada	$14.95	☐ New York State	$14.95
☐ Caribbean	$14.95	☐ Northwest	$16.95
☐ Cruises (incl. Alaska, Carib, Mex, Hawaii, Panama, Canada & US)	$14.95	☐ Portugal, Madeira & the Azores	$14.95
		☐ Scandinavia	$18.95
☐ California & Las Vegas	$14.95	☐ South Pacific	$14.95
☐ Egypt	$14.95	☐ Southeast Asia	$14.95
☐ England & Scotland	$14.95	☐ Southern Atlantic States	$14.95
☐ Florida	$14.95	☐ Southwest	$14.95
☐ France	$14.95	☐ Switzerland & Liechtenstein	$14.95

☐ USA $16.95

FROMMER'S $-A-DAY® GUIDES

(In-depth guides to sightseeing and low-cost tourist accommodations and facilities.)

☐ Europe on $40 a Day	$15.95	☐ Israel on $40 a Day	$13.95
☐ Australia on $40 a Day	$13.95	☐ Mexico on $35 a Day	$14.95
☐ Costa Rica; Guatemala & Belize on $35 a day	$15.95	☐ New York on $60 a Day	$13.95
		☐ New Zealand on $45 a Day	$14.95
☐ Eastern Europe on $25 a Day	$16.95	☐ Scotland & Wales on $40 a Day	$13.95
☐ England on $50 a Day	$13.95	☐ South America on $40 a Day	$15.95
☐ Greece on $35 a Day	$14.95	☐ Spain on $50 a Day	$15.95
☐ Hawaii on $60 a Day	$14.95	☐ Turkey on $30 a Day	$13.95
☐ India on $25 a Day	$12.95	☐ Washington, D.C. & Historic Va. on $40 a Day	$13.95
☐ Ireland on $35 a Day	$13.95		

FROMMER'S TOURING GUIDES

(Color illustrated guides that include walking tours, cultural and historic sites, and other vital travel information.)

☐ Amsterdam	$10.95	☐ New York	$10.95
☐ Australia	$10.95	☐ Paris	$8.95
☐ Brazil	$10.95	☐ Rome	$10.95
☐ Egypt	$8.95	☐ Scotland	$9.95
☐ Florence	$8.95	☐ Thailand	$10.95
☐ Hong Kong	$10.95	☐ Turkey	$10.95
☐ London	$10.95	☐ Venice	$8.95

(TURN PAGE FOR ADDITONAL BOOKS AND ORDER FORM)

FROMMER'S CITY GUIDES

(Pocket-size guides to sightseeing and tourist accommodations and facilities in all price ranges.)

☐ Amsterdam/Holland	$8.95	☐ Minneapolis/St. Paul	$8.95
☐ Athens	$8.95	☐ Montréal/Québec City	$8.95
☐ Atlanta	$8.95	☐ New Orleans	$8.95
☐ Atlantic City/Cape May	$8.95	☐ New York	$8.95
☐ Barcelona	$7.95	☐ Orlando	$8.95
☐ Belgium	$7.95	☐ Paris	$8.95
☐ Berlin	$8.95	☐ Philadelphia	$8.95
☐ Boston	$8.95	☐ Rio	$8.95
☐ Cancún/Cozumel/Yucatán	$8.95	☐ Rome	$8.95
☐ Chicago	$9.95	☐ Salt Lake City	$8.95
☐ Denver/Boulder/Colorado Springs	$7.95	☐ San Diego	$8.95
☐ Dublin/Ireland	$8.95	☐ San Francisco	$8.95
☐ Hawaii	$8.95	☐ Santa Fe/Taos/Albuquerque	$10.95
☐ Hong Kong	$7.95	☐ Seattle/Portland	$7.95
☐ Las Vegas	$8.95	☐ St. Louis/Kansas City	$9.95
☐ Lisbon/Madrid/Costa del Sol	$8.95	☐ Sydney	$8.95
☐ London	$8.95	☐ Tampa/St. Petersburg	$8.95
☐ Los Angeles	$8.95	☐ Tokyo	$8.95
☐ Mexico City/Acapulco	$8.95	☐ Toronto	$8.95
☐ Miami	$8.95	☐ Vancouver/Victoria	$7.95

☐ Washington, D.C. $8.95

SPECIAL EDITIONS

☐ Beat the High Cost of Travel	$6.95	☐ Motorist's Phrase Book (Fr/Ger/Sp)	$4.95
☐ Bed & Breakfast—N. America	$14.95	☐ Paris Rendez-Vous	$10.95
☐ California with Kids	$16.95	☐ Swap and Go (Home Exchanging)	$10.95
☐ Caribbean Hideaways	$14.95	☐ The Candy Apple (NY with Kids)	$12.95
☐ Honeymoon Destinations (US, Mex &		☐ Travel Diary and Record Book	$5.95
Carib)	$14.95	☐ Where to Stay USA (From $3 to $30 a	
☐ Manhattan's Outdoor Sculpture	$15.95	night)	$13.95

☐ Marilyn Wood's Wonderful Weekends (CT, DE, MA, NH, NJ, NY, PA, RI, VT) $11.95
☐ The New World of Travel (Annual sourcebook by Arthur Frommer for savvy travelers) $16.95

GAULT MILLAU

(The only guides that distinguish the truly superlative from the merely overrated.)

☐ The Best of Chicago	$15.95	☐ The Best of Los Angeles	$16.95
☐ The Best of France	$16.95	☐ The Best of New England	$15.95
☐ The Best of Hawaii	$16.95	☐ The Best of New Orleans	$16.95
☐ The Best of Hong Kong	$16.95	☐ The Best of New York	$16.95
☐ The Best of Italy	$16.95	☐ The Best of Paris	$16.95
☐ The Best of London	$16.95	☐ The Best of San Francisco	$16.95

☐ The Best of Washington, D.C. $16.95

ORDER NOW!

In U.S. include $2 shipping UPS for 1st book; $1 ea. add'l book. Outside U.S. $3 and $1, respectively.
Allow four to six weeks for delivery in U.S., longer outside U.S.
Enclosed is my check or money order for $_____

NAME_____

ADDRESS_____

CITY_____ STATE_____ ZIP_____

0391